INTERNATIONAL MARITIME BOUNDARIES

THE AMERICAN SOCIETY OF INTERNATIONAL LAW

International Maritime Boundaries

VOLUME IX

Edited by

COALTER G. LATHROP

BRILL | NIJHOFF

LEIDEN | BOSTON

Typeface for the Latin, Greek, and Cyrillic scripts: "Brill". See and download: brill.com/brill-typeface.

ISBN 978-90-04-73048-9 (hardback)

Copyright 2025 by The American Society of International Law and Koninklijke Brill BV, Plantijnstraat 2, 2321 JC Leiden, The Netherlands.
Koninklijke Brill BV incorporates the imprints Brill, Brill Nijhoff, Brill Schöningh, Brill Fink, Brill mentis, Brill Wageningen Academic, Vandenhoeck & Ruprecht, Böhlau and V&R unipress.
All rights reserved. No part of this publication may be reproduced, translated, stored in a retrieval system, or transmitted in any form or by any means, electronic, mechanical, photocopying, recording or otherwise, without prior written permission from the publisher.
Requests for re-use and/or translations must be addressed to Koninklijke Brill BV via brill.com or copyright.com.
For more information: info@brill.com.

This book is printed on acid-free paper and produced in a sustainable manner.

PRINTED BY DRUKKERIJ WILCO B.V. - AMERSFOORT, THE NETHERLANDS

Table of Contents

VOLUME IX

Preface   xxvii
Contributors   xxix
Introduction   xxxix
   Coalter G. Lathrop
Regional Maps   xli

BOUNDARY REPORTS
I. *North America*
1-4 (2)   Cuba – United States   5819
1-5 (4)   Mexico – United States   5841

II. *Middle America, Caribbean Sea*
2-8 (2)   Cuba – Mexico   5861
2-20   France (Saint Martin and Saint Barthelemy) – United
                 Kingdom (Anguilla) (Add. 2)   5881
2-37   Antigua and Barbuda – France (Saint Barthélemy,
                 Guadeloupe)   5889
2-38   Antigua and Barbuda – United Kingdom (Anguilla)   5901
2-39   Dominican Republic – Netherlands   5913
2-40   Barbados – Saint Lucia   5925
2-41   Saint Lucia – Saint Vincent and the Grenadines   5941
2-42   Saint Kitts and Nevis – Netherlands   5957

III. *South America*
None

IV. *Africa*
None

vi   *Table of Contents*

V. *Central Pacific, East Asia, Southeast Asia*
5-6   Fiji – France (Wallis and Futuna) (Add. 2)   5975
5-47   Federated States of Micronesia – Papua New Guinea   5981
5-48   Fiji – Tuvalu   6005
5-49   Fiji – Solomon Islands   6027

VI. *Indian Ocean*
6-22 (2)   Mauritius – Seychelles   6047
6-33   Mauritius – Maldives   6103

VII. *Persian Gulf*
None

VIII. *Mediterranean Sea, Black Sea*
8-4 (2)   Greece – Italy   6127
8-16   Algeria – Tunisia (Add. 1)   6139
8-24   Libya – Turkey   6159
8-25   Egypt – Greece   6181
8-26   Israel – Lebanon   6197
8-27   Croatia – Italy   6231

IX. *Northern and Western Europe*
9-26   Denmark/The Faroes – Iceland; Denmark/
The Faroes – Norway; Iceland – Norway (Add. 1)   6251

X. *Baltic Sea*
10-25   Denmark – Poland   6273

XI. *Caspian Sea*
None

Country-by-Country Index   6291

VOLUME I

Preface xiii
Contributors xv
Glossary of Terms xix
References xxi
Introduction and Conclusions xxiii
  Jonathan I. Charney

GLOBAL ANALYSES

I. Political, Strategic, and Historical Considerations 3
  Bernard H. Oxman
II. The Legal Regime of Maritime Boundary Agreements 41
  David Colson
III. Economic and Environmental Considerations in Maritime Boundary
  Delimitations 75
  Barbara Kwiatkowska
IV. Geographic Considerations in Maritime Delimitation 115
  Prosper Weil
V. Islands, Rocks, Reefs, and Low-Tide Elevations in Maritime
  Boundaries 131
  Derek Bowett
VI. Baseline Considerations 153
  Louis B. Sohn
VII. The Use of Geophysical Factors in the Delimitation of Maritime
  Boundaries 163
  Keith Highet
VIII. Method, Oppositeness and Adjacency, and Proportionality in
  Maritime Boundary Delimitation 203
  Leonard Legault and Blair Hankey
IX. Technical Considerations in Maritime Boundary Delimitations 243
  Peter Beazley

REGIONAL ANALYSES

REGION I. North American Maritime Boundaries 267
  Lewis M. Alexander
REGION II. Middle American and Caribbean Maritime
  Boundaries 271
  Kaldone G. Nweihed

viii *Table of Contents*

REGION III. South American Maritime Boundaries 285
Eduardo Jimenez de Arechaga
REGION IV. African Maritime Boundaries 293
Andronico O. Adede
REGION V. Central Pacific and East Asian Maritime Boundaries 297
Choon-Ho Park
REGION VI. Indian Ocean and South East Asian Maritime
Boundaries 305
J.R. Victor Prescott
REGION VII. Persian Gulf Maritime Boundaries 315
Lewis M. Alexander
REGION VIII. Mediterranean and Black Sea Maritime Boundaries 321
Tullio Scovazzi
REGION IX. Northern and Western European Maritime
Boundaries 331
D.H. Anderson
REGION X. Baltic Sea Maritime Boundaries 345
Erik Franckx

MARITIME BOUNDARY REPORTS AND DOCUMENTS
I. *North America*
1-1 Canada – Denmark (Greenland) (1973) 371
1-2 Canada – France (St. Pierre and Miquelon) (1972 and 1992) 387
1-3 Canada – United States (Gulf of Mexico) (1979 and 1984) 401
1-4 Cuba – United States (1977) 417
1-5 Mexico – United States (1970, 1976 and 1987) 427
1-6 United States – Soviet Union (1990) 447

II. *Middle America/The Caribbean*
2-1 Colombia – Costa Rica (1977) 463
2-2 Colombia – Dominican Republic (1978) 477
2-3 Colombia – Haiti (1978) 491
2-4 Colombia – Honduras (1986) 503
2-5 Colombia – Panama (1976) 519
2-6 Costa Rica – Panama (1980) 537
2-7 Cuba – Haiti (1977) 551
2-8 Cuba – Mexico (1976) 565
2-9 Dominican Republic – Venezuela (1979) 577

2-10	France (Martinique) – Saint Lucia (1981) 591
2-11	France (Guadeloupe and Martinique) – Venezuela (1980) 603
2-12	The Netherlands (Antilles) – Venezuela (1978) 615
2-13 (1)	Trinidad and Tobago – Venezuela (Gulf of Paria) (1942) 639
2-13 (2)	Trinidad and Tobago – Venezuela (1989) 655
2-13 (3)	Trinidad and Tobago – Venezuela (1990) 675
2-14	United States (Puerto Rico and the Virgin Islands) – Venezuela (1978) 691
2-15	Dominica – France (Guadeloupe and Martinique) (1987) 705

III. *South America*

3-1	Argentina – Chile (1984) 719
3-2	Argentina – Uruguay (1973) 757
3-3	Brazil – France (French Guiana) (1981) 777
3-4	Brazil – Uruguay (1972) 785
3-5	Chile – Peru (1952) 793
3-6	Colombia – Costa Rica (1984) 801
3-7	Colombia – Ecuador (1975) 809
3-8	Costa Rica – Ecuador (1985) 819
3-9	Ecuador – Peru (1952) 829

IV. *Africa*

4-1	Cameroon – Nigeria (1975) 841
4-2	The Gambia – Senegal (1975) 849
4-4	Guinea – Guinea – Bissau (1985) 857
4-4	Guinea – Bissau – Senegal (1989) 867
4-5	Kenya – Tanzania (1976) 875
4-6	Mauritania – Morocco (1976) 885
4-7	Mozambique – Tanzania (1988) 893

V. *Central Pacific/East Asia*

5-1	Australia – France (New Caledonia) (1982) 905
5-2	United Kingdom (Sarawak, North Borneo, Brunei) (1958) 915
5-3	Australia – Papua New Guinea (1978) 929
5-4	Australia – Solomon Islands (1988) 977
5-5	Cook Islands – United States (American Samoa) (1980) 985

x *Table of Contents*

5-6   Fiji – France (New Caledonia, Wallis and Futuna)
            (1983)   995
5-7   France (French Polynesia) – United Kingdom (Pitcairn,
            Henderson, Ducie and Oeno Islands) (1983)   1003
5-8   France (Wallis and Futuna) – Tonga (1980)   1011
5-9 (1)   Indonesia – Malaysia (Continental Shelf) (1969)   1019
5-9 (2)   Indonesia – Malaysia (Territorial Sea) (1970)   1029
5-10   Indonesia – Papua New Guinea (1980)   1039
5-11   Indonesia – Singapore (1973)   1049
5-12   Japan – South Korea (1974)   1057
5-13   Malaysia – Thailand (Territorial Sea) (1979)   1091
5-13   Malaysia – Thailand (Gulf of Thailand Continental Shelf)
            (1979)   1099
5-14   New Zealand (Tokelau) – United States (American Samoa)
            (1980)   1125
5-15 (1)   North Korea – Soviet Union (Territorial Sea) (1985)   1135
5-15 (2)   North Korea – Soviet Union (Exclusive Economic Zone
            and Continental Shelf) (1986)   1145
5-16   Papua New Guinea – Solomon Islands (1989)   1155
5-17   France (New Caledonia) – Solomon Islands (1990)   1167
5-18   Cook Islands – France (1990)   1175

VOLUME II

VI. *Indian Ocean/South East Asia*
6-1   Australia (Heard/McDonald Islands) – France (Kerguelen
            Islands) (1982)   1185
6-2 (1)   Australia – Indonesia (Seabed Boundaries) (1971)   1195
6-2 (2)   Australia – Indonesia (Timor and Arafura Seas)
            (1972)   1207
6-2 (3)   Australia (Papua New Guinea) – Indonesia (1973)   1219
6-2 (4)   Australia – Indonesia (Fisheries) (1981)   1229
6-2 (5)   Australia – Indonesia (Timor Gap) (1989)   1245
6-3   Burma (Myanmar) – India (1986)   1329
6-4   Burma (Myanmar) – Thailand (1980)   1341
6-5   France (Reunion) – Mauritius (1980)   1353
6-6 (1)   India – Indonesia (1974)   1363
6-6 (2)   India – Indonesia (Andaman Sea and Indian Ocean)
            (1977)   1371

6-7	India – Indonesia – Thailand (1978) 1379
6-8	India – Maldives (1976) 1389
6-9	India – Maldives – Sri Lanka (1976) 1401
6-10 (1)	India – Sri Lanka (Historic Waters) (1974) 1409
6-10 (2)	India – Sri Lanka (Gulf of Manaar and Bay of Bengal) (1976) 1419
6-11	India – Thailand (1978) 1433
6-12	Indonesia – Malaysia – Thailand (1971) 1443
6-13 (1)	Indonesia – Thailand (Malacca Strait and Andaman Sea) (1971) 1455
6-13 (2)	Indonesia – Thailand (Andaman Sea) (1975) 1465

VII. *Persian Gulf*

7-1	Abu Dhabi – Dubai (1968) 1475
7-2	Bahrain – Iran (1971) 1481
7-3	Bahrain – Saudi Arabia (1958) 1489
7-4	Dubai – Sharjah (1981) 1499
7-5	Iran – Oman (1974) 1503
7-6	Iran – Qatar (1969) 1511
7-7	Iran – Saudi Arabia (1968) 1519
7-8	Iran – United Arab Emirates (Dubai) (1974) 1533
7-9	Qatar – United Arab Emirates (Abu Dhabi) (1969) 1541
7-10	Sharjah – Umm al Qaywayn (1964) 1549

VIII. *Mediterranean/Black Sea*

8-1	Cyprus – United Kingdom (Akrotiri, Dhekelia) (1960) 1559
8-2	France – Italy (1986) 1571
8-3	France – Monaco (1984) 1581
8-4	Greece – Italy (1977) 1591
8-5	Italy – Spain (1974) 1601
8-6	Italy – Tunisia (1971) 1611
8-7 (1)	Italy – Yugoslavia (Continental Shelf) (1969) 1627
8-7 (2)	Italy – Yugoslavia (Territorial Sea) (1975) 1639
8-8	Libya – Malta (1986) 1649
8-9	Libya – Tunisia (1988) 1663
8-10 (1)	Turkey – Soviet Union (Territorial Sea) (1973) 1681
8-10 (2)	Turkey – Soviet Union (Continental Shelf) (1978) 1693
8-10 (3)	Turkey – Soviet Union (Exclusive Economic Zone) (1986 and 1987) 1701

xii *Table of Contents*

IX. *Northern and Western Europe*

9-1	Denmark (Faroe Islands) – Norway (1979) 1711
9-2	France – Spain (1974) 1719
9-3	France – United Kingdom (1975, 1982, 1988 and 1991) 1735
9-4	Iceland – Norway (1980 and 1981) 1755
9-5	Ireland – United Kingdom (1988) 1767
9-6	Norway – Soviet Union (1957) 1781
9-7	Portugal – Spain (1976) 1791
9-8	Denmark – Federal Republic of Germany (1965, 1967, 1969, and 1974) 1801
9-9	Denmark – Norway (1965) 1815
9-10	Denmark – United Kingdom (1966 and 1971) 1825
9-11	Federal Republic of Germany – The Netherlands (1962, 1964, 1967 and 1971) 1835
9-12	Federal Republic of Germany – United Kingdom (1971) 1851
9-13	The Netherlands – United Kingdom (1965 and 1971) 859
9-14	Norway – Sweden (1968) 1871
9-15	Norway – United Kingdom (1965 and 1978) 1879
9-16	Belgium – France (1990) 1891
9-17	Belgium – United Kingdom (1991) 1901

X. *Baltic Sea*

10-1	Denmark – Federal Republic of Germany (1965) 1915
10-2	Denmark – Sweden (1984) 1931
10-3	Finland – Sweden (1972) 1945
10-4 (1)	Finland – Soviet Union (Continental Shelf in the Gulf of Finland) (1965) 1959
10-4 (2)	Finland – Soviet Union (Continental Shelf in the North Eastern Baltic Sea) (1967) 1971
10-4 (3)	Finland – Soviet Union (Fishing in the North Eastern Baltic Sea) (1980) 1979
10-4 (4)	Finland – Soviet Union (the Economic Zone, the Fishery Zone, and the Continental Shelf in the Gulf of Finland and the North Eastern Baltic Sea) (1985) 1989
10-5	Federal Republic of Germany – German Democratic Republic (1974) 1997
10-6 (1)	German Democratic Republic – Poland (1989) 2005
10-6 (2)	Federal Republic of Germany – Poland (1990) 2023

10-7	German Democratic Republic – Sweden (1978) 2029
10-8	Poland – Soviet Union (1985) 2039
10-9	Sweden – Soviet Union (1988) 2057
10-10	Poland – Sweden (1989) 2077
10-11	Denmark – German Democratic Republic (1988) 2087
10-12	Poland – Sweden-Soviet Union (1989) 2097

Index   2105

VOLUME III

Preface   xiii
Contributors   xv
Introduction   xix
  Jonathan I. Charney

MARITIME BOUNDARY REPORTS AND DOCUMENTS

I. *North America*

| 1-2 | Canada – France (St. Pierre and Miquelon) (1992) (Add. 2)   2141 |

II. *Middle America/The Caribbean*

2-16	United Kingdom (British Virgin Islands) – United States (Puerto Rico and the US Virgin Islands) (1993) 2161
2-17	United Kingdom (Anguilla) – United States (US Virgin Islands) (1993) 2171
2-18	Colombia – Jamaica (1993) 2179
2-19	Cuba – Jamaica (1994) 2205
2-20	France (St. Martin and St. Barthelemy) – United Kingdom (Anguilla) (1996) 2219
2-21	France (Guadeloupe) – United Kingdom (Montserrat) (1996) 2227
2-22	Dominican Republic – United Kingdom (Turks and Caicos Islands) (1996) 2235

III. *South America*
None

xiv   *Table of Contents*

IV. *Africa*
4-1   Cameroon – Nigeria (1975) (Add.)   2249
4-4 (4) & (5)   Guinea – Bissau – Senegal (1993 and 1995)   2251
4-8   Cape Verde – Senegal (1993)   2279

V. *Central Pacific/East Asia*
5-7   United Kingdom (Pitcairn) – France (Polynesia)
                       (Add.)   2295
5-15 (3)   North Korea – Soviet Union (Territorial Sea) (1990)   2299
5-16 (2)   Papua New Guinea – Solomon Islands (1989)   2323
5-19   Malaysia – Vietnam (1992)   2335
5-20   Malaysia (Johor) – Singapore (1995)   2345
5-21   Cambodia – Vietnam (1982)   2357

VI. *Indian Ocean/South East Asia*
6-3, 6-4, 6-11   India – Myanmar (Burma) – Thailand (1993)
                       (Add. 1)   2369
6-11   India – Thailand (1993) (Add. 2)   2377

VII. *Persian Gulf*
7-4   Dubai – Sharjah (1981) (Add. 1)   2385
7-11   Iraq – Kuwait (1993)   2387

VIII. *Mediterranean/Black Sea*
8-6   Italy – Tunisia (1971) (Corr.)   2435
8-7 (3)   Adriatic Sea Update (1996)   2437
8-10 (4)   Black Sea Update (1996)   2443
8-11   Albania – Italy (1992)   2447
8-12   Israel – Jordan (1996)   2457

IX. *Northern and Western Europe*
9-3 (4)   France – United Kingdom (1991) (Corr.)   2465
9-3 (5)   France – United Kingdom (Guernsey) (1992)   2471
9-5 (2)   Ireland – United Kingdom (1992)   2487
9-18   Denmark – The Netherlands (1966)   2497
9-19   Denmark (Greenland) – Norway (Jan Mayen) (1995)   2507
9-20   Northern and Western Europe Update (1996)   2527

X. *Baltic Sea*
10-13   Finland – Sweden (Bogskär Area) (1995)   2539
10-14   Baltic Sea Update (1996)   2557

VOLUME IV

Preface xv
Contributors xvii
Introduction xxi
  Jonathan I. Charney

MARITIME BOUNDARY REPORTS AND DOCUMENTS

I. *North America*
1-5   Mexico – United States (1978) (Add)   2619
1-5 (2)   Mexico – United States (2000)   2621

II. *Middle America/The Caribbean*
None

III. *South America*
3-5   Chile – Peru (1952) (Corr. 1, Add. 1)   2639
3-6   Colombia – Costa Rica (1984) (Add. 1, Corr. 1)   2641

IV. *Africa*
4-8   Equatorial Guinea – Sao Tome and Principe (1999)   2647
4-9   Equatorial Guinea – Nigeria (2000)   2657

V. *Central Pacific/East Asia*
5-4   Australia – Solomon Islands (1988) (Add.)   2671
5-22   Niue – United States (American Samoa) (1997)   2673
5-23   Thailand – Vietnam (1997)   2683

VI. *Indian Ocean/South East Asia*
6-2 (6)   Australia – Indonesia (1997)   2697
6-14   Eritrea – Yemen (1999)   2729
6-15   Australia – United Nations Transitional Administration in
               East Timor (UNTAET) (2000)   2753
6-16   Saudi Arabia – Yemen (2000)   2797
6-17   Oman – Pakistan (2000)   2809

xvi *Table of Contents*

VII. *Persian Gulf*
7-4   Dubai – Sharjah (1981) (Add. 1)   2823
7-12   Kuwait – Saudi Arabia (2000)   2825
7-13   Bahrain – Qatar (2001)   2841

VIII. *Mediterranean/Black Sea*
8-6   Italy – Tunisia (1971) (Corr. 2)   2863
8-10 (5)   Georgia – Turkey (1997)   2865
8-11   Albania – Italy (1992) (Corr. 1)   2869
8-13   Bulgaria – Turkey (1997)   2871
8-14   Bosnia – Herzegovina – Croatia (1999)   2887

IX. *Northern and Western Europe*
9-4 (2)   Iceland – Norway (Jan Mayen) (1997)   2903
9-19 (2)   Denmark (Greenland) – Norway (Jan Mayen) (1997)   2913
9-21   Belgium – The Netherlands (1996)   2921
9-22   Denmark (Greenland) – Iceland (1997)   2941
9-23   Denmark (Faroe Islands) – United Kingdom (1999)   2955
9-24   France – United Kingdom (Jersey) (2000)   2979

X. *Baltic Sea*
10-15   Estonia – Latvia (1996)   2995
10-16   Estonia – Finland (1996)   3019
10-17   Estonia – Latvia – Sweden (1997)   3041
10-18 (1)   Lithuania – Russia (1997)   3057
10-18 (2)   Lithuania – Russia (1997)   3077
10-19   Estonia – Sweden (1998)   3089
10-20   Latvia – Lithuania (1999)   3107
10-21   Estonia – Finland – Sweden (2001)   3129

Cumulative Index   3141

VOLUME V

Preface   xix
Contributors   xxi
Introduction   xxvii
   David A. Colson

ESSAYS ON DEVELOPMENTS IN INTERNATIONAL MARITIME BOUNDARY PRACTICE

I.   Developments in Maritime Boundary Law and Practice   3199
      David Anderson
II.   Resource, Navigational and Environmental Factors in Equitable
      Maritime Boundary Delimitation   3223
      Barbara Kwiatkowska
III. Islands and Rocks and their Role in Maritime Delimitation   3245
      Victor Prescott/Gillian Triggs
IV.   The Legal Regime of Maritime Boundary Agreements   3281
      Don McRae/Cisse Yacouba
V.   Tripoint Issues in Maritime Boundary Delimitation   3305
      Coalter Lathrop
VI.   Some Thoughts on the Technical Input in Maritime
      Delimitation   3377
      Nuno Antunes

REGIONAL REPORTS

I.   North America   3401
      Editors
II.   Middle America/ The Caribbean   3405
      Carl Dundas
III. South America   3425
      Editors
IV.   Africa   3429
      Tim Daniel
V.   Central Pacific, East Asia, Southeast Asia   3439
      Ted McDorman
VI.   Indian Ocean   3453
      Victor Prescott
VII. Persian Gulf   3467
      Chris Carleton
VIII. Mediterranean/Black Sea   3477
      Tullio Scovazzi
IX.   Northern and Western Europe   3493
      Michael Wood
X.   Baltic   3507
      Erik Franckx
XI.   Caspian   3537
      Robert Smith/Ashley Roach

xviii *Table of Contents*

BOUNDARY REPORTS

I. *North America*

1-4	Cuba – United States (Add. 1) 3555

II. *Middle America/Caribbean*

2-4	Colombia – Honduras (Add. 1) 3561
2-20	France (St. Martin and St. Barthelemy) – United Kingdom (Anguilla) (Add. 1) 3562
2-21	France (Guadeloupe) – United Kingdom (Montserrat) (Add. 1) 3563
2-23	Honduras – United Kingdom (Cayman Islands) 3564
2-24	Honduras – Nicaragua 3575
2-25	Colombia – Nicaragua 3576
2-26	Barbados – Trinidad & Tobago 3577
2-27	Barbados – Guyana 3578

III. *South America*

3-10	Guyana – Suriname 3601

IV. *Africa*

4-1	Cameroon – Nigeria (Add. 2) 3605
4-3	Guinea – Guinea – Bissau (Add. 1/Corr. 1) 3621
4-9	Equatorial Guinea – Nigeria (Add. 1) 3623
4-9 (2)	Equatorial Guinea – Nigeria 3624
4-10	Nigeria – São Tomé & Príncipe 3638
4-11	Gabon – São Tomé & Príncipe 3683
4-12	Cape Verde – Mauritania 3694
4-13	Angola – Namibia 3709

V. *Central Pacific, East Asia, Southeast Asia*

5-6	Fiji – France (Add. 1/Corr. 1) 3729
5-20 (2)	Malaysia – Singapore 3733
5-22	Niue – United States (Add. 1) 3734
5-24	Cambodia – Thailand 3735
5-25	China – Vietnam 3745
5-26	Australia – New Zealand 3759

VI. *Indian Ocean*

6-3,6-4,6-11	India – Burma – Thailand (Add. 1) 3781
6-18	France – Seychelles 3784
6-19	Seychelles – Tanzania 3795

Table of Contents   xix

6-20 (1)(2)   Australia – East Timor   3806
6-20 (3)   Australia – East Timor   3867
6-21   Oman – Yemen   3900

VIII. *Mediterranean, Black Sea*
8-15   Cyprus – Egypt   3917
8-16   Algeria – Tunisia   3927
8-17   Romania – Ukraine   3939

IX. *Northern and Western Europe*
9-3 (4)   France – United Kingdom (Add. 1)   3943
9-15 (2-4)   Norway – United Kingdom   3944
9-17   Belgium – United Kingdom (Add. 1)   4005
9-24   France – United Kingdom (Jersey) (Add. 1)   4006

X. *Baltic*
10-18 (1&2)   Lithuania – Russia (Add. 1)   4009

XI. *Caspian Sea*
11-1   Kazakhstan – Russia   4013
11-2   Azerbaijan – Russia   4034
11-3   Azerbaijan – Kazakhstan   4042
11-4   Azerbaijan – Kazakhstan – Russia   4055

Country-by-Country Index   4057
  R. Smith

Cumulative Index   4073

VOLUME VI

Preface   xxi
Contributors   xxiii
Introduction   xxxi
  David A. Colson

xx   *Table of Contents*

ESSAYS ON DEVELOPMENTS IN INTERNATIONAL MARITIME BOUNDARY PRACTICE

I. Recent Decisions of Courts and Tribunals in Maritime Boundary Cases   4119
    David Anderson
II. Continental Shelf Delimitation Beyond 200 Nautical Miles: Approaches Taken by Coastal States before the Commission on the Limits of the Continental Shelf   4139
    Coalter Lathrop

BOUNDARY REPORTS

I. *North America*
1-4	Cuba – United States (Add. 2)	4165

II. *Middle America/Caribbean*
2-24	Honduras – Nicaragua (Add. 1)	4169
2-25	Colombia – Nicaragua (Add. 1)	4186
2-26	Barbados – Trinidad & Tobago (Add. 1)	4187
2-27	Barbados – Guyana (Add. 1)	4201
2-28	Honduras – Mexico	4202
2-29	United Kingdom (Anguilla and Virgin Islands)	4213
2-30	Barbados – France (Guadeloupe and Martinique)	4223

III. *South America*
3-5	Chile – Peru (Add. 2)	4235
3-10	Guyana – Suriname (Add. 1)	4236

IV. *Africa*
4-1	Cameroon – Nigeria (Add. 3)	4251
4-14	Benin – Nigeria	4256
4-15	Angola – Democratic Republic of the Congo	4270
4-16	Angola – Republic of Congo	4281

V. *Central Pacific, East Asia, Southeast Asia*
5-20 (2)	Malaysia – Singapore (Add. 1)	4299
5-26	Australia – New Zealand (Add. 1)	4300
5-27	Indonesia – Vietnam	4301
5-28	Federated States of Micronesia – Marshall Islands	4316
5-29	France (Wallis and Futuna) – Tuvalu	4330

| 5-30 | France (Wallis and Futuna) – New Zealand (Tokelau)   4339 |
| 5-31 | Federated States of Micronesia – Palau   4348 |

VI. *Indian Ocean*
6-17	Oman – Pakistan (Add. 1) 4365
6-20 (3)	Australia – East Timor (Add. 1) 4366
6-20 (4)	Australia – East Timor 4367
6-22	Mauritius – Seychelles 4391
6-23	Bangladesh – India 4403
6-24	Bangladesh – Myanmar 4404
6-25	France (Reunion) – Madagascar 4405

VII. *Persian Gulf*
| 7-14 | Qatar – Saudi Arabia   4417 |

VIII. *Mediterranean, Black Sea*
8-4	Greece – Italy (Add. 1/Corr. 1) 4431
8-15	Cyprus – Egypt (Add. 1) 4433
8-18	Romania – Ukraine 4434
8-19	Cyprus – Lebanon 4445
8-20	Croatia – Slovenia 4455
8-21	Albania – Greece 4462

IX. *Northern and Western Europe*
9-6 (2)	Norway – Russian Federation 4479
9-10 (2)	Denmark – United Kingdom 4488
9-13 (2)	The Netherlands – United Kingdom 4494
9-15 (5)	Norway – United Kingdom 4499
9-17 (2)	Belgium – United Kingdom 4506
9-25	Denmark/Greenland – Norway (Svalbard) 4513
9-26	Denmark/The Faroes – Iceland – Norway 4532
9-27	Denmark/The Faroes – Iceland 4553

X. *Baltic*
| 10-22 | Estonia – Russia   4567 |

XI. *Caspian Sea*
None

Country-by-Country Index   4585
R. Smith

xxii *Table of Contents*

VOLUME VII

Foreword   xxiii
  Bernard H. Oxman
Preface   xxv
Contributors   xxvii
Introduction   xxxvii
  Coalter G. Lathrop
Regional Maps   xli

BOUNDARY REPORTS
I. *North America*

1-4	Cuba – United States (Add. 3)	4607
1-4	Cuba – United States (Add. 4)	4611
1-5 (3)	Mexico – United States 4613	

II. *Middle America, Caribbean Sea*

2-13 (4)	Trinidad and Tobago – Venezuela 4649	
2-25 (2)	Colombia – Nicaragua 4683	
2-25	Colombia – Nicaragua (Add. 2)	4685
2-31	Grenada – Trinidad and Tobago	4705
2-32	Bahamas – Cuba 4721	
2-33	Cuba – Honduras 4735	
2-34	Costa Rica – Nicaragua 4745	

III. *South America*

3-5 (2)	Chile-Peru 4749	
3-7	Colombia – Ecuador (Add. 1)	4765
3-9	Ecuador – Peru (Add. 1)	4769

IV. *Africa*

4-5 (2)	Kenya – Tanzania 4781	
4-7 (2)	Mozambique – Tanzania 4793	
4-17	Kenya – Somalia 4807	
4-18	Ghana – Ivory Coast 4809	

V. *Central Pacific, East Asia, Southeast Asia*

5-11 (2)	Indonesia – Singapore 4813	

5-11 (3)	Indonesia – Singapore 4827
5-22	Niue – United States (American Samoa) (Add. 1, Corr. 1) 4839
5-25	China – Vietnam (Add. 1) 4841
5-32	Cook Islands – Kiribati 4847
5-33	Cook Islands – Niue 4859
5-34	Kiribati – Marshall Islands 4869
5-35	Kiribati – Nauru 4881
5-36	Kiribati – New Zealand (Tokelau) 4893
5-37	Kiribati – Tuvalu 4903
5-38	Marshall Islands – Nauru 4915
5-39	Kiribati – Marshall Islands – Nauru 4925
5-40	Kiribati – United States 4935
5-41	Indonesia – Philippines 4947
5-42	Federated States of Micronesia – United States (Guam) 4963
5-43	Cook Islands – New Zealand (Tokelau) 4973

VI. *Indian Ocean*

6-23	Bangladesh – India (Add. 1) 4985
6-24	Bangladesh – Myanmar (Add. 1) 4999
6-26	Comoros – Mozambique 5017
6-27	Comoros – Mozambique – Tanzania 5033
6-28	Comoros – Seychelles 5039
6-29	Comoros – Seychelles – Tanzania 5053
6-30	Comoros – Tanzania 5059

VII. *Persian Gulf*

7-14 (2)	Qatar – Saudi Arabia 5073

VIII. *Mediterranean Sea, Black Sea*

8-22	Cyprus – Israel 5091
8-23	Jordan – Saudi Arabia 5105

IX. *Northern and Western Europe*

9-3 (6)	France – United Kingdom 5115
9-4 (3)	Iceland – Norway (Jan Mayen) 5123
9-4	Iceland – Norway (Jan Mayen) (Add.1) 5143
9-5 (3)	Ireland – United Kingdom 5151
9-6 (3)	Norway – Russian Federation 5167

xxiv *Table of Contents*

9-13 (3)	Netherlands – United Kingdom 5205
9-15 (6)	Norway – United Kingdom 5213
9-17 (3)	Belgium – United Kingdom 5253
9-22 (2)	Denmark (Greenland) – Iceland 5259
9-23 (2)	Denmark (Faroe Islands) – United Kingdom 5275

X. *Baltic Sea*
None   5285

XI. *Caspian Sea*
None   5287

Country-by-Country Index   5289

VOLUME VIII

Preface   xxv
Contributors   xxvii
Introduction   xxxv
  Coalter G. Lathrop
Regional Maps   xxxvii

BOUNDARY REPORTS
I. *North America*

1-1	Canada – Denmark (Greenland) (Add. 1) 5341
1-2 (2)	Canada – France 5351
1-4	Cuba – United States (Add. 5) 5395
1-4	Cuba – United States (Add. 6) 5399

II. *Middle America, Caribbean Sea*

2-34	Costa Rica – Nicaragua (Add. 1) 5407
2-35	Barbados – Saint Vincent and the Grenadines 5433
2-36	France – Netherlands 5445

III. *South America*

| 3-8 (2) | Costa Rica – Ecuador   5461 |
| 3-11 | France (French Guiana) – Suriname   5473 |

Table of Contents xxv

IV. *Africa*
4-18   Ghana – Ivory Coast (Add. 1)   5489

V. *Central Pacific, East Asia, Southeast Asia*
5-29   France (Wallis and Futuna) – Tuvalu (Add. 1)   5503
5-44   France – Kiribati   5517
5-45   Solomon Islands – Vanuatu   5527
5-46   Fiji – France (Wallis and Futuna) – Tuvalu   5539

VI. *Indian Ocean*
6-20 (5)   Australia – Timor-Leste   5547
6-31   Iran – Oman   5605
6-32   Egypt – Saudi Arabia   5617

VII. *Persian Gulf*
None

VIII. *Mediterranean Sea, Black Sea*
8-2 (2)   France – Italy   5637
8-15 (2)   Cyprus – Egypt   5651
8-20   Croatia – Slovenia (Add. 1)   5667

IX. *Northern and Western Europe*
9-13 (4)   The Netherlands – United Kingdom   5685

X. *Baltic Sea*
10-23   Lithuania – Russia – Sweden   5731
10-24   Lithuania – Sweden   5743

XI. *Caspian Sea*
None

Country-by-Country Index   5763

Preface

The persons who contributed reports for this ninth volume of *International Maritime Boundaries* are identified at the end of each report, and a short biography of each author is provided in the front matter of this volume. The contributing authors are the backbone of this project which would not be possible without these experts, veterans and first-timers alike. Their efforts are greatly appreciated. Beret Dernbach provided exceptional editorial support. The maps that appear in this volume were prepared by International Mapping under the direction of the editor. This volume was produced under the auspices of the American Society of International Law.

Coalter G. Lathrop
November 2024

Contributors

Rosemarie Cadogan is an international lawyer and consultant with progressively responsible experience in Guyana, the Caribbean, West Africa, the Pacific, and Canada, supporting small island developing states and regional groupings in integrated ocean and environmental governance, maritime jurisdiction acquisition and management, maritime institutional strengthening, sustainable maritime transportation, and legislative reform. As legal negotiator, she represented Guyana in maritime enforcement (ship rider) negotiations and maritime delimitation negotiations with Suriname and Barbados. As Legal Adviser with the Commonwealth Secretariat, she supported member states' applications before the Commission on the Limits of the Continental Shelf, maritime delimitation negotiations among The Netherlands, Saint Kitts and Nevis, and Trinidad and Tobago, and the conclusion of six maritime boundary agreements among Antigua and Barbuda, France, the United Kingdom, Saint Lucia, Barbados, and Saint Vincent and the Grenadines. She is a member of the International Law Association's Alternative Dispute Resolution Committee.

Galo Carrera is an international consultant with extensive experience in the delimitation of international maritime boundaries via various dispute resolution mechanisms and the determination of the outer limits of maritime spaces under national jurisdiction, including the continental shelf beyond 200 nautical miles. He was an elected member of the Commission on the Limits of the Continental Shelf for four terms from 1997 to 2017. He is author and co editor of *The Law of the Sea: Training Manual for Delineation of the Outer Limits of the Continental Shelf Beyond 200 Nautical Miles and for Preparation of Submissions to the Commission on the Limits of the Continental Shelf* (United Nations, February 2007). He was a member of the Legal and Technical Commission of the International Seabed Authority from 2001 to 2006. He has been an invited lecturer in a large number of events organized by academic and government national institutions and international organizations in all continents, including the UN Open-ended Informal Consultative Process on Oceans and the Law of the Sea, the International Tribunal for the Law of the Sea, the International Seabed Authority, and the World Ocean Assessment III. He is an expert on marine scientific research according to Article 2 of Annex VIII (Special Arbitration) of the United Nations Convention on the Law of the Sea.

xxx *Contributors*

Perpétua B. Chéry is an associate in Debevoise & Plimpton's International Dispute Resolution and Public International Law groups. Ms. Chéry joined Debevoise in 2021. From 2020 to 2021, she served as a judicial fellow to H.E. Judge Mohamed Bennouna at the International Court of Justice. Ms. Chéry received a J.D. from Georgetown University Law Center, where she was a Global Law Scholar, and a Master's in Economic Law from the Institut d'Etudes Politiques de Paris (Sciences Po). Prior to law school, Ms. Chéry worked extensively with governments and non-state actors throughout West and Central Africa on issues related to peace and security, governance, and human rights.

Pierre-Emmanuel Dupont is a lawyer and a consultant in public international law, international investment law, and dispute resolution. His advisory services have involved issues of the law of the sea, international environmental law, international dispute settlement procedures, international responsibility, international economic sanctions, state immunity, international humanitarian law, human rights law, and disarmament and non-proliferation. Pierre-Emmanuel has served as legal adviser to the UN Special Rapporteur on unilateral sanctions (unilateral coercive measures) and has worked on several international arbitration cases including investor-state disputes under the ICSID Convention, the Energy Charter Treaty, and bilateral investment treaties. He is a Senior Lecturer at the Catholic Institute of Vendée (ICES) (France) and a member of the Board of Experts of the Hague Centre for Law and Arbitration.

Rolf Einar Fife is Special Adviser at the Norwegian Ministry of Foreign Affairs. He is an elected member of the UN International Law Commission (2023-2027). Prior to that, he was Norway's ambassador to the European Union (2019-2023), ambassador to France and Monaco (2014-2019), and the Director General of the Legal Department of the Ministry of Foreign Affairs (2002-2014). He was a member of the Arbitral Tribunal between the Republic of Croatia and the Republic of Slovenia (land and maritime boundary) (2015-2017). He has served as Chair of the Council of Europe Committee of Legal Advisers on Public International Law (2008-2010). He worked with the Norwegian Ministry of Justice (1984-1985) and joined the Ministry of Foreign Affairs in 1985, with postings in the Middle East (1988-1990) and at the Norwegian Mission to the United Nations in New York (1990-1993) and several positions in the Legal Department of the Ministry of Foreign Affairs. He has headed Norwegian delegations to multilateral and bilateral negotiations and has acted as Agent for Norway in cases before international courts. He was the chief negotiator on the Norwegian side for several treaties of maritime delimitation with neighboring states, including the 2010 delimitation and cooperation treaty with the Russian Federation. He headed the Norwegian team before the Commission on the Limits of the Continental Shelf. He is a member of the Permanent Court of Arbitration and of the Institut de droit international.

Erik Franckx is a professor at the Vrije Universiteit Brussel, honorary professor at the Nelson Mandela University, and professeur émérite at the Université libre de Bruxelles. He holds teaching assignments at the Sorbonne Université Abu Dhabi, United Arab Emirates, and the University of Akureyri, Iceland. Besides numerous articles on the law of the sea, he has also updated, together with John Noyes and Kristen Juras, two standard works of Louis B. Sohn in this domain, namely *The Law of the Sea in a Nutshell* (West, 2nd ed. 2010, 3rd ed. forthcoming) and *Cases and Materials on the Law of the Sea* (Brill, 2nd ed. 2014). He served between 2017 and 2022 as President of the Belgian Society for International Law and was appointed by Belgium as an expert in marine scientific research for use in special arbitration under the 1982 United Nations Convention on the Law of the Sea (1982 Convention) since 2004, as an expert in maritime boundary delimitation to the International Hydrographic Organization since 2005, and as an arbitrator under the 1982 Convention starting in 2014. Between 2006 and 2012, he was appointed by his country as a member of the Permanent Court of Arbitration. He served as a consultant to governments (foreign as well as the three levels of the Belgian state structure, i.e. the federal, regional, and community level), international, supra-national, and non-governmental organizations. He was legal counsel on behalf of the Netherlands in the *Arctic Sunrise Arbitration* against the Russian Federation (2013-2017).

McClean Hobson served in the capacity of Director of Maritime Affairs of Saint Kitts and Nevis between the period 2003 and 2020, with primary responsibility for overseeing the enforcement of the Merchant Shipping Act and the enforcement of laws for the prevention of pollution from ships. Mr. Hobson was one of the chief architects of the Saint Kitts and Nevis Ship Registry, serving as manager from 2005 to 2020. He was Focal Point for the International Maritime Organization (IMO) in Saint Kitts and Nevis and served as Chief Maritime Boundary Negotiator for Saint Kitts and Nevis from 2011 to 2020. He represented Saint Kitts and Nevis on the Organization of the Eastern Caribbean States (OECS) Ocean Governance Team from 2013 to 2020, chairing it from 2015 to 2017. Mr. Hobson led the development of Saint Kitts and Nevis' Yachting Policy, Yachting Strategic and Action Plan, Coastal Master Plan and Marine Spatial Plan, and the National Ocean Policy and Strategic Plan. Mr. Hobson is trained in IMO Hydrographic Surveys, IMO Regional Training Course for Auditors, the Legal Implementation of Regional Seas Conventions and related MEA's for Small Island Developing States, Law of the Sea and Ocean Governance in the Caribbean, Principles and Practice of Maritime Boundary Delimitation, and CARIS LOTS – Limits & Boundaries. Upon retirement, Mr. Hobson has continued to serve the maritime industry of Saint Kitts and Nevis in various capacities.

Coalter G. Lathrop directs Sovereign Geographic, an international law firm and cartography consultancy serving sovereign clients throughout the world. Over the last twenty-five years he has acted as counsel and advisor in multiple cases before the International Court of Justice, the International Tribunal for the Law of the Sea, and *ad hoc* tribunals on questions of territorial sovereignty, maritime delimitation, transboundary harm, and shared resources. Lathrop has provided negotiating support and advice on related matters to governments and private interests in Africa, Asia, the Middle East, and North and South America. Lathrop holds a degree in marine policy from the University of Washington and a J.D. and LL.M. in International and Comparative Law from Duke University. He presents and publishes on the law of the sea, the Arctic, island sovereignty, and maritime boundaries; teaches courses on Law of the Sea and International Environmental Law at Duke University; and has lectured at the Yeosu Academy, International Foundation for the Law of the Sea Summer Academy, and the International Boundaries Research Unit at Durham University. Lathrop served as the rapporteur of the International Law Association Baselines Committee, is the current chair of the Law of the Sea Committee of the American Branch of the International Law Association (ABILA), and is in his thirteenth year as the editor of *International Maritime Boundaries*, a De Gruyter Brill publication and project of the American Society of International Law (ASIL).

Oliver Lewis is an Assistant Legal Adviser in the US Department of State, Office of the Legal Adviser. He is an expert in a wide range of matters involving international law and foreign relations law, including having served as the lead attorney in the Department of State on law of the sea matters. In that capacity, he served as the Head of the US delegation for maritime boundary negotiations, including for the US-Cuba and US-Mexico maritime boundary treaties that were signed in 2018. Since joining the Department of State in 2007, he has advised and negotiated extensively on international agreements and other legal matters concerning climate change, conservation, protection of the environment, public health, Western Hemisphere affairs, international criminal law, law enforcement cooperation, counterterrorism, intelligence, information-sharing, and numerous other areas. He holds an A.B. and a J.D. from Harvard University.

Najib Messihi is a Ph.D. candidate at the Graduate Institute of International and Development Studies in Geneva where he is completing a doctoral thesis on the law of maritime delimitation between states with adjacent coasts under the supervision of Professor Marcelo G. Kohen. From 2015 to 2019, he served as a lecturer in international law at Sciences Po (Middle Eastern and Mediterranean Undergraduate College). In 2017, he acted as assistant counsel to the Republic of Costa Rica before the International Court of Justice in the two joined cases *Maritime Delimitation in the Caribbean Sea and the Pacific Ocean (Costa Rica* v. *Nicaragua)* and *Land Boundary in the Northern Part of Isla Portillos (Costa Rica* v. *Nicaragua)*. Between October 2020 and May 2021, he served as a member of the Lebanese delegation to the maritime boundary talks with Israel in the UN headquarters of Naqoura.

Alex G. Oude Elferink is the Director of the Netherlands Institute for the Law of the Sea (NILOS) and an associate of the Utrecht Centre for Oceans, Water and Sustainability Law (UCWOSL), School of Law, Utrecht University, the Netherlands. He is the author of *The Delimitation of the Continental Shelf between Denmark, Germany and the Netherlands; Arguing Law, Practicing Politics?* (Cambridge University Press, 2013) and the co-editor of *The Oxford Handbook of the Law of the Sea* (Oxford University Press, 2015) and *Maritime Boundary Delimitation: The Case Law; Is it Consistent and Predictable?* (Cambridge University Press, 2018). He has advised governments on various law of the sea issues and has acted as counsel for Nicaragua in a number of cases before the International Court of Justice.

Irini Papanicolopulu is British Academy Global Professor of International Law at SOAS, University of London and conducts research and teaches in international law and its different branches. She holds a Ph.D. in international law from the University of Milano and has previously worked at the University of Oxford, the University of Glasgow, and the University of

Milano-Bicocca. Irini is a visiting professor at Catolica University, Lisbon, Portugal, and St. Gallen University, Switzerland. She has published two monograph and various articles and book chapters on maritime delimitation, the law of the sea, and various other branches of international law. She is the Chair of the International Law Association Committee on Protection of People at Sea and a member of the Coordinating Committee of the Interest Group on the Law of the Sea of the European Society of International Law. Irini has been a member of the Italian delegation in negotiations concerning the law of the sea and occasionally advises states, international organizations, civil society organizations, and business actors on issues of international law, the law of the sea, human rights law, and environmental law.

Yuri Parkhomenko is a partner at Foley Hoag LLP, specializing in advising and representing states in international dispute resolution. He has represented states before the International Court of Justice, International Tribunal for the Law of the Sea, and other leading international dispute resolution fora in high-profile public international law cases. They resulted in landmark victories in disputes concerning sovereignty, land and maritime boundary delimitation, self-determination, use of force, reparation, human rights, humanitarian law, and environment. Since 2009, Mr. Parkhomenko acted as counsel in nearly all maritime delimitation cases before the ICJ, ITLOS and tribunals under Annex VII of UNCLOS. He offers extensive experience in providing advice and advocacy at all stages of international dispute resolution from strategic advice on an emerging dispute and selection of a dispute settlement body, to formulating claims and defenses, to managing evidence, to acting as advocate during oral hearings. In addition to contentious matters, Mr. Parkhomenko advises states on a wide range of international law issues to identify and manage risks in international disputes.

Martin Pratt is Director of Bordermap Consulting Ltd. He is a specialist in international boundary-making and dispute resolution and has advised more than one hundred governments, international organizations, and companies around the world on boundary and sovereignty issues. He has also provided technical support to governments in numerous maritime boundary negotiations and cases before the International Court of Justice and other judicial and arbitral bodies. He led the International Boundaries Research Unit at Durham University, United Kingdom, from 2002 to 2014 and remains an Honorary Professor of Geography at the university. He has also served as an advisor to the United Nations Geographic Information Working Group Task Force on International Boundaries and the African Union Border Programme.

Natalie L. Reid is a partner in Debevoise & Plimpton's International Dispute Resolution group, co-chair of the Public International Law group, and co-chair of the firm's Caribbean practice. Ms. Reid focuses on public international law, international arbitration, and complex commercial litigation matters in proceedings in US courts and a wide range of international fora, including the International Court of Justice and international arbitration tribunals. A Jamaican national, she regularly advises and represents states, multinational corporations, international organizations, and non-governmental organizations. Ms. Reid acts as counsel in commercial, treaty, and public international law arbitrations conducted under the rules of the major arbitral institutions and sits as an arbitrator in commercial cases. She currently serves as a board member of the London Court of International Arbitration (LCIA), President of the LCIA North America User's Council, a member of the ICC International Court of Arbitration, and a counsellor of the American Society of International Law (ASIL).

David P. Riesenberg is the founding partner of Pinna Goldberg's practice in Washington, DC. David has acted before ICSID and UNCITRAL tribunals, as well as the International Tribunal for the Law of the Sea. In 2022, he was recognized by International Financial Law Review as a Rising Star in Commercial Arbitration. David has litigated international disputes before US trial and appellate courts. With local counsel, he has advised clients regarding transnational disputes before the courts of Australia, Belgium, Canada, England, France, Germany, India, Ireland, Luxembourg, the Netherlands, Singapore, and Switzerland. David has been appointed to mediate commercial disputes and is accredited as a mediator by the Supreme Court of Virginia. He has authored or co-authored commentaries published by Oxford University Press, Brill, Kluwer, Thomson Reuters, and the American Society of International Law. He has taught international arbitration as an adjunct professor for University of Miami and made presentations for ICC-YAF and ICCA.

Cmdr. David Robin (ret'd) has acted in various national and regional capacities, most recently as Programme Director for Ocean Governance and Fisheries at the Commission of the Organisation of Eastern Caribbean States (OECS). In this capacity he has held lead responsibility for the strategic coordination of delimitation of maritime boundaries, sustainable ocean (blue economy) management, good governance, and clean coast and ocean within the indigenous integrated Island Management Systems Framework for Small Island Developing States in the Eastern Caribbean. David was Director of

Maritime Administration for Saint Vincent and the Grenadines from 2005 to 2016 and the Commander of its Coast Guard Service from 1994 to 2005. He has headed Saint Vincent and the Grenadines' delegations for the delimitation of maritime boundaries with neighboring states, including a treaty with Barbados in 2015, Saint Lucia in 2019, and the Barbados-Saint Vincent and the Grenadines-Saint Lucia tripoint finalized by the Barbados and Saint Lucia treaty of 2019. He prepared the OECS Eastern Caribbean Regional Ocean Policy (ECROP) in 2007 and coordinated preparation of the Revised Eastern Caribbean Regional Ocean Policy and Strategic Action Plan (Revised ECROP 2020). He developed the 2011 OECS Maritime Boundary Delimitation Strategy and Action Plan in collaboration with the OECS Commission and the Commonwealth Secretariat, which was approved by the OECS Heads of Government in 2012, and he spearheaded subsequent amendments of the Strategy and Action Plan in 2013 and 2017.

Benjamin Samson is a tenured assistant professor at the Catholic University of Paris, where he teaches international and EU law and heads the Master/ LL.M. in International and European Business Law. He holds a Ph.D. in public law from Université Paris Nanterre, where he is also an associate researcher at the Centre de droit international de Nanterre (CEDIN). He is the author and editor of various publications in the fields of the law of the sea, international economic and environmental law, international dispute settlement, and EU law. He was a visiting scholar at the George Washington University School of Law, Washington, DC, in 2017. Benjamin also has extensive experience acting as counsel for governments in proceedings before the International Court of Justice, the International Tribunal for the Law of the Sea, and the Permanent Court of Arbitration.

Clive Schofield is Professor at the Australian Centre for Ocean Resources and Security (ANCORS), University of Wollongong (UOW), Australia. He served as the inaugural Head of Research at the WMU-Sasakawa Global Ocean Institute, World Maritime University (WMU), Malmö, Sweden (2018-2023). He holds a Ph.D. in Geography from Durham University, United Kingdom and an LL.M. in International Law from the University of British Columbia, Canada. His research relates to the maritime jurisdictional aspects of the law of the sea, the determination of baselines along the coast in an era of sea-level rise, the delineation of the limits to maritime claims, and the delimitation of international maritime boundaries as well as boundary dispute resolution and ocean governance on which he has authored over 200 scholarly publications. Professor Schofield is a member of the International Law Association Committee on International Law and Sea-level Rise and serves as an International Hydrographic Office (IHO)-nominated Observer on the Advisory Board on the Law of the Sea (ABLOS). He has been involved in the peaceful settlement of boundary and territory disputes by providing advice to governments engaged in boundary negotiations and in dispute settlement cases. Additionally, he served as an independent expert witness in the 2016 international arbitration case between the Philippines and China.

Nawi Ukabiala is an associate in Debevoise & Plimpton's International Dispute Resolution and Public International Law groups. His practice focuses on international arbitration and litigation. Mr. Ukabiala has significant experience in the extractive industries and energy sectors, as well as human rights disputes. He regularly advises clients on complex issues related to jurisdiction and valuation of damages. Mr. Ukabiala clerked for the International Court of Justice. He is a leader in international law professional organizations, currently serving as a member of the Executive Council of the American Society of International Law (ASIL), a member of the Board of Directors of the American Branch of the International Law Association (ABILA), a member of the CPR Young Attorneys in International Dispute Resolution Steering Committee (CPR Y-ADR) and Arbitration Committee, and a member of the African Arbitration Association (AfAA). Mr. Ukabiala has broad and notable experience in international law. He has published numerous articles, regularly conducts trainings for governments and practitioners, and regularly presents at conferences on pertinent issues in the field.

Beatrice A. Walton is an associate in the Litigation Department at Debevoise & Plimpton LLP and a member of the firm's International Dispute Resolution and Public International Law groups. Ms. Walton joined Debevoise in 2022. From 2018 to 2019, she served as a judicial fellow at the International Court of Justice. Ms. Walton received a J.D. from Yale Law School in 2018, where she was awarded the Jerome Sayles Hess Prize in international law, the Ambrose Gherini Prize for best paper in international law, and the Oxford University Press Student Deák Award, presented at the ASIL annual meeting. Ms. Walton has also served as an assistant at the UN International Law Commission and to a defense team at the International Criminal Court. In fall 2023, she was a visiting lecturer at Yale Law School, co-teaching a course on international adjudication and advanced international law.

Romain Zamour is Vice President and General Counsel at The Lane Construction Corporation, the US subsidiary of global construction group Webuild. In that capacity, he leads the company's legal department, advising business leaders on a broad range of strategic legal matters and risk mitigation measures. Prior to that, he spent ten years in private practice in New York and Paris, focusing on the resolution of international disputes, including through international commercial and investment arbitration, international litigation, and public international law processes. Mr. Zamour is fluent in both the civil law and common law traditions and is admitted to practice in Paris and New York.

Introduction

COALTER G. LATHROP

This ninth volume of *International Maritime Boundaries* provides reports on maritime delimitations completed or publicized subsequent to the closing of Volume VIII in 2019, and it updates past reports where necessary. The country-by-country index at the back of this volume provides a complete listing of all agreements reported in the nine volumes of this series with updated entry into force dates and United Nations Treaty Series registration numbers. Several newly agreed maritime boundaries did not make the deadline for this volume, but reports covering those agreements are in preparation and will be published at the next opportunity. The reporting format remains the same as in previous volumes; however, some flexibility in form has been allowed for reports on tripoint agreements and second-generation agreements related to the sharing of straddling hydrocarbon resources.

Since its launch in 2012, *International Maritime Boundaries Online* has provided subscribers with a new set of digital maritime boundary reports toward the end of each calendar year. In essence this ninth volume is a compilation of the annual online updates from 2020, 2021, 2022, 2023, and 2024, with modifications to entry into force and publication information where that has become available in the interim.

This volume benefits from the efforts of authors who have been involved in the project for many years, including Erik Franckx, since the inception; Rolf Einar Fife, Irini Papanicolopulu, and Clive Schofield, beginning with Volume VI; Martin Pratt and David P. Riesenberg, beginning with Volume VII; and Pierre-Emmanuel Dupont, Najib Messihi, and Alex Oude Elferink, beginning with Volume VIII. In addition to these long-standing contributors, new contributors have been added with the goals of increasing author diversity, maintaining quality reporting, and including individuals with regional expertise or firsthand knowledge of a specific boundary. New authors include Rosemarie Cadogan, Galo Carrera, Perpétua B. Chéry, McClean Hobson, Oliver Lewis, Yuri Parkhomenko, Natalie L. Reid, David Robin, Nawi Ukabiala, Beatrice A. Walton, and Romain Zamour.

A few general observations are in order in light of what is reported in this volume. First, states continue to access third-party dispute settlement mechanisms in order to resolve their maritime boundary disputes, although only one of the boundaries reported in this volume falls into this category.[1] In the case concerning the maritime boundary between Colombia and Nicaragua, first reported in Volume VII, the International Court of Justice concluded that "there is no area of overlapping entitlement to be delimited in the present case."[2] Regrettably, the report on the judgment in the delimitation case between Kenya and Somalia was not completed before deadline. One maritime delimitation case is currently pending before international courts and tribunals – the case between Belize and Guatemala before the International Court of Justice. Second, new agreements continue to emerge from the Pacific and Caribbean regions, many of them completed with the assistance of organizations such as the Commonwealth Secretariat and the Secretariat of the Pacific Community. Nearly half of the reports in this volume come from those two geographic regions. Third, in regions where boundary delimitation has been underway for many decades, such as the Mediterranean and Northwestern Europe, existing boundaries are being augmented, extended into new zones, and adjusted to account for improved hydrographic information. Finally, extraordinary diplomatic efforts have resulted in maritime boundary agreements between adversarial states, including, most notably, the 2022 agreement between Israel and Lebanon.[3] It is hoped that peaceful means of dispute settlement, including in regard to maritime boundary disputes, will continue to prevail.

---

1   *See* Report Number 6-33 addressing the result of the case between Mauritius and Maldives.
2   Question of the Delimitation of the Continental Shelf between Nicaragua and Colombia beyond 200 Nautical Miles from the Nicaragua Coast (Nicaragua v. Colombia), Judgment (13 July 2023), para 91.
3   *See* Report Number 8-26.

Boundary Reports

I

North America

Cuba – United States

Report Number 1-4 (2)

Treaty between the United States of America and the Republic of Cuba on the Delimitation of the Continental Shelf in the Eastern Gulf of Mexico beyond 200 Nautical Miles

Signed: 18 January 2017
Entry into force: Not yet in force, applied provisionally
Published at: US Senate Treaty Doc. 118-1

I SUMMARY

The Treaty between the United States of America and the Republic of Cuba on the Delimitation of the Continental Shelf in the Eastern Gulf of Mexico beyond 200 Nautical Miles (the Treaty, or the 2017 Treaty) delimits, on the basis of equidistance, the parties' respective continental shelf entitlements beyond 200 nautical miles (M) in the eastern Gulf of Mexico. Using a single geodetic line spanning 30.1 M, the Treaty connects the western endpoint of the parties' existing, equidistance-based maritime boundary for areas within 200 M (provisionally applied since 1977) to an equidistant tripoint where the extended continental shelves[1] of the United States, Cuba, and Mexico meet in the eastern Gulf of Mexico. In addition, the Treaty establishes a regime for bilateral cooperation regarding possible transboundary hydrocarbon reservoirs beyond 200 M, including a moratorium through 2026 on permitting or authorizing drilling or exploitation activities in a 1.4-M-wide buffer zone on either side of the new boundary.

The Treaty was concluded following several rounds of negotiations hosted by the government of Mexico in 2016, in conjunction with simultaneous negotiations on US-Mexico and Cuba – Mexico maritime boundaries in the eastern Gulf of Mexico. These negotiations addressed the only remaining area in the Gulf of Mexico where maritime boundaries had not been agreed.

---

1 The term "extended continental shelf" is used in this report as a term of convenience to refer to areas of continental shelf beyond 200 M from the baselines from which the breadth of the territorial sea is measured.

Coalter G. Lathrop (ed.), International Maritime Boundaries, 5819-5839.
© *The American Society of International Law and Koninklijke Brill BV, Leiden 2025.*

5820 *Report Number 1-4 (2)*

The Treaty was signed on 18 January 2017, and, on the same day, the parties exchanged diplomatic notes effecting an agreement to provisionally apply the Treaty pending its entry into force. The Treaty will enter into force upon ratification by both countries, communicated by note verbale. For the United States, ratification is subject to the advice and consent of the United States Senate. To date, neither side has ratified the Treaty.

II CONSIDERATIONS

1 *Political, Strategic, and Historical Considerations*

Despite having severed diplomatic ties in 1961, Cuba and the United States signed an agreement in 1977 defining the majority of their maritime boundary.[2] That agreement has not entered into force, but it has been provisionally applied since its signature by periodic agreement of the parties.[3] The 1977 agreement, however, concerns only areas within 200 M of shore. Beyond the western end of that boundary is an approximately 18,000 km^2 pocket of high seas in the eastern Gulf of Mexico, sometimes referred to as the "Eastern Gap" or "Eastern Polygon," under which the continental shelves of the United States, Cuba, and Mexico extend.

On 17 December 2014, the United States and Cuba announced that they would restore diplomatic relations. On the same day, recalling that "[t]he United States, Cuba, and Mexico have extended continental shelf in an area within the Gulf of Mexico where the three countries have not yet delimited any boundaries," the United States announced that it was "prepared to invite the governments of Cuba and Mexico to discuss shared maritime boundaries in the Gulf of Mexico."[4] The United States and Cuba reestablished diplomatic relations and reopened their respective embassies on 20 July 2015.[5]

---

2 *See* Report Number 1-4, I IMB 417.
3 *See* Report Number 1-4 (Add. 1), V IMB 3555; Report Number 1-4 (Add. 2), VI IMB 4165; Report Number 1-4 (Add. 3), VII IMB 4607; Report Number 1-4 (Add. 4), VII IMB 4611; Report Number 1-4 (Add. 5), VIII IMB 5395; Report Number 1-4 (Add. 6), VIII IMB 5399.
4 *See* Press Release, White House Office of the Press Secretary, *Fact Sheet: Charting a New Course on Cuba* (17 December 2014), https://obamawhitehouse.archives.gov/the-press-office/2014/12/17/fact-sheet-charting-new-course-cuba.
5 *See, e.g.*, Press Release, US Department of State, Office of the Spokesperson, *Media Note: United States, Cuba, and Mexico: Resolving Maritime Boundaries* (7 July 2016), https://2009-2017.state.gov/r/pa/prs/ps/2016/07/259450.htm.

In 2016, the government of Mexico hosted the United States and Cuba for several rounds of negotiations that developed three bilateral maritime boundary agreements with respect to the continental shelf beyond 200 M in the eastern Gulf of Mexico.[6] The Treaty between the United States and Cuba was signed in Washington on 18 January 2017 by US Acting Assistant Secretary of State for Western Hemisphere Affairs Mari Carmen Aponte, and by Cuba's ambassador to the United States José Ramón Cabañas Rodríguez. The same day, the governments of Cuba and the United States exchanged diplomatic notes to agree that, pending the Treaty's entry into force, its terms would be applied provisionally. Specifically, the two parties agreed that "the terms of the Treaty be applied on a provisional basis for a three-year period, beginning on January 18, 2017, and thereafter provisionally applied for successive three-year periods unless, at least two months prior to the end of a given period, a written notice to terminate provisional application at the end of that period is given by one Party to the other Party or the Parties have agreed on a different period of application on a provisional basis." (Subsequently, in December 2017, the United States and Cuba agreed to provisionally apply their 1977 maritime boundary agreement for synchronized three-year periods under the same terms, rather than the two-year periods that had previously been renewed by exchanges of diplomatic notes each biennium since the 1970s.[7])

2 Legal Regime Considerations

Cuba is a state party to the United Nations Convention on the Law of the Sea (the Convention). The United States is not but considers that many of the Convention's provisions reflect customary international law, including paragraphs 1 through 7 of Article 76.

As the Treaty concerns only areas beyond 200 M from each country, the legal regime of the continental shelf applies. Accordingly, the Treaty refers to the boundary it delimits as a "continental shelf boundary," and Article III of the Treaty, which operationalizes the boundary line described in Article I, pertains to "sovereign rights or jurisdiction over the seabed and subsoil," not the water column. Article VII further provides that the Treaty is without prejudice to the parties' views concerning any other maritime area:

---

6 *See, e.g., id.*
7 *See* Report Number 1-4 (Add. 6), VIII IMB 5399.

"The continental shelf boundary established by this Treaty shall not affect or prejudice in any manner the positions of either Party with respect to the extent of internal waters, of the territorial sea, of the contiguous zone, of the exclusive economic zone, of the high seas, or with respect to sovereign rights or jurisdiction for any other purpose."

The Treaty does not provide for binding dispute settlement. Specifically, Article VI provides instead for consultation: "Upon written request by a Party through diplomatic channels, the Parties shall consult to discuss any issue regarding the interpretation or implementation of this Treaty."

3   *Economic and Environmental Considerations*

To date, there has not been any drilling for hydrocarbons in the eastern Gulf of Mexico beyond 200 M from any country. The last preambular paragraph of the Treaty nevertheless indicates the parties' attention to "the possibility that there could exist petroleum or natural gas reservoirs that extend across the continental shelf boundary, and the need for cooperation and periodic consultation between the Parties in protecting their respective interests in such circumstances."

Accordingly, Articles IV and V of the Treaty create a buffer zone running along the boundary line and extending 1.4 M to each side of it. In this area, the Treaty establishes a special regime with respect to hydrocarbon resources, noting "the possible existence of petroleum or natural gas reservoirs that may extend across the boundary set forth in Article I (hereinafter 'transboundary reservoirs')." Articles IV and V of the 2017 Treaty closely follow the model of the 2000 treaty between the United States and Mexico delimiting the extended continental shelf in the western Gulf of Mexico.[8] The provisions of the 2000 treaty led to the 2012 transboundary hydrocarbon agreement between the United States and Mexico that establishes a cooperative process for managing the maritime boundary region and promotes joint utilization of transboundary reservoirs. The treatment of transboundary hydrocarbons in the 2000 treaty between Mexico and the United States was viewed as a successful model, and the 2017 Treaty between Cuba and the United States repeats its relevant terms almost verbatim.

---

8   *See* Report Number 1-5 (2), IV IMB 2621.

Specifically, Articles IV and V impose a temporary moratorium on authorizing or permitting hydrocarbon drilling or exploitation in this buffer zone (extending through 31 December 2026, or such other date as might be mutually agreed by the parties through an exchange of diplomatic notes), along with certain related obligations regarding information-sharing, consultations and periodic meetings, notifications, and facilitation of requests from the other party to authorize geological and geophysical studies. During the moratorium period, among other provisions regarding information-sharing and cooperation, Article V(1)(b) further obligates the parties to seek to reach agreement for the efficient and equitable exploitation of transboundary hydrocarbon reservoirs. After the expiry of the moratorium period, Article V(2) obligates each party to "inform the other Party of its decisions to lease, license, grant concessions, or otherwise use or make available portions of the [buffer zone] on its side of the boundary for petroleum or natural gas exploration or development and shall also inform the other Party when petroleum or natural gas resources are to commence production," and also to "ensure that entities it authorizes to undertake activities within the Area shall observe the terms of this Treaty."

4 Geographic Considerations

The Preamble of the Treaty expressly clarifies the parties' desire to establish the continental shelf boundary "on the basis of equidistance." The equidistance-based boundary is defined in Article I and consists of a geodetic line connecting two points. As set out in Article II, the western endpoint "represents a 'tri-point,' equidistant from the United States, the Republic of Cuba, and a third State" (*i.e.*, Mexico). (The Cuba – Mexico and Mexico – US continental shelf boundaries that were negotiated simultaneously likewise terminate at this tripoint.) No separate trilateral agreement to specify the tripoint was deemed necessary; rather, the coordinates of this tripoint are the same in each of the bilateral treaties developed during the negotiations hosted by Mexico, and, for additional clarity, it is expressly described in each of the treaties as a tripoint.

The equidistant tripoint was measured from one contributing basepoint in each of Cuba and the United States (as well as a point in Mexico), and each of those contributing basepoints could serve as part of a normal baseline for measuring the breadth of the territorial sea. On the US side, this point is located slightly more than one nautical mile southwest of Loggerhead

Key, Florida, on a low-tide elevation depicted on an official, large-scale navigational chart published by the US National Oceanic and Atmospheric Administration (NOAA).[9] On the Cuban side, the contributing point is on a feature called Quebrado de Buenavista, which is above low tide and near the western coast of Cuba and reflected on an official Cuban chart.

The western terminus of the parties' 1977 maritime boundary was also calculated on the basis of equidistance,[10] and the parties agreed to complete the equidistance boundary beyond 200 M by connecting the tripoint described above to the western terminus of the 1977 boundary line using a single geodetic line.

5 Islands, Rocks, Reefs, and Low-tide Elevations Considerations

In determining the equidistance boundary line, the parties considered that both contributing basepoints were to be given full effect. In both cases, these basepoints appear to be on low-tide elevations located within 12 M of land above high tide – in Cuba's case, its mainland as well as other islands, and in the case of the United States, Loggerhead Key and other islands.

6 Baseline Considerations

The United States measures its maritime zones from the normal baseline. Cuba has claimed a system of straight baselines, which the United States does not recognize, objecting that the baselines do not comply with the specific requirements under international law governing where straight baselines may be drawn.[11] Quebrado de Buenavista, the feature used for the basepoint on the Cuban side that contributes to the equidistance line, is also used as turning point number 10 in Cuba's claimed system of straight baselines.[12]

---

9 See NOAA-NOS Chart 11438 (14th ed., Nov. 2012), available at https://www.historicalcharts.noaa.gov/image.php?filename=11438-11-2012.

10 See US Department of State, Bureau of Oceans and International Environmental and Scientific Affairs, Maritime Boundary Cuba – United States, Limits in the Seas, No.110 (21 February 1990), available at https://www.state.gov/wp-content/uploads/2019/12/LIS-110.pdf.

11 See, e.g., US Department of State, Bureau of Oceans and International Environmental and Scientific Affairs, Straight Baselines: Cuba, Limits in the Seas, No. 76 (28 October 1977), available at https://www.state.gov/wp-content/uploads/2019/11/LIS-76.pdf.

12 See Certification of 6 November 1985 (Cuba), available at http://www.un.org/Depts/los/LEGISLATIONANDTREATIES/PDFFILES/CUB_1985_Certification.pdf.

Cuba's claimed straight baselines are not relevant to this boundary, however. Their lawfulness, and the US objection to them, concern a separate question (governed by international law as reflected in Article 7 of the Convention) that is not affected by the use of this point for measuring equidistance for the maritime boundary (governed by international law as reflected in Article 83 of the Convention). Moreover, Quebrado de Buenavista, which is depicted on the relevant Cuban chart by the aid to navigation installed on top of it, is at least a low-tide elevation and is located within 12 M of the coast of mainland Cuba; as such it would serve as a point from which the breadth of the territorial sea could be measured under a system of normal baselines, consistent with international law as reflected in Article 13 of the Convention.[13] In addition, as noted above, Article VII of the Treaty expressly preserves each party's position with respect to the extent of maritime zones.

7   Geological and Geomorphological Considerations

In the Preamble of the Treaty, the parties affirmed "that the provisions of international law pertaining to the seaward extent of the continental shelf are reflected in Article 76 of the 1982 United Nations Convention on the Law of the Sea." Given that the United States is not a party to the Convention, this preambular provision indicates that both countries recognize the relevant parts of Article 76 as reflecting customary international law for delineating the outer limits of a coastal state's continental shelf. (Elsewhere, the United States has long confirmed that it considers paragraphs 1 through 7 of Article 76 to reflect customary international law.[14])

---

13 *See also Maritime Boundary Cuba – United States*, Limits in the Seas, No.110, *supra* note 10 at 3 (noting that "[t]he western portion of the [1977] boundary was not influenced by Cuba's straight baselines").

14 *See, e.g.*, The Treaties with the Republic of Cuba and the Government of the United Mexican States on the Delimitation of Maritime Boundaries, US-Mex. and US-Cuba, S. Treaty Doc. No. 118-1 (2023), https://www.congress.gov/118/cdoc/tdoc1/CDOC-118tdoc1.pdf at VI; US Department of State, Executive Summary: The Outer Limits of the Extended Continental Shelf of the United States of America, 2023, *available at* https://www.state.gov/wp-content/uploads/2023/12/ECS_Executive_Summary.pdf at 6 ("The Convention generally reflects customary international law binding on all countries, including the provisions in Article 76 pertaining to delineating the outer limits of the continental shelf. In this regard, the United States has delineated the outer limits of its extended continental shelf consistent with Article 76. A country's continental shelf rights are inherent under international law, including as reflected in Article 77 of the Convention, and *exist ipso facto and ab initio*." (emphasis in original)); US Department

5826 *Report Number 1-4 (2)*

In 2009, Cuba submitted information to the Commission on the Limits of the Continental Shelf under Article 76(8) of the Convention.[15] Perhaps in anticipation of future negotiations with the United States on the basis of equidistance, the northern limit of Cuba's continental shelf delineation described in this submission generally approximates the boundary line ultimately reflected in this Treaty. Also in the submission, as well as in a subsequent presentation to the Commission, Cuba expressly recognized that the submission "does not prejudice the final delimitation of the continental shelf."[16] Following Cuba's submission, the United States provided a diplomatic note to the UN noting the potential overlap between the continental shelves of the United States and Cuba in this area, recalling that the 1982 Convention and the Commission's rules of procedure provide that actions of the Commission shall not prejudice matters relating to delimitation of maritime boundaries, and confirming that the United States had no objection to the Commission considering the submission and making recommendations "to the extent that such recommendations are without prejudice to the establishment of the outer limits of its continental shelf by the United States, or to any final delimitation of the continental shelf concluded subsequently in this area between Cuba and the United States."[17] Mexico transmitted a similar diplomatic note with respect to its own continental shelf entitlement in response to Cuba's submission.[18] To date, Cuba's submission remains in the Commission's queue, and while the Commission has begun active

---

of State, Office of the Legal Adviser, Cumulative Digest of U.S. Practice in International Law 1981–1988, (1993) at 1878–79, *citing* Memorandum from Assistant Secretary John D. Negroponte to Deputy Legal Adviser Elizabeth Verville, 17 November 1987 (stating that "the delimitation provisions of Article 76 ... reflect customary international law and that the United States will use these rules when delimiting its continental shelf and in evaluating the continental shelf claims of other countries" and variously referring to paragraphs 1 to 7 of Article 76).

15 Republic of Cuba, Executive Summary: Submission to the Commission on the Limits of the Continental Shelf to Demonstrate the Natural Extension of the Continental Shelf of Cuba Beyond 200 Nautical Miles in the Eastern Sector of the Gulf of Mexico, 1 June 2009, *available at* http://www.un.org/depts/los/clcs_new/submissions_files/cub51_09/cub_2009execsummary.pdf.

16 *Id.*; *see also.* Commission on the Limits of the Continental Shelf, *CLCS/66 – Statement by the Chairperson of the Commission on the Limits of the Continental Shelf on the Progress of Work in the Commission – Twenty-Fifth Session,* 30 April 2010, *available at* https://documents.un.org/doc/undoc/gen/n10/337/97/pdf/n1033797.pdf (hereinafter "CLCS/66") at para. 85.

17 Diplomatic Note from the United States to the UN dated June 30, 2009, *available at* http://www.un.org/depts/los/clcs_new/submissions_files/cub51_09/usa_re_cuba_2009.pdf.

18 Diplomatic Note from Mexico to the UN dated 21 August 2009, *available at* http://www.un.org/depts/los/clcs_new/submissions_files/submission_cub_51_2009.htm.

consideration of it, it has not yet issued its recommendations.[19] (Mexico, too, has made a partial submission to the Commission concerning the eastern Gulf of Mexico, which also remains in the Commission's queue and has not yet led to recommendations.[20]) The United States announced the outer limits of its continental shelf beyond 200 M in December 2023, and in the relevant area of eastern Gulf of Mexico, the US continental shelf limits are defined by geographic coordinates that are identical to those contained in the Treaty.[21]

---

19 *See* CLCS/66, *supra* note 16 at para. 86; Commission on the Limits of the Continental Shelf, *CLCS 60/2 – Progress of Work in the Commission on the Limits of the Continental Shelf,* 21 March 2024, https://documents.un.org/doc/undoc/gen/n24/078/97/pdf/n2407897. pdf; Submissions, through the Secretary-General of United Nations, to the Commission on the Limits of the Continental Shelf, pursuant to article 76, paragraph 8 of the United Nations Convention on the Law of the Sea of 10 December 1982, *available at* https:// www.un.org/depts/los/clcs_new/commission_submissions.htm.
   The Commission has not yet begun active consideration of Mexico's submission in this area.
20 Mexico, Executive Summary: A Partial Submission of Data and Information on the Outer Limits of the Continental Shelf of the United Mexican States pursuant to Part VI of and Annex II to the United Nations Convention on the Law of the Sea, 19 December 2011, *available at* http://www.un.org/depts/los/clcs_new/submissions_files/submission_ mex58_2011.htm; Commission on the Limits of the Continental Shelf, *CLCS/74 – Progress of Work in the Commission on the Limits of the Continental Shelf- Statement by the Chairperson – Twenty-Ninth Session,* 30 April 2024, http://daccess-ods.un.org/ access.nsf/Get?Open&DS=CLCS/74&Lang=E at paras. 43-46.
   In 2007, Mexico made a submission to the Commission concerning a similar area of extended continental shelf in the western Gulf of Mexico where Mexico and the United States had agreed on a continental shelf boundary in 2000. The Commission considered the submission and made favorable recommendations in 2009. *See* Mexico, Executive Summary: A Partial Submission of Data and Information on the Outer Limits of the Continental Shelf of the United Mexican States Pursuant to Part VI of and Annex II to the United Nations Convention on the Law of the Sea, December 2007, *available at* https:// www.un.org/depts/los/clcs_new/submissions_files/mex07/part_i_executive_summary. pdf; CLCS, *Recommendations of the Commission on the Limits of the Continental Shelf in Regard to the Submission Made by Mexico in Respect of the Western Polygon in the Gulf of Mexico on 13 December 2007,* adopted on 31 March 2009, *available at* https:// www.un.org/depts/los/clcs_new/submissions_files/mex07/mex_rec.pdf; Commission on the Limits of the Continental Shelf, Progress of Work in the Commission on the Limits of the Continental Shelf- Statement by the Chairperson – Twenty-Third Session, 20 April 2009, https://documents-dds-ny.un.org/doc/UNDOC/GEN/N09/307/58/PDF/N0930758. pdf?OpenElement at paras. 22-26.
21 *See* Press Release, US Department of State, Office of the Spokesperson, *Media Note: Announcement of U.S. Extended Continental Shelf Outer Limits* (19 December 2023), https://www.state.gov/announcement-of-u-s-extended-continental-shelf-outer-limits/; US Department of State, Executive Summary: The Outer Limits of the Extended Continental Shelf of the United States of America, 2023, *available at* https://www.state.gov/ wp-content/uploads/2023/12/ECS_Executive_Summary.pdf at 33-37, 83 ("These outer limits correspond with the continental shelf boundaries set forth in treaties concluded in 2017 between the United States and Cuba and between the United States and Mexico.").

In the course of negotiating the Treaty, the parties shared and discussed scientific and technical information concerning the seabed and subsoil in the Gulf of Mexico and confirmed that each country passed the test of appurtenance, which is reflected in the Scientific and Technical Guidelines of the Commission on the Limits of the Continental Shelf.[22] Thus, they do indeed have an entitlement to extended continental shelf. Indeed, the especially thick sediment throughout the central Gulf of Mexico beyond 200 M leaves no doubt that, under international law as reflected in Article 76, the United States, Mexico, and Cuba are each entitled to continental shelf throughout the entire area on its side of the relevant maritime boundaries. (Thus, while the pocket of high seas overlying this area is sometimes called the "Eastern Gap," there is not any gap between the continental shelves of Cuba, Mexico, and the United States.) This lack of doubt about the three countries' entitlement to extended continental shelf in the relevant areas on each side of the equidistance boundaries removed any need to delay boundary negotiations until such time as the Commission makes its recommendations concerning the submissions of Cuba and Mexico (or of the United States, if in the future it makes a submission to the Commission based on the outer limits it announced in 2023).

8   *Method of Delimitation Considerations*

As described above, the delimitation was based on equidistance. All other maritime boundaries in the Gulf of Mexico had been resolved previously, and were also delimited on the basis of equidistance.

9   *Technical Considerations*

Article II of the 2017 Treaty clarifies that the World Geodetic System 1984 (WGS84) is "the geodetic and computational base used to determine the boundary set forth in Article I." Because the 2017 Treaty used as its eastern endpoint the western endpoint of the boundary delimited in the parties'

---

22 Commission on the Limits of the Continental Shelf, *CLCS/11 – Scientific and Technical Guidelines, available at* https://www.un.org/depts/los/clcs_new/commission_guidelines. htm at Section 2.2.

1977 agreement, a datum transformation was needed to reflect the 1977 western endpoint in WGS84. As described in Article II of the 2017 Treaty, "[b]oundary point number 1 is boundary point 27 (25° 12′ 25″ N, 86° 33′ 12″ W) of the 1977 Maritime Boundary Agreement. This point, which was originally determined with reference to the North American Datum 1927 and the Clarke 1866 ellipsoid, has been transformed to the WGS84 datum."

10   *Other Considerations*

The Treaty includes two annexes, consisting of maps that are expressly "for the purpose of illustration only." The first annex is a small-scale depiction of the boundary in relation both to the relevant coastlines of the two countries and to the 1977 boundary. The second annex is a larger-scale depiction of the boundary showing, in addition, the buffer zone that is 1.4 M wide on either side of the boundary.

III   CONCLUSIONS

This bilateral agreement between the United States and Cuba was developed through a diplomatic process in which the countries met together simultaneously with Mexico to resolve three outstanding maritime boundaries in the same general area, facilitating trilateral collaboration on the tripoint and other issues of common concern while allowing bilateral discussions and negotiations for other issues. The success in resolving these last outstanding maritime boundaries in the Gulf of Mexico was significantly aided by the existence of precedents among the three countries for maritime boundaries and transboundary frameworks elsewhere in the Gulf of Mexico, especially with respect to the use of an equidistance methodology and the regime for possible transboundary hydrocarbon reservoirs. The process was also aided by the lack of doubt about each country's legal entitlement to extended continental shelf in the entirety of its relevant area, especially given the thickness of the sediment throughout, notwithstanding that the Commission on the Limits of the Continental Shelf has yet to offer any recommendations with respect to the eastern Gulf of Mexico.

As provided in Article IX, the Treaty "shall enter into force on the date of the last note verbale in which the Parties indicate that their internal legal requirements have been satisfied." To date, neither side has provided such a note to the other. In the United States, the Treaty was transmitted in December 2023 to the US Senate for its advice and consent to ratification, where it remains pending.[23]

In the meantime, pursuant to the contemporaneous exchange of notes, the provisions of the Treaty are being provisionally applied, like those of the 1977 agreement between the United States and Cuba concerning the maritime boundary within 200 M of their coasts. The moratorium period in Article IV ends 31 December 2026 unless the parties mutually agree to modify it through an exchange of diplomatic notes. By spurring closer coordination between the relevant regulatory authorities in each country, these provisions could form a basis for closer cooperation and sharing best practices concerning the safety and efficiency of resource development, as well as environmental protection.[24]

IV   RELATED LAW IN FORCE

A   *Law of the Sea Conventions*

United States: Party to all four 1958 Geneva Conventions; recognizes many provisions of the 1982 United Nations Convention on the Law of the Sea Convention as reflecting customary international law, including paragraphs 1 through 7 of Article 76.

Cuba: Party to UNCLOS (signed 10 December 1982, ratified 15 August 1984).

B   *Maritime Jurisdiction Claimed at the Time of Signature*

United States: From normal baselines, 12 M territorial sea; 24 M contiguous zone; 200 M EEZ; continental shelf, including beyond 200 M.

---

23   *See* US Senate Treaty Doc. 118-1, *supra* note 14; *see also* Press Release, U.S. Department of State, Office of the Spokesperson, *Media Note: United States and Cuba Sign Maritime Boundary Treaty* (18 January 2017), *available at* https://2009-2017.state.gov/r/pa/prs/ps/2017/01/267117.htm ("Before entry into force, the treaty will warrant the advice and consent of the US Senate.").

24   *See, e.g.*, US Senate Treaty Doc. 118-1, *supra* note 14 at IX.

Cuba: 12 M territorial sea; 24 M contiguous zone; 200 M EEZ; continental shelf (CLCS submission concerning the Eastern Polygon region on 1 June 2009).

C Maritime Jurisdiction Claimed Subsequent to Signature

United States: No change, though as noted above, on 19 December 2023, the United States released the geographic coordinates defining the outer limits of its continental shelf in areas beyond 200 M, including in the relevant area of the Gulf of Mexico in a manner that matches the Treaty.[25]
Cuba: No change.

Prepared by Oliver Lewis

---

25 *See supra* note 21 and accompanying text.

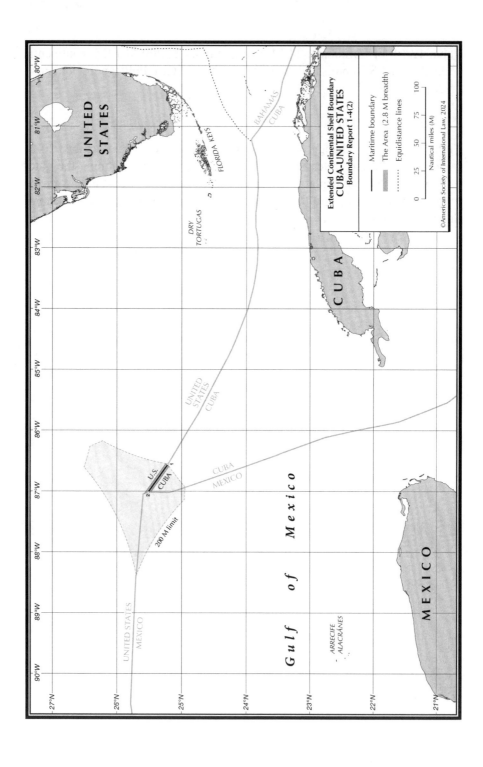

Treaty between the United States of America and the Republic of Cuba on the Delimitation of the Continental Shelf in the Eastern Gulf of Mexico beyond 200 Nautical Miles

The United States of America and the Republic of Cuba (hereinafter "the Parties");

Recalling the Maritime Boundary Agreement between the United States of America and the Republic of Cuba, signed on December 16, 1977 (the "1977 Maritime Boundary Agreement");

Desiring to establish, in accordance with international law, and on the basis of equidistance, the continental shelf boundary between the United States of America and the Republic of Cuba in the Eastern Gulf of Mexico beyond 200 nautical miles from the baselines from which the breadth of the territorial sea is measured;

Affirming that the provisions of international law pertaining to the seaward extent of the continental shelf are reflected in Article 76 of the 1982 United Nations Convention on the Law of the Sea; and

Taking into account the possibility that there could exist petroleum or natural gas reservoirs that extend across the continental shelf boundary, and the need for cooperation and periodic consultation between the Parties in protecting their respective interests in such circumstances;

Have agreed as follows:

Article I

The continental shelf boundary between the United States of America and the Republic of Cuba in the Eastern Gulf of Mexico beyond 200 nautical miles from the baselines from which the breadth of the territorial sea is measured shall be determined by geodetic lines connecting the following coordinates:

1. 25° 12′ 26.28″ N   86° 33′ 11.91″ W
2. 25° 29′ 16.44″ N   87° 00′ 49.44″ W

Article II

1.   The geodetic and computational base used to determine the boundary set forth in Article I is the World Geodetic System 1984 ("WGS84").

2.   For purposes of Article I:

   (a)   Boundary point number 1 is boundary point 27 (25° 12' 25" N, 86° 33' 12" W) of the 1977 Maritime Boundary Agreement. This point, which was originally determined with reference to the North American Datum 1927 and the Clarke 1866 ellipsoid, has been transformed to the WGS84 datum.
   (b)   Boundary point number 2 represents a "tri-point," equidistant from the United States, the Republic of Cuba, and a third State.

3.   For the purpose of illustration only, the boundary line in Article I is shown in Annex 1 to this Treaty.

Article III

South of the continental shelf boundary set forth in Article I, the United States of America shall not, and north of said boundary, the Republic of Cuba shall not, claim or exercise for any purpose sovereign rights or jurisdiction over the seabed and subsoil.

Article IV

1.   Due to the possible existence of petroleum or natural gas reservoirs that may extend across the boundary set forth in Article I (hereinafter referred to as "transboundary reservoirs"), the Parties, during a period ending December 31, 2026, shall not authorize or permit petroleum or natural gas drilling or exploitation of the continental shelf within one and four-tenths (1.4) nautical miles on each side of the boundary set forth in Article I. (This two and eight-tenths (2.8) nautical mile area hereinafter shall be referred to as the "Area".)

2.   For the purpose of illustration only, the Area set forth in paragraph 1 is shown in Annex 2 to this Treaty.

3. The Parties, by mutual agreement through an exchange of diplomatic notes, may modify the period set forth in paragraph 1.

4. With respect to the Area on its side of the boundary (1.4 nautical miles), each Party, in accordance with its national laws and regulations, shall facilitate requests from the other Party to authorize geological and geophysical studies to help determine the possible presence and distribution of transboundary reservoirs.

5. With respect to the Area in its entirety (2.8 nautical miles), each Party, in accordance with its national laws and regulations, shall share geological and geophysical information in its possession in order to determine the possible existence and location of transboundary reservoirs.

6. If a Party has knowledge of the existence or possible existence of a transboundary reservoir in the Area, it shall notify the other Party.

Article V

1. With respect to the Area in its entirety (2.8 nautical miles), during the period set forth in paragraph 1 of Article IV:

(a) as geological and geophysical information is generated that facilitates the Parties' knowledge about the possible existence of transboundary reservoirs, including notifications by Parties, in accordance with paragraphs 5 and 6 of Article IV, the Parties shall meet at least once per year for the purpose of identifying, locating and determining the geological and geophysical characteristics of such reservoirs;

(b) the Parties shall seek to reach agreement for the efficient and equitable exploitation of such transboundary reservoirs; and

(c) the Parties shall, within sixty days of receipt of a written request by a Party through diplomatic channels, consult to discuss matters related to possible transboundary reservoirs.

2. With respect to the Area in its entirety (2.8 nautical miles), following the expiry of the period set forth in paragraph 1 of Article IV:

(a) a Party shall inform the other Party of its decisions to lease, license, grant concessions, or otherwise use or make available portions of the Area on its side of the boundary for petroleum or natural gas exploration or development and shall also inform the other Party when petroleum or natural gas resources are to commence production; and

(b) a Party shall ensure that entities it authorizes to undertake activities within the Area shall observe the terms of this Treaty.

Article VI

Upon written request by a Party through diplomatic channels, the Parties shall consult to discuss any issue regarding the interpretation or implementation of this Treaty.

Article VII

The continental shelf boundary established by this Treaty shall not affect or prejudice in any manner the positions of either Party with respect to the extent of internal waters, of the territorial sea, of the contiguous zone, of the exclusive economic zone, of the high seas, or with respect to sovereign rights or jurisdiction for any other purpose.

Article VIII

Any dispute concerning the interpretation or application of this Treaty shall be resolved by negotiation or other peaceful means as may be agreed upon by the Parties.

Article IX

This Treaty shall enter into force on the date of the last note verbale in which the Parties indicate that their internal legal requirements have been satisfied.

IN WITNESS WHEREOF, the undersigned, having been duly authorized by their respective Governments, have signed this Treaty.

DONE at Washington, this 18th day of January, 2017, in duplicate, in the English and Spanish languages, both texts being equally authentic.

FOR THE UNITED STATES   FOR THE REPUBLIC
OF AMERICA: OF CUBA:
(signed)   *(signed)*

5838 *Report Number 1-4 (2)*

Agreement between the United States of America and Cuba on Provisional Application of the Treaty of January 18, 2017

Effected by Exchange of Notes at Washington and Havana
January 18, 2017

Note No. 18/08 from Department of State of the United States to Ministry of Foreign Affairs of the Republic of Cuba

No. 18/08

The Department of State presents its compliments to the Ministry of Foreign Affairs of the Republic of Cuba and refers to the Treaty between the United States of America and the Republic of Cuba on the Delimitation of the Continental Shelf in the Eastern Gulf of Mexico beyond 200 Nautical Miles, signed on January 18, 2017 (the Treaty). On behalf of the United States of America, the Department proposes that the terms of the Treaty be applied on a provisional basis for a three-year period, beginning on January 18, 2017, and thereafter provisionally applied for successive three-year periods unless, at least two months prior to the end of a given period, a written notice to terminate provisional application at the end of that period is given by one Party to the other Party or the Parties have agreed on a different period of application on a provisional basis. In any event, the period of provisional application shall terminate when the Treaty enters into force.

If this proposal is acceptable to the Republic of Cuba, the Department of State proposes that this note and the affirmative reply from the Ministry of Foreign Affairs of the Republic of Cuba shall constitute an Agreement between the United States and the Republic of Cuba, which shall enter into force on the date of the reply.

The Department avails itself of this opportunity to renew to the Ministry of Foreign Affairs of the Republic of Cuba the assurances of its highest consideration.

Department of State, [*initialed*]
Washington, January 18, 2017.

Note No. 136 from Ministry of Foreign Affairs of the Republic of Cuba to Department of State of the United States

Republic of Cuba
Ministry of Foreign Affairs

Note Verbale No. 136

The Ministry of Foreign Affairs presents its compliments to the Department of State of the United States of America and has the honor to refer to Department note No. 18/08 of January 18, 2017, regarding the Treaty Between the United States of America and the Republic of Cuba on the Delimitation of the Continental Shelf in the Eastern Gulf of Mexico beyond 200 Nautical Miles, signed on January 18, 2017 (the Treaty), which reads as follows:

> [The Spanish translation of Department Note No. 18/08 agrees in all respects with the original English text.]

The Ministry of Foreign Affairs, on behalf of the Republic of Cuba, is pleased to inform the Department of State of the United States that the proposal set forth in Note No. 18/08 of January 18, 2017 is acceptable to the Republic of Cuba, and to confirm that this note and the note from the Department of State shall constitute an agreement between the Republic of Cuba and the United States of America, which shall enter into force on the date of this note.

[Complimentary close]
[Initialed]

Havana, January 18, 2017

United States Department of State

Mexico – United States

Report Number 1-5 (4)

Treaty between the Government of the United Mexican States and the Government of the United States of America on the Delimitation of the Maritime Boundary in the Eastern Gulf of Mexico

Signed: 18 January 2017
Entry into force: Not yet in force
Published at: US Senate Treaty Doc. 118-1

I SUMMARY

The Treaty between the Government of the United Mexican States and the Government of the United States on the Delimitation of the Maritime Boundary in the Eastern Gulf of Mexico (the Treaty, or the 2017 Treaty) delimits, on the basis of equidistance, the parties' respective continental shelf entitlements beyond 200 nautical miles (M) in the eastern Gulf of Mexico. Using a series of geodetic lines connecting seven points defined by geodetic coordinates (and spanning approximately 79 M), the Treaty connects the eastern endpoint of the parties' existing, equidistance-based maritime boundary for areas within 200 M to an equidistant tripoint where the extended continental shelves of the United States, Mexico, and Cuba meet in the eastern Gulf of Mexico.[1]

The Treaty was concluded following several rounds of negotiations hosted by the government of Mexico in 2016, in conjunction with simultaneous negotiations on bilateral US-Cuba and Mexico-Cuba maritime boundary agreements for the eastern Gulf of Mexico. These negotiations addressed the only remaining area in the Gulf of Mexico where maritime boundaries had not been agreed. The Treaty was signed on 18 January 2017 and will enter into force thirty days after the parties exchange instruments of ratification. Under both Mexican and US law, there are requirements for legislative approval

---

1   The term "extended continental shelf" is used in this report as a term of convenience to refer to areas of continental shelf beyond 200 M from the baselines from which the breadth of the territorial sea is measured.

Coalter G. Lathrop (ed.), International Maritime Boundaries, 5841-5857.
© *The American Society of International Law and Koninklijke Brill BV, Leiden 2025.*

before ratification; the Mexican Senate approved the Treaty on 24 April 2018,[2] and it was transmitted to the US Senate for its advice and consent on 18 December 2023.[3] To date, the Treaty has not entered into force.

II CONSIDERATIONS

1 Political, Strategic, and Historical Considerations

Mexico and the United States have three previous agreements that establish their maritime boundaries in the Gulf of Mexico. In 1970, Mexico and the United States concluded a treaty delimiting their maritime boundaries out to 12 M from their baselines, on the basis of equidistance.[4] In 1978, the two countries concluded another treaty to delimit their maritime boundaries between 12 and 200 M, again on the basis of equidistance.[5] In the Gulf of Mexico, there are two enclaves of high seas beyond the outer limits of the 200 M exclusive economic zones of the coastal states under which extend the continental shelves of Mexico, the United States, and, in the eastern enclave, Cuba.[6] In 2000, Mexico and the United States delimited an equidistance-based boundary for the extended continental shelf in the western enclave of the Gulf of Mexico,[7] leaving the extended continental shelf boundaries in the eastern enclave of the Gulf of Mexico as the region of their last unresolved maritime boundary.

On 17 December 2014, recalling that "[t]he United States, Cuba, and Mexico have extended continental shelf in an area within the Gulf of Mexico where the three countries have not yet delimited any boundaries," the United

---

2   Tratado Entre el Gobierno de Los Estados Unidos Mexicanos y el Gobierno de Los Estados Unidos de Américe Sobre la Delimitación de la Frontera Marítima en la Región Oriental del Golfo de México, Gaceta del Senado 26-04-2018, (Mex.), https://www.senado.gob.mx/65/gaceta_del_senado/documento/80700.

3   *See* The Treaties with the Republic of Cuba and the Government of the United Mexican States on the Delimitation of Maritime Boundaries, US-Mexico and US-Cuba, S. Treaty Doc. No. 118-1 (2023), https://www.congress.gov/118/cdoc/tdoc1/CDOC-118tdoc1.pdf; *see also* Press Release, White House Office of the Press Secretary, *Message to the Senate Transmitting Two Maritime Treaties* (18 December 2023), https://www.whitehouse.gov/briefing-room/presidential-actions/2023/12/18/message-to-the-senate-transmitting-two-maritime-treaties/.

4   *See* Report Number 1-5, I IMB 427.

5   *See* Report Number 1-5, I IMB 427.

6   These pockets of high seas are sometimes referred to as the "Western Gap" and the "Eastern Gap," or "Western Polygon" and "Eastern Polygon".

7   *See* Report Number 1-5 (2), IV IMB 2621.

States announced that it was "prepared to invite the governments of Cuba and Mexico to discuss shared maritime boundaries in the Gulf of Mexico."[8]

In 2016, the government of Mexico hosted the United States and Cuba for several rounds of negotiations that developed three bilateral maritime boundary agreements with respect to the continental shelf beyond 200 M in the eastern Gulf of Mexico.[9] The Treaty was signed on 18 January 2017 in Washington, DC, by the US Acting Assistant Secretary of State for Western Hemisphere Affairs, Mari Carmen Aponte, and by Mexico's ambassador to the United States, Carlos Manuel Sada Solana.[10]

2   Legal Regime Considerations

Mexico is a state party to the United Nations Convention on the Law of the Sea (the Convention). The United States is not but considers that many of the Convention's provisions reflect customary international law, including paragraphs 1 through 7 of Article 76.

As the Treaty is focused only on areas beyond 200 M from each country, the legal regime of the continental shelf applies. Accordingly, the Treaty refers to the boundary it delimits as a "continental shelf boundary," and

---

8   *See* Press Release, White House office of the Press Secretary, *Fact Sheet: Charting a New Course on Cuba* (17 December 2014), https://obamawhitehouse.archives.gov/the-press-office/2014/12/17/fact-sheet-charting-new-course-cuba.

9   *See* Press Release, US Department of State, Office of the Spokesperson, *Media Note: United States, Cuba, and Mexico: Resolving Maritime Boundaries* (7 July 2016), https://2009-2017.state.gov/r/pa/prs/ps/2016/07/259450.htm; *see also* Press Release, Secretaría de Relaciones Exteriores, *Communicado No. 301: Cuba, Estados Unidos y México, celebraron ronda de consultas para la delimitación de la plataforma continental en el Golfo de México* (7 July 2016), https://www.gob.mx/sre/prensa/cuba-estados-unidos-y-mexico-celebraron-la-primera-ronda-de-consultas-para-la-delimitacion-de-la-plataforma-continental-en-el-golfo-de-mexico?idiom=es; Press Release, Secretaría de Relaciones Exteriores, *Communicado No. 432: Segunda ronda de consultas entre Cuba, Estados Unidos de América y México para la delimitación de la plataforma continental* (30 September 2016), https://www.gob.mx/sre/prensa/segunda-ronda-de-consultas-entre-cuba-estados-unidos-de-america-y-mexico-para-la-delimitacion-de-la-plataforma-continental-mas-alla-de-las-doscientas-millas-nauticas-en-el-golfo-de-mexico.

10 Press Release, Secretaría de Relaciones Exteriores, *Memoria Documental: Tratado de Delimitación entre los Estados Unidos Mexicanos y la República de Cuba sobre la Delimitación de la plataforma continental en el Polígono Oriental del Golfo de México más allá de las 200 millas náuticas y Tratado entre el Gobierno de los Estados Unidos Mexicanos y el Gobierno de los Estados Unidos de América sobre la Delimitación de la Frontera Marítima en la Región Oriental del Golfo de México* (2018), https://www.gob.mx/cms/uploads/attachment/file/426907/MD_Tratados_delimitaci_n_Golfo_de_M_xico.pdf.

Article III of the Treaty, the primary article which operationalizes the boundary described in Article I, pertains to "sovereign rights or jurisdiction over the seabed and subsoil," not the water column.

Nevertheless, Article IV clarifies that, to the extent that any part of the boundary ever falls within 200 M of the coastal baselines, the boundary also applies with respect to sovereign rights or jurisdiction over the "waters," in addition to the seabed and subsoil. Both Mexico and the United States use the normal baseline along their relevant coastal areas, so this provision serves to future-proof the treaty line in case ambulatory coastlines someday bring any part of the new boundary within 200 M, such that for those areas it would become an all-purpose boundary applicable to exclusive economic zones as well as the continental shelf. Indeed, where the new boundary connects to the endpoint of the 1978 boundary, it may already fall slightly within 200 M of shore owing to coastal changes or improved technical calculations since 1978. Article IV is the only provision of the 2017 Treaty that also, by its terms, applies with respect to the boundary set forth in the parties' 2000 treaty regarding the western Gulf of Mexico. While problems in the absence of Article IV may not have been likely as a practical matter (and there is no indication that they have arisen with respect to the 2000 boundary), such a provision will help avoid ambiguity. It also indicates careful attention by the parties to both the legal and technical considerations relevant to the junction of their 1978 all-purpose (exclusive economic zone and continental shelf) boundary with a boundary that applies to the extended continental shelf.

Article VII provides that the Treaty is without prejudice to the parties' views concerning any other maritime area: "The continental shelf boundary established by this Treaty shall not affect or prejudice in any manner the positions of either Party with respect to the extent of internal waters, of the territorial sea, of the high seas or of sovereign rights or jurisdiction for any other purpose."

The Treaty does not provide for binding dispute settlement. Specifically, Article VI provides instead for consultation: "Upon written request by a Party through diplomatic channels, the Parties shall consult to discuss any issue regarding the interpretation or implementation of this Treaty."

3   *Economic and Environmental Considerations*

The Preamble of the Treaty indicates that the parties were "bearing in mind the importance of cooperation to protect the marine environment, including with respect to pollution contingency plans and areas in the Gulf of Mexico beyond 200 nautical miles from shore."

The parties' 2000 treaty delimiting the extended continental shelf boundary in the western Gulf of Mexico created a buffer zone running along the boundary and a moratorium and related provisions regarding possible transboundary hydrocarbon reservoirs. As discussed in an earlier report in this series, "[t]he intent of the moratorium [in the 2000 treaty] . . . was to provide a window for the negotiation and entry into force of an agreement to address the exploitation of transboundary resources."[11] Indeed, the parties ultimately agreed to, and the moratorium they originally imposed was terminated by, the 2012 transboundary hydrocarbon agreement between Mexico and the United States that establishes a cooperative process for managing the maritime boundary region and promotes joint utilization of transboundary reservoirs.[12] The provisions of the 2012 transboundary hydrocarbon agreement will apply with respect to the boundary in the 2017 Treaty upon the latter's entry into force, and, therefore, there was no need to include such provisions in the 2017 Treaty.[13]

Specifically, the 2012 transboundary hydrocarbon agreement applies with respect to the "Delimitation Line," which Article 2 of that agreement defines as "the maritime boundaries in the Gulf of Mexico delimited in the 1970 Treaty, the 1978 Treaty on Maritime Boundaries and the 2000 Treaty on the Continental Shelf, *and any future maritime boundary in the Gulf of Mexico delimited between the Parties*, as agreed."[14] Accordingly, Article

---

11 *See* Report Number 1-5 (3), VII IMB 4613, 4616. The mandate to conclude such an agreement during the moratorium period is found in Article V(1)(b) of the 2000 treaty: during the moratorium period "the Parties shall seek to reach agreement for the efficient and equitable exploitation of such transboundary reservoirs."

12 *See* Report Number 1-5 (3), VII IMB 4613. *See also, e.g.*, Press Release, US Department of State, Office of the Spokesperson, *Fact Sheet: U.S.-Mexico Transboundary Hydrocarbons Agreement* (20 February 2012), https://2009-2017.state.gov/r/pa/prs/ps/2012/02/184235. htm. Article 24 of the 2012 agreement, titled "Termination of the Moratorium on Hydrocarbon Activity in the Boundary Area in the Western Gap of the Gulf of Mexico," provides: "Upon entry into force of this Agreement, the period of any moratorium on the authorization or permitting of petroleum or natural gas drilling or exploration of the continental shelf within the boundary "Area" as established by Article 4, paragraph 1, of the 2000 Treaty on the Continental Shelf and extended by any subsequent exchanges of notes shall be terminated."

13 This is in contrast to the simultaneously concluded bilateral agreements between Cuba and the United States and Cuba and Mexico, both of which create buffer zones along the respective continental shelf boundaries. *See* Report Number 1-4 (2), in this volume; Report Number 2-8 (2), in this volume.

14 *See* Report Number 1-5 (3), VII IMB 4613, 4627 (emphasis added).

V of the 2017 Treaty clarifies that "[t]he maritime boundary set forth in Article I will constitute a delimitation line as defined in Article 2 of the 2012 Transboundary Hydrocarbon Reservoirs Agreement, such that the provisions of that Agreement become applicable to the maritime boundary upon entry into force of this Treaty."

4 Geographic Considerations

The Preamble of the Treaty recalls that the maritime boundary agreements signed on 23 November 1970, 4 May 1978, and 9 June 2000, were concluded on the basis of equidistance, and it expressly clarifies the parties' desire to establish the continental shelf boundary "on the basis of equidistance." The equidistance-based boundary is defined in Article I and consists of geodetic lines connecting seven points defined by geodetic coordinates equivalent in the WGS84 and ITRF2008 reference systems. As set out in Article II, the easternmost endpoint "represents a 'tri-point,' equidistant from the United States, the United Mexican States, and a third State" (*i.e.*, Cuba). (The Cuba – Mexico and Cuba – US continental shelf boundaries that were negotiated simultaneously likewise terminate at this tripoint.) No separate trilateral agreement to specify the tripoint was deemed necessary; rather, the coordinates of this tripoint are the same in each of the bilateral treaties developed during the negotiations hosted by Mexico, and for additional clarity it is expressly described in each of the treaties as a tripoint. Article II also clarifies that the westernmost endpoint is the same as the eastern terminus of the parties' 1978 boundary treaty.

The equidistance line between the United States and Mexico was measured from several contributing basepoints along the parties' coasts, each of which as charted could serve as part of a normal baseline for measuring the breadth of the territorial sea. On the US side, these points are located on a low-tide elevation near Loggerhead Reef, Florida, at the edge of a charted feature near South Pass, Louisiana, and at the end of a jetty near Southwest Pass, Louisiana, all as depicted on official, large-scale navigational charts published by the US National Oceanic and Atmospheric Administration (NOAA).[15] On the Mexican side, the contributing points are located on Alacrán, which includes islands and low tide elevations, located north of

---

15 *See* NOAA-NOS Chart 11361 (77th ed., May 2013), https://www.historicalcharts.noaa.gov/image.php?filename=11361-05-2013; NOAA-NOS Chart 11438 (14th ed., Nov. 2012), https://www.historicalcharts.noaa.gov/image.php?filename=11438-11-2012.

the Yucatan Peninsula, as shown on current official charts issued by the Hydrographic Directorate of the Mexican Navy.

5 Islands, Rocks, Reefs, and Low-tide Elevations Considerations

In determining the equidistance boundary, the parties considered that all contributing basepoints were to be given full effect. Specifically, the basepoints on Alacrán and near Loggerhead Reef were given full effect, consistent with their treatment in other maritime boundary agreements between the parties and with Cuba.

6 Baseline Considerations

The United States and Mexico both measure their maritime zones in the Gulf of Mexico from the normal baseline.

7 Geological and Geomorphological Considerations

In 2011, Mexico made a partial submission to the Commission on the Limits of the Continental Shelf concerning its extended continental shelf in the eastern Gulf of Mexico.[16] The northern limit of Mexico's continental shelf delineation in that submission easily encompasses the entirety of the area on Mexico's side of the Mexico – US boundary line subsequently agreed in the 2017 Treaty.

In the submission, as well as in a subsequent presentation to the Commission, Mexico emphasized that its submission does not prejudice the final delimitation of the continental shelf.[17] The United States did not submit a note to the UN in response to Mexico's 2011 submission to the

---

16 Mexico, Executive Summary: A Partial Submission of Data and Information on the Outer Limits of the Continental Shelf of the United Mexican States pursuant to Part VI of and Annex II to the United Nations Convention on the Law of the Sea, 19 December 2011, *available at* http://www.un.org/depts/los/clcs_new/submissions_files/submission_mex58_2011.htm.

17 *Id.; see also* Commission on the Limits of the Continental Shelf, *CLCS/74 – Progress of Work in the Commission on the Limits of the Continental Shelf- Statement by the Chairperson – Twenty-Ninth Session*, 30 April 2024, http://daccess-ods.un.org/access.nsf/Get?Open&DS=CLCS/74&Lang=E at para. 45.

5848 *Report Number 1-5 (4)*

Commission. However, following Cuba's 2009 submission to the Commission regarding its extended continental shelf in the eastern Gulf of Mexico, the United States provided a diplomatic note to the UN noting the potential overlap between the continental shelves of the United States and Cuba in this area, recalling that the Convention and the Commission's rules of procedure provide that actions of the Commission shall not prejudice matters relating to delimitation of maritime boundaries, and confirming that the United States had no objection to the Commission considering the submission and making recommendations "to the extent that such recommendations are without prejudice to the establishment of the outer limits of its continental shelf by the United States, or to any final delimitation of the continental shelf concluded subsequently in this area between Cuba and the United States."[18] (Mexico transmitted a similar diplomatic note with respect to its own continental shelf entitlement in response to Cuba's submission.[19]) Although the US note predated Mexico's submission and addressed only Cuba's submission, Mexico's submission cited both the Cuban submission and the US note as reflecting that all three countries shared "a clear understanding that, in accordance with article 76, paragraph 10, the provisions of article 76 are without prejudice to the question of delimitation of the continental shelf between States with opposite or adjacent coasts in the Gulf of Mexico."[20] To date, Mexico's submission remains in the Commission's queue, and the Commission has not yet addressed it in substance or issued its recommendations.[21] (Cuba's submission also remains in the Commission's

---

18 Diplomatic Note from the United States to the UN dated June 30, 2009, *available at* http://www.un.org/depts/los/clcs_new/submissions_files/cub51_09/usa_re_cuba_2009.pdf.

19 Diplomatic Note from Mexico to the UN dated Aug. 21, 2009, *available at* http://www.un.org/depts/los/clcs_new/submissions_files/submission_cub_51_2009.htm.

20 Mexico Executive Summary (2011), *supra* note 16 at 8.

21 *See* Commission on the Limits of the Continental Shelf, *CLCS/74 – Progress of Work in the Commission on the Limits of the Continental Shelf- Statement by the Chairperson – Twenty-Ninth Session*, 30 April 2024, http://daccess-ods.un.org/access.nsf/Get?Open&DS=CLCS/74&Lang=E at paras. 43-46; *see also* Submissions, through the Secretary-General of United Nations, to the Commission on the Limits of the Continental Shelf, pursuant to article 76, paragraph 8 of the United Nations Convention on the Law of the Sea of 10 December 1982, *available at* https://www.un.org/depts/los/clcs_new/commission_submissions.htm.

In 2007, Mexico made a submission to the Commission concerning a similar area of extended continental shelf in the western Gulf of Mexico, where Mexico and the United States had agreed on a continental shelf boundary in 2000. The Commission considered the submission and made favorable recommendations in 2009. *See* Mexico, Executive Summary: A Partial Submission of Data and Information on the Outer Limits of the Continental Shelf of the United Mexican States Pursuant to Part VI of and Annex II to the United Nations Convention on the Law of the Sea, December 2007, *available at* https://

queue, and while the Commission has begun active consideration of it, it has not yet issued recommendations.[22]) The United States, although not a party to the Convention, has long confirmed that it considers paragraphs 1 through 7 of Article 76 to reflect customary international law.[23] The United States announced the outer limits of its continental shelf beyond 200 M in December 2023, and, in the relevant area of eastern Gulf of Mexico, the US continental shelf limits are defined by geographic coordinates that are identical to those forming the boundary in the 2017 Treaty.[24]

---

www.un.org/depts/los/clcs_new/submissions_files/mex07/part_i_executive_summary. pdf; CLCS, *Recommendations of the Commission on the Limits of the Continental Shelf in Regard to the Submission Made by Mexico in Respect of the Western Polygon in the Gulf of Mexico on 13 December 2007*, adopted on 31 March 2009, *available at* https:// www.un.org/depts/los/clcs_new/submissions_files/mex07/mex_rec.pdf; Commission on the Limits of the Continental Shelf, Progress of Work in the Commission on the Limits of the Continental Shelf- Statement by the Chairperson – Twenty-Third Session, 20 April 2009, https://documents-dds-ny.un.org/doc/UNDOC/GEN/N09/307/58/PDF/N0930758. pdf?OpenElement at paras. 22-26.

22 *See* Commission on the Limits of the Continental Shelf, *CLCS/66 – Statement by the Chairperson of the Commission on the Limits of the Continental Shelf on the Progress of Work in the Commission – Twenty-Fifth Session,* 30 April 2010, para. 86, *available at* https://documents.un.org/doc/undoc/gen/n10/337/97/pdf/n1033797.pdf; Commission on the Limits of the Continental Shelf, *CLCS 60/2 – Progress of Work in the Commission on the Limits of the Continental Shelf,* 21 March 2024, https://documents.un.org/doc/ undoc/gen/n24/078/97/pdf/n2407897.pdf and *Commission on the Limits of Continental Shelf Concludes Its Sixtieth Session,* 11 March 2024, *available at* https://press.un.org/ en/2024/sea2194.doc.htm; *see also* Submissions, through the Secretary-General of United Nations, to the Commission on the Limits of the Continental Shelf, pursuant to article 76, paragraph 8 of the United Nations Convention on the Law of the Sea of 10 December 1982, *available at* https://www.un.org/depts/los/clcs_new/commission_submissions.htm. It has not yet begun active consideration of Mexico's submission in this area.

23 *See, e.g.*, US Senate Treaty Doc. No. 118-1, *supra* note 3 at VI; US Department of State, Executive Summary: The Outer Limits of the Extended Continental Shelf of the United States of America, 2023, *available at* https://www.state.gov/wp-content/ uploads/2023/12/ECS_Executive_Summary.pdf at 6 ("The Convention generally reflects customary international law binding on all countries, including the provisions in Article 76 pertaining to delineating the outer limits of the continental shelf. In this regard, the United States has delineated the outer limits of its extended continental shelf consistent with Article 76. A country's continental shelf rights are inherent under international law, including as reflected in Article 77 of the Convention, and *exist ipso facto and ab initio.*" (emphasis in original)); US Department of State, Office of the Legal Adviser, Cumulative Digest of U.S. Practice in International Law 1981–1988, (1993) at 1878– 79, *citing* Memorandum from Assistant Secretary John D. Negroponte to Deputy Legal Adviser Elizabeth Verville, 17 November 1987 (stating that "the delimitation provisions of Article 76 ... reflect customary international law and that the United States will use these rules when delimiting its continental shelf and in evaluating the continental shelf claims of other countries" and variously referring to paragraphs 1 to 7 of Article 76).

24 *See* Press Release, US Department of State, Office of the Spokesperson, *Media Note: Announcement of U.S. Extended Continental Shelf Outer Limits* (19 December 2023), https://www.state.gov/announcement-of-u-s-extended-continental-shelf-outer-limits/; US

In the course of negotiating the Treaty, the parties shared and discussed scientific and technical information concerning the seabed and subsoil in the Gulf of Mexico and confirmed that each country passed the test of appurtenance, which is reflected in the Scientific and Technical Guidelines of the Commission on the Limits of the Continental Shelf.[25] Thus, they do indeed have an entitlement to extended continental shelf. Mexico's submission to the Commission relies on the formula provided in Article 76(4)(a)(ii) of the Convention (*i.e.*, by reference to fixed points not more than 60 nautical miles from the foot of the continental slope). In any event, the especially thick sediment throughout the central Gulf of Mexico beyond 200 M leaves no doubt that, under international law as reflected in Article 76 (including the alternative formula based on sediment thickness, set forth in paragraph 4(a)(i)), the United States, Mexico, and Cuba are each entitled to continental shelf throughout the entire area on its side of the relevant maritime boundaries. (Thus, while the pocket of high seas overlying this area is sometimes called the "Eastern Gap," there is not any gap between the continental shelves of Cuba, Mexico, and the United States.) This lack of doubt about the three countries' continental shelf entitlements in the relevant areas on each side of the equidistance boundaries removed any need to delay boundary negotiations until such time as the Commission makes its recommendations concerning the submissions of Mexico and Cuba (or of the United States if, in the future, it makes a submission to the Commission based on the outer limits it announced in 2023).

8 *Method of Delimitation Considerations*

As described above, the delimitation was based on equidistance. All the parties' other maritime boundaries in the Gulf of Mexico had been resolved previously, and were also delimited on the basis of equidistance.

Department of State, Executive Summary: The Outer Limits of the Extended Continental Shelf of the United States of America, 2023, *available at* https://www.state.gov/wp-content/uploads/2023/12/ECS_Executive_Summary.pdf at 33-37, 83 ("These outer limits correspond with the continental shelf boundaries set forth in treaties concluded in 2017 between the United States and Cuba and between the United States and Mexico.").

25 Commission on the Limits of the Continental Shelf, *CLCS/11 – Scientific and Technical Guidelines, available at* https://www.un.org/depts/los/clcs_new/commission_guidelines.htm at Section 2.2.

9 Technical Considerations

Article II of the 2017 Treaty clarifies that "[t]he geodetic and computational bases used to determine the boundary set forth in Article I are the World Geodetic System of 1984 ("WGS84") and the International Terrestrial Reference Frame 2008 ("ITRF2008")," and that "[f]or purposes of Article I ... WGS84 and ITRF2008 shall be considered to be identical." Because the 2017 Treaty used as its western endpoint the easternmost endpoint of the boundary delimited in the parties' 1978 agreement, a datum transformation was needed to reflect the 1978 eastern endpoint in WGS84 and ITRF2008. As described in Article II of the 2017 Treaty, "[b]oundary point number 1 is boundary point GM.E-3 (25° 41' 56.52" N., 88° 23' 05.54" W.) of the 1978 Treaty on Maritime Boundaries. This point, which was originally determined with reference to the North American Datum of 1927, has been transformed to the WGS84 and ITRF2008 reference frames."

10 Other Considerations

The Treaty includes an annex consisting of a map that is expressly "for the purpose of illustration only." The map is a small-scale depiction of the new boundary, showing also the parties' 1970, 1978, and 2000 maritime boundaries in the Gulf of Mexico.

III CONCLUSIONS

This bilateral agreement between Mexico and the United States was developed through a diplomatic process in which the countries met together simultaneously with Cuba to resolve three outstanding maritime boundaries in the same general area, facilitating trilateral collaboration on the tripoint and other issues of common concern while allowing bilateral discussions and negotiations for other issues. The success in resolving these last outstanding maritime boundaries in the Gulf of Mexico was significantly aided by the existence of precedents among the three countries for maritime boundaries and transboundary frameworks elsewhere in the Gulf of Mexico, especially with respect to the use of an equidistance methodology and the regime for possible transboundary hydrocarbon reservoirs. The process was also aided by the lack of doubt about each country's legal entitlement to extended continental shelf in the entirety of its relevant area, especially given the thickness of the sediment throughout, notwithstanding that the Commission on the Limits of the Continental Shelf has yet to offer any recommendations with respect to the eastern Gulf of Mexico.

As provided in Article IX, the Treaty will enter into force 30 days after the date on which the parties exchange instruments of ratification. In Mexico, the Senate approved the Treaty on 24 April 2018, and Mexico has completed its internal steps necessary to proceed to ratification. In the United States, on 18 December 2023, the Treaty was transmitted to the US Senate for its advice and consent to ratification, where it remains pending.[26]

IV RELATED LAW IN FORCE

A *Law of the Sea Conventions*

United States: Party to all four 1958 Geneva Conventions; not a party to UNCLOS but recognizes many provisions of the 1982 United Nations Convention on the Law of the Sea Convention as reflecting customary international law, including paragraphs 1 through 7 of Article 76.

Mexico: Party to UNCLOS (signed 10 December 1982, ratified 18 March 1983).

B *Maritime Jurisdiction Claimed at the Time of Signature*

United States: 12 M territorial sea; 24 M contiguous zone; 200 M EEZ; continental shelf, including beyond 200 M.

Mexico: 12 M territorial sea; 24 M contiguous zone; 200 M EEZ; continental shelf (CLCS submission concerning the Western Polygon region on 13 December 2007 and CLCS submission concerning the Eastern Polygon region on 19 December 2011).

C *Maritime Jurisdiction Claimed Subsequent to Signature*

United States: No change, though as noted above, on December 19, 2023, the United States released the geographic coordinates defining the outer limits of its continental shelf in areas beyond 200 M, including in the relevant area of the Gulf of Mexico in a manner that matches the Treaty.[27]

Mexico: No change.

Prepared by Oliver Lewis and Galo Carrera

---

26 *See* US Senate Treaty Doc. No. 118-1, *supra* note 3.
27 *See* US Executive Summary *supra* note 23 and accompanying text.

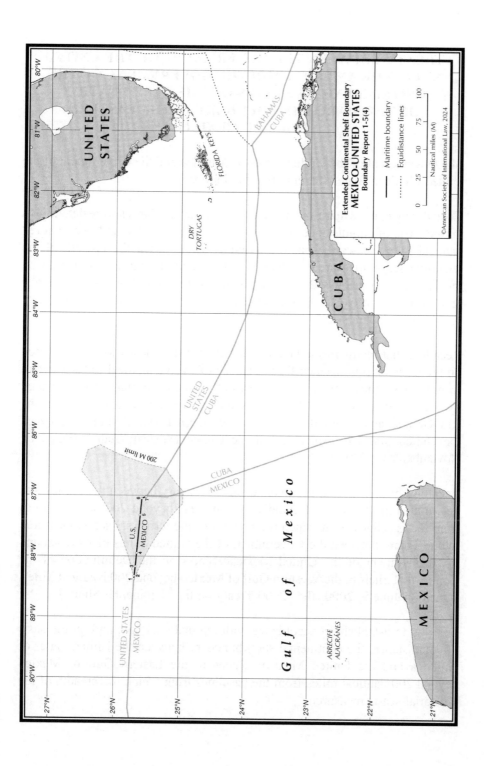

5854   *Report Number 1-5 (4)*

TREATY BETWEEN THE GOVERNMENT OF THE UNITED STATES OF AMERICA AND THE GOVERNMENT OF THE UNITED MEXICAN STATES ON THE DELIMITATION OF THE MARITIME BOUNDARY IN THE EASTERN GULF OF MEXICO

The Government of the United States of America and the Government of the United Mexican States (hereinafter "the Parties");

Considering that the maritime boundaries between the Parties were determined on the basis of equidistance for a distance between twelve and two hundred nautical miles seaward from the baselines from which the breadth of the territorial sea is measured in the Gulf of Mexico and the Pacific Ocean by the Treaty on Maritime Boundaries between the United States of America and the United Mexican States, signed on May 4, 1978 (the "1978 Treaty on Maritime Boundaries");

Recalling that the maritime boundaries between the Parties were determined on the basis of equidistance for a distance of twelve nautical miles seaward from the baselines from which the breadth of the territorial sea is measured by the Treaty to Resolve Pending Boundary Differences and Maintain the Rio Grande and Colorado River as the International Boundary between the United States of America and the United Mexican States, signed on November 23, 1970;

Recalling further that the continental shelf boundary between the Parties was determined on the basis of equidistance in areas beyond 200 nautical miles from the baselines from which the breadth of the territorial sea is measured by the Treaty between the Government of the United States of America and the Government of the United Mexican States on the Delimitation of the Continental Shelf in the Western Gulf of Mexico beyond 200 Nautical Miles, signed on June 9, 2000 (the "2000 Treaty on the Continental Shelf");

Desiring to establish, in accordance with international law, and on the basis of equidistance, the continental shelf boundary between the United States of America and the United Mexican States in the Eastern Gulf of Mexico beyond 200 nautical miles from the baselines from which the breadth of the territorial sea is measured;

Taking into account the possibility that there could exist petroleum or natural gas reservoirs that extend across the continental shelf boundary, and the need for cooperation and periodic consultation between the Parties in protecting their respective interests in such circumstances;

Recalling the Agreement between the United States of America and the United Mexican States Concerning Transboundary Hydrocarbon Reservoirs in the Gulf of Mexico, signed on February 20, 2012 (the "2012 Transboundary Hydrocarbon Reservoirs Agreement");

Bearing in mind the importance of cooperation to protect the marine environment, including with respect to pollution contingency plans and areas in the Gulf of Mexico beyond 200 nautical miles from shore;

Have agreed as follows:

Article I

The continental shelf boundary between the United States of America and the United Mexican States in the Eastern Gulf of Mexico beyond 200 nautical miles from the baselines from which the breadth of the territorial sea is measured shall be determined by geodetic lines connecting the following coordinates:

1. 25° 41' 57.90" N   88° 23' 05.62" W
2. 25° 41' 54.18" N   88° 20' 02.64" W
3. 25° 41' 07.43" N   88° 10' 18.18" W
4. 25° 40' 02.86" N   87° 57' 09.24" W
5. 25° 36' 49.79" N   87° 19' 30.71" W
6. 25° 35' 24.99" N   87° 03' 05.03" W
7. 25° 29' 16.44" N   87° 00' 49.44" W

Article II

1. The geodetic and computational bases used to determine the boundary set forth in Article I are the World Geodetic System of 1984 ("WGS84") and the International Terrestrial Reference Frame 2008 ("ITRF2008").

5856   *Report Number 1-5 (4)*

2.   For purposes of Article I:

(a)   WGS84 and ITRF2008 shall be considered to be identical; and
(b)   Boundary point number 1 is boundary point GM.E-3 (25° 41′ 56.52″N., 88° 23′ 05.54″W.) of the 1978 Treaty on Maritime Boundaries. This point, which was originally determined with reference to the North American Datum of 1927, has been transformed to the WGS84 and ITRF2008 reference frames.
(c)   Boundary point number 7 represents a "tri-point," equidistant from the United States of America, the United Mexican States, and a third State.

3.   For the purpose of illustration only, the boundary line in Article I is drawn on the map that appears as the Annex to this Treaty.

Article III

South of the continental shelf boundary set forth in Article I, the United States of America shall not, and north of said boundary, the United Mexican States shall not claim or exercise for any purpose sovereign rights or jurisdiction over the seabed and subsoil.

Article IV

To the extent that any portion of the boundary lines between the United States of America and the United Mexican States set forth in Article I or in the 2000 Treaty on the Continental Shelf delimits at any time an area within 200 nautical miles of the baselines from which the breadth of the territorial sea is measured, such portion of the boundary line shall apply with respect to sovereign rights and jurisdiction over the seabed, subsoil, and waters.

Article V

The maritime boundary set forth in Article I will constitute a delimitation line as defined in Article 2 of the 2012 Transboundary Hydrocarbon Reservoirs Agreement, such that the provisions of that Agreement become applicable to the maritime boundary upon entry into force of this Treaty.

Article VI

Upon written request by a Party through diplomatic channels, the Parties shall consult to discuss any issue regarding the interpretation or implementation of this Treaty.

Article VII

The continental shelf boundary established by this Treaty shall not affect or prejudice in any manner the positions of either Party with respect to the extent of internal waters, of the territorial sea, of the high seas or of sovereign rights or jurisdiction for any other purpose.

Article VIII

Any dispute concerning the interpretation or application of this Treaty shall be settled by negotiation or other peaceful means as may be agreed upon by the Parties.

Article IX

This Treaty shall enter into force 30 (thirty) days after the date on which the Parties exchange instruments of ratification.

IN WITNESS WHEREOF, the undersigned, having been duly authorized by their respective Governments, have signed this Treaty.

DONE at Washington, this 18th day of January, 2017, in duplicate, in the English and Spanish languages, both texts being equally authentic.

FOR THE GOVERNMENT
OF THE UNITED STATES
OF AMERICA:
(signed)

FOR THE GOVERNMENT
OF THE UNITED
MEXICAN STATES:
(signed)

II

Middle America, Caribbean Sea

Cuba – Mexico

Report Number 2-8 (2)

Treaty between the Government of the United Mexican States and the Government of the Republic of Cuba on the Delimitation of the Continental Shelf in the Eastern Polygon of the Gulf of Mexico

Signed: 18 January 2017
Entry into force: 27 July 2018
Published at: UNTS (I-55481); Diario Oficial de la Federación (Mexico), DOF: 26/07/2018

I SUMMARY

The Treaty between the Government of the United Mexican States and the Government of the Republic of Cuba on the Delimitation of the Continental Shelf in the Eastern Polygon of the Gulf of Mexico (the Treaty, or the 2017 Treaty) delimits, on the basis of equidistance, the parties' respective continental shelf entitlements beyond 200 nautical miles (M) in the eastern Gulf of Mexico. Using a series of geodetic lines connecting four points defined by geodetic coordinates (and spanning approximately 33.5 M), the Treaty connects the northern endpoint of the parties' existing, equidistance-based maritime boundary for areas within 200 M to an equidistant tripoint where the extended continental shelves of Cuba, Mexico, and the United States meet in the eastern Gulf of Mexico.[1]

The Treaty was concluded following several rounds of negotiations hosted by the government of Mexico in 2016, in conjunction with simultaneous negotiations on bilateral Mexico – US and Cuba – US maritime boundary agreements for the eastern Gulf of Mexico. These negotiations addressed the only remaining area in the Gulf of Mexico where maritime boundaries had not been agreed. The Treaty was signed on 18 January 2017 and entered into

---

1   The term "extended continental shelf" is used in this report as a term of convenience to refer to areas of continental shelf beyond 200 M from the baselines from which the breadth of the territorial sea is measured.

Coalter G. Lathrop (ed.), International Maritime Boundaries, 5861-5879.
© *The American Society of International Law and Koninklijke Brill BV, Leiden 2025.*

5862   *Report Number 2-8 (2)*

force on 27 July 2018,[2] thirty days after the parties exchanged instruments of ratification.

II   CONSIDERATIONS

1   *Political, Strategic, and Historical Considerations*

In 1976, Cuba and Mexico concluded an exchange of notes constituting an agreement on the delimitation of the exclusive economic zone of Mexico in the sector adjacent to Cuban maritime areas out to a distance of 200 M from the baselines from which the breadth of the territorial sea is measured, on the basis of equidistance.[3] In the Gulf of Mexico, there are two enclaves of high seas beyond the outer limits of the 200 M exclusive economic zones of the coastal states. The continental shelves of Mexico and the United States extend in the western enclave, and the continental shelves of Cuba, Mexico, and the United States extend in the eastern enclave.[4] Mexico and the United States delimited an equidistance-based boundary for the extended continental shelf in the western enclave of the Gulf of Mexico in 2000,[5] leaving the extended continental shelf boundaries in the eastern enclave of the Gulf of Mexico as the region of their last unresolved maritime boundaries among them and with Cuba.

On 17 December 2014, recalling that "[t]he United States, Cuba, and Mexico have extended continental shelf in an area within the Gulf of Mexico where the three countries have not yet delimited any boundaries," the United States announced that it was "prepared to invite the governments of Cuba and Mexico to discuss shared maritime boundaries in the Gulf of Mexico."[6]

In 2016, the government of Mexico hosted the United States and Cuba for several rounds of negotiations that developed three bilateral maritime boundary agreements with respect to the continental shelf beyond 200 M

---

2   GOC-2018-855-O42, Gaceta Oficial de la República de Cuba No. 42 Ordinaria de 2018 (Cuba), *available at* https://www.gacetaoficial.gob.cu/es/proclama-sn-de-2018-de-consejo-de-estado-6.

3   *See* Report Number 2-8, I IMB 565.

4   These pockets of high seas are sometimes referred to as the "Western Gap" and the "Eastern Gap," or "Western Polygon" and "Eastern Polygon".

5   *See* Report Number 1-5 (2), IV IMB 2621.

6   *See* Press Release, White House Office of the Press Secretary, *Fact Sheet: Charting a New Course on Cuba* (17 December 2014), https://obamawhitehouse.archives.gov/the-press-office/2014/12/17/fact-sheet-charting-new-course-cuba.

in the eastern Gulf of Mexico.[7] The Treaty between Cuba and Mexico was signed in Habana on 18 January 2017 by the Director of International Law of Cuba's Ministry of Foreign Affairs Anet Pinero Rivero, and by Mexico's ambassador to Cuba Enrique Martínez y Martínez.[8] Under both Cuban and Mexican law, there are requirements for legislative approval before ratification. The Cuban Council of Ministers approved the Treaty on 13 April 2017 and submitted it for ratification to the State Council of the National Assembly, and the Cuban State Council ratified the Treaty on 8 May 2017. The Mexican Senate approved the Treaty on 26 April 2018,[9] and it entered into force on 27 July 2018.

2 Legal Regime Considerations

Cuba and Mexico are both states parties to the United Nations Convention on the Law of the Sea (the Convention). As the Treaty is focused only on areas beyond 200 M from each country, the legal regime of the continental shelf applies. Accordingly, the Treaty refers to the boundary it delimits as a "continental shelf boundary," and Article III of the Treaty, the primary article which operationalizes the boundary line described in Article I, pertains

---

7   See Press Release, US Department of State, Office of the Spokesperson, *Media Note: United States, Cuba, and Mexico: Resolving Maritime Boundaries* (7 July 2016), https://2009-2017.state.gov/r/pa/prs/ps/2016/07/259450.htm; *see also* Press Release, Secretaría de Relaciones Exteriores, *Communicado No. 301: Cuba, Estados Unidos y Mexico, celebraron ronda de consultas para la delimitación de la plataforma continental en el Golfo de México* (7 July 2016), https://www.gob.mx/sre/prensa/cuba-estados-unidos-y-mexico-celebraron-la-primera-ronda-de-consultas-para-la-delimitacion-de-la-plataforma-continental-en-el-golfo-de-mexico?idiom=es; Press Release, Secretaría de Relaciones Exteriores, *Communicado No. 432: Segunda ronda de consultas entre Cuba, Estados Unidos de América y México para la delimitación de la plataforma continental* (30 September 2016), https://www.gob.mx/sre/prensa/segunda-ronda-de-consultas-entre-cuba-estados-unidos-de-america-y-mexico-para-la-delimitacion-de-la-plataforma-continental-mas-alla-de-las-doscientas-millas-nauticas-en-el-golfo-de-mexico.

8   Press Release, Secretaría de Relaciones Exteriores, *Memoria Documental: Tratado de Delimitación entre los Estados Unidos Mexicanos y la República de Cuba sobre la Delimitación de la plataforma continental en el Polígono Oriental del Golfo de México más allá de las 200 millas náuticas y Tratado entre el Gobierno de los Estados Unidos Mexicanos y el Gobierno de los Estados Unidos de América sobre la Delimitación de la Frontera Marítima en la Región Oriental del Golfo de México* (2018), https://www.gob.mx/cms/uploads/attachment/file/426907/MD_Tratados_delimitaci_n_Golfo_de_M_xico.pdf.

9   Tratado Entre el Gobierno de Los Estados Unidos Mexicanos y el Gobierno de Los Estados Unidos de Américe Sobre la Delimitación de la Frontera Marítima en la Región Oriental del Golfo de México, Gaceta del Senado 26-04-2018, (Mex.), https://www.senado.gob.mx/65/gaceta_del_senado/documento/80700.

to "sovereign rights or jurisdiction over the seabed and subsoil," not the water column.

Due to the possible existence of oil or natural gas deposits that may extend across the boundary, Article IV provides for a moratorium of five years from the date of entry into force on the drilling or exploitation by the parties within 1.4 M on either side of the boundary. The period of this moratorium may be extended by mutual agreement through the exchange of diplomatic notes.

The Treaty does not provide for binding dispute settlement. Specifically, Article VII provides instead for consultation: "The Parties shall consult on any matter relating to the interpretation or execution of this Treaty, upon written request of either Party, through diplomatic channels."

Article VIII provides that the Treaty is without prejudice to the parties' views concerning any other maritime area: "The continental shelf boundary established by this Treaty shall not affect or prejudice, in any manner, the positions of either Party with respect to the extent of internal waters, the territorial sea, the contiguous zone, of the exclusive economic zone and the high seas, or with respect to its sovereign rights or jurisdiction for any other purpose.

3   Economic and Environmental Considerations

The Preamble of the Treaty indicates that the parties acknowledge the importance of developing, at the bilateral and regional levels, "additional measures for prevention, attention and mitigation in the event of possible environmental contingencies that could occur in the marine environment of the Gulf of Mexico." Cuba, Mexico, and the US are among twenty-six parties to the Convention for the Protection and Development of the Marine Environment of the Wider Caribbean Region,[10] which covers the marine environment of the Gulf of Mexico, the Caribbean Sea, and the areas of the Atlantic Ocean adjacent thereto, south of 30° north latitude and within 200 M of the Atlantic coasts of the states. This environmental convention is

---

10   Convention for the Protection and Development of the Marine Environment of the Wider Caribbean Region, *adopted* 24 March 1983, *entered into force* 11 October 1986, 1506 UNTS 157.

supported by three protocols, including the Protocol Concerning Co-operation in Combating Oil Spills in the Wider Caribbean Region.[11]

Article IV(4) of the Treaty provides an avenue for the facilitation of applications by either party in order to conduct geological and geophysical studies within the drilling and exploitation moratorium buffer zone in order to determine the possible presence and distribution of transboundary oil and gas resources. The Treaty also provides for information sharing of these studies and results.

Article IV(7) provides a mandate to conduct future negotiations towards the conclusion of an additional agreement on transboundary deposits for the efficient and equitable exploitation of oil and gas resources throughout the maritime boundary.

4 Geographic Considerations

The Preamble of the Treaty recalls that the 1976 exchange of notes constituting an agreement on the delimitation of the exclusive economic zone of Mexico in the sector adjacent to Cuban maritime areas out to a distance of 200 M from the baselines from which the breadth of the territorial sea is measured, was concluded on the basis of equidistance. Considering that all relevant circumstances remained unchanged, both parties agreed to continue the determination of their continental shelf boundary beyond 200 M using the same methodology.

The equidistance-based boundary is defined in Article I and consists of geodetic lines connecting four points defined by geodetic coordinates equivalent in the WGS84 and ITRF2008 reference systems. As set out in Article II, the northernmost endpoint "represents a 'tri-point,' equidistant from the Republic of Cuba, the United Mexican States, and a third State" (*i.e.*, the United States). (The Cuba – US and Mexico – US continental shelf boundaries that were negotiated simultaneously likewise terminate at this tripoint.) No separate trilateral agreement to specify the tripoint was deemed necessary; rather, the coordinates of this tripoint are the same in each of the bilateral treaties developed during the negotiations hosted by Mexico, and

---

11 Protocol Concerning Co-operation in Combating Oil Spills in the Wider Caribbean Region, *adopted* 24 March 1983, *entered into force* 11 October 1986, 1506 UNTS 157. Cuba, Mexico, and the US became contracting Parties to the Protocol on 15 September 1988, 11 April 1985, and 31 October 1984, respectively. *See* UN Environment Programme, *Cartagena Convention*, https://www.unep.org/cep/who-we-are/cartagena-convention.

for additional clarity it is expressly described in each of the treaties as a tripoint. Article II also clarifies that the southernmost endpoint is the same as the northern terminus of the parties' 1976 boundary agreement.

The equidistance line between Cuba and Mexico was measured from several contributing basepoints along the coast of each country. On the Cuba side, these points are turning points on Cuba's straight baselines,[12] which could also be considered to be normal baseline points determined at the low-water line for measuring the breadth of the territorial sea. On the Mexican side, the contributing points are located on Alacrán, which includes several islands and low-tide elevations, located north of the Yucatan Peninsula, as shown on current official charts issued by the Hydrographic Directorate of the Mexican Navy.

5 Islands, Rocks, Reefs, and Low-tide Elevations Considerations

In determining the equidistance boundary, the parties considered that all contributing basepoints were to be given full effect. Specifically, the basepoints on Mexico's Alacrán and Cuba's main and other western islands were given full effect, consistent with their treatment in other maritime boundary agreements between the parties and with the US.

6 Baseline Considerations

Cuba measures the breath of its maritime zones in the Gulf of Mexico from a system of straight baselines. Mexico measures the breath of its maritime zones in the Gulf of Mexico from the normal baseline. Only the turning points of Cuba's straight baselines contributed to the determination of the equidistant boundary. No points on the intervening segments of Cuba's system of straight baselines were used to determine this boundary.

---

12 Decreto-Ley No. 1 del 24 de febrero de 1977 referente a la anchura del mar territorial de Cuba, Gaceta Oficial N° 6, 26 de febrero de 1977 (Cuba), *available at* https://faolex.fao. org/docs/pdf/cub1242.pdf, *English translation available at* https://www.un.org/Depts/los/ LEGISLATIONANDTREATIES/PDFFILES/CUB_1977_Decree1.pdf, at 15–17.

7 Geological and Geomorphological Considerations

In 2011, Mexico made a partial submission to the Commission on the Limits of the Continental Shelf concerning its extended continental shelf in the eastern Gulf of Mexico.[13] This was Mexico's second partial submission. The first concerned areas of extended continental shelf in the western Gulf of Mexico.[14] The limit of Mexico's continental shelf delineation in its second submission easily encompasses the entirety of the area on Mexico's side of the Mexico – US and Cuba – Mexico boundary lines subsequently agreed in their respective treaties.

In the submission, as well as in a subsequent presentation to the Commission, Mexico emphasized that its submission does not prejudice the final delimitation of the continental shelf.[15] The UN has not received any note from any state in response to Mexico's 2011 submission to the Commission.

In 2009, Cuba made a submission to the Commission concerning its extended continental shelf in the eastern Gulf of Mexico.[16] The limit of Cuba's continental shelf delineation in that submission does not conform with area on Cuba's side of the Cuba – Mexico and Cuba – US boundary lines subsequently agreed in their respective treaties.

In its submission, as well as in a subsequent presentation to the Commission, Cuba emphasized that the submission does not prejudice the final delimitation of the continental shelf.[17] However, in response to Cuba's

---

13 Mexico, Executive Summary: A Partial Submission of Data and Information on the Outer Limits of the Continental Shelf of the United Mexican States pursuant to Part VI of and Annex II to the United Nations Convention on the Law of the Sea, 19 December 2011, *available at* http://www.un.org/depts/los/clcs_new/submissions_files/submission_mex58_2011.htm.

14 Mexico, Executive Summary: A Partial Submission of Data and Information on the Outer Limits of the Continental Shelf of the United Mexican States Pursuant to Part VI of and Annex II to the United Nations Convention on the Law of the Sea, December 2007, *available at* https://www.un.org/depts/los/clcs_new/submissions_files/mex07/part_i_executive _summary.pdf.

15 *Id.*; Commission on the Limits of the Continental Shelf, *CLCS/74 – Progress of Work in the Commission on the Limits of the Continental Shelf- Statement by the Chairperson – Twenty-Ninth Session*, 30 April 2024, http://daccess-ods.un.org/access. nsf/Get?Open&DS=CLCS/74&Lang=E.

16 Republic of Cuba, Executive Summary: Submission to the Commission on the Limits of the Continental Shelf to Demonstrate the Natural Extension of the Continental Shelf of Cuba Beyond 200 Nautical Miles in the Eastern Sector of the Gulf of Mexico, 1 June 2009, *available at* http://www.un.org/depts/los/clcs_new/submissions_files/cub51_09/cub_2009execsummary.pdf.

17 *Id.* at ES1; Commission on the Limits of the Continental Shelf, *CLCS/66 – Statement by the Chairperson of the Commission on the Limits of the Continental Shelf on the Progress*

5868   *Report Number 2-8 (2)*

submission, the United States provided a diplomatic note to the UN noting the potential overlap between the continental shelves of the United States and Cuba in this area, recalling that the Convention and the Commission's rules of procedure provide that actions of the Commission shall not prejudice matters relating to delimitation of maritime boundaries, and confirming that the United States had no objection to the Commission considering the submission and making recommendations "to the extent that such recommendations are without prejudice to the establishment of the outer limits of its continental shelf by the United States, or to any final delimitation of the continental shelf concluded subsequently in this area between Cuba and the United States."[18] Mexico transmitted a similar diplomatic note with respect to its own continental shelf entitlement in response to Cuba's submission.[19] Although the US note predated Mexico's submission and addressed only Cuba's submission, Mexico's second partial submission cited both the Cuban submission and the US note as reflecting that all three countries shared "a clear understanding that, in accordance with article 76, paragraph 10, the provisions of article 76 are without prejudice to the question of delimitation of the continental shelf between States with opposite or adjacent coasts in the Gulf of Mexico."[20]

To date, the Commission has begun active consideration of Cuba's submission, but it has not yet issued its recommendations.[21] The second partial submission made by Mexico remains in the Commission's queue,

---

    of Work in the Commission – Twenty-Fifth Session, 30 April 2010, para. 86, *available at* https://documents.un.org/doc/undoc/gen/n10/337/97/pdf/n1033797.pdf.

18 Diplomatic Note from the United States to the UN dated 30 June 2009, *available at* http://www.un.org/depts/los/clcs_new/submissions_files/cub51_09/usa_re_cuba_2009.pdf.

19 Diplomatic Note from Mexico to the UN dated 21 August 2009, *available at* http://www.un.org/depts/los/clcs_new/submissions_files/submission_cub_51_2009.htm and https://www.un.org/depts/los/clcs_new/submissions_files/cub51_09/mex_re_cub_clcs51_s.pdf.

20 Mexico Executive Summary (2011), *supra* note 13 at 8.

21 *See* Commission on the Limits of the Continental Shelf, *CLCS/66 – Statement by the Chairperson of the Commission on the Limits of the Continental Shelf on the Progress of Work in the Commission – Twenty-Fifth Session,* 30 April 2010, *available at* https://documents.un.org/doc/undoc/gen/n10/337/97/pdf/n1033797.pdf at para. 86; Commission on the Limits of the Continental Shelf, *CLCS 60/2 – Progress of Work in the Commission on the Limits of the Continental Shelf,* 21 March 2024, https://documents.un.org/doc/undoc/gen/n24/078/97/pdf/n2407897.pdf; Submissions, through the Secretary-General of United Nations, to the Commission on the Limits of the Continental Shelf, pursuant to article 76, paragraph 8 of the United Nations Convention on the Law of the Sea of 10 December 1982, *available at* https://www.un.org/depts/los/clcs_new/commission_submissions.htm.

and the Commission has not yet addressed it in substance or issued its recommendations.[22]

In the course of negotiating the Treaty, the parties shared and discussed scientific and technical information concerning the seabed and subsoil in the Gulf of Mexico and confirmed that each country passed the test of appurtenance, which is reflected in the Scientific and Technical Guidelines of the Commission on the Limits of the Continental Shelf.[23] Thus, they do indeed have an entitlement to extended continental shelf in this area.

The submissions made by Cuba and Mexico in the eastern region of the Gulf of Mexico rely on the formula provided in Article 76(4)(a)(ii) of the Convention (*i.e.*, by reference to fixed points not more than 60 nautical miles from the foot of the continental slope). In any event, the especially thick sediment throughout the central Gulf of Mexico beyond 200 M leaves no doubt that, under international law as reflected in Article 76 (including the alternative formula based on sediment thickness, set forth in paragraph 4(a)(i)), Cuba, Mexico, and the United States[24] are each entitled to continental shelf throughout the entire area on its side of the relevant maritime boundaries. (Thus, while the pocket of high seas overlying this area is sometimes called the "Eastern Gap," there is not any gap between the continental shelves of Cuba, Mexico, and the United States.) This lack of doubt about the three countries' entitlement to extended continental shelf in the relevant areas on each side of the equidistance boundaries removed any need to delay boundary

---

22 *See* Submissions, through the Secretary-General of United Nations, to the Commission on the Limits of the Continental Shelf, pursuant to article 76, paragraph 8 of the United Nations Convention on the Law of the Sea of 10 December 1982, *available at* https://www.un.org/depts/los/clcs_new/commission_submissions.htm.

In 2007, Mexico made its first partial submission to the Commission concerning a similar area of extended continental shelf in the western Gulf of Mexico where Mexico and the United States had agreed on a continental shelf boundary in 2000. The Commission considered the submission and made favorable recommendations in 2009. *See* Mexico Executive Summary (2007), *supra* note 14; CLCS, *Recommendations of the Commission on the Limits of the Continental Shelf in Regard to the Submission Made by Mexico in Respect of the Western Polygon in the Gulf of Mexico on 13 December 2007*, adopted on 31 March 2009, *available at* https://www.un.org/depts/los/clcs_new/submissions_files/mex07/mex_rec.pdf; Commission on the Limits of the Continental Shelf, Progress of Work in the Commission on the Limits of the Continental Shelf- Statement by the Chairperson – Twenty-Third Session, 20 April 2009, https://documents-dds-ny.un.org/doc/UNDOC/GEN/N09/307/58/PDF/N0930758.pdf?OpenElement at paras. 22-26.

23 Commission on the Limits of the Continental Shelf, *CLCS/11 – Scientific and Technical Guidelines, available at* https://www.un.org/depts/los/clcs_new/commission_guidelines.htm at Section 2.2.

24 US Department of State, Executive Summary: The Outer Limits of the Extended Continental Shelf of the United States of America, 2023, *available at* https://www.state.gov/wp-content/uploads/2023/12/ECS_Executive_Summary.pdf.

negotiations until such time as the Commission makes its recommendations concerning the submissions of Mexico and Cuba (or of the United States if, in the future, it makes a submission to the Commission based on the outer limits it announced in 2023).

8 Method of Delimitation Considerations

As described above, the delimitation was based on equidistance. All the parties' other maritime boundaries in the Gulf of Mexico had been resolved previously and were also delimited on the basis of equidistance.

9 Technical Considerations

Article II of the 2017 Treaty clarifies that "[t]he geodetic and computational bases used to determine the boundary set forth in Article I are the World Geodetic System of 1984 ("WGS84") and the International Terrestrial Reference Frame 2008 ("ITRF2008")," and that "[f]or purposes of Article I . . . WGS84 and ITRF2008 shall be considered to be identical." Because the southernmost endpoint of the new boundary uses the northernmost endpoint of the boundary delimited in the parties' 1976 agreement, a datum transformation was needed to reflect the 1976 northern terminus in WGS84 and ITRF2008. As described in Article II(2)(b) of the Treaty, "[b]oundary point number 1, described in Article I, is boundary point 1 (24° 56' 28.83" N., 86° 56' 16.69" W.) of the 1976 Agreement on Maritime Boundaries. This point, which was originally determined with reference to the North American Datum of 1927, has been transformed to the WGS84 and ITRF2008 reference frames."

10 Other Considerations

The Treaty includes an annex consisting of two small-scale maps that are expressly "for the purpose of illustration only." One map depicts the continental shelf boundary determined by four points and the other shows the moratorium "Area" along their boundary as defined in Article IV(1).

III   CONCLUSIONS

This bilateral agreement between Cuba and Mexico was developed through a diplomatic process in which the countries met together with the United States to resolve three outstanding maritime boundaries in the same general area, facilitating trilateral collaboration on the tripoint and other issues of common concern while allowing bilateral discussions and negotiations for other issues.

The success in resolving these last outstanding maritime boundaries in the Gulf of Mexico was significantly aided by the existence of precedents among the three countries for maritime boundaries and transboundary frameworks elsewhere in the Gulf of Mexico, especially with respect to the use of an equidistance methodology and the regime for possible transboundary hydrocarbon reservoirs. The process was also aided by the lack of doubt about each country's legal entitlement to extended continental shelf in the entirety of its relevant area, especially given the thickness of the sediment throughout, notwithstanding that the Commission on the Limits of the Continental Shelf has yet to offer any recommendations with respect to the eastern Gulf of Mexico.

As provided in Article XI, the Treaty entered into force 30 days after the date on which the parties exchange instruments of ratification.

IV   RELATED LAW IN FORCE

A   *Law of the Sea Conventions*

Cuba: Party to UNCLOS (signed 10 December 1982, ratified 15 August 1984)

Mexico: Party to UNCLOS (signed 10 December 1982, ratified 18 March 1983)

B   *Maritime Jurisdiction Claimed at the Time of Signature*

Cuba: 12 M territorial sea; 24 M contiguous zone; 200 M EEZ; continental shelf (CLCS submission concerning the Eastern Polygon region on 1 June 2009).

Mexico: 12 M territorial sea; 24 M contiguous zone; 200 M EEZ; continental shelf (CLCS submission concerning the Western Polygon region on 13 December 2007 and CLCS submission concerning the Eastern Polygon region on 19 December 2011).

C *Maritime Jurisdiction Claimed Subsequent to Signature*

Cuba: No change.
Mexico: No change.

Prepared by Galo Carrera

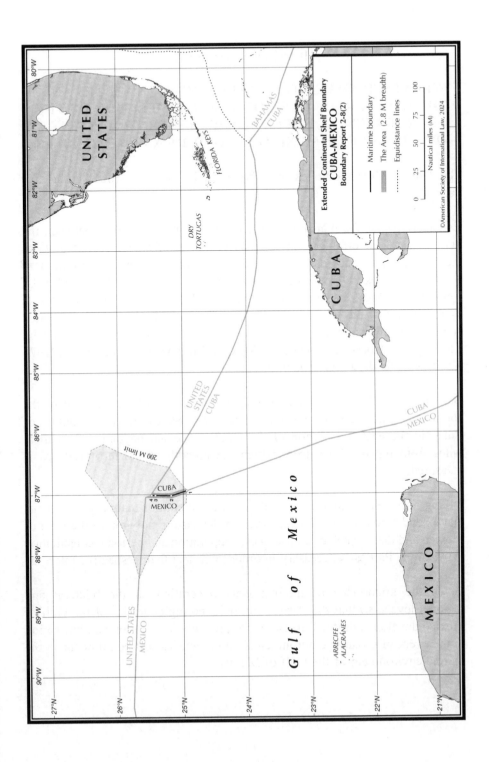

[unofficial translation]

TREATY BETWEEN THE UNITED MEXICAN STATES AND THE REPUBLIC OF CUBA ON THE DELIMITATION OF THE CONTINENTAL SHELF IN THE EASTERN POLYGON OF THE GULF OF MEXICO BEYOND 200 NAUTICAL MILES

The United Mexican States and the Republic of Cuba (hereinafter "the Parties");

Considering that the maritime limits up to 200 nautical miles between the Parties were determined on the basis of equidistance counted from the baselines, in accordance with the Agreement on the Delimitation of Maritime Spaces between the United Mexican States and the Republic of Cuba, in the Areas in which such Spaces will be adjacent by virtue of the establishment of the Exclusive Economic Zone of Mexico and the eventual creation of an Economic Zone of Cuba (or its equivalent), concluded by exchange of Notes exchanged in Mexico City on July 26, 1976 ("1976 Maritime Boundary Agreement");

Desiring to establish, in accordance with international law, the limit of the continental shelf between the United Mexican States and the Republic of Cuba, in the eastern polygon of the Gulf of Mexico beyond 200 nautical miles from the baselines from which the breadth of the territorial sea is measured;

Taking into account that there could exist petroleum or natural gas deposits that extend across the continental shelf in the eastern polygon of the Gulf of Mexico and that in such circumstances, cooperation and periodic consultation between the Parties is necessary in order to protect their respective interests;

Given the importance of international cooperation, at the bilateral and regional levels, so that the Parties and neighboring countries of the Gulf of Mexico develop additional measures for prevention, attention and mitigation in the event of possible environmental contingencies that could occur in the marine environment of the Gulf of Mexico;

Considering the United Mexican States and the Republic of Cuba are Parties to the United Nations Convention on the Law of the Sea, adopted in Montego Bay, Jamaica, on December 10, 1982; and

Considering that the practice of good neighborliness has strengthened the friendly and cooperative relations between the Parties,

Have agreed as follows:

Article I

The limit of the continental shelf of the United Mexican States and the Republic of Cuba in the eastern polygon of the Gulf of Mexico, beyond 200 nautical miles counted from the baselines from which the breadth of the territorial sea is measured, shall be determined by the geodetic lines connecting the following coordinates:

1. 24° 56′ 30.25″ N. 86° 56′ 16.60″ W.
2. 25° 10′ 58.30″ N. 87° 01′ 12.37″ W.
3. 25° 25′ 46.92″ N. 87° 00′ 54.45″ W.
4. 25° 29′ 16.44″ N. 87° 00′ 49.44″ W.

Article II

1. The geodetic reference systems used to determine the boundary established in Article I are the World Geodetic System of 1984 (WGS84) and the International Terrestrial Reference Frame 2008 (ITRF2008).

2. For the purposes of Article I:

    (a) The WGS84 and ITRF reference systems are considered identical.
    (b) Point number 1, described in Article I, is boundary point 1 of the Maritime Boundary Agreement of 1976 (24° 56′ 28.83″ N., 86° 56′ 16.69″ W.). The coordinates of this point, which were originally determined with reference to the North American Data of 1927

(NAD27) have been transformed to the WGS84 and ITRF2008 Reference Frames.

(c) The coordinates at point 4 represent a triple point, equidistant between the Republic of Cuba, the United Mexican States and a third State.

3. For the purposes of illustration only, the limit referred to in Article I is shown in Annex 1 to this Treaty.

Article III

The United Mexican States, to the East of the limit of the continental shelf established in the dividing line formed by the union of the boundary points identified in Article I, and the Republic of Cuba, to the West of said limit, shall not claim, nor exercise for any purpose, sovereignty rights or jurisdiction over the seabed and subsoil.

Article IV

1. By virtue of the possible existence of oil or natural gas deposits that may extend across the boundary set forth in Article I (hereinafter referred to as "transboundary deposits"), the Parties, for a period of five (5) years from the date of entry into force of this Treaty, shall not authorize the drilling or exploitation of or permit petroleum or natural gas on the continental shelf within one and four tenths nautical mile (1.4M) on either side of the boundary set forth in Article I. This Area of two and eight tenths nautical miles (2.8M) shall hereinafter be referred to as the "Area".

2. For the purpose of illustration only, the Area set forth in paragraph 1 is shown in Annex 2 to this treaty.

3. The parties, by mutual agreement through an exchange of diplomatic notes, may modify the period set forth in paragraph 1.

4. With respect to its side within the Area set forth in Article I, each Party, in accordance with its national legislation, shall facilitate requests by the other Party to authorize geological and geophysical surveys to help determine the possible presence and distribution of transboundary deposits.

5. With respect to the Area in its entirety (2.8M), as of the date of entry into force of this Treaty, each Party, in accordance with its national legislation, shall share the geological and geophysical information it has in order to determine the possible existence and location of transboundary deposits.

6. Upon entry into force of this Treaty, if a Party has knowledge of the existence or possible existence of a transboundary deposit, it shall notify the other Party.

7. The Parties shall carry out negotiations in order to conclude a Transboundary Deposits Agreement for the efficient and equitable exploitation of these deposits in the maritime limits of the United Mexican States and the Republic of Cuba in the Gulf of Mexico.

Article V

1. During the period established in paragraph 1 of Article IV, with respect to the Area in its entirety (2.8M):

    (a) As geological and geophysical information is generated that facilitates the Parties' knowledge about the possible existence of transboundary deposits, including notifications by Parties in accordance with Article IV, paragraphs 5 and 6, the Parties shall meet at least once per year for the purpose of identifying, locating, and determining the geological and geophysical characteristics of such deposits,

    (b) The Parties shall, within sixty (60) days of receipt of written request by a Party through diplomatic channels, consult to discuss matters relating to possible transboundary deposits.

2. At the end of the period set forth in paragraph 1 of Article IV, with respect to the Area in its entirety (2.8M):

    (a) The Parties shall inform each other of their decisions to lease, license, grant concessions or otherwise make use of portions of the Area on its side of the boundary for petroleum or natural gas exploration or development and shall also inform the other Party when it commences production of petroleum or natural gas resources; and

(b) Each Party shall ensure that the entities it authorizes to carry out activities within the Area observe the terms of this Treaty.

Article VI

The Parties shall adopt, within a period not exceeding three (3) years from the signature of this Treaty, a joint bilateral cooperation plan for the preparation, response and cooperation in the face of marine pollution by spills of hydrocarbons and other harmful substances, as well as other incidents that may have adverse impacts on the marine environment.

Article VII

The Parties shall consult on any matter relating to the interpretation or execution of this Treaty, upon written request of either Party, through diplomatic channels.

Article VIII

The continental shelf boundary established by this Treaty shall not affect or prejudice, in any manner, the positions of either Party with respect to the extent of internal waters, the territorial sea, the contiguous zone, of the exclusive economic zone and the high seas, or with respect to its sovereign rights or jurisdiction for any other purpose.

Article IX

The provisions of this Treaty shall not affect the rights and obligations of the Parties under the United Nations Convention on the Law of the Sea.

Article X

Any dispute concerning the interpretation or application of this Treaty shall be resolved by negotiation or other peaceful means as may be agreed upon by the Parties.

Article XI

This Treaty shall enter into force thirty (30) days after the date of receipt of the last note received through diplomatic channels in which the Parties communicate to each other the fulfillment of their internal legal requirements for entry into force.

IN WITNESS WHEREOF, the undersigned, being duly authorized, have signed this Treaty.

DONE at Havana, Cuba, this eighteenth day of January, two thousand seventeen, in two original copies in the Spanish language, both texts being equally authentic.

<table>
<tr><td>FOR THE UNITED
MEXICAN STATES
(signed)
Enrique Martinez y Martinez
Ambassador Extraordinary and
Plenipotentiary to the Republic of Cuba</td><td>FOR THE REPUBLIC
OF CUBA
(signed)
Anet Pino Rivero
Director of International Law
Ministry of Foreign Affairs</td></tr>
</table>

France (Saint Martin and Saint Barthelemy) – United Kingdom (Anguilla)

Report Number 2-20 (Add. 2)

Exchange of Notes between the Government of the United Kingdom of Great Britain and Northern Ireland in respect of Anguilla and the Government of the French Republic concerning Arrangements relating to the Tripoint between the Maritime Areas Under the Jurisdictions of the United Kingdom of Great Britain and Northern Ireland (in respect of Anguilla), Antigua and Barbuda, and the French Republic (in respect of Saint Martin and Saint-Barthélemy) (The "Tripoint")

Signed:	29 January 2021 and 4 March 2021
Entry into force:	4 March 2021
Published at:	United Kingdom Treaty Series No. 17 (2021), CP 527

The United Kingdom (Anguilla) and France (Saint Martin and Saint Barthélemy) signed a maritime boundary agreement in 1996 that entered into force in 1997 (1996 Agreement).[1] The 1996 Agreement created an equidistance boundary consisting of eight turning points connected by geodetic lines and stretching approximately 83 nautical miles (M) from Point 1 in the west near the tripoint with Saba Island (Netherlands) to Point 8 in the east near the tripoint with Antigua and Barbuda. As the parties to the 1996 Agreement noted in Article 3:

> It has not been possible, for the time being, to complete the maritime delimitation before point 1 and beyond point 8. It is, however, agreed between the Parties that the delimitation: ... from point 8 to the tripoint between the limits of the maritime areas under the respective jurisdiction of the Parties and of Antigua and Barbuda, shall be completed at the appropriate time by applying the same methods as those used to determine the limit between the points 1 and 8.

---

1   *See* Report Number 2-20, III IMB 2219; Report Number 2-20 (Add. 1), V IMB 3562.

Coalter G. Lathrop (ed.), International Maritime Boundaries, 5881-5888.
© *The American Society of International Law and Koninklijke Brill BV, Leiden 2025.*

5882 *Report Number 2-20 (Add. 2)*

With the successful negotiation of a boundary between France and Antigua and Barbuda in 2017[2] and with negotiations between the United Kingdom and Antigua and Barbuda nearing completion,[3] the "appropriate time" arrived in early 2021.

The 2021 exchange of notes between the United Kingdom and France agreed an eastern endpoint at the point with coordinates 18° 18′ 36.1″N, 062° 13′ 37.3″W (WGS84). The parties refer to this new point as the "tripoint". The 670-meter geodetic line connecting Point 8 with this new point completes the eastern end of the 1996 boundary, and the new point ties into the two related boundaries with Antigua and Barbuda.

The first of those, the 2017 boundary between France and Antigua and Barbuda, also hedged with respect to its endpoint, in this case its northern endpoint. The northern end of the France-Antigua and Barbuda boundary continues from the last specified point, Point A1, "along a loxodrome of 11.2 degrees until it reaches the maritime zones of the United Kingdom with respect to Anguilla."[4] The 2021 exchange of notes refers to the 2017 boundary and its relationship to the new point: "In accordance with the aforementioned France-Antigua and Barbuda Maritime Boundary Agreement, the delimitation of the maritime spaces between France and Antigua and Barbuda from point A1 is a loxodrome of azimuth 11.2 degrees which extends to the tripoint."

The second of those boundaries, the boundary between the United Kingdom (Anguilla) and Antigua and Barbuda agreed in July 2021, was finalized after the January/March 2021 exchange of notes between the United Kingdom and France. Although the notes do not refer to the later boundary agreement, they do refer to the maritime boundary negotiations between the United Kingdom and Antigua and Barbuda, "as well as the exchanges between officials from the Governments of the United Kingdom, of Antigua and Barbuda and of the French Republic concerning the proposed tripoint." The precise content of these exchanges is not known, but it is clear that a mutual understanding was reached with respect to the location of their shared endpoint. This is evidenced by the language of the July 2021 agreement between the United Kingdom and Antigua and Barbuda which describes its southernmost point, Point 1, as "the tripoint between the Parties and the Republic of France, as has been accepted in an exchange of diplomatic notes

---

2   *See* Report Number 2-37, in this volume.
3   *See* Report Number 2-38, in this volume.
4   Report Number 2-37, in this volume, Article 3(2).

by the Republic of France."[5] Point 1 of the July 2021 agreement shares the same coordinates and geodetic reference system as the new endpoint agreed between the United Kingdom and France.

With the 2021 exchange of notes between the United Kingdom and France, the eastern end of their boundary has been completed, and its relationship with the endpoints of the two related boundaries with Antigua and Barbuda has been clarified. Even in the absence of a trilateral agreement, the three coordinated bilateral agreements leave no doubt where the United Kingdom-France-Antigua and Barbuda tripoint is located.

Prepared by Coalter G. Lathrop

---

5   Report Number 2-38, in this volume, Article 1(5).

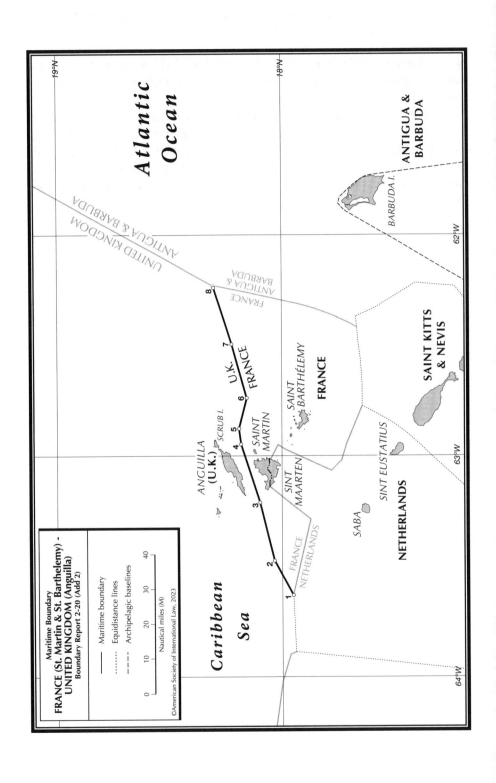

France (Saint Martin and Saint Barthelemy) – United Kingdom (Anguilla) 5885

AGREEMENT IN THE FORM OF AN EXCHANGE OF NOTES BETWEEN THE GOVERNMENT OF THE UNITED KINGDOM OF GREAT BRITAIN AND NORTHERN IRELAND IN RESPECT OF ANGUILLA AND THE GOVERNMENT OF THE FRENCH REPUBLIC CONCERNING ARRANGEMENTS RELATING TO THE TRIPOINT BETWEEN THE MARITIME AREAS UNDER THE JURISDICTIONS OF THE UNITED KINGDOM OF GREAT BRITAIN AND NORTHERN IRELAND (IN RESPECT OF ANGUILLA), ANTIGUA AND BARBUDA, AND THE FRENCH REPUBLIC (IN RESPECT OF SAINT-MARTIN AND SAINT-BARTHÉLEMY) (THE "TRIPOINT")

No. 1

From Her Britannic Majesty's Embassy Paris to the Ministry for Europe and Foreign Affairs of the French Republic

Paris
29th January 2021

Note Verbale No 003/2021

Her Britannic Majesty's Embassy Paris presents its compliments to the Ministry for Europe and Foreign Affairs of the French Republic on behalf of the Government of the United Kingdom of Great Britain and Northern Ireland (in respect of itself and the Government of Anguilla) and has the honour to propose the following arrangements relating to the tripoint between the maritime areas under the jurisdictions of the United Kingdom of Great Britain and Northern Ireland (in respect of Anguilla), Antigua and Barbuda, and the French Republic (in respect of Saint- Martin and Saint-Barthélemy) (the **"tripoint"**).

The Embassy has the honour to refer to the Agreement on maritime delimitation between the Government of the French Republic and the Government of the United Kingdom of Great Britain and Northern Ireland concerning Saint-Martin and Saint-Barthélemy on the one hand, and Anguilla on the other, done at London on 27 June 1996 (UN registration number 36144) (the **"United Kingdom (Anguilla) – France Maritime Boundary**

Agreement"). Article 3(b) of that Agreement states: *"the delimitation... from point 8 to the tripoint between the limits of the maritime areas under the respective jurisdiction of the parties and of Antigua and Barbuda, shall be completed at the appropriate time by applying the same methods as those used to determine the limit between points 1 and 8."*

The Embassy also has the honour to refer to the Agreement between the Government of the French Republic and the Government of Antigua and Barbuda on the delimitation of maritime space between France and Antigua and Barbuda in the Caribbean region, done at St John's on 15 March 2017 (the **"France – Antigua and Barbuda Maritime Boundary Agreement"**). Article 3(2) of that Agreement states:

"From Point A1, the delimitation extends along a loxodrome with an azimuth of 11.2 degrees until it reaches the maritime zones of the United Kingdom with respect to Anguilla."

The Embassy has the further honour to refer to recent negotiations between representatives of the Government of the United Kingdom and the Government of Antigua and Barbuda in respect of the maritime boundary between the United Kingdom (in respect of Anguilla) and Antigua and Barbuda, as well as the exchanges between officials from the Governments of the United Kingdom, of Antigua and Barbuda and the French Republic concerning the proposed tripoint.

The Embassy confirms that during the negotiations with Antigua and Barbuda, the two delegations considered that the tripoint envisaged below was compatible with the United Kingdom (Anguilla) – France Maritime Boundary Agreement and the France – Antigua and Barbuda Maritime Boundary Agreement.

Accordingly, the Embassy has the honour to propose that the maritime boundary between the United Kingdom (in respect of Anguilla) and the French Republic (in respect of Saint-Martin and Saint-Barthélemy) beyond point 8 described in the United Kingdom (Anguilla) – France Agreement shall consist of a geodesic line from point 8 to the coordinates set out in the table below (using the WGS 84 geodetic reference system), which shall constitute the tripoint:

Latitude	Longitude
18° 18′ 36.1″ N	062° 13′ 37.3″ W

If the foregoing is acceptable to the Government of the French Republic, the Embassy proposes that this Note, together with the reply from the Ministry for Europe and Foreign Affairs, shall constitute an agreement between the Government of the United Kingdom of Great Britain and Northern Ireland (in respect of Anguilla) and the Government of the French Republic, which shall enter into force on the date of the reply of the Ministry for Europe and Foreign Affairs.

In accordance with the aforementioned France – Antigua and Barbuda Maritime Boundary Agreement, the delimitation of the maritime spaces between France and Antigua and Barbuda from point A1 is a loxodrome of azimuth 11.2 degrees which extends to the tripoint.

Her Britannic Majesty's Embassy Paris avails itself of the opportunity to renew to the Ministry for Europe and Foreign Affairs of the French Republic the assurances of its highest consideration.

Translation of No.2

From the Ministry for Europe and Foreign Affairs of the French Republic to Her Britannic Majesty's Embassy Paris

Paris
le 4 mars 2021

N° 2021-0109106

The Ministry for Europe and Foreign Affairs of the French Republic presents its compliments to Her Britannic Majesty's Embassy Paris. The Ministry has the honour to acknowledge receipt of Note. No. 003/2021 received on January 29, 2021 relating to the tripoint between the maritime areas under the jurisdictions of the French Republic (in respect of Saint-Martin and Saint-Barthélemy), the United Kingdom of Great Britain and Northern Ireland (in respect of Anguilla) and Antigua and Barbuda (the "**tripoint**") and which reads as follows:

5888   *Report Number 2-20 (Add. 2)*

[see text of Note. No. 003/2021]

The Ministry for Europe and Foreign Affairs has the honour to inform the Embassy that the foregoing proposal is acceptable to the Government of the French Republic and therefore that Note No. 003/2021 and the present reply shall constitute an agreement between the two Governments which shall enter into force on the date of this reply.

The Ministry for Europe and Foreign Affairs of the French Republic avails itself of the opportunity to renew to Her Britannic Majesty's Embassy Paris the assurances of its highest consideration.

Antigua and Barbuda – France
(Saint Barthélemy, Guadeloupe)

Report Number 2-37

Agreement Between the Government of the Republic of France and the Government of Antigua and Barbuda on the Delimitation of Maritime Space Between France and Antigua and Barbuda in the Caribbean Region

Signed:	15 March 2017
Entry into force:	1 October 2018
Published at:	UNTS (I-55817); 101 LOS Bull. 33 (2019)

I SUMMARY

On 15 March 2017, France and Antigua and Barbuda agreed on two maritime boundaries between their opposite coasts separating their exclusive economic zone and continental shelf. The boundaries separate Barbuda from Saint Barthélemy to the west and Antigua from Guadeloupe to the south. The agreed boundaries are both simplified equidistant lines of unequal length.

With this agreement, France completed lateral delimitations with respect to Guadeloupe. Guadeloupe's maritime boundaries with Dominica and the United Kingdom (Montserrat) were agreed, respectively, on 7 September 1987[1] and 27 June 1996.[2] France has also defined the outer limit of its continental shelf beyond 200 nautical miles (M).[3] Although it has not yet communicated the coordinates of its outer limit to the Secretary-General of the United Nations, the entire maritime area of Guadeloupe is now clearly defined. As concerns Saint Barthélemy, France delimited its maritime boundaries with the United Kingdom (Anguilla) and the Netherlands (Sint

---

1 *See* Report Number 2-15, I IMB 705.
2 *See* Report Number 2-21, III IMB 2227.
3 *See* Decree No. 2015-1180 of 25 September 2015 defining the outer limits of the continental shelf off the territory of Martinique and Guadeloupe, JORF 27 September 2015, no. 0224, *available at* https://www.legifrance.gouv.fr/jorf/id/JORFTEXT000031224442.

Coalter G. Lathrop (ed.), International Maritime Boundaries, 5889-5899.
© *The American Society of International Law and Koninklijke Brill BV, Leiden 2025.*

5890 *Report Number 2-37*

Maarten) by agreement, respectively, on 27 June 1996[4] and 6 April 2016.[5] Only the maritime delimitation with Saint Kitts and Nevis remains to be completed.

Antigua and Barbuda delimited its maritime boundary to the north with Anguilla by agreement on 27 July 2021.[6] This leaves the delimitations to the west with Saint Kitts and Nevis and with the Montserrat.

II CONSIDERATIONS

1 *Political, Strategic and Historical Considerations*

The 2017 agreement between the parties concerning their maritime delimitation (the Agreement) concludes a long-standing maritime dispute between France and Antigua and Barbuda and aims at reinforcing the good relations between them. It provides a solution to problems related to fisheries, as fishermen from both parties were fishing in the same areas.[7]

Third-state interests in the region have affected the boundaries agreed by France and Antigua and Barbuda. The parties did not define fixed endpoints of the boundary between Saint Barthélemy and Barbuda and simply indicated that the line extends beyond Point A8 until it reaches the maritime areas of Saint Kitts and Nevis to the south and beyond Point A1 until it reaches those of the Anguilla to the north (Article 3(2) & (3)). In 2021, France and the United Kingdom agreed to extend their 1996 maritime boundary between Saint Martin and Saint Barthélemy and Anguilla to a fixed point which will function as the tripoint among France, Antigua and Barbuda, and the United Kingdom as contemplated by the extension north of Point A1 in the France-Antigua and Barbuda Agreement.[8] No such tripoint has been defined with Saint Kitts and Nevis. Similarly, the line between the opposite coasts of Antigua and Guadeloupe has no endpoint in the west and runs until it reaches Montserrat's maritime space (Article 4(2)). In the east, the endpoint was left open to account for possible changes to baselines and thus to outer limits measured from those baselines.

---

4   *See* Report Number 2-20, III IMB 2219.
5   *See* Report Number 2-36, VIII IMB 5445.
6   *See* Report Number 2-38, in this volume.
7   *Gov't safeguards twin island's maritime boundaries*, THE DAILY OBSERVER (16 March 2017), https://antiguaobserver.com/govt-safeguards-twin-islands-maritime-boundaries/.
8   *See* Report Number 2-20 (Add. 2), in this volume.

2 Legal Regime Considerations

The Agreement establishes two boundaries delimiting the exclusive economic zone and continental shelf of the parties (Article 1(1)). Although continental shelf beyond 200 M is not expressly referred to, both states claim a continental shelf to the outer edge of the continental margin and the delimitation line between Antigua and Barbuda and Guadeloupe has no endpoint to the east. While France has established the outer limit of its continental shelf in areas east of Guadeloupe, Antigua and Barbuda does not seem to claim shelf areas beyond 200 M. It is therefore likely that the boundary with Guadeloupe stops at 200 M from the parties' baselines.

The Preamble of the Agreement expressly and solely refers to the United Nations Convention on the Law of the Sea (UNCLOS). The Agreement specifies that any dispute should be settled by means of consultations or negotiations (Article 6).

3 Economic and Environmental Considerations

Notwithstanding that the Agreement settles fishery-related issues between the parties, no economic consideration appears to have influenced the construction of the delimitation lines. In the Preamble, the parties recalled the importance of the marine environment to their respective people. However, this has not led the parties to modify their equidistance boundary lines.

4 Geographic Considerations

Both maritime boundaries are between islands of unequal size. The size difference had, however, no influence on the position of the boundaries, as they were not moved closer to one party or the other.

To the west, the delimitation line separates the maritime areas of the islands of Saint Barthélemy (24 km^2) and Barbuda (160 km^2). Although the western portion of Barbuda's coast is concave, this had no influence on the direction of the line as it was constructed from the archipelagic baselines of the island. To the south, the boundary delimits the maritime zones of Antigua (281 km^2) and Guadeloupe (1628 km^2). The configuration of the parties' coasts had no real influence on the direction of the line as it was drawn from Antigua's archipelagic baselines and Guadeloupe's straight baselines.

5 Islands, Rocks, Reefs, and Low-tide Elevations Considerations

Both agreed equidistance boundary lines separate islands. However, no insular feature caused the parties to shift the equidistance lines. Antigua and Barbuda's small and uninhabited insular feature named Redonda, which complicates the negotiations with Montserrat and with Saint Kitts and Nevis, had no bearing on the delimitation with Guadeloupe or Saint Barthélemy.

6 Baseline Considerations

Baselines played a decisive role in the maritime delimitation between France and Antigua and Barbuda. The latter has established archipelagic baselines encircling the islands of Antigua, Barbuda and Redonda.[9] Although it is not specified in the Agreement, both boundary lines were constructed on the basis of these baselines, which explains why they were depicted on the map annexed to the Agreement. Similarly, Guadeloupe's and Saint Barthélemy's straight baselines were used for the construction of the equidistance line with Antigua and Barbuda.[10]

It is not uncommon for states to use their archipelagic or straight baselines for the purpose of constructing their common maritime boundary.[11]

7 Geological and Geomorphological Considerations

No geological or geomorphological considerations appear to have influenced the direction of the boundary.

---

9 Act No. 18 of 17 August 1982, Maritime Areas Act, Sections 2(B) & 4 (Antigua and Barbuda) *available at* https://www.un.org/Depts/los/LEGISLATIONANDTREATIES/PDFFILES/ATG_1982_18.pdf. For a depiction of Antigua and Barbuda's archipelagic baselines, *see* United Nations, *Antigua and Barbuda: Archipelagic Baselines*, UN Map No. 3496, November 1988, *available at* https://digitallibrary.un.org/record/1484147?ln=fr.

10 Decree No. 2017-1511 of 30 October 2017 defining the baselines from which the territorial sea adjacent to the French Antilles is measured, JORF 1 November 2017, no. 0256, Articles 3 & 4, *available at* https://www.un.org/Depts/los/LEGISLATIONANDTREATIES/PDFFILES/DEPOSIT/2017-1511_en.pdf.

11 L.B. Sohn, *Baseline Considerations*, *in* I INTERNATIONAL MARITIME BOUNDARIES 155 (J.I. Charney & L.M. Alexander eds., 1993).

8 Method of Delimitation Considerations

As expressly indicated in the Agreement, the parties used the equidistance method for both delimitation lines because they considered that it achieved an equitable result in this case (Article 1(2)). The parties thus scrupulously followed the rule embodied in Articles 74 and 83 of UNCLOS and applicable to the delimitation of the exclusive economic zone and the continental shelf. This approach conforms to the general state practice as regards maritime delimitation between opposite islands.

The coastal relationship between Saint Barthélemy and Barbuda remains one of oppositeness for the entire length of the boundary. As concerns the coastal relationship between Antigua and Guadeloupe, it is one of oppositeness from point B1 to point B5. From point B5 it becomes one of adjacency. This however had no bearing on the direction of the line, as the parties did not shift the equidistance line.

9 Technical Considerations

For both boundaries, the equidistance line has been simplified. The 43 M line between Saint Barthélemy and Barbuda is formed by seven loxodromic segments which connect eight turning points (Article 3). The boundary between Antigua and Guadeloupe is more than 230 M long and is also composed of loxodromic segments that link ten turning points (Article 4). A rhumb line azimuth is specified for the purpose of extending the boundary lines beyond each of the four fixed endpoints.

The geographical coordinates of the points used to define the maritime boundaries are referred to the World Geodetic System 1984 (WGS 84). The delimitation line is depicted for purposes of illustration on a map annexed to the Agreement (Article 5).

10 Other Considerations

None.

5894 *Report Number 2-37*

III CONCLUSIONS

The 2017 Agreement between France and Antigua and Barbuda ends a long-standing dispute between the two countries. It establishes two boundaries, one between Saint Barthélemy (France) and Barbuda and another between Antigua and Guadeloupe (France). Both are simplified equidistance lines constructed from the parties' straight or archipelagic baselines.

IV RELATED LAW IN FORCE

A *Law of the Sea Conventions*

France: Party to UNCLOS (ratified 11 April 1996).
Antigua and Barbuda: Party to UNCLOS (ratified 2 February 1989)

B *Maritime Jurisdiction Claimed at the Time of Signature*

France (Saint-Barthélemy and Guadeloupe): 12 M territorial sea; 24 M contiguous zone; 200 M EEZ; continental shelf to the outer edge of the continental margin for Guadeloupe only (submission to the CLCS on 5 February 2009; recommendations adopted on 9 April 2012).
Antigua and Barbuda: Archipelagic waters; 12 M territorial sea; 24 M contiguous zone; 200 M EEZ; 200 M fishery zone; continental shelf to the outer edge of the continental margin.

C *Maritime Jurisdiction Claimed Subsequent to Signature*

France: No change
France: No change.

Prepared by Benjamin Samson

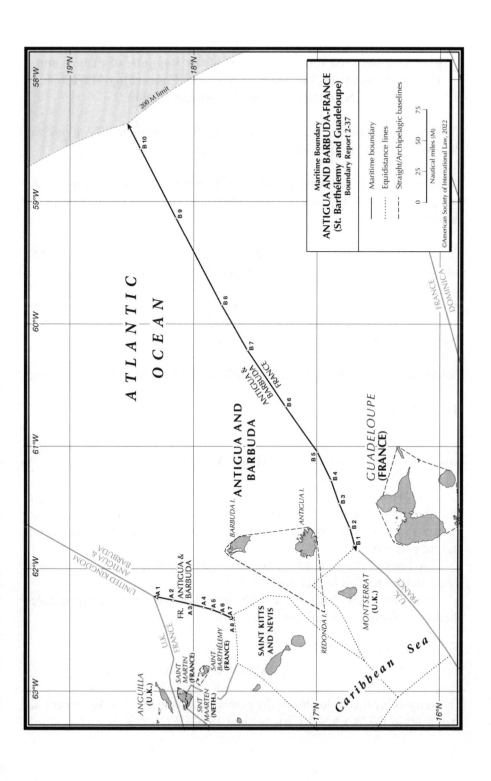

5896 *Report Number 2-37*

Agreement between the Government of the Republic of France and the Government of Antigua and Barbuda Concerning Maritime Delimitation in the Caribbean Region

The Government of the French Republic and the Government of Antigua and Barbuda, hereinafter referred to as "the Parties",

Considering that it is desirable to delimit the maritime zones over which the two States respectively exercise their sovereign rights or jurisdiction in the Caribbean region;

Considering that the relations between the French Republic and Antigua and Barbuda are based on the principle of good neighbourliness;

Having regard to the United Nations Convention on the Law of the Sea, concluded at Montego Bay on 10 December 1982, to which the French Republic and Antigua and Barbuda are Parties;

Conscious of the importance of the maritime environment to their peoples;

Have agreed as follows:

Article 1

1. The maritime delimitation between the French Republic and Antigua and Barbuda established in this Agreement is the delimitation of the maritime zones over which the two States exercise their sovereign rights and jurisdiction.
2. The lines of delimitation are based on equidistance, which is considered an equitable solution in this case.
3. A decision of a Party to establish, extend or amend its maritime zones shall be in accordance with this Agreement.

Article 2

The geographical coordinates of the points established in this Agreement are expressed in the World Geodetic System 1984 (WGS 84).

Article 3

1. The delimitation line between Saint-Barthélemy on the one hand and Antigua and Barbuda on the other hand, comprises loxodromes joining the following points identified by their geographical coordinates, in the order in which they are given:

Point	Latitude (North)	Longitude (West)
A1	18° 17′ 37.0″	062° 13′ 49.6″
A2	18° 09′ 38.3″	062° 15′ 28.4″
A3	18° 01′ 30.4″	062° 17′ 19.5″
A4	17° 55′ 03.7″	062° 18′ 51.3″
A5	17° 51′ 07.2″	062° 20′ 01.2″
A6	17° 46′ 20.8″	062° 21′ 51.7″
A7	17° 41′ 46.2″	062° 24′ 03.8″
A8	17° 40′ 34.9″	062° 24′ 47.1″

2. From Point A1, the delimitation extends along a loxodrome with an azimuth of 11.2 degrees until it reaches the maritime zones of the United Kingdom with respect to Anguilla.
3. From Point A8, the delimitation extends along a loxodrome with an azimuth of 210.2 degrees until it reaches the maritime zones of Saint Kitts and Nevis.

Article 4

1. The delimitation line between Guadeloupe on the one hand and Antigua and Barbuda on the other hand, comprises loxodromes joining the following points identified by their geographical coordinates in the order in which they are given:

Point	Latitude (North)	Longitude (West)
B1	16° 41′ 32.1″	061° 48′ 25.4″
B2	16° 43′ 49.2″	061° 40′ 04.9″
B3	16° 49′ 04.7″	061° 27′ 52.0″
B4	16° 53′ 02.1″	061° 16′ 30.4″
B5	16° 59′ 43.2″	061° 02′ 46.3″
B6	17° 15′ 27.3″	060° 40′ 22.1″
B7	17° 34′ 03.1″	060° 12′ 46.0″

B8	17° 46' 37.0"	059° 50' 33.3"
B9	18° 08' 33.2"	059° 08' 04.0"
B10	18° 25' 46.1"	058° 34' 02.8"

2. From Point B1, the delimitation line extends along a loxodrome with an azimuth of 254.1 degrees until it reaches the maritime zones of the United Kingdom with respect to Montserrat.

3. From Point B10, the delimitation extends along a loxodrome with an azimuth of 62.2 degrees to the outer limit of the maritime zones of Guadeloupe and Antigua and Barbuda.

Article 5

The delimitation lines as established in Articles 3 and 4 of this Agreement are depicted for illustration purposes only on the map in the Annex to this Agreement.

Article 6

Any dispute between the Parties in relation to the interpretation or the application of this Agreement shall be settled peacefully by consultation or negotiation between the Parties, in accordance with international law.

Article 7

The Parties shall notify each other in writing of the completion of their domestic procedures necessary to bring this Agreement into force. This Agreement shall enter into force on the first day of the second month following the date of receipt of the last notification.

In witness whereof the undersigned, duly authorized by their respective Governments, have signed this Agreement.

Done at Saint John's, on March 15, 2017, in the English and French language, both texts being equally authentic.

For the Government of the French Republic: H.E. Philippe Ardanaz, Ambassador of France to the OECS Member States	For the Government of Antigua and Barbuda: Hon. Gaston Browne, Prime Minister of Antigua and Barbuda

Antigua and Barbuda – United Kingdom (Anguilla)

Report Number 2-38

Treaty between the Government of the United Kingdom of Great Britain and Northern Ireland and the Government of Antigua and Barbuda establishing a Maritime Boundary between Anguilla and Antigua and Barbuda

Signed: 27 July 2021
Entry into force: Not yet in force
Published at: United Kingdom Command Paper No. CP 526

I SUMMARY

Antigua and Barbuda is an archipelagic state in the Eastern Caribbean lying opposite and southeast of the British island territory of Anguilla and the French island territories of Saint Martin and Saint Barthélemy. Anguilla is an internally self-governing British Overseas Territory in the Eastern Caribbean.

The maritime delimitation treaty between Antigua and Barbuda and the United Kingdom, with respect to Anguilla (the Treaty), establishes an all-purpose maritime boundary covering the water column, the seabed, and the subsoil (Article 1(1)). The parties concluded the Treaty "[h]aving regard to the United Nations Convention on the Law of the Sea [UNCLOS]" (Preamble), which establishes the rules applicable to maritime boundary delimitation between opposite and adjacent coastal states. The two states delimited the boundary line using the equidistance methodology, which they "considered an equitable solution in this case" (Article 1(3)). The boundary extends for 177 nautical miles (M) in a northeasterly direction from the tripoint with the French islands of Saint Martin and Saint Barthélemy in the south to the outer limit of the maritime jurisdiction of Anguilla and Antigua and Barbuda.

The Treaty, which was achieved with the support of the Commonwealth Secretariat, is the result of two rounds of negotiations, which occurred

---

Coalter G. Lathrop (ed.), International Maritime Boundaries, 5901-5911.
© *The American Society of International Law and Koninklijke Brill BV, Leiden 2025.*

5902   *Report Number 2-38*

in 2019 and 2020.[1] It was signed in St. John's, Antigua and Barbuda on 27 July 2021.[2]

II CONSIDERATIONS

1   Political, Strategic, and Historical Considerations

Antigua and Barbuda is an archipelagic state in the Eastern Caribbean, which gained independence from the United Kingdom on 1 November 1981. It is a member of the Caribbean Community (CARICOM), the Organisation of Eastern Caribbean States (the OECS), and the Commonwealth of Nations (the Commonwealth). Anguilla is an internally self-governing British Overseas Territory and, therefore, is recognized internationally as a territory for whose international relations the United Kingdom is responsible. Anguilla is an associate member of both CARICOM and the OECS.

The Treaty marks an important accomplishment in a maritime boundary delimitation initiative that Antigua and Barbuda developed in the preceding years. In 2014, Antigua and Barbuda's National Oceans Governance Committee requested assistance from the Commonwealth Secretariat in implementing a maritime boundary negotiation strategy.[3] Supported by a combination of legal advice, training, and technical assistance, including the provision of software and imagery to support the delimitation process, Antigua and Barbuda concluded a maritime delimitation agreement in 2017 with France with respect to Guadeloupe and Saint Barthélemy.[4]

Antigua and Barbuda's maritime boundary delimitation initiative continued with negotiations with the United Kingdom with respect to the boundary with Anguilla, also supported by the Commonwealth Secretariat. Negotiations occurred in two rounds; the first in 2019 and the second of 2020.

---

1   Press Release, Commonwealth Secretariat, *Antigua and Barbuda, UK Sign Maritime Boundary Agreement* (19 August 2021), https://thecommonwealth.org/news/antigua-and -barbuda-uk-sign-maritime-boundary-agreement.
2   Foreign, Commonwealth and Development Office, *Explanatory Memorandum on the Treaty between the Government of the United Kingdom of Great Britain and Northern Ireland and the Government of Antigua and Barbuda Establishing a Maritime Boundary between Anguilla and Antigua and Barbuda* (Command Paper No. 526, 2021) (United Kingdom) para. 3.1, *available at* https://www.gov.uk/government/publications/ukantigua -and-barbuda-treaty-establishing-a-maritime-boundary-between-anguilla-and-antigua -and-barbuda-cs-antigua-barbuda-no12021.
3   Commonwealth 2021, *supra* note 1.
4   Commonwealth 2021, *supra* note 1; *see also* Report Number 2-37, in this volume.

In parallel with the negotiations, the parties consulted France and reached an agreement on the tripoint between Anguilla, Antigua and Barbuda, and St. Martin and St. Barthélemy by an exchange of diplomatic notes between the United Kingdom and France on 4 March 2021.[5] The tripoint was adopted as the southwestern point (Point 1) of the boundary line in the Treaty. The parties signed the Treaty in St. John's on 27 July 2021. The government of Anguilla was "involved at all stages of negotiation of the Treaty" and approved the final version of the Treaty prior to signature.[6] As of writing, the Treaty has not entered into force.

2   Legal Regime Considerations

Antigua and Barbuda and the United Kingdom became parties to UNCLOS in 1989 and 1997, respectively. Both parties have adopted legislation pertaining to their maritime zones. Antigua and Barbuda started the process of establishing its maritime jurisdiction with the Maritime Areas Act of 1982, in which it claimed a 12 M territorial sea, a 24 M contiguous zone, and a 200 M exclusive economic zone, and provided for the drawing of archipelagic baselines.[7] Pursuant to this act, Antigua and Barbuda established the coordinates of its archipelagic baselines and designated certain waters as internal.[8]

The United Kingdom extended Anguilla's fishery limits to 200 M pursuant to Proclamation No. 28 of 1981.[9] In 2007, the United Kingdom issued an order extending Anguilla's territorial sea to 12 M.[10]

Article 1 of the Treaty establishes an all-purpose maritime boundary covering the water column, the seabed, and the subsoil. Article 2 states that the Treaty does not "prejudice in any manner either Party's position

---

5   *See* Report Number 2-20 (Add. 2), in this volume; *see also* Explanatory Memorandum, *supra* note 2 at para. 10.3. It is not known whether Antigua and Barbuda and France have exchanged notes related to the tripoint.
6   Explanatory Memorandum, *supra* note 2 at para. 10.2.
7   Act No. 18 of 17 August 1982, Maritime Areas Act, Sections 2(B) & 4 (Antigua and Barbuda) *available at* https://www.un.org/Depts/los/LEGISLATIONANDTREATIES/PDFFILES/ATG_1982_18.pdf.
8   US Department of State, *Antigua and Barbuda: Archipelagic and other Maritime Claims and Boundaries*, Limits in the Seas No. 133 (28 March 2014) 1.
9   US Department of State, *United States – United Kingdom Maritime Boundaries in the Caribbean*, Limits in the Seas No. 115 (11 April 1994) 2.
10   The Anguilla (Territorial Sea) Order 2007 (Statutory Instrument 2007 No. 2916) (10 October 2007), Article 2(1).

with respect to the rules of international law relating to the law of the sea." This suggests that while Antigua and Barbuda and the United Kingdom have agreed how to separate their respective sovereign rights and maritime jurisdictions, they may not necessarily agree on particular claims that the other party maintains with respect to the international law of the sea. Article 3 is a dispute resolution clause providing that any dispute over the interpretation or application of the Treaty will be settled by consultation and negotiation.

3   Economic and Environmental Considerations

The parties did not find any economic or environmental consideration to be significant enough to influence the boundary line, and the Treaty contains no provisions on maritime environmental protection or non-living marine resources. Nevertheless, the Preamble recognizes "the importance of the marine environment to th[e] peoples" of the United Kingdom and Antigua and Barbuda. The Treaty is conducive to both parties' ability to exploit ocean resources and implement environmental protections within their respective boundaries. In particular, Antigua and Barbuda has committed to a transition to the "Blue Economy", the aim of which "is to support the sustainable use of ocean resources for economic growth and improved livelihoods, while protecting ocean health."[11] Antigua and Barbuda is a co-champion of the Commonwealth Blue Charter Action Group on the Sustainable Blue Economy and has recognized the importance of maritime boundary delimitation agreements in realizing the full economic potential of ocean resources.[12]

4   Geographic Considerations

Anguilla is made up of one main island, with an area of 91 km^2, and many small islets. Antigua and Barbuda lies opposite and to the southeast of Anguilla and the French island territories of Saint Martin and Saint Barthélemy. It consists of three main islands: Antigua (280 km$^{2)}$; Barbuda (161 km^2), which lies 40 kilometers north of Antigua; and the uninhabited island of Redonda

---

11   Press Release, Commonwealth Secretariat, *Antigua & Barbuda to Co-Champion Blue Economy Action for the Commonwealth* (24 November 2020), https://thecommonwealth .org/news/antigua-barbuda-co-champion-blue-economy-action-commonwealth.
12   *Id.*; Commonwealth 2021, *supra* note 1.

(1.25 km^2), which lies 40 kilometers southwest of Antigua. The parties did not deem any specific geographic considerations significant enough to affect the course of the boundary line.

5 Islands, Rocks, Reefs, and Low-tide Elevations Considerations

Base points on the northeastern coast of Anguilla's Scrub Island and the northern baselines of Barbuda would have had the only influence on the course of the equidistant line that forms the boundary. The northern coast of the island of Barbuda is fringed by an extensive reef system, including Goat Reef and Cobb Reef, which impacts Antigua and Barbuda's basepoints in the region. These reefs have never been systematically surveyed. Therefore, the Parties established the base points on the northwestern coast of Barbuda on a pragmatic basis, taking account of Antigua and Barbuda's archipelagic baselines and the best available geographic information concerning the outer edge of the fringing reefs.

6 Baseline Considerations

Antigua and Barbuda is an archipelagic state and, pursuant to Article 47 of UNCLOS, has established archipelagic baselines encompassing the islands of Antigua, Barbuda, and Redonda.[13] The end result is a 142 M archipelagic baseline system made up of 22 line segments, ranging from 0.5 nautical miles to 52.9 nautical miles in length.[14] The baseline system the United Kingdom has established for Anguilla generally uses the low-water line along the coast.[15]

7 Geological and Geomorphological Considerations

Geologic and geomorphological factors did not affect the boundary.

---

13 1982 Maritime Areas Act, *supra* note 7 at Art. 4; Limits in the Seas No. 133, *supra* note 8 at 1-2.
14 Limits in the Seas No. 133, *supra* note 8 at 2.
15 2007 Territorial Sea Order, *supra* note 10 at Article 3.

8 *Method of Delimitation Considerations*

Antigua and Barbuda and the United Kingdom delimited the boundary line using a strict application of the equidistance methodology, which they recognized was an "equitable solution". The first point on the boundary line is defined as the tripoint between the parties and France, with respect to Saint Martin and Saint Barthélemy (Article 1(5)). The boundary extends through 14 additional points for 177 M in a northeasterly direction. Beyond Point 15, it extends along a line with a geodetic azimuth of 28.3 degrees until it reaches the outer limit of the maritime jurisdiction of the parties (Article 1(4)).[16]

9 *Technical Considerations*

The parties used the World Geodetic System, 1984 (WGS 84) to define the 15 turning points. Geodetic lines connect the points to form the boundary.

10 *Other Considerations*

None.

III CONCLUSIONS

The Treaty marks a milestone in both parties' efforts to delimit their respective maritime boundaries in the Caribbean and to pursue the development and preservation goals associated with the Blue Economy. It was the first maritime boundary delimitation that the United Kingdom had agreed in the Caribbean since the early 2000s and the third that Antigua and Barbuda agreed in the preceding five-year period.[17] At the time of writing, Anguilla's only maritime boundary remaining to be negotiated is

---

16 There is no indication that either party claims or intends to claim areas of continental shelf lying beyond 200 M from their coasts. Instead, this provision is understood to account for possible changes to baselines and to EEZ limits measured therefrom.

17 Explanatory Memorandum, *supra* note 2 at para. 3.1 (in regard to the boundaries of Anguilla); Commonwealth 2021, *supra* note 1 (in regard to the boundaries of Antigua and Barbuda). *See* Report Number 2-37, in this volume, covering the single agreement between Antigua and Barbuda and France that creates two boundary lines, one with Guadeloupe and one with Saint Barthélemy.

in the southwest with Saba, an overseas territory of the Netherlands. Of Antigua and Barbuda's five maritime boundaries, only those with St. Kitts and Nevis and with Monserrat (United Kingdom) remain to be negotiated. Upon signing the Treaty, the Prime Minister of Antigua and Barbuda stated that his "Government is pledged to ensuring that the outstanding boundaries are completed in the shortest reasonable time in order to position Antigua and Barbuda to continue to lead within the OECS on the development and implementation of the blue economy and blue growth."[18]

IV   RELATED LAW IN FORCE

A   Law of the Sea Conventions

United Kingdom: Party to UNCLOS (ratified 25 July 1997).
Antigua and Barbuda: Party to UNCLOS (acceded 2 February 1989).

B   Maritime Jurisdiction Claimed at the Time of Signature of this boundary agreement

Antigua and Barbuda: Archipelagic waters; 12 M territorial sea; 24 M
  contiguous zone; 200 M EEZ; continental shelf.
United Kingdom: 12 M territorial sea and a 200 M fisheries zone with respect
  to Anguilla.

C   Maritime Jurisdiction Claimed Subsequent to Signature

No change.

Prepared by Natalie L. Reid, Nawi Ukabiala, Perpétua B. Chéry

---

18 Commonwealth 2021, *supra* note 1; *Antigua and Barbuda PM Browne Signs Maritime Boundary Agreement with Anguilla,* Associates Times (31 July 2021), https://associatestimes.com/antigua-and-barbuda-pm-browne-signs-maritime-boundary-agreement-with-anguilla/.

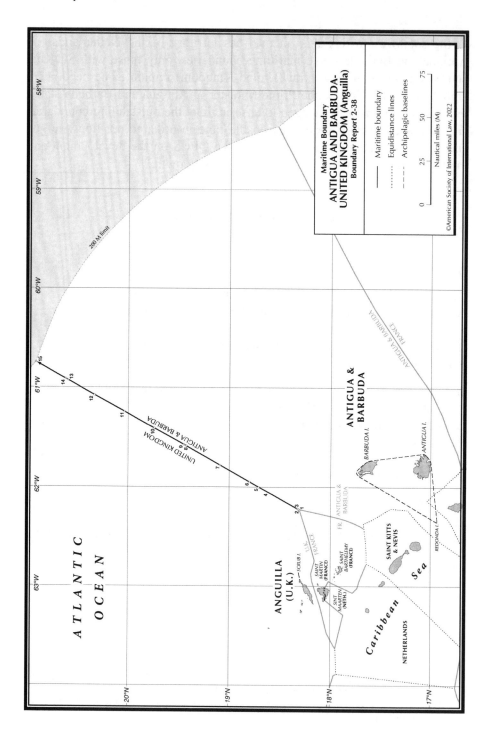

Treaty between the Government of the United Kingdom of Great Britain and Northern Ireland and the Government of Antigua and Barbuda Establishing a Maritime Boundary between Anguilla and Antigua and Barbuda

The Government of the United Kingdom of Great Britain and Northern Ireland, in respect of itself and Anguilla, and the Government of Antigua and Barbuda (the "Parties");

Conscious of the cordial relations between the Parties based on the principles of good neighbourliness and the importance of the marine environment to their peoples;

Having regard to the United Nations Convention on the Law of the Sea, concluded at Montego Bay on 10th December 1982, to which Antigua and Barbuda and the United Kingdom are Parties;

Desiring to establish an all-purpose maritime boundary between the United Kingdom, in respect of Anguilla, and Antigua and Barbuda;

Have agreed as follows:

ARTICLE 1

Maritime Boundary

1) The boundary is understood to be an all-purpose boundary covering the water column, seabed and subsoil.

2) The maritime boundary between Anguilla and Antigua and Barbuda shall be formed by geodesic lines connecting the following points:

Point	Latitude	Longitude
1	18° 18′ 36.1″ N	062° 13′ 37.3″ W
2	18° 18′ 45.2″ N	062° 13′ 37.3″ W
3	18° 19′ 25.7″ N	062° 13′ 14.3″ W
4	18° 37′ 04.1″ N	062° 03′ 11.3″ W
5	18° 42′ 33.2″ N	062° 00′ 03.3″ W
6	18° 48′ 02.3″ N	061° 56′ 55.1″ W

7	19° 05′ 39.8″ N	061° 46′ 48.8″ W
8	19° 25′ 49.0″ N	061° 35′ 12.4″ W
9	19° 27′ 09.0″ N	061° 34′ 27.4″ W
10	19° 44′ 51.5″ N	061° 24′ 28.5″ W
11	20° 02′ 33.4″ N	061° 14′ 27.4″ W
12	20° 20′ 14.7″ N	061° 04′ 24.1″ W
13	20° 35′ 59.6″ N	060° 55′ 24.7″ W
14	20° 37′ 15.2″ N	060° 54′ 41.4″ W
15	20° 54′ 55.3″ N	060° 44′ 33.7″ W

3) The line of delimitation is based on equidistance which is considered an equitable solution in this case.

4) After Point 15, the maritime boundary between Anguilla and Antigua and Barbuda shall extend along a line with a geodetic azimuth of 28.3 degrees until it reaches the outer limit of the maritime jurisdiction of the Parties.

5) Point 1 shall be the tripoint between the Parties and the Republic of France, as has been accepted in an exchange of diplomatic notes by the Republic of France.

6) The geodetic reference system used to calculate the position of the points listed in the table in Article 1(2) is WGS 84.

7) The boundary has been drawn, for the purposes of illustration only, on the map contained in the Annex to this Treaty.

ARTICLE 2

Parties' Positions on International Law of the Sea

The maritime boundary established by this Treaty shall not affect or prejudice in any manner either Party's position with respect to the rules of international law relating to the law of the sea, including those concerned with the exercise of sovereignty, sovereign rights, or jurisdiction with respect to the water column, seabed or subsoil.

ARTICLE 3

Dispute Resolution

Any dispute between the Parties in relation to the interpretation or the application of this Treaty shall be settled peacefully by consultation and negotiation between the Parties, in accordance with international law.

ARTICLE 4

Amendment

This Treaty may only be amended by mutual written agreement of the Parties.

ARTICLE 5

Entry into Force

The Parties shall notify each other in writing of the completion of their domestic procedures necessary to bring this Treaty into force. This Treaty shall enter into force 30 days after the receipt of the last notification of completion of the respective internal procedures.

IN WITNESS WHEREOF the undersigned, being duly authorised by their respective Governments, have signed this Treaty.

DONE in duplicate at St John's this 27th day of July 2021

For the Government of the United Kingdom of Great Britain and Northern Ireland:

For the Government of Antigua and Barbuda:

LINDSY THOMPSON

GASTON BROWNE

Dominican Republic – Netherlands

Report Number 2-39

Agreement between the Kingdom of the Netherlands and the Dominican Republic Concerning Maritime Delimitation

Signed: 5 July 2021
Entry into force: Not yet in force
Published at: *Tractatenblad* (Netherlands Treaty Series) 2021, 103

I SUMMARY

The Agreement between the Kingdom of the Netherlands and the Dominican Republic Concerning Maritime Delimitation (2021 Agreement) delimits the maritime zones of the Dominican Republic and the Netherlands territories of Aruba and Curaçao. The boundary, which is located between the opposite coasts of the parties and measures some 42 nautical miles (M), is an all-purpose maritime boundary. The shortest distance between the land territory of the Dominican Republic and the island of Aruba is just over 300 M and the distance from the former to the island of Curaçao is some 340 M. The maritime boundary between the Dominican Republic and the Netherlands aligns with the termini of the maritime boundary between the Netherlands and Venezuela that was established in 1978 (1978 Treaty)[1] and nearly coincides with the termini of the maritime boundary between the Dominican Republic and Venezuela, which was defined by a treaty concluded in 1979 (1979 Treaty).[2]

---

1   *See* Report Number 2-12, I IMB 615, providing analysis and text of *Boundary Delimitation Treaty between the Republic of Venezuela and the Kingdom of the Netherlands*, 31 March 1978, 1140 UNTS 324 (1978 Treaty).
2   *See* Report Number 2-9, I IMB 577, providing analysis and text of *Treaty on the Delimitation of Marine and Submarine Areas between the Republic of Venezuela and the Dominican Republic*, 3 March 1979 (1979 Treaty).

Coalter G. Lathrop (ed.), International Maritime Boundaries, 5913-5924.
© *The American Society of International Law and Koninklijke Brill BV, Leiden 2025.*

5914 *Report Number 2-39*

II CONSIDERATIONS

1 *Political, Strategic and Historical Considerations*

The Netherlands had proposed negotiations on this maritime boundary in the past, but the actual negotiations leading up to the conclusion of the 2021 Agreement were initiated after an invitation of the Dominican Republic to start negotiations in March of 2020.[3] A first meeting took place on 23 November 2020, and the Agreement was signed on 5 July 2021. On the part of the Kingdom of the Netherlands, Aruba and Curaçao, two of the four countries that make up the Kingdom, were involved in the negotiations, because the delimitation is concerned with the maritime areas of these two countries.[4] The 2021 Agreement is not relevant for the delimitation of the maritime areas of the Netherlands island of Bonaire, which is a special municipality of the country of the Netherlands, because the internal delimitation between the country of Curaçao and Bonaire does not extend up to the median line boundary between the Netherlands and the Dominican Republic.[5]

The maritime boundary between the Netherlands and the Dominican Republic fits in with the delimitation agreements both states concluded with Venezuela in 1978 and 1979 respectively. The end points of the maritime boundary between the Netherlands and the Dominican Republic are aligned with the corresponding end points of the maritime boundary between the Netherlands and Venezuela. The end points of the maritime boundary between Venezuela and the Dominican Republic are slightly to the northeast of the corresponding end points of the maritime boundary between the latter and the Netherlands. This discrepancy likely is explained by the use of a different geodetic datum in the two bilateral treaties with Venezuela (see further below at section 9).

---

3 Explanatory Memorandum to the Bill for approval of the Agreement submitted to the Netherlands Parliament (*Memorie van Toelichting*), Parliamentary Paper 36 017 (R2159), No. 3), 1, *available at* https://zoek.officielebekendmakingen.nl/kst-36017-3.pdf.
4 Explanatory Memorandum, *supra* note 3 at 1.
5 *See* Royal Netherlands Navy, Hydrographic Service, *Maritime limits and boundaries of the Kingdom of the Netherlands*, 2018, *available at* https://english.defensie.nl/binaries /large/content/gallery/defence/content-afbeeldingen/topics/hydrography/maritime-limits /zonegrenzen_benedenwinds_2018_en.jpg.

2 Legal Regime Considerations

The Dominican Republic and the Netherlands are parties to the United Nations Convention on the Law of the Sea (Convention). The 2021 Agreement refers to this fact in its preamble and provides that the parties have regard to the Convention. The Agreement establishes an all-purpose maritime boundary. Article 1(1) provides that it "shall establish the delimitation of all maritime zones in the Caribbean Sea between the Parties." Article 1(2) further adds that "[a] decision of a Party to establish, extend or amend its maritime zones shall be in accordance with this Agreement." Due to its location, the 2021 Agreement currently delimits the continental shelf and exclusive economic zone of the parties.

The 2021 Agreement contains a number of provisions on transboundary cooperation. Article 3 deals with transboundary hydrocarbon deposits and requires the parties to make their best efforts to enter into cooperative arrangements. It provides that "the cost and benefits related to [exploitation] activities shall be equitably and reasonably apportioned in accordance with [the Convention] and other relevant rules of international law." Article 4 of the 2021 Agreement requires the parties to "promote and facilitate the development and conduct of marine scientific research in their maritime zones." In this connection, reference is made to Article 239 of the Convention, which contains an identically-worded provision on scientific cooperation. This provision was included upon the request of the Dominican Republic.[6] The Agreement does not contain any specific provisions on transboundary cooperation in the field of fisheries.[7]

Article 5(1) provides that "[a]ny dispute regarding the interpretation or application of this Agreement shall be settled peacefully by negotiation, in accordance with international law." Paragraph 2 provides that when "no agreement can be reached within a reasonable period of time, either Party may have recourse to the provisions on dispute settlement provided by Part XV" of the Convention. This includes recourse to compulsory dispute settlement under section 2 of Part XV. Neither party at the time of writing has made a declaration under Article 298 of the Convention excluding delimitation disputes from such settlement.

---

6 Explanatory Memorandum, *supra* note 3 at 3.
7 The Explanatory Memorandum does observe that the boundary may be of relevance for fisheries management, *supra* note 3 at 11.

5916 *Report Number 2-39*

3 *Economic and Environmental Considerations*

There is no indication that economic or environmental considerations played a role in determining the location of the maritime boundary.

4 *Geographic Considerations*

The 2021 Agreement indicates that the boundary is based on equidistance (Article 2(1)). The boundary consists of a single-segment geodetic line that connects two points defined in geographical coordinates referenced to WGS84 (Article 2(2)). The western end point of the boundary (Point 1) is controlled by basepoints on the coast of Aruba and the Dominican Republic's mainland and island of Saona, while the eastern endpoint (Point 2) is equidistant between basepoints on Aruba and Curaçao and the island of Saona.

5 *Islands, Rocks, Reefs, and Low-tide Elevations Considerations*

The maritime boundary is located between the mainland of the Dominican Republic, which is located on the eastern half of the island of Hispaniola, and smaller islands adjacent to the Dominican mainland, on the one hand, and the islands of Aruba and Curaçao, on the other hand. All of these features have received full weight in determining the equidistant maritime boundary between the parties (see further section 8).

6 *Baseline Considerations*

As is noted in section 5, the maritime boundary is an equidistance line that gives full effect to the mainland of the Dominican Republic and its adjacent islands and the islands of Aruba and Curaçao. However, the boundary is not an equidistance line if the straight baselines established by the Dominican Republic are taken into account. The Dominican Republic declared itself to be an archipelagic state and established archipelagic straight baselines in 2007.[8] If these straight baselines had been taken into account, an equidistance

---

8 Act 66-07 of 22 May 2007 on archipelagic baselines, Arts. 1 and 2 (Dominican Republic), English translation *available at* https://www.un.org/Depts/los/LEGISLATIONAND

line would be located slightly to the south of the maritime boundary in the 2021 Agreement for most of its course, except for a small area at the eastern end of the maritime boundary. A couple of points may be noted in this connection. Straight baselines do not always receive the same treatment as normal baselines in determining maritime boundaries, and, as was noted above, the parties to the 2021 Agreement had already concluded bilateral maritime boundary agreements with Venezuela in 1978 and 1979. The termini of those earlier agreements were based on equidistance using the normal baseline. Using a different baseline for the 2021 Agreement would have required agreeing on how to link the boundary of that agreement to the existing boundaries.

7 Geological and Geomorphological Considerations

Geological and geomorphological considerations have not played a role in the determination of the maritime boundary between the parties. The entire area concerned is located within the 200 M limit.

8 Method of Delimitation Considerations

As was noted above in section 6, the method of delimitation is the equidistance method. As far as can be ascertained, oppositeness and proportionality have not affected the delimitation. Nonetheless, it is of interest to note the difference in the lengths of the relevant coasts of the Dominican Republic and the Netherlands. The south-facing coast of the Dominican Republic measures around 460 kilometers. The north- and northeast-facing coasts of Aruba and Curaçao measure approximately 23 and 62 kilometers. The ratio between these relevant coasts is 5.4:1.[9] It may, moreover, be noted that the islands of

---

TREATIES/PDFFILES/DOM_2007_Act_frombulletin65.pdf. For an analysis of the straight baselines established by the Dominican Republic see US Department of State, *Dominican Republic Archipelagic and other Maritime Claims and Boundaries,* Limits in the Seas No. 130 (31 January 2014); S. Kopela, *2007 Archipelagic Legislation of the Dominican Republic: An Assessment,* 24 (200) INTERNATIONAL JOURNAL OF MARINE AND COASTAL LAW 501.

9   It could, however, be argued that the island of Bonaire for delimitation purposes should also be taken into account. The north-facing coast of Bonaire measures some 28 kilometers. In this case the ratio between the relevant coast of the Dominican Republic and that of the Netherlands would still be around 4.1:1.

Aruba, Curaçao and Bonaire received less than full weight in the adjacent segments of the delimitation between the Netherlands and Venezuela.

Two considerations may in particular explain why the issue of (dis)proportionality did not play any role in delimiting the maritime boundary between the Dominican Republic and the Netherlands. First, the delimitation between the Netherlands and Venezuela was effected between the islands of Aruba, Curaçao, and Bonaire and the Venezuelan mainland coast. While the delimitation between the Dominican Republic is also effected between a longer mainland coast and the islands of Aruba, Curaçao, and Bonaire, the broader geographical context indicates that there would be limited room for adjusting an equidistance line toward Aruba and Curaçao, as the islands are located at a close distance from the Venezuelan mainland coast, which is also opposite the coast of the Dominican Republic. Second, and perhaps more importantly, the Dominican Republic had already accorded Aruba and Curaçao full weight in its 1979 Treaty with Venezuela.[10] This treatment of third-state territory resulted in end points on the 1979 Dominican Republic-Venezuela boundary that are equidistant from the Dominican Republic and Aruba and Curaçao.[11] In that light, it might have been difficult for the Dominican Republic to convince the Netherlands to accept giving less weight to the islands in their bilateral delimitation.

9   Technical Considerations

The 2021 Agreement provides that "[t]he geographical coordinates of the points established in [it] are expressed in the geodetic reference system WGS 84 (World Geodetic System 1984)." The boundary is defined as a geodesic line. As was mentioned above, the end points of the boundary align with the corresponding end points of the maritime boundary between the Netherlands and Venezuela, but the end points of the maritime boundary between Venezuela and the Dominican Republic are slightly to the northeast. It may be noted that the geographical coordinates of the end points as defined in the earlier treaties with Venezuela are identical. However, the geodetic datums to which they are referenced are different, meaning the points are not

---

10 Report Number 2-9, I IMB 577, 581.

11 Although the islands of Aruba, Curaçao, and Bonaire were accorded limited weight in establishing the lateral boundaries between Venezuela and the Netherlands, the northern termini of those boundaries are similarly equidistant between the islands and the Dominican Republic.

in the same location despite having the same coordinates. The treaty between the Netherlands and Venezuela uses the Provisional South American Datum 1956, and the agreement between the Dominican Republic and Venezuela uses the North American Datum 1927.[12] Due to differences between these two datums, there is a distance of approximately 500 meters between the end points defined in these two earlier agreements. This small difference most likely was not intentional.[13] The 2021 Agreement resolves the geodetic datum issue by converting the 1978 coordinates to WGS84. Consequently the 2021 endpoints are in the same locations as their 1978 counterparts even though their geographic coordinates are different. With this approach the maritime boundaries of the Netherlands in this region are completely consistent with each other, while there remains a small gap between the two tripoints and the bilateral boundary of the Dominican Republic and Venezuela.

10 *Other Considerations*

None.

III CONCLUSIONS

The 2021 Agreement accords with the large majority of maritime boundary agreements in applying equidistance as the method of delimitation and fits in with the bilateral maritime boundaries previously established by the parties and Venezuela.

---

12 1978 Treaty, Art. 3 (1); 1979 Treaty, Art. 3.

13 It may be noted that the treaty between the Netherlands and Venezuela uses both the Provisional South American Datum 1956 (for sectors A, B and C involving the Venezuelan mainland) and the North American Datum 1927 for sector D between the Venezuelan island of Aves and the Netherlands islands of Saba and Sint Eustatius. While the treaty between Venezuela and the Dominican Republic uses the same coordinates as the treaty between the Netherlands and Venezuela in defining the boundary, it uses the datum of that treaty that was used for a different sector of the boundary between the Netherlands and Venezuela (between the Venezuelan island of Aves and the Netherlands islands of Saba and Sint Eustatius). 1978 Treaty, Art. 3 (2).

5920 *Report Number 2-39*

IV RELATED LAW IN FORCE

A *Law of the Sea Conventions*

Dominican Republic: Party to UNCLOS (ratified 10 July 2009).
Netherlands: Party to UNCLOS (ratified 28 June 1996).

B *Maritime Jurisdiction Claimed at the Time of Signature*

Dominican Republic: Archipelagic waters; 12 M territorial sea; 12 M contiguous zone; 200 M EEZ; continental shelf.
Netherlands: 12 M territorial sea; 12 M contiguous zone; 200 M EEZ; continental shelf.

C *Maritime Jurisdiction Claimed Subsequent to Signature*

Dominican Republic: No change.
Netherlands: No change.

Prepared by Alex G. Oude Elferink

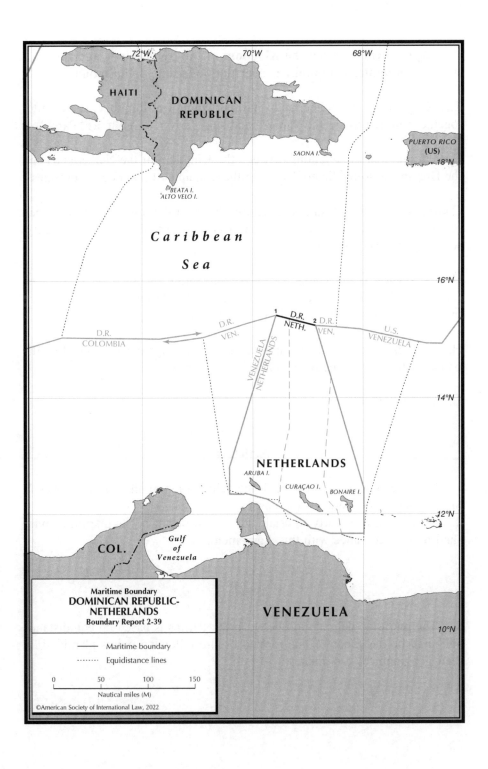

Agreement between the Kingdom of the Netherlands and the Dominican Republic concerning maritime delimitation

The Kingdom of the Netherlands and the Dominican Republic, (hereinafter together referred to as "the Parties" and singularly referred to as "Party");

Considering that the relations between the Kingdom of the Netherlands and the Dominican Republic are based on the principle of good neighbourliness;

Considering that it is desirable to delimit the maritime zones in the Caribbean region over which the two States respectively exercise their sovereignty, sovereign rights or jurisdiction;

Having regard to the United Nations Convention on the Law of the Sea ("UNCLOS"), concluded at Montego Bay on 10 December 1982, to which the Kingdom of the Netherlands and the Dominican Republic are Parties;

Having regard to the maritime border delimitation agreements signed by the parties with their respective neighboring countries;

Have agreed as follows:

Article 1

1.   This Agreement shall establish the delimitation of all maritime zones in the Caribbean Sea between the Parties.
2.   A decision of a Party to establish, extend or amend its maritime zones shall be in accordance with this Agreement.

Article 2

1.   The maritime delimitation between the Parties is based on equidistance and shall be the geodesic line formed by the following points identified by their geographical coordinates:

Point	North Latitude	West Longitude
1	15° 24′ 37″	69° 34′ 45″
2	15° 14′ 17″	68° 51′ 51″

2. The geographic coordinates of the points established in paragraph 1 are expressed in the geodetic reference system WGS 84 (World Geodetic System 1984).

3. For illustrative purposes, this delimitation is shown on nautical chart INT402 annexed to this Agreement.

Article 3

In the event that a single geological structure or mineral field containing oil or natural gas should extend across the line established in Article 2, and a part of said structure or field that is situated on one side of the line could be exploited totally or partially from the other side of the line, the Parties, after holding technical consultations, will make their best efforts to seek to reach agreement regarding the most effective way of exploiting said structure or field, and on the way in which the cost and benefits related to such activities shall be equitably and reasonably apportioned in accordance with UNCLOS and other relevant rules of international law.

Article 4

In accordance with Article 239 of UNCLOS, the Parties shall promote and facilitate the development and conduct of marine scientific research in their maritime zones, and may, if appropriate, make arrangements.

Article 5

1. Any dispute regarding the interpretation or application of this Agreement shall be settled peacefully by negotiation, in accordance with international law.

2. In the event that no agreement can be reached within a reasonable period of time, either Party may have recourse to the provisions on dispute settlement provided by Part XV UNCLOS.

Article 6

This Agreement shall enter into force on the first day of the second month following the date of receipt of the last written notification, through diplomatic channels, by which the Parties shall have notified each other that all necessary internal procedures for entry into force of this Agreement have been completed.

IN WITNESS WHEREOF, the representatives of the Parties, being duly authorized for this purpose, have signed this Agreement.

DONE at Santo Domingo this 05th day of July 2021, in two original copies, in the Dutch, Spanish and English languages, all texts being equally authentic. In case of divergence in the interpretation of this Agreement, the English version shall prevail.

For the Kingdom of the Netherlands,   *For the Dominican Republic,*

ANNEMIEKE ALEXANDRA VERRIJP   ROBERTO ÁLVAREZ

Barbados – Saint Lucia

Report Number 2-40

Agreement between the Government of Barbados and the Government of Saint Lucia on the Delimitation of the Maritime Boundary between Barbados and Saint Lucia

Signed: 6 July 2017
Entry into force: 1 September 2019
Published at: UNTS (I-56440)

I SUMMARY

The maritime boundary agreement between Barbados and Saint Lucia (the Agreement), is one of three maritime boundary agreements negotiated within 2015 to 2017 among Barbados, Saint Lucia, and Saint Vincent and the Grenadines. The agreement between Barbados and Saint Vincent and the Grenadines was concluded in 2015 (the 2015 Agreement).[1] The agreement between Saint Lucia and Saint Vincent and the Grenadines was concluded on the same day as the Barbados and Saint Lucia Agreement.[2] These three independent Caribbean states are members of the Caribbean Community (CARICOM) and, except for Barbados, are members of the Organisation of Eastern Caribbean States (OECS). Both regional institutions played a substantial role in reaching the Agreement.

The Agreement establishes Barbados' fifth maritime boundary. At the time of its conclusion, Barbados possessed considerable experience and familiarity with delimitation issues, having established an Exclusive Economic Cooperation Zone with Guyana in 2003,[3] determined its maritime boundary with Trinidad and Tobago through arbitration in 2006,[4] and negotiated single-purpose maritime boundaries with France in 2009[5] and Saint Vincent and the

---

1   *See* Report Number 2-35, VIII IMB 5433.
2   *See* Report Number 2-41, in this volume.
3   *See* Report Number 2-27, V IMB 3578.
4   *See* Report Number 2-26 (Add.1), VI IMB 4187.
5   *See* Report Number 2-30, VI IMB 4223.

Coalter G. Lathrop (ed.), International Maritime Boundaries, 5925-5939.
© *The American Society of International Law and Koninklijke Brill BV, Leiden 2025.*

5926   *Report Number 2-40*

Grenadines in 2015.[6] Barbados' last remaining maritime boundary issues are implicated by the ongoing territorial issues between Guyana and Venezuela and the outcomes of submissions to the Commission on the Limits of the Continental Shelf by Suriname, Trinidad and Tobago and Guyana.

The Agreement is one of three maritime boundaries concluded by Saint Lucia in more than thirty years, the first having been signed with France two years after achieving independence on 22 February 1979. The delimitation agreement between Saint Lucia and Saint Vincent and the Grenadines rounds out Saint Lucia's delimitations to date. Saint Lucia's last remaining maritime boundary issues are implicated by the effect to be given to Venezuela's Aves Island.[7]

The single-purpose maritime boundary established by the Agreement delimiting the exclusive economic zones (EEZ) and continental shelves of Barbados and Saint Lucia utilizes the equidistance method and comprises 21 points joined by geodetic lines. Points 1 and 21 are intended to be coincident with the end points of the related boundaries with France and Saint Vincent and the Grenadines thereby creating tripoints in the north with France and in the south with Saint Vincent and the Grenadines.

II   CONSIDERATIONS

1   *Political, Strategic, and Historical Considerations*

As indicated in the Preamble, regional institutions played an important role in reaching the Agreement. Between 2011 and 2013, the OECS revised its Maritime Boundary Delimitation Negotiating Strategy (the Revised Strategy), which aligns with international best practices under Articles 74 and 83 of the United Nations Convention on the Law of the Sea (UNCLOS). The Agreement is a tangible outcome of the Revised Strategy. The Preamble of the Agreement refers to UNCLOS and to regional integration instruments and strategies relating to economic union, fisheries management, and ocean policy.[8] Reference in the Preamble to the Eastern Caribbean Regional

---

6   *See* Report Number 2-35, VIII IMB 5433.
7   In this report, the Venezuelan feature will be referred to as Aves Island. This does not connote any significance as to its geographical or legal status or its entitlements under UNCLOS.
8   The Preamble refers to:
     Revised Treaty of Chaguaramas Establishing the Caribbean Community including the Single Market and Economy (available at https://treaty.caricom.org/);

Oceans Policy (ECROP) incorporates ECROP Priority 1 on securing access to resources[9] and includes Goal 1.1 addressing delimitation by member states for the protection of their rights and jurisdiction over maritime areas.[10]

In pursuance of the Revised Strategy and by common agreement, technical discussions on maritime boundary delimitation took place among Barbados, Saint Lucia, and Saint Vincent and the Grenadines in May 2015. This meeting resulted in Barbados and Saint Vincent and the Grenadines signing the 2015 Agreement on 31 August 2015.[11] A follow-up round of negotiations to develop a draft maritime boundary agreement between Barbados and Saint Lucia was held in Barbados from 1-4 March 2016 resulting in a draft agreement being reached on 4 March 2016. At that meeting, discussions were also held between Saint Vincent and the Grenadines and Saint Lucia on options for finalizing tripoints among the three states (in the south) and with France (in the north). Saint Lucian technical officials at the 2016 negotiations were also part of the regional OECS Ocean Governance Team, further reflecting the importance of regional institutions in this process.[12]

Both the Barbados – Saint Lucia Agreement and the agreement between Saint Lucia and Saint Vincent and the Grenadines were signed the next year at the 38th Regular Meeting of the Conference of Heads of Government of CARICOM in St George's, Grenada on 6 July 2017. The three delimitations

---

Revised Treaty of Basseterre Establishing the Organisation of Eastern Caribbean States Economic Union (*available at* https://www.oecs.org/en/our-work/knowledge/library /revised-treaty-of-basseterre/download);
Caribbean Community Common Fisheries Policy (http://extwprlegs1.fao.org/docs/pdf /mul167228.pdf);
Organisation of Eastern Caribbean States Fisheries Management and Development Strategy (unpublished);
Barbados Fisheries Sector Management and Development Policy (unpublished);
Eastern Caribbean Regional Ocean Policy (ECROP) of the Organization of Eastern Caribbean States (*available at* https://clmeplus.org/doculibrary/eastern-caribbean-regional -ocean-policy/). ECROP 2020 (a revised version of ECROP 2013) is awaiting final endorsement by the OECS Authority.

9   Priority 1 articulates that the outer legal limits of maritime jurisdiction have been established through the delimitation of maritime boundaries in accordance with the provisions of the United Nations Convention on the Law of the Sea (UNCLOS) which allows for the exercise of rights accorded to nations under international law.

10   Goal 1.1 provides that OECS member states formalize and define maritime boundaries in order to secure, exercise and protect their rights and jurisdiction over their maritime area and resources.

11   Press Release, CARICOM, *Barbados & St. Vincent Sign Maritime Agreement* (6 September 2015) https://caricom.org/barbados-st-vincent-sign-maritime-agreement/. *See also* Report Number 2-35, VIII IMB 5433.

12   This is a body established under ECROP 2013 to strengthen regional coordinating mechanisms for ocean governance, including the finalization of unresolved maritime boundaries among member states.

(the 2015 Agreement, and each of the agreements concluded in 2017) utilize the same model language, with paragraphs repeated *mutatis mutandis*. These agreements are intended to set precedent for future OECS delimitation agreements and activities where the equidistance method is applied. There were no special or relevant circumstances nor any overriding national interests to warrant departure from the essentially trilateral nature of the agreements, making this a harmonized approach adopted by the parties.[13]

Regional and international technical assistance played a significant role in the conclusion of the Agreement. Saint Lucia, like other OECS states, benefitted from legal, technical, and logistical support provided by the Dalhousie Ocean Studies Programme (DOSP) through the Canadian International Development Agency (CIDA) in the 1980s and, in later years, assistance from the Commonwealth Secretariat and the United Kingdom Hydrographic Office (UKHO) in the form of preliminary legal and technical assessments and hydrographic studies. Barbados and Saint Lucia participated in the OECS Commission/Commonwealth Secretariat Regional Working Session in Saint Lucia in 2014 where delimitation options were illustrated in a non-binding context and good practice examples were shared by Barbados, The Bahamas, Jamaica, and Trinidad and Tobago as regional states at more advanced stages of maritime boundary delimitation. In 2016, a follow-up Regional Maritime Boundaries and Ocean Governance Working Session among independent Caribbean states and territories provided opportunities for further delimitation training, increased awareness of current jurisprudence, and appreciation of integrated ocean management practices.

These efforts in 2014, 2015, and 2016 helped overcome the earlier hesitation among OECS states to complete the maritime boundary delimitation process. In earlier consultations on law of the sea matters facilitated by the OECS Commission in November 2007 in Barbados, Barbados proposed that maritime boundary delimitation issues and collaborative approaches to managing marine space with OECS member states be pursued either bilaterally or multilaterally within the context of the CARICOM Common Fisheries Policy regime and measures for the exploitation of non-living

---

13 A goal of the Revised OECS Maritime Boundary Delimitation Strategy elucidated in January 2011, is that OECS member states should settle outstanding maritime boundaries among themselves and engage in maritime boundary negotiations with non-OECS states, provided that member states shall consult with other member states before agreeing to a maritime boundary with a non-OECS state that is less favorable than a median line solution.

resources (i.e., oil and gas). However, subsequent to the 2007 consultations and further diplomatic communications, the OECS Commission weighed Barbados' greater state of readiness. Due to OECS states' lack of relevant data regarding the presence of hydrocarbons in the vicinity of the boundary and given that information on its non-living resources potential, particularly oil and gas deposits might impact an assessment of whether a delimitation would produce an equitable solution, the OECS Commission indicated to Barbados that it was not ready to commence delimitation in 2007.

Barbados' historical practice of using the provisional median line to define its offshore concession areas on maps was taken into consideration during the 2016 negotiations. Although this state practice by Barbados in the area adjacent to Saint Lucia was stated to be without prejudice to the final delimitation of the maritime boundary with Saint Lucia, it was noted during the negotiations.

Previously agreed maritime boundaries among Barbados, Saint Lucia, France, and Saint Vincent and the Grenadines were taken into consideration, as were Barbados' perspectives from its arbitration with Trinidad and Tobago and its stated preference for peaceful dispute resolution. The parties appreciated that their negotiations would set the tone for the upcoming Saint Lucia – Saint Vincent and the Grenadines negotiations and aimed to reach agreement on tripoints where possible. There were no disputes among the parties regarding the area to be delimited.

2 Legal Regime Considerations

The Agreement establishes a single, all-purpose boundary delimiting the EEZ and continental shelf between Barbados and Saint Lucia. The parties have no overlapping areas of territorial sea. Article 3 supports collaboration between the parties on marine environmental protection and conservation and the management of living resources, whilst Article 4 addresses the unitization of any future straddling deposits.

Article 5 provides for any dispute between the parties regarding the interpretation or application of the Agreement to be settled by peaceful means according to international law, including by recourse to the dispute settlement provisions of Part XV of UNCLOS, to which both states are party. These provisions reflect the same model language as employed in the agreements between Saint Vincent and the Grenadines and Barbados respectively.

3 Economic and Environmental Considerations

Barbados' need to consolidate and maximize utilization of its marine space regarding living and non-living resources is matched by the importance of fisheries resources for OECS member states. Based on the limited living and non-living resource activities in the area to be delimited, there were no prevailing economic, environmental, or resource considerations weighing on the parties' deliberations. In that sense, the provisions of Article 3 relating to the coordination of activities regarding the protection and preservation of the marine environment and conservation and management of living resources, as well as Article 4 regarding the unitization of future joint deposits, were included in the Agreement in an abundance of caution. Most of Barbados' agreements and the related OECS maritime boundary agreements adopt these provisions as a matter of course.

4 Geographic Considerations

Barbados lies east of the volcanic Winward Islands chain, of which Saint Lucia forms a part. Barbados is situated approximately 80 nautical miles (M) east of Saint Lucia. Saint Lucia is the larger of the two island states with a land area of 617 km^2, while Barbados possesses a land area of 432 km^2.

Barbados and Saint Lucia are both single-island states with coasts in a position of oppositeness. There were no specific geographic factors affecting the location of the boundary, and the slightly concave sections of the Saint Lucia coastline were not critical for identifying basepoints for measuring the extent of its territorial sea or delimiting its EEZ and continental shelf.

5 Islands, Rocks, Reefs, and Low-tide Elevations Considerations

Saint Lucia's Maria Islands, two uninhabited islets just off the southeast coast of the main island of Saint Lucia, do not contribute basepoints for the equidistance line between the two states and were therefore not relevant to discussions concerning the alignment of the boundary.

6 Baseline Considerations

Both Barbados and Saint Lucia use normal baselines. During initial technical discussions in Barbados in May 2015, Barbados provided details of their normal baseline to Saint Lucia. There were no historic or archipelagic waters necessitating the use of straight baseline segments to arrive at the location of the boundary.

7 Geological and Geomorphological Considerations

There was no need for the parties to invoke these concepts.

8 Method of Delimitation Considerations

Technical discussions and informal exchanges of views in May 2015 towards negotiations for the 2015 Agreement resulted in the subsequent equidistant boundary delimitation between Barbados and Saint Vincent and the Grenadines. The parties reconvened in Barbados in September 2015 and from 1-4 March 2016 for trilateral discussions on the remaining maritime boundaries between Barbados and Saint Lucia, and Saint Lucia and Saint Vincent and the Grenadines.

At the negotiations in March 2016, as with previous discussions, the parties agreed on the equidistance principle being used to guide the negotiations. Since the states are in a position of oppositeness with similar coastal lengths, coastal proportionality was not a factor. To maximize progress during face-to-face negotiations, the parties had previously exchanged draft negotiating texts. The parties generated their respective equidistance lines from their normal baselines as the starting point for negotiations and shared their respective median line coordinates which were found to be identical. As such, it was considered that an accurate maritime boundary between the two states could be generated.

The parties then considered whether there were any compelling reasons to move the provisional median line. Cognizance was taken of the fact that the parties to the 2015 Agreement had utilized normal and archipelagic baselines and adopted the equidistance methodology. No compelling reasons were found to depart from the provisional median line, and an equidistance boundary was "considered to be an equitable solution in this case" (Article 1).

It was further agreed that best efforts would be used to agree on a tripoint with France in the north. The agreed boundary established by the 1981 agreement between Saint Lucia and France comprises 18 points,[14] and it was

---

14 *See* Report Number 2-10, I IMB 591.

expected that the eastern endpoint (Point L18) would be close to a tripoint between France, Saint Lucia, and Barbados. A review of the Barbados-France median line indicated that the southern endpoint of this line (Point 1) was coincident with Point L18.[15] These formerly-agreed points were not, however, coincident with the northern endpoint of the provisional median line constructed by Barbados and Saint Lucia.

It was considered that if the parties were to use a different endpoint this might complicate maritime domain enforcement, pollution prevention, or create navigational errors. Consequently, identifying a single tripoint coincident with the end points in the respective treaties each party had already concluded with France was considered an acceptable solution. This was accomplished by a slight adjustment to the northern segment of the provisional median line connecting the penultimate turning point (Point 2) with the final northern endpoint of the Barbados – Saint Lucia boundary (Point 1).[16]

In the south, the related boundary between Barbados and Saint Vincent and the Grenadines delimited by the 2015 Agreement ended their median line boundary at a point (Point 2) short of where a tripoint among Barbados, Saint Vincent and the Grenadines, and Saint Lucia would be located, thus leaving "[t]he coordinates of a Point number 1 [to] be established with a third State along an azimuth of 358° 13' 22" from Point number 2 ... ." With that third state's participation (i.e., Saint Lucia's) and the conclusion of the second (and simultaneously the third) related boundary, the parties to the Agreement were able to define the southern endpoint of their boundary (Point 21) at the intersection of the Barbados – Saint Vincent and the Grenadines azimuth line with Saint Lucia's maritime area.

9 *Technical Considerations*

Using available Admiralty Raster Chart Service (ARCS) charts detailing the Saint Lucia coastline, normal baselines were constructed for Saint Lucia. Satellite imagery acquired by the Commonwealth Secretariat and computations using Caris LOTS software were used to select certain features

---

15 These points are coincident, but they do not share the same coordinates because they are referenced to different geodetic systems. The earlier agreement between France and Saint Lucia is referenced to geodetic system adopted by the French National Geographic Institute for Martinique in 1953 while the later agreement between Barbados and France is referenced to WGS84.

16 This minor adjustment only affected 13.8 km of the 109 km boundary.

along the relevant coastline and to identify basepoint coordinates relevant to the delimitation. These were compared using the relevant large-scale charts for the area. Barbados used the normal baseline data shared during the earlier technical discussions.

The difference between the northern endpoint of the provisional median line and the endpoint agreed with France in 1981 (Saint Lucia) and 2009 (Barbados) prompted the construction of a modern hypothetical median line between Saint Lucia and France. The result was very close to that of the line in the 1981 agreement. This satisfied Saint Lucia and Barbados and allowed them to adjust their northern endpoint to coincide with Point L18 of the 1981 agreement and Point 1 of the 2009 agreement. After consultations with France, it was considered that the slightly modified line resulted in a Barbados-France-Saint Lucia tripoint. The resulting boundary consists of geodetic lines connecting 21 turning points the coordinates of which are provided to the nearest one-hundredth of an arc second. All coordinates are referenced to the WGS84 datum.

10 *Other Considerations*

None.

III CONCLUSIONS

The Agreement is uncontroversial in many respects: it follows the model set by the 2015 Agreement and uses a northern endpoint previously agreed with a third state. Additionally, it is set in a relatively uncomplicated geographic situation conducive to an unadjusted equidistance boundary. The spirit of regional collaboration that existed prior to the negotiations among Barbados and Saint Lucia as CARICOM states, together with the targeted assistance from regional and international institutions, allowed for the relatively rapid conclusion of this straightforward maritime boundary delimitation. Close communication with France and Saint Vincent and the Grenadines simplified fixing the locations of Point 1 and Point 21 of the Agreement coincident with the endpoints of the treaties each party had with France, and with a point on the azimuth specified in the earlier agreement between Barbados and Saint Vincent and the Grenadines. The Agreement entered into force on 1 September 2019 in accordance with Article 6(2).

5934 *Report Number 2-40*

IV RELATED LAW IN FORCE

A *Law of the Sea Conventions*

Barbados: Party to UNCLOS (ratified 12 October 1993).
Saint Lucia: Party to UNCLOS (ratified 27 March 1985).

B *Maritime Jurisdiction Claimed at the Time of Signature*

Barbados: 12 M territorial sea; 12 M contiguous zone; 200 M EEZ; continental
shelf submission to the CLCS on 8 May 2008, recommendations adopted
on 15 April 2010.
Saint Lucia: 12 M territorial sea; 12 M contiguous zone; 200 M EEZ; 200M
continental shelf.

C *Maritime Jurisdiction Claimed Subsequent to Signature*

Barbados: No change.
Saint Lucia: No change.

Prepared by Rosemarie Cadogan, Cmdr. David Robin (ret'd)

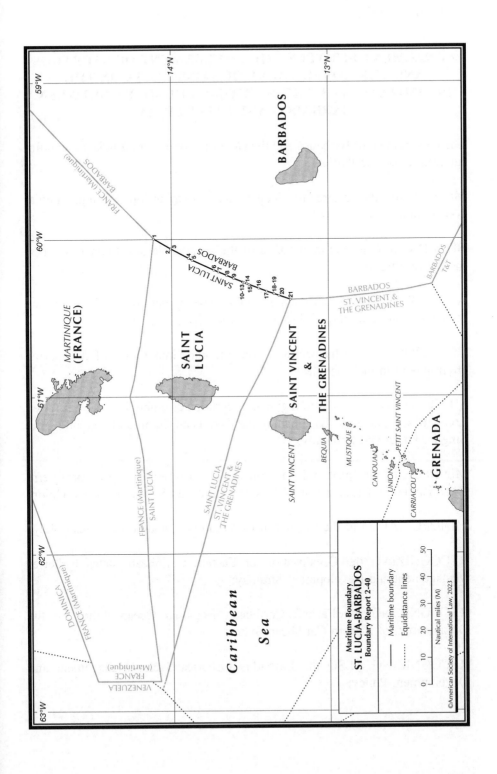

5936 *Report Number 2-40*

AGREEMENT BETWEEN THE GOVERNMENT OF BARBADOS AND THE GOVERNMENT OF SAINT LUCIA ON THE DELIMITATION OF THE MARITIME BOUNDARY BETWEEN BARBADOS AND SAINT LUCIA

The Government of Barbados and the Government of Saint Lucia, hereinafter referred to as "the Parties",

MOVED by the desire to deepen their relationship through mutual cooperation;

BEARING in mind the importance of the sustainable development of their marine resources;

ACKNOWLEDGING that the sustainable development of adjoining marine resources can be promoted through collaboration;

CONSCIOUS of the historic and contemporary importance of the marine environment to their peoples;

SHARING a commitment to regional integration as embodied in the Revised Treaty of Chaguaramas Establishing the Caribbean Community including the Single Market and Economy;

MINDFUL of the spirit and principles in the Revised Treaty of Basseterre Establishing the Organisation of Eastern Caribbean States Economic Union;

MINDFUL ALSO of the Caribbean Community Common Fisheries Policy;

RECOGNIZING the Organisation of Eastern Caribbean States Fisheries Management and Development Strategy;

RECOGNIZING the Eastern Caribbean Regional Ocean Policy of the Organization of Eastern Caribbean States;

RECOGNIZING ALSO the Barbados Fisheries Sector Management and Development Policy;

NOTING the importance of the delimitation of maritime boundaries by agreement in accordance with international law in providing clarity and certainty for the exercise of jurisdiction over their respective maritime zones;

UNDERLINING the importance of the United Nations Convention on the Law of the Sea to which both States are party.

The Parties agree as follows:

Article 1

1. This Agreement establishes a single maritime boundary for delimitation of the maritime space between Barbados and Saint Lucia.
2. The line of delimitation is based on equidistance which is considered an equitable solution in this case. This line is calculated from the baselines, as defined by their respective national laws, from which the territorial seas of Barbados and Saint Lucia are measured.

Article 2

1. The line of delimitation of the maritime space between Barbados and Saint Lucia is a geodetic line defined by the coordinates listed below, expressed with reference to the World Geodetic System 1984 (WGS 84):

List of coordinates

Point Number	Latitude	Longitude
1	14-06-56.80N	59-59-45.60W
2	14-00-23.78N	60-03-32.84W
3	14-00-18.59N	60-03-35.75W
4	13-53-27.50N	60-07-14.01W
5	13-52-02.01N	60-07-59.65W
6	13-43-44.80N	60-11-45.57W
7	13-42-01.58N	60-12-28.08W
8	13-38-53.05N	60-13-49.32W
9	13-36-11.46N	60-14-58.83W
10	13-32-52.71N	60-16-18.44W

11	13-32-43.45N	60-16-22.14W
12	13-32-38.35N	60-16-24.19W
13	13-32-06.15N	60-16-37.15W
14	13-31-10.25N	60-16-59.40W
15	13-30-21.56N	60-17-18.81W
16	13-26-42.21N	60-18-43.13W
17	13-23-43.58N	60-19-51.80W
18	13-20-54.56N	60-20-49.42W
19	13-20-51.52N	60-20-50.51 W
20	13-18-59.47N	60-21-29.15W
21	13-14-37.99N	60-22-59.31 W

2.   The coordinates of Point number 1 are coincident with Point number L18, as described in the Agreement on the Delimitation between the Government of Saint Lucia and the Government of the French Republic of 4 March 1981; and Point number 1, as described in the Agreement between the Government of Barbados and the Government of the French Republic on the Delimitation of the Maritime Space between Barbados and France of 15 October 2009.
3.   Point number 21 is on the geodetic line, which has an initial azimuth of 358° 13′ 22″ from Point number 2, as described in the Agreement between the Government of Barbados and the Government of Saint Vincent and the Grenadines on the Delimitation of the Maritime Boundary between Barbados and Saint Vincent and the Grenadines of 31 August 2015.
4.   For illustrative purposes, the line of delimitation is depicted on the map annexed to this Agreement.

Article 3

The Parties shall, as appropriate, adopt measures and coordinate their activities in accordance with international law for the protection and preservation of the marine environment and the conservation and management of the living resources therein.

Article 4

If any single oil or gas structure or field or any other mineral deposit extends across the line of delimitation established in Article 2 and any part of such structure, field or deposit which is situated on one side of the line is exploitable, wholly or in part, from the other side of the line, the Parties shall, after holding the appropriate technical consultations, make every effort to reach agreement on the manner in which any such structure, field or deposit shall be most effectively exploited and on the equitable sharing of the costs and benefits arising from such exploitation.

Article 5

Any dispute between the Parties in relation to the interpretation or the application of this Agreement shall be settled by peaceful means in accordance with international law, including recourse to the dispute settlement provisions of Part XV of the United Nations Convention on the Law of the Sea.

Article 6

1. The Parties shall inform each other by exchange of diplomatic note of the completion of their domestic law procedures required for the entry into force of this Agreement.
2. The Agreement shall enter into force on the first day of the second month following the date of the last notification.

IN WITNESS WHEREOF the undersigned, duly authorized by their respective Governments, have signed this Agreement.

Done in duplicate at St. George's on this 6th day of July 2017.

<table>
<tr><td>For the Government of
SAINT LUCIA</td><td>For the Government of
BARBADOS</td></tr>
<tr><td>The Hon. Allen M. Chastanet</td><td>The Rt. Hon. Freundel J. Stuart,
Q.C. M.P.</td></tr>
<tr><td>Prime Minister of Saint Lucia</td><td>Prime Minister of Barbados</td></tr>
</table>

Saint Lucia – Saint Vincent and the Grenadines

Report Number 2-41

Agreement Between the Government of Saint Lucia and the Government of Saint Vincent and the Grenadines on the Delimitation of the Maritime Boundary between Saint Lucia and Saint Vincent and The Grenadines

Signed:	06 July 2017
Entry into force:	01 May 2019
Published at:	UNTS (I-56460)

I SUMMARY

The maritime boundary delimitation agreement between Saint Lucia and Saint Vincent and the Grenadines (the Agreement) establishes a single maritime boundary dividing the maritime spaces of the parties, including a small area of overlapping territorial sea and their exclusive economic zones (EEZs) and continental shelf. The Agreement was signed 6 July 2017 at the same time as the signing of the maritime boundary agreement between Barbados and Saint Lucia.[1] The two 2017 agreements are based on the model language used in the related 2015 agreement between Barbados and Saint Vincent and the Grenadines.[2] As with these related agreements, the Agreement between Saint Lucia and Saint Vincent and the Grenadines utilizes the equidistance method and, in the east, coordinates its endpoint (Point 1) with the two related agreements. The boundary consists of 27 points numbered east to west, with a final point (Point 28) to be established with a third state along a specified azimuth based on the same principles used to determine the other 27 points.

Coordination within the Organisation of Eastern Caribbean States (OECS) and the Caribbean Community (CARICOM) facilitated the completion of this agreement, as did assistance from the Commonwealth Secretariat. The

---

1   *See* Report Number 2-40, in this volume.
2   *See* Report Number 2-35, VIII IMB 5433.

Coalter G. Lathrop (ed.), International Maritime Boundaries, 5941-5956.
© *The American Society of International Law and Koninklijke Brill BV, Leiden 2025.*

5942   Report Number 2-41

Preamble notes the importance of regional organizations and instruments and the United Nations Convention on the Law of the Sea (UNCLOS), to which both are states party.

II   CONSIDERATIONS

1   *Political, Strategic, and Historical Considerations*

Saint Lucia and Saint Vincent and the Grenadines share common ties and similar patterns of occupation. Saint Lucia became a Crown colony in 1814 after changing hands among British, Spanish, and French settlers. Saint Vincent and the Grenadines became a Crown colony in 1877. Both countries became independent in 1979.

Both states are members of the OECS, a subregional organization formed in 1981 by the Treaty of Basseterre, and of CARICOM, a regional organization established in 1973 by the Treaty of Chaguaramas. Maritime boundary delimitation is viewed as a means of securing access to marine areas and resources, exercising rights and jurisdiction, supporting sustainable growth from the utilization of ocean resources, and transitioning to a sustainable ocean (blue) economy. The Agreement is a tangible outcome of the Revised OECS Maritime Boundary Negotiating Strategy which makes delimitation a priority for OECS member states.[3] Saint Lucia and Saint Vincent and the Grenadines are also represented on the OECS Ocean Governance Team (OGT), a body established under the Eastern Caribbean Regional Oceans Policy (ECROP) 2013.[4] Under this strategic ocean policy instrument, certainty over the limits of national maritime jurisdiction is prioritized. The OGT's wide mandate includes the development of a regional integrated ocean governance framework; facilitating political engagement and effective coordination; and supporting ocean governance activities at international, regional, and national levels. As such, negotiations for the conclusion of this agreement were characterized by a high degree of cooperation and coordination.

---

3   A goal of the Revised OECS Maritime Boundary Delimitation Strategy elucidated in January 2011, is that OECS member states should settle outstanding maritime boundaries among themselves and engage in maritime boundary negotiations with non-OECS States, provided that member states shall consult with other member states before agreeing to a maritime boundary with a non-OECS State that is less favorable than a median line solution.

4   ECROP 2020 has replaced ECROP 2013.

Within this context, the Agreement is one of four maritime boundary agreements negotiated among OECS states, independent member states of CARICOM, and metropolitan states within 2015 to 2017.[5] The Agreement accords with international best practice and good governance principles from the international development agenda, including UNCLOS, the 2030 Agenda for Sustainable Development, and the SAMOA Pathway, to which both states adhere.

International support in maritime boundaries during the 1980s from the Canadian International Development Agency (CIDA) and Dalhousie Ocean Studies Programme (DOSP) was subsequently reinforced by technical assistance in formulating preliminary legal and technical assessments and hydrographical studies by the Commonwealth Secretariat and the United Kingdom Hydrographic Office (UKHO). Regional participation by other Caribbean states – The Bahamas, Barbados, Jamaica, and Trinidad and Tobago – in an OECS Commission/Commonwealth Secretariat Regional Working Session in Saint Lucia in 2014 helped identify commonalities and potential solutions in a non-binding setting. OECS states were able to review their positions and engage in training sessions during a follow up Working Session held by the Commonwealth Secretariat in London in July 2016.

The Commonwealth Secretariat provided legal and technical support to Saint Lucia and Saint Vincent and the Grenadines ahead of the negotiations.[6] Similar support by the Secretariat allowed Saint Vincent and the Grenadines to settle the first of its five maritime boundaries by agreement with Barbados in 2015 and facilitated the agreement between Barbados and Saint Lucia in 2017.

The Agreement establishes Saint Lucia's third maritime boundary. Delimitation for Saint Lucia has been sporadic. Its first maritime boundary was agreed with France in 1981 two years after Saint Lucia became independent.[7] After a hiatus of more than thirty years, trilateral discussions among Barbados, Saint Lucia, and Saint Vincent and the Grenadines took place in March 2016. Further negotiations in May 2017 resulted in the conclusion of Saint Lucia's second and third maritime boundary agreements

---

5   Antigua and Barbuda, an OECS member state, concluded its first maritime boundary agreement with France in December 2016 in respect of Martinique and Guadeloupe. Antigua and Barbuda subsequently concluded its second maritime boundary with the United Kingdom in respect of Anguilla in July 2021.

6   The Secretariat's Good Offices process allows for provision of impartial advice on legal and technical issues on an equal footing to both states. Advisors act as intermediaries in the negotiations to facilitate a boundary that is fair and equitable.

7   See Report Number 2-10, I IMB 591.

with Barbados and Saint Vincent and the Grenadines respectively on the same day in July 2017.[8]

The Agreement establishes Saint Vincent and the Grenadines' second maritime boundary, the first having been concluded with Barbados in 2015. Saint Vincent and the Grenadines has unresolved maritime boundaries with Grenada and Trinidad and Tobago. Saint Lucia and Saint Vincent and the Grenadines also have unresolved issues with Venezuela, including at the western end of their agreed boundary.

Under Article 4.1(d) of the Revised Treaty of Basseterre Establishing the Organisation of Eastern Caribbean States Economic Union, states parties agree "to seek to adopt wherever possible, common positions on international issues," including, pursuant to Article 4.2, "endeavour[ing] to co-ordinate, harmonise and undertake joint actions and pursue joint policies particularly in ... matters relating to the sea and its resources." The adoption of harmonized action at the negotiations between Saint Lucia and Saint Vincent and the Grenadines was of significance for the OECS and specifically for the parties to the Agreement, both of which are impacted by unresolved delimitations with Venezuela.

Venezuela is a dominant regional economic and political power possessing the world's largest proven oil reserves[9] and wielding significant geopolitical and strategic influence among world powers and independent island states in the Caribbean Sea. Venezuela asserts ownership of Aves Island, or Bird Rock as it is sometimes referred to within the OECS,[10] and

---

8 The agreements were signed at the 38th Regular Meeting of the Conference of Heads of Government of CARICOM in Saint George's, Grenada on 6 July 2017.

9 The US Geological Survey estimated undiscovered, technically recoverable mean continuous resources of 656 million barrels of oil and 5.7 trillion cubic feet of gas in the Maracaibo Basin Province of Venezuela and Colombia. US Geological Survey, National and Global Petroleum Assessment, *Assessment of Continuous Oil and Gas Resources of the Maracaibo Basin Province of Venezuela and Colombia, 2016*, Fact Sheet 2017-3011 (March 2017), https://pubs.usgs.gov/fs/2017/3011/fs20173011.pdf.

Caribbean countries (including Saint Lucia and Saint Vincent and the Grenadines) have at various times accessed crude oil at discounted prices through Venezuela's PetroCaribe, under which Saint Vincent and the Grenadines also has arrangements for fertilizer, asphalt and housing. *Saint Vincent: PertroCaribe agreements being finalised*, Loop News (5 October 2022), https://caribbean.loopnews.com/content/st-vincent-petrocaribe-agreements-being-finalised.

Barbados and Venezuela entered into joint cooperation agreements to strengthen their relations in the fields of oil and agriculture in June 2023. *President Maduro meets with Barbadian Prime Minister Mottley*, TeleSUR (10 July 2023), https://www.telesurenglish.net/news/President-Maduro-Meets-With-Barbadian-Prime-Minister-Mottley-20230710-0008.html.

10 In this report, this Venezuelan feature will be referred to as Aves Island. This does not connote any significance as to its geographical or legal status or its entitlements under UNCLOS.

establishes an EEZ along the coasts of its mainland and islands.[11] Aves Island is a small, low-lying sand and coral feature situated 380 nautical miles (M) north of mainland Venezuela. Previous agreements with France in respect of Guadeloupe and Martinique,[12] the Netherlands Antilles,[13] and to a lesser extent the United States in respect of Puerto Rico and the United States Virgin Islands,[14] accord full status and maritime zone entitlements to Aves Island and treat the feature as an "island" and not a "rock" in the context of Article 121 of UNCLOS. In contrast, OECS states consider Aves Island to be an Article 121(3) feature with no entitlements to an EEZ or continental shelf beyond 12 M. They lodged international protests to this effect in July and August 1997, depositing copies with the UN Secretary-General for circulation in keeping with UN practice. Consistent with the Revised OECS Maritime Boundary Delimitation Strategy, OECS states which share maritime boundaries with Venezuela have refrained from commencing bilateral negotiations with Venezuela until the OECS reaches a common position regarding such delimitation.

In 2015, political considerations loomed large when Venezuela issued decrees extending its security jurisdiction over large areas of the Caribbean Sea.[15] These decrees incorporated military operations within a new territorial defense system of territorial armed units, or ZODIMAIN.[16] Of particular

---

11 Act establishing an Exclusive Economic Zone along the coasts of the Mainland and Islands (26 July 1978) (Venezuela), *available at* https://www.un.org/Depts/los/LEGIS LATIONANDTREATIES/PDFFILES/VEN_1978_Act.pdf.
12 Report Number 2-11, I IMB 603.
13 Report Number 2-12, I IMB 615.
14 Report Number 2-14, I IMB 691.
15 *See* Decree No 1.787 of 26 May 2015 (reprinted 8 June 2015 due to errors in the original) establishing Comprehensive Operational Defense Zones (ZODI) (with coordinates) and Comprehensive Defense Areas (ADI), Gaceta Oficial, 27 May 2015, No. 40.669 at 420.896 (Venezuela); Decree No 1.859 of 6 July 2015 (repealing and replacing Decree No 1.787) establishing Comprehensive Operational Defense Zones (ZODI) (without coordinates) and Comprehensive Defense Areas (ADI), Gaceta Oficial, 6 July 2015, No. 40.696 at 421.916 (Venezuela).

Decree 1.859 does not provide coordinates but does provide verbal descriptions of the ZODIMAIN which leave their scope and implications substantially the same as the earlier Decree 1.787. Although Decree 1.859 states that it does not aim to establish territorial boundaries, delimitation or any other process for drawing demarcation lines and does not purport to make any announcement regarding territorial aspects which is beyond its scope, it states that its only purpose and scope is to protect the country from any threats, risks and other vulnerabilities and that "[t]he State has the obligation of preserving territorial integrity, sovereignty, security, defense ... national territory shall never be relinquished, transferred, rented, or otherwise sold, not even temporal or partially, to Foreign States or other bodies of International Law."
16 ZODIMAIN stands for Zona Operative de Defensa Integral Marítima Insular or, loosely, Marine and Island Comprehensive Operational Defense Zone.

relevance here was the establishment of Venezuela's "ZODIMAIN Oriental" which would impact the maritime entitlements of six OECS states and territories, including Saint Vincent and the Grenadines and, to a much smaller degree, Saint Lucia.[17] The ZODIMAIN Oriental encroaches beyond an equidistance line (giving full effect to Aves Island) between Saint Vincent and the Grenadines and Venezuela to the extent of approximately 3,000 km^2, and an additional 3,000 km^2 if Aves Island were treated as a "rock". The treatment of Aves Island in any future delimitation between Saint Vincent and the Grenadines (and other impacted OECS members) and Venezuela remains of utmost importance. Consequently, the weight that the parties to the Agreement accorded to Aves Island assumed particular significance. This was noted during the conclusion of the Agreement and is reflected in the treatment of the extension beyond Point 27 to the as-yet-undefined western endpoint, Point 28.

CARICOM responded to Venezuela's decrees at their 36th Heads of Government Meeting in July 2015 and met with Venezuelan officials to discuss the issue. In their communiqué, CARICOM leaders noted the negative implications of the decrees for several other CARICOM countries and called for adherence to accepted principles of international law in relation to the delineation and delimitation of the EEZ and continental shelf in the region. They further noted that CARICOM states do not accept any unilateral proclamation which is inconsistent with international law, emphasizing that CARICOM states have legitimate territorial and maritime entitlements that conform to international law and that must be respected.[18]

2   Legal Regime Considerations

The Agreement establishes a single, all-purpose maritime boundary delimiting the maritime space between Saint Lucia and Saint Vincent and the Grenadines. This includes a small overlap of territorial seas and larger areas of EEZ and continental shelf. The Agreement applies the same

---

17 "ZODIMAIN Oriental" refers to an area of the eastern Caribbean that encompasses Aves Island and surrounding waters. The other OECS states and territories impacted by Venezuela's ZODIMAIN Oriental are St. Kitts and Nevis, Montserrat (UK), Dominica, and Grenada.

18 Press Release, CARICOM, *Communique Issued at the Conclusion of the 36th Regular Meeting of the Heads of Government of the Caribbean Community* (5 July 2015), https://caricom.org/communique-issued-at-the-conclusion-of-the-36th-regular-meeting-of-the-heads-of-government-of-the-caribbean-community/.

model language as employed in negotiations between Saint Vincent and the Grenadines and Barbados, and between Barbados and Saint Lucia, and does not distinguish between the section of the boundary delimiting territorial sea and those parts delimiting areas beyond 12 M from the coast.

As states parties to UNCLOS, both parties apply Articles 15, 74, and 83 to the delimitation of their territorial sea, EEZ, and continental shelf. Article 1 of the Agreement identifies the use of equidistance to construct the boundary and acknowledges that an equidistance line achieves an equitable solution.

Cooperation in relation to protection and preservation of the marine environment and regarding straddling hydrocarbon deposits is included in Articles 3 and 4, respectively. Article 5 contemplates dispute settlement through peaceful means according to international law including recourse to the dispute settlement provisions in Part XV of UNCLOS.

3 Economic and Environmental Considerations

Mechanisms exist for economic cooperation and marine environment resource management under the Revised Treaty of Basseterre and within the OECS Commission's institutional structure.[19] Although there were no prevailing economic or environmental factors affecting the location of the boundary, the parties adopted the provisions in Articles 3 and 4 from the model employed in their respective delimitations with Barbados. Article 3 provides for the adoption of measures and coordination of activities regarding marine environmental protection and the conservation and management of living resources.

Article 4 provides for unitization of any straddling deposits through technical consultations and agreement on effective exploitation and equitable cost sharing of benefits. The possible presence of commercial quantities of hydrocarbon and other non-living resources in the area to be delimited was not ascertained, and this consideration did not affect negotiations on the location of the boundary.

---

19 *See generally* OECS Commission, *Ocean Governance and Blue Economy in the Eastern Caribbean*, https://oecs.org/en/blue-economy-eastern-caribbean-ocean-governance.

5948 *Report Number 2-41*

4 *Geographic Considerations*

Saint Vincent and the Grenadines is an archipelagic state forming part of the Lesser Antilles with an area of approximately 389 km² and a population of approximately 109,000. Saint Lucia is a single-island state with an area of approximately 620 km² and a population of approximately 180,000.

Saint Vincent and the Grenadines consists of the main island of Saint Vincent and, to the south, a chain of islands comprising the Grenadines. The area to be delimited was located between Saint Lucia and the main island of Saint Vincent, and the relevant coastlines were the northeast coastline of Saint Vincent and the southwest coastline of Saint Lucia.

The relevant coastline length of Saint Vincent was 23 M, and the relevant coastline length for Saint Lucia was 37 M, resulting in a coastline length ratio of 0.62:1. Relevant maritime areas of 1,347 km² for Saint Vincent and the Grenadines and 958 km² for Saint Lucia, resulted in a ratio of 1:1.40. The parties did not consider any disparity between the coastline lengths ratio and the ratio of the apportioned maritime areas as justification for modification of the median line. The relative population sizes and political or economic status of the parties were not considered relevant to the delimitation.

5 *Islands, Rocks, Reefs, and Low-tide Elevations Considerations*

Only the two closest islands, Saint Lucia and the main island of Saint Vincent, were relevant to the construction of the equidistance line. No smaller islands or low-tide elevations affected the equidistance line.

6 *Baseline Considerations*

The parties approached the delimitation from the respective standpoints of Saint Vincent and the Grenadines as an archipelagic state with archipelagic baselines and Saint Lucia as a single-island state with normal baselines.

Saint Vincent and the Grenadines' archipelagic baselines, published in 2014, consist of 33 line segments extending from Saint Vincent in the north to Petit Saint Vincent in the south and enclosing an area of approximately 1,485 km², around 400 km² of which is land territory. Points 12-33, which wrap the north coast of Saint Vincent, closely follow the low-water line of the island. Due to this close correspondence of the archipelagic baseline with the low-water line along the relevant coast of Saint Vincent, the archipelagic baselines had minimal effect on the construction of the median line with Saint Lucia.

7 Geological and Geomorphological Considerations

Geological and geomorphological considerations were not relevant to this delimitation.

8 Method of Delimitation Considerations

The main island of Saint Vincent lies approximately 20 M southwest of Saint Lucia in a position of oppositeness. Due to their proximity in the semi-enclosed Caribbean Sea, neither Saint Lucia or Saint Vincent and the Grenadines can enjoy a full 200 M EEZ or continental shelf. In these confined circumstances, an unadjusted equidistance boundary presented an equitable solution, and the parties agreed that the delimitation line would function as a single-purpose boundary dividing all maritime zones between them.

The eastern end of the median line begins over 40 M from the coasts of the parties at Point 1, a tripoint at the intersection of the three boundaries agreed among Saint Vincent and the Grenadines, Saint Lucia, and Barbados.

The western end of the median line boundary has not been determined pending resolution of the Aves Island question.[20] The parties established the coordinates of their penultimate turning point, Point 27, and proceeded on the basis that the delimitation would continue west beyond Point 27 using equidistance. The direction of this continuation is set in the Agreement at an initial azimuth of 286° 15' 36", and Article 2.3 of the Agreement provides

---

20 In contrast, the 1981 agreement between Saint Lucia and France (Martinique), takes a different approach to the Aves Island question. Instead of calling for the possible future extension of the boundary west beyond the last agreed point (here, Point L1), it stops the line at longitude 62° 48' 50" W (IGN Martinique 1953). (*See* Report Number 2-10, I IMB 591). This limit corresponds to the French and Venezuelan positions vis-à-vis Aves Island. This does not preclude Saint Lucia from claiming maritime areas west of that meridian which France has disavowed in a separate agreement with Venezuela. (*See* Report Number 2-11, I IMB 603).

that the coordinates of Point 28 will be established with a third state in accordance with the same principles used to determine Points 1 to 27.[21]

9   Technical Considerations

For Saint Lucia, an independent digitization of its southern coastline was conducted in the absence of declared baselines or basepoints. Saint Lucia's normal baseline was used for the construction of median line options, with the Caris LOTs median line tool applying various weight factors to specific points. The archipelagic baselines of Saint Vincent and the Grenadines were used for the construction of the provisional median line. These basepoints were verified during technical meetings between the parties in March 2016.

The agreed boundary follows a series of geodetic lines connecting turning points defined by coordinates referred to the WGS 84 coordinate system and quoted to the nearest one-hundredth second of arc.

10   Other Considerations

None.

III   CONCLUSIONS

The Agreement all but completes Saint Lucia's delimitation of its maritime boundaries, leaving only the question of Aves Island and its impact in the western reaches of Saint Lucia's maritime space. It also brings Saint Vincent and the Grenadines one boundary closer to finalizing its maritime boundaries, leaving outstanding boundaries with Grenada, Trinidad and Tobago, and Venezuela. By pursuing collective and harmonized action through this agreement and the others concluded from 2015 to 2021, OECS member states continue to implement the Revised OECS Maritime Boundary Delimitation Strategy.

---

21   The elongated arrow on the map attached to the Agreement indicates a section at the western end of the Saint Lucia – Saint Vincent and the Grenadines boundary the endpoint of which is yet to be determined.

IV RELATED LAW IN FORCE

A *Law of the Sea Conventions*

Saint Lucia: Party to UNCLOS (ratified 27 March 1985).
Saint Vincent and the Grenadines: Party to UNCLOS (ratified 1 October 1993).

B *Maritime Jurisdiction Claimed at the Time of Signature*

Saint Lucia: 12 M territorial sea; 12 M contiguous zone; 200 M EEZ; continental shelf.
Saint Vincent and the Grenadines: 12 M territorial sea; 12 M contiguous zone; 200 M EEZ; 200M continental shelf

C *Maritime Jurisdiction Claimed Subsequent to Signature*

Country A: No change.
Country B: No change

V REFERENCES AND ADDITIONAL READINGS

Ronald Sanders, *Venezuela in the Caribbean: Expanding its sphere of influence*, 96 THE ROUND TABLE 465 (2007).

INTERVENTION, BORDER AND MARITIME ISSUES IN CARICOM (Kenneth O. Hall & Myrtle Chuck-A-Sang eds., 2007).

Prepared by Rosemarie Cadogan, Cmdr. David Robin (ret'd)

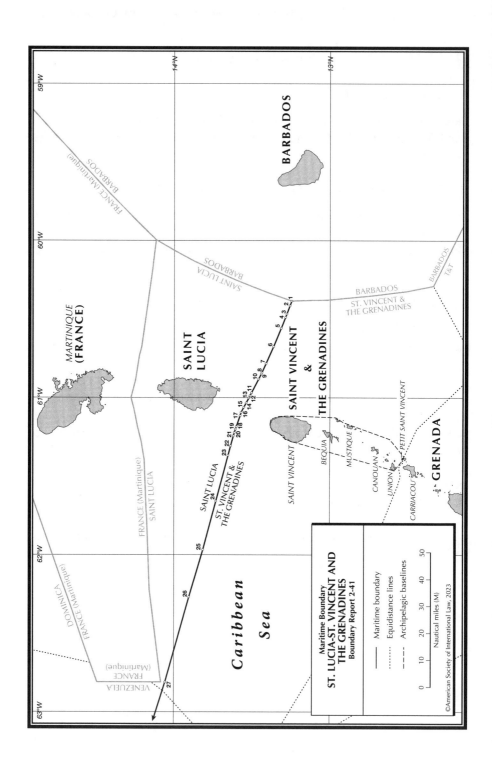

AGREEMENT BETWEEN THE GOVERNMENT OF SAINT LUCIA AND THE GOVERNMENT OF SAINT VINCENT AND THE GRENADINES ON THE DELIMITATION OF THE MARITIME BOUNDARY BETWEEN SAINT LUCIA AND SAINT VINCENT AND THE GRENADINES

The Government of Saint Lucia and the Government of Saint Vincent and the Grenadines, hereinafter referred to as "The Parties",

MOVED by the desire to deepen their relationship through mutual cooperation;

CONSCIOUS of the historical and contemporary value of the marine environment to their peoples, and the importance of marine resources to sustainable development;

ACKNOWLEDGING that the sustainable development of adjoining marine resources can be promoted through collaboration;

BEARING in mind the international development agenda, including the SAMOA Pathway and the Sustainable Development Goals, in particular Goal 14;

MINDFUL of the commitment to regional integration embodied in the Revised Treaty of Basseterre Establishing the Organisation of Eastern Caribbean States Economic Union;

SHARING the spirit and principles enshrined in the Revised Treaty of Chaguaramas Establishing the Caribbean Community including the Single Market and Economy;

RECOGNISING the Eastern Caribbean Regional Ocean Policy of the Organisation of the Eastern Caribbean States;

RECOGNISING ALSO the Caribbean Community Common Fisheries Policy;

NOTING the importance of the delimitation of maritime boundaries in accordance with international law in providing certainty for the exercise of jurisdiction over their respective maritime zones;

UNDERLINING the importance of the United Nations Convention on the Law of the Sea to which both States are party;

AGREE AS FOLLOWS:

Article 1

1. This Agreement establishes a single maritime boundary for delimitation of the maritime space between Saint Lucia and Saint Vincent and the Grenadines.
2. The line of delimitation is based on equidistance which is considered an equitable solution in this case. This line is calculated from the baselines, as defined by their respective national laws, from which the territorial seas of Saint Lucia and of Saint Vincent and the Grenadines are measured.

Article 2

1. The line of delimitation of the maritime space between Saint Lucia and Saint Vincent and the Grenadines is a geodetic line defined by the coordinates listed below, expressed with reference to the World Geodetic System 1984 (WGS 84):

List of Coordinates

Point no.	Latitude	Longitude
1	13-14-37.99N	60-22-59.31W
2	13-15-17.92N	60-24-50.04W
3	13-16-29.33N	60-27-58.93W
4	13-16-57.95N	60-29-14.75W
5	13-18-39.73N	60-33-24.69W
6	13-21-32.99N	60-40-25.02W
7	13-24-28.59N	60-46-54.32W
8	13-26-02.13N	60-50-20.21W
9	13-26-17.06N	60-50-53.14W
10	13-27-18.45N	60-52-50.41W
11	13-30-03.53N	60-58-05.19W
12	13-30-39.12N	60-59-12.62W
13	13-31-04.83N	61-00-03.83W
14	13-32-04.47N	61-01-56.16W

15	13-32-58.63N	61-03-36.34W
16	13-34-00.99N	61-05-33.81W
17	13-34-22.33N	61-06-48.75W
18	13-35-48.83N	61-10-57.47W
19	13-36-09.88N	61-11-55.57W
20	13-36-35.32N	61-13-14.55W
21	13-36-57.98N	61-14-28.79W
22	13-38-02.38N	61-18-22.90W
23	13-39-01.27N	61-22-00.02W
24	13-43-41.68N	61-39-25.49W
25	13-48-43.75N	61-58-00.39W
26	13-54-03.92N	62-16-06.01W
27	14-03-21.17N	62-48-37.29W

2. The coordinates of Point Number 1 are coincident with Point Number 21, as agreed between the Government of Saint Lucia and the Government of Barbados, and on the geodetic line, which has an initial azimuth of 358° 13′ 22″ from Point Number 2, as described in the Agreement between the Government of Barbados and the Government of Saint Vincent and the Grenadines on the Delimitation of the Maritime Boundary between Barbados and Saint Vincent and the Grenadines of 31 August 2015.
3. The coordinates of Point Number 28 will be established with a third State along an azimuth of 286° 15′ 36″ from Point Number 27 in accordance with the same principles used to determine Point Numbers 1 through 27.
4. For illustrative purposes, the line of delimitation is depicted on the map annexed to this Agreement.

Article 3

The Parties shall, as appropriate, adopt measures and coordinate their activities, in accordance with international law, for the protection and preservation of the marine environment and the conservation and management of the living resources therein.

Article 4

If any single oil or gas structure or field or any other mineral deposit extends across the line of delimitation established in Article 2 and any part of such structure, field or deposit which is situated on one side of the line is exploitable, wholly, or in part, from the other side of the line, the Parties shall, after holding the appropriate technical consultations, make every effort to reach agreement on the manner in which any such structure, field or deposit shall be most effectively exploited and on the equitable sharing of the cost and benefits arising from such exploitation.

Article 5

Any dispute between the Parties in relation to the interpretation or the application of this Agreement shall be settled by peaceful means in accordance with international law including recourse to the dispute settlement provisions of Part XV of the United Nations Convention on the Law of the Sea.

Article 6

1. The parties shall inform each other by exchange of diplomatic note of the completion of their domestic law procedures required for the entry into force of this Agreement.
2. The Agreement shall enter into force on the first day of the second month following the date of the last notification.

In witness whereof the undersigned, duly authorized by their respective governments, have signed this Agreement.

Done in duplicate at St. George's on 6 this day of July 2017

For the Government of Saint Lucia
<signed>

For the Government of Saint Vincent and the Grenadines
<signed>

Saint Kitts and Nevis – Netherlands

Report Number 2-42

Agreement between the Federation of Saint Christopher and Nevis and the Kingdom of the Netherlands concerning Maritime Delimitation

Signed: 4 April 2024
Entry into force: Not yet in force
Published at: Currently unpublished

I SUMMARY

The Agreement between the Federation of Saint Christopher and Nevis and the Kingdom of the Netherlands concerning Maritime Delimitation (the Treaty) was initialed on 12 September 2014 and signed on 4 April 2024. The Treaty establishes an agreed maritime boundary delimiting the maritime zones between the Federation of Saint Christopher and Nevis (Saint Kitts and Nevis) and Sint Eustatius, a special municipality of the Kingdom of the Netherlands.

The Treaty is the first maritime boundary agreement to be finalized by Saint Kitts and Nevis, an independent member of the Caribbean Community (CARICOM) and the Organisation of Eastern Caribbean States (OECS), and is the sixth such agreement to be concluded by an OECS state during the ten-year period 2015 to 2024.[1] Saint Kitts and Nevis has unresolved maritime boundaries with the United Kingdom (Montserrat), France (Saint Barthélemy), Antigua and Barbuda, and Venezuela (Aves Island).[2]

---

1 *See* Report Number 2-35, VIII IMB 5433 (Barbados – Saint Vincent and the Grenadines); Report Number 2-37, in this volume (Antigua and Barbuda – France (Guadeloupe and Saint Barthélemy)); Report Number 2-38, in this volume (Antigua and Barbuda – United Kingdom (Anguilla)); Report Number 2-40, in this volume (Barbados – Saint Lucia); Report Number 2-41, in this volume (Saint Lucia – Saint Vincent and the Grenadines).
2 In this report, the Venezuelan feature will be referred to as Aves Island. This usage is without any significance as to the feature's geographical or legal status or its entitlement under the 1982 United Nations Convention on the Law of the Sea.

Coalter G. Lathrop (ed.), International Maritime Boundaries, 5957-5968.
© The American Society of International Law and Koninklijke Brill BV, Leiden 2024.

5958 *Report Number 2-42*

The Treaty is the third maritime boundary agreement to be concluded by the Netherlands in respect of its territory in this area (Sint Maarten, Saba, and Sint Eustatius).[3] In respect of this territory, the Netherlands has outstanding boundaries with the United Kingdom (Anguilla) and the United States (US Virgin Islands).

As is the case with the other agreements concluded among the OECS states, the Treaty utilizes the equidistance method and establishes a single-purpose maritime boundary between the islands of Saint Kitts and Sint Eustatius.

II CONSIDERATIONS

1 *Political, Strategic, and Historical Considerations*

The Netherlands has been reengaging in maritime boundary delimitation in the Caribbean region, recently completing a maritime boundary agreement with France in respect of Saint Martin and Saint Barthélemy, and continuing its outreach with the United Kingdom in respect of Anguilla.

Saint Kitts and Nevis, acting in pursuance of the newly revised OECS Maritime Boundary Delimitation Negotiating Strategy, and in the interest of good international relations, effective marine resource management and law enforcement, finalized its Maritime Boundary Delimitation Strategy in 2011.

Following the dissolution of the Netherlands Antilles in October 2010, Sint Eustatius became a special municipality (*bijzondere gemeenten*) of the Kingdom of the Netherlands,[4] making it part of the Caribbean Netherlands.[5]

---

3   *See* Report No. 2-12, I IMB 615 (Venezuela (Aves Island)); Report Number 2-36, VIII IMB 5445 (France (Saint Martin and Saint Barthélemy)).
4   By virtue of the Public Entities Bonaire, St. Eustatius and Saba Act of May 17, 2010 and as provided for by Article 123 of the Constitution of the Kingdom of the Netherlands, 2018.
   Wet openbare lichamen Bonaire, Sint Eustatius en Saba van 17 mei 2010, Stb. 2010, 345 (Neth.), *English translation available* at https://www.statiagovernment.com/governance/documents/decrees-orders-and-decisions/2010/05/17/the-public-entities-bonaire-st.-eustatius-and-saba-act; Gw. [Constitution] art. 123 (2018).
5   The Caribbean Netherlands, composed of the special municipalities of the islands of Bonaire, Sint Eustatius, and Saba, constitutes a public body (*openbaar lichaam*). The central Government of the Kingdom of the Netherlands exercises defense and foreign affairs jurisdiction regarding Sint Eustatius, including the negotiation and conclusion of bilateral treaties. *See* Government of the Netherlands, *Carribean Parts of the Kingdom: Governance of Bonaire, St Eustatius and Saba,* https://www.statiagovernment.com/governance/documents/decrees-orders-and-decisions/2010/05/17/the-public-entities-

Accordingly, negotiations with Saint Kitts and Nevis were conducted by the Netherlands, with the Island Governor of Sint Eustatius being invited to participate in the discussions as a part of the Netherlands delegation.

With the support of the Commonwealth Secretariat, Saint Kitts and Nevis commenced work towards the settlement of outstanding maritime boundaries with the Netherlands in respect of Sint Eustatius. Diplomatic outreach to the Netherlands resulted in a series of information exchanges and technical discussions at the Commonwealth Secretariat in London in October 2013. The parties exchanged draft proposals and agreed to enter into formal negotiations in Saint Kitts and Nevis in September 2014.

One round of negotiations was held, culminating in the initialing of a draft treaty, which was formally signed in April 2024 after the parties resolved internal issues and obtained the requisite approvals.

2 Legal Regime Considerations

The distance between the coasts of the nearest territory of Saint Kitts and Sint Eustatius is less than 7 nautical miles (M), creating overlaps of their 12 M territorial seas, exclusive economic zones, and continental shelves. Article 1 of the Treaty indicates the parties' intent to establish a single-purpose maritime boundary, whilst the Preamble reflects the parties' intention to establish an equitable delimitation of all maritime zones between them. Most of the boundary between Points 1 and 7 delimits overlapping territorial seas. A short segment of the boundary north of Point 1 to the future tripoint with France delimits overlapping exclusive economic zones, as does the extension of this boundary to the south of Point 7.

Both Saint Kitts and Nevis and the Netherlands are parties to the 1982 United Nations Convention on the Law of the Sea (UNCLOS or the Convention). Specific reference is made to UNCLOS in the Preamble to the Treaty, and the conduct of negotiations between the parties reflected adherence to the relevant provisions of the Convention.

As regards dispute settlement, in Article 5 the parties agreed on a *modus operandi* whereby, in the first instance, they would adopt consultation and negotiation as the peaceful means of settling any dispute in relation to the interpretation or application of the Treaty. Failing this, if no agreement were

---

bonaire-st.-eustatius-and-saba-act; Government of the Netherlands, *Carribean Parts of the Kingdom: Responsibilities of the Netherlands, Aruba, Curaçao and St Maarten, See* Government of the Netherlands, *Carribean Parts of the Kingdom.*

reached within a reasonable time, either party could resort to the dispute settlement provisions under Part XV of UNCLOS.

3 Economic and Environmental Considerations

The parties recognized the need for the Treaty to reflect their differing competencies in managing the marine resources of the area delimited. Due to the relationship of association between the European Union and Sint Eustatius as an overseas territory, Sint Eustatius' waters are considered to be European Union fishing waters, and management is shared with the island government. As an independent state, Saint Kitts and Nevis manages its marine environment and resources in the waters under its jurisdiction. Accordingly, Article 3 provides for consultation between the parties on marine governance issues consistent with their international obligations and with due regard to the transfer of competencies to the European Union by the Netherlands.

In consideration of any potential non-living resources in the area delimited, Article 4 of the Treaty calls upon the parties to hold technical consultations to seek agreement on the most effective way of exploiting, unitizing, and apportioning the costs and benefits of any straddling or shared deposits of oil, natural gas, and other minerals that might straddle or extend across the delimitation line established by Article 2 of the Treaty.

The marine environment around Saba Bank has been recognized as a protected area of high biological diversity and productivity.[6] Although there were no marine environmental nor non-living resource considerations between the parties at the time of the negotiations, these "anticipatory" provisions regarding the utilization of potential marine resources and non-living reserves are to be found in the five OECS maritime boundary agreements concluded after the initialing of the Treaty in 2014. In this regard, Saint Kitts and Nevis initiated this practice within the OECS.

---

6   Int'l Maritime Org. [IMO], *Particularly Sensitive Sea Areas*, https://www.imo.org/en/ OurWork/Environment/Pages/PSSAs.aspx; Dutch Caribbean Nature Alliance, *Saba Bank gains PSSA status,* https://dcnanature.org/saba-banks-pssa-status-fully-implemented/.

4 Geographic Considerations

The two islands of Saint Kitts and Nevis, separated by a narrow channel, form part of the Lesser Antilles islands in the semi-enclosed Caribbean Sea. With a population of approximately 48,000[7] and land territory of approximately 270 km^2, it is the smallest independent nation in the Western Hemisphere based on population size and territory. Saint Kitts, the larger of the two islands, spans approximately 174 km^2, and its sister island of Nevis covers an area of approximately 93 km^2.[8]

Sint Eustatius, with a surface area of 21 km^2 and population of just over 3,000, is the nearest territory of the Netherlands to Saint Kitts and Nevis and lies to the immediate northwest of Saint Kitts.[9] The northwest coast of Saint Kitts is approximately twice as long as the southeast coast of Sint Eustatius. It was agreed early in the negotiations that there were no relevant circumstances sufficient to require departure from the use of equidistance as an equitable solution. The parties also agreed that there were no relevant basepoints on either Nevis or Saba, the smallest special municipality of the Netherlands. Accordingly, only the islands of Saint Kitts and Sint Eustatius were relevant to the determination of the single maritime boundary.

To the north of the parties lie the French territories of Saint Barthélemy and Saint Martin, to the east Antigua and Barbuda, to the southeast Montserrat (United Kingdom), and to the south-southwest the Venezuelan territory of Aves Island. The Netherlands, in respect of Sint Maarten, Saba, and Sint Eustatius, has delimited with France, in respect of Saint Martin and Saint Barthélemy,[10] and has delimited with Venezuela in respect of Aves Island.[11] The boundary established in the Treaty will interact with these previous delimitations at its northern and southern ends, respectively.

5 Islands, Rocks, Reefs, and Low-tide Elevations

The geography of the relevant area of delimitation is relatively unremarkable. No maritime features such as islands, rocks, reefs, or low-tide elevations

---

7   World Bank, *St. Kitts and Nevis*, http://data.worldbank.org/country/st-kitts-and-nevis.
8   University of the West Indies Seismic Research Centre, *St. Kitts*, https://uwiseismic.com/island-profiles/st-kitts/.
9   St. Eustatius Government, *About St. Eustatius*, https://www.statiagovernment.com/about-st.-eustatius.
10 *See* Report Number 2-36, VIII IMB 5445.
11 *See* Report Number 2-12, I IMB 615.

5962 *Report Number 2-42*

were considered to have a bearing on the line, making it a comparatively straightforward delimitation exercise.

6 *Baseline Considerations*

The delimitation line established under Article 2 of the Treaty applied the principle of equidistance by reference to basepoints located on Saint Kitts and Sint Eustatius. An identification of suitable basepoints was carried out prior to the commencement of negotiations, with 9 basepoints on the low-water line of Saint Kitts and 27 basepoints selected on the smoother low-water line of Sint Eustatius.

7 *Geological and Geomorphological Considerations*

No geological or geomorphological considerations assumed any prominence during the negotiations. Given that there were no prevailing resource considerations of an economic nature, Article 4 can be considered precautionary.

8 *Method of Delimitation Considerations*

The delimitation line comprises eight fixed points, joined by geodesics, commencing at latitude 17° 35' 58.77" N and 62° 48' 15.30" W (Point 1), and terminating at latitude 17° 04' 03.32"N and 63° 14' 32.30" W (Point 8). The eight points are all located on the equidistance line between the nearest basepoints identified by the two countries. The initial calculated equidistance line contained 35 turning points, but the majority of those points had no material impact on the alignment of the line, so the parties agreed to reduce the number of points defining the boundary to eight.

Beyond Points 1 and 8 the boundary extends "until the delimitation with a third state is reached" (Article 2(3&4)). To the north, the third state will be France. The Netherlands was engaged in concurrent negotiations with France in respect of Saint Martin and Saint Barthélemy, and the resulting agreement identifies Saint Kitts and Nevis as the third state at the eastern end of their boundary.[12] During the exchanges of information between the

---

12 Report Number 2-36, VIII IMB 5445, 5457.

parties prior to the start of and during formal negotiations of the Treaty, the parties raised the potential of a tripoint between themselves and France. Although they did not fix that tripoint, Article 2(3) provides that the agreed line of delimitation continues beyond Point 1 in a northeasterly direction along a geodetic azimuth of 26.55 degrees to the delimitation with a third state. Consideration was also given to the future delimitation between Saint Kitts and Nevis and France's Saint Barthélemy.

Article 2(4) provides that the line of delimitation continues beyond Point 8 in a southwesterly direction along an azimuth of 222.74 degrees until the delimitation with a third state is reached. The question of third states and the extension of the boundary will require consideration of the Venezuelan territory of Aves Island and the implications of the maritime boundary agreement between the Netherlands and Venezuela.

9 Technical Considerations

The Treaty confirms in Article 2(2) that the points defining the geodetic coordinates are based on the World Geodetic System (WGS84).

10 Other Considerations

The prior agreement between the Netherlands (Saba and Sint Eustatius) and Venezuela (Aves Island) accorded Aves Island full-effect,[13] as did the agreement between the United States (Puerto Rico and Virgin Islands) and Venezuela (Aves Island).[14] More recently, Venezuela's Zodimain Oriental Decree, issued in 2015, accords Aves Island full weight as against the territory of the six surrounding OECS states, including Saint Kitts and Nevis, Montserrat (United Kingdom), Dominica, Saint Lucia, Saint Vincent and the Grenadines, and Grenada. The implication of the previous agreements and the Zodimain Decree is that Aves Island enjoys the maritime zone entitlements of an island with economic and geographic significance. CARICOM has engaged in discussions with Venezuela regarding the Zodimain Decree and the status of Aves Island.[15]

---

13 Report Number 2-12, I IMB 615, 623.
14 Report Number 2-14, I IMB 691, 692. The boundary between France (Guadeloupe and Martinique) and Venezuela (Aves Island) is constructed using a meridian of longitude which, in effect, gives Aves Island slightly less than full weight. *See* Report Number 2-11, I IMB 603.
15 *See* Report Number 2-41, in this volume.

Saint Kitts and Nevis, in keeping with the OECS Maritime Boundary Delimitation Negotiation Strategy, adopted the position that negotiations with Venezuela in respect of Aves Island will be addressed on a regional basis after the conclusion of its other delimitations. At the appropriate time, if such delimitation negotiations are conducted, Saint Kitts and Nevis will have to consider the weight it accords to Aves Island.

III CONCLUSIONS

The Treaty was negotiated in an atmosphere of goodwill and cooperation by the parties and strengthens the relationship between the two nations. It brings the Netherlands closer to completing its Caribbean maritime delimitations in this sector, and with its first maritime boundary concluded, Saint Kitts and Nevis is better positioned to resolve its outstanding maritime boundaries.

IV RELATED LAW IN FORCE

A *Law of the Sea Conventions*

Saint Kitts and Nevis: Party to UNCLOS (signed 7 December 1984, ratified 1 July 1993).
The Netherlands: Party UNCLOS (signed 10 December 1982, ratified 28 June 1996).

B *Maritime Jurisdiction Claimed at Time of Signature*

Saint Kitts and Nevis: 12 M territorial sea; archipelagic waters; 24 M contiguous zone; 200 M exclusive economic zone; continental shelf to the outer edge of the continental margin or 200 M where the outer edge of the continental margin does not extend up to that distance.
The Netherlands: 12 M territorial sea; 200 M exclusive economic zone; continental shelf.

C *Maritime Jurisdiction Claimed Subsequent to Signature*

None.

Prepared by Rosemarie Cadogan and McClean Hobson

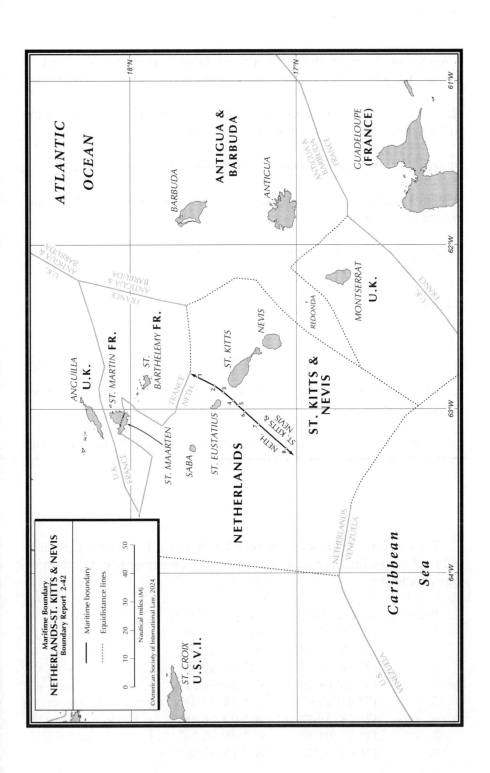

5966 *Report Number 2-42*

Agreement between the Federation of Saint Christopher and Nevis and the Kingdom of the Netherlands concerning Maritime Delimitation

The Federation of Saint Christopher and Nevis and the Kingdom of the Netherlands, hereinafter referred to as 'the Parties';

Desiring to strengthen the bonds of friendship between the Parties;

Desiring to establish an equitable delimitation of all maritime zones belonging to each of the Parties;

Recalling the relevant provisions of the United Nations Convention on the Law of the Sea of 10 December 1982;

Have agreed as follows:

Article 1

1. This Agreement shall establish the delimitation of all maritime zones between the Parties.

2. A decision of a Party to establish, extend or amend its maritime zones shall be in accordance with this Agreement.

Article 2

1. The maritime delimitation between the Parties is based on equidistance and shall be the line formed by the geodesics connecting points defined by their coordinates:

Point	Latitude North	Longitude West
1.	17° 35′ 58.77″	62° 48′ 15.30″
2.	17° 29′ 41.88″	62° 51′ 28.66″
3.	17° 26′ 33.27″	62° 53′ 48.63″
4.	17° 23′ 08.49″	62° 56′ 51.25″
5.	17° 21′ 23.97″	62° 58′ 37.43″
6.	17° 18′ 58.27″	63° 00′ 56.35″
7.	17° 14′ 01.32″	63° 05′ 30.24″
8.	17° 04′ 03.32″	63° 14′ 32.30″

2. The points defined by geographic coordinates are expressed in World Geodetic System 1984 (WGS 84).

3. From point 1 the delimitation extends along a geodetic azimuth of 26.55 degrees until the delimitation with a third state is reached.

4. From point 8 the delimitation extends along a geodetic azimuth of 222.74 degrees until the delimitation with a third state is reached.

5. For illustrative purposes, this delimitation is depicted on a chart annexed to this Agreement.

Article 3

The Parties will, as appropriate, and consistent with their international obligations and with due regard to the transfer of competencies to the European Union, consult with respect to marine governance issues of concern to them.

Article 4

In the event that a single geological structure or mineral field containing oil or natural gas should extend across the line established in Article 2, and a part of said structure or field that is situated on one side of the line could be exploited totally or partially from the other side of the line, the Parties, after holding technical consultations, will seek to reach agreement regarding the most effective way of exploiting said structure or field, and on the way in which the costs and benefits in relation to such activities shall be apportioned.

Article 5

1. Any dispute concerning the interpretation or application of this Agreement shall be settled peacefully by consultation and negotiation, in accordance with international law.

2. In the event that no agreement can be reached within a reasonable period of time, either Party may have recourse to the dispute settlement provisions provided by Part XV of the United Nations Convention on the Law of the Sea.

Article 6

This Agreement shall enter into force on the first day of the second month after both parties have notified each other in writing that the legal requirements for entry into force have been complied with.

IN WITNESS WHEREOF, the representatives of the Parties, being duly authorized for this purpose, have signed this Agreement.

Done at Basseterre this 04 day of April 2024, in duplicate, in the English language.

FOR THE FEDERATION OF
SAINT CHRISTOPHER AND NEVIS
(*signed*)

FOR THE KINGDOM OF THE
NETHERLANDS
(*signed*)

III

South America

IV

Africa

V

Central Pacific, East Asia, Southeast Asia

Fiji – France (Wallis and Futuna)

Report Number 5-6 (Add. 2)

Exchange of Letters between the Government of the French Republic and the Government of the Republic of Fiji concerning the Delimitation of Maritime Spaces under their Jurisdiction

Signed:	16 September 2015
Entry into force:	25 November 2022
Published at:	Journal Officiel de la République française, 31 December 2022, NOR: EAEJ2236398D

Fiji and France delimited equidistance-based exclusive economic zone boundaries between Fiji and the French territories of New Caledonia and Wallis and Futuna in January 1983.[1] In November 1990 the parties agreed a codicil which slightly modified the geographic coordinates of the Fiji-Wallis and Futuna boundary.[2] All five points defining the boundary were shifted, but none by more than 2.5 minutes of latitude or longitude.

In late 2014 Tuvalu agreed maritime boundaries with Fiji (17 October 2014)[3] and France (9 December 2014),[4] the latter agreement identifying coordinates for the equidistance line that had been agreed in principle as the boundary between the parties in 1985.[5] The conclusion of those agreements allowed for a trilateral agreement concerning the location of the Fiji – France (Wallis and Futuna) – Tuvalu tripoint, which was also concluded on 9 December 2014.[6]

These three 2014 agreements identified boundary coordinates with reference to the World Geodetic System 1984 (WGS84). Because the Fiji – Wallis and Futuna boundary delimited in 1983 and 1990 used coordinates referred to World Geodetic System 1972 (WGS72), Fiji and France agreed at the meeting of 9 December 2014 to update their bilateral boundary

---

1   *See* Report Number 5-6, I IMB 995.
2   *See* Report Number 5-6 (Add. 1/Corr. 1), V IMB 3729.
3   *See* Report Number 5-48, in this volume.
4   *See* Report Number 5-29 (Add. 1), VIII IMB 5503.
5   *See* Report Number 5-29, VI IMB 4330.
6   *See* Report Number 5-46, VIII IMB 5539.

Coalter G. Lathrop (ed.), International Maritime Boundaries, 5975-5980.
© *The American Society of International Law and Koninklijke Brill BV, Leiden 2025.*

coordinates to WGS84. This agreement was formalized in an exchange of notes between the two governments on 16 September 2015 which converted the coordinates of Points 1-4 of the 1990 line to WGS 84, and slightly shifted Point 5 to the recently-agreed tripoint with Tuvalu.

The change from WGS72 to WGS84 did not change the location of Points 1-4 on the surface of the earth; it just updated the coordinates to the coordinate reference system used for other maritime boundaries in the region (which is also the most widely used geocentric coordinate reference system around the world today). The difference between WGS72 and WGS84 is significant to geodesists but minor in terms of boundary coordinates: the latitude coordinates for Points 1-4 were unaltered by the conversion, and the longitude coordinates only changed by one second of arc. Nevertheless, the conversion is useful for mapping and geospatial data management purposes.

The September 2015 exchange of notes noted that the minutes of the December 2014 meeting at which the conversion to WGS84 was agreed contained an error concerning the coordinates of Point 5 of the Fiji – France boundary. The error was not specified, but the exchange of notes corrected it and confirmed that Point 5 of the boundary is located at the Fiji – France – Tuvalu tripoint at 13° 14′ 27.28″ S, 179° 32′ 05.12″ E (WGS84).

The agreement was to enter into force on the date of the last notification by the two governments confirming that the conditions for the entry into force of the agreement have been fulfilled. A French Decree of 30 December 2022 published in the Official Journal of the French Republic indicated that the agreement entered into force on 25 November 2022.[7]

Prepared by Martin Pratt

---

7   Decree No. 2022-1742 of 30 December 2022 publishing the agreement in the form of an exchange of letters between the Government of the French Republic and the Government of the Republic of Fiji relating to the delimitation of their maritime areas under jurisdiction (together two annexes), signed in Suva on September 16, 2015, JORF 31 December 2022, no 0303, *available at* https://www.legifrance.gouv.fr/jorf/id/JORFTEXT000046846709.

Unofficial Translation

AGREEMENT IN THE FORM OF AN EXCHANGE OF LETTERS BETWEEN THE GOVERNMENT OF THE FRENCH REPUBLIC AND THE GOVERNMENT OF THE REPUBLIC OF FIJI RELATING TO THE DELIMITATION OF THE MARITIME AREAS UNDER THEIR JURISDICTION (WITH TWO ANNEXES), SIGNED AT SUVA ON 16 SEPTEMBER 2015

THE AMBASSADOR

Suva, 16 September 2015
H. E. Ratu Inoke Kubuabola
Minister of Foreign Affairs
of the Republic of Fiji

Subject: Agreement in the form of an exchange of letters between the Government of the French Republic and the Government of the Republic of Fiji concerning the delimitation of the maritime areas under their jurisdiction

Mr. Minister,

I have the honour to refer:
1 – to the United Nations Convention on the Law of the Sea, signed at Montego Bay on 10 December 1982, which provides in articles 74 and 83 that the delimitation of maritime areas under the jurisdiction of States whose coasts are adjacent or opposite each other shall be effected by agreement in accordance with international law, in order to arrive at an equitable solution;
2 – to the amendment to the Convention of 19 January 1983 between the Government of the French Republic and the Government of the Republic of Fiji relating to the delimitation of their economic zones, signed in Suva on 8 November 1990;
3 – to the minutes of the concluding technical negotiation meeting held at the Commonwealth Secretariat General headquarters in London on 9 December 2014, initialed by the heads of the delegations of the Republic of France and the Republic of Fiji, as well as to the tripartite minutes signed on the same day by the heads of the delegations of the French Republic, the Republic of Fiji and the Government of Tuvalu.

I have the honour to confirm that the line delimiting the maritime areas under the jurisdiction of France and Fiji respectively, as agreed in London on 9 December 2014 on the basis of equidistance, is the line joining the points expressed in the geodetic system "World Geodetic System 1984" (WGS 84) mentioned in the attached Annex I, which forms an integral part of this agreement. This line is shown on the map in Annex II for information purposes only.

I note an error in the minutes of the concluding technical negotiation meeting of 9 December 2014 concerning the coordinates of point 5. The correct coordinates of point 5 are 13° 14′ 27.28″ S and 179° 32′ 05.12″ E, which corresponds to the tri-junction point between France, Fiji and Tuvalu.

Furthermore, I have the honour to confirm that any dispute which may arise between the Government of the French Republic and the Government of the Republic of Fiji concerning the interpretation or application of this agreement will be settled through bilateral consultations, in accordance with international law.

If the foregoing provisions meet with the approval of the Government of the Republic of Fiji, I have the honour to propose that this letter and your reply to this letter constitute an agreement between the Government of the French Republic and the Government of the Republic of Fiji, which will enter into force on the date of the last notification from the two governments confirming that the conditions for entry into force of the agreement have been met.

I take this opportunity to renew to Your Excellency the assurances of my highest consideration.

MICHEL DJOKOVIC

Suva, 16 September 2015
H.E. Mr. Michel Djokovic
Ambassador of France to Fiji Suva

Subject: Agreement in the form of an exchange of letters between the Government of the French Republic and the Government of the Republic of Fiji relating to the delimitation of the maritime zones under their jurisdiction

Mr. Ambassador,

I have the honor to acknowledge receipt of your letter dated 16 September 2015 and its two annexes, which read as follows:

[See text of previous note]

In reply, I have the honour to confirm that the proposal formulated in your letter meets with the approval of the Government of the Republic of Fiji and that, consequently, your letter and this reply constitute an agreement between the Government of the French Republic and the Government of the Republic of Fiji, which will enter into force on the date of the last notification from the two governments confirming that the conditions for entry into force of the agreement have been met.

MS. LITIA MAWI
Fiji's Roving Ambassador
to Polynesia and Micronesia

ANNEX I

The line delimiting the maritime areas under the jurisdiction of the French Republic (Wallis and Futuna) and the Republic of Fiji is the line successively joining by geodetic lines the points defined below by their geographical coordinates referred to the geodetic system "World Geodetic System 1984" (WGS 1984).

Identifier	Latitude	Longitude
1	15° 53′ 56″ S	177° 25′ 03″ W
2	15° 17′ 44″ S	178° 29′ 41″ W
3	14° 47′ 33″ S	179° 14′ 43″ W
4	13° 19′ 04″ S	179° 30′ 19″ E
5	13° 14′ 27.28″ S	179° 32′ 05.12″ E

ANNEX II

[map not reproduced]

Federated States of Micronesia – Papua New Guinea

Report Number 5-47

**Treaty between the Federated States of Micronesia
and the Independent State of Papua New Guinea concerning
maritime boundaries between the Federated States of
Micronesia and the Independent State of Papua New Guinea
and co-operation on related matters**

Signed: 29 July 1991
Entry into force: 18 March 2016
Published at: UNTS (I-54917); 96 LOS BULL. 21 (2018)

**Amendment to the Treaty between the Federated States of
Micronesia and the Independent State of Papua New Guinea**

Signed: 7 September 2015
Entry into force: 18 March 2016
Published at: UNTS (A-54917); 96 LOS BULL. 24 (2018)

I SUMMARY

The 426 nautical mile-long boundary between the Federated States of
Micronesia (FSM) and Papua New Guinea (PNG) is an equidistance line
separating the exclusive economic zones (EEZs) of the two states located
between two pockets of high seas to the west and east. It is defined by means
of 38 points numbered from the intersection of the two states' 200 nautical
mile (M) EEZ limits in the west, to the intersection of their 200 M EEZ
limits in the east.

Whilst an agreement on the delimitation of EEZ (or exclusive fishing zone)
and seabed and subsoil rights was concluded in July 1991 (the Treaty or 1991
Treaty), the 1991 Treaty did not come into force until after an amendment
to the treaty was signed in 2015 (the Amendment or 2015 Amendment).
The 2015 Amendment to the 1991 Treaty, signed on 7 September 2015,
replaced Annex 1 of the Treaty, which contained the coordinates defining
the boundary line, with Annex 1-A containing a revised list of coordinates.

Coalter G. Lathrop (ed.), International Maritime Boundaries, 5981-6003.
© *The American Society of International Law and Koninklijke Brill BV, Leiden 2025.*

The Amendment also included three illustrative maps designated Annex 2-A. The purpose of the Amendment, as stated in the preamble, was "to reflect the accurate and updated information on their maritime boundary." The amended list of coordinates reportedly took into account improved survey techniques in order to deliver improvements in the construction and definition of the boundary line.

The amended agreement came into force on 18 March 2016 in accordance with Article 9 of the Treaty. With this agreement, both states have completed all maritime delimitations within 200 M with neighboring states.

II CONSIDERATIONS

1 *Political, Strategic, and Historical Considerations*

FSM and PNG are both island states. FSM spans around 2,900 km east to west and consists of a federation of four major island groups – Kosrae, Pohnpei, Chuuk and Yap – which collectively total over 600 insular features.

FSM was formerly a United Nations Trust Territory of the Pacific Islands under United States administration, which gained independence on 3 November 1986 and is now a federal republic in free association with the United States (renewed in May 2004). Under the original Compact of Free Association (1986-2001), the United States provided US$1.3 billion in grants and aid. Under the renewed compact (2004-2023), the United States will provide a total of approximately US$2.1 billion to FSM with a trust fund also being established to provide a comparable income stream after 2023.

PNG comprises the eastern half of the island of New Guinea, together with numerous smaller islands including those fringing the Bismarck Sea. There is a considerable contrast between FSM and PNG in terms of land area, populations, and size of economy. While FSM has a land area of just over 700 km^2, PNG has a land area of just under 463,000 km^2. Similarly, there is a considerable disparity between the two states in terms of population: FSM has a population of around 115,000 while that of PNG is about 8.94 million.[1] Moreover, the gross domestic product of FSM at US$348 million is around 1% of the gross domestic product of PNG at over US$30 billion. These

---

1   World Population Review, *2020 World Population by Country*, https://worldpopulation review.com/ (last visited 18 October 2020).

Federated States of Micronesia – Papua New Guinea 5983

disparities do not, however, appear to have had an impact on the course of the maritime boundary between them.

Both states are members of regional bodies including the Pacific Islands Forum, the Pacific Islands Forum Fisheries Agency (FFA), the Secretariat of the Pacific Community (SPC), and the Western and Central Pacific Fisheries Commission (WCPFC), and they enjoy a cooperative bilateral relationship.

2 Legal Regime Considerations

The preamble to the 1991 Treaty takes into account the United Nations Convention on the Law of the Sea (LOSC) "regarding the regime of the continental shelf and exclusive economic zone." Article 1(a) of the Treaty defines "Exclusive Economic Zone or fishing zone" as being "the area over which each party has sovereign rights for the purpose of exploring, exploiting, conserving and managing the natural resources, whether living or non-living, of the waters within the areas not exceeding 200 nautical miles from the base lines from which the Territorial Sea is measured in accordance with the United Nations Convention on the Law of the Sea." Meanwhile, Article 1(b) of the Treaty defines "Seabed jurisdiction" as the "sovereign rights over the seabed, subsoil and the superjacent waters in accordance with international law."

The maritime boundary line defined by the list of coordinates contained in Annex 1 of the Treaty is defined as being "between the area of the seabed and subsoil that is adjacent to and appertains to" FSM and PNG and "shall be the boundary of the exclusive economic zone or fishing zone" between FSM and PNG. This language may have been deemed necessary because, in 1991, PNG had yet to claim an EEZ: for FSM the boundary related to the EEZ, for PNG it concerned its fishing zone. However, it is clear that the parties intended that the same line should also divide their continental shelf entitlements such that the agreement can be considered to establish a 'single' maritime boundary. The 2015 Amendment omits reference to fishing zones, instead stating that the delimitation line is "between the exclusive economic zones and the areas of seabed and subsoil over which each Party respectively exercises sovereign rights in accordance with international law." The boundary line is far enough removed from the coasts of the parties that it does not involve delimitation of the territorial sea or contiguous zone.

Any disputes between the parties "arising out of the interpretation or implementation" of the Treaty are "to be settled by consultation or negotiation" in accordance with Article 6, and Article 7 calls for mandatory consultation "at the request of either [party], on any matters relating to this Treaty."

3   Economic and Environmental Considerations

The preamble to the 1991 Treaty indicates that the purpose of the agreement is to "settle permanently the area within which the Federated States of Micronesia and the Independent State of Papua New Guinea shall respectively exercise sovereign rights with respect to the exploration and exploitation of their respective sea and seabed resources".

Article 3 deals with cross-boundary oil, gas or other minerals and indicates that if any "single accumulation" of "liquid hydrocarbons or natural gas" or "any other mineral deposit beneath the seabed" extends across the "line defining seabed jurisdiction" between the parties, then the parties "shall consult with a view to reaching agreement" on the effective exploitation and equitable sharing of the benefits to be derived from such exploitation. Article 3 therefore effectively provides for negotiations towards a unitization type arrangement for straddling seabed resources. The mention of "liquid" hydrocarbon resources would seem to indicate conventional oil and gas resources were the type of seabed resources primarily in view for the drafters of the agreement, but the mention of "any other mineral deposit" gives the article wider effect, for instance to seabed mineral deposits such as cobalt crusts or seafloor massive sulfide deposits.

Articles 4 and 5 of the 1991 Treaty deal with cooperation on living resources and protection of the marine environment, respectively. Here it can be observed that fisheries resources and therefore the marine environment that supports them are of considerable significance to both FSM and PNG which have similarly-sized EEZs: both are approximately 3 million km^2. For both countries small-scale subsistence fishing remains vital to the food security requirements of coastal communities, especially those located on small, isolated islands. Commercial fishing is also important for both countries and is dominated by the tuna fishery. For FSM access fees from foreign vessels contribute an estimated 10% of all government revenue, and fisheries contribute over 10% of GDP.[2] Fisheries are of lesser relative importance to

---

2   The contribution of fisheries to FSM's GDP ranged from 10%-14.3% over the period 2009-2014. Food and Agriculture Organization of the United Nations, *Fishery and Aquaculture Country Profiles: the Federated States of Micronesia*, Table 9 (March 2018), http://www.fao.org/fishery/facp/FSM/en.

PNG's more land-based economy, representing an estimated 2.7% of GDP but remain important in terms of livelihoods and food security.[3]

Accordingly, Article 4 of the Treaty states that FSM and PNG will "consult with a view to co-operating in the management, conservation and utilization of the living resources" within their exclusive zones with "particular regard to highly migratory species and the participation by third Parties in the exploitation of the living resources of such zones." The second half of this one-sentence article is a clear acknowledgement of the importance of tuna and tuna-like species to both states as well as the salient role of distant-water foreign fishing in their exploitation. Further, Article 5 of the 1991 Treaty provides that FSM and PNG "shall consult where appropriate with a view to co-ordinating their policies in accordance with international law on the protection of the marine environment and the conduct of marine research in their respective economic zones or fishing zones."

At the ceremony formalizing their maritime boundary agreement on the sidelines of the Pacific Islands Forum meeting in Port Moresby in September 2015, the leaders of both countries emphasized that the improved delineation of their boundaries would enhance the management and enforcement of their waters and fishery resources.[4] Beyond this general agreement between the parties concerning the value of delimiting their maritime boundary from a marine resources management perspective, it does not appear that economic and environmental considerations influenced the course of the maritime boundary line between them.

4 Geographic Considerations

The primary geographic considerations relate to the opposite coasts of their islands and the construction of an equidistance line between them.

3　An estimated 250,000-500,000 people participate in PNG's coastal subsistence fishery. Food and Agriculture Organization of the United Nations, *Fishery and Aquaculture Country Profiles: Independent State of Papua New Guinea* (June 2018), http://www.fao.org/fishery/facp/PNG/en.

4　*FSM and PNG sign amendment to maritime boundaries*, KASELEHLIE PRESS (4 October 2015), http://www.kpress.info/index.php?option=com_content&view=article&id=155:fsm-and-png-sign-amendment-to-maritime-boundaries&catid=8&Itemid=103.

5986   *Report Number 5-47*

5   *Islands, Rocks, Reefs, and Low-tide Elevations Considerations*

As both FSM and PNG are island states, islands were fundamental to delimitation of the maritime boundary between them. The southernmost territory of FSM, Kapingamarangi, is a large atoll on which 33 small islands are located. Kapingamarangi is the sole FSM insular feature relevant to the maritime delimitation with PNG and the only FSM feature referred to in the Amendment. The British Admiralty Sailing Directions indicate that the feature includes "more than 30 densely wooded islands" located on the eastern side of the atoll with the western side of the atoll being described as "almost submerged" at high water and that the islands are inhabited.[5] The combined land area of the islands has been recorded as 0.521 square miles (0.84 km²) and the lagoon area as 22.01 square miles (35.42 km²).[6]

On the PNG side, the islands fringing the northern coast of New Ireland face FSM to the north-east and are the relevant PNG features in this delimitation. According to Annex 1-A of the 2015 Amendment the islands involved on the PNG side are Namotu, Paona, Mahur, Simberi, Enus and Mussau Islands.

It has been suggested that PNG might argue that an equidistance-based delimitation line would not be equitable in light of the relatively isolated character of Kapingamarangi, 160 M from the nearest FSM feature to the north, as compared to the relatively larger and more numerous islands of PNG forming a compact group to the south.[7] It is not known whether this argument was made, but, if it was, it did not prevail. Instead, the insular features of both FSM and PNG have been accorded full weight in the construction of the boundary line.

6   *Baseline Considerations*

The key feature for FSM for the delimitation of a maritime boundary with PNG was Kapingamarangi with the southern seaward low-water line of the

---

5   United Kingdom Hydrographic Office, *Pacific Islands Pilot*, Volume 1, NP60 (11th edition, 2007) at 424.

6   School of Naval Administration, Hoover Institute, Stanford University, HANDBOOK ON THE TRUST TERRITORY OF THE PACIFIC ISLANDS 8 (Navy Department, Office of the Chief of Naval Operations 1948). *See also* William A. Niering, *Terrestrial Ecology of Kapingamarangi Atoll, Caroline Islands*, 33 (2) ECOLOGICAL MONOGRAPHS 131, 131-132 (Spring 1963).

7   J.R.Victor Prescott & Clive H. Schofield, THE MARITIME POLITICAL BOUNDARIES OF THE WORLD 415 (Martinus Nijhoff Publishers 2005).

reef providing the baseline on the FSM side in keeping with Article 6 of the LOSC.

PNG claims a system of archipelagic baselines, established through its National Seas Act of 1977, Offshore Seas Proclamation of 1978, and Declaration of the Baselines by Method of Coordinates of Base Points for Purposes of the Location of Archipelagic Baselines of 25 July 2002.[8] However, the archipelagic baseline segments facing FSM were not used in the construction of the maritime boundary between FSM and PNG. Instead, basepoints on the normal baselines of PNG's islands facing FSM were used for this purpose.

7 Geological and Geomorphological Considerations

Geophysical factors concerning the geology and geomorphology of the sea floor did not influence this equidistance-based delimitation line dividing areas within 200 M of the parties' coasts. However, as noted above, the 2015 Amendment made it clear that the delimitation line related to both the parties' EEZ rights and their sovereign rights over "areas of seabed and subsoil." It can also be noted that both parties have made submissions to the Commission on the Limits of the Continental Shelf (CLCS) with respect to areas of continental shelf located beyond 200 M to both the east and west of their boundary termini, Point 38 and Point 1, respectively.

To the east, on 5 May 2009, FSM, PNG, and the Solomon Islands made a joint submission concerning the Ontong Java Plateau regarding which the CLCS issued recommendations on 17 March 2017.[9] Once the outer limits of the continental shelf beyond 200 M are delineated on the basis of the

---

8   U.S. Department of State, Office of Ocean and Polar Affairs, Bureau of Oceans and International Environmental and Scientific Affairs, *Papua New Guinea Archipelagic and Other Maritime Claims and Boundaries*, Limits in the Seas, No.138 (23 May 2014).

9   Federated States of Micronesia, Papua New Guinea & Solomon Islands, Joint Submission to the Commission on the Limits of the Continental Shelf concerning the Ontong Java Plateau by the Federated States of Micronesia, Papua New Guinea and the Solomon Islands, 5 May 2009, *available at* https://www.un.org/Depts/los/clcs_new/submissions_ files/fmpgsb32_09/exsumdocs/fmpgsb2009executivesummary.pdf; Commission on the Limits of the Continental Shelf, *Summary of Recommendations of the Commission on the Limits of the Continental Shelf in regard to the Joint Submission made by The Federated States of Micronesia, Papua New Guinea and Solomon Islands Concerning the Ontong Java Plateau On 5 May 2009*, approved by the Subcommission on 12 August 2016 and approved by the Commission with amendments on 17 March 2017,*available at* https:// www.un.org/Depts/los/clcs_new/submissions_files/fmpgsb32_09/2017_03_17_OJP_ SumRec_COM_for%20website_10-06-2019.pdf.

Commission's recommendations, these three states will need to delimit this area of continental shelf between them. The northwestern portion of this area will presumably require FSM and PNG to delimit a continental shelf boundary continuing to the east from Point 38 of their current boundary line with the potential for a tripoint with the Republic of Nauru should Nauru prove to have continental shelf rights in this area.[10]

To the west, on 30 August 2013, FSM made a submission in respect of the Eauripik Rise which, at the time of writing, had yet to be considered by the CLCS. PNG has yet to make a full submission covering this area but has provided preliminary information concerning the Eauripik Rise and Mussau Ridge.[11] These areas of continental shelf lie between of the 200 M limits of both FSM and PNG. Here it can be noted that, at the time of writing, FSM had yet to make a submission to the CLCS concerning the Mussau Ridge region. It can therefore be anticipated that, should PNG make a full submission and FSM do likewise, when and if these submissions receive favorable recommendations from the CLCS, FSM and PNG will require delimitation of a continental shelf boundary in areas west of Point 1 of their current boundary line. It also appears that further west in the Eurapik Rise area the delimitation of continental shelf boundaries seawards of 200 M between FSM and PNG may involve the determination of a tripoint with Indonesia.[12]

8 Method of Delimitation Considerations

The maritime boundary between FSM and PNG defined by the 1991 Treaty and the 2015 Amendment is an equidistance line between basepoints located on the normal baselines of each state. As a result of the 2015 revisions, slight inconsistencies exist at both ends of the boundary line where short diversions

---

10 At the time of writing Nauru had not made a preliminary or full submission to the CLCS relating to the Ontong Java Plateau area.

11 Papua New Guinea, Preliminary Information Indicative of the Outer Limits of the Continental Shelf Beyond 200 Nautical Miles for the Mussau Ridge and Eauripik Rise Areas Submitted by Papua New Guinea, 5 May 2009, *available at* https://www.un.org/depts/los/clcs_new/submissions_files/preliminary/png_preliminaryinfo.pdf.

12 Indonesia made a submission to the CLCS on 11 April 2019 concerning an area that encompasses a large portion of the Eauripik Rise. Republic of Indonesia, Continental Shelf Submission of the Republic of Indonesia – Partial Submission with respect to the Area of North of Papua, 2018, *available at* https://www.un.org/Depts/los/clcs_new/submissions_files/idn1_83_19/2019-02-01_IDN-Executive_Summary.pdf.

are required to meet the intersecting 200 M limits of the two states.[13] This suggests that the part of the boundary between Point 2 and Point 37 may depart, if only marginally, from strict equidistance.

9 Technical Considerations

The 1991 maritime boundary agreement was problematic from a technical perspective. In particular it provided coordinates of the boundary terminus and turning points with extremely high precision but without specifying a geodetic datum for the coordinates listed at Annex 1. As the geodetic datum positions and orients the geodetic reference system for geographical coordinates, the absence of a specified datum leads to positional uncertainty concerning the coordinates involved. The 2015 Amendment rectifies these technical deficits by defining the boundary terminus and turning points to a reasonable degree of precision, specifying the reference system to be World Geodetic System 1984 (WGS84),[14] and defining the line segments making up the boundary as geodesic lines. As noted in the preamble, the purpose of the 2015 Amendment was "to amend the Treaty in order to reflect the accurate and updated information on their maritime boundary." Improved technical survey standards, coupled with the use of high-resolution satellite imagery and additional field work, allowed for a better definition of the boundary line and conclusion of the 2015 Amendment with the support of the Regional Maritime Boundaries Unit of the SPC.[15] The 2015 Amendment replaced Annex 1 of the 1991 Treaty, which contained the coordinates of 36 points defining the boundary line, with a revised list of coordinates of 38 points (Annex 1-A) and three illustrative maps (Annex 2-A). The majority

---

13 These slight diversions, or dog-legs, measure 0.35 nautical miles (650 m) between Points 1 and 2 at the western end of the boundary line and 0.03 nautical miles (52 m) between Points 37 and 38 at the eastern end of the boundary line. These diversions are illustrated on the maps included in Annex 2-A of the 2015 Amendment to the 1991 Treaty.

14 Defined in the 2015 Amendment, Annex 1-A, as "a spheroid having its centre at the centre of the Earth, and a Semi-major axis (a) of 6,378,137.0000 meters, a Semi-minor axis (b) of 6,356,752.3142 meters and a flattening ratio (f)=(a-b)/a of 1/298.257 223 563."

15 Pacific Community, *Papua New Guinea completes mapping of its maritime boundaries* (15 September 2015), https://gsd.spc.int/component/content/article/631-papua-new-guinea-completes-mapping-of-its-maritime-boundaries.

The SPC's Regional Maritime Boundaries Unit was established in 2001 and works in partnership with Geoscience Australia and Australia's Attorney General's Department under the Enhanced Pacific Ocean Governance (EPOG) grant from the Government of Australia. Other contributors include the University of Sydney, the Commonwealth Secretariat, the Pacific Islands Forum Fisheries Agency, and UNEP-GRID Arendal.

5990 *Report Number 5-47*

(Points 2-37) of the points contained in the 2015 Amendment are reflective of those in the 1991 Treaty.[16] The additional terminal points (Points 1 and 38) provided in 2015 connect to the intersection of the parties' 200 M limits. Consequently, the location of the overall line remained unchanged except for relatively minor adjustments at either end to accommodate the intersection of recalculated EEZ limits.

10 *Other Considerations*

None.

III CONCLUSIONS

The 1991 Treaty between FSM and PNG provides for a fairly straight forward equidistance-based boundary dividing areas within 200 M between the parties. Technical issues prevented the agreement from entering into force until an amendment to the agreement was reached in 2015 based on more recent surveys and technical support. Once the 2015 Amendment was concluded, the 1991 Treaty, as amended, entered into force in 2016. Both FSM and PNG have now deposited lists of the geographic coordinates of their baselines, limits of their maritime claims, and their boundaries with the United Nations Secretary-General, pursuant to Article 16(2) and Article 75(2) of the LOSC.[17] It can be observed here that this action is part of a coordinated effort on the part of Pacific island states and is in keeping with the first strategic priority of the Pacific Oceanscape Framework which addresses jurisdictional rights and responsibilities. The Framework urges Pacific island countries and territories to deposit coordinates and charts delineating their maritime zones with the United Nations with the explicit objective that, once established, these areas "could not be challenged and reduced due to climate change and sea level rise."[18] It can be observed that this practice appears to

---

16 The coordinates provided in the 2015 Amendment reflect those in the 1991 Treaty but are rounded to the nearest second of arc. This suggests a realization that the coordinates provided in the 1991 Treaty were defined to an unnecessary level of detail.

17 *See* United Nations Division of Ocean Affairs and the Law of the Sea, *Deposit of Charts*, https://www.un.org/Depts/los/LEGISLATIONANDTREATIES/depositpublicity.htm (last visited 18 October 2020).

18 Cristelle Pratt & Hugh Govan, *Our Sea of Islands, Our Livelihoods, Our Oceania. Framework for A Pacific Oceanscape: A catalyst for implementation of ocean policy* 57-58 (Pacific Islands Forum Secretariat, November 2010), http://www.forumsec.org/

conflict with the traditional view that normal baselines can change location or "ambulate" over time.[19] It therefore remains to be seen whether this – what might be termed progressive interpretation of the baseline provisions of the LOSC – will prevail and prove to be opposable to other states.

IV RELATED LAW IN FORCE

A *Law of the Sea Conventions*

Federated States of Micronesia: Party to UNCLOS (acceded 29 April 1991).
Papua New Guinea: Party to UNCLOS (ratified 14 January 1997).

B *Maritime Jurisdiction Claimed at the Time of Signature* [of 1991 Treaty]

Federated States of Micronesia: 12 M territorial sea; 200 M EEZ; continental shelf.
Papua New Guinea: 12 M territorial sea; archipelagic waters; 200 M fishing zone; continental shelf.

C *Maritime Jurisdiction Claimed Subsequent to Signature* [of 1991 Treaty]

Federated States of Micronesia: 24 M contiguous zone; continental margin/ 200M continental shelf (CLCS submissions Ontong Java Plateau 5 May 2009 and Eauripik Rise 3 August 2013).
Papua New Guinea: 24 M contiguous zone; 200 M EEZ; continental margin/200M continental shelf (CLCS submission Ontong Java Plateau 5 May 2009).

> *Prepared by Clive Schofield (with technical assistance from*
> *Robert van de Poll)*

---

wp-content/uploads/2018/03/Framework-for-a-Pacific-Oceanscape-2010.pdf (last visited 18 October 2020). *See also*, Clive H. Schofield & David Freestone, *Islands Awash Amidst Rising Seas?: Sea Level Rise and Insular Status under the Law of the Sea*, 34 INT'L J. MARINE & COASTAL L. 391, 406 (2019).

19   Michael W. Reed, 3 SHORE AND SEA BOUNDARIES: THE DEVELOPMENT OF INTERNATIONAL MARITIME BOUNDARY PRINCIPLES THROUGH UNITED STATES PRACTICE 185 (U.S. Department of Commerce, National Oceanic and Atmospheric Administration, 2000). *See also, Baselines under the International Law of the Sea: Reports of the International Law Association Committee on Baselines under the International Law of the Sea*, BRILL RESEARCH PERSPECTIVES ON THE LAW OF THE SEA 58 (Coalter G. Lathrop, J. Ashley Roach & Donald R. Rothwell eds., Brill 2019).

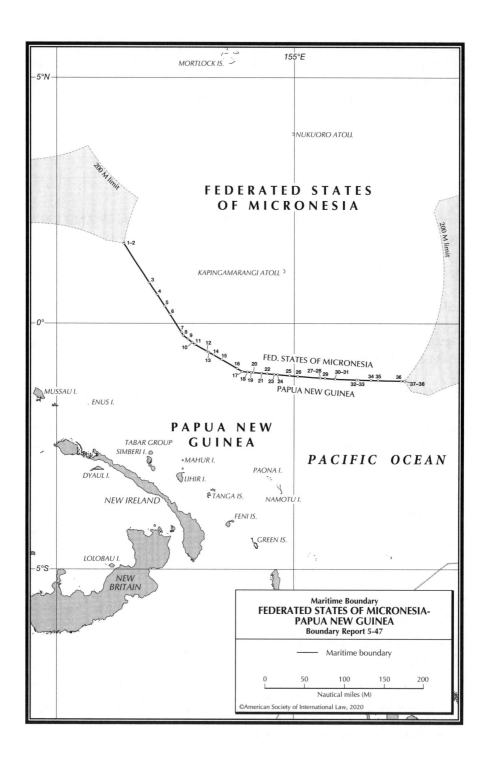

Treaty between the Federated States of Micronesia and the Independent State of Papua New Guinea concerning maritime boundaries between the Federated States of Micronesia and the Independent State of Papua New Guinea and co-operation on related matters

THE FEDERATED STATES OF MICRONESIA and THE INDEPENDENT STATE OF PAPUA NEW GUINEA,

DESIRING to establish maritime boundaries and to provide for certain other related matters in the area between the two countries;

RESOLVING, as good neighbours and in a spirit of co-operation and friendship, to settle permanently the limits of the area within which the Federated States of Micronesia and the Independent State of Papua New Guinea shall respectively exercise sovereign rights with respect to the exploration and exploitation of their respective sea and seabed resources;

TAKING INTO ACCOUNT the United Nations Convention on the Law of the Sea regarding the regime of the continental shelf and exclusive economic zone;

HAVE AGREED as follows:

Article 1
Definitions

In this Treaty

(a) "Exclusive Economic Zone or fishing zone" means the area over which each party has sovereign rights for the purpose of exploring and exploiting, conserving and managing the natural resources, whether living or non-living, of the waters within the areas not exceeding 200 nautical miles from the base lines from which the breadth of the Territorial Sea is measured in accordance with the United Nations Convention on the Law of the Sea.

(b) "Seabed jurisdiction" means sovereign rights over the seabed, subsoil, and the superjacent waters in accordance with international law.

Article 2
Maritime Jurisdiction

1. The maritime boundary between the area of seabed and subsoil that is adjacent to and appertains to the Federated States of Micronesia and the area of seabed and subsoil that is adjacent to and appertains to the Independent State of Papua New Guinea shall be the line described in Annex 1 to this Treaty. The line so described is shown on the map annexed to this Treaty as Annex 2.

2. The maritime boundary line referred to in paragraph 1 of this Article shall be the boundary of the exclusive economic zone or fishing zone between the Federated States of Micronesia and the Independent State of Papua New Guinea.

Article 3
Exploitation of Certain Seabed Deposits

If any single accumulation of liquid hydrocarbons or natural gas, or if any other mineral deposit beneath the seabed, extends across any line defining the limits of seabed jurisdiction of the Parties, and if the part of such accumulation or deposit that is situated on one side of such a line is recoverable in fluid form wholly or in part from the other side, the Parties shall consult with a view to reaching agreement on the manner in which the accumulation or deposit may be most effectively exploited and on the equitable sharing of the benefits from such exploitation.

Article 4
Co-operation on Living Resources

The Parties shall consult with a view to co-operating in the management, conservation and utilization of the living resources of their respective exclusive economic zones or fishing zones with particular regard to highly migratory species and the participation by third Parties in the exploitation of the living resources of such zones.

Federated States of Micronesia – Papua New Guinea 5995

Article 5
Protection of Marine Environment

The Parties shall consult where appropriate with a view to co-ordinating their policies in accordance with international law on the protection of the marine environment and the conduct of marine research in their respective economic zones or fishing zones.

Article 6
Settlement of Disputes

Any disputes between the Parties arising out of the interpretation or implementation of this Treaty shall be settled by consultation or negotiation.

Article 7
Consultations

The Parties shall consult, at the request of either, on any matters relating to this Treaty.

Article 8
Annexes

The Annexes to this Treaty shall have force and effect as integral parts to this Treaty.

Article 9
Ratification

This Treaty is subject to ratification and shall enter into force on the exchange of the instruments of ratification.

IN WITNESS WHEREOF, the undersigned being duly authorized have signed this Treaty.

DONE IN DUPLICATE at Palikir, Pohnpei, this 29th day of July, One thousand nine hundred and ninety-one.

[*signed*]   [*signed*]

FOR THE FEDERATED STATES   FOR THE INDEPENDENT STATE
OF MICRONESIA   OF PAPUA NEW GUINEA

ANNEX I

To the Treaty between the Federated States of Micronesia and the Independent State of Papua New Guinea concerning Maritime Boundaries between the Federated States of Micronesia and the Independent State of Papua New Guinea

Maritime and Seabed Boundaries between the Federated States of Micronesia and Papua New Guinea

The boundary line referred to in Article 2 of the Treaty shall be a continuous line:

commencing at the point of Latitude 01° 37' 09".8450 N, Longitude 151° 25' 24".4562 E (Point 1).

running thence South easterly along the geodesic to the point of Latitude 00° 49° 52".4841 N, [Longitude] 151° 56' 52".5917 E (Point 2).

thence South easterly along the geodesic to the point of Latitude 00° 35' 03".6124 N, Longitude 152° 06' 44".0304 E (Point 3).

thence South easterly along the geodesic to the point of Latitude 00° 20' 45".4167 N, Longitude 152° 16' 15".1987 E (Point 4).

thence South easterly along the geodesic to the point of Latitude 00° 10' 47".8691 N, Longitude 152° 22' 52".4576 E (Point 5).

thence South easterly along the geodesic to the point of Latitude 00° 10' 49".4145 S, Longitude 152° 37' 15".4357 E (Point 6).

thence South easterly along the geodesic to the point of Latitude 00° 14′ 44″.3028 S, Longitude 152° 39′ 51″.7836 E (Point 7).

thence South easterly along the geodesic to the point of Latitude 00° 19′ 14″.3931 S, Longitude 152° 45′ 52″.2049 E (Point 8).

thence South easterly along the geodesic to the point of Latitude 00° 23′ 13″.3709 S, Longitude 152° 51′ 10″.7148 E (Point 9).

thence South easterly along the geodesic to the point of Latitude 00° 25′ 41″.4053 S, Longitude 152° 54′ 28″.4061 E (Point 10),

thence South easterly along the geodesic to the point of Latitude 00° 33′ 53″.8933 S, Longitude 153° 09′ 37″.7150 E (Point 11).

thence South easterly along the geodesic to the point of Latitude 00° 35′ 14″.4954 S, Longitude 153° 12′ 06″.1340 E (Point 12).

thence South easterly along the geodesic to the point of Latitude 00° 38′ 36″.0189 S, Longitude 153° 18′ 15″.6166 E (Point 13).

thence South easterly along the geodesic to the point of Latitude 00° 44′ 19″.7484 S, Longitude 153° 28′ 46″.8789 E (Point 14).

thence South easterly along the geodesic to the point of Latitude 00° 55′ 14″.1565 S, Longitude 153° 48′ 13″.4663 E (Point 15).

thence South easterly along the geodesic to the point of Latitude 00° 58′ 49″.6570 S, Longitude 153° 54′ 37″.3067 E (Point 16).

thence South easterly along the geodesic to the point of Latitude 00° 59′ 22″.5533 S, Longitude 154° 01′ 14″.7473 E (Point 17).

thence South easterly along the geodesic to the point of Latitude 00° 59′ 45″.4030 S, Longitude 154° 05′ 49″.0414 E (Point 18).

thence Easterly along the geodesic to the point of Latitude 00° 59′ 59″.9281 S, Longitude 154° 08′ 44″.1522 E (Point 19).

5998   *Report Number 5-47*

thence Easterly along the geodesic to the point of Latitude 01° 00′ 51″.6962 S, Longitude 154° 19′ 00″.1954 E (Point 20).

thence Easterly along the geodesic to the point of Latitude 01° 01′ 26″.8520 S, Longitude 154° 25′ 55″.0000 E (Point 21).

thence Easterly along the geodesic to the point of Latitude 01° 02′ 12″.6413 S, Longitude 154° 34′ 59″.9227 E (Point 22).

thence Easterly along the geodesic to the point of Latitude 01° 02′ 35″.4054 S, Longitude 154° 39′ 28″.6383 E (Point 23).

thence Easterly along the geodesic to the point of Latitude 01° 03′ 50″.5123 S, Longitude 154° 54′ 25″.7589 E (Point 24).

thence Easterly along the geodesic to the point of Latitude 01° 04′ 41″.6785 S, Longitude 155° 04′ 41″.1551 E (Point 25).

thence Easterly along the geodesic to the point of Latitude 01° 06′ 34″.5459 S, Longitude 155° 31′ 53″.5317 E (Point 26).

thence Easterly along the geodesic to the point of Latitude 01° 06′ 39″.6364 S, Longitude 155° 33′ 06″.7447 E (Point 27).

thence Easterly along the geodesic to the point of Latitude 01° 07′ 03″.2282 S, Longitude 155° 38′ 48″.3096 E (Point 28).

thence Easterly along the geodesic to the point of Latitude 01° 07′ 55″.0730 S, Longitude 155° 50′ 44″.9008 E, (Point 29).

thence Easterly along the geodesic to the point of Latitude 01° 07′ 59″.1480 S, Longitude 155° 51′ 39″.9295 E (Point 30).

thence Easterly along the geodesic to the point of Latitude 01° 08′ 59″.9626 S, Longitude 156° 18 ' 08″.1125 E (Point 31).

thence Easterly along the geodesic to the point of Latitude 01° 09′ 03″.2404 S, Longitude 156° 20′ 33″.3143 E (Point 32).

thence Easterly along the geodesic to the point of Latitude 01° 09′ 24″.4277 S, Longitude 156° 36′ 04″.4562 E (Point 33).

thence Easterly along the geodesic to the point of Latitude 01° 09′ 36″.3268 S, Longitude 156° 45′ 05″.1780 E (Point 34).

thence Easterly along the geodesic to the point of Latitude 01° 10′ 11″.4569 S, Longitude 157° 14′ 27″.7721 E (Point 35).

thence Easterly along the geodesic to the point of Latitude 01° 10′ 16″.0536 S, Longitude 157° 18′ 24″.8537 E (Point 36).

Amendment to the Treaty between the Federated States of Micronesia and the Independent State of Papua New Guinea

WHEREAS, the Parties signed the Treaty between the Federated States of Micronesia and the Independent State of Papua New Guinea Concerning Maritime Boundaries and Co-operation on Related Matters (the "Treaty") on July 29, 1991, in Palikir, Pohnpei, FSM; and

WHEREAS, the Parties have mutually agreed to amend the Treaty in order to reflect the accurate and updated information on their maritime boundary.

NOW THEREFORE, the Parties have amended their Treaty in the following respects:

ANNEX 1-A

To the Treaty between the Federated States of Micronesia and the Independent State of Papua New Guinea concerning Maritime Boundaries between the Federated States of Micronesia and the Independent State of Papua New Guinea

Maritime and Seabed Boundaries between the Federated States of Micronesia and the Independent State of Papua New Guinea

1. The line of delimitation referred to in Article 2 of the Treaty between the exclusive economic zones and the areas of sea bed and subsoil over which each Party respectively exercises sovereign rights in accordance with

6000 *Report Number 5-47*

international law lies seaward of the islands of Kapingamarangi, on the one hand and the islands of Namotu (Southern Nuguria group of Islands), Paona, (Malum group of Islands), Mahur, Simberi, Enus and Mussau Islands, on the other hand, along the geodesics connecting the following points, defined by their coordinates, in the order stated:

a. commencing at the point of Latitude 1°37′32.59″ North, Longitude 151°25′26.58″ East (Point 1);

b. running thence at the point of Latitude 01°37′11.67″ North, Longitude 151°25′23.24″ East (Point 2);

c. thence South easterly along the geodesic to the point of Latitude 00°49′52″ North, Longitude 151°56′53″ East (Point 3);

d. thence South easterly along the geodesic to the point of Latitude 00°35′04″ North, Longitude 152°06′44″ East (Point 4);

e. thence South easterly along the geodesic to the point of Latitude 00°20′45″ North, Longitude 152°16′15″ East (Point 5);

f. thence South easterly along the geodesic to the point of Latitude 00°10′48″ North, Longitude 152°22′52″ East (Point 6);

g. thence South easterly along the geodesic to the point of Latitude 00°10′49″ South, Longitude 152°37′15″ East (Point 7);

h. thence South easterly along the geodesic to the point of Latitude 00°14′44″ South, Longitude 152°39′52″ East (Point 8);

i. thence South easterly along the geodesic to the point of Latitude 00°19′14″ South, Longitude 152°45′52″ East (Point 9);

j. thence South easterly along the geodesic to the point of Latitude 00°23′13″ South, Longitude 152°51′11″ East (Point 10);

k. thence South easterly along the geodesic to the point of Latitude 00°25′41″ South, Longitude 152°54′28″ East (Point 11);

l. thence South easterly along the geodesic to the point of Latitude 00°33′54″ South, Longitude 153°09′38″ East (Point 12);

Federated States of Micronesia – Papua New Guinea 6001

m. thence South easterly along the geodesic to the point of Latitude 00°35′14″ South, Longitude 153°12′06″ East (Point 13);

n. thence South easterly along the geodesic to the point of Latitude 00°38′36″ South, Longitude 153°18′16″ East (Point 14);

o. thence South easterly along the geodesic to the point of Latitude 00°44′20″ South, Longitude 153°28′47″ East (Point 15);

p. thence South easterly along the geodesic to the point of Latitude 00°55′14″ South, Longitude 153°48′13″ East (Point 16);

q. thence South easterly along the geodesic to the point of Latitude 00°58′50″ South, Longitude 153°54′37″ East (Point 17);

r. thence South easterly along the geodesic to the point of Latitude 00°59′23″ South, Longitude 154°01′15″ East (Point 18);

s. thence South easterly along the geodesic to the point of Latitude 00°59′45″ South, Longitude 154°05′49″ East (Point 19);

t. thence Easterly along the geodesic to the point of Latitude 01°00′00″ South, Longitude 154°08′44″ East (Point 20);

u. thence Easterly along the geodesic to the point of Latitude 01°00′52″ South, Longitude 154°19′00″ East (Point 21);

v. thence Easterly along the geodesic to the point of Latitude 01°01′27″ South, Longitude 154°25′55″ East (Point 22);

w. thence Easterly along the geodesic to the point of Latitude 01°02′13″ South, Longitude 154°35′00″ East (Point 23);

x. thence Easterly along the geodesic to the point of Latitude 01°02′35″ South, Longitude 154°39′29″ East (Point 24);

y. thence Easterly along the geodesic to the point of Latitude 01°03′51″ South, Longitude 154°54′26″ East (Point 25);

z. thence Easterly along the geodesic to the point of Latitude 01°04′42″ South, Longitude 155°04′41″ "East (Point 26);

6002 *Report Number 5-47*

aa. thence Easterly along the geodesic to the point of Latitude 01°06′35″ South, Longitude 155°31′54″ East (Point 27);

bb. thence Easterly along the geodesic to the point of Latitude 01°06′40″ South, Longitude 155°33′07″ East (Point 28);

cc. thence Easterly along the geodesic to the point of Latitude 01°07′03″ South, Longitude 155°38′48″ East (Point 29);

dd. thence Easterly along the geodesic to the point of Latitude 01°07′55″ South, Longitude 155°50′45″ East (Point 30);

ee. thence Easterly along the geodesic to the point of Latitude 01°07′59″ South, Longitude 155°51′40″ East (Point 31);

ff. thence Easterly along the geodesic to the point of Latitude 01°09′00″ South, Longitude 156°18′08″ East (Point 32);

gg. thence Easterly along the geodesic to the point of Latitude 01°09′03″ South, Longitude 156°20′33″ East (Point 33);

hh. thence Easterly along the geodesic to the point of Latitude 01°09′24″ South, Longitude 156°36′04″ East (Point 34);

ii. thence Easterly along the geodesic to the point of Latitude 01°09′36″ South, Longitude 156°45′05″ East (Point 35);

jj. thence Easterly along the geodesic to the point of Latitude 01°10′11″ South, Longitude 157°14′28″ East (Point 36);

kk. thence Easterly along the geodesic to the point of Latitude 01°10′16.04″ South, Longitude 157°18′24.17″ East (Point 37);

ll. thence Easterly along the geodesic to the point of Latitude 01°10′17.36″ South, Longitude 157°18′25.23″ East (Point 38).

2. The geographical coordinates referred to in this Annex are expressed in terms of the World Geodetic System 1984 (WGS84). Where for the purpose of this Agreement it is necessary to determine the position on the surface of the Earth of a point, line or area, that position may be determined by

reference to WGS84 in respect of a spheroid having its centre at the centre of the Earth, and a Semi-major axis (a) of 6,378,137.0000 meters, a Semi-minor axis (b) of 6,356,752.3142 meters and a flattening ratio (f)=(a-b)/a of 1/298.257 223 563 as depicted below.

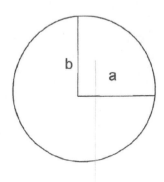

a=6378137m which is the semi major axis
b=6356752.3142m which is the semi minor axis
a flattening ratio of 1/298.257 223 563

(1) Annex 1 to the Treaty is deleted and replaced with the attached ANNEX 1-A. This is the annex referred to in article 2, paragraph 1, of the Treaty.

(2) Annex 2 to the Treaty is deleted and replaced with the attached ANNEX 2-A.

(3) The Treaty, as amended, shall enter into force on the exchange of instruments of ratification.

Done in duplicate at Port Moresby on this 7th day of September Two Thousand Fifteen]

[signed]

FOR THE FEDERATED
STATES OF MICRONESIA

[signed]

FOR THE INDEPENDENT STATE
OF PAPUA NEW GUINEA

ANNEX 2-A

[maps not included]

Fiji – Tuvalu

Report Number 5-48

Agreement Between the Government of Fiji and the Government of Tuvalu Concerning their Maritime Boundaries

Signed: 17 October 2014
Entry into force: 17 October 2014
Published at: UNTS (I-56867)

Exchange of Notes Constituting an Agreement Between the Government of Fiji and the Government of Tuvalu Amending Article 1 of the Agreement Between the Government of Fiji and the Government of Tuvalu Concerning their Maritime Boundaries

Signed: 4 April 2019 and 26 October 2020
Entry into force: 26 October 2020
Published at: UNTS (A-56867)

I SUMMARY

The Agreement Between the Government of Fiji and the Government of Tuvalu Concerning their Maritime Boundaries (Fiji – Tuvalu Treaty or 2014 Treaty) provides for the establishment of a maritime boundary delimiting the exclusive economic zone (EEZ) and continental shelves between the Republic of Fiji and Tuvalu, based on the principle of equidistance. Signed on 17 October 2014 in Suva, Fiji, the Treaty supplies the coordinates of 31 turning points along the maritime boundary, beginning in the northwest at the intersection of the two states' 200 nautical mile (M) limits and stretching approximately 370 M in the southeast direction, with significant turns at 78 M and 137 M. At its southeastern end, the maritime boundary line approaches a tripoint with the French overseas collectivity Wallis and Futuna. To account for the presence of a third state, the Treaty specifies that the identification of Point 31 is without prejudice to any further negotiations with France.

Coalter G. Lathrop (ed.), International Maritime Boundaries, 6005-6026.
© *The American Society of International Law and Koninklijke Brill BV, Leiden 2025.*

6006 *Report Number 5-48*

Following the entry into force of the Fiji – Tuvalu Treaty, representatives of Fiji, Tuvalu, and France met at the Commonwealth Secretariat offices in London on 9 December 2014 and agreed on the coordinates of their tripoint point.[1] On the basis of the agreed minutes from this meeting, Fiji and Tuvalu also agreed on the same day to amend the table of turning point coordinates in Article 1 of their Treaty to include Point 32 which "represents the agreed tri-junction point" between the three states.[2] The agreed tripoint is very close to, but not exactly coincident with, Point 31 originally specified in the Fiji – Tuvalu Treaty.[3]

In the wake of these agreements, Fiji and Tuvalu proceeded to formalize their boundary agreement to account for the settled tripoint. On 16 January 2015, Fiji sent a *note verbale* proposing to amend Article 1 of the Fiji – Tuvalu Treaty to include Point 32, which Tuvalu accepted on 15 September 2015.[4] On 16 September 2015, the three states met in Suva for a signing ceremony confirming the tripoint agreement reached in London in December 2014. Finally, on 4 April 2019, Fiji sent a note to Tuvalu suggesting that "the tri-point needs to be annexed to the [Fiji – Tuvalu Treaty]"; Tuvalu responded and agreed on 26 October 2020.[5] The 2014 Treaty and the 2019–2020 Exchange of Notes have been deposited with the UN Secretariat.

The conclusion of the Fiji – Tuvalu Treaty marks the culmination of efforts in recent years by the two island states to delimit their maritime boundaries. It was achieved in part through the support of the Commonwealth Secretariat and the Secretariat of the Pacific Community,[6] and technical expertise

---

1 *See* Report Number 5-46, VIII IMB 5539; *see also* Press Release, Commonwealth Secretariat, *Agreement Reached between Fiji, Tuvalu and France on Maritime Boundaries* (12 December 2014), https://thecommonwealth.org/news/agreement-reached-between-fiji -tuvalu-and-france-maritime-boundaries.

2 *See* Minutes of the Meeting between the Delegation of the Republic of Fiji and the Delegation of Tuvalu modifying the Agreement between the Government of the Republic of Fiji and the Government of Tuvalu concerning their Maritime Boundaries signed in Suva on the 17th October 2014 (signed 9 December 2014), reproduced at the end of this report.

3 Tuvalu and France also agreed to the coordinates of a maritime boundary on 9 December 2014. *See* Report Number 5-29 (Add. 1), VIII IMB 5503.

4 *See* Ministry of Foreign Affairs, Fiji, Note No. 21/2015 (16 January 2015); Ministry of Foreign Affairs, Government of Tuvalu, MFAT:3 14/15 (15 September 2015), reproduced at the end of this report.

5 *See* Exchange of notes constituting an agreement between the Government of Fiji and the Government of Tuvalu amending Article 1 of the Agreement between the Government of Fiji and the Government of Tuvalu concerning their maritime boundaries (entry into force on 26 October 2020 by the exchange of notes), UNTS A-56867, reproduced at the end of this report.

6 *See* Press Release, *supra* note 1.

offered by other regional entities. The Treaty was also concluded against the backdrop of growing concern about climate change. At the September 2015 trilateral signing ceremony, the Prime Minister of Tuvalu recalled the issue of sea-level rise and climate change, and noted the importance of the agreement for ensuring each state's maritime resources.[7] While the Fiji – Tuvalu Treaty does not refer to these challenges directly, a relatively uncommon provision in Article 4 records the two states' agreement to adjust their boundary based on the same principles as those in the existing agreement, should new surveys or resulting charts and maps indicate changes in base points "sufficiently significant to require adjustments of the maritime boundary." The impact of this provision may depend in part on ongoing debates over how to assess maritime boundaries in light of rising sea levels, as well as whether base point coordinates are to remain constant in the event of the submergence of land territory.[8]

II CONSIDERATIONS

1 Political, Strategic, and Historical Considerations

Fiji and Tuvalu are both archipelagic states. Fiji, an independent state since 1970, is located in the South Pacific and is composed of approximately 300 islands, more than 100 of which are inhabited. Fiji possesses an EEZ of approximately 1,280,000 km². Its total land area is approximately 18,300 km², with a maximum height of 1,325 meters above sea level reached at Mount Tomanivi, an extinct volcano located on Viti Levu, the largest island in Fiji at 10,400 km².[9] Viti Levu, home to the capital city of Suva, along with Vanua Levu, the second largest island at 5,600 km², together account for roughly three-quarters of the total land area of Fiji. Some 87% of Fiji's total population of 896,450 are resident on these two mountainous islands. Overall, the islands of Fiji are divided into nine major groups, the smallest of which is the Conway Reef Islands (also known as Ceva-i-Ra) and Skerries, and the largest of which is the Vanua Levu Group. The northernmost

---

7 Fijian Government, YouTube, *Fiji, France and Tuvalu signs Delimitation of Maritime Boundaries* (16 September 2015), https://www.youtube.com/watch?v=r_YxtMcR72E.
8 *See International Law and Sea Level Rise: Report of the International Law Association Committee on International Law and Sea Level Rise*, BRILL RESEARCH PERSPECTIVES (D Vidas et al. eds., 2019), 38-40.
9 Pacific Community, *Members: Fiji*, https://www.spc.int/our-members/fiji/details.

cluster of islands is the Rotuma Group. Fiji has historically maintained a large agriculture sector, along with tourism, forestry, fishing, and mineral extraction. Fiji has maritime boundaries with France (New Caledonia, Wallis and Futuna), Tuvalu, Tonga, Vanuatu, and Solomon Islands.

Tuvalu, which achieved independence in 1978, is a South Pacific state consisting of three reef islands and six small coral atolls. Tuvalu, like Fiji, also has an EEZ many times larger than its land area. While Tuvalu's land mass measures only around 26 km^2, its accompanying EEZ is some 750,000 km^2.[10] The largest atoll in Tuvalu is Funafuti, which consists of a narrow strip of land between 20 to 400 meters wide encircling a large central lagoon around 18 kilometers long and 14 kilometers wide. Funafuti is home to the capital of Tuvalu and some 60% of Tuvalu's total population of approximately 12,000. The economy of Tuvalu is based in significant part on licensing foreign fishing vessels, with tuna being one of the primary fish caught.

Tuvalu has maritime boundaries with France (Wallis and Futuna), Fiji, and Kiribati. Tuvalu established a maritime boundary with Kiribati (Gilbert Islands Group) in August 2012.[11] Tuvalu and France also agreed to minutes providing the coordinates of their maritime boundary in December 2014.[12] Accordingly, with the subsequent exchange of notes between Fiji and Tuvalu in 2015 and their 2019–2020 Exchange of Notes updating the 2014 Fiji – Tuvalu Treaty, Tuvalu has now delimited boundaries with all of its neighbors with overlapping EEZs.

With an average height above sea level of 2 meters, Tuvalu faces an existential threat from climate change-related sea-level rise. The maximum elevation of Tuvalu, 4.6 meters above sea level, is reached on Niulakita, the southernmost point of Tuvalu and Tuvalu's smallest island. Tuvalu has already suffered from loss of shoreline and saltwater intrusion of freshwater resources.

The Fiji – Tuvalu Treaty was concluded with the technical assistance and support of the Pacific Community's Regional Maritime Boundaries Unit, the Commonwealth Secretariat, and other regional entities. Tuvalu and Fiji are both Members of the Pacific Community, the Commonwealth of Nations,

---

10 Pacific Community, *Members: Tuvalu*, https://www.spc.int/our-members/tuvalu/details.

11 *See* Report Number 5-37, VII IMB 4903.

12 *See* Report Number 5-29 (Add. 1), VIII IMB 5503. These minutes were formalized in an unpublished exchange of letters on 16 September 2015. *See* LN No. 7 of November 2015 on Declaration on the Outer Limits of the Exclusive Economic Zone (Tuvalu), p. 6, *available at* https://isa.org.jm/files/files/documents/0237_001.pdf.

and the Alliance of Small Island States (AOSIS).[13] In recent years, several such organizations have addressed their members on the importance of depositing geographic coordinates of maritime points with the UN Secretary-General as soon as possible. AOSIS has also taken several positions relevant to the maritime boundaries of small-island states. In AOSIS's September 2021 Leaders' Declaration, AOSIS state leaders declared that there is no obligation under UNCLOS "to keep baselines and outer limits of maritime zones under review nor to update charts or lists of geographical coordinates once deposited with the Secretary-General of the United Nations," as well as that "maritime zones and the rights and entitlements that flow from them shall continue to apply without reduction, notwithstanding any physical changes connected to climate change-related sea-level rise."[14] The leaders of the Pacific Islands Forum (PIF) have made similar pronouncements, including in their August 2021 Declaration on Preserving Maritime Zones in the Face of Climate Change-related Sea-Level Rise, which concluded that: (1) a state's maritime zones may not be reduced in light of climate change-related sea-level rise once those zones have been notified to the UN Secretary-General; (2) states need not review and update the baselines and outer limits of their maritime zones as a consequence of climate change-related sea-level rise; and (3) maritime zones and entitlements shall continue to apply without reduction, notwithstanding any physical changes connected to climate change-related sea-level rise.[15]

In light of these declarations, it is notable that Article 4 of the Treaty calls for the parties to make adjustments to the maritime boundary "[i]f new surveys or resulting charts and maps should indicate that changes in the base points co-ordinates are sufficiently significant." This provision may reflect the relative difficulty of accurately determining the basepoint coordinates of low-water lines, particularly along the outer limits of fringing reefs. At the same time, it may also be relevant to the issue of sea-level rise, depending on what changes are taken to be "significant" under the Treaty.

---

13 Tuvalu also signed the Agreement for the establishment of the Commission of Small Island States on Climate Change and International Law in October 2021.

14 Alliance of Small Island States, *Leaders' Declaration* (22 September 2021), https://www.aosis.org/launch-of-the-alliance-of-small-island-states-leaders-declaration/.

15 Pacific Islands Forum, *Declaration on Preserving Maritime Zones in the Face of Climate Change-related Sea-level Rise* (6 August 2021), https://www.forumsec.org/2021/08/11/declaration-on-preserving-maritime-zones-in-the-face-of-climate-change-related-sea-level-rise/.

2 *Legal Regime Considerations*

Tuvalu declared the coordinates of its baseline and EEZ limit in the 2012 Maritime Zones Act, and the reach of its territorial sea in its 2012 Declaration of Territorial Sea Baselines. Fiji declared the coordinates of its archipelagic baselines and EEZ, and its territorial sea, in its 2012 Marine Spaces Act. There is no area of overlapping territorial seas in need of division between Fiji and Tuvalu. The boundary agreed in the Fiji – Tuvalu Treaty divides areas of continental shelf and EEZ.

In light of the presence of Wallis and Futuna, the Fiji – Tuvalu Treaty contemplated that further negotiations with France would be needed before the maritime boundary could be settled. As a result, Article 2 expressly provided that Point 31—the last point agreed in the Treaty as of its signing in October 2014—was without prejudice to "any further negotiations with France." The tripoint was ultimately fixed 37 meters away from Point 31 in the agreed minutes of Fiji, Tuvalu, and France on 9 December 2014 in London. To account for this discrepancy, Fiji and Tuvalu added the tripoint (13° 14′ 27.28″ S, 179° 32′ 05.12″ E) as Point 32 of the Treaty through agreed minutes on 9 December 2014, keeping Point 31 (13° 14′ 26.34″ S, 179° 32′ 04.37″ E) in place.

The agreed tripoint was incorporated as Point 13 of the France (Wallis and Futuna)-Tuvalu maritime boundary.[16] The agreed tripoint is "quite close to, but not precisely coincident with Point 5 of the maritime boundary between Fiji and France."[17] Accordingly, Fiji and France may need to update their own existing maritime boundary agreement (currently set out in a 1990 Codicil) to incorporate the agreed tripoint.

3 *Economic and Environmental Considerations*

While the Fiji – Tuvalu Treaty does not refer to any economic or environmental considerations directly, several such considerations appear to have played a role in the delimitation. First, as noted above, both states appear to have been motivated by the desire to solidify maritime boundaries amidst rising sea levels.

---

16 *See* Report Number 5-29 (Add. 1), VIII IMB 5503.
17 Report Number 5-46, VIII IMB 5539, 5540.

Second, both states appear to have shared the goal of removing jurisdictional "grey-zones." This motivation is particularly relevant to the issue of illegal, unlicensed, and unregulated (IUU) fishing, which is an ongoing challenge for regional and global fisheries, as well as trafficking and other cross-border illegal activities. Tuvalu and Fiji are both parties to several treaties concerning monitoring and control of fishing, including the Western and Central Pacific Fisheries Convention, the Niue Treaty, and the Wellington Treaty.

Along similar lines, both states may have sought to secure their entitlements to hydrocarbon and other resources. Tuvalu's EEZ has potentially high cobalt and polymetallic content, and it is notable that the Tuvalu Seabed Minerals Act was enacted on 19 December 2014, shortly after minutes were agreed on the tripoint.[18] Fiji also has potential deep-sea mineral resources and has developed its laws on such deposits in recent years.[19] No provision is made in the Treaty for any resource deposits which may be found along the boundary line.

4 Geographic Considerations

The geography of the two states, including their opposite orientation, is well-suited to application of the equidistance method. While Fiji contains a larger total land mass compared to Tuvalu, by a scale of 700:1, only features in Fiji's small Rotuma Group were relevant to the boundary with Tuvalu. The relatively large distance between the two states and the wide geographic spread of islands in Tuvalu further counter any effect of this size disparity.

5 Islands, Rocks, Reefs, and Low-tide Elevations Considerations

Islands and reefs featured prominently in this delimitation. The Tuvaluan features of Niulakita, Nukalaelae, Funafuti, Nukufetau, and Nui likely

---

18 *See* Report Number 5-29 (Add. 1), VIII IMB 5503, 5507; Pacific Community, *Tuvalu prepares to dig deep for seabed mineral wealth* (28 March 2017), https://www.spc.int/updates/blog/2017/03/tuvalu-prepares-to-dig-deep-for-seabed-mineral-wealth#:~:text=Tuvalu%20is%20the%20fourth%20Pacific,via%20sponsorship%20of%20a%20State.

19 *See* Decree No. 21 of 2013 on International Seabed Mineral Management, Government of Fiji Gazette, vol. 14, no. 58, (12 July 2013), *available at* https://www.isa.org.jm/files/documents/EN/NatLeg/Fiji2013.pdf.

influenced the delimitation as the features closest to Fiji. Of these points, Niulakita and Nukulaelae are farthest south. Niulakita is a reef island covering 0.4 km², with a population of less than 50. Nukulaelae is an atoll with two major insular features and a dozen other islets, and a population of about 400. Nui, an atoll with a population of approximately 600, is the northernmost point affecting the delimitation line. In Fiji, only features in the Rotuma Group of islands would have an effect on the course of the equidistance line. The Rotuma Group has an approximate area of 50 km² and a population of about 1,600.

Without specifying that they are the only sources of basepoints, Article 1(1) of the Treaty provides that the line of delimitation between the EEZs and continental shelves of Fiji and Tuvalu "lies seaward of Rotuma Islands in Fiji on the one hand and Niulakita, Nukalaelae, Funafuti, Nukufetau, Nui in Tuvalu Islands on the other hand, along the geodesics connecting" the points as stated in the Treaty.

6 Baseline Considerations

Both Tuvalu and Fiji have declared archipelagic state status and have identified archipelagic straight baselines. The archipelagic baseline system established by Tuvalu in 2012 includes four main segments joining the Nukufetau, Funafuti, and Nukulaelae atolls, but not encompassing other features to the north and south.[20] The system includes sixty segments of lengths ranging from 0.01 M to 67.57 M connecting the outermost points of seaward drying reefs in the archipelago.[21] Under the provisions of the 1982 United Nations Convention on the Law of the Sea, Tuvalu was not able to draw one archipelagic baseline system to include the entirety of its features. Tuvalu has accordingly provided normal baselines, drawn from the low-water line of the fringing reef, for six of its islands: Niulakita, Nanumea, Nanumanga, Niutao, Nui, and Vaitupu.[22]

---

20 LN No. 7 of 22 November 2012 on Declaration of Archipelagic Baselines (Tuvalu), *available at* https://www.un.org/depts/los/LEGISLATIONANDTREATIES/PDFFILES /tuv_declaration_archipelagic_baselines2012_1.pdf; LN No. 6 of 22 November 2012 on Declaration of Territorial Sea Baselines (Tuvalu), *available at* https://www.un.org /Depts/los/LEGISLATIONANDTREATIES/PDFFILES/tuv_declaration_territorial_sea _baselines2012_1.pdf.

21 US Department of State, *Tuvalu: Archipelagic and other Maritime Claims and Boundaries*, Limits in the Seas, No. 139 (23 May 2014), 2-3.

22 *Id.* at 3; Maritime Zones Act 2012 of 4 May 2012, Art. 7 (1) (Tuvalu), https://www.un.org /depts/los/LEGISLATIONANDTREATIES/PDFFILES/tuv_maritime_zones_act _2012_1.pdf; Territorial sea baselines declaration (Tuvalu), *supra* note 20 at 23.

Fiji amended its archipelagic and normal baseline coordinates in 2012.[23] The Fijian archipelagic baselines system encompasses the islands of Vanua Levu and Viti Levu and comprises line segments connecting 69 basepoints on the outermost islands and drying reefs.[24] Like in Tuvalu, Fiji's baselines system separates features not capable of falling within the archipelago on account of their relative distance. Fiji's declaration accordingly provides normal baselines for Ceva-i-Ra, an uninhabited coral atoll to the far south-east.[25] Fiji notably refers to the Rotuma Group as an archipelago in its 2012 declaration and provides baselines connecting points along the fringing reefs of small features in that group, including Afgaha, Hautiu, Uea, Hafhaveiag, Hofliua, and Solnohu.[26]

No reference is made in the Treaty to the baselines relied on in the delimitation, or to the baselines as publicly declared by Tuvalu and Fiji. It is nonetheless assumed that the parties likely took the basepoints identified in each state's public declarations as the starting point for the delimitation.[27]

7 Geological and Geomorphological Considerations

Geological and geomorphological considerations do not appear to have influenced the delimitation.

8 Method of Delimitation Considerations

As stated in Article 1(2) of the Treaty, the delimitation was based on the principle of equidistance. The Treaty provides the coordinates of 31 turning

---

23 Marine Spaces (Territorial Seas) (Rotuma and its Dependencies) (Amendment) Order 2012, Government of Fiji Gazette Supplement, no. 40, (9 November 2012), 347-48, *available at* https://www.un.org/Depts/los/LEGISLATIONANDTREATIES/PDFFILES/DEPOSIT /fji_mzn113_2015.pdf; Marine Spaces (Archipelagic Baselines and EEZ) (Amendment) Order 2012, Government of Fiji Gazette Supplement, no. 40, (9 November 2012), 348-51, *available at* https://www.un.org/Depts/los/LEGISLATIONANDTREATIES/PDFFILES /DEPOSIT/fji_mzn113_2015.pdf.

24 *See* Marine Spaces (Archipelagic Baselines and EEZ), *supra* note 23 at 348–51; *see also* US Department of State, *Fiji's Maritime Claims*, Limits in the Seas, No. 101 (30 November 1984), 2-3.

25 *See* Marine Spaces (Archipelagic Baselines and EEZ), *supra* note 23 at 350-51.

26 Marine Spaces (Territorial Seas), *supra* note 23 at 347-48.

27 Tuvalu initially declared 34 points along the outer limits of its EEZ with Fiji in 2012. *See* LN No. 12 of 24 December 2012 on Declaration of the Outer Limits of the Exclusive Economic Zone, 28-30 (Tuvalu), *available at* https://www.un.org/depts/los/LEGISLATION ANDTREATIES/PDFFILES/tuv_declaration_outer_limits_eez2012_1.pdf.

6014   *Report Number 5-48*

points and a chart depicting the delimitation line is annexed for illustrative purposes. Point 32 was added to the boundary between Fiji and Tuvalu through a series of trilateral and bilateral agreements. Point 1 is located at the equidistant intersection of the 200 M outer limits of Fiji and Tuvalu and Point 32 is "equidistant from the nearest points on the coasts of Fiji, the French Republic (Wallis and Futuna) and Tuvalu."[28] The equidistant line connecting these endpoints is relatively smooth and includes two major turning points (Points 9 and 12). It appears that the only features influencing two-thirds of the line from Point 12 to Point 32 are Fiji's Rotuma Group and Tuvalu's tiny Niulakita.

9   *Technical Considerations*

As amended, the Fiji – Tuvalu Treaty provides coordinates for 32 turning points. These coordinates are identified to the nearest one-hundredth of an arc second determined by reference to the World Geodetic System 1984 (WGS 84). Geodesics connect these points to form the maritime boundary. Technical support was provided by the South Pacific Applied Geoscience Commission, working with relevant authorities, in the lead-up to the conclusion of the Fiji – Tuvalu Treaty.

10   *Other Considerations*

Article 5 of the Treaty provides for dispute resolution. Specifically, it states that the parties shall settle any dispute concerning the interpretation or application of the agreement "peacefully through consultation and negotiation in accordance with international law." Both states also agreed in Article 4 to pursue adjustments to the maritime boundary based on the principle of equidistance and the coordinates set out in the Treaty should new surveys or resulting charts and maps indicate changes in the coordinates of the base points "sufficiently significant to require adjustments of the maritime boundary."

---

28   Report Number 5-46, VIII IMB 5539, 5543.

III CONCLUSIONS

With the delimitation of the maritime boundary between Fiji and Tuvalu, two-thirds of the approximately 48 overlapping EEZs in the Pacific Islands region have now been delimited.[29] The delimitation between Fiji and Tuvalu was made possible by improvements in technical charting and mapping, in relation to which the parties appear to have cooperated extensively. The delimitation also appears to have been carried out in a relatively friendly manner, with both states taking the conclusion of the agreement as an opportunity to highlight the critical issue of sea-level rise, among other regional concerns. Against this background, the delimitation will hopefully offer a degree of surety in relation to each state's maritime entitlements.

IV RELATED LAW IN FORCE

A *Law of the Sea Conventions*

Tuvalu: Party to UNCLOS (ratified 9 December 2002).
Fiji: Party to UNCLOS (ratified 10 December 1982).

B *Maritime Jurisdiction Claimed at the Time of Signature*

Tuvalu: Archipelagic waters; 12 M territorial sea; 24 M contiguous zone; 200 M EEZ; continental shelf (joint submission to the Commission on the Limits of the Continental Shelf by Tuvalu, the Republic of France, and New Zealand (Tokelau) in relation to the Robbie Ridge, 7 December 2012).
Fiji: Archipelagic waters; 12 M territorial sea; 24 M contiguous zone; 200 M EEZ; continental shelf (submission to the Commission on the Limits of the Continental Shelf, 28 April 2009, updated 30 April 2012) (joint submission of preliminary information to the Commission on the Limits of the Continental Shelf by Vanuatu, Solomon Islands, and the Republic of the Fiji Islands on the North Fiji Basin).

---

29 *See* Pacific Community, Geoscience Division, *Fiji and Tuvalu Sign Maritime Boundary Agreement* (24 October 2014), https://gsd.spc.int/media-releases/1-latest-news/594-fiji-and-tuvalu-sign-maritime-boundary-agreement.

6016 *Report Number 5-48*

C *Maritime Jurisdiction Claimed Subsequent to Signature*

Tuvalu: No change.
Fiji: No change.

V REFERENCES AND ADDITIONAL READINGS

Malcolm D. Evans, *Maritime Boundary Delimitation, in* THE OXFORD HANDBOOK OF THE LAW OF THE SEA 254 (D Rothwell et al. eds., 2015).
Coalter G. Lathrop, *Tripoint Issues in Maritime Boundary Delimitation*, V INTERNATIONAL MARITIME BOUNDARIES 3305 (2005).

Prepared by Natalie Reid, Romain Zamour, Beatrice Walton

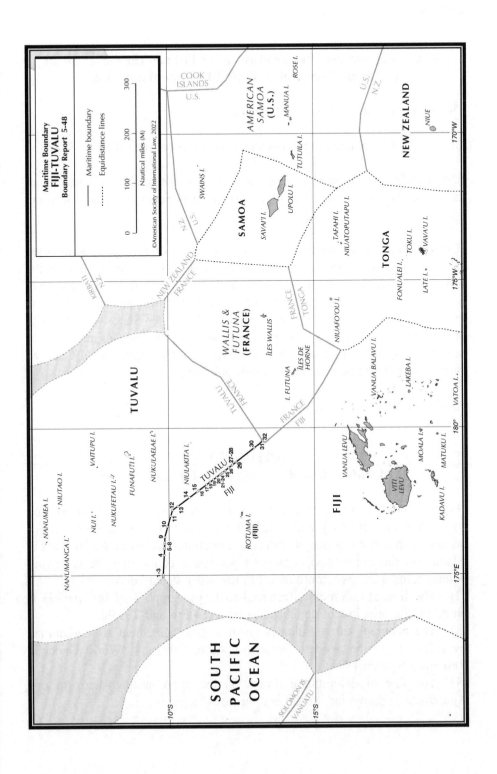

Agreement between the Government of Fiji and the Government of Tuvalu Concerning Their Maritime Boundaries

The Sovereign States of Fiji and Tuvalu

DESIRING to strengthen the bonds of friendship between the two States,

RECOGNIZING the need to effect a precise and equitable delimitation of the respective maritime areas in which the two States exercise sovereign rights, and,

BASING themselves on the rules and principles of relevant international law, as they are expressed in the United Nations Convention Law of the Sea, 10 December 1982 to which both Fiji and Tuvalu are a party, and, in particular Article 74 and 83 which provide that the delimitation of the exclusive economic zone and continental shelf between States with opposite or adjacent coasts shall be effected by agreement on the basis of international law, as referred to in Article 38 of the Statute of the International Court of Justice, in order to achieve an equitable solution,

HAVE AGREED AS FOLLOWS:

ARTICLE 1
Maritime Boundaries between Fiji and Tuvalu

(1)   The line of delimitation between the exclusive economic zones and continental shelves of Fiji and Tuvalu lies seaward of Rotuma Islands in Fiji on one hand and Niulakita, Nukulaelae, Funafuti, Nukufetau, Nui in Tuvalu Islands on the other hand, along the geodesics connecting the following points, defined by their coordinates, in the order stated below.
(2)   The line of delimitation referred to in paragraph 1 of this Article is based on the principle of equidistance between Fiji and Tuvalu.
(3)   The geographical coordinates given in this Agreement are determined by reference to the geodetic reference system WGS84 (World Geodetic Reference System 1984)
(4)   The line of delimitation drawn on the chart in the Annex to this Agreement is drawn for illustrative purposes only.

Point Identifier	Latitude (WGS 84)	Longitude (WGS 84)
FJ_TV MB 1	9° 47' 00.56" S	174° 54' 48.69" E
FJ_TV MB 2	9° 47' 04.60" S	174° 56' 37.67" E
FJ_TV MB 3	9° 47' 09.01" S	174° 58' 26.24" E
FJ_TV MB 4	9° 48' 40.98" S	175° 38' 48.82" E
FJ_TV MB 5	9° 49' 09.00" S	175° 51' 27.72" E
FJ_TV MB 6	9° 49' 11.87" S	175° 52' 53.41" E
FJ_TV MB 7	9° 49' 27.34" S	176° 00' 34.16" E
FJ_TV MB 8	9° 49' 33.79" S	176° 03' 46.63" E
FJ_TV MB 9	9° 49' 54.44" S	176° 14' 09.46" E
FJ_TV MB 10	9° 56' 07.46" S	176° 35' 09.93" E
FJ_TV MB 11	10° 02' 48.76" S	176° 57' 50.08" E
FJ_TV MB 12	10° 06' 42.36" S	177° 11' 06.89" E
FJ_TV MB 13	10° 17' 53.03" S	177° 18' 48.12" E
FJ_TV MB 14	10° 42' 26.68" S	177° 36' 51.54" E
FJ_TV MB 15	10° 58' 21.85" S	177° 48' 35.43" E
FJ_TV MB 16	11° 02' 02.90" S	177° 51' 18.50" E
FJ_TV MB 17	11° 17' 58.90" S	178° 03' 04.52" E
FJ_TV MB 18	11° 25' 19.89" S	178° 08' 30.81" E
FJ_TV MB 19	11° 32' 18.07" S	178° 13' 40.49" E
FJ_TV MB 20	11° 38' 39.35" S	178° 18' 27.76" E
FJ_TV MB 21	11° 45' 52.21" S	178° 23' 54.23" E
FJ_TV MB 22	11° 47' 48.11" S	178° 25' 21.78" E
FJ_TV MB 23	11° 50' 15.58" S	178° 27' 13.39" E
FJ_TV MB 24	11° 52' 19.35" S	178° 28' 47.64" E
FJ_TV MB 25	11° 56' 35.94" S	178° 32' 03.05" E
FJ_TV MB 26	12° 04' 30.60" S	178° 38' 04.69" E
FJ_TV MB 27	12° 11' 06.84" S	178° 43' 06.09" E
FJ_TV MB 28	12° 11' 57.42" S	178° 43' 44.58" E
FJ_TV MB 29	12° 19' 15.46" S	178° 49' 21.96" E
FJ_TV MB 30	12° 56' 07.47" S	179° 17' 51.29" E
FJ_TV MB 31	13° 14' 26.34" S	179° 32' 04.37" E

ARTICLE 2
Without Prejudice

It is agreed by both Parties that 'Point 31' (FJ_TV MB 31) in Article 1 of this Agreement will not prejudice any further negotiations with France.

6020 *Report Number 5-48*

ARTICLE 3
Sovereign Rights

The lines described in Article 1 of this Agreement shall be the maritime boundary between the areas referred to in the Article 1 in which the Parties, in accordance with international law, exercise any sovereign right or jurisdiction.

ARTICLE 4
Adjustments to Maritime Boundary

If new surveys or resulting charts and maps should indicate that changes in the base points co-ordinates are sufficiently significant to require adjustments of the maritime boundary, the Parties agree that an adjustment will be carried out on the basis of the same principles as those used in determining the maritime boundary, and such adjustments shall be provided for in a Protocol to this Agreement.

ARTICLE 5
Dispute Resolution

Any dispute between the parties concerning the interpretation or application of this Agreement shall be settled peacefully through consultation and negotiation in accordance with international law.

ARTICLE 6
Agreement Deposit

Upon the completion of all national procedures bringing this Agreement into force, each party shall take all the necessary steps to lodge this Agreement, including the coordinates in Article 1, with the appropriate International Bodies.

ARTICLE 7

Each Party shall notify the other of the completion of its national procedures to bring this Agreement into force.

This Agreement shall enter into force on the date of its signature.

IN WITNESS WHEREOF, the representatives of the two Governments, being duly authorized for this purpose, have signed this Agreement and have affixed thereto their seals.

DONE at Suva on the 17th day of October in the year Two Thousand and Fourteen (2014), in two originals, each in the English language.

For the Government of the
Republic of Fiji

For the Government
of Tuvalu

Mr. Josaia Voreqe Bainimarama
Honorable Prime Minister

Mr. Enele Sopoaga
Honorable Prime Minister

Minutes of the Meeting between the Delegation of the Republic of Fiji and the Delegation of Tuvalu modifying the Agreement between the Government of the Republic of Fiji and the Government of Tuvalu concerning their Maritime Boundaries signed in Suva on the 17th October 2014

Both Delegations,

Have agreed to amend Article 1 of the *Agreement between the Government of Fiji and the Government of Tuvalu concerning their Maritime Boundaries* signed in Suva on the 17th October 2014 by exchange of Diplomatic Notes to include the following additional point:

Article 1

Point Identifier	Latitude (WGS 84)	Longitude (WGS 84)
FJ_TV MB 32	13° 14' 27.28" S	179° 32' 05.12" E

This point represents the agreed tri-junction point between the Republic of Fiji, Tuvalu and the French Republic (Wallis and Futuna).

Each party shall notify the other of the completion of its national procedures necessary to bring this Amendment into force. The Amendment shall enter into force on the date of receipt of the later of those notifications.

IN WITNESS WHEREOF, the undersigned, have signed these Minutes. RECORDED at the Fiji High Commission, London on the 9th of December 2014 in two originals, in the English language.

Head of the Delegation of the Republic of Fiji	Head of the Technical Delegation for the Government of Tuvalu
H.E. Solo Mara, Fiji's High Commissioner to the United Kingdom	Mr Faatasi Malologa, Director, Department of Lands & Survey, Ministry of Natural Resources

Fiji – Tuvalu 6023

Note from Fiji Ministry of Foreign Affairs to Tuvalu High Commission, 16 January 2015

<u>Note No. 21/2015</u>

The Government of the Republic of Fiji presents its compliments to the Government of Tuvalu and has the honour to refer to the *Agreement between the Government of Fiji and the Government of Tuvalu Concerning their Maritime Boundaries*, done at Suva on 17 October 2014 ('the Agreement').

With respect to the agreed Minutes of the trilateral meeting held by Fiji, France and Tuvalu on 9 December 2014 in London (refer attachment), and noting that the Agreement has yet to enter into force, the Government of the Republic of Fiji wishes to propose that Article 1 of the Agreement be amended to include the following additional point:

Point Identifier	Latitude (WGS 84)	Longitude (WGS 84)
FJ_TV MB 32	13° 14' 27.28" S	179° 32' 05.12" E

The point denoted as FJ_TV MB 32 represents the provisionally agreed tri-junction point between the Republic of Fiji, Tuvalu and the French Republic (Wallis and Futuna).

Should the Government of Tuvalu agree to accept this proposal, the Government of the Republic of Fiji has the further honour to advise that the Exchange of Notes shall constitute an Agreement between the two Parties which will come into force on the date of receipt of the Government of Tuvalu's formal response to this Note.

The Government of the Republic of Fiji avails itself of this opportunity to renew to the Government of Tuvalu the assurances its highest consideration.

6024 *Report Number 5-48*

Note from Tuvalu Ministry of Foreign Affairs
to Fiji Ministry of Foreign Affairs
15 September 2015

<u>MFAT:314/15</u>

The Ministry of Foreign Affairs, Trade, Tourism, Environment and Labour of the Government of Tuvalu presents its compliments to the Ministry of Foreign Affairs of the Government of the Republic of Fiji and has the honour to refer to the Agreement between the Government of Tuvalu and the Government of Fiji concerning their Maritime Boundaries, done at Suva on 17 October 2014.

Tuvalu has the honour to acknowledge receipt of your letter of 16 January 2015 concerning the maritime boundary delimiting the exclusive economic zones and continental shelves between Tuvalu and the Republic of Fiji.

Tuvalu has the honour to agree to your Government's proposal that your letter, the Minutes attached to it, and this letter in reply constitute an Agreement between our two Governments delimiting the maritime boundary between Tuvalu and the Republic of Fiji.

Tuvalu will notify Fiji on completion of its domestic procedures to bring the agreement into force.

The Ministry of Foreign Affairs, Trade, Tourism, Environment and Labour of the Government of Tuvalu avails itself of the opportunity to renew to the Ministry of Foreign Affairs the assurances of its highest consideration.

Fiji – Tuvalu   6025

Exchange of Notes Constituting an Agreement between the Government of Fiji and the Government of Tuvalu Amending Article 1 of the Agreement Between the Government of Fiji and the Government of Tuvalu Concerning Their Maritime Boundaries. Suva, 4 April 2019, And Funafuti, 26 October 2020

Note No. 348/2019

The Ministry of Foreign Affairs of the Government of the Republic of Fiji presents its compliments to the Tuvalu High Commission in Suva and has the honour to refer to the "Agreement" signed by the Government of the Republic of Fiji and the Government of Tuvalu in Suva on 17 October 2014, concerning the Parties shared maritime boundaries.

The Ministry has the honour to inform that following consultation between officials of the Government of Fiji, Tuvalu and France, the officials noted that the coordinates denoted below as FJ_TV MB 32 represent an agreed tri-junction point between the Government of Fiji, Government of Tuvalu and the Government of France (Wallis and Futuna) signed in Suva on 16 September 2015.

The tri-point needs to be annexed to the Agreement signed by the Government of Fiji and the Government of Tuvalu. The Ministry in this connection wishes to propose the amendment of the Agreement to include the agreed tri-junction point below:

Point Identifier	Latitude (WGS 84)	Longitude (WGS 84)
FJ_TV MB 32	13° 14′ 27.28″ S	179° 32′ 05.12″ E

The Ministry advises that should the Government of Tuvalu agree to accept this proposal, the Exchange of Notes shall constitute an Agreement between the two Parties which shall come into force on the date of receipt of the Government of Tuvalu's official response to this Note Verbale.

Accordingly, the Ministry intends to deposit the amended Agreement with the United Nations Division of Ocean Affairs and the Law of the Sea.

The Ministry would appreciate the High Commission's assistance in the conveyance of this Note to the relevant authority in Funafuti.

The Ministry of Foreign Affairs of the Republic of Fiji avails itself of this opportunity to renew to the Tuvalu High Commission the assurances its highest consideration.

TUV:9/20/FJ

The Ministry of Justice, Communication and Foreign Affairs of the Government of Tuvalu presents its compliments to the Ministry of Foreign Affairs of the Government of the Republic of Fiji and with reference to Note No. 348/2019 regarding the *Agreement between the Government of Fiji and the Government of Tuvalu Concerning their Maritime Boundaries* ("Agreement"), done at Suva on the 17 October 2014, has the honour to advise that the Government of Tuvalu has agreed to the proposed amendment for the agreed tri-junction point to be annexed to the "Agreement".

The Ministry has further the honour to confirm that this Note shall constitute an Agreement between the Government of Fiji and the Government of Tuvalu to the agreed tri-junction point to be annexed to the "Agreement" and will organise the depository of the amended Agreement with the UN DOALOS.

The Ministry of Justice, Communication and Foreign Affairs of the Government of Tuvalu avails itself of this opportunity to renew to Ministry of Foreign Affairs of the Government of the Republic of Fiji the assurances of its highest consideration.

Fiji – Solomon Islands

Report Number 5-49

Agreement Between the Republic of Fiji and Solomon Islands Concerning Their Maritime Boundary

Signed: 11 July 2022
Entry into force: 22 February 2023
Published at: UNTS (I-57923); 113 LOS BULL. 16 (2024); Solomon Islands Gazette, No. 9 (January 31, 2023)

I SUMMARY

The Agreement Between the Republic of Fiji and the Solomon Islands Concerning their Maritime Boundary (Fiji – Solomon Islands Agreement or Agreement), signed on 11 July 2022, establishes a maritime boundary delimiting a relatively small area of overlap between the exclusive economic zones (EEZ) and continental shelves within 200 nautical miles (M) of each state. Located in the North Fiji Basin, the boundary extends approximately 45 M from Point MB 1 to MB 6 in a south-southwest direction and is described as lying seaward of the island of Fatutaka, in the Solomon Islands, and Rotuma, in Fiji (understood here to mean the Rotuma Archipelago as defined in Fiji's Marine Spaces Act amended in 2012).[1] The median line boundary consists of geodesics connecting six points. The delimitation line resolves a small overlap between the parties' 200 M arcs.[2]

Concluded in Suva, Fiji, on the sidelines of the 51st Pacific Islands Forum (PIF) summit, the Fiji – Solomon Islands Agreement marks the latest in a series of boundary agreements reached by Pacific Island states as part

---

1 Marine Spaces (Territorial Seas) (Rotuma and its Dependencies) (Amendment) Order 2012, Government of Fiji Gazette Supplement, no. 40, (9 November 2012), *available at* https://www.un.org/Depts/los/LEGISLATIONANDTREATIES/PDFFILES/DEPOSIT /fji_mzn113_2015.pdf.
2 *See* Fiji Government, Appendices, *Agreement between the Republic of Fiji and Solomon Islands concerning their Maritime Boundary*, *available at* https://www.parliament.gov.fj /wp-content/uploads/2020/12/Appendices-Agreement-between-the-Republic-of-Fiji-and -Solomon-Islands-concerning-their-Maritime-Boundary.pdf, p. 23.

Coalter G. Lathrop (ed.), International Maritime Boundaries, 6027-6044.
© *The American Society of International Law and Koninklijke Brill BV, Leiden 2025.*

6028   *Report Number 5-49*

of a decade-long push to delimit boundaries in the region, particularly amidst growing threats from climate change and rising sea levels, as well as threats to the security of maritime natural resources. At the signing of the Agreement, the Prime Minister of Fiji recalled the challenges posed by climate change to his country, noting that the delimitation marked "a step toward a brighter and bluer future" for both states.[3] As with other maritime boundary agreements concluded in the Pacific region in recent years, support for the Fiji – Solomon Islands Agreement came from the Secretariat of the Pacific Community (SPC)[4] among other regional and national partners. The Agreement entered into force on 22 February 2023 following an exchange of notes by both states indicating that they had completed their national procedures for bringing the Agreement into force. On 15 August 2023, the Solomon Islands registered the Agreement with the United Nations.

II   CONSIDERATIONS

1   *Political, Strategic, and Historical Considerations*

Fiji and the Solomon Islands are two archipelagic states located in the southwest Pacific. Fiji, which gained independence from the United Kingdom in 1970, is composed of approximately 300 islands, more than 100 of which are inhabited. Its total land area is approximately 18,300 km^2 and its EEZ amounts to approximately 1,290,000 km^2. Viti Levu, the largest island in Fiji at 10,400 km^2 is home to Fiji's capital city of Suva. Vanua Levu, the second largest island, has an area of approximately 5,600 km^2. These two main islands account for the overwhelming majority of Fiji's population of 948,000.

Several major island groupings exist in Fiji. Approximately 300 M north of Fiji's two main islands lies the Rotuma Group of volcanic islands, with a population of approximately 1,600 and an approximate area of 50 km^2. Other groups include the southern Kadavu Group, with a population of approximately 10,900; the southeastern Lau Islands, with a population of approximately 9,500; and the eastern Lomaiviti Islands, with a population

---

3   *Maritime boundary agreed between Fiji, Solomon Islands*, RNZ (12 July 2022), *available at* https://www.rnz.co.nz/international/pacific-news/470785/maritime-boundary-agreed -between-fiji-solomon-islands.

4   *See* Fiji Government, Appendices, *supra* note 2 at 5-6.

of approximately 15,700.[5] The Mamanuca Islands and the Yasawa Islands lie towards the northwest and west, respectively.

Fiji has committed to concluding agreements on all of its maritime boundaries by 2025.[6] While Fiji has concluded maritime boundary agreements with France (with respect to New Caledonia and Wallis and Futuna)[7] and Tuvalu,[8] negotiations remain ongoing with Tonga and Vanuatu.[9]

The Solomon Islands, which gained independence from the United Kingdom in 1978,[10] has a population of approximately 720,000 and consists of roughly 1,000 islands and other features (some 340 of which are inhabited) amounting to a total land area of approximately 28,900 km².[11] The EEZ of the Solomon Islands, like that of Fiji, covers a vast expanse of approximately 1,589,000 km² and reaches boundaries with Australia,[12] France (New Caledonia),[13] Papua New Guinea,[14] Vanuatu,[15] and Fiji, all of which have now been delimited.

Two parallel chains of mountainous and heavily forested volcanic islands form the principal and most populated island group in the Solomon Islands. The southern chain includes the Solomon Islands' largest island, Guadalcanal, which is home to the capital city of Honiara and the Solomon Islands' tallest peak, Mount Popomanaseu, reaching 2,300 meters above sea level. Also in this group are the islands of Vella Lavella, Savo, and the New Georgia Islands. The northern chain includes the islands of Choiseul, Santa Isabel, and Malaita. San Cristobal Island, in the southeast, marks the convergence of these two major chains. Ontong Java Atoll, an exceptionally large coral atoll spread across 122 small islands, is situated to the north of the main

---

5   Fiji Government, Bureau of Statistics, *2017 Population and Housing Census*, (21 September 2018), *available at* https://www.statsfiji.gov.fj/component/finder/search.html?q =2017+census&Itemid=435.

6   *See* Fiji Government, Appendices, *supra* note 2 at 60.

7   Report Number 5-6 (Add.1/Corr. 1), V IMB 3729; Report Number 5-6, I IMB 995.

8   Report Number 5-48, in this volume; Report Number 5-46, VIII IMB 5539.

9   Fiji Government, Appendices, *supra* note 2 at 38.

10   Prior to becoming a British protectorate at the end of World War II, the northern Solomon Islands fell under an Australian mandate, and the southern islands under British protectorate.

11   Solomon Islands Government, *Provisional Count: 2019 National Population and Housing Census*, (16 November 2020), *available at* https://www.statistics.gov.sb/images /SolomonFiles/Social-and-Demography-Statistics/2019_National_Population_and_Hous ing_Census/Provisional_Count-2019_Census_Result.pdf.

12   *See* Report Number 5-4, I IMB 977.

13   Report Number 5-17, I IMB 1167.

14   Report Number 5-16, I IMB 1155.

15   Report Number 5-45, VIII IMB 5527.

6030 *Report Number 5-49*

Solomon Islands group. Some 2,000 inhabitants live on this atoll, though only approximately 12 km² of its total area of 1,400 km² is land.

To the south of the main Solomon Islands group lie Rennell and Bellona islands, which have a combined population of approximately 4,000. Closest to the boundary line with Fiji are the Santa Cruz Islands, with a total area of 13,200 km². The largest island in the Santa Cruz Islands is Nendö, with an area of about 800 km², while the smallest island, the uninhabited Fatutaka, has an area of less than 1 km². Northeast of the Santa Cruz Islands is the much smaller and less populous group of the Duff Islands.

Both Fiji and the Solomon Islands are considerably vulnerable to climate change-related sea-level rise. In the Solomon Islands, some 80% of the population is estimated to live in low-lying rural areas prone to flooding and damage from high tides, despite the country's relatively mountainous terrain.[16] In 2016, five small islands in the north of the country ranging in size from one to five hectares reportedly disappeared entirely following cyclones and storms, while other islands have reported significant destruction of villages and losses of territory in recent years.[17] Fiji faces similar issues and in November 2022 identified 42 villages believed to be in need of relocation in the next five to ten years.[18]

This background served as an impetus for Fiji and the Solomon Islands to formalize their maritime boundary. Both states are members of the Pacific Community, the Commonwealth of Nations, the Alliance of Small Island States (AOSIS), and the PIF, all of which have encouraged their members to deposit the geographic coordinates of their baselines and boundaries with the United Nations. AOSIS and PIF have also taken the position that doing so will help prevent any change to those boundaries in the event of the submergence of land territory. In its September 2021 Leaders' Declaration, for example, AOSIS state leaders declared that there is no obligation under UNCLOS "to keep baselines and outer limits of maritime zones under review nor to update charts or lists of geographical coordinates once deposited with the Secretary-General of the United Nations," and that "maritime zones

---

16 *See* United Nations Development Programme, *Sea-level rise mapping: An eye-opener for a Solomon Islands community*, (8 August 2014), *available at* https://stories.undp.org /af-solomon-islands.

17 *Five Pacific islands lost to rising seas as climate change hits*, THE GUARDIAN (10 May 2016), https://www.theguardian.com/environment/2016/may/10/five-pacific-islands-lost -rising-seas-climate-change.

18 Kate Lyons, *How to move a country: Fiji's radical plan to escape rising sea levels*, THE GUARDIAN (8 November 2022), https://www.theguardian.com/environment/2022/nov/08 /how-to-move-a-country-fiji-radical-plan-escape-rising-seas-climate-crisis.

and the rights and entitlements that flow from them shall continue to apply without reduction, notwithstanding any physical changes connected to climate change-related sea-level rise."[19] The August 2021 PIF Declaration on Preserving Maritime Zones in the Face of Climate Change-related Sea-Level Rise likewise declared that a state's maritime zones and entitlements may not be reduced in light of climate change-related sea-level rise once those zones have been notified to the UN Secretary-General. It also asserted that states do not have an obligation to review and update the baselines and outer limits of their maritime zones in response to sea-level rise.[20] The Prime Minister of Fiji alluded to this issue at the signing in Suva, where he indicated that the Agreement established the boundary between the two states as permanent, "irrespective of climate change-related sea-level rise and its potential impact on maritime boundaries."[21]

In addition to the issue of climate change, solidifying boundary agreements may also help curb threats from illegal fishing and various forms of illegal trafficking.[22]

2   Legal Regime Considerations

Fiji declared the coordinates of its archipelagic baselines and EEZ, as well as its territorial sea, in its 2012 Marine Spaces Act.[23] The Solomon Islands declared its territorial sea and EEZ in 1978,[24] and its archipelagic baselines in

---

19   Alliance of Small Island States, *Leaders' Declaration* (22 September 2021), https://www .aosis.org/launch-of-the-alliance-of-small-island-states-leaders-declaration/.

20   Pacific Islands Forum, *Declaration on Preserving Maritime Zones in the Face of Climate Change-related Sea-level Rise* (6 August 2021), https://www.forumsec.org/2021/08/11 /declaration-on-preserving-maritime-zones-in-the-face-of-climate-change-related-sea -level-rise/.

21   RNZ, *supra* note 3.

22   *See* Pacific Islands Forum, *2050 Strategy for the Blue Pacific Continent* (2022), https:// www.forumsec.org/wp-content/uploads/2022/08/PIFS-2050-Strategy-Blue-Pacific -Continent-WEB-5Aug2022.pdf; *see* Fiji Government, Appendices, *supra* note 2 at 28.

23   Marine Spaces (Territorial Seas), *supra* note 1 at 347-48; Marine Spaces (Archipelagic Baselines and EEZ) (Amendment) Order 2012, Government of Fiji Gazette Supplement, no. 40, (9 November 2012), 348-51, *available at* https://www.un.org/Depts/los /LEGISLATIONANDTREATIES/PDFFILES/ DEPOSIT/fji_mzn113_2015.pdf. Fiji also previously declared EEZ boundaries under the Marine Spaces Act of 1978. *See* Marine Spaces Act, 1977, Act. No. 18 of 15 December 1977, as amended by the Marine Spaces (Amendment) Act 1978, Act No. 15 of 6 October 1978, *available at* https://www.un.org /depts/los/ LEGISLATIONANDTREATIES/PDFFILES/FJI_1978_Act.pdf.

24   Act No. 32 of 21 December 1978, Delimitation of Marine Waters Act (Solomon Islands) *available at* https://www.un.org/Depts/los/LEGISLATIONANDTREATIES/PDFFILES /SLB_1978_Act.pdf.

1979.[25] Both states have filed submissions with the Commission on the Limits of the Continental Shelf (CLCS) claiming areas of continental shelf beyond 200 M, but those areas are not in the vicinity of this boundary. However, both states have also submitted Preliminary Information documents to the CLCS indicating possible future submissions related to areas immediately north of Point MB 1 (the Charlotte Bank Region)[26] and immediately south of Point MB 6 (the North Fiji Basin).[27] So, while there is no area of overlapping territorial seas, and only a small area of overlapping EEZ and continental shelf within 200 M between Fiji and the Solomon Islands, future developments could bring additional areas of overlapping continental shelf beyond 200 M and a further need for delimitation.

A key legal question surrounding this agreement, like others concluded in the region, is what effect, if any, climate change-related sea-level rise will have on agreed maritime boundaries. This question remains unresolved in international law as of this writing.[28] At the same time, states throughout the region have been working to conclude boundary agreements with the aim of ensuring their maritime entitlements ahead of any geological changes imposed by climate change. PIF and regional leaders have also taken the position that maritime boundary points are to remain constant in the face of sea-level rise.[29] In the present Agreement, Article 6 provides that the two states agree that an "adjustment will be carried out on the basis of the same

---

25 Legal Notice No. 41 of 1979, Declaration of Archipelagic Baselines pursuant to section 4 (2) of Delimitation of Marine Waters Act, 1978 (Solomon Islands) *available at* https://www.un.org/Depts/los/LEGISLATIONANDTREATIES/PDFFILES/SLB_1979_Notice.pdf.

26 Fiji and the Solomon Islands submitted a joint Preliminary Information document to the CLCS in April 2009 with respect to the Charlotte Bank Region. *See* Preliminary Information submitted by the Solomon Islands and the Republic of the Fiji Islands on the Charlotte Bank Region, 19 April 2009, *available at* https://www.un.org/depts/los/clcs_new/submissions_files/preliminary/ fji_slb_2009_preliminaryinfo.pdf.

27 Fiji, the Solomon Islands, and Vanuatu submitted a joint Preliminary Information document to the CLCS in April 2009 with respect to the area beyond each state's 200 M baseline in the North Fiji Basin. *See* Preliminary Information submitted by the Republic of Vanuatu, Solomon Islands and the Republic of the Fiji Islands on the North Fiji Basin, 19 April 2009, *available at* https://www.un.org/depts/los/clcs_new/submissions_files/preliminary/ fji_slb_vut_2009_preliminaryinfo.pdf.

28 Efforts are currently underway to clarify this issue. *See, e.g.,* International Law Commission, *Sea-Level Rise in relation to International Law: First Issues Paper,* Bogdan Aurescu and Nilüfer Oral, Co-Chairs of the Study Group on Sea-Level Rise in relation to International Law, UN Doc. A/CN.4/740 (28 February 2020); International Law Commission, *Sea-Level Rise in relation to International Law: Second Issues Paper,* Patrícia Galvão Teles and Juan José Ruda Santolaria, Co-Chairs of the Study Group on Sea-Level Rise in relation to International Law, UN Doc. A/CN.4/752 (19 April 2022).

29 *See* Fiji Government, Appendices, *supra* note 2 at 7.

principles as those used in determining the maritime boundary" where "changes in the base point coordinates are sufficiently significant to require adjustments of the maritime boundary." Concern about this provision, which mirrors a provision in the Fiji – Tuvalu maritime boundary agreement concluded in 2014,[30] was raised during government deliberations on the Fiji side, with some calling for reconsideration of its inclusion on the ground that it might imply that the maritime boundary is "ambulatory" in response to geological changes.[31] A proposal was made, but ultimately not accepted, to include a provision stating that the line is "final and binding."[32]

3 Economic and Environmental Considerations

The potential for the discovery and exploitation of hydrothermal deposits,[33] including seafloor massive sulphides and cobalt-rich ferromanganese crusts, as well as deposits of other metals and minerals,[34] may have played a role in the conclusion of the Agreement. Article 8 provides that "[i]f any single accumulation or deposit of liquid hydrocarbon, natural gas, or other mineral lies on the maritime boundary median line, the accumulation or deposit of such resources shall be effectively exploited by either or both Parties." Further, "both Parties shall equitably share the benefits of such resource exploitation." While similar provisions have appeared in other maritime boundary agreements concluded in the region,[35] unlike some, Article 8 notably does not call for consultation ahead of exploitation, but instead for the "effective[]" exploitation of the resource and the sharing of benefits.

The issue of deep-seabed mining, both within and beyond national jurisdiction, has become a source of some disagreement in the region. Along with Palau and Samoa, Fiji has led a group of states since the 2022 UN Oceans Conference calling for a ten-year moratorium on deep-sea mining so that appropriate scientific study can be completed.[36] Fiji has also expressed

---

30 *See* Report Number 5-48, in this volume.
31 *See* Fiji Government, Appendices, *supra* note 2 at 7, 17.
32 *Id.* at 64-65.
33 *Id.* at 10.
34 *See* Blue Ocean Law and the Pacific Network on Globalization, *Resource Roulette: How Deep Sea Mining and Inadequate Regulatory Frameworks Imperil the Pacific and its Peoples*, https://www.savethehighseas.org/wp-content/uploads/2018/05/Blue-oceans-law -Resource_Roulette.pdf.
35 *See, e.g.*, Report Number 5-16 (2), III IMB 2323.
36 *'Not worth the risk': Palau, Fiji call for deep-sea mining moratorium*, Reuters (27 June 2022), https://www.reuters.com/business/environment/not-worth-risk-palau-fiji-call-deep -sea-mining-moratorium-2022-06-27.

its support for applying the moratorium in relation to deep-seabed mining within its national waters.[37] For its part, the Solomon Islands has not yet agreed to that moratorium. A leaked 2022 memorandum of understanding between the Solomon Islands and the People's Republic of China notably also appears to "encourage businesses to conduct investment cooperation" in relation to the "[e]xploration and development of offshore oil, gas and mineral resources."[38]

No provision is made in the Agreement concerning environmental protection of living marine resources,[39] though tuna stocks are of crucial economic importance in this area. Both states are members of the Pacific Islands Forum Fisheries Agency (FFA), which was established to help countries sustainably manage tuna fisheries falling within their EEZ,[40] as well as the Western and Central Pacific Fisheries Convention, Niue Treaty, and Wellington Treaty.

4 Geographic Considerations

The geographic circumstances under which this maritime boundary agreement was concluded allow for few options other than the application of the equidistance method. The 200 M arcs drawn from the nearest features, Fatutaka and Rotuma, overlap by no more than 4.3 kilometers leaving almost no room for adjustment.[41] Even in the event of a larger area of overlap, equidistance would have been an appropriate and commonly-used method

---

37 *See* Press Release, Government of Fiji, *Fiji Supports Moratorium on Deep Sea Mining* (29 June 2022), *available at* https://www.fiji.gov.fj/Media-Centre/News/FIJI-SUPPORTS -MORATORIUM-ON-DEEP-SEA-MINING; Aqela Susu, *Fiji Backs 10-year ban on seabed mining*, Fiji Times (16 August 2019), *available at* https://www.fijitimes.com/fiji -backs-10-year-ban-on-seabed-mining/.
38 *Memorandum of Understanding on Deepening Blue Economy Cooperation between the Ministry of Commerce of the People's Republic of China and the Ministry of XXX of Solomon Islands*, (unsigned draft), *available at* https://origin.go.theaustralian.com.au /wp-content/uploads/2022/05/DocScan_05_06_2022.pdf, p. 2. *See also* Press Release, Solomon Islands Government, *Solomon Islands and People's Republic of China Deepened Relations with the Signing of More Development Cooperation* (27 May 2022), https:// solomons.gov.sb/solomon-islands-and-peoples-republic-of-china-deepened-relations- with-the-signing-of-more-development-cooperation/.
39 Compare with the Papua New Guinea-Solomon Islands maritime agreement. *See* Report Number 5-16, I IMB 1155.
40 *See* Pacific Islands Forum Fisheries Agency (FFA), *available at* https://www.ffa.int /about.
41 Fiji Government, Appendices, *supra* note 2 at 79.

for delimiting a boundary between opposite, small, mid-ocean islands nearly 400 M from each other located far from the main territories of either state.

5 Islands, Rocks, Reefs, and Low-tide Elevations Considerations

Article 3(1) of the Agreement indicates that the line of delimitation "lies seaward of Fatutaka in the Solomon Islands and Rotuma in Fiji" indicating that these are the closest features to the delimitation. Fatutaka is an uninhabited small volcanic island of less than 1 km^2 located in the Santa Cruz Islands, southeast of the main islands of the Solomon Islands. The Rotuma Group consists of the northwesternmost features of Fiji. The Rotuma archipelagic baselines encompass two small features to the west of the main island of Rotuma: Uea Island and Hafhaveiag Island. Basepoints on one or both of these small features are likely to have influenced the delimitation. No other maritime features appear to have been relevant to the negotiation and delimitation of the maritime boundary.

6 Baseline Considerations

Fiji and the Solomon Islands have both declared archipelagic state status. Fiji's archipelagic baselines system encompasses the islands of Vanua Levu and Viti Levu and comprises line segments connecting 69 basepoints on the outermost islands and drying reefs. While Fiji's declaration provides normal baselines for Ceva-i-Ra, an uninhabited coral atoll to the far south-east,[42] it refers to the Rotuma Group as an archipelago in its 2012 declaration and provides baselines connecting points along the fringing reefs of small features in that group, including Afgaha, Hautiu, Uea, Hafhaveiag, Hofliua, and Solnohu.[43]

In the Solomon Islands, 83 line segments establish an archipelagic baselines system around five groups of islands and other features, namely, the Russell Islands; the Rennell, Bellona and Indispensable Reef Atoll; the Ontong Java Group Archipelago; the Santa Cruz Islands Archipelago; and the Duff Islands Archipelago. The longest of these line segments is

---

42 Marine Spaces (Archipelagic Baselines and EEZ), *supra* note 23.
43 Marine Spaces (Territorial Seas), *supra* note 1.

approximately 124 M and the shortest is .31 M.[44] Fatutaka is not included in the Solomon Islands archipelagic baselines system.

In relation to the Fiji – Solomon Islands Agreement, it appears that both states worked together and exchanged data during workshops leading up to the agreement,[45] and that the line of equidistance was likely calculated from the base points declared by each state. While normal baselines would have been used for Fatutaka, archipelagic baselines were likely used for the Rotuma Archipelago. Once the baselines were updated and agreed and the equidistance line was calculated, there does not appear to have been dispute about the delimitation method or the resulting line.[46]

7 Geological and Geomorphological Considerations

Geological and geomorphological considerations do not appear to have influenced the delimitation.

8 Method of Delimitation Considerations

Article 3(2) of the Fiji – Solomon Islands Agreement indicates that the delimitation line is the equidistance line between Fiji and the Solomon Islands. The preamble also notes that both states are party to UNCLOS and accordingly that they "bas[ed]" the delimitation on the "rules and principles" expressed therein, specifically Article 74 providing for delimitation of the EEZ. The Agreement provides the coordinates of six points, and the equidistant line connecting these points is short with no significant turning points.

---

44 US Department of State, *Solomon Islands: Archipelagic and other Maritime Claims and Boundaries*, Limits in the Seas, No. 136 (28 March 2014), *available at* https://www.state.gov/wp-content/uploads/2019/12/LIS-136.pdf, p. 2.

45 *See* Fiji Government, Appendices, *supra* note 2 at 23.

46 Parliament of the Government of Fiji, *Agreement Between the Republic of Fiji and Solomon Islands Concerning their Maritime Boundary*, Written Analysis, https://www.parliament.gov.fj/wp-content/uploads/2021/02/Written-Analysis-SOI-and-FJ-Agreement-FINAL-2-1.pdf, p. 2.

9 Technical Considerations

The Agreement provides six points joined by geodetic lines which form the maritime boundary. The five line segments are short, ranging in length from just over approximately 1 M with the longest stretching approximately 22 M. These coordinates are identified to the nearest one-hundredth of an arc second determined by reference to the World Geodetic System 1984 (WGS 84). Technical support for this delimitation and the conclusion of the Agreement was received from the Geoscience, Energy and Maritime Division (GEM) of the SPC. According to a GEM submission to the Fiji Parliament, the median line calculation used baseline data for Rotuma and Fatutaka updated in 2010 and 2007, respectively, and "[t]he equidistant median line was computed using maritime boundaries delimitation software recognised by UNDOALOS."[47] A chart is annexed to the Agreement for illustrative purposes.

10 Other Considerations

Article 7 provides that any dispute between the parties concerning the interpretation or application of the Agreement "shall be settled peacefully through consultation and negotiations between the Parties or through negotiation in accordance with international law as agreed to by the Parties." It remains to be seen how these two references to "negotiation" would be interpreted.[48]

The Agreement does not address areas beyond 200 M which may explain the references in the Preamble only to the delimitation provisions of UNCLOS Article 74 (but not of Article 83) and, in Article 5, only to the sovereign rights and jurisdiction conferred by UNCLOS Article 56 (but not by Article 77).[49] However, Article 4 alludes to "further negotiations . . . relating to . . . seabed or areas of continental shelf," among other topics.[50] Depending upon the outcome of the parties' efforts before the CLCS, there

---

47 Fiji Government, Appendices, *supra* note 2 at 79.

48 There also appears to be a typographical mistake in Article 9, where reference is made to the coordinates specified in Article 1, when such coordinates are instead specified in Article 3.

49 Of course, UNCLOS Articles 83 and 77 also apply to the continental shelf within 200 M.

50 Notably, Article 4, the "without prejudice" provision of this treaty, applies only to "any further negotiations with Solomon Islands." Fiji is not mentioned. This imbalance is highly unusual, and the reason for this construction is not known to the authors.

may be cause for further boundary negotiation in areas beyond 200 M to the north and south of the present boundary.

III CONCLUSIONS

The conclusion of the Fiji – Solomon Islands Agreement marks an important milestone for the Solomon Islands, which has now finalized all of its EEZ boundaries. Fiji is also well on its way to concluding agreements on all of its maritime boundaries by its goal of 2025. Region-wide, only a dozen of the approximately 48 overlapping EEZs in the Pacific Islands region remain to be delimited.[51] The level of cooperation required to meet these milestones is admirable, particularly against the background of the incredible challenges posed by climate change to this region. The Fiji – Solomon Islands Agreement is one more piece of this complex puzzle, albeit a very small one.

IV RELATED LAW IN FORCE

A *Law of the Sea Conventions*

Fiji: Party to UNCLOS (ratified 10 December 1982).
Solomon Islands: Party to UNCLOS (ratified 23 June 1997).

B *Maritime Jurisdiction Claimed at the Time of Signature*

Fiji: Archipelagic waters; 12 M territorial sea; 24 M contiguous zone; 200 M EEZ; continental shelf (submission to the Commission on the Limits of the Continental Shelf, 28 April 2009, updated 30 April 2012) (joint submission of preliminary information to the Commission on the Limits of the Continental Shelf by Vanuatu, Solomon Islands, and the Republic of the Fiji Islands on the North Fiji Basin).
Solomon Islands: Archipelagic waters; 12 M territorial sea; 24 M contiguous zone; 200 M EEZ; continental shelf (Joint submission to the CLCS by the Federated States of Micronesia, Papua New Guinea and Solomon Islands

---

51 RNZ, *supra* note 3.

concerning the Ontong Java Plateau, 5 May 2009; recommendations adopted on 17 March 2017. Preliminary information submitted to the CLCS: Fiji and Solomon Islands on the Charlotte Bank Region, 21 April 2009; Fiji, Solomon Islands and Vanuatu on the North Fiji Basin, 21 April 2009; Solomon Islands in respect to a high seas enclave at the junction of the Solomon Islands, Papua New Guinea and Australia Exclusive Economic Zones, 5 May 2009).

C   *Maritime Jurisdiction Claimed Subsequent to Signature*

Fiji: No change.
Solomon Islands: No change.

Prepared by Natalie L. Reid, Romain Zamour, Beatrice A. Walton

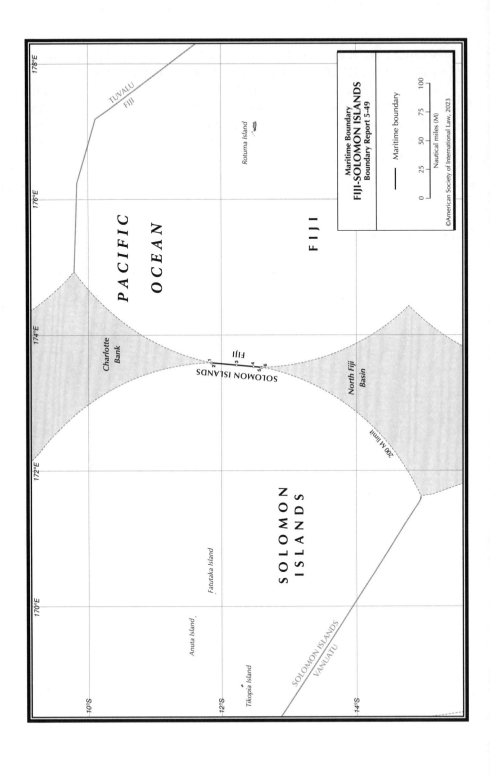

AGREEMENT BETWEEN THE REPUBLIC OF FIJI AND SOLOMON ISLANDS CONCERNING THEIR MARITIME BOUNDARY

The Sovereign states of the Republic of Fiji ('Fiji') and Solomon Islands;

DESIRING to strengthen the bonds of friendship between the two States;

RECOGNIZING the need to effect a precise and equitable delimitation of the respective maritime areas in which the two States exercise sovereign rights;

BASING themselves on the rules and principles of relevant international law, as they are expressed in the United Nations Convention Law of the Sea, 10 December 1982 to which both Fiji and the Solomon Islands are a party, and, in particular Article 74 which provide that the delimitation of the exclusive economic zone between States with opposite or adjacent coasts shall be effected by agreement on the basis of international law, as referred to in Article 38 of the Statute of the International Court of Justice, in order to achieve an equitable solution; and

DESIROUS of establishing a clear maritime boundary between the Republic of Fiji and the Solomon Islands;

HAVE AGREED AS FOLLOWS:

ARTICLE 1
Interpretation

In this Agreement unless the context otherwise requires:

"**Agreement**" means this Agreement;

"**continental shelf**" in accordance with Part VI of UNCLOS, includes the seabed and subsoil of the submarine areas that extend beyond its territorial sea throughout the natural prolongation of its land territory to the outer edge of the continental margin, or to a distance of 200 nautical miles from the baselines from which the breadth of the territorial sea is measured where the outer edge of the continental margin does not extend up to that distance in accordance with Part VI of UNCLOS;

6042 *Report Number 5-49*

"**EEZ**" means the Exclusive Economic Zones measured 200 nautical miles from the baselines of each Party as referred to under with Part V of UNCLOS; "**Parties**" means the Republic of Fiji and the Solomon Islands; and

"**UNCLOS**" means the United Nations Convention on the Law of the Sea 1982.

ARTICLE 2
Purpose

The purpose of this Agreement is to establish in accordance with international law, the maritime boundary between the Republic of Fiji and the Solomon Islands.

ARTICLE 3
Maritime Boundary between Fiji and Solomon Islands

(1) The line of delimitation between the exclusive economic zones and continental shelves over which each State respectively exercises sovereign rights and jurisdiction in accordance with international law lies seaward of Fatutaka in the Solomon Islands and Rotuma in Fiji respectively, along geodesics connecting the following geographical coordinates of points ('points'), defined by their coordinates in the order stated below:

Point Identifier	Latitude	Longitude
FJ_SB MB 1	11°50′ 53.09″ S	173° 35′ 34.62″ E
FJ _SB MB 2	11°51′ 53.09″ S	173°35′ 29.20″ E
FJ_ SB MB 3	12°13′ 30.64″ S	173°33′ 33.05″ E
FJ _SB MB 4	12°28′ 31. 76″ S	173°32′ 12.15″ E
FJ_ SB MB 5	12°35′ 08.29″ S	173°31′ 36.49″ E
FJ_ SB MB 6	12°36′ 08.29″ S	173°31′ 31.09″ E

(2) The line of delimitation referred to in paragraph 1 of this Article is the equidistance line between Fiji and the Solomon Islands.
(3) The geographical coordinates given in this Agreement are determined by reference to the geodetic reference system WGS 84 (World Geodetic Reference System 1984).

(4) The boundary line drawn on the chart in the Annexure to this Agreement is drawn for illustrative purposes only.

ARTICLE 4
Without Prejudice

This Agreement will not prejudice any further negotiations with Solomon Islands relating to international law, the law of the sea including those to do with the regional cooperation, waters, seabed or areas of continental shelf areas.

ARTICLE 5
Sovereign Rights

The lines described in Article 3 of this Agreement shall be the maritime boundary between the areas referred to in Article 3 in which Parties, in accordance with international law and Article 56 of UNCLOS shall exercise their sovereign rights or jurisdiction.

ARTICLE 6
Adjustments to Maritime Boundary

If new surveys or resulting charts and maps should indicate that changes in the base point coordinates are sufficiently significant to require adjustments of the maritime boundary, the Parties agree that an adjustment will be carried out on the basis of the same principles as those used in determining the maritime boundary, and such adjustments shall be provided for in a Protocol to this Agreement.

ARTICLE 7
Dispute Resolution

Any dispute between the parties concerning the interpretation or application of this Agreement shall be settled peacefully through consultation and negotiations between the Parties or through negotiation in accordance with international law as agreed to by the Parties.

ARTICLE 8
Equitable Benefit from Resource Exploitation

If any single accumulation or deposit of liquid hydrocarbon, natural gas, or other mineral lies on the maritime boundary median line, the accumulation or deposit of such resources shall be effectively exploited by either or both Parties and both Parties shall equitably share the benefits of such resource exploitation.

ARTICLE 9
Agreement Deposit

Upon the completion of all national procedures bringing this Agreement into force, each party shall take all the necessary steps to lodge this Agreement, including the coordinates in Article 1 [*sic*], with the appropriate international bodies.

ARTICLE 10
Entry into Force

Each Party shall notify the other of the completion of its national procedures to bring this Agreement into force. This Agreement shall enter into force on the date of the later note in an exchange of notes between Parties indicating that each Party has completed its national procedures for the entry into force of this Agreement.

IN WITNESS WHEREOF, the representatives of the two Governments, being duly authorized for this purpose, have signed this Agreement and have affixed thereto their seals.

DONE at Suva, Fiji on the eleventh-day of July in the year 2022 in two originals, each in the English language.

<table>
<tr><td>For the Government of
Solomon Islands</td><td>For the Government of the
Republic of Fiji</td></tr>
<tr><td>**HON. MANASSEH D.
SOGAVARE**
Prime Minister of Solomon Islands</td><td>**HON. JOSAIA V.
BAINIMARAMA**
Prime Minister of the Republic
of Fiji</td></tr>
</table>

VI

Indian Ocean

Mauritius – Seychelles

Report Number 6-22 (2)

Treaty Concerning the Joint Exercise of Sovereign Rights over the Continental Shelf in the Mascarene Plateau Region between the Government of the Republic of Mauritius and the Government of the Republic of Seychelles

Signed: 13 March 2012
Entry into force: 18 June 2012
Published at: 2847 UNTS 277 (I-49782); 79 LOS BULL. 26 (2013)

Treaty Concerning the Joint Management of the Continental Shelf in the Mascarene Plateau Region between the Government of the Republic of Mauritius and the Government of the Republic of Seychelles

Signed: 13 March 2012
Entry into force: 18 June 2012
Published at: 2847 UNTS 307 (I-49783); 79 LOS BULL. 41 (2013)

I SUMMARY

The Republic of Mauritius and the Republic of Seychelles entered into two bilateral treaties on 13 March 2012, thereby establishing the largest offshore joint management area (JMA) in the world. The parties' JMA covers approximately 400,000 square kilometers of maritime space,[1] which is greater than the total land area of Japan or Norway. In addition to its striking size, the JMA is noteworthy as the first such zone in history to be located entirely at a distance of more than 200 nautical miles (M) from the mainland

---

1 Press Release, Commonwealth Secretariat, *Mauritius and Seychelles secure and manage joint seabed rights through continental shelf submission*, https://thecommonwealth .org/project/mauritius-and-seychelles-secure-and-manage-joint-seabed-rights-through -continental-shelf (last visited 4 October 2021).

Coalter G. Lathrop (ed.), International Maritime Boundaries, 6047-6102.
© *The American Society of International Law and Koninklijke Brill BV, Leiden 2025.*

or insular coasts of any state. The establishment of the JMA followed the delimitation of the parties' exclusive economic zones (EEZs) in 2008.[2]

The pragmatic objective of the JMA is to enable Mauritius and Seychelles to avoid deadlock over their remaining boundary delimitation issues in this area, while proceeding to begin development of the potentially significant natural resources of the Mascarene Plateau. Petroleum geologists have suspected for decades that this vast region may contain offshore hydrocarbon deposits, although these predictions have neither been proven nor disproven as of 2021.

The Mascarene Plateau is an immense maritime feature in the Indian Ocean located between 4° S and 21° S, more than one thousand kilometers east of the African continent. It comprises a series of continuous, submerged banks and seafloor highs extending for several thousand kilometers along a generally north-south axis in an arcuate formation taking the shape of a boomerang. The relevant part of Seychelles is located at the northwest end of the formation. The eponymous main island of Mauritius lies toward the formation's southwest end near the French island of Réunion. The JMA is located to the east of both states' nearest insular territory, in the center of the "boomerang." The JMA is dominated by the expansive middle segment of the Mascarene Plateau known as the Saya de Malha Bank. This bank is relatively flat and covered by seagrass beds and coral reefs with depths ranging from 10 to 100 meters, creating a massive region of mid-ocean shallow water uninterrupted by insular features.

As detailed below, the first of the two 2012 treaties has the narrow purpose of identifying the JMA's geographic perimeter based largely upon a 2011 recommendation from the Commission on the Limits of the Continental Shelf (CLCS). This agreement is the Treaty Concerning the Joint Exercise of Sovereign Rights over the Continental Shelf in the Mascarene Plateau Region (the Sovereign Rights Treaty). The parties' second treaty establishes a specialized legal regime and institutional structure designed to govern economic and environmental issues in the JMA during its anticipated 30-year duration. This agreement is the Treaty Concerning the Joint Management of the Continental Shelf in the Mascarene Plateau Region (the Joint Management Treaty).

---

2   *See* Report Number 6-22, VI IMB 4391. This report by Victor Prescott and Gillian Triggs provides additional context regarding the parties' history and relationship and additional information about the geography of these states' insular territories.

Both treaties are explicitly provisional arrangements pursuant to Article 83(3) of the United Nations Convention on the Law of the Sea (UNCLOS). Unless the parties choose to renew the provisional arrangement, it will be terminated at the end of a 30-year term or upon the parties' delimitation of a permanent maritime boundary dividing their areas beyond 200 M.

II CONSIDERATIONS

1 *Political, Strategic, and Historical Considerations*

Mauritius and Seychelles are both island states located at a great distance from the African mainland coast. Mauritius exercises territorial sovereignty over the principal island of Mauritius, as well as more than 100 smaller islands, islets, and rocks, whereas Seychelles exercises territorial sovereignty over 115 islands and numerous smaller features. Mauritius has a population of nearly 1.4 million, concentrated on the principal island.[3] Seychelles has a population of nearly 100,000, concentrated on the island of Mahé.[4]

Most of the islands now possessed or claimed by Mauritius and Seychelles were acquired by the French in the 1700s and then transferred to British control after the defeat of Napoleon in 1814.[5] Mauritius gained independence in 1968, and Seychelles gained independence in 1976. Both states are presently members of the African Union, the Southern African Development Community, and the Commonwealth of Nations, as well as parties to UNCLOS.

For 20 years, Mauritius and Seychelles have worked carefully to avoid deadlock over their respective maritime entitlements and offshore natural resources. This period of cooperation began as early as 2002 when Mauritius and Seychelles commenced negotiation of a boundary to delimit their respective EEZs.[6] That negotiation was concluded on 29 July 2008 with the parties' Agreement on the Delimitation of the Exclusive Economic Zone Between the Two States (the EEZ Treaty). The EEZ Treaty established

---

3 CIA, The World Factbook: Mauritius, https://www.cia.gov/the-world-factbook/countries/mauritius/ (last visited 4 October 2021).
4 CIA, The World Factbook: Seychelles, https://www.cia.gov/the-world-factbook/countries/seychelles/ (last visited 4 October 2021).
5 Jeremy Black, Europe and the World: 1650-1830 78, 140 (Routledge 2002).
6 *See supra* note 2 at 4398, Preamble (explicitly describing "negotiations which took place between the two States between April 2002 and July 2008").

6050   *Report Number 6-22 (2)*

a simple all-purpose boundary based on an equidistance line defined by 33 points.[7]

Two months later, on 18 September 2008, Mauritius and Seychelles concluded another bilateral agreement: the Treaty on the Framework for a Joint Submission to the United Nations Commission on the Limits of the Continental Shelf.[8] Pursuant to this agreement, the parties worked together to make a joint submission to the CLCS in accordance with Article 76(8) of UNCLOS. Filed on 1 December 2008, the joint submission requested the CLCS to provide recommendations as to the delineation of the outer continental shelf resulting from the natural prolongation of the parties' insular territory beyond 200 M associated with the Mascarene Plateau and the Saya de Malha Bank, in particular. On 30 March 2011, the CLCS published its recommendations.[9] The CLCS adopted most of the parties' methodology and analysis but disagreed or requested additional data in several instances. The recommendations ultimately delineated the outer limit of the continental shelf based upon a line connecting 453 points defined by geographic coordinates referenced to the WGS 84 datum.

About one year later, the parties' cooperation entered yet another phase with the finalization and adoption of the Sovereign Rights Treaty and the Joint Management Treaty in 2012. While preparing the joint submission to the CLCS, and throughout negotiation of the 2012 treaties, Mauritius and Seychelles received legal and technical assistance from the Commonwealth Secretariat, which provided a budget of GBP 160,000 for the project and "also assumed a critical 'good offices' role."[10]

The parties' cooperation is still actively ongoing. The Joint Commission established by the Joint Management Treaty has generally met at least twice each year to discuss and implement different aspects of the JMA. Since 2018, the JMA's advancement has been supported by the United Nations Development Programme (UNDP), which has allocated a total budget of

---

7   *Id.* at 4399, Art. 2 ("Description of Delimitation Line").

8   This 2008 treaty is unpublished, but it is referenced in the preambles of both 2012 treaties discussed in this report.

9   CLCS, *Summary of the Recommendations of the Commission on the Limits of the Continental Shelf in regard to the Joint Submission made by Mauritius and Seychelles concerning the Mascarene Plateau region on 1 December 2008*, adopted on 30 March 2011, *available at* https://www.un.org/depts/los/clcs_new/submissions_files/submission_musc.htm (last visited 4 October 2021).

10   *Supra* note 1.

more than \$2 million to the project.[11] The parties remain optimistic regarding the potential for eventual discovery of economically viable hydrocarbon deposits, although the most ambitious plans are presently stalled due to low oil prices and the COVID-19 pandemic.

2 Legal Regime Considerations

The Sovereign Rights Treaty is straightforward and concise. The Preamble and Article 1 confirm that the agreement relates only to sovereign rights "for the purpose of exploring the continental shelf and exploiting its natural resources." The agreement thus does not purport to concern any rights to the superjacent water column, fisheries, or any natural resources located above the continental shelf. The agreement confirms that the parties shall exercise their sovereign rights "jointly" with respect to the entire "Joint Zone" (Article 1), the area of which is described in Article 2. In turn, the JMA "is established in respect of the Joint Zone described in Article 2 of the [Sovereign Rights Treaty]" (Article 3(a) of the Joint Management Treaty). In other words, the Joint Zone and JMA refer to the same geographic area.

Under Article 2 and Annex 1 of the Sovereign Rights Treaty, the Joint Zone is defined as the area enclosed by the 453-point line identified by the CLCS (the zone's "outer limits" to the north and east) and the relevant sections of the outer limits of the parties' respective EEZs (the zone's "inner limits" to the south and west). The EEZ limits are identified using 15 points defining the Mauritius EEZ, a further 5 points defining the Seychelles EEZ, and a "tripoint" where the Joint Zone meets the eastern end of the parties' 2008 EEZ boundary at Point MS1 of that line.[12] The Preamble to the Sovereign Rights Treaty acknowledges its status as a "provisional arrangement[]" of a practical nature" under Article 83(3) of UNCLOS. Article 3 provides that the agreement shall not prejudice the parties' legal position or rights concerning any future delimitation of a permanent maritime boundary.

The Joint Management Treaty establishes the JMA and addresses a wide range of administrative, economic, and environmental issues applicable to that area. Five aspects warrant particular attention:

---

11 UNDP, Project Document: Demonstrating Innovative Ocean Governance Mechanisms and Delivering Best Practices and Lessons for Extended Continental Shelf Management within the Western Indian Ocean Large Marine Ecosystems (11 January 2018).

12 See supra note 2 at 4399, Art. 2 (providing coordinates of turning points of 2008 EEZ boundary).

6052 *Report Number 6-22 (2)*

(i) *Equal Sharing of Revenue and Expenses* – In Article 5, the parties commit to sharing equally in all "revenue received in respect of natural resource activities" in the JMA according to a 50-50 split. The parties likewise agree to share equally in the management costs. The parties exclude from this arrangement any revenue pertaining to a potentially unitized "reservoir of petroleum or unitary mineral deposit" extending across the boundary of the JMA and either party's EEZ (Article 10). If such transboundary resources are ultimately discovered, the parties undertake to work expeditiously and in good faith to agree as to the effective and equitable treatment of such transboundary resources (Article 10(b)).

(ii) *Institutional Structure* – Article 4 of the Joint Management Treaty provides for the establishment of a "three-tiered joint administrative structure consisting of a Ministerial Council, a Joint Commission and a Designated Authority," which are collectively responsible for managing economic and environmental issues in the JMA. The Designated Authority—once it is established—will implement "the day-to-day regulation and management of natural resource activities in the JMA," including with respect to granting contracts to private operators. The Joint Commission will oversee the work of the Designated Authority, and is responsible for promulgating policies and regulations in accordance with the directives of the Ministerial Council. The Ministerial Council is the highest political authority within the JMA, and it resolves matters where the Joint Commission is unable to agree on a resolution. The powers of the Joint Commission and Designated Authority are further elaborated in Annexes C and D, respectively.

(iii) *Supplemental Codes and Regulations* – Many provisions of the Joint Management Treaty anticipate promulgation of additional normative instruments to govern economic and environmental activities in the JMA. These include express references to a Taxation Code (Article 6), Natural Resource Codes (Article 8), and health and safety standards (Article 15). During subsequent years, the Joint Commission has also agreed to a model petroleum agreement, marine scientific research code, and environmental code of practice. In other provisions of the Joint Management Treaty, the parties also agree more generally to cooperate with respect to constructing and operating pipelines, conducting surveys, protecting the seabed marine environment, applying customs laws, and performing search and rescue operations within the JMA.

(iv) *Provisional Status* – Like Article 3 of the Sovereign Rights Treaty, Article 2 of the Joint Management Treaty reiterates that the JMA is a provisional arrangement without prejudice to the final delimitation of a permanent maritime boundary for the parties' continental shelf entitlements. Article 23(a) further provides that the Joint Management Treaty will terminate automatically 30 years after the date of entry into force, or upon the conclusion of a permanent agreement governing the maritime boundary. Article 23(b) provides, however, that the JMA may be renewed by agreement, while Article 23(c) ensures a degree of economic certainty for prospective operators by providing that "[n]atural resource projects commenced under this Treaty shall continue" even after the JMA's termination.

(v) *Settlement of Disputes* – Article 21 provides that disputes will be settled "as far as possible...through mutual consultation." If such consultations fail, then either of the parties may refer a dispute to an Arbitral Tribunal. Procedures for the constitution of the Arbitral Tribunal and the conduct of the arbitration are elaborated in Annex B. Notably, Annex B designates the President of the International Tribunal for the Law of the Sea (ITLOS) as the potential appointing authority if a Chairman of the Arbitral Tribunal cannot be selected by agreement of the two party-appointed arbitrators or if the Chairman is not approved by the parties. The Arbitral Tribunal is mandated to deliver a decision within six months of being convened by the Chairman. The Arbitral Tribunal is empowered to determine its own procedures.

A number of aspects of the Joint Management Treaty appear to have been inspired by the 2002 Timor Sea Treaty,[13] which is now superseded by a subsequent agreement.[14] The general structure of both treaties is noticeably similar, and comparable language is used to describe the allocation of responsibilities amongst the three "Regulatory Bodies." The two treaties' annexes on dispute resolution are also similar, with only minor variations.

---

13 *See* Report Number 6-20 (1) & (2), V IMB 3806. The similarities are potentially attributable to the involvement and participation of the Commonwealth Secretariat.
14 *See* Report Number 6-20 (5), VIII IMB 5547.

6054   *Report Number 6-22 (2)*

3   *Economic and Environmental Considerations*

For decades, petroleum geologists have made optimistic predictions about the possibility of discovering viable hydrocarbon deposits on or around Saya de Malha Bank.[15] These predictions have been neither proven nor disproven. Sufficient exploration and study have not taken place due to obstacles resulting from the challenging geography and geomorphology, as well as the region's delicate environment and biodiversity. In recent years, progress has been further impeded by low oil prices and the COVID-19 pandemic, as well as the broader issue of the JMA's unique and unprecedented nature, both legally and administratively. Many aspects of the JMA have required innovation.

The Joint Commission meets regularly, but the Designated Authority has yet to be established, even though more than nine years have passed since the JMA's creation. During this time, foreign vessels have reportedly engaged in fishing within the water column superjacent to the JMA, as well as bottom trawling activities and collection of sedentary species on the seabed of the JMA. Although international law permits fishing within the water column superjacent to areas of extended continental shelf without authorization by the coastal state, any such activities affecting sedentary species "on or under the seabed" would necessarily violate the rights of Mauritius and Seychelles under Article 77 of UNCLOS if conducted without their authorization.

On 11 January 2018, the UNDP concluded an agreement with Mauritius and Seychelles to provide support by "developing and demonstrating new management approaches" for the JMA.[16] The UNDP is contributing a total of $2.2 million to this ongoing project. The project was originally scheduled for completion in January 2022, although the deadline has been extended due to COVID-19. The project's four components are (1) building technical and management capacity, (2) developing a data and information system, (3) implementing a marine spatial planning approach to effective decision-making, and (4) monitoring and evaluating sustainability.

---

15   *E.g.*, Press Release, Spectrum Geo, *Landmark Seychelles-Mauritius Agreement* (25 January 2018), https://www.spectrumgeo.com/press-release/landmark-agreement-paves-the-way-for-new-seychelles-mauritius-jma-seismic (last visited 4 October 2021) ("[B]asin modelling puts the potential Seychelles style pre-volcanic source rocks into the oil window," as "corroborated by the presence of high quality oil slicks . . . captured on satellite data.").
16   *Supra* note 11.

4 Geographic Considerations

The JMA encompasses the Saya de Malha Bank and its slopes to the north, east, and southwest. The elevated seafloor extends the prolongation of the two states' continental shelf entitlements into a region where their spatial relationship becomes one of adjacency, rather than oppositeness. In this region, there are no islands to generate any territorial sea or EEZ entitlements.

5 Islands, Rocks, Reefs, and Low-tide Elevations Considerations

The western and southern limits of the JMA are identified by 21 points following the arcs of the parties' 200 M EEZs measured from their coastal baselines. In this region, the Mauritius EEZ is generated by basepoints on the island of Agalega and the atoll of Saint Brandon (Cargados Carajos Shoals).[17] The relevant section of the Seychelles EEZ is generated by basepoints on the islands of Coëtivy and Frégate, a feature east of the main island of Mahé.[18] The baseline of Coëtivy was also used by the parties and the CLCS to construct the arcs for applying the 350 M distance constraint under Article 76(5) of UNCLOS.

6 Baseline Considerations

In the relevant area, Mauritius has established normal baselines around Agalega, and archipelagic baselines around the atoll of Saint Brandon (Cargados Carajos Shoals).[19] These baselines are described in Mauritius' 2005 Maritime Zones (Baselines and Delineating Lines) Regulations.[20] Seychelles has established normal baselines around the relevant islands of Coëtivy and Frégate, as described in Seychelles' 2008 Maritime Zones

---

17 *See* Regulation of 5 August 2005 concerning maritime zones (baselines and delineating lines) (Mauritius), *reprinted in* 67 LOS BULL. 13 (2008), *available at* https://www.un.org/Depts/los/doalos_publications/LOSBulletins/bulletinpdf/bulletin67e.pdf (last visited 4 October 2021).
18 *See* Presidential Order S.I. 88 of 6 November 2008 concerning maritime zones (baselines) (Seychelles), *reprinted in* 70 LOS BULL. 16 (2009), *available at* https://www.un.org/Depts/los/doalos_publications/LOSBulletins/bulletinpdf/bulletin70e.pdf (last visited 4 October 2021).
19 *Supra* note 17.
20 *Id.*

6056 *Report Number 6-22 (2)*

(Baselines) Order.[21] These baselines were used to establish the limits of the parties' EEZs (the "inner limits" of the JMA), but they played only a small role in defining the "outer limits" of the JMA area.[22]

7 Geological and Geomorphological Considerations

The northern and eastern limits of the JMA are determined by the 453-point line identified in the CLCS recommendations. The location of this line reflects geomorphological considerations resulting from the application of Article 76 of UNCLOS.

As explained in the 2011 recommendations, the CLCS accepted most of the analysis proposed by the parties in their joint submission.[23] The CLCS agreed with the joint proposals regarding the location of 8 of the 14 relevant foot-of-slope (FOS) points to be "determined as the point of maximum change in the gradient" at the base of the continental shelf in accordance with Article 76(4)(b). Adjustments were then made to the remaining FOS points after consultation with the parties and collection of additional data.[24]

The CLCS essentially accepted all of the parties' remaining submissions. First, the CLCS accepted the parties' use of the FOS points to construct 60 M arcs, thus establishing the outer edge of the continental margin under Article 76(4)(a)(ii).[25] Second, the CLCS accepted the parties' application of the distance and depth constraints under Article 76(5). In 18 instances, the final points of delineation were adjusted landward because the continental margin extended beyond 350 M from the states' baselines.[26] In 173 instances, the final points of delineation were adjusted landward because the continental margin extended beyond 100 M from the 2,500 meter isobaths associated with the Saya de Malha Bank.[27] These adjustments produced the 453-point line adopted in the Sovereign Rights Treaty.

---

21 *Supra* note 18.
22 Of the 453 points on the outer limit of the JMA, only Points ECS107 to ECS123 are located on the 350 M constraint line.
23 *Supra* note 9.
24 *Id.* at paras. 30-37.
25 *Id.* at paras. 40-43.
26 *Id.* at Table 3 (identifying Points ECS 107 to ECS 123 as "350 M constraint point[s]").
27 *Id.* at Table 3 (identifying 173 "Depth constraint point[s]").

8 *Method of Delimitation Considerations*

Neither the Sovereign Rights Treaty nor the Joint Management Treaty delimits any maritime boundaries. Both are expressly characterized as provisional arrangements without prejudice to a future delimitation.

9 *Technical Considerations*

The Sovereign Rights Treaty describes the Joint Zone using coordinates of points for which latitude and longitude are referenced to the WGS 84 datum and are provided to the nearest 0.00000001 of a degree. The lines connecting these points are geodesics.

10 *Other Considerations*

Mauritius and Seychelles are located in a region of the world with a substantial number of intractable disputes over territorial sovereignty and maritime rights—generally involving the United Kingdom, France, and one or more former colonies.[28] In this context, it is notable that Mauritius and Seychelles have remained committed to the collaborative reconciliation of their respective interests in potential maritime resources for the past 20 years.

III CONCLUSIONS

The Sovereign Rights Treaty and Joint Management Treaty represent the first example in international practice where two coastal states have established a joint management arrangement consistent with Article 83 of UNCLOS in respect of an area of continental shelf extending beyond 200 M from their coastal baselines.

---

28 For example, Mauritius is itself a participant in the ongoing dispute over the Chagos Archipelago, among other territorial features. *See* Victor Prescott, *Region VI, Indian Ocean Boundaries,* V IMB 3453, 3462–3465. The JMA does not affect any of these disputes, however, because it lies at considerable distance from the relevant territories.

IV RELATED LAW IN FORCE

A Law of the Sea Conventions

Mauritius: Party to UNCLOS (ratified 4 November 1994)
Seychelles: Party to UNCLOS (ratified 16 September 1991)

B Maritime Jurisdiction Claimed at the Time of Signature

Mauritius: 12 M territorial sea; 24 M contiguous zone; 200 M EEZ; continental shelf (CLCS joint submission with Seychelles 1 December 2008, recommendations 30 March 2011; and CLCS submission (Rodrigues Island) 6 May 2009).

Seychelles: 12 M territorial sea; 24 M contiguous zone; 200 M EEZ; continental shelf (CLCS joint submission with Mauritius 1 December 2008, recommendations 30 March 2011; CLCS submission (Northern Plateau Region) 7 May 2009, recommendations 27 August 2018; and CLCS preliminary information (Aldabra Island) 8 May 2009).

C Maritime Jurisdiction Claimed Subsequent to Signature

On 26 March 2019 and 24 May 2021, Mauritius submitted further information concerning the outer limits of the extended continental shelf in the Chagos Archipelago Region. Mauritius had previously submitted preliminary information relating to the Chagos Archipelago Region on 6 May 2009.

Prepared by David P. Riesenberg

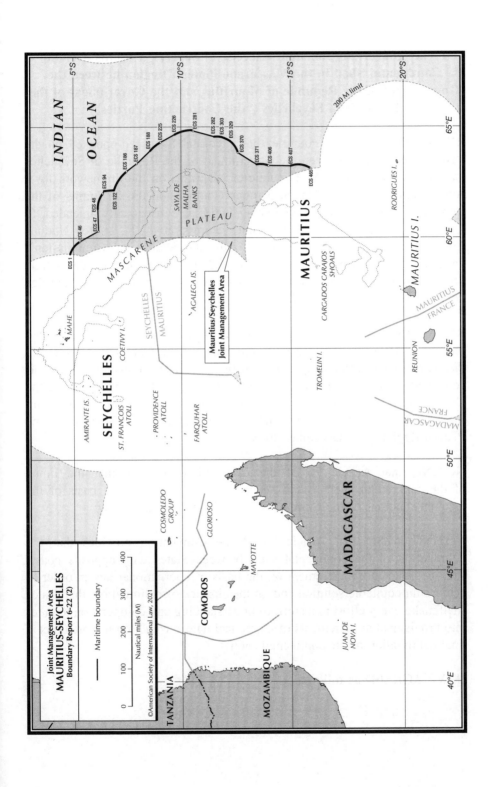

6060 *Report Number 6-22 (2)*

Treaty concerning the Joint Exercise of Sovereign Rights over the Continental Shelf in the Mascarene Plateau Region between the Government of the Republic of Mauritius and the Government of the Republic of Seychelles ("the Contracting Parties")

RECALLING that both countries being coastal States co-operated on the basis of the Treaty between the Government of the Republic of Seychelles and the Government of the Republic of Mauritius on the Framework for a Joint Submission to the United Nations Commission on the Limits of the Continental Shelf dated 18 September 2008, as subsequently amended, to lodge on 1 December 2008 the Joint Submission to the United Nations Commission on the Limits of the Continental Shelf ('the Commission') concerning the Mascarene Plateau region ("Joint Submission") under Article 76, paragraph 8 of the United Nations Convention on the Law of the Sea done at Montego Bay on 10 December 1982 ("the Convention");

RECALLING ALSO that on 30 March 2011, the Commission adopted recommendations confirming the entitlement of the Contracting Parties to the area of continental shelf submitted by them in the Joint Submission, as contained in the Commission document entitled Recommendations of the Commission on the Limits of the Continental Shelf in regards to the Joint Submission made by Mauritius and Seychelles in respect of the Mascarene Plateau Region on 1 December 2008;

NOTING that Article 76 of the Convention provides that the limits of the continental shelf established by coastal States on the basis of the recommendations of the Commission shall be final and binding;

NOTING ALSO that Article 83 of the Convention provides that the delimitation of the continental shelf between States with opposite coasts shall be effected by agreement on the basis of international law in order to achieve an equitable solution and, in the absence of delimitation, that States shall make every effort in a spirit of understanding and co-operation to enter into provisional arrangements of a practical nature which do not prejudice a final delimitation of the continental shelf;

HAVE AGREED as follows:

Article 1: Joint Exercise of Sovereign Rights over the Continental Shelf

The Contracting Parties shall exercise sovereign rights jointly for the purpose of exploring the continental shelf and exploiting its natural resources in the area described in Article 2 ('the Joint Zone').

Article 2: Delineation of the Joint Zone

The Joint Zone is defined by the following points, the coordinates of latitude and longitude [referred to the World Geodetic System (WGS84)] of which are set out at Annex 1 to this Treaty, and as illustrated in the map at Annex 2 of this Treaty:

Commencing at point ECS1 on Seychelles Exclusive Economic Zone Boundary, the boundary line runs through points ECS2 to ECS44, thence to point ECS45, thence to point ECS46, thence through points ECS47 to ECS105, thence to point ECS106, thence through points ECS107 to ECS123, thence through points ECS124 to ECS186, thence to point ECS187, thence to point ECS188, thence through points ECS189 to ECS220, thence to point ECS221, thence through points ECS222 to ECS269, thence through points ECS270 to ECS275, thence to point ECS276, thence through points ECS277 to ECS296, thence through points ECS297 to ECS321, thence through points ECS322 to ECS362, thence to point ECS363, thence through points ECS364 to ECS395, thence to point ECS396, thence through points ECS397 to ECS453 on Mauritius Exclusive Economic Zone boundary, thence along Mauritius Exclusive Economic Zone boundary to point 34, thence through points 35 to 41, thence through points 42 to 47, thence through point 48 to MS1 on the intersection of the Seychelles and Mauritius Exclusive Economic Zone boundaries, thence along the Seychelles Exclusive Economic Zone boundary through points EZI to EZ5, thence along the Seychelles Exclusive Economic Zone boundary to the starting point at ECS1 on Seychelles Exclusive Economic Zone boundary.

The boundary line between the above listed points is a geodesic.

Article 3: Treaty without Prejudice

Nothing contained in this Treaty, and no act taking place whilst this Treaty is in force, shall be interpreted as prejudicing or affecting the legal position or rights of the Contracting Parties concerning any future delimitation of the continental shelf between them in the Mascarene Plateau Region.

Article 4: Entry into Force

(a)   Each Contracting Party shall notify the other, by means of exchange of diplomatic notes, the completion of the procedures required by its law for the bringing into force of this Treaty. The Treaty shall enter into force on the date of receipt of the later notification.

(b)   Upon entry into force, the Treaty shall be taken to have effect, and all of its provisions shall be taken to have applied, from the date of signature.

IN WITNESS WHEREOF the undersigned, being duly authorised thereto by their respective Governments, have signed this Treaty.

DONE at Clarisse House, Vacoas, Mauritius in duplicate on this 13th day of March Two Thousand and Twelve in the English language.

For the Government of the Republic of Mauritius

Dr. the Hon Navinchandra
Ramgoolam, GCSK, FRCP
Prime Minister

For the Government of the Republic of Seychelles

H.E. Mr. James Alix Miche
President

ANNEX 1

Geographical coordinates (DATUM WGS 84) delineating the Seychelles-Mauritius Joint Zone

Coordinates ID	Latitude (decimal deg)	Longitude (decimal deg)
ECS 1	-4.90806007	59.27680588
ECS 2	-4.90956497	59.28105164
ECS 3	-4.91540956	59.29670334
ECS 4	-4.92151403	59.31225586
ECS 5	-4.92787600	59.32770157
ECS 6	-4.93449545	59.34303665
ECS 7	-4.94137001	59.35826111
ECS 8	-4.94849682	59.37337112
ECS 9	-4.95587683	59.38836288
ECS 10	-4.96350431	59.40323257
ECS 11	-4.97137928	59.41796875
ECS 12	-4.97949934	59.43257141
ECS 13	-4.98786354	59.44704437
ECS 14	-4.99646616	59.46137238
ECS 15	-5.00530624	59.47555161
ECS 16	-5.01438284	59.48958588
ECS 17	-5.02369118	59.50346756
ECS 18	-5.03323078	59.51719284
ECS 19	-5.04299784	59.53075790
ECS 20	-5.05298948	59.54415894
ECS 21	-5.06320477	59.55739212
ECS 22	-5.07363844	59.57045746
ECS 23	-5.08429050	59.58334732
ECS 24	-5.09515572	59.59605789
ECS 25	-5.10623217	59.60858536
ECS 26	-5.11751652	59.62093353
ECS 27	-5.12900496	59.63308716
ECS 28	-5.14069462	59.64505005
ECS 29	-5.15258312	59.65681839

Coordinates ID	Latitude (decimal deg)	Longitude (decimal deg)
ECS 30	-5.16466522	59.66838837
ECS 31	-5.17693901	59.67975616
ECS 32	-5.18940115	59.69091797
ECS 33	-5.20204639	59.70186615
ECS 34	-5.21487331	59.71261215
ECS 35	-5.22787952	59.72314072
ECS 36	-5.24105835	59.73344803
ECS 37	-5.25440645	59.74353409
ECS 38	-5.26792240	59.75340271
ECS 39	-5.28160143	59.76304626
ECS 40	-5.29543781	59.77246094
ECS 41	-5.30942869	59.78164291
ECS 42	-5.32357216	59.79058838
ECS 43	-5.33786345	59.79930496
ECS 44	-5.35229826	59.80777740
ECS 45	-6.04989910	60.20489120
ECS 46	-6.33353949	61.16790390
ECS 47	-6.33209372	61.17536163
ECS 48	-6.32918072	61.19184875
ECS 49	-6.32654333	61.20837402
ECS 50	-6.32418060	61.22494888
ECS 51	-6.32209444	61.24155807
ECS 52	-6.32028484	61.25819778
ECS 53	-6.31875229	61.27486801
ECS 54	-6.31749725	61.29155731
ECS 55	-6.31652117	61.30826569
ECS 56	-6.31582165	61.32498932
ECS 57	-6.31540155	61.34172058
ECS 58	-6.31525993	61.35845566
ECS 59	-6.31539631	61.37519073
ECS 60	-6.31581163	61.39192200
ECS 61	-6.31650543	61.40864563
ECS 62	-6.31747723	61.42535400
ECS 63	-6.31872654	61.44204330

Coordinates ID	Latitude (decimal deg)	Longitude (decimal deg)
ECS 64	-6.32025385	61.45871353
ECS 65	-6.32205820	61.47535324
ECS 66	-6.32413960	61.49196243
ECS 67	-6.32649660	61.50853348
ECS 68	-6.32912970	61.52506638
ECS 69	-6.33203697	61.54154968
ECS 70	-6.33521795	61.55797958
ECS 71	-6.33867264	61.57435989
ECS 72	-6.34240007	61.59067917
ECS 73	-6.34639788	61.60693741
ECS 74	-6.35066462	61.62312317
ECS 75	-6.35520077	61.63923264
ECS 76	-6.36000395	61.65526581
ECS 77	-6.36507416	61.67122269
ECS 78	-6.37040901	61.68709183
ECS 79	-6.37600660	61.70286560
ECS 80	-6.38186646	61.71854782
ECS 81	-6.38798571	61.73412704
ECS 82	-6.39436436	61.74960709
ECS 83	-6.40099859	61.76497269
ECS 84	-6.40788794	61.78023148
ECS 85	-6.41503096	61.79537201
ECS 86	-6.42242527	61.81039810
ECS 87	-6.43006754	61.82529068
ECS 88	-6.43795681	61.84006119
ECS 89	-6.44609165	61.85469437
ECS 90	-6.45446777	61.86919403
ECS 91	-6.46308422	61.88354874
ECS 92	-6.47193909	61.89775848
ECS 93	-6.48102808	61.91181564
ECS 94	-6.49035025	61.92572784
ECS 95	-6.49990320	61.93947983
ECS 96	-6.50968266	61.95307159
ECS 97	-6.51968861	61.96650314

Coordinates ID	Latitude (decimal deg)	Longitude (decimal deg)
ECS 98	-6.52991676	61.97976303
ECS 99	-6.54036427	61.99285126
ECS 100	-6.55102587	62.00576401
ECS 101	-6.56190205	62.01849747
ECS 102	-6.57298803	62.03104782
ECS 103	-6.58428144	62.04341125
ECS 104	-6.59578037	62.05558777
ECS 105	-6.60747910	62.06757355
ECS 106	-6.64228535	62.14421082
ECS 107	-6.64349413	62.14431381
ECS 108	-6.66018200	62.14571762
ECS 109	-6.67687464	62.14706802
ECS 110	-6.69357014	62.14837265
ECS 111	-6.71026993	62.14962769
ECS 112	-6.72697210	62.15083694
ECS 113	-6.74367857	62.15199661
ECS 114	-6.76038790	62.15311050
ECS 115	-6.77710056	62.15417862
ECS 116	-6.79381609	62.15519714
ECS 117	-6.81053400	62.15616989
ECS 118	-6.82725477	62.15709305
ECS 119	-6.84397793	62.15797043
ECS 120	-6.86070395	62.15879440
ECS 121	-6.87743282	62.15957642
ECS 122	-6.89416313	62.16030884
ECS 123	-6.90895700	62.16091537
ECS 124	-6.91269541	62.17265320
ECS 125	-6.91794109	62.18856430
ECS 126	-6.92334414	62.20442963
ECS 127	-6.92890596	62.22024155
ECS 128	-6.93462420	62.23598862
ECS 129	-6.94049788	62.25168228
ECS 130	-6.94652843	62.26731491
ECS 131	-6.95271444	62.28289032

Coordinates ID	Latitude (decimal deg)	Longitude (decimal deg)
ECS 132	-6.95905590	62.29840469
ECS 133	-6.96554995	62.31385040
ECS 134	-6.97219896	62.32923508
ECS 135	-6.97900009	62.34455109
ECS 136	-6.98595285	62.35979462
ECS 137	-6.99305725	62.37496948
ECS 138	-7.00031376	62.39007950
ECS 139	-7.00771809	62.40510941
ECS 140	-7.01527262	62.42007065
ECS 141	-7.02297592	62.43495178
ECS 142	-7.03082609	62.44975662
ECS 143	-7.03882408	62.46448517
ECS 144	-7.04696798	62.47912598
ECS 145	-7.05525827	62.49369049
ECS 146	-7.06369352	62.50817871
ECS 147	-7.07227278	62.52257156
ECS 148	-7.08099365	62.53688812
ECS 149	-7.08985615	62.55110931
ECS 150	-7.09886122	62.56524277
ECS 151	-7.10800505	62.57928848
ECS 152	-7.11728811	62.59323883
ECS 153	-7.12671137	62.60710144
ECS 154	-7.13627148	62.62086487
ECS 155	-7.14596748	62.63453293
ECS 156	-7.15579844	62.64810181
ECS 157	-7.16576481	62.66157913
ECS 158	-7.17586517	62.67495346
ECS 159	-7.18609715	62.68822861
ECS 160	-7.19646263	62.70139694
ECS 161	-7.20695877	62.71446228
ECS 162	-7.21758318	62.72742462
ECS 163	-7.22833681	62.74028015
ECS 164	-7.23921728	62.75302505
ECS 165	-7.25022507	62.76566696

Coordinates ID	Latitude (decimal deg)	Longitude (decimal deg)
ECS 166	-7.26135778	62.77819824
ECS 167	-7.27261400	62.79061127
ECS 168	-7.28399372	62.80291367
ECS 169	-7.29549551	62.81510544
ECS 170	-7.30711746	62.82718277
ECS 171	-7.31886101	62.83914566
ECS 172	-7.33071995	62.85098267
ECS 173	-7.34269810	62.86270523
ECS 174	-7.35479164	62.87430954
ECS 175	-7.36700201	62.88578796
ECS 176	-7.37932396	62.89714813
ECS 177	-7.39175987	62.90838623
ECS 178	-7.40430641	62.91949844
ECS 179	-7.41696167	62.93048477
ECS 180	-7.42972660	62.94134140
ECS 181	-7.44259834	62.95207214
ECS 182	-7.45557690	62.96267700
ECS 183	-7.46866083	62.97314835
ECS 184	-7.48184776	62.98348999
ECS 185	-7.49513769	62.99370193
ECS 186	-7.50852728	63.00377655
ECS 187	-7.91089344	63.30073547
ECS 188	-8.63939953	63.99520874
ECS 189	-8.64674473	64.00283813
ECS 190	-8.65851116	64.01480865
ECS 191	-8.67039585	64.02666473
ECS 192	-8.68239594	64.03840637
ECS 193	-8.69451237	64.05001831
ECS 194	-8.70674229	64.06151581
ECS 195	-8.71908665	64.07288361
ECS 196	-8.73154259	64.08412933
ECS 197	-8.74411106	64.09525299
ECS 198	-8.75678825	64.10624695
ECS 199	-8.76957417	64.11711884

Coordinates ID	Latitude (decimal deg)	Longitude (decimal deg)
ECS 200	-8.78246784	64.12786102
ECS 201	-8.79546642	64.13847351
ECS 202	-8.80856991	64.14895630
ECS 203	-8.82177639	64.15930176
ECS 204	-8.83508396	64.16952515
ECS 205	-8.84849358	64.17960358
ECS 206	-8.86200142	64.18955231
ECS 207	-8.87560654	64.19937134
ECS 208	-8.88930893	64.20904541
ECS 209	-8.90310764	64.21858215
ECS 210	-8.91699982	64.22798157
ECS 211	-8.93098354	64.23724365
ECS 212	-8.94505882	64.24636841
ECS 213	-8.95922375	64.25534821
ECS 214	-8.97347832	64.26418304
ECS 215	-8.98781776	64.27288055
ECS 216	-9.00224400	64.28143311
ECS 217	-9.01675510	64.28984070
ECS 218	-9.03134918	64.29809570
ECS 219	-9.04602337	64.30621338
ECS 220	-9.06077766	64.31417847
ECS 221	-9.72202778	64.66599274
ECS 222	-9.73690510	64.67373657
ECS 223	-9.75185776	64.68132782
ECS 224	-9.76688576	64.68877411
ECS 225	-9.78198719	64.69606781
ECS 226	-9.79715919	64.70320892
ECS 227	-9.81239986	64.71019745
ECS 228	-9.82771015	64.71703339
ECS 229	-9.84308815	64.72371674
ECS 230	-9.85853100	64.73023987
ECS 231	-9.87403774	64.73661041
ECS 232	-9.88960648	64.74282837
ECS 233	-9.90523720	64.74888611

6070 *Report Number 6-22 (2)*

Coordinates ID	Latitude (decimal deg)	Longitude (decimal deg)
ECS 234	-9.92092419	64.75479126
ECS 235	-9.93666935	64.76053619
ECS 236	-9.95247269	64.76611328
ECS 237	-9.96832848	64.77153778
ECS 238	-9.98423862	64.77680206
ECS 239	-10.00019836	64.78191376
ECS 240	-10.0162096	64.78685760
ECS 241	-10.03226757	64.79164124
ECS 242	-10.04837227	64.79626465
ECS 243	-10.06452084	64.80072021
ECS 244	-10.08071423	64.80502319
ECS 245	-10.09694862	64.80915070
ECS 246	-10.11322403	64.81312561
ECS 247	-10.12953854	64.81693268
ECS 248	-10.14588833	64.82057953
ECS 249	-10.16227436	64.82405090
ECS 250	-10.17869282	64.82736206
ECS 251	-10.19514370	64.83051300
ECS 252	-10.21162510	64.83348846
ECS 253	-10.22813511	64.83630371
ECS 254	-10.24467182	64.83895874
ECS 255	-10.26123428	64.84143829
ECS 256	-10.27782059	64.84375000
ECS 257	-10.29442883	64.84589386
ECS 258	-10.31105804	64.84787750
ECS 259	-10.32770443	64.84968567
ECS 260	-10.34436989	64.85132599
ECS 261	-10.36104870	64.85280609
ECS 262	-10.37774277	64.85411072
ECS 263	-10.39444828	64.85524750
ECS 264	-10.41116428	64.85622406
ECS 265	-10.42788887	64.85702515
ECS 266	-10.44462109	64.85765076
ECS 267	-10.46135712	64.85812378

Coordinates ID	Latitude (decimal deg)	Longitude (decimal deg)
ECS 268	-10.47809792	64.85841370
ECS 269	-10.49031353	64.85850525
ECS 270	-10.49157715	64.85778809
ECS 271	-10.50604057	64.84926605
ECS 272	-10.52036285	64.84049225
ECS 273	-10.53453636	64.83148956
ECS 274	-10.54855919	64.82224274
ECS 275	-10.56242657	64.81275940
ECS 276	-11.53587055	64.56176758
ECS 277	-11.54926395	64.56311798
ECS 278	-11.56594849	64.56450653
ECS 279	-11.58265495	64.56561279
ECS 280	-11.59937763	64.56644440
ECS 281	-11.61611176	64.56698608
ECS 282	-11.63285160	64.56725311
ECS 283	-11.64959335	64.56723022
ECS 284	-11.66633320	64.56692505
ECS 285	-11.68306541	64.56633759
ECS 286	-11.69978523	64.56546783
ECS 287	-11.71648884	64.56431580
ECS 288	-11.73317146	64.56288147
ECS 289	-11.74982834	64.56115723
ECS 290	-11.76645279	64.55915833
ECS 291	-11.78304386	64.55688477
ECS 292	-11.79959488	64.55432129
ECS 293	-11.81610012	64.55148315
ECS 294	-11.83255959	64.54836273
ECS 295	-11.84896374	64.54496002
ECS 296	-11.85276985	64.54411316
ECS 297	-11.86732674	64.53952789
ECS 298	-11.88326836	64.53433990
ECS 299	-11.89915848	64.52898407
ECS 300	-11.91499519	64.52346039
ECS 301	-11.93077564	64.51778412

Coordinates ID	Latitude (decimal deg)	Longitude (decimal deg)
ECS 302	-11.94649982	64.51194763
ECS 303	-11.96216488	64.50595093
ECS 304	-11.97776890	64.49979401
ECS 305	-11.99331379	64.49347687
ECS 306	-12.00879383	64.48699951
ECS 307	-12.02420902	64.48036957
ECS 308	-12.03956032	64.47357941
ECS 309	-12.05484200	64.46662903
ECS 310	-12.07005405	64.45952606
ECS 311	-12.08519459	64.45227814
ECS 312	-12.10026455	64.44486237
ECS 313	-12.11526108	64.43729401
ECS 314	-12.13018131	64.42958069
ECS 315	-12.14502525	64.42170715
ECS 316	-12.15979004	64.41368866
ECS 317	-12.17447376	64.40551758
ECS 318	-12.18907642	64.39720154
ECS 319	-12.20359898	64.38872528
ECS 320	-12.21803570	64.38011169
ECS 321	-12.22765923	64.37423706
ECS 322	-12.22867489	64.37349701
ECS 323	-12.24215317	64.36339569
ECS 324	-12.25546074	64.35307312
ECS 325	-12.26859665	64.34251404
ECS 326	-12.28155994	64.33174133
ECS 327	-12.29434299	64.32074738
ECS 328	-12.30694199	64.30953217
ECS 329	-12.31935501	64.29811096
ECS 330	-12.33158112	64.28647614
ECS 331	-12.34361267	64.27463531
ECS 332	-12.35544777	64.26259613
ECS 333	-12.36708546	64.25035095
ECS 334	-12.37851810	64.23790741
ECS 335	-12.38974571	64.22527313
ECS 336	-12.40076351	64.21245575

Mauritius – Seychelles 6073

Coordinates ID	Latitude (decimal deg)	Longitude (decimal deg)
ECS 337	-12.41156864	64.19944763
ECS 338	-12.42216015	64.18625641
ECS 339	-12.43253326	64.17288208
ECS 340	-12.44268513	64.15933228
ECS 341	-12.45261288	64.14561462
ECS 342	-12.46231174	64.13173676
ECS 343	-12.47178364	64.11769104
ECS 344	-12.48102188	64.10347748
ECS 345	-12.49002647	64.08911133
ECS 346	-12.49879360	64.07460022
ECS 347	-12.50732136	64.05993652
ECS 348	-12.51560688	64.04513550
ECS 349	-12.52364826	64.03018188
ECS 350	-12.53144264	64.01510620
ECS 351	-12.53898716	63.99989319
ECS 352	-12.54628086	63.98455811
ECS 353	-12.55332184	63.96909332
ECS 354	-12.56010818	63.95351791
ECS 355	-12.56663799	63.93782425
ECS 356	-12.57290745	63.92202377
ECS 357	-12.57891941	63.90611267
ECS 358	-12.58466625	63.89011002
ECS 359	-12.59015179	63.87400436
ECS 360	-12.59537029	63.85780716
ECS 361	-12.60032272	63.84152603
ECS 362	-12.60500622	63.82516098
ECS 363	-13.46895790	63.30273819
ECS 364	-13.48847485	63.30590820
ECS 365	-13.50505543	63.30826950
ECS 366	-13.52167130	63.31034470
ECS 367	-13.53831768	63.31214142
ECS 368	-13.55499172	63.31365204
ECS 369	-13.57168865	63.31488419
ECS 370	-13.58840275	63.31582642
ECS 371	-13.60513020	63.31648254

Coordinates ID	Latitude (decimal deg)	Longitude (decimal deg)
ECS 372	-13.62186623	63.31686020
ECS 373	-13.63860512	63.31694412
ECS 374	-13.65534401	63.31674576
ECS 375	-13.67207718	63.31626511
ECS 376	-13.68880081	63.31549835
ECS 377	-13.70550919	63.31444550
ECS 378	-13.72219753	63.31311035
ECS 379	-13.73886299	63.31148529
ECS 380	-13.75549793	63.30958176
ECS 381	-13.77209949	63.30739594
ECS 382	-13.78866482	63.30492020
ECS 383	-13.80518627	63.30216599
ECS 384	-13.82166004	63.29912949
ECS 385	-13.83808231	63.29581070
ECS 386	-13.85444927	63.29221344
ECS 387	-13.87075520	63.28833771
ECS 388	-13.88699532	63.28418350
ECS 389	-13.90316677	63.27975082
ECS 390	-13.91926098	63.27504349
ECS 391	-13.93527794	63.27006149
ECS 392	-13.95121098	63.26480484
ECS 393	-13.96705627	63.25927734
ECS 394	-13.98280811	63.25347900
ECS 395	-13.99846554	63.24740982
ECS 396	-15.00259304	63.22919846
ECS 397	-15.01154613	63.23255157
ECS 398	-15.02736378	63.23817825
ECS 399	-15.04327106	63.24353790
ECS 400	-15.05926418	63.24862289
ECS 401	-15.07533455	63.25342941
ECS 402	-15.09148216	63.25796509
ECS 403	-15.10770130	63.26222229
ECS 404	-15.12398624	63.26620483
ECS 405	-15.14033318	63.26990509
ECS 406	-15.15673828	63.27332306

Coordinates ID	Latitude (decimal deg)	Longitude (decimal deg)
ECS 407	-15.17319489	63.27646255
ECS 408	-15.18970108	63.27931213
ECS 409	-15.20625210	63.28188705
ECS 410	-15.22284031	63.28417969
ECS 411	-15.23946476	63.28618240
ECS 412	-15.25611877	63.28790283
ECS 413	-15.27279758	63.28933334
ECS 414	-15.28949738	63.29048157
ECS 415	-15.30621433	63.29133606
ECS 416	-15.32294273	63.29191208
ECS 417	-15.33967781	63.29219437
ECS 418	-15.35641479	63.29219437
ECS 419	-15.37314892	63.29190826
ECS 420	-15.38987637	63.29132843
ECS 421	-15.40659332	63.29046631
ECS 422	-15.42329121	63.28931046
ECS 423	-15.43997192	63.28787613
ECS 424	-15.45662403	63.28615189
ECS 425	-15.47324753	63.28414154
ECS 426	-15.48983574	63.28184128
ECS 427	-15.50638485	63.27925873
ECS 428	-15.52288914	63.27639389
ECS 429	-15.53934574	63.27324677
ECS 430	-15.55574894	63.26981354
ECS 431	-15.57209492	63.26609802
ECS 432	-15.58837700	63.26210403
ECS 433	-15.60459232	63.25782776
ECS 434	-15.62073612	63.25327301
ECS 435	-15.63680649	63.24843979
ECS 436	-15.65279388	63.24332809
ECS 437	-15.66869640	63.23794174
ECS 438	-15.68451118	63.23228836
ECS 439	-15.70023251	63.22635269
ECS 440	-15.71585274	63.22015381
ECS 441	-15.73137283	63.21368790

Coordinates ID	Latitude (decimal deg)	Longitude (decimal deg)
ECS 442	-15.74678612	63.20695114
ECS 443	-15.76208591	63.19994736
ECS 444	-15.77727318	63.19268036
ECS 445	-15.79233932	63.18515778
ECS 446	-15.80728149	63.17736816
ECS 447	-15.82209682	63.16932678
ECS 448	-15.83677864	63.16102982
ECS 449	-15.85132599	63.15247726
ECS 450	-15.86573219	63.14367294
ECS 451	-15.87999344	63.13462830
ECS 452	-15.89410686	63.12532806
ECS 453	-15.89661980	63.12361526
34	-15.79002778	63.10013889
35	-15.59972222	63.04955556
36	-15.22291667	62.91305556
37	-14.99580556	62.80525000
38	-14.37400000	62.46211111
39	-13.48758333	61.56097222
40	-12.98025000	60.39572222
41	-12.93102778	59.04275000
42	-12.93450000	59.02105556
43	-11.61919444	59.89227778
44	-11.40336111	59.96177778
45	-10.48425000	60.08894444
46	-10.02905556	60.05661111
47	-9.41155556	59.90933333
48	-9.26716667	59.85652778
MS1	-8.43648564	59.38658331
EZ1	-7.95331969	59.54675947
EZ2	-7.47748800	59.63139861
EZ3	-6.74310167	59.62970689
EZ4	-6.42679378	59.57978517
EZ5	-5.41164578	59.19109953

ANNEX 2

Area of the Mauritius – Seychelles Joint Zone

[Map not included]

6078 *Report Number 6-22 (2)*

Treaty Concerning the Joint Management of the Continental Shelf in the Mascarene Plateau Region

THE GOVERNMENT OF THE REPUBLIC OF MAURITIUS
and
THE GOVERNMENT OF THE REPUBLIC OF SEYCHELLES
("the Contracting Parties")

SEEKING to promote the sustainable and long-term economic and social development of their respective small island countries for the benefit of present and future generations;

COMMITTED to maintaining, renewing and further strengthening the mutual respect, goodwill, friendship and co-operation between their two countries;

ACKNOWLEDGING the existence of an overlapping area of continental shelf extending beyond the Exclusive Economic Zone boundaries established by their two countries under the *Treaty between the Government of the Republic Mauritius and the Government of the Republic of Seychelles on the Delimitation of the Exclusive Economic Zone between the two States* dated 29 July 2008;

RECALLING that both countries co-operated on the basis of the *Treaty between the Government of the Republic of Seychelles and the Government of the Republic of Mauritius on the Framework for a Joint Submission to the United Nations Commission on the Limits of the Continental Shelf* dated 18 September 2008, as subsequently amended, to lodge on 1 December 2008 the Joint Submission to the United Nations Commission on the Limits of the Continental Shelf ("the Commission") concerning the Mascarene Plateau region ("Joint Submission") under Article 76, paragraph 8 of the United Nations Convention on the Law of the Sea done at Montego Bay on 10 December 1982 ("the Convention");

RECALLING ALSO on 30 March 2011, the Commission adopted recommendations confirming the entitlement of their two countries to the area of continental shelf as contained in the Commission document entitled

Recommendations of the Commission on the Limits of the Continental Shelf in regard to the Joint Submission made by Mauritius and Seychelles in respect of the Mascarene Plateau Region on 1 December 2008;

CONSCIOUS that the Convention provides in Article 83 that the delimitation of the continental shelf between States with opposite coasts shall be effected by agreement on the basis of international law in order to achieve an equitable solution and, in the absence of delimitation, that States shall make every effort in a spirit of understanding and co-operation to enter into provisional arrangements of a practical nature which do not prejudice a final determination of the extended continental shelf delimitation;

RECOGNISING the importance of providing an equitable and co-operative legal basis for the exercise by their two countries of their sovereign rights and jurisdiction over the continental shelf in the Mascarene Plateau Region in accordance with international law;

REAFFIRMING the *Treaty Concerning the Joint Exercise of Sovereign Rights over the Continental Shelf in the Mascarene Plateau Region* of 13 March 2012, under which the Contracting Parties established the outer limits of the continental shelf in the Mascarene Plateau Region and agreed to exercise sovereign rights jointly for the purpose of exploring the continental Shelf and exploiting its natural resources;

MINDFUL of the importance of jointly managing the natural resources of the continental shelf in Mascarene Plateau Region in a manner that is sustainable and consistent with the precautionary principle and the protection of the marine environment and the biological diversity of the continental shelf;

DESIRING to enter into an international agreement to provide an effective and equitable framework to govern the joint management of the continental shelf in the Mascarene Plateau Region;

HAVE AGREED as follows:

PART 1: PRELIMINARY

Article 1: Definitions

For the purposes of this Treaty:

(a)   "Authority" means the Designated Authority established in Article 4 of this Treaty;

(b)   "bioprospecting" means the examination of biological resources for features including but not limited to chemical compounds, genes and their products and physical properties that may be of value for commercial development;

(c)   "Commission" means the Joint Commission established under Article 4 of this Treaty;

(d)   "continental shelf" has the meaning contained in Article 76 of the Convention;

(e)   "contractor" means a corporation, company or other legal entity or entities with limited liability that enter into a contract with the Designated Authority and which are duly regulated;

(f)   "Convention" means the United Nations Convention on the Law of the Sea done at Montego Bay on 10 December 1982;

(g)   "criminal law" means any law in force in the territory of either of the Contracting Parties, whether substantive or procedural, that makes provision for, or in relation to offences, or for or In relation to the investigation or prosecution of offences or the punishment of offenders, including the carrying out of a penalty imposed by a court. For this purpose, "investigation" includes entry to an installation or structure in the JMA, the exercise of powers of search and questioning and the apprehension of a suspected offender;

(h)   "Council" means the Ministerial Council established in Article 4 of this Treaty;

(i)   "initially processed" means processing of petroleum to a point where it is ready for off-take from the production facility and may include such processes as the removal of water, volatiles and other impurities;

(j)   "JMA" means the Joint Management Area established in Article 3 of this Treaty;

(k)   "minerals" means any naturally occurring element, compound or substance, amorphous or crystalline (including liquid crystalline compounds), formed through geological or biogeochemical processes and any naturally occurring mixture of substances, including in the form of coal, clay, evaporates, gravel, limestone, oil-shale, sand, shale, rock, and polymetallic nodules;

(l)   "natural resources" means the mineral, petroleum and other non-living resources of the seabed and subsoil of the continental shelf together with living organisms belonging to sedentary species that are at the harvestable stage either immobile on or under the seabed or are unable to move except in constant physical contact with the seabed or subsoil;

(m)   "natural resource activities" means all activities authorised or contemplated under a contract, permit or license that are undertaken to explore and exploit natural resources in the JMA including but not limited to development, initial processing, harvesting, production, transportation and marketing, as well as the planning and preparation for such activities;

(n)   "natural resource codes" means codes referred to in Article 8 of this Treaty;

(o)   "natural resource project" means any natural resource activity taking place with the approval of the Designated Authority in a specified area of the JMA;

(p)   "petroleum" means any naturally occurring hydrocarbon, whether in a gaseous, liquid, or solid state and any naturally occurring mixture of hydrocarbons, whether in a gaseous, liquid or solid state, together with other substances produced in association with such hydrocarbons, and includes any petroleum that has been returned to a reservoir;

(q)   "petroleum produced" means initially processed petroleum extracted from a reservoir through petroleum activities;

(r)   "reservoir" means an accumulation of petroleum in a geological unit limited by rock, water or other substances without pressure communication through liquid or gas to another accumulation of petroleum;

(s)   "Taxation Code" means the Code referred to in Article 6 of this Treaty;

(t)   "Treaty" means this Treaty, including Annexes A-D and any Annex that may subsequently be agreed by the Contracting Parties to form a part of this Treaty.

Article 2: Treaty without Prejudice

(a)   This Treaty gives effect to international law as reflected in the Convention which under Article 83 requires States with opposite or adjacent coasts to make every effort to enter into provisional arrangements of a practical nature pending agreement on the final delimitation of the continental shelf between them in a manner consistent with international law. This Treaty is intended to adhere to such obligation.

(b)   Nothing contained in this Treaty, and no act taking place while this Treaty is in force, shall be interpreted as prejudicing or affecting the legal position or rights of the Contracting Parties concerning their respective continental shelf entitlements or the delimitation of the continental shelf.

PART 2: THE JOINT MANAGEMENT AREA

Article 3: Joint Management Area

(a)   The Joint Management Area (JMA) is established in respect of the Joint Zone described in Article 2 of the Treaty Concerning the Joint Exercise of Sovereign Rights over the Continental Shelf in the

Mascarene Plateau Region, done on 13 March 2012 and as depicted in the map at Annex A.

(b) The Contracting Parties shall jointly control, manage and facilitate the exploration of the continental shelf within the JMA and the conservation, development and exploitation of its natural resources.

(c) Natural resource activities in the JMA shall be carried out under the direction of the Designated Authority, by such means as it may determine in accordance with this Treaty, including where appropriate through the issue of licences or pursuant to contracts between the Authority and a contractor. This provision shall also apply to the successors or assignees of such contractors.

(d) The Contracting Parties shall each make it an offence under their respective national laws for any person to conduct resource activities in the JMA otherwise than in accordance with this Treaty.

PART 3: INSTITUTIONAL AND REGULATORY ARRANGEMENTS

Article 4: Regulatory Bodies

(a) A three-tiered joint administrative structure consisting of a Ministerial Council, a Joint Commission and a Designated Authority, is established.

(b) Ministerial Council

    i.   A Ministerial Council for the JMA is hereby established. The Ministerial Council shall consistent of an equal number of Ministers designated by the Contracting Parties.

    ii.   The Ministerial Council shall consider any matter relating to the operation of this Treaty that is referred to it by either of the Contracting Parties. It shall also consider any matter referred to under sub-paragraph (c)(iii).

iii. The Ministerial Council shall meet at the request of either Contracting Party or at the request of the Commission.

iv. All decisions of the Ministerial Council shall be adopted by consensus. In the event the Council is unable to resolve a matter, either of the Contracting Parties may invoke the dispute resolution procedure provided under Article 21.

v. No decision of the Ministerial Council shall be valid unless it is recorded in writing and signed by at least one member from each Contracting Party.

vi. The Ministerial Council shall establish its own procedures, including those in relation to taking decisions out of session and for conducting meetings by means of telephonic and electronic communication.

(c) Joint Commission:

i. The Joint Commission shall consist of an equal number of commissioners appointed by the Contracting Parties. The Joint Commission shall establish policies and regulations relating to petroleum and other natural resource activities in the JMA and shall oversee the work of the Authority.

ii. A non-exhaustive list of more detailed powers and functions of the Joint Commission is set out in Annex C. This list may be amended from time to time as necessary.

iii. The Joint Commission may at any time refer to a matter to the Ministerial Council for resolution.

iv. The Joint Commission shall meet at least once a year in the Contracting Parties on an alternate basis, or otherwise as agreed, and each meeting shall be co-chaired.

v. Decisions of the Joint Commission shall be made by consensus.

(d)   Designated Authority:

    i.   the Joint Commission shall establish the Designated Authority ("Authority").

    ii.   The Authority shall have juridical personality and such legal capacities under the law of the Contracting Parties as are necessary for the exercise of its powers and the performance of its functions. It shall have the capacity to contract, to acquire and dispose of movable and immovable property and to institute and be party to legal proceedings.

    iii.   The Authority shall be responsible to the Joint Commission and shall carry on the day-to-day regulation and management of natural resource activities in the JMA.

    iv.   A non-exhaustive list of more detailed powers and functions of the Authority is contained in Annex D. The Annexes to this Treaty may identify other additional powers and functions of the Authority. The Authority also has such other powers and functions as may be conferred upon it by the Commission.

    v.   The Authority shall be financed on an equal basis by the Contracting Parties, including eventually through the remittance of fees collected under natural resource codes.

    vi.   The Authority shall be exempt from:

        (1)   income tax or business tax, as the case may be; and

        (2)   customs duties, excise tax, Value Added Tax (VAT), levy and other similar taxes on imports for official use, imposed under the law in force in the territory of each of the Contracting Parties, as well as any identical or substantially similar taxes that are imposed after the date of signature of this Treaty in addition to, or in place of, the existing taxes.

vii. Personnel of the Authority:

(1) shall be subject to taxation in the Contracting Party of which they are a national and in accordance with the tax law of that Contracting Party in respect of salaries, allowances and other payments made to them by the Authority in connection with their employment with the Authority. For the purposes of this paragraph the term "national" includes a resident of either Contracting Party as defined in the income tax law of that Contracting Party; and

(2) shall, at the time of the first taking up the post with the Authority located in either of the Contracting Parties in which they are not resident, be exempt from customs duties, excise tax, VAT, levy and other similar taxes and other such charges (except payments for services) in respect of imports of furniture and other household and personal effects including one motor vehicle in their ownership or possession or already ordered by them and intended for their personal use or for their establishment, subject to terms and conditions established by the Joint Commission. Such goods shall be imported within six months of an officer's first entry but in exceptional circumstances an extension of time shall be granted by the Contracting Parties respectively. Goods that have been acquired or imported by officers and to which exemptions under this sub-paragraph apply shall not be given away, sold, lent or hired out, or otherwise disposed of except under conditions agreed in advance depending on in which country the officer is located.

(e) No member of the Ministerial Council, Joint Commission and personnel of the Authority shall have any financial or personal interest in any natural resource project in the JMA.

Article 5: Sharing of Revenue

(a) The Contracting Parties shall share revenue received in respect of natural resource activities carried out in the JMA equally, whereby fifty (50) *per cent* of revenue received shall be remitted to Mauritius and fifty (50) *per cent* of revenue received shall be remitted to Seychelles.

(b) To the extent that fees referred to in Article 4(d)(v) and other income are adequate to cover the expenditure of the Authority in relation to this Treaty, that expenditure shall be borne by each of the Contracting Parties in the same proportion as set out in paragraph (a).

(c) Paragraph (a) shall not apply to the equitable sharing of the benefits arising from unitization under Article 10 unless mutually agreed by the Contracting Parties.

Article 6: Taxation Code

(a) The Contracting Parties shall agree upon a Taxation Code applicable to income derived from natural resource activities in the JMA.

(b) Neither Contracting Party may during the life of a natural resource project vary any of the provisions of the Taxation Code applicable to it except by mutual agreement.

Article 7: Application of Domestic Law

For the purposes of the application of the domestic laws of each Contracting Party related directly or indirectly to:

i. the exploration of the continental shelf within the JMA and the development and exploitation of natural resources in the JMA; and

ii. acts, matters, circumstances and things touching, concerning, arising out of or connected with, natural resource activities in the JMA,

the JMA shall be deemed to be and treated by each Contracting Party as forming part of its respective territory.

Article 8: Natural Resource Codes

(a) The Contracting Parties may agree upon natural resource codes concerning the exploration of the continental shelf within the JMA and the development, exploitation, harvesting, conservation and export of natural resources from the JMA.

(b) The Commission shall, where necessary, adopt interim arrangements to be applied pending the adoption of natural resource codes in accordance with paragraph (a).

PART 4: PIPELINES AND UNITISATION

Article 9: Pipelines

(a) The construction and operation of a pipeline within the JMA for the purposes of exporting petroleum from the JMA shall be subject to the approval of the Commission.

(b) The Contracting Parties shall consult each other on the terms and conditions for laying of pipelines exporting petroleum from the JMA to the point of landing.

(c) A pipeline landing in the territory of a Contracting party shall be under the jurisdiction of the country of landing.

(d) In the event of a pipeline is constructed from the JMA to the territory of either of the Contracting Parties, the country where the pipeline lands may not object to or impede decisions of the Commission regarding that pipeline except where the construction of a pipeline would have an adverse economic or physical impact upon an existing natural resource project in the JMA.

(e) Petroleum from the JMA and from fields which straddle the boundaries of the JMA shall at all times have priority of carriage along any pipeline carrying petroleum from and within the JMA.

(f) There shall be open access to pipelines for petroleum from the JMA. The open access arrangements shall be in accordance with good international regulatory practice. If one Contracting Party has jurisdiction over the pipeline, it shall consult with the other Contracting Party over access to the pipeline.

Article 10: Unitisation

(a) Any reservoir of petroleum or unitary mineral deposit that extends across or straddles the boundary of the JMA into the Exclusive Economic Zone of either or both Contracting Parties shall be treated as a single entity for exploration, development and management purposes.

(b) The Contracting Parties shall work expeditiously and in good faith to reach agreement on the manner in which the petroleum field or mineral deposit referred to in paragraph (a) will be most effectively managed and developed and on the equitable sharing of revenue arising from such development.

Article 11: Surveys

Each of the Contracting Parties has a right to conduct surveys including hydrographic, geological, geophysical and seismic surveys to facilitate natural resource activities in the JMA. In the exercise of such right, the Contracting Parties shall:

i.   notify the Authority of any proposed survey;

ii.   cooperate on the conduct of such surveys, including the provision of necessary onshore facilities; and

iii. exchange information relevant to natural resource activities in the JMA.

PART 5: PROTECTION OF THE ENVIRONMENT, BIODIVERSITY AND BIOPROSPECTING

Article 12: Protection of the Seabed Marine Environment

(a) The Contracting Parties shall co-operate to protect natural resources in the JMA so as to secure seabed biodiversity and prevent pollution and other risks of harm

(b) The Contracting Parties shall apply the precautionary principle in co-operating to conserve and protect the environment and biodiversity of the seabed in the JMA. This shall include measures concerning fishing activity in the waters superjacent to the seabed in the JMA where such activity is having a direct impact upon, or poses a significant risk to, the natural resource of the seabed and subsoil in the JMA.

(c) The Contracting Parties shall co-operate to protect seabed marine habitats and associated ecological communities of the seabed in the JMA. This shall include the identification of environmental benchmarks and the identification of seabed marine protected areas, having regard to the following

    i.   geographical distribution of seabed marine species and biological communities;

    ii.   the structure of these communities;

    iii.   their relationship with the physical and the chemical environment;

    iv.   the natural ecological and genetic variability; and

    v.   the nature and the effect of the anthropogenic influences including fishing and natural resource activities on these ecosystem components.

(d) Where pollution of the marine environment occurring in the JMA spreads beyond the JMA, the Contracting Parties shall co-operate in taking prompt and effective action to prevent, mitigate and eliminate such pollution in accordance with international best practices, standards and procedures.

(e) The Authority shall issue regulations to protect the living natural resources and seabed environment in the JMA. It shall establish a contingency plan for combating pollution from natural resource activities in the JMA.

(f) Contractors shall be liable for damage or expenses incurred as a result of pollution of the marine environment arising out of natural resource activities within the JMA in accordance with:

  i. their contract, licence or permit or other form of authority issued pursuant to this Treaty; and,

  ii. he law of jurisdiction of the Contracting Party in which the claim is brought.

Article 13: Biological Surveys and Bioprospecting

(a) Each of the Contracting Parties has the right to carry out biological surveys for the purposes of Article 12 of this Treaty and to engage in bioprospecting to identify and examine living natural resources that may be of value for commercial development in the JMA or of conservation significance.

(b) The Contracting Parties shall:

  i.   notify the Authority of any proposed survey;

  ii. co-operate in the conduct of such biological surveys and bioprospecting, including the provision of necessary on-shore facilities; and

  iii. exchange information relevant to biological surveys and bioprospecting in the JMA.

PART 6: EMPLOYMENT, HEALTH AND SAFETY AND APPLICATION OF DOMESTIC LAWS

Article 14: Employment

The Contracting Parties shall take appropriate measures to ensure that preference is given in employment in the JMA to nationals of both Contracting Parties and to facilitate, as a matter of priority, training and employment opportunities for those nationals.

Article 15: Health and Safety for Workers

(a) The Authority shall develop, and contractors shall apply where required, occupational health and safety standards and procedures for persons employed on installations and structures in the JMA in accordance with internationally accepted standards and best practices.

(b) Similar occupational health, safety standards and procedures shall apply to all workers engaged in natural resource activities in the JMA

Article 16: Criminal Jurisdiction

(a) The Contracting Parties shall examine different options for addressing offences committed in the JMA. Pending the completion of such exercise, the provisions of this Article shall apply with respect to offences committed in the JMA.

(b) A national or resident of a Contracting Party shall be subject to the criminal law of the country of nationality or residence in respect of acts or omissions occurring in the JMA connected with or arising out of natural resource activities.

(c) Notwithstanding paragraph (e), a national of a third state, not being a resident of either Contracting Party, shall be subject to the criminal law of either Contracting Party in respect of acts or omissions occurring in the JMA connected with or arising out of natural resource activities. Such person shall not be subject to criminal proceedings under the law of either Contracting Party if he or she has already been tried and discharged or acquitted by a competent tribunal or already undergone punishment for the same act or omission under the law of the other country or where the competent authorities of one country, in accordance with its law, have decided in the public interest to refrain from prosecuting the person for that act or omission.

(d)   In cases referred to in paragraph (c), the Contracting Parties shall, as and when necessary, consult each other to determine which criminal law is to be applied, taking into account the nationality of the victim and the interests of the country most affected by the alleged offence.

(e)   The criminal law of the flag state shall apply in relation to acts or omissions on board vessels operating in the waters superjacent to the JMA.

(f)   The Contracting Parties shall provide assistance to and co-operate with each other, including through agreements or arrangements as appropriate, for the purposes of enforcement of criminal law under this Article, including the obtaining of evidence and information.

(g)   The Contracting Parties each recognise the interest of the other country where a victim of an alleged offence is a national of that other country and shall keep that other country informed, to the extent permitted by its law, of action being taken with regard to the alleged offence.

(h)   The Contracting Parties may make arrangements permitting officials of one country to assist in the enforcement of the criminal law of the other country. Where such assistance involves the detention of a person who under paragraph (b) is subject to the jurisdiction of the other country, that detention may only continue until it is practicable to hand the person other to the relevant officials of that other country.

Article 17: Customs, Migration and Quarantine

(a)   The Contracting Parties may, subject to paragraphs (c), (e), (f) and (g), apply customs, migration and quarantine laws in accordance with international accepted standards and best practices to persons, equipment and goods entering its territory from, or leaving its territory for, the JMA. The Contracting Parties may adopt arrangements to facilitate such entry and departure.

(b)   Contractors shall ensure, unless otherwise authorised by the Contracting Parties, that persons, equipment and goods do not enter structures in the JMA without first entering the Contracting Parties, and that their employees and the employees of their subcontractors are authorised by the Authority to enter the JMA.

(c)   Either Contracting Party may request consultations with the other Contracting party in relation to the entry of particular persons, equipment and goods to structures in the JMA aimed at controlling the movement of such persons, equipment and goods.

(d)   Nothing in this Article prejudices the right of either Contracting Party to apply customs, migration and quarantine controls to persons, equipment and goods entering the JMA without the authority of either Contracting Party. The Contracting Parties may adopt arrangements to coordinate the exercise of such rights.

(e)   Goods and equipment entering the JMA for purposes related to natural resource activities shall not be subject to customs duties, excise tax, VAT, levy and other similar taxes.

(f)   Goods and equipment leaving or in transit through the territory of the Contracting Parties for the purpose of entering the JMA for purposes related to natural resource activities shall not be subject to customs duties, excise tax, VAT, levy and other similar taxes.

(g)   Goods and equipment leaving the JMA for the purpose of being permanently transferred to a part of the territory of the Contracting Parties may be subject to customs duties, excise tax, VAT, levy and other similar tax of that Contracting Party.

Article 18: Safety, Operating Standards and Crewing of Resource Industry Vessels

(a) Except as otherwise provided in this Treaty, vessels of the nationality of a Contracting Party engaged in natural resource activities in the JMA shall be subject to the law of their nationality in relation to safety and operating standards and crewing regulations.

(b) Vessels flying the flag of States other than the Contracting Parties and which are engaged in natural resource activities in the JMA shall be subject to the relevant international safety and operating standards and crewing regulations.

PART 7: SURVEILLANCE, SECURITY AND RESCUE

Article 19: Surveillance and Security Measures

(a) For purposes of this Treaty, the Contracting Parties shall have the right to carry out surveillance activities in the JMA in relation to natural resource activities.

(b) The Contracting Parties shall co-operate on and co-ordinate any surveillance activities carried out in accordance with paragraph (a) and shall exchange information on likely threats to, or security incidents relating to, natural resource activities in the JMA.

(c) The Contracting Parties shall make arrangements for responding promptly and effectively to security incidents in the JMA.

Article 20: Search and Rescue

The Contracting Parties shall, at the request of the Authority and consistent with this Treaty, co-operate and assist in the conduct of search and rescue operations in the JMA, taking into account generally accepted international rules, regulations and procedures established through competent international organizations.

PART 8: SETTLEMENT OF DISPUTES, DURATION AND ENTRY INTO FORCE

Article 21: Settlement of Disputes

(a)   With the exception of disputes falling within the scope of the Taxation Code referred to in Article 6 of this Treaty and which shall be settled in accordance with that Code as agreed by the Contracting parties, any dispute concerning the interpretation or application of this Treaty shall, as far as possible, be settled amicably through mutual consultation.

(b)   Any dispute which is not settled in the manner set out in paragraph (a) and any unresolved matter relating to the operation of this Treaty under Article 4(b)(ii) shall, at the request of either of the Contracting Parties, be submitted to an Arbitral Tribunal established in accordance with the procedure set out in Annex B.

Article 22: Amendment

This Treaty may be amended at any time by written agreement between the Contracting Parties.

Article 23: Duration of the Treaty

(a)   This Treaty shall remain in force until a permanent delimitation of the continental shelf is agreed between the Contracting Parties or for thirty (30) years from the date of its entry into force, whichever is sooner.

(b)   This Treaty may be renewed by agreement between the Contracting Parties.

(c)   Natural resource projects commenced under this Treaty shall continue, notwithstanding that this Treaty is no longer in force, under conditions that are consistent with those that are provided for under this Treaty.

Article 24: Entry into Force

(a)   Each of the Contracting Parties shall notify the other, by means of exchange of diplomatic notes, the completion of the procedures required by its law for the bringing into force of this Treaty. The Treaty shall enter into force on the date of receipt of the later notification.

(b)   Upon entry into force, the Treaty shall be taken to have effect, and all of its provisions shall be taken to have applied, from the date of signature.

IN WITNESS WHEREOF the undersigned, being duly authorised thereto by their respective Governments, have signed this Treaty.

DONE at Clarisse House, Vacoas, Mauritius in duplicate on this 13th day of March Two Thousand and Twelve in the English Language.

<table>
<tr><td>For the Government of the
Republic of Mauritius</td><td>For the Government of the
Republic of Seychelles</td></tr>
<tr><td>Dr the Hon Navichandra
RAMGOOLAM GCSK, FRCP
Prime Minister</td><td>H.E. Mr. James Alix MICHEL
President</td></tr>
</table>

Annex A under Article 3 of this Treaty
Designation and Description of the JMA

The JMA referred to in Article 3 comprises the area of continental shelf set out in Article 2 of the Treaty Concerning the Joint Exercise of Sovereign Rights over the Continental Shelf in the Mascarene Plateau Region, done on 13 March 2012, as depicted in the map below –

[Map not included]

Annex B under Article 21 of this Treaty
Dispute Resolution Procedure

(a) An Arbitral Tribunal ("Tribunal") to which a dispute is submitted pursuant to Article 21 (b) shall consist of three persons appointed as follows:

    i. the Contracting Parties shall each appoint one arbitrator;

    ii. the arbitrators appointed by the Contracting Parties shall, within sixty (60) days of the appointment of the second of them, by agreement, select a third arbitrator who shall be a citizen, or permanent resident of a third country which has diplomatic relations with both the Contracting Parties; and

    iii. the Contracting Parties shall, within sixty (60) days of the selection of the third arbitrator, approve the selection of that arbitrator who shall act as Chairman of the Tribunal.

(b) Arbitration proceedings shall be instituted upon notice being given through the diplomatic channel by the Contracting Party instituting such proceedings to the other Contracting Party. Such notice shall contain:

    i. a statement setting forth in summary form the grounds of the claim;

    ii. the nature of the relief sought; and

    iii. the name of the arbitrator appointed by the Contracting Party instituting such proceedings.

Within sixty (60) days after the giving of such notice, the respondent Contracting Party shall notify the Contracting Party instituting proceedings of the name of the arbitrator appointed by the respondent Contracting Party.

(c) If, within the time limits provided for in sub-paragraphs (a) (ii) and (iii) and paragraph (b) of this Annex, the required appointment has not been made or the required approval has not been given, the Contracting Parties may request the President of the International Tribunal of the

Law of the Sea ("ITLOS") to make the necessary appointment. If the President is a citizen or permanent resident of the Contracting Parties or is otherwise unable to act, the Vice-President shall be invited to make the appointment. If the Vice-President is a citizen or permanent resident of the Contracting Parties or is otherwise unable to act, the Member of the ITLOS next in seniority who is not a citizen or permanent resident of the Contracting Parties shall be invited to make their appointment.

(d)   In case any arbitrator appointed as provided for in this Annex resigns or becomes unable to act, another arbitrator shall be appointed in the same manner as prescribed for the appointment of the original arbitrator and the new arbitrator shall have all the powers and duties of the original arbitrator.

(e)   The Tribunal shall convene at such time and place as shall be fixed by the Chairman of the Tribunal. Thereafter, the Tribunal shall determine where and when it shall sit.

(f)   The Tribunal shall decide all questions relating to its competence and shall, subject to any agreement between the Contracting Parties, determine its own procedures.

(g)   Before the Tribunal makes a decision, it may at any stage of the proceedings propose to the Contracting Parties that the dispute be settled amicably. The Arbitral Tribunal shall reach its award by majority vote, taking into account the provisions of this Treaty and relevant international law.

(h)   Each Contracting Party shall bear the costs incurred in relation to its appointed arbitrator and its own costs in preparing and presenting cases. The cost incurred in relation to the Chairman of the Tribunal and the expenses associated with the conduct of the arbitration shall be borne in equal parts by the Contracting Parties.

(i)   The Tribunal shall afford to the Contracting Parties a fair hearing. It may render an award on the default of either of the Contracting Parties. In any case, the Arbitral Tribunal shall render its award within six (6) months from the date it is convened by the Chairman of the Tribunal. Any award shall be rendered in writing and shall state its legal basis. A signed counterpart of the award shall be transmitted to the Contracting Parties.

(j)   An award of the Tribunal shall be final and binding on the Contracting Parties.

Annex C under Article 4(c)(ii) of this Treaty
Powers and Functions of the Joint Commission

1.   The powers and functions of the Joint Commission shall include:

(a)   establishing the Authority;

(b)   giving directions to the Authority on the exercise of its powers and performance of its functions;

(c)   conferring additional powers and functions to the Authority;

(d)   adopting taxation and natural resource codes applicable to the JMA including amendments and interim arrangement as necessary;

(e)   approving financial estimates of income and expenditure of the Authority;

(f)   approving rules, regulations and procedures for the effective functioning of the Authority;

(g)   calling for the auditing of the Authority's books and accounts;

(h)   considering and adopting the annual report of the Authority.

Annex D under Article 4(d)(iv) of this Treaty
Powers Functions of the Authority

The powers and functions of the Authority shall include:

(a) day-to-day management and regulation of natural resource activities in accordance with this Treaty and any instruments made or entered into under this Treaty, including directions given by the Joint Commission;

(b) preparation of annual estimates of income and expenditure of the Authority for submission to the Joint Commission. Any expenditure shall only be made in accordance with estimates approved by the Joint Commission or otherwise in accordance with regulations and procedures approved by the Joint Commission;

(c) preparation of annual reports for submission to the Joint Commission;

(d) requesting assistance from the appropriate authorities consistent with this Treaty;

    i. for search and rescue operations in the JMA;

    ii. in the event of piracy or terrorist threats to vessels and structures engaged in natural resource petroleum operations in the JMA;

(e) requesting assistance with pollution prevention measures, equipment and procedures from the appropriate authorities or other bodies or persons;

(f) establishment of safety zones and restrictied zones, consistent with international law, to ensure the safety of navigation connected with natural resource activities;

(g) controlling movements into, within and out of the JMA of vessels, aircraft, structures and other equipment engaged in natural resource activities in a manner consistent with international law; and, subject to Article 15, authorizing the entry of employees and contractors and their subcontractors and other persons into the JMA;

(h)   applying regulations and giving directions as approved by the Commission under this Treaty, on all matters related to the supervision and control of natural resource activities including on health, safety, environmental protection and assessments and work practices, pursuant to natural resource codes;

(i)   acting as a repository of all data and information pertaining to the JMA;

(j)   conducting inspections and audits concerning natural resource activities in the JMA; and

(k)   such other powers and functions as may be identified by the Contracting Parties or as may be conferred on it by the Joint Commission.

Mauritius – Maldives

Report Number 6-33

Dispute concerning delimitation of the maritime boundary between Mauritius and Maldives in the Indian Ocean (Mauritius/Maldives)

Decision:	Judgment of the Special Chamber of the International Tribunal for the Law of the Sea in Dispute concerning Delimitation of the Maritime Boundary between Mauritius and Maldives in the Indian Ocean (Mauritius/Maldives)
Entry into force:	28 April 2023
Published at:	ITLOS, List of cases: No. 28, *available at* www.itlos.org

I SUMMARY

On 23 August 2019, the Republic of Mauritius informed the President of the International Tribunal for the Law of the Sea (the Tribunal or ITLOS) of the institution of arbitral proceedings by Mauritius against the Republic of the Maldives pursuant to Annex VII to the United Nations Convention on the Law of the Sea (the Convention or UNCLOS) to establish a maritime boundary delimiting the exclusive economic zone (EEZ) and continental shelf.

Following consultations held by the President of the Tribunal with representatives of Mauritius and the Maldives in Hamburg on 17 September 2019, the two states concluded a Special Agreement on 24 September 2019 to submit their maritime boundary dispute to a special chamber of ITLOS to be formed pursuant to Article 15(2) of the Statute of ITLOS.[1] By Order of 27 September 2019, the Tribunal accepted the Parties' request to form a special chamber, which consisted of nine judges: President Paik; Judges Jesus, Pawlak, Yanai, Bouguetaia, Heidar, Chadha; and Judge *ad hoc*

---

1   The Special Agreement and Notification between Mauritius and the Maldives dated 24 September 2019.

Coalter G. Lathrop (ed.), International Maritime Boundaries, 6103-6121.
© *The American Society of International Law and Koninklijke Brill BV, Leiden 2025.*

6104 *Report Number 6-33*

Oxman, appointed by the Maldives, and Judge *ad hoc* Schrijver, appointed by Mauritius.

The maritime area delimited in this case lies in the Indian Ocean between the southern territory of the Maldives and the Chagos Archipelago of Mauritius, both archipelagic states.

Before effecting delimitation, the Special Chamber had to address the Maldives' preliminary objections and rejected them in the Judgment on Preliminary Objections on 28 January 2021.[2] The Special Chamber then proceeded to the merits and established a maritime boundary delimiting the parties' entitlements within 200 nautical miles (M) but decided not to proceed with delimitation in the area of the continental shelf beyond 200 M.[3]

II CONSIDERATIONS

1 *Political, Strategic, and Historical Considerations*

The Special Chamber had to consider the legal status of the Chagos Archipelago to determine whether Mauritius is the coastal state in respect of

---

2 *Dispute concerning delimitation of the maritime boundary between Mauritius and Maldives in the Indian Ocean (Mauritius/Maldives)*, Case No. 28, Preliminary Objections, Judgment of 28 January 2021 (Preliminary Objections). In operative paragraph 354 of the Judgment, the Special Chamber decided as follows: "(1) Unanimously, Rejects the first preliminary objection raised by the Maldives on the grounds that the United Kingdom is an indispensable third party to the present proceedings. (2) By 8 votes to 1, Rejects the second preliminary objection raised by the Maldives on the grounds that the Special Chamber lacks jurisdiction to determine the disputed issue of sovereignty over the Chagos Archipelago ... (3) By 8 votes to 1, Rejects the third preliminary objection raised by the Maldives relating to articles 74 and 83 of the Convention. ... (4) Unanimously, Rejects the fourth preliminary objection raised by the Maldives based on the non-existence of a dispute between the Parties. (5) Unanimously, Rejects the fifth preliminary objection raised by the Maldives based on an abuse of process. (6) By 8 votes to 1, Finds that it has jurisdiction to adjudicate upon the dispute submitted to it by the Parties concerning the delimitation of the maritime boundary between them in the Indian Ocean and that the claim submitted by Mauritius in this regard is admissible; defers, however, to the proceedings on the merits questions regarding the extent to which the Special Chamber may exercise its jurisdiction, including questions arising under article 76 of the Convention. ... (7) Unanimously, Reserves for consideration and decision in the proceedings on the merits the question of jurisdiction and admissibility with respect to Mauritius' claim stated in paragraph 28 of its Notification concerning the obligations under article 74, paragraph 3, and article 83, paragraph 3, of the Convention."

3 *Dispute concerning delimitation of the maritime boundary between Mauritius and Maldives in the Indian Ocean (Mauritius/Maldives)*, Case No. 28, Judgment of 28 April 2023 (Judgment).

the Chagos Archipelago for the purpose of delimiting a maritime boundary with the Maldives.

This question was put before the Special Chamber by the Maldives. It stated that, since 1814 and following the establishment of the British Indian Ocean Territory in 1965, "the United Kingdom has consistently claimed sovereignty over the Chagos Archipelago," and that "since at least 1980, Mauritius has claimed that it is sovereign over the Chagos Archipelago."[4] On this basis, the Maldives raised two preliminary objections. First, the Maldives argued that the United Kingdom was an indispensable third party to the proceedings, and, because the United Kingdom was not a party to the proceedings, the Special Chamber had no jurisdiction to delimit a maritime boundary between Mauritius and the Maldives.[5] Second, the Maldives argued that the Special Chamber had no jurisdiction to determine the disputed issue of sovereignty over the Chagos Archipelago, which it would necessarily have to do if it were to determine Mauritius' maritime claims to the EEZ and continental shelf.[6] Both preliminary objections ultimately failed.

Before addressing them, the Special Chamber examined the legal status of the Chagos Archipelago in light of both the advisory opinion that the International Court of Justice (ICJ) rendered on 25 February 2019 in the *Legal Consequences of the Separation of the Chagos Archipelago from Mauritius in 1965*[7] and resolution 73/295 adopted by the United Nations General Assembly on 22 May 2019 regarding the *Chagos* advisory opinion.[8] As to the *Chagos* advisory opinion, the ICJ determined in its operative part, *inter alia*, that "the process of decolonization of Mauritius was not lawfully completed when that country acceded to independence in 1968, following the separation of the Chagos Archipelago," and that "the United Kingdom is under an obligation to bring to an end its administration of the Chagos Archipelago as rapidly as possible."[9] These determinations, according to the Special Chamber, "have legal effect and clear implications for the legal status of the Chagos Archipelago,"[10] such that the United Kingdom's continued claim to sovereignty over the Chagos Archipelago "is contrary to those

---

4   Preliminary Objections, *supra* note 2 at para. 61.
5   *Id.* at paras. 81-89.
6   *Id.* at paras. 101-105.
7   Legal Consequences of the Separation of the Chagos Archipelago from Mauritius in 1965, Advisory Opinion, 2019 ICJ Rep. 95 (Feb. 25) (*Chagos* Advisory Opinion).
8   G.A. Res. 73/295, Advisory opinion of the International Court of Justice on the legal consequences of the separation of the Chagos Archipelago from Mauritius in 1965 (22 May 2019).
9   *Chagos* Advisory Opinion, *supra* note 7 at para. 183.
10   Preliminary Objections, *supra* note 2 at para. 246.

determinations."[11] The Special Chamber concluded that "[w]hile the process of decolonization has yet to be completed, Mauritius' sovereignty over the Chagos Archipelago can be inferred from the ICJ's determinations."[12] As to UN General Assembly resolution 73/295, the Special Chamber noted that this resolution "demanded that the United Kingdom withdraw its administration over the Chagos Archipelago within six months from its adoption," and the fact that "the time-limit set by the General Assembly has passed without the United Kingdom complying with this demand" further strengthened the Special Chamber's finding that the United Kingdom's "claim to sovereignty over the Chagos Archipelago is contrary to the authoritative determinations made in the advisory opinion."[13]

In rejecting the first preliminary objection, the Special Chamber concluded that "the United Kingdom is not an indispensable party" to the maritime boundary delimitation proceedings between Mauritius and the Maldives because "whatever interests the United Kingdom may still have with respect to the Chagos Archipelago, they would not render the United Kingdom a State with sufficient legal interests, let alone an indispensable third party, that would be affected by the delimitation of the maritime boundary around the Chagos Archipelago."[14]

In rejecting the second preliminary objection, the Special Chamber stated that "even before the process of the decolonization of Mauritius is completed," Mauritius can be regarded as "the State with an opposite or adjacent coast to the Maldives within the meaning of article 74, paragraph 1, and article 83, paragraph 1, of the Convention and the concerned State within the meaning of paragraph 3 of the same articles."[15] To treat Mauritius as such state, in the Special Chamber's view, "is consistent with the determinations made in the *Chagos* advisory opinion which were acted upon by UNGA resolution 73/295."[16]

---

11 *Id.*
12 *Id.*
13 *Id.*
14 *Id.* at paras. 247, 248.
15 *Id.* at para. 251.
16 *Id.* at para. 250.

2 Legal Regime Considerations

The parties disagreed on the scope of the dispute before the Special Chamber. The Maldives argued that the dispute concerned only the delimitation of the maritime boundary in the parties' EEZ and continental shelves *within* 200 M, and the overlap arising from the Maldives' claim to the continental shelf beyond 200 M and Mauritius' claim to the EEZ in the relevant area.[17] The Maldives also contended that Mauritius' claim in respect of its outer continental shelf entitlement was inadmissible.[18] Mauritius submitted that the Special Chamber had jurisdiction to delimit the maritime boundary between the parties, both *within* and *beyond* 200 M, and that its claim to a continental shelf beyond 200 M was admissible.[19]

The Special Chamber decided that its jurisdiction covered the continental shelf in its entirety, both within and beyond 200 M, for two reasons. First, the Special Chamber observed that the Special Agreement defined the subject matter of the dispute in "comprehensive terms as a 'dispute concerning the delimitation of the maritime boundary between [the Parties] in the Indian Ocean'," and, therefore, nothing in this language "suggests, expressly or implicitly, that delimitation of the maritime boundary between the Parties should exclude the continental shelf beyond 200 nm."[20] Second, the Special Chamber reaffirmed the well-established jurisprudence that "there is in law only a single 'continental shelf' rather than an inner continental shelf and a separate extended or outer continental shelf."[21] The Special Chamber recalled that, in *Bangladesh/Myanmar*, ITLOS found it had jurisdiction to delimit the continental shelf in its entirety because "[a]rticle 76 of the Convention embodies the concept of a single continental shelf," and "[i]n accordance with article 77, paragraphs 1 and 2, of the Convention, the coastal State exercises exclusive sovereign rights over the continental shelf in its entirety without any distinction being made between the shelf within 200 nm and the shelf beyond that limit."[22] For all those reasons, the Special Chamber held that "the portion of the continental shelf beyond 200 nm should not be treated as a separate and different maritime area of the coastal State, entailing two separate disputes."[23]

---

17 Judgment, *supra* note 3 at para. 83.
18 *Id.*
19 *Id.* at para. 82.
20 *Id.* at para. 331.
21 *Id.* at para. 338, citing to *Barbados v. Trinidad and Tobago*, at para. 213.
22 *Id.* at para. 339, citing to *Bangladesh/Myanmar*, at para. 361.
23 *Id.* at para. 340.

However, the Special Chamber ultimately found that, in the circumstances of the case, it was "not in a position to determine the entitlement of Mauritius to the continental shelf beyond 200 nm in the Northern Chagos Archipelago Region" and thus decided "not...to delimit the continental shelf between Mauritius and the Maldives beyond 200 nm."[24]

3 Economic and Environmental Considerations

Economic and environmental considerations did not affect this delimitation. However, the established maritime boundary clarified the limits of the parties' sovereign rights and jurisdiction that can be exercised in those areas, including with respect to economic activities and environmental protection.

4 Geographic Considerations

The delimitation area lies in the Indian Ocean between the Maldives and the Chagos Archipelago of Mauritius. The Maldives consists of an archipelago of 1,190 coral islands which are grouped within 26 atolls. The Chagos Archipelago is located over 250 M south of the Maldives' southernmost territory of Addu Atoll and over 1,100 M northeast in relation to the Island of Mauritius. The Chagos Archipelago is composed of various islands, banks, and reefs, many of these features clustered together in ring-shaped coral atolls.

5 Islands, Rocks, Reefs, and Low-tide Elevations Considerations

The Special Chamber had to address important issues concerning Blenheim Reef, a feature forming part of the Chagos Archipelago. A geodetic survey conducted by Mauritius in 2022 showed the existence of extensive areas of drying reef along the northern, eastern, and western flanks of Blenheim Reef's seaward perimeter.[25] According to that geodetic survey, Blenheim Reef is some 10.6 M east-northeast of Salomon Islands Atoll; it covers approximately 36 square kilometers; it extends for 9.6 kilometers from north

---

24 *Id.* at para. 466 (4). The reasons underlying this decision are explained below in Section 7 on *Geological and Geomorphological Considerations.*

25 *Id.* at para. 158.

to south, while at its widest point, from east to west, it spans 4.7 kilometers.[26] The discovery of extensive areas of drying reef at Blenheim Reef, according to Mauritius, should have a significant impact on Blenheim Reef's legal status under UNCLOS and the maritime area it generates in the context of overlapping maritime entitlements. The geography of Blenheim Reef gave rise to three questions bearing on selecting basepoints for a provisional equidistance line.

The first question was whether Blenheim Reef is a single low-tide elevation or a feature comprising multiple low-tide elevations. At high tide, Blenheim Reef is completely submerged, but some of it appears above water at low tide. On that basis, the Maldives argued that each part of the feature exposed at low tide constitutes a separate low-tide elevation within the meaning of Article 13(1) of UNCLOS.[27] Mauritius disagreed, arguing that because those parts are connected through an underwater structure, they should be considered a single low-tide elevation.[28] The Special Chamber decided that the definition of a low-tide elevation under Article 13(1) of UNCLOS has nothing indicating that separate "parts" or "patches" exposed at low tide, connected through an "underwater structure", constitute a single low-tide elevation.[29] Therefore, the Special Chamber concluded that Blenheim Reef consists of a number of low-tide elevations, only one of which is situated within 12 M of Île Takamaka, the nearest island.[30]

The next question was whether Blenheim Reef can be a site of basepoints for constructing a provisional equidistance line. Although the Special Chamber observed that there is no general rule for disregarding a low-tide elevation in selecting basepoints for the purpose of delimitation,[31] it found it appropriate in the circumstances of the case not to place a basepoint on the part of Blenheim Reef situated within 12 M from Île Takamaka because its impact on a provisional equidistance line was "by no means insubstantial."[32]

Finally, the Special Chamber had to address a question of whether archipelagic turning points around Blenheim Reef should be used as basepoints for constructing the provisional equidistance line and whether they should be given full effect. Mauritius asserted that Blenheim Reef is not only a low-tide elevation within 12 M of an island for the purpose of Article 13(1)

---

26 *Id.* at para. 158.
27 *Id.*
28 *Id.* at para. 215.
29 *Id.* at para. 216.
30 *Id.* at para. 219.
31 *Id.* at para. 152.
32 *Id.* at para. 154.

of UNCLOS, but also a "drying reef" within the meaning of Article 47(1) of the Convention. According to Mauritius, such status of Blenheim Reef entails significant consequences for delimitation because "a drying reef that is located on a properly drawn archipelagic baseline is to be treated like other land having entitlements to a full maritime area."[33] The Special Chamber concluded that treating Blenheim Reef as a drying reef, or drying reefs, within the meaning of Article 47(1) of UNCLOS cannot change its finding that no basepoints can be located on Blenheim Reef for the construction of the provisional equidistance line.[34] According to the Special Chamber, although Article 47 of the Convention allows placing appropriate points on outermost islands and drying reefs in drawing archipelagic baselines, it has nothing suggesting that such points should also be used as basepoints for constructing the provisional equidistance line, or that they should be given full effect in delimitation of the EEZ and the continental shelf, or that drying reefs should be treated like islands for the purpose of delimitation.[35]

For all those reasons, the Special Chamber decided not to place basepoints on any part of Blenheim Reef in constructing the provisional equidistance line.[36]

6 Baseline Considerations

Mauritius and the Maldives are two of 22 states that have declared themselves archipelagic states under Article 46 of UNCLOS. The Special Chamber decided to measure the parties' 200 M limits in the area relevant to delimitation from the respective archipelagic baselines published by each party, except for the archipelagic baselines at Blenheim Reef.[37]

For Blenheim, the Special Chamber had to address the question of whether the requirements of Article 47(4) of UNCLOS[38] apply to drawing Mauritius' archipelagic baselines at this feature. Mauritius argued that these requirements do not apply because Blenheim Reef is a drying reef within

---

33 *Id.* at para. 162.
34 *Id.* at para. 192.
35 *Id.* at para. 184
36 *Id.* at para. 230.
37 *Id.* at para. 235.
38 Article 47(4) of UNCLOS reads: "Such baselines shall not be drawn to and from low-tide elevations, unless lighthouses or similar installations which are permanently above sea level have been built on them or where a low-tide elevation is situated wholly or partly at a distance not exceeding the breadth of the territorial sea from the nearest island." United Nations Convention on the Law of the Sea, Dec. 10, 1982, 1833 UNTS 397, art 47 (4).

the meaning of Article 47(1).[39] The Maldives objected, arguing that because Blenheim Reef consists of many low-tide elevations it is subject to such requirements, with the effect that the 200 M limit of Mauritius must be measured only from those low-tide elevations of Blenheim Reef that are situated within 12 M of Île Takamaka.[40] The Special Chamber concluded that because "a drying reef is a low-tide elevation," Article 47(4) that applies to low-tide elevations should also "apply when archipelagic baselines are drawn joining the outermost points of outermost islands and 'drying reefs'."[41] Therefore, the 200 M limit of Mauritius "must be measured from a low-tide elevation of Blenheim Reef that is situated wholly or partly within 12 M of Île Takamaka."[42]

On that basis, the Special Chamber measured the 200 M limit of Mauritius from the northern intersection point of the low-water line of a low-tide elevation of Blenheim Reef located with the 12 M limit measured from the low-water line of Île Takamaka.[43]

7 Geological and Geomorphological Considerations

As discussed above, the Special Chamber decided its jurisdiction covered the continental shelf in its entirety, both within and beyond 200 M, because "there is in law only a single 'continental shelf' rather than an inner continental shelf and a separate extended or outer continental shelf."[44] However, the Special Chamber decided not to delimit the continental shelf between Mauritius and the Maldives beyond 200 M for two main reasons.

The first reason was based on the requirement that "a coastal State must demonstrate a natural prolongation of *its* submerged land territory to the outer edge of *its* continental margin beyond 200 M"[45] and "cannot validly claim an entitlement to a continental shelf beyond 200 M based on the natural prolongation through another State's uncontested continental shelf."[46] According to one of the arguments by Mauritius, its natural prolongation from the Chagos Archipelago extended northwards from the islands of Peros

---

39 Judgment, *supra* note 3 at paras. 194-199.
40 *Id.* at paras. 201-212.
41 *Id.* at para. 222.
42 *Id.* at para. 229.
43 *Id.*
44 *Id.* at para. 338, citing to *Barbados* v. *Trinidad and Tobago*, at para. 213.
45 *Id.*
46 *Id.*

6112 *Report Number 6-33*

Banhos Atoll, Salomon Islands Atoll, and Blenheim Reef along the Chagos-Laccadive Ridge.[47] However, the Special Chamber found that this route "passes within the continental shelf of the Maldives within 200 nm that is uncontested by Mauritius"[48] and, therefore, rejected such approach.

The second reason for not delimiting the continental shelf beyond 200 M was "significant uncertainty" as to whether two other approaches presented by Mauritius "could form a basis for its natural prolongation" beyond 200 M.[49] Given the significant uncertainty, the Special Chamber concluded that it was "not in a position to determine the entitlement of Mauritius to the continental shelf beyond 200 nm in the Northern Chagos Archipelago Region."[50]

The decision not to delimit the continental shelf beyond 200 M between Mauritius and the Maldives was an exercise of caution that, in the view of the Special Chamber, was "called for" because "there may be a risk of prejudice to the interests of the international community in the Area and the common heritage principle."[51]

8 *Method of Delimitation Considerations*

The Special Chamber reaffirmed the long line of international jurisprudence that "equidistance/relevant circumstances" is the methodology for delimiting the EEZ and the continental shelf unless recourse to it is not feasible or appropriate. While not mandatory, this methodology, as the Special Chamber stressed, "not only leads to an equitable solution in most cases but also brings transparency and predictability to the process of delimitation."[52]

Because the parties agreed to the application of this methodology and because there were no circumstances or factors that would make its application inappropriate or unfeasible, the Special Chamber agreed to apply it, proceeding in well-established three stages.

The first stage involves constructing a provisional equidistance line based on the geography of the coasts of the parties and mathematical calculations. At this stage, the Special Chamber decided not to select any basepoint on Blenheim Reef given the jurisprudence according to which international

---

47 *Id.* at para. 393.
48 *Id.* at para. 444.
49 *Id.* at para. 448.
50 *Id.* at para. 450.
51 *Id.* at para. 453.
52 *Id.* at para. 96.

courts and tribunals have rarely placed basepoints on a low-tide elevation for the construction of the provisional equidistance line. It also considered that the effect Blenheim Reef would have on the provisional equidistance line, if basepoints were to be placed on it, would by no means be insubstantial. The Special Chamber's provisional equidistance line starts, in the west, at a point on the intersection of the 200 M limits of Mauritius and the Maldives[53] and runs in an easterly direction until it reaches the 200 M limit of the Maldives. It is defined by a series of 47 turning points which are connected by geodetic lines, as described in paragraph 236 of the Judgment and depicted on the map at page 87 of the Judgment.

The second stage of the delimitation process requires determining whether there are any relevant circumstances calling for the adjustment of the provisional equidistance line and, if so, making an adjustment of the provisional equidistance line to ensure an equitable solution. At this stage, the Special Chamber considered that ignoring Blenheim Reef completely would not lead to an equitable solution given the presence of extensive areas of drying reefs as shown by the geodetic survey carried out by Mauritius. It also noted that such drying reefs amount to "other natural features" within the meaning of Article 46(b) of the Convention and, together with a group of islands and interconnecting waters, form the Chagos Archipelago.[54] The Special Chamber thus found that Blenheim Reef constitutes a relevant circumstance, requiring an adjustment of the provisional equidistance line.

According to the Special Chamber, the adjustment should give half effect to Blenheim Reef by shifting the line northward beginning between Points PEL-36 and PEL-37 at a point with coordinates 3° 07' 28.9" S and 73° 19' 11.0" E.[55] From this point the adjusted line continues as a single-segment geodetic line until the endpoint in the east, which is the intersection of the 200 M limits of the parties.[56]

As a result of such adjustment, the delimitation line for the EEZ and the continental shelves of the parties starts in the west at Point 1, the intersection point of the 200 M limits of Mauritius and the Maldives measured from

---

53 The 200 M limits of the Parties in the area relevant to this delimitation was measured from the respective archipelagic baselines published by each Party, with the exception of the archipelagic baselines at Blenheim Reef. For Blenheim Reef, the 200 M limit was measured from the northern intersection point of the low-water line of Blenheim Reef with the 12 M limit measured from the low-water line of Île Takamaka, for the reasons discussed above in Section 5 on *Islands, Rocks, Reefs, and Low-tide Elevations Considerations. See id.* at para. 235.

54 *Id.* at para. 245.

55 *Id.* at para. 247.

56 *Id.*

archipelagic baselines published by each party.[57] The delimitation line runs in an easterly direction until it reaches Point X (Point 37) with coordinates 3° 07' 28.9" S and 73° 19' 11.0" E.[58] From Point X, the delimitation line runs to Point Y (Point 38), the intersection point of the 200 M limits of Mauritius and the Maldives measured from archipelagic baselines published by each party, with the exception of the parts of Blenheim Reef located beyond 12 M from Île Takamaka. The Special Chamber's delimitation line is defined by the turning points described in paragraphs 249 and 250 and depicted on the map on page 93 of the Judgment.

The third stage of the delimitation process requires checking whether the delimitation line results in any significant disproportion between the ratio of the respective coastal lengths and the ratio of the maritime areas allocated to each party. The Special Chamber found that the relevant area in this case comprises the area of overlap resulting from the maritime entitlements of both parties up to a distance of 200 M, which measures approximately 92,563 km^2.[59] The Special Chamber established that the ratio of the lengths of the parties' relevant coasts – with Mauritius' relevant coast being 40.3 kilometers and the Maldives' relevant coast 39.0 kilometers – is 1:1.033.[60] The adjusted delimitation line allocates to Mauritius 45,331 km^2 and to the Maldives 47,232 km^2 of the relevant area. Because the ratio of the areas allocated to the parties is 1:0.960,[61] the Special Chamber found that there is no significant disproportion between this ratio and the ratio of the lengths of the respective coasts of the parties.[62]

9 Technical Considerations

In this case, Mauritius presented three different routes for natural prolongation to its foot of slope point FOS-VIT31B, on which it based its claim of entitlement to the continental shelf beyond 200 M in the Northern Chagos Archipelago Region.[63] The Special Chamber decided that the first route was

---

57 *Id.* at para. 248.
58 *Id.* at para. 249.
59 *Id.* at para. 254.
60 *Id.* at para. 253.
61 *Id.* at para. 255.
62 *Id.* at para. 256.
63 *See id.* at paras. 436-450 for the Special Chamber discussion of the three routes presented by Mauritius.

impermissible on legal grounds under Article 76 of the UNCLOS, and that significant scientific uncertainty called into question whether the second and third routes could form a basis for Mauritius' natural prolongation to the critical foot of slope point. In this regard, this case was markedly different from *Bangladesh/Myanmar*, where the ITLOS proceeded to delimit the overlapping entitlements in the continental shelf beyond 200M, even though the outer limits of that area were not yet delineated by the Commission on the Limits of the Continental Shelf (CLCS). Uncontested scientific evidence regarding the unique nature of the Bay of Bengal and information submitted during the proceedings satisfied the Tribunal that both Bangladesh and Myanmar had entitlements to a continental shelf extending beyond 200 M.

The Special Chamber asked the parties whether it would be necessary to arrange for an expert opinion pursuant to Article 82 of the Rules of ITLOS on scientific and technical issues concerning the delimitation of the continental shelf beyond 200 M. However, the Maldives took the position that caused the Special Chamber to conclude that, in the circumstances of this case, it would not be appropriate to arrange for such an opinion.[64] However, the Special Chamber encouraged the parties to contemplate giving their consent to the CLCS allowing it to consider each other's submissions.[65]

10 *Other Considerations*

None.

---

64 *Id.* at para. 454. Specifically, in response to the Registrar's letter of 16 August 2022 requesting the Parties' views on the necessity of arranging for an expert opinion, the Maldives set out the following reasons against arranging an expert opinion regarding scientific and technical issues concerning the delimitation of the continental shelf beyond 200 M: (i) as a matter of fact, it was unnecessary to arrange an expert opinion because there was no evidence on which an expert could meaningfully comment; (ii) as a matter of law, the question of entitlement beyond 200 M is legal in nature, not technical, and there was thus no need for any further expert report for the Special Chamber; and (iii) it would manifestly encroach on the functions of the CLCS because to pronounce on Mauritius' claim of natural prolongation an expert would have to establish the precise location of the continental margin, and this would constitute delineation of the outer limits of the continental shelf, which is beyond the jurisdiction of the Special Chamber. *Id.* at paras. 424-426.

65 *Id.* at para. 456.

III CONCLUSIONS

The proceedings in this case were instituted by the Special Agreement whereby Mauritius and the Maldives, following constructive consultations with the President of ITLOS, agreed to transfer the arbitral proceedings initially instituted by Mauritius under Annex VII of UNCLOS to a Special Chamber of the Tribunal. It highlighted once again the Tribunal's institutional importance for dispute resolution under the Convention.

In resolving the parties' dispute, the Special Chamber provided authoritative guidance on the interpretation and application of the Convention by making the following important determinations:

- First, the Special Chamber decided that Mauritius can be regarded as the state with an opposite or adjacent coast to the Maldives within the meaning of Article 74(1) and Article 83(1) of the Convention and as the concerned state within the meaning of paragraph 3 of the same articles even before the process of the decolonization of Mauritius with respect to the Chagos Archipelago is completed.
- Second, the Special Chamber authoritatively interpreted Article 47 of UNCLOS and clarified its application for placing archipelagic basepoints and drawing archipelagic baselines. It also made clear that although Article 47 allows placing appropriate points on outermost islands and drying reefs for drawing archipelagic baselines, this provision does not provide that such points should also be basepoints for the construction of a provisional equidistance line, or should be given full effect in delimitation of the EEZ and the continental shelf, or that drying reefs should be treated like islands for the purpose of delimitation.
- Third, the Special Chamber authoritatively clarified the meaning of Article 13 of UNCLOS by holding that even though parts or patches of land exposed at low tide are connected through an underwater structure, they must be treated not as a single low-tide elevation but as separate low-tide elevations, with a result that maritime jurisdiction of a coastal state must be measured from those low-tide elevations wholly or partly situated within 12 M of an insular feature.
- Fourth, the Special Chamber reaffirmed that "equidistance/relevant circumstances" is the methodology for delimiting the EEZ and the continental shelf unless recourse to it is not feasible or appropriate. In applying this methodology, the Special Chamber clarified the role that low-tide elevations may play in delimiting these maritime areas.

Although the Special Chamber decided not to select any basepoint on Blenheim Reef to construct its provisional equidistance line, the Special Chamber found no rule or principle requiring *a priori* disregard of low-tide elevations in this exercise. Everything will depend on the unique geographic context in each case. In the specific geographic circumstances of this case, the Special Chamber excluded Blenheim Reef as a basepoint in constructing its provisional equidistance line to avoid the outsized effect this feature would have on the provisional equidistance line. However, to ensure an equitable result, the Special Chamber then adjusted the provisional equidistance line by giving half-effect to Blenheim Reef because of its extensive drying areas that form an integral part of the Chagos Archipelago. This is the first decision in international maritime delimitation jurisprudence where a low-tide elevation was given any effect in delimiting the EEZ and the continental shelf.

- Fifth, the Special Chamber reaffirmed and clarified some important aspects relating to the legal regime of the continental shelf and its delimitation. It held that the portion of the continental shelf beyond 200 M should not be seen and treated as a separate and different maritime area of a coastal state, entailing two separate disputes. In so doing, the Special Chamber reaffirmed that Article 76 of the Convention embodies the concept of a single continental shelf and that under Article 77(1 & 2) of the Convention a coastal state exercises exclusive sovereign rights over the continental shelf in its entirety without any distinction being made between the shelf within 200 M and the shelf beyond that limit.

- Finally, the Special Chamber clarified that a coastal state cannot validly claim an entitlement to continental shelf beyond 200 M based on the natural prolongation through another state's uncontested continental shelf; it must demonstrate a natural prolongation of *its* submerged land territory to the outer edge of *its* continental margin beyond 200 M. The Special Chamber also reaffirmed the application of the standard of "significant uncertainty" for determining whether a coastal state has a natural prolongation beyond 200 M. Based on this standard, the Special Chamber decided not to delimit the continental shelf beyond 200 M, thus prudently acting both to minimize the risk that the CLCS in its recommendations might later take a different position and to protect the interests of the international community in the Area and the common heritage principle.

In conclusion, the Special Chamber's Judgments on preliminary objections and on maritime boundary delimitation – both rigorously reasoned – will occupy an important place in international jurisprudence and will have an authoritative and lasting impact well beyond the resolution of the dispute submitted by the parties.

IV   RELATED LAW IN FORCE

A   *Law of the Sea Conventions*

Mauritius: Party to UNCLOS (ratified 4 November 1994).
Maldives: Party to UNCLOS (ratified 7 September 2000).

B   *Maritime Jurisdiction Claimed at the Time of Judgment*

Mauritius: 12 M territorial sea; 12 M contiguous zone; 200 M EEZ; continental shelf (CLCS submission concerning the Southern Chagos Archipelago region on 26 March 2019 and CLCS submission concerning the Northern Chagos Archipelago region on 12 April 2022, on which there is no recommendation as of the date of this publication).
Maldives: 12 M territorial sea; 12 M contiguous zone; 200 M EEZ; continental shelf (CLCS submission on 26 July 2010, on which there is no recommendation as of the date of this publication).

C   *Maritime Jurisdiction Claimed Subsequent to Judgment*

No changes noted.

Prepared by Yuri Parkhomenko

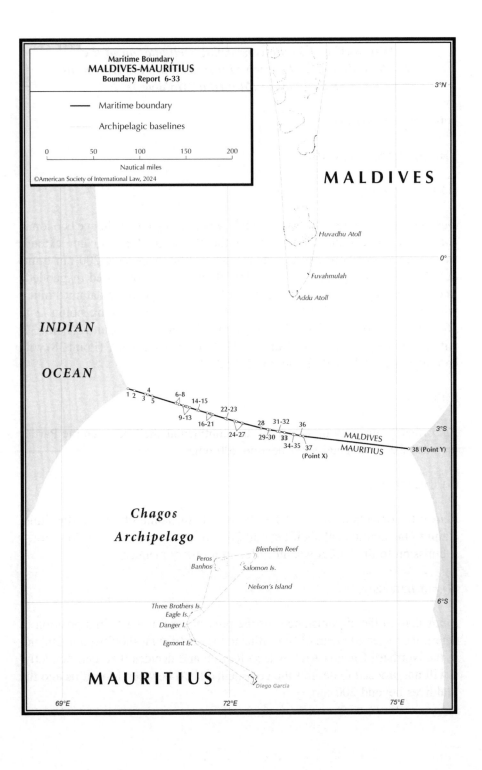

6120 *Report Number 6-33*

Dispositif in *Dispute concerning Delimitation of the Maritime Boundary between Mauritius and Maldives in the Indian Ocean (Mauritius/Maldives)*

466. For these reasons,

THE SPECIAL CHAMBER,

(1) Unanimously,

Decides that the single maritime boundary delimiting the exclusive economic zones and the continental shelves of the Parties within 200 nm extends from west to east between the intersections of the respective 200 nm limits determined in paragraphs 248 and 250 above and is composed of geodetic lines connecting the following points in WGS 84 as geodetic datum: Point 1 with coordinates 2° 17' 21.4" S and 70° 11' 56.2" E; turning points 2 to 36 with the coordinates identified in paragraph 249 above; Point X (Point 37) with coordinates 3° 07' 28.9" S and 73° 19' 11.0" E; and Point Y (Point 38) with coordinates 3° 20' 54.8" S and 75° 12' 52.1" E.

(2) Unanimously,

Finds that its jurisdiction to delimit the continental shelf between the Parties includes the continental shelf beyond 200 nm.

(3) Unanimously,

Rejects the objection raised by the Maldives to the admissibility of Mauritius' claim to the continental shelf beyond 200 nm on the grounds that Mauritius' submission to the CLCS was not filed in a timely manner.

(4) Unanimously,

Finds that, in the circumstances of the present case, it is not in a position to determine the entitlement of Mauritius to the continental shelf beyond 200 nm in the Northern Chagos Archipelago Region and decides that, consequently, it will not proceed to delimit the continental shelf between Mauritius and the Maldives beyond 200 nm.

Done in English and in French, both texts being equally authoritative, in the Free and Hanseatic City of Hamburg, this twenty-eighth day of April, two thousand and twenty-three, in three copies, one of which will be placed in the archives of the Tribunal and the others transmitted to the Government of the Republic of Mauritius and to the Government of the Republic of the Maldives.

(*signed*)
Jin-Hyun PAIK,
President of the Special Chamber

VII

Persian Gulf

VIII

Mediterranean Sea, Black Sea

Greece – Italy

Report Number 8-4 (2)

Agreement between the Italian Republic and the Hellenic Republic on the Delimitation of Their Respective Maritime Zones

Signed: 9 June 2020
Entry into force: Not yet in force
Published at: 108 LOS BULL. 16 (2022); Gazzetta Ufficiale della Repubblica Italiana, Serie generale – n. 149 p. 5 (24 June 2021)

I   SUMMARY

The 2020 Agreement between the Italian Republic and the Hellenic Republic on the Delimitation of Their Respective Maritime Zones (the 2020 Agreement or the Agreement) confirms that in the Mediterranean Sea the boundary between the maritime zones wherein Greece and Italy exercise sovereign rights or jurisdiction will follow the same course as the line delimiting their continental shelves established in the 1977 Agreement on the Delimitation of the Zones of the Continental Shelf Belonging to Each of the Two States (the 1977 Agreement).[1] The Agreement is part of a package, which also includes a joint communication by Greece and Italy to the European Commission concerning the rights of Italian fishers in the Greek territorial sea and a joint declaration on the resources of the Mediterranean Sea.

II   CONSIDERATIONS

1   *Political, Strategic, and Historical Considerations*

Greece and Italy are located in the central Mediterranean Sea; they have long coastlines and various islands. They also share the fact that they have yet

---

1   *See* Report Number 8-4, II IMB 1591.

Coalter G. Lathrop (ed.), International Maritime Boundaries, 6127-6138.
© *The American Society of International Law and Koninklijke Brill BV, Leiden 2025.*

to delimit maritime boundaries with several neighboring states, so they both must consider the effects of maritime boundary agreements on future delimitations in different contexts. The two countries have friendly relations and are both members of the European Union (EU) and of the North Atlantic Treaty Organization (NATO).

Greece and Italy had already delimited their continental shelves in the Ionian Sea in 1977. Their agreed continental shelf boundary was a modified equidistance line that gave full effect to most Greek islands and included minor spatial compensations to counterbalance the reduced effect of small Greek islands at the north and south of the boundary line. The 1977 boundary was adopted at a time when Italy was settling its continental shelf boundaries and Greece was involved in the still-ongoing dispute with Turkey concerning delimitation of the continental shelf in the Aegean Sea and Eastern Mediterranean Sea.

In recent years, Greece and Italy had tried to settle the boundary delimiting their superjacent waters, but their positions seemed irreconcilable. Italy objected to an extension of the seabed boundary to the superjacent waters because simply adopting an existing seabed boundary as the line to divide the water column would create a precedent that could jeopardize Italy's fishing interests in areas around its Pelagian Islands and the island of Pantelleria in the context of its maritime boundary with Tunisia. Greece insisted on the adoption of a single maritime boundary to delimit the continental shelf and the superjacent waters: a line like the agreed continental shelf boundary based, in principle, upon equidistance.

These conflicting positions were influenced, in part, by delimitations pending with third states. Italy had settled its continental shelf boundaries with Albania,[2] the former Yugoslavia[3] (now succeeded by Croatia and Montenegro), Spain,[4] and Tunisia[5] but still needed to agree whether those seabed boundaries would also apply to the waters above. Italy considers the extension to the superjacent waters of the continental shelf boundary agreed with Tunisia to be especially problematic because the seabed boundary enclaves Italy's Pelagian Islands and the island of Pantelleria, giving those features no effect on the direction of the boundary. Italy was concerned an agreement with Greece to adopt the same line to delimit both the seabed and the water column could create a negative precedent.

---

2 *See* Report Number 8-11, III IMB 2447.
3 *See* Report Number 8-7 (1), II IMB 1627.
4 *See* Report Number 8-5, II IMB 1601.
5 *See* Report Number 8-6, II IMB 1611.

As for Greece, its ongoing controversy with Turkey shapes to a great extent its foreign policy, including policy related to maritime delimitation. Greece and Turkey must still delimit their maritime zones in the Aegean Sea and the Eastern Mediterranean Sea.[6] While Greece calls for the application of equidistance giving full effect to the numerous Greek islands, Turkey negates the influence of islands in maritime delimitation and advocates a mainland-to-mainland approach in the delimitation of maritime boundaries. The latter approach was used to the detriment of Greece in the 2019 memorandum of understanding between Turkey and Libya (2019 MoU), which ignored the maritime zones generated by the Greek islands, including the large island of Crete.[7] Greece's insistence on the principle of giving full-effect to islands in equidistance delimitations with all of its neighbors is therefore instrumental in consolidating its position vis-à-vis Turkey and any other states which might contest the full entitlement of Greek islands.

Both Greece and Italy had recently experienced failures in the ratification of agreed boundaries making the conclusion of this agreement more difficult. In 2009, Greece entered into a delimitation agreement with Albania for an all-purpose maritime boundary that would delimit the territorial sea and the other zones between the two states.[8] However, the ratification process in Albania was interrupted following a Constitutional Court ruling in 2010. In 2015, Italy agreed with France its first all-purpose maritime boundary.[9] The agreement made use of a modified equidistance line, attributing to France waters where Italian fishermen had traditionally fished. Following two incidents involving Italian fishing vessels arrested by French authorities, Italy's ratification of this treaty was put on hold.

The successful conclusion of negotiations in 2020 may be attributed, in part, to the wider situation in the Mediterranean Sea. Considering the imminent extension of Greece's territorial sea from 6 nautical miles (M) to 12 M in the Ionian Sea, Italy needed to safeguard fishing traditionally carried out by its fleet in the affected part of the Ionian Sea. Italy also needed to elaborate a model for allowing its fishing fleet to exploit the resources located in waters attributed to other states. Following the conclusion of the 2019 MoU between Libya and Turkey, Greece was particularly keen to enter into bilateral delimitation treaties that would promote its own principles

---

6   The two states are at variance also with respect to other issues, such as the extension of the territorial sea and of the airspace above.
7   *See* Report Number 8-24, in this volume.
8   *See* Report Number 8-21, VI IMB 4462.
9   *See* Report Number 8-2 (2), VIII IMB 5637.

concerning delimitation of maritime boundaries and that would prove to Turkey that other coastal states in the region shared Greece's principles.

The 2020 Agreement is part of a package which also includes a joint communication by Greece and Italy to the European Commission and a joint declaration on the resources of the Mediterranean Sea. The joint communication concerns the authorization of Italian fishers to fish specific species in the territorial sea of Greece, in the area between 6 M and 12 M. The joint declaration identifies actions by the two states to protect the marine environment in the part of the Mediterranean Sea located between their coasts. With the joint communication and joint declaration, the Agreement allowed both states to safeguard their essential interests. Greece secured a maritime delimitation treaty that makes use of an equidistance line and gives full effect to most Greek islands, and Italy secured preferential rights for its fishers within Greek territorial waters, as detailed in the joint communication and as referred to indirectly in Article 3 of the Agreement.

2 Legal Regime Considerations

The 2020 Agreement constitutes a distinct treaty from the 1977 Agreement, although it makes express reference to the line established by the latter (Article 1). In contrast to the 1977 Agreement, the 2020 Agreement does not contain any clause concerning transboundary deposits; rather, it provides that it is without prejudice to fishing activities carried out in conformity with applicable EU rules and regulations and with the provisions of Article 58 of UNCLOS (Article 3). As the 2020 Agreement does not expressly terminate the 1977 Agreement, and in light of the different focus of the two treaties, they both continue to be in force, and the 2020 Agreement supersedes the previous treaty only in those parts where there is a formal incompatibility between their provisions, such as the geodetic datum to which the coordinates are referenced.

To date, neither party has claimed an exclusive economic zone, and the water column delimited by the Agreement is still formally part of the high seas. In 2006, Italy enacted framework legislation allowing for the creation of ecological protection zones[10] and, in 2011, instituted the first of these

---

10 Law No. 61 of 8 February 2006 on the establishment of an ecological protection zone beyond the outer limit of the territorial sea, G.U. 3 March 2006, n. 52 (Italy), *available at* https://www.un.org/Depts/los/LEGISLATIONANDTREATIES/PDFFILES/ITA_2006 _Law.pdf.

zones in areas of the northwestern Mediterranean Sea, the Ligurian Sea, and the Tyrrhenian Sea.[11] Within this zone, Italy has claimed jurisdiction concerning the protection of the marine environment and of underwater cultural heritage. However, Italy has so far not claimed any such zone in the Ionian Sea, the area in which the Agreement applies. In June 2021 the Italian Parliament adopted a law authorizing the President of the Republic to create an exclusive economic zone,[12] and it is expected that this zone will be created in the coming months. At the time of signature, Greece had a territorial sea of 6 M. After the signature of the 2020 Agreement, Greece established a system of straight baselines along its western coast[13] and extended its territorial sea from 6 to 12 M in the same area.[14]

The Agreement provides that the parties will try to settle disputes through negotiations. If negotiations do not solve the issue within a four-month period, either party may refer the issue to the International Court of Justice.

3 Economic and Environmental Considerations

Italy's fishing interests played a significant role in the formulation of the Agreement and the associated joint declaration to the European Commission.

According to EU law, vessels flying the flag of any EU member state have equal access to all EU waters, which comprise both the territorial sea and the exclusive economic zone.[15] However, in "the waters up to 12 nautical miles from baselines under their sovereignty or jurisdiction, Member States shall be authorised, until 31 December 2022, to restrict fishing to fishing vessels

---

11 Presidential Decree No. 209 of 27 October 2011 on regulations establishing ecological protection zones in the north-west Mediterranean, the Ligurian Sea and the Tyrrhenian Sea, G.U. 17 December 2011, n. 293 (Italy), *available at* https://www.un.org/Depts/los/LEGISLATIONANDTREATIES/PDFFILES/ITA_2011_Decree.pdf.

12 Law No. 91 of 14 June 2021 on the institution of an exclusive economic zone beyond the external limit of the territorial sea, G.U. 23 June 2021, n. 148 (Italy), *available at* https://www.un.org/Depts/los/LEGISLATIONANDTREATIES/PDFFILES/law9114jun21eez.pdf.

13 Presidential Decree No. 107 of 25 December 2020 on the closing of gulfs and the drawing of straight baselines in the sea area of the Ionian and the Ionian Islands up to Cape Tenaron of the Peloponnese, FEK A' 258 27 December 2020 (Greece).

14 Law No. 4767 of 21 January 2021 on the establishment of the breadth of the territorial sea in the sea area of the Ionian and Ionian Islands up to Cape Tenaron of the Peloponnese, FEK A' 9 21 January 2021 (Greece).

15 Council Regulation 1380/2013 of 11 December 2013 on the Common Fisheries Policy (as amended), 2013 O.J. (L 354) 22, Article 5(1), *available at* https://eur-lex.europa.eu/legal-content/EN/TXT/?uri=uriserv:OJ.L_.2013.354.01.0022.01.ENG.

6132 *Report Number 8-4 (2)*

that traditionally fish in those waters from ports on the adjacent coast."[16] If an EU member state exercises this power, then the vessels of other states may fish in that zone only if there is an agreement between the two states, to be included in Annex I of Regulation 1380/2013.

Absent any such agreement between Greece and Italy, Italian fishermen had been able to fish close to the Greek coast because Greece claimed a narrow territorial sea measuring 6 M from the coast and no exclusive economic zone. Among other species, the fishery in this area includes the valuable red prawn.[17] The proposed extension of the Greek territorial sea up to 12 M and the intention to claim an exclusive economic zone could have limited Italian fishing in this area, since Greece could have exercised its power under the EU fisheries rules to claim that fishing within the zone up to 12 M would be reserved to Greek vessels from nearby ports. This was likely to cause serious economic, social, and political consequences in Italy.

In order to take this circumstance into account, the Agreement provides that it is without prejudice to fishing activities carried out in conformity with applicable EU rules and regulations (Article 3). Furthermore, the joint communication adopted at the same time as the Agreement regulates fishing by Italian fishers in the territorial sea of Greece by requesting the EU to amend Annex I of Regulation 1380/2013 to allow Italian fishers to fish within the 6-12 M belt of the Greek territorial sea. In particular, Italian fishers are allowed to catch four species, including the red prawn, with an upper limit of 68 vessels and with the obligation to respect the Greek standards concerning fisheries.

Intensive fishing activities and projects to exploit offshore mineral deposits have drawn the attention of the two states and the public to the need to protect the marine environment in the region. The joint declaration on the resources of the Mediterranean Sea, adopted at the same time as the Agreement, promotes the balanced and sustainable management of such resources aimed at their conservation.

---

16 *Id.*, Article 5, para 2. The final date for such measures has already been extended more than once and currently is 31 December 2022.

17 Fishing activity in this area had intensified following the closure of Libyan waters as a consequence of the creation of the Libyan exclusive economic zone, the danger posed by the Libyan civil war, and the robust law enforcement actuated by the Libyan Coast Guard.

4 Technical Considerations

The 1977 Agreement between Greece and Italy did not specify the datum used to express the coordinates of the turning points, although it did state that the lines connecting them were great circle arcs. The resulting line was depicted on two charts, Hellenic nautical chart No. II, 1956 edition, on a scale of 1 : 1,000,000 at 38° N, and Italian nautical chart No. 436 L(C), 1975 edition, on a scale of 1 : 1,000,000 at 41° N. In the 2020 Agreement the opportunity was taken to express the coordinates of the 1977 turning points in WGS 84.

III CONCLUSIONS

The 2020 Agreement is an example of delimitation of future maritime zones in which the parties are entitled to exercise their sovereign rights and jurisdiction once those zones have been established. Neither Greece nor Italy has yet advanced claims to the waters superjacent to their continental shelves in this area, so the Agreement has set their maritime boundary preemptively, in anticipation of such claims, thus avoiding future disputes. The package, of which the Agreement is a part, has allowed both states to advance their priority interests (delimitation method for Greece and fishing interests for Italy) while settling, in a definitive way, their shared maritime boundary.

IV RELATED LAW IN FORCE

A *Law of the Sea Conventions*

Greece: Party to UNCLOS (ratified 21 July 1995).
Italy: Party to UNCLOS (ratified 13 January 1995)

B *Maritime Jurisdiction Claimed at the Time of Signature*

Greece: 6 M territorial sea; continental shelf.
Italy: 12 M territorial sea; continental shelf; ecological protection zones.

C *Maritime Jurisdiction Claimed Subsequent to Signature*

Greece: 12 M territorial sea, extended solely in the Ionian Sea.
Italy: No change.

V REFERENCES AND ADDITIONAL READINGS

Aris Marghelis, *The Maritime Delimitation Agreement between Greece and Italy of 9 June 2020: An Analysis in the Light of International Law, National Interest and Regional Politics*, 126 MARINE POLICY (2021) *available at* https://doi.org/10.1016/j.marpol.2021.104403.

Prepared by Irini Papanicolopulu

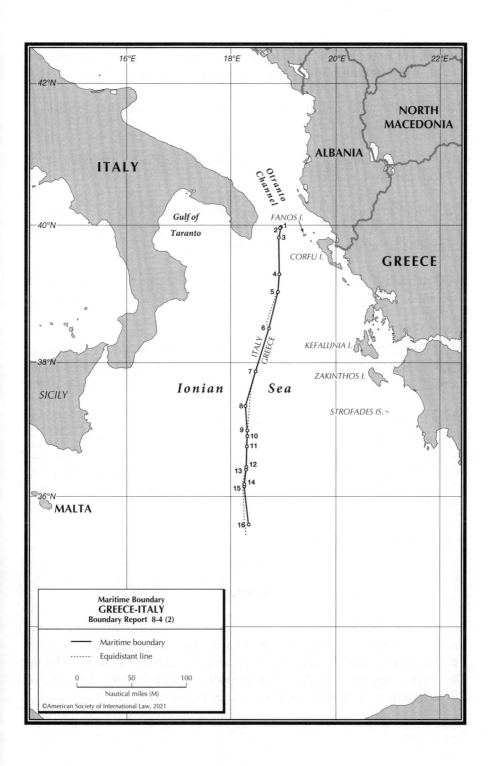

6136 *Report Number 8-4 (2)*

Agreement between the Italian Republic and the Hellenic Republic on the Delimitation of Their Respective Maritime Zones

The Italian Republic and the Hellenic Republic (hereinafter the "Parties" or the "countries");

DESIRING to strengthen the ties of good-neighbourliness and cooperation between the two countries;

AWARE of the need to delimit precisely the maritime zones over which the two countries are entitled to exercise, respectively, their sovereign rights or jurisdiction in accordance with international law;

TAKING INTO ACCOUNT the relevant provisions of the United Nations Convention on the Law of the Sea (1982), to which the two countries are parties;

REAFFIRMING the Agreement between the Italian Republic and the Hellenic Republic on the delimitation of their respective continental shelves, signed on the 24th of May 1977 and entered into force on 12th of November 1980;

RECALLING that the above Agreement establishes a boundary for the delimitation of the continental shelves between the two countries;

WISHING to apply the above continental shelf boundary for the delimitation of other maritime zones to which the two countries are entitled under international law;

HAVE AGREED upon the following:

Article 1

1. The boundary line of the maritime zones to which the two countries are entitled to exercise, respectively, their sovereign rights or jurisdiction under international law shall be the continental shelf boundary established under the 1977 Agreement between the Italian Republic and the Hellenic Republic on the delimitation of their respective continental shelves.

2. The coordinates of the above boundary line expressed in the WGS-84 datum are as follows:

A/A	LAI (WGS 84)	LON (WGS 84)
1	39° 57′ 38.46″ N	18° 57′ 27.29″ E
2	39° 52′ 20.45″ N	18° 56′ 03.29″ E
3	39° 48′ 56.44″ N	18° 54′ 51.29″ E
4	39° 17′ 14.40″ N	18° 55′ 33.31″ E
5	39° 01′ 56.39″ N	18° 53′ 57.32″ E
6	38° 29′ 56.34″ N	18° 43′ 51.32″ E
7	37° 51′ 56.29″ N	18° 28′ 33.33″ E
8	37° 21′ 14.26″ N	18° 16′ 57.33″ E
9	36° 59′ 26.23″ N	18° 19′ 03.34″ E
10	36° 54′ 20.23″ N	18° 19′ 09.35″ E
11	36° 44′ 56.22″ N	18° 18′ 33.35″ E
12	36° 26′ 26.20″ N	18° 17′ 57.36″ E
13	36° 24′ 02.19″ N	18° 17′ 39.36″ E
14	36° 10′ 56.18″ N	18° 15′ 39.37″ E
15	36° 08′ 56.18″ N	18° 15′ 39.37″ E
16	35° 34′ 08.15″ N	18° 20′ 39.39″ E

3. The delimitation, for the moment, shall not be intended to go beyond the point 1, to the North, and beyond the point 16, to the South. This delimitation shall be extended in either direction up to the junction points of the maritime zones of the respective neighboring States, once the relevant agreements will be concluded.

Article 2

Once a Party has taken the initiative to proclaim a maritime zone extending up to the boundary line of article 1 of this Agreement, it shall inform the other Party as early as possible.

Article 3

This Agreement is without prejudice to:

a. fishing activities carried out in conformity with applicable EU rules and regulations;
b. the provisions of article 58 of the United Nations Convention on the Law of the Sea regarding the rights, freedoms and duties of other States in the exclusive economic zone of the Parties as provided for in the above article.

Article 4

1. The Parties shall endeavour to settle, through diplomatic means, any dispute which may arise concerning the interpretation or application of this Agreement.
2. If such a dispute is not settled within four months from the date on which one of the Parties gave notice of its intention to initiate the procedure provided for in the preceding paragraph, it shall be referred, at the request of either Party, to the International Court of Justice or to any other international body chosen by mutual consent.

Article 5

1. This Agreement shall be subject to ratification.
2. This Agreement shall enter into force on the date of exchange of the instruments of ratification.

DONE at Athens, on 9 June 2020, in two originals, each in the Italian, Greek and English languages, all texts being equally authentic. In case of divergence in the interpretation of this Agreement, the text in English shall prevail.

For the Italian Republic	For the Hellenic Republic
<signed>	*<signed>*
Luigi Di Maio	Nikolaos – Georgios S.Dendias
Minister of Foreign Affairs and International Cooperation	Minister of Foreign Affairs

Algeria – Tunisia

Report Number 8-16 (Add. 1)

Annex to the Agreement on Provisional Arrangements for the Delimitation of the Maritime Boundary between the Republic of Tunisia and the People's Democratic Republic of Algeria

Signed: 7 August 2002
Entry into force: 23 November 2003
Published at: 2238 UNTS 211 (I-39821)

Convention Regarding Delimitation of the Maritime Boundaries between the People's Democratic Republic of Algeria and the Tunisian Republic

Signed: 11 July 2011
Entry into force: 16 September 2013[1]
Published at: Journal Officiel de la République Algérienne, No. 46, 22 Sept 2013, 3; Journal Officiel de la République Tunisienne, No. 82, 28 Oct 2011, 2326.

I SUMMARY

The 2011 Convention Regarding Delimitation of the Maritime Boundaries between the People's Democratic Republic of Algeria and the Tunisian Republic (the 2011 Agreement) sets out the final all-purpose delimitation of the maritime zones of the two adjacent countries. The 2011 Agreement supersedes the Agreement on Provisional Arrangements for the Delimitation of the Maritime Boundaries between Algeria and Tunisia, concluded in Algiers on 11 February 2002, which entered into force on 23 November 2003 (the 2002 Provisional Agreement).

---

1   This is the date of Algeria's ratification following Tunisia's ratification on 22 October 2011. It is not known when the instruments of ratification were exchanged pursuant to Article 8 of the 2011 Agreement.

Coalter G. Lathrop (ed.), International Maritime Boundaries, 6139-6158.
© *The American Society of International Law and Koninklijke Brill BV, Leiden 2025.*

6140　*Report Number 8-16 (Add. 1)*

The 2002 Provisional Agreement received careful analysis in an earlier report,[2] but the annex to that agreement containing important technical information was not available at that time. That annex constitutes an integral part of the 2002 Provisional Agreement, and it is referenced in the preamble of the 2011 Agreement. The 2002 annex is reproduced following this report and merits some comment as it provides the technical foundation for the final delimitation.

The boundary line as determined by the 2011 Agreement is identical to the provisional line described in the 2002 Provisional Agreement, so many of the observations from the earlier report apply to the boundary delimited in this final agreement. Like the provisional line, the agreed boundary is composed of a first segment extending approximately 53 nautical miles (M) from the land boundary terminus (point P1) through point P2 to point P3 and a second segment extending approximately 30 M from point P3 to point P4, near the notional tripoint among Algeria, Tunisia, and Italy. The boundary line departs from equidistance in order to mitigate the effect on the delimitation of La Galite, a small non-coastal island belonging to Tunisia.

II　CONSIDERATIONS

1　*Political, Strategic, and Historical Considerations*

Algeria and Tunisia first proceeded with the settlement of their land boundary by means of two agreements signed on 6 January 1970 and 19 March 1983.[3] The latter agreement established the land boundary terminus on the Mediterranean coast and the starting point for the two states' maritime boundary. Point P1 of the subsequent maritime boundary agreements corresponds to the location of land boundary marker Number 001.

Algeria and Tunisia entered into negotiations on their maritime boundary in 1995 and concluded their provisional maritime boundary arrangement in 2002.[4] This provisional arrangement appeared necessary in particular to

---

2　Report Number 8-16, V IMB 3927.

3　Agreement on the Frontier Line between Algeria and Tunisia from Bir Romane to the Lybian Frontier, Algeria – Tunisia, 6 Jan 1970, 1760 UNTS 321 (determining the southern part of the land border); Agreement on the Emplacement of Boundary Markers from the Mediterranean Sea to Bir Rouman, Algeria – Tunisia, 19 Mar 1983, 1936 UNTS 3 (determining the northern part of the land border, including the land boundary terminus).

4　Scheyma Djaziri, *La délimitation des espaces maritimes entre la Tunisie et l'Algérie*, 22 ANNUAIRE DU DROIT DE LA MER 43-64, 44 (2017) (noting the first negotiations were held in July 1995 in Tunis and in September 1995 in Algiers).

prevent the repetition of certain maritime incidents involving alleged illicit fishing activities in Tunisian territorial waters.[5] According to the preamble of the Provisional Agreement, the negotiation of the provisional arrangement involved ten work sessions of the Joint Commission for the Delimitation of the Maritime Boundaries, the most important of which was held in Algiers on 27 June 2001.

It is not known whether the parties formally extended the 2002 Provisional Agreement upon its six-year expiration in 2008 (Articles 9 and 10), but it appears by that time Algeria and Tunisia were already engaged in the process of negotiating their final agreement. One commentator has asserted that the 2011 Agreement was first "adopted by the negotiators" on 1 March 2009 in Algiers, then initialed by the Ministers of Foreign Affairs on 30 October 2009 in Tunis (along with an exchange of letters to extend the validity of the provisional arrangement until the final agreement was signed).[6] One could speculate that the civil unrest and change of government that occurred in Tunisia during the Arab Spring might have delayed the signing. In any event, the 2011 Agreement, as subsequently ratified by both parties, was signed on 11 July 2011 in Algiers by the Ministers of Foreign Affairs of Tunisia and Algeria.

In the preamble to the 2011 Agreement the parties declare themselves "desirous of consolidating the relations of brotherhood, cooperation and good-neighborliness existing between the two fraternal countries and peoples and based on common historical ties."

The existence of a bilateral agreement on the delimitation of the continental shelf between Tunisia and Italy would have had an influence on the determination of the final point of the boundary line between Algeria and Tunisia.[7]

---

5 Id.
6 Habib Slim, *La délimitation des espaces maritimes entre la Tunisie et l'Algérie, in* LE DROIT DE LA MER FACE AUX "MÉDITERRANÉES": QUELLE CONTRIBUTION DE LA MÉDITERRANÉE ET DES MERS SEMI-FERMÉES AU DROIT INTERNATIONAL DE LA MER? 57, 62 (Nathalie Ros & Florence Galletti eds., 2016). *See also* Habib Slim & Tullio Scovazzi, *Study of the current status of ratification implementation and compliance with maritime agreements and conventions applicable to the Mediterranean Sea Basin*, Part 2: Regional Report (European Commission, Europe-Aid Cooperation Office, Dec 2009).
7 *See* Report Number 8-6, II IMB 1611.

2 Legal Regime Considerations

Like the line established under the 2002 Provisional Agreement, the parties agreed that the final delimitation line would be an all-purpose boundary delimiting the full range of existing maritime zones, as well as "any other maritime zone newly created or that may be created in accordance with the United Nations Convention on the Law of the Sea of 1982 and international law" (Article 2).

It is to be noted that the 2002 Provisional Agreement initially defined an all-purpose line which, in the absence of exclusive economic zone (EEZ) claims by either party, defined a boundary between their territorial seas and their continental shelves. The line also divided Tunisia's contiguous zone from Algeria's 52 M fishing zone, and it defined the eastern limit of Algeria's fishing zone vis-à-vis an area of high seas to the east of the provisional line.[8] Beyond point P3, the provisional line divided only the seabed. Since 2002, both countries have established EEZs – Tunisia in 2005,[9] after the 2002 Provisional Agreement, and Algeria in 2018,[10] after the 2011 Agreement. These claims, and Algeria's establishment of a contiguous zone in 2004,[11] have changed the legal regime applicable to the boundary line.

It is also noteworthy that Algeria's fishing zone, which was instrumental in determining the location of point P3,[12] has been, for all practical purposes, superseded by the subsequent EEZ claim of Algeria, so that the location of point P3 may be an artifact of an earlier but now *de facto* extinct claim.

The 2011 Agreement, following the legal terminology found in the 1982 Law of the Sea Convention, clearly specifies in Article 3 – as the 2002

---

8 Report Number 8-16, V IMB 3927, 3929; *but see*, David Attard, *Mediterranean Maritime Jurisdictional Claims: A Review*, 23 HAMBURG STUDIES ON MARITIME AFFAIRS 89, 96 (2012) (indicating that Tunisia had not declared a contiguous zone, but instead an archaeological protection zone).

9 Act No. 50/2005 of 27 June 2005 concerning the exclusive economic zone off the Tunisian coasts (Tunisia), *reprinted in* 58 LOS BULL. 19 (2005).

10 Presidential Decree No. 18-96 of 2 Rajab A.H. 1439, corresponding to 20 March A.D. 2018, establishing an exclusive economic zone off the coast of Algeria (Algeria), Official Gazette of the Republic of Algeria, No. 18, 3 Rajab A.H. 1439 (21 March A.D. 2018), *available at* https://www.un.org/Depts/los/LEGISLATIONANDTREATIES/PDFFILES/DZA_2018_Decree_1896_en.pdf.

11 Presidential Decree No. 04-344 of of 23 Ramadan 1425 (6 November 2004) Establishing a Zone Contiguous to the Territorial Sea (Algeria), *reprinted in* 57 LOS BULL. 116 (2005).

12 The 2002 Provisional Agreement, Article 1, describes point P3 as "the point of intersection of the line connecting points P1 and P2 with the line situated 52 nautical miles away delimiting in the north the Algerian exclusive fishing zone and measured from Algerian baselines." *Reprinted in* Report Number 8-16, V IMB 3927, 3936.

Provisional Agreement also did – that the delimitation relates to areas where sovereignty, sovereign rights, or jurisdiction can be exercised by the parties, and it further specifies that these are exercised by Algeria to the west of the line and by Tunisia to the east of the line.

Article 7 of the 2011 Agreement calls for the creation of a joint maritime boundaries commission "which will be entrusted with the task of the follow-up of the present convention and to ease the difficulties that may result from its application."

3 Economic and Environmental Considerations

The 2011 Agreement incorporates undertakings of information and cooperation regarding certain economic activities carried out in areas located close to the boundary line. Article 4 provides for an obligation of notification of "surveying work with a view to exploration or exploitation of the mineral resources located in the immediate vicinity of the line of maritime boundaries." Article 5 provides for an obligation of exchange of information and an obligation to seek to reach an agreement on "arrangements concerning exploitation of [straddling] resources." These obligations apply in situations where "a geological structure or an oil well or natural gas well or other non-living natural resources would be located on both sides of the line," and "if the structure or the well located on one side of the line can be exploited, in full or in part, from the other side of the said line."

It can be noted that, whereas the 2002 Provisional Agreement in its Article 6, contained an undertaking of the parties to cooperate and coordinate their activities in various areas, including the "conservation of natural resources and in particular of living resources," no similar reference to the marine environment and resources is found in the 2011 Agreement, except as regards non-living resources. The reason behind this omission is not known, but it can be noted that Tunisia and Algeria are both parties to the 1995 Barcelona Convention for the Protection of the Marine Environment and the Coastal Region of the Mediterranean, which provides for a framework of co-operation for the benefit of the marine and coastal environment.

4 Geographic Considerations

In the region where this lateral delimitation occurs, the coastlines of the two countries run in a rather regular east to west direction without well-marked

6144　*Report Number 8-16 (Add. 1)*

concavities or headlands. It does not appear that the mainland coastal configuration created any disagreement. Instead, the geographic circumstance that played a major role in the negotiations was the presence of the Tunisian island of La Galite.

As with most coastal states on the Mediterranean Sea, Algeria and Tunisia do not enjoy the full extent of their potential 200 M zones. In this zone-locked geography, the delimitation between Algeria and Tunisia had to take into consideration the existence of the prior continental shelf delimitation agreement between Italy and Tunisia. It has been reported that the Tunisian side was especially concerned by the need to have the final point of their boundary with Algeria correspond with "point Zero": the westernmost point of the Italy-Tunisia continental shelf boundary.[13] This ultimately proved acceptable to Algeria, and point P4 "is very close to the Algeria-Italy-Tunisia equidistant tripoint."[14] It may be assumed the location of point P4 would also be acceptable to Italy. However, west and north of point P4 Algeria's claimed EEZ outer limit has been opposed by Italy (and, further west, by Spain) which has asserted that Algeria's EEZ "unduly overlaps on zones of legitimate and exclusive Italian national interest."[15]

5   *Islands, Rocks, Reefs, and Low-tide Elevations Considerations*

Three different maritime features could theoretically have affected the location of the boundary: (i) a shoal known as Le Sec Bank (in French "banc le sec"), (ii) the Reefs of the Sorelles, and (iii) the island of La Galite. The impact of these features on the boundary line had already been provisionally agreed in 2002, and no change has occurred in that respect in the 2011 Agreement.

First, Le Sec Bank, a shoal in approximately 50 meters of water depth, located between 18 M and 20 M from the Algerian coast, was previously claimed by Tunisia as part of its maritime zone.[16] As a result of the delimitation agreement, it is now located on the Algerian side of the boundary.

13　Djaziri, *supra* note 4, at 50.
14　Report Number 8-16, V IMB 3927, 3931.
15　Note verbale *dated 28 November 2018 from the Permanent Mission of Italy to the United Nations addressed to the Secretary-General, available at* https://www.un.org/Depts/los/LEGISLATIONANDTREATIES/PDFFILES/2018_NV_Italy.pdf. *See also,* Note verbale *dated 20 June 2019 from the Ministry of Foreign Affairs of Algeria to the Embassy of the Republic of Italy, available at* https://www.un.org/Depts/los/LEGISLATIONANDTREATIES/PDFFILES/AlgItaly.pdf.
16　*See* Djaziri, *supra* note 4. Le Sec Bank has been reported to be a rich fishing location by oceanographic surveys conducted in 1957-60. *See* Claude Maurin, *Etude des fonds*

Second, the Reefs of the Sorelles are now located on the Tunisian side of the boundary. This feature has been described as "a low-tide elevation that cannot produce any coastal zone by its own"[17] (presumably because it is located beyond the territorial sea), and Tunisia claims a normal baseline along "the low-water mark of the reefs of the Sorelles."[18] However, other sources indicate that the Sorelles are fully submerged at low tide and do not qualify as a low-tide elevation.[19] Regardless of their status, the Sorelles were given no effect in terms of an equidistance calculation, but they were used to determine the direction of the first segment of the boundary between points P1 and P3. Point P2, which sets the direction of that segment, is "the point situated 4 nautical miles west of the Sorelles rocks."[20] And the final determination of the boundary turning point coordinates was "based on data obtained form [sic] the hydrographical survey of the Sorelles reef of 4 July 2002 by the joint technical group."[21]

Third, La Galite is a small non-coastal island (about 5.3 kilometers long and 2 kilometers wide) located about 20 M from the Tunisian coast. It is surrounded by six rocks, including Galitons de l'Ouest to the southwest and Galitons de l'Est to the north. It would have had a marked influence on the drawing of an equidistance boundary in favor of Tunisia, starting at a point approximately 25 M from shore and increasingly so as an equidistance delimitation proceeded further from the mainland. While Tunisia preferred a delimitation based on strict equidistance, Algeria could not accept a line giving full effect to La Galite and advocated for a more northerly line giving no effect to La Galite.[22] The agreed line is a compromise between these two positions. La Galite is given no effect out to point P3. However, it is given

---

chalutables de la Méditerranée occidentale (écologie et pêche), 26 (2) REVUE DES TRAVAUX DE L'INSTITUT DES PÊCHES MARITIMES 163, 195 (1962).

17 Report Number 8-16, V IMB 3927, 3931.

18 Decree No. 73-527 of 3 November 1973 concerning baselines, Article 1 (Tunisia), available at https://www.un.org/Depts/los/LEGISLATIONANDTREATIES/PDFFILES/TUN_1973_Decree.pdf.

19 Report Number 8-6, II IMB 1611, 1616 ("The Joint Technical Commission decided to make an inspection to ascertain the precise nature of certain Tunisian insular formations. It determined that the rock Le Sorelle . . . was not above water at low tide and disregarded it as a land point."); see also, National Geospatial-Intelligence Agency, Pub. 131, SAILING DIRECTIONS (ENROUTE), WESTERN MEDITERRANEAN (17th ed. 2017) at 138 ("Ecueil des Sorelles . . . consisting of two shallow rocky patches").

20 2002 Provisional Agreement, Article 1, reprinted in Report Number 8-16, V IMB 3927, 3936.

21 Annex to the Agreement on Provisional Arrangements for the Delimitation of the Maritime Boundary between the Republic of Tunisia and the People's Democratic Republic of Algeria, Algeria – Tunisia, 7 Aug 2002, 2238 UNTS 211 (reprinted following this report).

22 Report Number 8-16, V IMB 3927-3938, 3931.

6146   *Report Number 8-16 (Add. 1)*

full effect for the purpose of locating point P4 (as it was in the determination of the westernmost point agreed between Italy and Tunisia), and therefore influences the direction of the line between points P3 and P4.

6   *Baseline Considerations*

The straight baselines of Algeria, as established in 1984 and which span the coast of Algeria from the Algeria – Morocco land boundary to the Algeria – Tunisia land boundary,[23] were taken into account in determining the location of point P3. That point is described in the 2002 Provisional Agreement, Article 1, as "the point of intersection of the line connecting points P1 and P2 with the line situated 52 nautical miles away delimiting in the north the Algerian exclusive fishing zone and measured from Algerian baselines." Tunisia uses the low water line in the relevant area of the coast. Tunisia's baselines are not mentioned in either agreement, and it is not clear whether baselines influenced the direction of the delimitation line.

7   *Geological and Geomorphological Considerations*

Geological and geomorphological considerations do not seem to have influenced the drawing of the boundary line.

8   *Method of Delimitation Considerations*

The 2002 Provisional Agreement and 2011 Agreement do not specify what method of delimitation has been followed, but it is clear the parties rejected equidistance in drawing the first segment of their boundary from point P1 to point P3, giving no effect to La Galite for the first 53 M. Instead this segment of the boundary appears to be based on considerations of equity, constructed on the basis of three agreed geographic criteria: the segment would start at the demarcated land boundary terminus (P1), pass 4 M to the west of the Sorelles (P2), and end at the point where it intersected the outer limit of Algeria's 52 M fishing zone (P3). This seems to reflect a narrowing

---

23   Decree No. 84-181 of 4 August 1984 defining the baselines for measuring the breadth of the maritime zones under national jurisdiction (Algeria), *available at* https://www.un.org/Depts/los/LEGISLATIONANDTREATIES/PDFFILES/DZA_1984_Decree.pdf.

of differences between the parties, during the course of negotiating the 2002 Provisional Arrangement, on the effect to be given to La Galite and to the reefs of the Sorelles, specifically on the distance that should exist between the Sorelles and the boundary line.[24]

Seaward of point P3, the method of delimitation in this negotiated solution changes, apparently in order to accommodate the westernmost point of the delimitation concluded in 1971 by Italy and Tunisia. As the authors of the report on the 2002 Provisional Agreement note:

> From P3 the boundary changes direction to the west, in order to reach point P4. This point (38° 00' N, 7° 50' E) is very close to the Algeria-Italy-Tunisia equidistant tripoint, as established under the 1971 continental shelf agreement between Italy and Tunisia (38° 00.6' N, 7° 49' E). In other words, La Galite was given almost full effect only as regards the determination of the final point of the provisional boundary line (and not as regards the drawing of the line itself up to that point).[25]

In contrast, La Galite (and the even smaller Galitons de l'Est) was given full effect by Italy and Tunisia when defining the western terminal of their maritime boundary.[26] This different treatment of the same feature may reflect the distinction between the effect of islands in opposite and adjacent delimitations.

9 Technical Considerations

The coordinates of the land boundary terminus and three turning points, provided in the 2002 annex and adopted in the 2011 Agreement, are given in eastings and northings in the Universal Transverse Mercator projection system (UTM 32) and referenced to WGS-84. In addition to the UTM coordinates, the 2002 annex provides that "in order to avoid any ambiguity when marking these four points on nautical charts based on different geodesic systems and projection systems, these points shall be defined in terms of the azimuth and distance from point P1." The 2011 Agreement, Article 1(3), adopts similar language, and both the annex and agreement set out the azimuth and distance from point P1 to each of points P2, P3, and P4. The azimuths for points P2 and P3 are the same confirming that the line segment from point P1 to point

---

24 *See* Djaziri, *supra* note 4, at 51-52.
25 Report Number 8-16, V IMB 3927-3938, 3931.
26 *See* Report Number 8-6, II IMB 1611; Report Number 8-6 (Corr.), III IMB 2435.

6148 *Report Number 8-16 (Add. 1)*

P3 is essentially a single segment with point P2 acting as a guide point but not a turning point.

10 *Other Considerations*

None.

III CONCLUSIONS

As was already the case for the 2002 Provisional Agreement, the final delimitation appears to be characterized by a spirit of compromise and realism, especially as regards Tunisia's acceptance to give only reduced effect to La Galite, an isolated non-coastal island. One commentator notes the following about the boundary line:

> [It] is a compromise line between the Algerian and Tunisian claims. In that compromise, indeed, Tunisia has given up its claims on a pure equidistance line between points P1 and P4, and at the same time its claims on the Banc Le Sec, in exchange for the safeguarding of its rights over the Sorelles as well as on point Zero [i.e. the point of departure of the Tunisia-Italy delimitation] which is an equidistance point.[27]

From a more general perspective, the 2002 Provisional Agreement had been quoted favorably as a relatively uncommon instance of inter-state cooperation in seeking a provisional solution to a disputed maritime boundary, pursuant to the obligations enshrined in Articles 74 (3) and 83 (3) of UNCLOS,[28] and had been hailed by some commentators as "an

---

27 Slim, *supra* note 6, at 63 ("ce tracé est un tracé de compromis entre les prétentions algériennes et tunisiennes. En effet, dans ce compromis, la Tunisie a abandonné ses prétentions sur une ligne d'équidistance pure tracée entre le point P1 et le point P4 et en même temps ses prétentions sur le Banc Le Sec, contre la sauvegarde de ses droits sur les Sorelles et sur le point Zéro qui est un point d'équidistance").

28 For further analysis of the 2002 Provisional Agreement, *see,* Enrico Milano & Irini Papanicolopulu, *State Responsibility in Disputed Areas on Land and at Sea,* 71 ZEITSCHRIFT FÜR AUSLÄNDISCHES ÖFFENTLICHES RECHT UND VÖLKERRECHT 587, 614 (2011); Florence Galletti, *Notion et pratique de "l'arrangement provisoire" prévu aux articles 74 § 3 et 83 § 3 de la Convention sur le droit de la mer. Une contribution marginale du droit de la délimitation maritime?* 9 ANNUAIRE DE DROIT DE LA MER 115 (2004); Louis Savadogo, *Le paragraphe 3 des articles 74 et 83 de la CMB: une contribution à l'Accord sur les arrangements provisoires relatifs à la délimitation des frontières maritimes entre la République tunisienne et la République algérienne démocratique et populaire,* 7 ANNUAIRE DE DROIT DE LA MER 239 (2002); Victor Luis Gutiérrez Castillo, EL MAGREB

interesting example for States willing to test a boundary line before adopting it definitely."[29]

The unfolding of the settlement of the Algeria – Tunisia maritime boundary also appears, from a practical viewpoint, as an instructive instance of a seemingly proactive and efficient interplay between the legal (and political) and the technical sides of the negotiating process of a maritime boundary. A three-step process was followed. First, the political agreement on the potential mutually acceptable (provisional) boundary line was reached under the 2002 Provisional Agreement. The two countries then entrusted a technical body (the joint technical group) with the specific mandate "to establish the coordinates of points P1, P2, P3 and P4 using the [WGS 84] and draw on charts the line defined in article 1 [of the 2002 Provisional Agreement]" with a six-month deadline to complete its work.[30] The outcome of the work of the joint technical group, under the form of a *procès-verbal* annexed to and deemed to be an integral part of the 2002 Provisional Agreement,[31] was in turn submitted to the parties, which incorporated it in the final 2011 Agreement.

IV   RELATED LAW IN FORCE

A   *Law of the Sea Conventions*

Algeria: Party to UNCLOS (ratified on 11 June 1996).
Tunisia: Party to UNCLOS (ratified on 24 April 1985).

B   *Maritime Jurisdiction Claimed at the Time of Signature*

Algeria: 12 M territorial sea; 24 M contiguous zone; 32 M (West) or 52 M (East) fishing zone.

Y SUS FRONTERAS EN EL MAR: CONFLICTOS DE DELIMITACIÓN Y PROPUESTAS 137 (Huygens Editorial 2009); Mitja Grbec, EXTENSION OF COASTAL STATE JURISDICTION IN ENCLOSED AND SEMI-ENCLOSED SEAS 63 (Routledge 2014); British Institute of International and Comparative Law, *Report on the Obligations of States under Articles 74 (3) and 83 (3) of UNCLOS in respect of Undelimited Maritime Areas* 83-84 (2016).

29   Irini Papanicolopulu, *The Mediterranean Sea*, in THE OXFORD HANDBOOK OF THE LAW OF THE SEA 604, 615 (Donald R. Rothwell et al. eds., Oxford 2015).

30   2002 Provisional Agreement, Article 2, *reprinted in* Report Number 8-16, V IMB 3927, 3936.

31   Id.

6150   *Report Number 8-16 (Add. 1)*

Tunisia: 12 M territorial sea; fishing zone in the south under the 50-meter depth criterion; 200M exclusive economic zone.

C   *Maritime Jurisdiction Claimed Subsequent to Signature*

Algeria: 200M EEZ.
Tunisia: No change.

V   REFERENCES AND ADDITIONAL READINGS

Irini Papanicolopulu, *A Note on Maritime Delimitation in a Multizonal Context: The Case of the Mediterranean*, 38 OCEAN DEVELOPMENT & INTERNATIONAL LAW 381 (2007).

Prepared by Pierre-Emmanuel Dupont

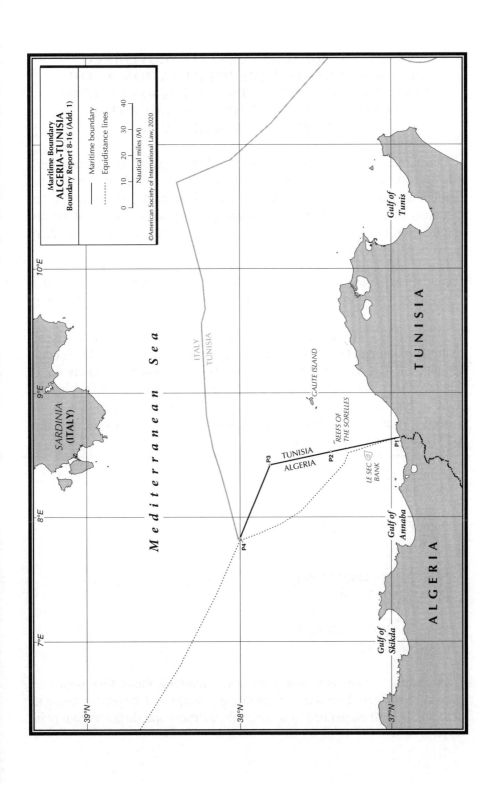

6152 *Report Number 8-16 (Add. 1)*

ANNEX TO THE AGREEMENT ON PROVISIONAL ARRANGEMENTS FOR THE DELIMITATION OF THE MARITIME BOUNDARY BETWEEN THE REPUBLIC OF TUNISIA AND THE PEOPLE'S DEMOCRATIC REPUBLIC OF ALGERIA

Pursuant to the provisions of article 2 of the Agreement on provisional arrangements for the delimitation of the maritime boundary between the Republic of Tunisia and the People's Democratic Republic of Algeria, signed at Algiers on 11 February 2002, the undersigned plenipotentiaries of the two countries have adopted the following procès-verbal containing the results of the work of the joint technical group:

PROCÈS-VERBAL OF THE MEETING OF THE JOINT ALGERIAN-TUNISIAN TECHNICAL GROUP HELD IN TUNIS, 1 TO 8 JULY 2002

In accordance with article 2 of the Agreement on provisional arrangements for the delimitation of the maritime boundary between the People's Democratic Republic of Algeria and the Republic of Tunisia, signed at Algiers on 11 February 2002, the four points forming the provisional line delimiting the maritime boundary between the two countries are calculated using the World Geodetic System 1984 (WGS 84) and the Universal Transverse Mercator (UTM) projection system as follows:

Point P1 (X=468128.71)
(Y=4088378.99)

Point P2 (X=457962.5)
(Y=4139213.5)

Point P3 (X=449023.8594)
(Y=4183909.7453)

Point P4 (X=397568.0535)
(Y=4206457.1241)

In order to avoid any ambiguity when marking these four points on nautical charts based on different geodesic systems and projection systems, these points shall be defined in terms of the azimuth and distance from point

P1, representing boundary marker No. 001 of the Algerian-Tunisian land boundary.

Point P2: Azimuth = 3480 28' 23" distance = 51860.9625 m

Point P3: Azimuth = 3480 28' 23" distance = 97459.2693 m

Point P4: Azimuth = 3280 55' 07" distance = 137601.2365 m

The determination of the aforementioned points was based on data obtained form [sic] the hydrographical survey of the Sorelles reef of 4 July 2002 by the joint technical group, as shown in the chart attached to this annex.

For the Tunisian technical group:
FETHI SETTAY
Marine commander

For the Algerian technical group:
COLONEL ABD-ENNOUR ABDERRAHMANE AOUN

Done at Algiers, on 7 August 2002, in two original copies in the Arabic language, both texts being equally authentic and constituting an integral part of the Agreement on provisional arrangements for the delimitation of the maritime boundary between the two countries.

For the plenipotentiary of the Republic of Tunisia:
ABDELMAJID BAOUAB
Director-General of Consular Affairs
Ministry of Foreign Affairs

For the plenipotentiary of the People's Democratic Republic of Algeria:
NADIR LARBAOUI
Director of Legal Affairs
Ministry of Foreign Affairs

6154   *Report Number 8-16 (Add. 1)*

Convention Regarding Delimitation of the Maritime Boundaries between the People's Democratic Republic of Algeria and the Tunisian Republic

The People's Democratic Republic of Algeria and the Tunisian Republic, hereinafter referred to as "the Parties";

Desirous of consolidating the relations of brotherhood, cooperation and good-neighborliness existing between the two fraternal countries and peoples and based on common historical ties;

Constantly striving to strengthen the distinguished relations between the two countries in all areas on the basis of brotherhood, solidarity and the promotion of common interests;

Wishing to consolidate the building of the Arab Maghreb Union by strengthening the relations of brotherhood and cooperation between them;

Conscious of the necessity to work for the protection of the Mediterranean and the safeguard of its natural resources, biological and non-biological, for the benefit of contemporary and future generations;

Inspired by the spirit of brotherhood and concord underlying the Agreement between the two countries on the emplacement of boundary markers, signed at Tunis on 19 March 1983 and ratified by the two Parties;

Motivated by the strong desire to settle questions relating to the delimitation of the maritime boundaries between the two countries in a spirit of understanding, cooperation and equity;

Considering the provisions of the United Nations Convention on the Law of the Sea, adopted at Montego Bay on 10 December 1982 and ratified by the two Parties, and international law;

Based on the Agreement on Provisional Arrangements for the Delimitation of the Maritime Boundaries between the two Parties, concluded in Algiers on 11 February 2002 and adopted by the two Parties, as well as on the minutes of the works of the Algerian-Tunisian joint technical team, signed in Algiers on 7 August 2002;

The two Parties have agreed on the definitive delimitation of the maritime boundaries between the People's Democratic Republic of Algeria and the Tunisian Republic, according to the following provisions:

Article 1

1. The course of the line of the maritime boundaries between the two countries shall consist of segments of straight lines connecting points P1, P2, P3 and P4, the coordinates of which are as follows, according to the projection system UTM32 (Universal Transverse Mercator):

P1 :   X = 468128.71
                      Y = 4088378.99

P2 :   X = 457962.5
                      Y = 4139213.5

P3 :   X = 449023.8594
                      Y = 4183909.7453

P4 :   X = 397568.0535
                      Y = 4206457.1241

2. The above-mentioned coordinates shall be defined according to the World Geodetic System 1984 (WGS 84).

3. In order to materialize the four points referred to above on maritime charts under different geodetic systems and projection systems, these points shall be defined according to azimuth and distance, starting from point 1 (Pl) which represents the boundary marker No. 001 for the Algeria – Tunisia land boundaries

Point 2 (P2) azimuth = 23″ 28′ 348° distance = m 51860.9625

Point 3 (P3) azimuth = 23″ 28′ 348° distance = m 97459.2693

Point 4 (P4) azimuth = 07″ 55′ 328° distance = m 137601.2365

6156 *Report Number 8-16 (Add. 1)*

4. For the purpose of deduction, the delimitation line shall be drawn as defined in the first paragraph of the present article, on the international maritime chart No. 3208.

Article 2

The course of the delimitation line of contingent maritime spaces constitutes the boundary of the territorial sea, of the contiguous zone, of the continental shelf, of the exclusive economic zone as well as of any other maritime zone newly created or that may be created in accordance with the United Nations Convention on the Law of the Sea of 1982 and international law.

Article 3

The People's Democratic Republic of Algeria exercises, west of the line of maritime boundaries, its sovereignty, its sovereign rights or its jurisdiction. The Tunisian Republic exercises, east of the line of maritime boundaries, its sovereignty, its sovereign rights or its jurisdiction

Article 4

In case where one of the Parties decides or authorizes the conduct of surveying work with a view to exploration or exploitation of the mineral resources located in the immediate vicinity of the line of maritime boundaries, it shall inform the other Party.

Article 5

In case where a geological structure or an oil well or natural gas well or other non-living natural resources would be located on both sides of the line of the maritime boundaries referred to in Article 1 of the present convention, and if the structure or the well located on one side of the line can be exploited, in full or in part, from the other side of the said line, the Parties shall exchange all relevant information and determine, by agreement, the arrangements concerning exploitation of these resources.

Article 6

Any dispute arising between the Parties concerning the interpretation or application of the present convention shall be settled by negotiations. Failing that, they shall have recourse to any other peaceful means agreed by the Parties in accordance with international law.

Article 7

1. The two Parties will create a joint maritime boundaries commission which will be entrusted with the task of the follow-up of the present convention and to ease the difficulties that may result from its application.

2. The joint maritime boundaries commission will be composed of a representative of either Party who will be assisted by advisors or experts.

3. The joint maritime boundaries commission will meet in ordinary sessions every two (2) years alternatively in either country. It will gather further to the express request of one of the Parties within two (2) months as of the date of this request.

4. The joint maritime boundaries commission shall formulate recommendations to be submitted to the two Parties. In case where these are adopted by the Parties, these recommendations shall become mandatory. In case where these have not been adopted by either Party, the provisions of Article 6 above shall apply.

Article 8

The present convention shall be ratified according to the constitutional procedures of either Party and it shall come into force as of the date of exchange of the instruments of ratification.

Article 9

The two Parties shall proceed jointly with the registration of the present convention with the United Nations Secretariat-General, in accordance with Article 102 of the United Nations Charter.

Done in Algiers, on 11 July 2011 in two original copies in Arabic language, each of which are equally authentic.

For the People's Democratic
Republic of Algeria
Mourad MEDELCI
Minister for Foreign Affairs

For the Tunisian Republic
Mohammed AL MOULDI AL KAFI
Minister for Foreign Affairs

(Unofficial translation by Pierre-Emmanuel Dupont)

Libya – Turkey

Report Number 8-24

Memorandum of Understanding between the Government of the Republic of Turkey and the Government of National Accord-State of Libya on Delimitation of the Maritime Jurisdiction Areas in the Mediterranean

Signed: 27 November 2019
Entry into force: 8 December 2019
Published at: UNTS (I-56119); Official Gazette of the Republic of Turkey, No. 30971, 7 December 2019, Decision No. 1815

I SUMMARY

The Memorandum of Understanding between the Government of the Republic of Turkey and the Government of National Accord-State of Libya on Delimitation of the Maritime Jurisdiction Areas in the Mediterranean (the MoU) delimits by a single line the continental shelf and exclusive economic zone (EEZ) between Libya and Turkey in the Mediterranean Sea following the equidistance method. It was met with rejection, objection, and protestation by the neighboring countries and the European Union on the grounds that it infringes upon the sovereign rights of third states and violates internal Libyan constitutional rules relating to the conclusion of treaties.

II CONSIDERATIONS

1 *Political, Strategic, and Historical Considerations*

The negotiation and conclusion of the MoU as well as the location of the maritime boundary it delineates must be envisaged against a dual context: the ongoing civil war in Libya and the geopolitical tensions in the Eastern Mediterranean over the delimitation of maritime boundaries and the exploration and exploitation of oil and gas resources.

Coalter G. Lathrop (ed.), International Maritime Boundaries, 6159-6179.
© *The American Society of International Law and Koninklijke Brill BV, Leiden 2025.*

After the 2011 overthrow and killing of Moammar Gadhafi, who had ruled the country for more than 40 years, Libya plunged into chaos and instability. Since 2016, the administration of its territory has been split between two rival authorities: the Government of National Accord (GNA), led by Prime Minister Fayez al-Sarraj and considered by the United Nations to be the sole legitimate government of Libya,[1] and the Libyan National Army (LNA), led by Field Marshal Khalifa Haftar and backed by the Libyan House of Representatives. While the former controls the northwestern part of the country, including the capital Tripoli, the latter controls the remaining part of Libya: the east and its chief town Benghazi; the central region where most of the country's oil and gas wells are located; and the south with the exception of a relatively small stretch controlled by different non-Arab armed groups.

On 4 April 2019, Field Marshal Haftar and the LNA launched a large-scale military campaign against Tripoli with the objective of extending their control over the entire Libyan territory and its capital city. By October 2019, the front seemed to have stabilized outside Tripoli. Nevertheless, the GNA feared that the balance of power was tipping in favor of Haftar's forces because of their aerial and technological superiority. Indeed, the LNA is supported directly and indirectly by the air forces of Egypt and the United Arab Emirates, as well as the Wagner Group, a private Russian military company.

Faced with this situation, the GNA turned to its main regional ally, Turkey, seeking an intensification of Turkey's military support and involvement on the battlefield. Turkey responded positively by concluding on 27 November 2019, with the GNA, a Memorandum of Understanding on Security and Military Cooperation.[2] It was on the basis of this military cooperation agreement that the Turkish Parliament passed a bill on 2 January 2020 authorizing the Turkish government to deploy troops in Libya. The deployment started a few days later and consisted in sending to Libya Syrian fighters, Turkish military experts, and advanced military equipment, including modern air defense systems and drones.

Interestingly, this military cooperation agreement was concluded on the same day as the signing of the MoU which is the object of the present report. Therefore, the delimitation agreement could be considered part of a *quid pro quo* between Turkey and Libya: the former agreeing to support militarily the legitimate government of the latter in exchange for the conclusion of a

---

1   Security Council Res. 2259, para. 3, UN Doc. S/RES/2259 (23 December 2015).
2   The text of this agreement is *available at* https://www.nordicmonitor.com/wp-content/uploads/2019/12/Turkey_Libya_military_deal_english.pdf.

maritime delimitation agreement that strengthens the position of Turkey in the Eastern Mediterranean.

The MoU was also concluded against the background of increasing geopolitical tensions in the region related to the delimitation of maritime boundaries and to the exploration and exploitation of offshore hydrocarbon resources. At the end of the 1990s and the beginning of the 2000s, many oil and gas discoveries offshore Egypt, Palestine, and Israel prompted the coastal countries of the Eastern Mediterranean to delimit their maritime boundaries and enhance their cooperation on energy issues. However, Turkey was somewhat left aside in this process.

The Cypriot government concluded delimitation agreements with Egypt in 2003,[3] Lebanon in 2007,[4] and Israel in 2010[5] without consulting or involving the Turkish Cypriot authorities. Turkey considers the Cypriot government not competent to represent jointly the Greek and Turkish Cypriots and consequently Cyprus as a whole.[6] Turkey holds the same view of the granting by Cyprus of oil and gas licenses to international companies in the EEZ claimed by the island state.[7]

Additionally, the three aforementioned agreements applied the equidistance principle and gave full effect to the island of Cyprus, thereby contradicting the longstanding Turkish approach to maritime delimitation in the Eastern Mediterranean which is based, in part, on the limited effect of islands, including Cyprus, on the delimitation of their maritime boundaries with continental territory.[8] In particular, by extending the delimitation

---

3   Report Number 8-15, V IMB 3917. This agreement was followed in 2013 by the conclusion of a framework agreement related to the development of transboundary hydrocarbons resources. *See* Report Number 8-15 (2), VIII IMB 5651.

4   Report Number 8-19, VI IMB 4445. This agreement is not in force.

5   Report Number 8-22, VII IMB 5091.

6   *See Information note by Turkey, concerning its objection to the Agreement between the Republic of Cyprus and the Arab Republic of Egypt on the Delimitation of the Exclusive Economic Zone* [of] *17 February 2003* (2 March 2004), *reprinted in* 54 LOS BULL. 127 (2004).

7   *Letter dated 30 May 2014 from the Chargé d'affaires a.i. of the Permanent Mission of Turkey to the United Nations addressed to the Secretary-General*, UN Doc. A/68/902, *available at* https://undocs.org/A/68/902.

8   *Letter dated 15 June 2016 from the Chargé d'affaires a.i. of the Permanent Mission of Turkey to the United Nations addressed to the Secretary-General*, UN Doc. A/70/945–S/2016/541, *available at* https://undocs.org/A/70/945.

    This approach is not new. Turkey had advocated the limited effect of islands in maritime delimitation on the occasion of its dispute with Greece in the Aegean Sea in the 1970s as well as during the Third United Nations Conference on the Law of the Sea. Turkey was among the four states that voted against the adoption of the UNCLOS notably because its Article 121, paragraph 2, provided for an equal treatment of insular and land territories in terms of maritime areas.

6162   *Report Number 8-24*

line west of the meridian 32° 16′ 18″E, the Cyprus-Egypt agreement of 2003 encroached on maritime areas claimed by Turkey on the basis of its geographical situation as the country with the longest coastline in the Eastern Mediterranean and the cut-off effect generated by the island of Cyprus on the seaward projections of this coastline.[9]

In view of the above, the Libya – Turkey MoU should be understood as an attempt to break Turkey's relative confinement in the Eastern Mediterranean through the conclusion of a delimitation treaty that upholds the Turkish approach to maritime delimitation in the region. Indeed, on the eve of the conclusion of the present MoU, the only agreement of this type in the region was the very controversial delimitation agreement concluded on 21 September 2011 between Turkey and the Turkish Republic of Northern Cyprus, an entity whose creation was deemed illegal by the United Nations Security Council and which is only recognized as a state by Turkey itself.[10] This agreement delimits the continental shelf with an equidistance line adjusted in favor of Turkey in order to accommodate the greater length of its continental shoreline and uphold the principle of limited effect of islands that it advocates. In keeping with this principle, the Libya – Turkey agreement follows a strict equidistance line between the continental coasts of Libya and Turkey, presupposing that Cyprus and the Greek islands of Crete, Casos, Carpathos, and Rhodes only generate a territorial sea but not an EEZ or continental shelf.

On 14 January 2019, Egypt, Cyprus, Greece, Israel, Italy, Jordan, and Palestine established the Eastern Mediterranean Gas Forum, a cooperation platform based in Cairo that aims to "create a regional gas market that serves the interests of its members by ensuring supply and demand, optimizing resource development, rationalizing the cost of infrastructure, offering competitive prices and improving trade relations."[11] Turkey was excluded

---

9   *Information note by Turkey, supra* note 6. For additional explanations on the legal basis of Turkey's position with regard to the delimitation of its maritime boundaries in the Mediterranean, *see also Letter dated 18 March 2019 from the Permanent Representative of Turkey to the United Nations addressed to the Secretary-General*, UN Doc. A/73/804, *available at* https://undocs.org/en/A/73/804; *Letter dated 18 March 2020 from the Permanent Representative of Turkey to the United Nations addressed to the Secretary-General*, UN Doc. A/74/757, *available at* https://undocs.org/en/A/74/757.

10 *See* Nikolaos A. Ioannidis, *The Continental Shelf Delimitation Agreement Between Turkey and "TRNC"*, EJIL:Talk! (26 May 2014), https://www.ejiltalk.org/the-continental-shelf-delimitation-agreement-between-turkey-and-trnc/.

11 *Eastern Mediterranean countries to form regional gas market*, Reuters (14 January 2019), https://www.reuters.com/article/us-egypt-energy-gas/eastern-mediterranean-countries-to-form-regional-gas-market-idUSKCN1P81FG.

from this initiative which probably prompted it to seek out other Mediterranean partners such as Libya with its tremendous oil and gas resources.

Finally, on 20 March 2019, the president of Cyprus and the prime ministers of Greece and Israel met in Jerusalem to discuss trilateral cooperation with the presence of the United States Secretary of State Mike Pompeo. On this occasion statements of support were issued for the establishment of an Eastern Mediterranean (EastMed) pipeline connecting the Cypriot and Israeli gas fields to Western Europe through Greece.[12] If constructed as planned, this pipeline would cross maritime areas claimed by Turkey and would compete with the Trans-Anatolian and the TurkStream pipelines – both of which aim to convey Azerbaijani and Russian gas to Europe through Turkey – thereby threatening Turkey's position as the main Mediterranean transit territory for gas into Europe. By adopting a boundary located approximately 45 nautical miles (M) south of the Greek island of Crete, this agreement places the EastMed Pipeline within the area of continental shelf claimed by Turkey, which would allow the latter to hinder its establishment since international law grants coastal states several prerogatives with regard to the laying of pipelines on their continental shelf.[13]

2 Legal Regime Considerations

The MoU delimits the EEZ and continental shelf between Libya and Turkey. Neither state is a party to the United Nations Convention on the Law of the Sea (UNCLOS) nor to the 1958 Geneva Convention on the Continental Shelf.

Libya issued an official declaration in 2009 by which it claimed an EEZ.[14] Interestingly, Turkey has not, for the time being, claimed an EEZ in the Mediterranean Sea.[15] Therefore, the MoU is in line with the unusual practice of some Eastern Mediterranean states, notably Cyprus, Israel, and Lebanon,

---

12 Press Release, U.S. Embassy in Cyprus, *Remarks by Secretary Pompeo with Israeli Prime Minister Netanyahu, Cyprus President Anastasdiades, and Greek Prime Minister Tsipras* (20 March 2019), https://cy.usembassy.gov/ (last visited 19 October 2020).

13 *See, e.g.*, UNCLOS, Article 79, paras. 3 and 4.

14 General People's Committee Decision No. 260 of A.J. 1377 (A.D. 2009) concerning the declaration of the exclusive economic zone of the Great Socialist People's Libyan Arab Jamahiriya (Libya), *reprinted in* 72 LOS BULL. 78 (2010), *available at* https://www.un.org/Depts/los/LEGISLATIONANDTREATIES/PDFFILES/lby_2009_declaration_e.pdf.

15 Turkey has only claimed an EEZ in the Black Sea. Decree by the Council of Ministers, No. 86/11264 (17 December 1986) (Turkey), *available at* https://www.un.org/Depts/los/LEGISLATIONANDTREATIES/PDFFILES/TUR_1986_Decree.pdf.

6164 *Report Number 8-24*

which consists in concluding bilateral EEZ delimitation agreements before claiming an EEZ.[16]

The Preamble refers to the decision of the parties to "determine a precise and equitable delimitation ... in accordance with applicable rules of international law taking into account all relevant circumstances" and to their willingness "to achieve equitable and mutually acceptable solutions." Therefore, Libya and Turkey seem to have undertaken their delimitation on the basis of customary international law as it has been expressed in the case law of the International Court of Justice, according to which the delimitation of the EEZ/continental shelf must be effected by the application of equitable principles, taking into account all relevant circumstances in order to achieve an equitable solution.[17]

With regard to the settlement of disputes, Article IV(1) of the MoU stipulates that any dispute arising out of the interpretation or implementation of the MoU "shall be settled through diplomatic channels in a spirit of mutual understanding and cooperation in accordance with Article 33 of the Charter of the United Nations."

3 Economic and Environmental Considerations

No economic or environmental considerations seem to have affected the location of the maritime boundary between Libya and Turkey. However, Article IV(2) of the MoU provides that: "In case there are natural resources extending from the Economic Exclusive Zone [*sic*] of one Party to the Exclusive Economic Zone of the other, the two Parties could cooperate in

---

16 Cyprus delimited its EEZ with Egypt in 2003 and declared its EEZ in 2004. *See* Report Number 8-15, V IMB 3917; Law to provide for the Proclamation of the Exclusive Economic Zone by the Republic of Cyprus (2 April 2004) (Cyprus), *available at* https://www.un.org/Depts/los/LEGISLATIONANDTREATIES/PDFFILES/cyp_2004_eez_proclamation.pdf.

Lebanon concluded and EEZ delimitation agreement with Cyprus in 2007 (not in force) and claimed its EEZ in 2011. *See* Report Number 8-19, VI IMB 4445; Law No. 163/2011 on the Delineation and Declaration of the maritime areas of the Lebanese Republic (18 August 2011) (Lebanon), No. 39 Lebanese Official Journal, 3100.

Israel delimited its EEZ with Cyprus in 2010 without having previously claimed such a zone. *See* Report Number 8-22, VII IMB 5091.

On this Eastern Mediterranean practice and its legal implications, *see* Haritini Dipla, *Ressources énergétiques et limites maritimes en Méditerranée orientale*, 16 ANNUAIRE DU DROIT DE LA MER 63 (2011).

17 *See, e.g., Continental Shelf (Libyan Arab Jamahiriya/Malta), Judgment, I.C.J. Reports 1985*, 38, para. 45.

order to reach an agreement on the modalities of the exploitation of such resources."

4 Geographic Considerations

The relevant coasts of the parties, that is the coasts which generate overlapping seaward projections and face the relevant delimitation area, are in a relationship of oppositeness and have approximately the same length. These geographic characteristics have certainly played a role in the adoption of the equidistance method for the purpose of reaching an equitable solution for the delimitation of the EEZ/continental shelf between Libya and Turkey. However, it is notable that between the opposite coasts of Libya and Turkey from which this agreed line is equidistant are substantial Greek islands and the maritime areas they are entitled to under international law. The MoU and the boundary delimited by it presuppose that these third-state territories generate very limited maritime zones.

5 Islands, Rocks, Reefs, and Low-tide Elevations Considerations

Turkish and Libyan islands, rocks, and low-tide elevations played little if any role in this delimitation. Five of the 18 basepoints listed for Turkey were placed on coastal islands, rocks and low-tide elevations. These are basepoints 6, 8, 12, 13, and 14. None of these basepoints is the nearest point to the agreed equidistance line.

Instead, the consideration in this delimitation related to islands is the treatment of Greek islands. As shown in the sketch-map annexed to the present report, the agreed delimitation line lies well beyond the notional equidistance lines between the parties and Greece. It follows that Libya and Turkey assumed that the neighboring Greek islands of Crete, Casos, Carpathos, and Rhodes generate a very limited maritime area. This is confirmed by the letter sent by Turkey on 18 March 2020 to the United Nations Secretary-General, to which was annexed a map showing the outer limits of the continental shelf claimed by Turkey in the Mediterranean, as well as a list of coordinates of the main turning points that define the limits of the Turkish shelf.[18] In this map, the aforementioned Greek islands are only

---

18 *Letter dated 18 March 2020 from the Permanent Representative of Turkey to the United Nations addressed to the Secretary-General*, UN Doc. A/74/757, *available at* https://undocs.org/en/A/74/757.

given a territorial sea of 6 M, and the limit between the Greek islands and the Turkish continental shelf is drawn following the semi-enclave method.[19]

In a letter dated 9 December 2019 and addressed to the United Nations Secretary-General, Greece protested against the Libya – Turkey delimitation agreement *inter alia* on the grounds that it "disregards the presence of the Greek islands … including the island of Crete, and violates their right to generate maritime zones as any land territory, as article 121 of the United Nations Convention on the Law of the Sea clearly stipulates."[20] It also added that the boundary "openly infringe[s] on Greece's sovereign rights."[21]

Similarly, in a letter dated 20 January 2020, also addressed to the United Nations Secretary-General, Cyprus stated that the MoU signed between Turkey and Libya delimits the EEZ/continental shelf between their coasts in complete disregard of the nearby islands. It also added in this respect that: "Article 121 (2) of the United Nations Convention on the Law of the Sea explicitly provides for the entitlement of islands to a territorial sea, contiguous zone, continental shelf and EEZ. This entitlement constitutes a rule of customary international law and, as such, is opposable also to States which are not parties to the Convention, like Turkey."[22]

Likewise, on 12 December 2019, the European Council issued the following statement: "The Turkey-Libya Memorandum of Understanding on the delimitation of maritime jurisdictions in the Mediterranean Sea infringes upon the sovereign rights of third States, does not comply with the Law of the Sea and cannot produce any legal consequences for third States."[23]

Ascertaining whether the Libya – Turkey agreement constitutes, by itself, a violation of the international law of the sea and a breach of Greece's sovereign rights is beyond the scope of the present report. The same can be said regarding the customary character of UNCLOS Article 121 (2) and its opposability to Turkey which has persistently objected to the regime

---

19 Greece fixed the extent of its territorial sea at 6 M from the coast in 1936. Law No. 230 of 17 September 1936, Article 1 (Greece), *available at* https://www.un.org/Depts/los/LEGISLATIONANDTREATIES/PDFFILES/GRC_1936_Law.pdf.

20 *Letter dated 9 December 2019 from the Permanent Representative of Greece to the United Nations addressed to the Secretary-General*, UN Doc. A/74/706, *available at* https://undocs.org/en/A/74/706.

21 Id.

22 *Letter dated 20 January 2020 from the Permanent Representative of Cyprus to the United Nations addressed to the Secretary-General*, UN Doc. A/74/660-S/2020/50, *available at* https://undocs.org/en/A/74/660.

23 European Council, *European Council Meeting – Conclusions*, para. 19 (12 December 2019), *available at* https://www.consilium.europa.eu/media/41768/12-euco-final-conclusions-en.pdf.

of islands set out by this provision.[24] Nevertheless, it suffices here to say that pursuant to the *pacta tertiis nec nocent nec prosunt* rule, the Libya – Turkey MoU is *res inter alios acta* and cannot bind Greece or affect its legal rights and position with respect to the extent of its maritime areas and their delimitation with the neighboring countries.[25] The same can be said with regard to Cyprus and any other state in the region.

6 Baseline Considerations

The coordinates of the basepoints used to establish the equidistance line are reproduced in Annex 2 of the MoU. This annex contains two tables with 18 basepoints each, the first table listing the basepoints that were placed on the Turkish coasts and the second listing those that were defined on the Libyan coasts. Only a small subset of one or two basepoints on each coast would actually have had an influence on the location of the single-segment equidistance boundary.

In 2005, Libya established a system of straight baselines from which the maritime zones of the country are to be measured and transmitted the decision to the United Nations.[26] The Libyan system connects 64 points with straight lines and stretches to the border between Libya and Egypt. Some of the Libyan basepoints listed in Annex 2 appear to have been placed on Libya's claimed straight baselines, while many others, including Basepoint 18, are located, for unknown reasons, a few hundred meters apart from the said baselines. Basepoint 18, the easternmost of the Libya's listed basepoints, appears to be the nearest basepoint to the equidistance boundary and, therefore, the only Libyan basepoint relevant to this delimitation.

---

24 *See* Stefan Talmon & Mary Lobo, *The intricacies of maritime boundary delimitation: Germany's one-sided response to the Turkey-Libya MoU on delimitation of the maritime jurisdiction areas in the Mediterranean*, GERMAN PRACTICE IN INTERNATIONAL LAW (9 March 2020, revised 22 July 2020), https://gpil.jura.uni-bonn.de/2020/03/the-intricacies-of-maritime-boundary-delimitation-germanys-one-sided-response-to-the-turkey-libya-mou-on-delimitation-of-the-maritime-jurisdiction-areas-in-the-mediterranean/.

25 *See* Vienna Convention on the Law Treaties art. 34, 23 May 1969, 1155 UNTS 332. For an application of this principle in a maritime delimitation context *see also Maritime Delimitation in the Caribbean Sea and the Pacific Ocean (Costa Rica v. Nicaragua)* and *Land Boundary in the Northern Part of Isla Portillos (Costa Rica v. Nicaragua), Judgment, I.C.J. Reports 2018*, 187, para. 123.

26 General People's Committee Decision No. 104 of the year 1373 from the death of the Prophet (AD 2005) concerning straight baselines for measuring the breadth of the territorial sea and maritime zones of the Libyan Arab Jamahiriya (Libya), *reprinted in* 59 LOS BULL. 15 (2005).

Unlike Libya, Turkey has not established a straight baseline system. Consequently, the basepoints on its side were placed on normal baselines, more specifically on the tip of coastal promontories and on the extremity of maritime features. Here too, only one or two of the listed basepoints, Basepoints 2 and 3 on the southern coast of the Datça Peninsula, are the nearest basepoints to the boundary. It is worth noting that the Greek islands of Tilos, Carpathos, and Casos sit directly between this section of Turkey's normal baseline and the boundary agreed with Libya.

7 Geological and Geomorphological Considerations

No geological or geomorphological factors seem to have influenced the drawing of the boundary line.

8 Method of Delimitation Considerations

The maritime boundary line between Libya and Turkey was drawn following the equidistance method.

The resulting single-segment line is described in Article I(1) of the MoU as a line connecting Point A (34° 16' 13.720"N – 026° 19' 11.640"E) with Point B (34° 09' 07.9"N – 026° 39' 06.3"E). This line, which measures approximately 18 M, is straight and has no intermediate turning points. Consequently, it cannot have been drawn on the basis of all 36 basepoints (18 on each side) provided in Annex 2 of the agreement, because this would have produced a multi-segment line with many turning points. Instead, the delimitation line was most probably drawn using only one or two basepoints on each side. Libyan Basepoint 18 and Turkish Basepoints 2 and 3 are the nearest basepoints to the line.

Besides their coordinates, the Libya – Turkey agreement does not contain any further information with regard to the location of the end points of the boundary. Point A – the western endpoint of the boundary – seems to correspond to the point of intersection between the equidistance line and the meridian passing through the easternmost point of the island of Crete. In this respect, it is worth noting that Turkey used the same method to determine the starting point of its claimed median line with Egypt which is located at the intersection of that line with the meridian passing through the westernmost point of the island of Cyprus.[27] As for Point B – the eastern endpoint of the boundary line – it appears to correspond to the equidistant tripoint between the Turkish, Libyan, and Egyptian coasts.

9   Technical Considerations

The boundary line is shown on the map that constitutes Annex 1 of the Libya – Turkey agreement. This map is based on the INT 308 Nautical Chart, which corresponds to the British Admiralty 183 Chart (Ed. 1992) and is at a scale of 1:1,102,000. The geographical coordinates of the aforementioned Point A and Point B appear on the map and in Article I(1) of the MoU and are expressed in terms of the World Geodetic System 1984 (WGS-84). The coordinates of the basepoints used to generate the equidistance line and which are enlisted in Annex 2 of the MoU are also referenced to WGS-84.

10   Other Considerations

In separate letters addressed to the United Nations Secretary-General respectively on 9 and 23 December 2019, Greece and Egypt submitted that the MoU is null and void and without legal effect because, by concluding it without the endorsement of the Libyan House of Representatives, the GNA violated the Libyan Political Agreement concluded in Skhirat, Morocco on 17 December 2015.[28] This internal agreement, signed under the auspices of the United Nations, aimed at putting an end to the then political division of Libya between the General National Congress and the House of Representatives: two rival parliaments resulting respectively from the Libyan general elections of 2012 and 2014. The constitutional value of the Libyan Political Agreement is confirmed by several of its provisions, including

---

27 *Letter dated 18 March 2020 from the Permanent Representative of Turkey to the United Nations addressed to the Secretary-General*, UN Doc. A/74/757, *available at* https://undocs.org/en/A/74/757. *See also* Report Number 8-15, V IMB 3918.

28 *Letter dated 9 December 2019 from the Permanent Representative of Greece to the United Nations addressed to the Secretary-General*, UN Doc. A/74/706, *available at* https://undocs.org/en/A/74/706; Note verbale *dated 23 December 2019 from the Permanent Mission of Egypt to the United Nations addressed to the Secretary-General*, UN Doc. A/74/628, *available at* https://undocs.org/en/A/74/628.

Article 65 which stipulates that the Constitutional Declaration, issued by the Interim Transitional National Council on 3 August 2011, shall be amended in accordance with the stipulations of the Libyan Political Agreement. With regard to the conclusion of international agreements, Article 8 (2)(f) of the said agreement provides that "the Presidency Council of the Council of Ministers ... shall ... conclude international agreements and conventions provided that they are endorsed by the House of Representatives." In a letter dated 2 December 2019, the president of the House of Representatives, Aguila Saleh Issa, informed the United Nations Secretary-General of the House's disapproval of the Libya – Turkey delimitation agreement. He also denounced its qualification as a "Memorandum of Understanding" instead of an "agreement" as a suspicious attempt to circumvent the abovementioned provision.[29] However, the United Nations Secretary-General was more nuanced in his report of 15 January 2020 on the United Nations Support Mission in Libya, in which he stated that: "On 4 January, a group of members of the House of Representatives based in Tobruk declared the memorandums of understanding illegal, while another group of members of the House of Representatives based in Tripoli had previously endorsed them."[30] In an explanatory note addressed to the United Nations Secretary-General on 26 December 2019, the Chargé d'affaires *ad interim* of the Permanent Mission of Libya to the United Nations advocated the validity of the Libya – Turkey MoU and emphasized the right of the Presidency Council of the GNA to sign memorandums of understanding as the supreme executive authority in Libya.[31]

The validity or invalidity of the Turkey-Libya delimitation agreement under Libyan and international law remains an open question.[32] Answering it is beyond the scope of the present study.

---

29 For the text of the letter, *see Aguila Saleh to the UN Security Council: We Demand 3 Urgent Steps Including Withdrawing Recognition of the GNA*, Al Marsad (2 December 2019),https://almarsad.co/en/2019/12/02/aguila-saleh-to-the-un-security-council-we-demand-3-urgent-steps-including-withdrawing-recognition-of-the-gna/.

30 The Secretary-General, *Report of the Secretary-General on the United Nations Support Mission in Libya*, para. 7, UN Doc. S/2020/41 (15 January 2020), *available at* https://unsmil.unmissions.org/sites/default/files/sg_report_to_sc_15_january_2020_eng.pdf.

31 *Letter dated 26 December 2019 from the Chargé d'affaires a.i. of the Permanent Mission of Libya to the United Nations addressed to the Secretary-General*, UN Doc. A/74/634, *available at* https://undocs.org/en/A/74/634.

32 On the invalidity of treaties concluded in violation of provisions of internal law regarding competence to conclude treaties *see* Vienna Convention on the Law Treaties art. 46, 23 May 1969, 1155 UNTS 332.

III CONCLUSIONS

The conclusion of the maritime delimitation agreement between Libya and Turkey exacerbated the already existing tensions in the Eastern Mediterranean. The MoU was met with objection by Egypt, Cyprus, the European Union, and especially Greece, which responded by expelling the Libyan ambassador.[33] It also led to the acceleration and consolidation of the different projects, dynamics, and initiatives that Turkey had intended to hinder by agreeing with Libya on a common maritime boundary. On 2 January 2020, the prime ministers of Greece and Israel and the president of Cyprus signed a formal agreement on the construction of the EastMed pipeline.[34] In the same vein, on 16 January 2020, the member states of the EastMed Gas Forum decided to conclude a "foundation charter" thereby turning their cooperation platform into a permanent regional organization.[35] Finally, on 7 August 2020, Egypt and Greece concluded an agreement for the delimitation of their EEZ following an equidistance line that gives full effect to Greek islands.[36]

Turkey, for its part, responded by expanding its oil and gas exploration activities in different disputed areas of the Eastern Mediterranean. After having registered and published on 30 May 2020 a number of hydrocarbon exploration license applications filed by the state-owned Turkish Petroleum Corporation concerning areas located south and southeast of the Greek islands of Rhodes, Carpathos, Casos, and Crete and claimed by Greece as part of its continental shelf,[37] Turkey dispatched its survey ship *Oruç Reis* to the areas in question on 10 August 2020, escorted by five gunboats, for the

---

33 *Greece to expel Libyan ambassador over Turkey-Libya accord*, REUTERS (6 December 2019), https://www.reuters.com/article/greece-libya-turkey-diplomacy/greece-to-expel-libyan-ambassador-over-turkey-libya-accord-idUSA8N23200F.

34 Press Release, Israel Ministry of Foreign Affairs, *EastMed Gas pipeline agreement signed at trilateral summit between PM Benjamin Netanyahu, Greek PM Kyriakos Mitsokakis and Cypriot Pres. Nicos Anastasiades* (2 January 2020), https://mfa.gov.il/ (last visited 19 October 2020).

35 Kostis Geropoulos, *East Med Gas Forum makes Cairo HQ*, NEWEUROPE (17 January 2020), https://www.neweurope.eu/article/east-med-gas-forum-makes-cairo-hq/.

36 For an early account of this agreement, *see* Constantinos Yiallourides, *Part I: Some Observations on the Agreement between Greece and Egypt on the Delimitation of the Exclusive Economic Zone*, EJIL:TALK! (25 August 2020), https://www.ejiltalk.org/18969-2/.

37 *Letter dated 1 June 2020 from the Permanent Representative of Greece to the United Nations addressed to the Secretary-General*, UN Doc. A/74/872, *available at* https://undocs.org/en/a/74/872.

purpose of carrying out a seismic survey.[38] Similarly, on 15 August 2020, Turkey extended to 15 September 2020 the exploratory activities conducted since October 2019 by its drillship *Yavuz* southwest of Cyprus in a maritime area claimed by that island state as part of its EEZ.[39]

Beyond regional disapproval and opposition, the MoU is also weakened by the fact that it was concluded with an authority that, irrespective of its international legitimacy, only controls a limited part of the Libyan territory and which does not include the coast relevant to the present delimitation. The fate and viability of the MoU will therefore additionally depend on the outcome of the current Libyan civil war which, at the time of writing, remains uncertain.

IV   RELATED LAW IN FORCE

A   *Law of the Sea Conventions*

Libya: None.
Turkey: None.

B   *Maritime Jurisdiction Claimed at the Time of Signature*

Libya: 12 M territorial sea; 12 M contiguous zone; 200 M EEZ; continental shelf.
Turkey: 12 M territorial sea; 12 M contiguous zone; 200 M EEZ (in the Black Sea only); continental shelf.

---

38 Andrew Norris, *Troubled Waters in the Eastern Mediterranean*, EJIL:TALK! (24 August 2020), https://www.ejiltalk.org/troubled-waters-in-the-eastern-mediterranean/.

39 Andria Kades, *Cyprus issues anti-Navtex countering Turkey's notice extending gas exploration*, CYPRUS MAIL (16 August 2020), https://cyprus-mail.com/2020/08/16/cyprus-issues-anti-navtex-countering-turkeys-notice-extending-gas-exploration/. *See also Letter dated 30 April 2020 from the Permanent Representative of Cyprus to the United Nations addressed to the Secretary-General*, UN Doc. A/74/832–S/2020/350, *available at* https://www.undocs.org/pdf?symbol=en/A/74/832.

C *Maritime Jurisdiction Claimed Subsequent to Signature*

No change.

V REFERENCES AND ADDITIONAL READINGS

None.

Prepared by Najib Messihi

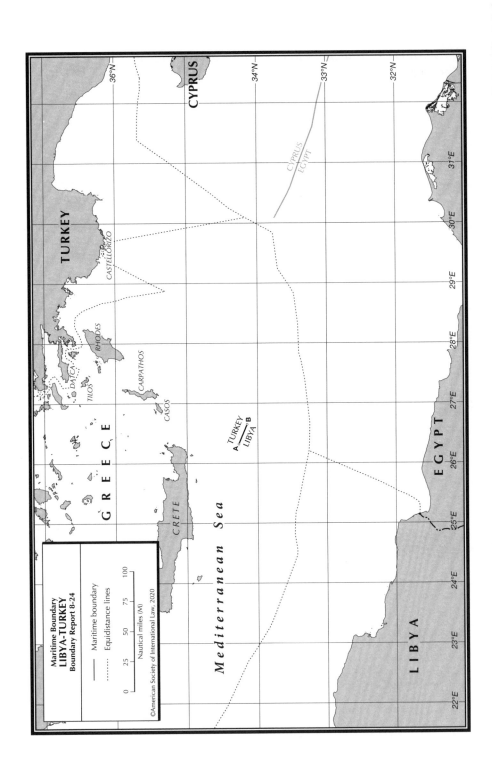

Memorandum of Understanding between the Government of the Republic of Turkey and the Government of National Accord-State of Libya on Delimitation of the Maritime Jurisdiction Areas in the Mediterranean

The Government of the Republic of Turkey and the Government of the National Accord-State of Libya (hereinafter referred to as "the Parties"),

Confirming their commitment to the aims and principles of the Charter of the United Nations,

Having decided to determine a precise and equitable delimitation of their respective maritime areas in the Mediterranean in which the Parties exercise sovereignty, sovereign rights and/or jurisdiction in accordance with applicable rules of international law taking into account all relevant circumstances,

Taking into account the willingness of the Parties to achieve equitable and mutually acceptable solutions to the above-mentioned issues through constructive negotiations and in the spirit of good-friendly relations,

Convinced that this Memorandum of Understanding will contribute to the strengthening of the relations and encourage further cooperation between the Parties in the interest of two brotherly countries,

Have agreed as follows:

Article I
The Boundaries of Continental Shelf and Exclusive Economic Zone

1. The boundaries of the Continental Shelf and the Exclusive Economic Zone in the Mediterranean between the Republic of Turkey and the Government of National Accord-State of Libya begins at Point A (34° 16' 13.720" N – 026° 19' 11.640" E) and ends at the Point B (34° 09' 07.9" N – 026° 39' 06.3" E).

The Parties have agreed on these boundaries.

2. The boundaries of the Continental Shelf and the Exclusive Economic Zone determined in Article I, paragraph 1 of this Memorandum of Understanding are shown on the Maritime Chart INT 308 (Data Source: BA Chart Edition

1992), scale 1:1 102 000 (Annex 1). The coordinates are shown in the chart at Annex 1 in its coordinate system. The geographical coordinates referred to in Article I of this Memorandum of Understanding are expressed in terms of the World Geodetic System 1984 (WGS84).

3. Base points coordinates that are used to determine the equidistance line are shown in Annex [2]

Article II
Annexes to the Memorandum of Understanding

The annexes indicated in the second and third paragraphs of Article I constitute integral part of this Memorandum of Understanding.

Article III
Registration

Upon its entry into force, this Memorandum of Understanding shall be registered with the Secretariat of the United Nations pursuant to Article 102 of the Charter of the United Nations.

Article IV
Settlement of Disputes

1. Any dispute between the Parties arising out of the interpretation or implementation of this Memorandum of Understanding shall be settled through diplomatic channels in a spirit of mutual understanding and cooperation in accordance with Article 33 of the Charter of the United Nations.

2. In case there are natural resources extending from the Economic Exclusive Zone [sic] of one Party to the Exclusive Economic Zone of the other, the two Parties could cooperate in order to reach an agreement on the modalities of the exploitation of such resources.

3. If either of the two Parties is engaged in negotiations aimed at the delimitation of its Exclusive Economic Zone with another State, that Party,

before reaching a final agreement with the other State, shall notify and consult the other Party.

Article V
Amendment and Review

Either party may propose amendment or review of this MoU through diplomatic channels, if deemed necessary except Article I and Article II. Amendments are made with the consensus of the parties.

Article VI
Entry into Force

This Memorandum of Understanding shall enter into force on the date of receipt of the last written notification by which the Parties notify each other through diplomatic channels of the completion of their internal legal procedures required for the entry into force of the Memorandum of Understanding.

This Memorandum of Understanding was done in Istanbul on 27 November 2019, in two original copies in Turkish, Arabic and English languages, all texts being equally authentic. In case of divergence of interpretation, the English text shall prevail.

On behalf of the Government of the
Republic of Turkey
Mevlüt ÇAVUŞOĞLU
Minister of Foreign Affairs

On behalf of the Government of
National Accord-State of Libya
Mohamed Taher SIYALA
Minister of Foreign Affairs

6178 *Report Number 8-24*

Annex 1

Maritime Chart INT 308: Map of the Mediterranean with the boundary
of the continental shelf and the exclusive economic zone between the
Republic of Turkey and the Government of National Accord-State of Libya

[Map not included]

Annex 2

Base points for Turkey-Libya continental shelf/EEZ coordinates list

1. Turkish Coasts

	LATITUDE	LONGITUDE
1	36° 40′ 50″.287 N	27° 22′ 27″.873 E
2	36° 39′ 45″.969 N	27° 24′ 19″.359 E
3	36° 38′ 50″.428 N	27° 28′ 38″.882 E
4	36° 39′ 28″.639 N	27° 40′ 42″.469 E
5	36° 33′ 12″.889 N	27° 58′ 44″.128 E
6	36° 33′ 16″.661 N	28° 02′ 07″.031 E
7	36° 34′ 56″.051 N	28° 05′ 18″.361 E
8	36° 35′ 43″.847 N	28° 07′ 42″.814 E
9	36° 41′ 20″.260 N	28° 13′ 30″.287 E
10	36° 43′ 12″.400 N	28° 17′ 25″.494 E
11	36° 41′ 54″.779 N	28° 37′ 38″.668 E
12	36° 37′ 35″.654 N	28° 45′ 41″.864 E
13	36° 34′ 01″.991 N	28° 49′ 29″.785 E
14	36° 32′ 16″.733 N	29° 01′ 22″.266 E
15	36° 23′ 16″.073 N	29° 06′ 04″.195 E
16	36° 20′ 27″.209 N	29° 09′ 58″.078 E
17	36° 19′ 24″.623 N	29° 12′ 27″.635 E
18	36° 14′ 48″.669 N	29° 18′ 50″.685 E

2. Libyan Coasts

	LATITUDE	LONGITUDE
1	32-50-06.873 N	22-27-00.194 E
2	32-49-43.717 N	22-28-11.254 E
3	32-48-07.040 N	22-32-41.368 E
4	32-46-26.472 N	22-37-39.116 E
5	32-46-09.093 N	22-38-33.969 E
6	32-44-07.238 N	22-44-28.857 E
7	32-42-43.985 N	22-48-54.607 E
8	32-38-32.161 N	23-05-48.986 E
9	32-38-20.558 N	23-06-27.841 E
10	32-37-49.615 N	23-07-06.696 E
11	32-06-44.158 N	23-58-05.833 E
12	32-01-28.159 N	24-40-27.392 E
13	32-01-34.000 N	24-43-00.941 E
14	32-01-18.423 N	24-44-59.999 E
15	32-01-10.634 N	24-45-38.854 E
16	32-01-10.634 N	24-45-45.570 E
17	31-58-13.028 N	24-58-55.688 E
18	31-58-05.234 N	24-59-34.543 E

3. Coordinates are by WGS-84 system.

Egypt – Greece

Report Number 8-25

Agreement between the Government of the Hellenic Republic and the Government of the Arab Republic of Egypt on the Delimitation of the Exclusive Economic Zone between the Two Countries

Signed: 6 August 2020
Entry into force: 2 September 2020
Published at: UNTS (I-56237)

I SUMMARY

The 2020 agreement between Egypt and Greece (the Agreement) delimits by a single line the maritime areas of Egypt and Greece in the Eastern Mediterranean Sea, including the exclusive economic zone of Egypt, the continental shelf of Greece, and any future zones that Greece may proclaim. The boundary consists in a modified equidistance line that favors the Egyptian mainland, while at the same time giving significant effect to the Greek islands. The Agreement and the boundary established by it clarify entitlement to maritime zones, as between the parties, in view of future exploration and exploitation activity in an area promising in terms of mineral resources. Furthermore, the Agreement may be seen as a response to the 2019 memorandum of understanding between Libya and Turkey (the MoU or the 2019 MoU) and the implication that Greek islands in the area should not be allowed any continental shelf or exclusive economic zone.[1]

---

1   *See* Report Number 8-24, in this volume.

Coalter G. Lathrop (ed.), International Maritime Boundaries, 6181-6196.
© *The American Society of International Law and Koninklijke Brill BV, Leiden 2025.*

6182 *Report Number 8-25*

II CONSIDERATIONS

1 *Political, Strategic, and Historical Considerations*

Egypt and Greece are opposite states located in the eastern part of the Mediterranean Sea with generally friendly relationships. This is the first maritime boundary agreed by Greece with respect to the Eastern Mediterranean Sea, while Egypt entered into an agreement with Cyprus delimiting their exclusive economic zones in 2003 followed by a framework agreement for sharing transboundary hydrocarbon deposits in 2013.[2]

Negotiations for the delimitation of the maritime boundary between Egypt and Greece started in 2005 following the discovery of substantial mineral resources in the Eastern Mediterranean. Negotiations were affected by the geography of the area, which sees a number of Greek islands opposite the Egyptian mainland coast, and by the presence of third states.

Both states agreed in principle that the delimitation should be effected taking into account the Egyptian coast, on the one side, and the Greek islands, on the other. However, they disagreed on the weight to be accorded to the Greek islands. Greece has a significant number of islands spread across the Aegean Sea, from the Greek mainland to the Turkish mainland, ranging from the large island of Crete to small islets and rocks. Consequently, Greece has always claimed that islands are entitled to the same treatment as mainland territory in the delimitation of maritime boundaries. Egypt, which had agreed on an equidistance boundary with the island nation of Cyprus in the same region, was, however, not ready to entirely accept the Greek position and considered that, while Greek islands should be taken into account, not all of them should be given full effect. The final boundary between Egypt and Greece, which appears to be a modified equidistant line, is somewhat closer to the Greek coast than to the Egyptian coast.

Among the third states in the region, Turkey's presence to the east and north of the delimitation line and its long-held position on the role of islands in maritime delimitation would have been important considerations throughout these negotiations. For many decades, Greece has maintained the position that its islands should be given full effect in the delimitation of maritime areas, including vis-à-vis Turkey, with which there is an ongoing controversy concerning delimitation of maritime zones in the Aegean Sea

---

2 *See* Report Number 8-15, V IMB 3917; Report Number 8-15 (2), VIII IMB 5651.

and in the Eastern Mediterranean Sea.[3] While Greece calls for the application of equidistance giving full effect to Greek islands, Turkey's position negates the influence of islands and advocates a mainland-to-mainland approach to the delimitation of maritime boundaries.[4]

Turkey's presence in the area and its ongoing dispute with Greece complicated negotiations between Egypt and Greece.[5] In particular, the disagreement between Greece and Turkey as to the effect (if any) that the Greek islands should have on the maritime boundary between Greece and Turkey has a concrete bearing upon the delimitations among Greece, Turkey, Libya, Egypt, and Cyprus. For example, if the Greek island of Kastellorizo were given full effect in a delimitation between Greece and Cyprus, this would eliminate the possibility of a maritime boundary between Egypt and Turkey. Even if Kastellorizo were to be given only partial effect, the effect of other Greek islands, such as Rhodes and Karpathos, would diminish the length of the maritime boundary between Egypt and Turkey. And, if the Greek island of Crete and its neighboring features were given even partial effect, there would be no remaining maritime space for a boundary between Turkey and Libya. For quite some time, Egypt adopted a cautious position on the dispute between Greece and Turkey, waiting for the two states to settle their maritime boundaries before establishing its boundaries with either.

The conclusion in November 2019 of the MoU on the delimitation of maritime jurisdictional areas between Libya and Turkey signaled a turning point in the negotiations. Both Egypt and Greece declared the 2019 MoU null and void and requested the UN Secretary General not to register it.[6] Greece protested strongly against the continental shelf and exclusive economic

---

3 The two states are at variance also with respect to other issues, such as the breadth of the territorial sea and of the airspace above.

4 The mainland-to-mainland approach was applied in the delimitation between Turkey and Libya to the detriment of Greece. *See* Report Number 8-24, in this volume. It is interesting to note that Egypt, if it sought to maximize its maritime area, could have adopted Turkey's position with respect to islands, including Cyprus and the Greek islands. This may have provided Egypt with some leverage and may have been a consideration in the compromise reached between Egypt and Greece.

5 The relationships between Turkey and, respectively, Greece and Egypt are rather complicated. Greece and Turkey are both NATO members and thus allies; however, they have longstanding disputes with historical roots and from time to time they verge on conflict. Egypt and Turkey are also opposed on a number of fronts, including the Libyan civil war (where Egypt had supported the military commander Khalifa Haftar while Turkey has sided with the internationally recognised Government of National Accord), leadership in the Eastern Mediterranean region, in particular with respect to Muslim countries, and the energy market.

6 Note verbale *dated 23 December 2019 from the Permanent Mission of Egypt to the United Nations addressed to the Secretary-General*, UN Doc. A/74/628; *Letter dated*

6184   *Report Number 8-25*

zone boundaries established by the MoU asserting that, by disregarding the presence of all Greek islands in the area, including Crete, they were "fictitious, unlawful, arbitrary and provocative, and openly infringe on Greece's sovereign rights."[7] Egypt also rejected the MoU and the delimitation between Turkey and Libya.[8]

The situation in the Eastern Mediterranean became even more tense in the months following the conclusion of the 2019 MoU when Turkey undertook exploratory drilling operations, accompanied by military escort, in areas of the Eastern Mediterranean claimed by Cyprus.[9] This activity generated a response from Cyprus, other coastal states, and the European Union.[10] This situation likely prompted Greece and Egypt to resume their delimitation negotiations, and it is likely that the MoU and subsequent drilling spurred Egypt and Greece to conclude a legally binding instrument delimiting the maritime areas enjoyed by Greece and Egypt in Eastern Mediterranean.

In addition to defining their maritime areas, an agreement would serve to strengthen the agendas of both states. Greece could seize the momentum created by its 2020 agreements with Egypt and Italy[11] to demonstrate that it was able to conclude delimitation agreements with neighboring states that took due account of its position with respect to islands. For Egypt, the 2020 Agreement was one more move towards establishing its leadership in the Eastern Mediterranean region and the Middle East and consolidating its geopolitical position vis-à-vis Libya and Turkey. Furthermore, the Agreement appears to reflect the Egyptian boundary position vis-à-vis Libya, as Point E is located closer to Libya than to Egypt. At the same time, Egypt has not accepted to extend the boundary eastwards of Point A, presumably in order to avoid entering into areas of continental shelf claimed by Turkey.[12]

---

9 December 2019 from the Permanent Representative of Greece to the United Nations addressed to the Secretary-General, UN Doc. A/74/706.

7   *See* UN Doc. A/74/706, *supra* note 6.

8   *See* UN Doc. A/74/628, *supra* note 6.

9   *Letter dated 20 January 2020 from the Permanent Representative of Cyprus to the United Nations addressed to the Secretary-General*, UN Doc. A/74/660 - S/2020/50.

10 *See, e.g., Letter dated 19 February 2020 from the Permanent Representative of Greece to the United Nations addressed to the Secretary-General*, UN Doc. A/74/710–S/2020/129.

11 *See* Report Number 8-4 (2), in this volume. A new agreement would also confirm the positive trend in establishing Greece's maritime boundaries after the failure of the 2009 agreement with Albania to enter into force following the adverse ruling of the Albanian Constitutional Court and also – it has been often submitted – pressures by Turkey on Albania. *See* Report Number 8-21, VI IMB 4462.

12 Point A of the 2020 Agreement between Egypt and Greece is within 1 nautical mile of Point A of Turkey's claimed continental shelf: the westernmost point of Turkey's claim. Turkey has reserved the right to extend that claim further to the west. For Turkey's

The agreed boundary between Egypt and Greece is in direct conflict with the earlier delimitation between Libya and Turkey: it delimits essentially the same maritime area but on the basis of entirely different principles. Although the agreed boundary line does not appear to enter areas claimed by Turkey, Turkey has protested the 2020 Agreement as a violation of Turkey's continental shelf.[13]

2 Legal Regime Considerations

The Agreement "establishes a partial delimitation of the maritime boundary between the two parties" (Article 1.a). This partial boundary will be completed through consultations between the two parties beyond Point A and Point E "in accordance with international law" (Article 1.a). Egypt and Greece have specified that Point A (the easternmost point) may be extended only eastwards and Point E (the westernmost point) only westwards (Article 1.e). The Agreement furthermore requires the parties to notify and consult each other before reaching any delimitation agreement with a third state (Article 1.e).

The Agreement provides that the boundary delimits the exclusive economic zones of the two parties (Article 1.b). Upon ratification of the Law of the Sea Convention in 1983, Egypt declared that it would "exercise as from this day the rights attributed to it by the provisions of parts V and VI of the United Nations Convention on the Law of the Sea in the exclusive economic zone situated beyond and adjacent to its territorial sea in the Mediterranean Sea and in the Red Sea."[14] In the following years, it has not been clear whether Egypt was actually exercising such rights. In 2003, when the delimitation agreement with Cyprus was signed, it was considered that Egypt was exercising exclusive economic zone rights, and Egypt has made express

---

continental shelf claim, *see* Annex to *Letter dated 13 November 2019 from the Permanent Representative of Turkey to the United Nations addressed to the Secretary-General*, UN Doc. A/74/550.

13 Note verbale *dated 14 August 2020 from the Permanent Mission of Turkey to the United Nations addressed to the Secretary-General*, UN Doc. A/74/990.

14 Declaration concerning the exercise by Egypt of its rights in the Exclusive Economic Zone made upon ratification of the United Nations Convention on the Law of the Sea, 1983, *reprinted in* Food and Agriculture Organization of the United Nations, *Regional compendium of fisheries legislation (Indian Ocean Region)*, FAO Legislative Study 42/1, 254 (1986).

reference to the 1983 declaration more recently.[15] Greece has not established an exclusive economic zone and claims only continental shelf rights, which exist *ipso facto* and *ab initio,* in the area delimited by the Agreement. Until Greece claims an exclusive economic zone, it is assumed that the Agreement delimits the exclusive economic zone of Egypt and the continental shelf of Greece. The Agreement thus follows the regional practice of delimiting future zones before they are established in order to have a settled boundary once the zone is proclaimed.[16] Due to the distance between the respective coasts there cannot be any territorial sea or contiguous zone boundary between Egypt and Greece.

In its preamble, the Agreement recalls the Law of the Sea Convention, to which both states are parties, as well as "the importance of reaching an agreement based on international law." The Agreement furthermore contains a clause according to which it "shall not be subject to denunciation, withdrawal or suspension for any reason" (Article 4.a) and provides that it "may be amended only by agreement between the two parties" (Article 4.b). These two provisions seem redundant in a delimitation agreement, which by its very nature is not subject to denunciation or withdrawal.[17] Furthermore, any bilateral treaty can be amended solely with the consent of both parties, as provided for in Article 39 of the Vienna Convention on the Law of Treaties.[18] Article 4 may have been included *ad abundantiam* and in order to signal the will of the two states not to revise their maritime boundary, irrespective of future developments in the area, including those involving third states.

With regard to the settlement of disputes, Article 3 of the Agreement provides that disputes concerning its interpretation or implementation will be settled through negotiations. No judicial settlement is envisaged.

3 *Economic and Environmental Considerations*

In recent years, significant deposits of mineral resources have been discovered in the Eastern Mediterranean Sea. Gas deposits have been identified close

---

15 *See e.g., Letter dated 1 August 2020 from the Permanent Representative of Egypt to the United Nations addressed to the Secretary-General,* UN Doc. A/74/978.

16 *See, e.g.,* the delimitation agreements between Cyprus and Egypt (Report Number 8-15, V IMB 3917), Cyprus and Israel (Report Number 8-22, VII IMB 5091), and Cyprus and Lebanon (Report Number 8-19, VI IMB 4445). Greece has followed this practice also in the recently adopted exclusive economic zone delimitation agreement with Italy. Report Number 8-4 (2), in this volume.

17 *See* Vienna Convention on the Law of Treaties, Art. 56, 23 May 1969, 1155 UNTS 331.

18 *Id.*

to the coasts and further offshore of Egypt, but no discoveries of mineral resources have been announced in the proximity of the boundary established by the Agreement. In the preamble, Egypt and Greece have recognized "the importance of the delimitation of their Exclusive Economic Zone for the purpose of development in the two countries." However, no economic or environmental considerations seem to have affected the location of the maritime boundary thus established. The parties have inserted in the Agreement a general provision according to which, in the case of transboundary natural resources, including hydrocarbons reservoirs, they shall cooperate in order to reach an agreement on the modalities for their exploitation (Article 2).

4 Geographic Considerations

Egypt and Greece are opposite states. The western part of the Egyptian mainland faces the Greek islands of Crete, Kasos, Karpathos, Rhodes, and Kastellorizo and other islands and islets. The boundary has been drawn between the Egyptian mainland and the Greek islands. The presence of third states has caused the parties to adopt a partial boundary to be completed following negotiations with other states in the area. To the west, the third state is Libya. To the east, the geography is more complex, and any extension in that direction could involve either Cyprus or Turkey.

5 Islands, Rocks, Reefs, and Low-tide Elevations Considerations

The presence of numerous Greek islands has affected the location of the boundary, which appears to be a modified equidistance line between the mainland territory of Egypt, on one hand, and the Greek islands, on the other.

The main Greek islands facing Egypt in the area delimited by the Agreement are Crete, Kasos, Karpathos, and Rhodes. Crete is the largest Greek island and the fifth largest in the Mediterranean Sea, with an area of 8,336 km². It has a population of 623,065 inhabitants, which makes it the fifth most populous region of Greece according to the 2011 census. The small islands of Chrysi and Koufonisi, which are surrounded by some islets and rocks, are located south of the easternmost part of Crete opposite Egypt. Rhodes, which is located on the eastern side of the Dodecanese and very close to the Turkish coast, is the largest island of this archipelago, with an area of 1,400 km². It is 79 km long and 38 km wide. Its population amounts to 115,490 inhabitants. Karpathos, the second biggest island of the Dodecanese, has an area of 324 km². It has a long and narrow shape (49 km long and 11 km wide) and is located 47 km southwest of Rhodes, roughly midway between Rhodes and Crete. Karpathos has a population of 6,226 inhabitants. Kasos is located southwest of Karpathos. It has a surface of 49 km² and a population of 1084 inhabitants.

The boundary established by the Agreement is located between the Greek islands and the Egyptian coast, and at a significant distance from mainland Greece. It gives substantial effect to the Greek islands and confirms their entitlement to maritime zones, including an exclusive economic zone and continental shelf. However, they were not given full effect, since the boundary line is located closer to the Greek islands than to the Egyptian coast. In the text of the Agreement, the parties have not specified the exact effect given to the Greek islands. There does not seem to have been a consistent method for determining the exact effect given to the islands, and it is not possible to establish the effect given, if any, to small islands, islets and rocks.

6   Baseline Considerations

Egypt adopted a system of straight baselines in 1990.[19] The parties have not indicated in their agreement the baselines used for the measurement of the boundary line. In any case, given the geographic characteristics of the relevant coastline of Egypt, the straight baselines would not have influenced the establishment of the maritime boundary in an appreciable way.

Greece, which upon signature of the Agreement had not established any straight baselines, adopted such a system in December 2020.[20] Greece's straight baselines, however, apply only to the Ionian coast, and do not concern the area relevant to the Agreement with Egypt.

---

19   Presidential Decree No. 27 of 9 January 1990 concerning the baselines of the maritime areas of the Arab Republic of Egypt, *available at* https://www.un.org/Depts/los/LEGISLATIONANDTREATIES/PDFFILES/EGY_1990_Decree.pdf.

20   Presidential Decree No. 107 of 25 December 2020 on the closing of gulfs and the drawing of straight baselines in the sea area of the Ionian and the Ionian Islands up to Cape Tenaron of the Peloponnese, FEK A' 258 27 December 2020 (Greece).

7 Geological and Geomorphological Considerations

Geological and geomorphological considerations do not seem to have influenced the drawing of the boundary line.

8 Method of Delimitation Considerations

The Agreement does not specify the method used for drawing the boundary line and only provides that this is a partial boundary to be completed through consultations between the parties beyond the two endpoints, A and E (Article 1.a).

Egypt and Greece are opposite states, and the boundary between them appears to be a median line modified to give less than full effect to the Greek islands. All turning points are located closer to the nearest points on the coast of Greece than to points on the coast of Egypt. For example, Point A is 100 nautical miles (M) from Greece and 153 M from Egypt, and Point E is 88 M from Greece and 107 M from Egypt. Similarly, Points B, C and D are all closer to Koufonisi than to the Egyptian coast. It is difficult to determine whether the modifications follow a uniform criterion, such as a ratio to consistently reduce the effect for the Greek islands along the length of the agreed line.

Regardless of the exact method used, it is clear that this delimitation is more favorable to Egypt than a strict equidistance line giving full effect to all features and more favorable to Greece than a line drawn using a mainland-to-mainland approach.

The method used to determine the locations of the boundary endpoints is also subject to some speculation. In the west, Point E is located beyond the equidistance line between Egypt and Libya and, presumably, reflects Egypt's position vis-à-vis its boundary with Libya. In the east, Point A is located within 1 M of the endpoint of Turkey's claimed continental shelf limit. Therefore, the location of Point A may have been guided less by delimitation methodology and more by diplomatic concerns.

9 Technical Considerations

The Agreement lists the geographical coordinates of five points, A to E, that are joined by four segments running in a generally east-west direction from approximately meridian 28° E to meridian 26° E. The geographical coordinates are expressed in terms of the World Geodetic System 1984 (WGS-84). The boundary line thus drawn appears on the hydrographic chart attached to the Agreement as Annex II, which constitutes an integral part thereof.

10   *Other Considerations*

None

III   CONCLUSIONS

The Agreement signed on 6 August 2020 by Egypt and Greece delimits the exclusive economic zone of Egypt and the future exclusive economic zone of Greece. The boundary appears to be based on an equidistance line modified in favor of Egypt. At the same time, the boundary line gives significant but not full effect to the Greek islands vis-à-vis the Egyptian coastline. This is the second agreement entered into by Egypt in the Eastern Mediterranean Sea and the first one to be concluded by Greece in this area, which is currently witnessing rapid developments. While it could be seen as a reply to the claims advanced by Libya and Turkey with the conclusion of their 2019 MoU, the Agreement also clarifies the extension of the maritime zones of Egypt and Greece and consolidates the latter's claim that islands are to be accorded significant effect in the drawing of maritime boundaries.

IV   RELATED LAW IN FORCE

A   *Law of the Sea Conventions*

Egypt: Party to UNCLOS (ratified 23 August 1983).
Greece: Party to UNCLOS (ratified 21 July 1995).

B   *Maritime Jurisdiction Claimed at the Time of Signature*

Egypt: 12 M territorial sea; 200 M EEZ; continental shelf.
Greece: 6 M territorial sea; continental shelf.

C Maritime Jurisdiction Claimed Subsequent to Signature

Egypt: No change.
Greece: 12 M territorial sea, extended solely in the Ionian Sea.

V REFERENCES AND ADDITIONAL READINGS

None

Prepared by Irini Papanicolopulu

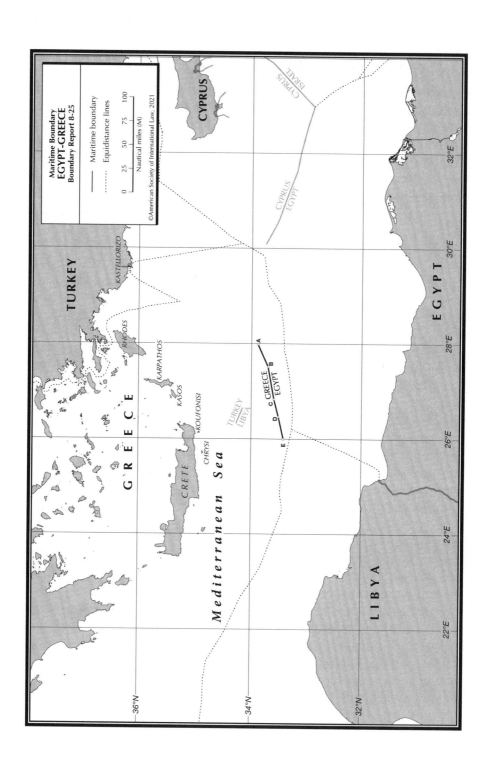

Agreement between the Government of the Arab Republic of Egypt and the Government of the Hellenic Republic on the Delimitation of the Exclusive Economic Zone between the two countries

The Government of the Arab Republic of Egypt and the Government of the Hellenic Republic (hereinafter referred to, individually as the "party", and jointly as the "two parties");

Recalling the principles and purposes of the Charter of the United Nations; Desiring to contribute to the stability of the region in good faith and in accordance with international law;

Desiring to strengthen the neighborly relations, bonds of friendship and mutual cooperation;

Aware of the need for each of the two parties to delimit its Exclusive Economic Zone, over which this party is entitled to exercise its sovereign rights and jurisdiction in accordance with international law;

Recognizing the importance of the delimitation of their Exclusive Economic Zone for the purpose of development in the two countries;

Cognizant of the United Nations Convention on the Law of the Sea of December 10, 1982, which entered into force on November 16, 1994, to which both countries are party;

Conscious of the importance of reaching an agreement based on international law;

Have agreed as follows:

Article (1)

(a) This agreement establishes a partial delimitation of the maritime boundary between the two parties. The completion of this delimitation shall be conducted, where appropriate, through consultations between the two parties beyond point (A) and point (E), in accordance with international law.

(b) The partial delimitation line between the Exclusive Economic Zone of each of the two parties is defined by points (A East) to (E West), in accordance with the list of geographical coordinates attached hereto as Annex I, which constitutes an integral part of this agreement. The part of the delimitation line between the Exclusive Economic Zone of each of the two parties from point (A East) and point (E West) is binding and final.

(c) The delimitation line, as determined in paragraph 1(b) above, appears graphically on the Hydrographic Chart attached hereto as Annex II, which constitutes an integral part of this agreement.

(d) The geographical coordinates of point (A) may be reviewed towards the East and point (E) towards the West, by an agreement between the two parties, in case of future delimitation of the Exclusive Economic Zone with other concerned neighboring States, provided that the revision is limited in this regard to point (A) extending Eastward and point (E) extending Westward.

(e) Without prejudice to the provision of Article 1 (d), if either of the two parties is engaged in negotiations aimed at the delimitation of its Exclusive Economic Zone with another State that shares with the two parties their maritime zones, that party, before reaching the final agreement with the third State, shall notify and consult the other party.

Article (2)

In case there are natural resources, including hydrocarbons reservoirs, extending from the Exclusive Economic Zone of one party to the Exclusive Economic Zone of the other, the two parties shall cooperate in order to reach an agreement on the modalities of the exploitation of such resources.

Article (3)

Any dispute arising from the interpretation or implementation of this Agreement shall be settled through the diplomatic channels in a spirit of understanding and cooperation.

Article (4)

(a)   This Agreement shall not be subject to denunciation, withdrawal or suspension for any reason.

(b)   This Agreement may be amended only by agreement between the two parties.

Article (5)

(a)   This Agreement is subject to ratification according to the constitutional procedures in each of the two parties.

(b)   This Agreement shall enter into force on the date of exchange of instruments of ratification by the two parties.

Done at Cairo, on August 6, 2020, in two originals each in Arabic, Greek and English languages, all texts being equally authentic. In case of divergence of interpretation of the texts, the English version shall prevail.

For The Arab Republic of Egypt
<signed>
Sameh Shoukry
Minister of Foreign Affairs

For The Hellenic Republic
<signed>
Nikolaos-Georgios S. Dendias
Minister for Foreign Affairs

ANNEX I

The list of the geographical coordinates

The geographical coordinates (WGS84)		Point
Latitude	Longitude	
33-53-05.00N	027-59-02.00E	A
33-41-56.41N	027-30-42.47E	B
33-35-24.09N	026-49-34.27E	C
33-30-26.24N	026-27-35.54E	D
33-24-56.14N	026-00-00.00E	E

Israel – Lebanon

Report Number 8-26

Exchange of Letters Constituting a Maritime Agreement between the State of Israel and the Lebanese Republic

Signed: 27 October 2022
Entry into force: 27 October 2022
Published at: UNTS (I-57582)

I SUMMARY

The exchange of letters of 27 October 2022 (the 2022 Delimitation Agreement or the Agreement) between the United States and Israel and the United States and Lebanon put an end to a twelve-year dispute between the two enemy states over their maritime boundary. The agreed delimitation line consists of four turning points starting from a point at sea, following an approximate equidistance line in the territorial sea, before veering south in the exclusive economic zone (EEZ) and following a straight line with a bearing of 290.40° until reaching the final point at or near the median line with the opposite coast of Cyprus. The boundary corresponds almost entirely to the line claimed by Lebanon and deposited with the United Nations Secretariat in 2010 and 2011. In the EEZ, the agreed boundary does not give effect to Israeli islets located near the land boundary terminus, a point of significant disagreement between the parties. The dispute and subsequent agreement involved a relatively small geographic area: an area located in the midst of a fraught political, strategic, and historical relationship between the parties.

II CONSIDERATIONS

1 *Political, Strategic, and Historical Considerations*

The dispute between Israel and Lebanon over their maritime boundary can be traced back to the years 2010 and 2011. On 15 July 2010, Lebanon deposited

---

Coalter G. Lathrop (ed.), International Maritime Boundaries, 6197-6229.
© *The American Society of International Law and Koninklijke Brill BV, Leiden 2025.*

the geographical coordinates of the southern limit of its maritime areas with the UN Secretary-General.[1] This limit roughly followed an equidistance line from the shore up until the external limit of the 12-nautical mile (M) territorial sea, before veering south in the EEZ and following a straight line with a bearing of approximately 290.40° until meeting the median line between the opposite coasts of Lebanon and Cyprus at a point called "Point 23". Lebanon's 2010 claim became known as "Line 23". On 17 December 2010, Cyprus and Israel concluded an agreement on the delimitation of their EEZ.[2] The agreed Cyprus-Israel line started in the north at a point called "Point 1" which corresponded to the southernmost point of the delimitation line between Cyprus and Lebanon which was agreed in 2007 but which Lebanon never ratified and which has never entered into force.[3] Since Point 1 was located approximately 9.2 M north of Lebanon's Point 23, the Cyprus-Israel agreement implied an Israeli claim to rights north of the maritime limit claimed by Lebanon. This was confirmed on 12 July 2011 when Israel transmitted to the UN Secretariat the geographical coordinates of the northern limit of its territorial sea and EEZ.[4] The Israeli northern limit, known as "Line 1", roughly followed the equidistance line over a distance of 18 M before bending north and following a straight line to Point 1. Lebanon officially protested the 2010 agreement between Cyprus and Israel and the geographical coordinates transmitted by the latter to the UN.[5] Moreover, on 19 October 2011, Lebanon reaffirmed its claim by depositing the geographical coordinates of the limits of its entire EEZ which included

---

1   Note verbale *dated 14 July 2010 from the Permanent Mission of Lebanon to the United Nations to the United Nations Secretary-General, available at* https://www.un.org/depts /los/LEGISLATIONANDTREATIES/PDFFILES/DEPOSIT/lbn_mzn79_2010.pdf.
2   *See* Report Number 8-22, VII IMB 5091.
3   *See* Report Number 8-19, VI IMB 4445.
4   Communication *dated 12 July 2011 from the Permanent Mission of Israel to the United Nations to the Secretariat of the United Nations, available at* https://www.un.org/depts /los/LEGISLATIONANDTREATIES/PDFFILES/isr_eez_northernlimit2011.pdf.
5   *Letter dated 20 June 2011 from the Minister for Foreign Affairs and Emigrants of Lebanon addressed to the Secretary-General of the United Nations concerning the Agreement between the Government of the State of Israel and the Government of the Republic of Cyprus on the Delimitation of the Exclusive Economic Zone, signed in Nicosia on 17 December 2010, available at* https://www.un.org/depts/los/LEGISLATIONANDTREATIES/PDF FILES/communications/lbn_re_cyp_isr_agreement2010.pdf; *Letter dated 3 September 2011 from the Minister for Foreign Affairs and Emigrants of Lebanon addressed to the Secretary-General of the United Nations concerning the geographical coordinates of the northern limit of the territorial sea and the exclusive economic zone transmitted by Israel,* 77 LOS BULL. 33 (2012), *available at* https://www.un.org/depts/los/LEGISLA TIONANDTREATIES/PDFFILES/communications/lbn_re_isr__listofcoordinates_e.pdf.

those it had previously deposited in 2010.[6] The opposing claims of Lebanon and Israel gave rise to an 882 km^2 disputed maritime area in the shape of a narrow triangle extending from the land boundary separating their adjacent coastal territory.

Despite the existence of an armistice agreement between them since 1949 and the non-participation of Lebanon in the Arab-Israeli wars of 1967 and 1973, the relationship between Israel and Lebanon has been marred by violence and conflict as recently as 2006 involving, in particular, the Israel Defense Forces and Hizballah. It was therefore feared that the nascent maritime dispute could trigger a new armed conflict between Israel and Hizballah which could escalate into a regional war due to the close ties between the latter and the Islamic Republic of Iran as well as the Syrian regime. At the same time, both Israel and Lebanon had an interest in settling their maritime border conflict peacefully, if only in order to be able to explore and exploit the natural resources of the subsoil of the disputed area which was assumed to encompass oil and gas deposits. However, if maritime delimitation disputes are normally resolved through direct talks and negotiations between the parties, this option was not available here due to two imperatives of Lebanon's foreign policy towards Israel: the non-recognition of Israel as a state and the non-normalization of relations with Israel, which prohibits any contact, cooperation, or relationship between the institutions or nationals of the two sides pending the resolution of the Palestinian question.

In view of the above, the US volunteered to act as a mediator between Israel and Lebanon in an attempt to find an agreed solution to their border dispute. From 2011 to 2012, this task was entrusted to the US Special Envoy to Syria, Frederic C. Hof.[7] After months of shuttle diplomacy between the two parties, Ambassador Hof proposed a compromise based on the adoption of a strict equidistance line giving full effect to all relevant maritime features on both sides. This line was to start from a point located 3 M off the shoreline in order to avoid pronouncing on one of the most contentious aspects of the dispute: the location of the land boundary terminus which would normally constitute the starting point of the maritime border. The "Hof Line" ran between the claims of the parties, leaving 55% of the disputed area to

---

6   Note verbale *dated 19 October 2011 from the Permanent Mission of Lebanon to the United Nations addressed to the Secretary-General of the United Nations*, 77 LOS BULL. 18 (2012), *available at* https://www.un.org/depts/los/LEGISLATIONANDTREATIES /PDFFILES/DEPOSIT/lbn_mzn85_2011.pdf.

7   For a detailed account of Frederic Hof's mediation see, Frederic C. Hof, *Parting the Seas: Maritime Mediation between Lebanon and Israel*, NEW LINES MAGAZINE (4 December 2020), https://newlinesmag.com/first-person/parting-the-seas/.

Lebanon and the remaining 45% to Israel. Israel accepted the Hof Line, but Lebanon rejected it insisting that it should get the entire disputed triangle.

After the failure of this first attempt, Hof was replaced by the US Special Envoy and Coordinator for International Energy Affairs, Amos Hochstein, who suggested to turn the disputed area into a joint development zone. The oil and gas resources of the area would be explored and exploited by foreign companies and the revenues split between Israel and Lebanon. This proposal was rejected by Lebanon because it implied a certain degree of economic cooperation with Israel which would have been inconsistent with the Lebanese policy of non-normalization. Moreover, Lebanon was not ready to split the revenues stemming from resources to which it claimed full ownership. Hochstein's mission ended in 2016 with the end of Barack Obama's tenure and the election of Donald Trump as the new US president.

From 2017 to 2019, the American mediation efforts were carried out by the Acting Assistant Secretary for Near Eastern Affairs, David Satterfield. During his first visits to the region, Ambassador Satterfield suggested two alternative solutions: adopt the Hof Line as a maritime boundary between the two countries or arbitrate. Both suggestions were disapproved by Lebanon which insisted on its claim to Line 23 and feared that its participation in arbitral proceedings would be tantamount to tacit recognition of Israel. Faced with these rejections, Satterfield tried to facilitate, through shuttle diplomacy between Beirut and Jerusalem, the conclusion of an agreement between the two sides on a common framework for holding talks on their maritime dispute. However, by the end of his tenure in summer 2019, he had not succeeded in securing such agreement due to the differing views of the parties on several key issues, including the duration of the talks, whether they should extend to land boundary questions, and the nature of the possible role to be played by the UN. By 2019, it was clear the American mediation had reached a stalemate.

This situation did not come as a surprise. By insisting on getting the entirety of its claimed area, Lebanon was rendering any settlement almost impossible. Indeed, by definition, any successful negotiation whether direct or through a mediator involves a readiness for compromise and mutual concessions. Moreover, as will be explained below, it was not clear that Lebanon's claim was based on any recognized principle of delimitation. Therefore, the American mediator and Israel had no compelling reasons to back the Lebanese position and accept it as a solution to the dispute. Finally, since all of Israel's discovered gas fields were located outside the disputed area, Israel had no real incentive to concede any, much less all, of the disputed area to Lebanon. Indeed, Karish, the northernmost Israeli gas field, was located several kilometers south of the disputed area, and none of Israel's ongoing oil and gas activities were impacted by the existence of the dispute. In contrast, Lebanon had no offshore commercial discoveries, and the development of its oil and gas sector seemed to be hindered by the dispute with Israel. Consequently, the deadlock was likely to perdure unless a fundamental change occurred in the positions of the stakeholders.

The change occurred in the summer of 2020 when local press reports revealed that Lebanon was envisaging a modification of its southern maritime boundary claim. The new line advocated by Lebanon would correspond to an equidistance line between the mainland coasts of Lebanon and Israel (i.e., giving no effect to several Israeli islets) and would lie significantly south of Line 23. The new line, which came to be known as "Line 29", would add approximately 1430 km^2 to the disputed area. More importantly, the new claim would cut across the Karish field, thus turning it into a disputed deposit and calling into question its scheduled unilateral exploitation by Israel. Two events confirmed the seriousness of the press leaks: the July 2020 attempt by the Lebanese President Michel Aoun to include the amended claim in the agenda of the Council of Ministers and his September 2020 signing of a letter to the UN Secretary-General notifying him of the new Lebanese line. (This letter was never sent to its addressee.) These developments prompted the US Assistant Secretary of State for Near Eastern Affairs, David Schenker, to visit Lebanon to try to resurrect the project of a framework agreement for Israeli-Lebanese negotiations over the delimitation of the maritime boundary that had been unsuccessfully discussed in the previous years.

On 1 October 2020, the Speaker of the Lebanese Parliament, Nabih Berri, who had handled the Lebanon-Israel maritime border file in the previous years, announced that, as a result of US mediation efforts, a framework agreement (the 2020 Framework Agreement, or Framework Agreement) had been reached on 29 September 2020 between Lebanon and Israel concerning the delimitation of their maritime boundary. Pursuant to the Framework Agreement, the talks would be held at the UN headquarters at Naqoura located in the vicinity of the land boundary separating the two sides. These talks would be hosted by the Office of the UN Special Coordinator for Lebanon (UNSCOL) and facilitated and mediated by the US.

The rapid conclusion of the Framework Agreement was primarily in response to Lebanon's intention to modify its maritime border claim, which would have strengthened Lebanon's negotiating position and threatened Israel's exploitation of Karish. Indeed, by initiating negotiations over the dispute before the formalization by Lebanon of its new position and its notification to the UN, Israel, backed by the US, had hoped to neutralize

Lebanon's plans and prevent it from moving forward with its new claim because otherwise Lebanon would have been accused of irresponsibly undermining the nascent negotiations.

Other regional and domestic factors may have played a role in reaching the Framework Agreement. On 15 September 2020, two weeks before its announcement, Israel, the United Arab Emirates, and Bahrain signed, at the White House, the Abraham Accords by which the two Arab states recognized Israel as a sovereign state and normalized relations with it. This first Arab-Israeli normalization event since the Israel-Jordan peace treaty of 1994 constituted a great foreign policy achievement for the Trump Administration on the eve of the 2020 presidential elections. By bringing delegations from Lebanon and Israel, two enemy states, to the same table, the US wanted to further strengthening the dynamic of normalization it had recently initiated.

In Beirut, the Lebanese ruling political class viewed the conclusion of the Framework Agreement as a means to relieve it from some external and internal pressures. On the one hand, several high-ranking officials had been sanctioned recently by the US Department of the Treasury's Office of Foreign Assets Control (OFAC) for engaging in corruption and supporting Hizballah.[8] Therefore, Lebanese decision-makers hoped that by contributing to the success of the American maritime mediation, they might prevent the US from targeting additional Lebanese officials. On the other hand, the internal legitimacy of the ruling class had been weakened in the preceding months by the severe financial crisis that hit the country in October 2019 (which led to a popular uprising) and by the explosion at the Port of Beirut in August 2020. By moving forward with the negotiations on the maritime border, Lebanese rulers intended to signal to the public that they were doing their best to find new sources of revenue, namely from offshore oil and gas.[9]

Pursuant to the terms of the Framework Agreement, negotiations started in Naqoura on 14 October 2020. Despite the fact that Lebanon's maritime claim deposited with the UN remained unchanged, the Lebanese delegation, acting upon the instructions of the president and the Army's commander-in-chief, adopted the more aggressive Line 29 as an opening negotiating position. Line 29 started from the land boundary terminus at the tip of

---

8   Press Release, US Department of the Treasury, *Treasury Targets Hizballah's Enablers in Lebanon* (8 September 2020), https://home.treasury.gov/news/press-releases/sm1116.
9   It was nevertheless well-known that Lebanon would have to wait for years of exploration and development, after the settlement of the dispute, before receiving any income from oil and gas activities and that the solution to the financial crisis rather lied in the swift adoption of long-awaited structural economic and administrative reforms.

the promontory of Ras Naqoura, as provided for in the 1923 delimitation agreement between France and Great-Britain, and followed the equidistance line constructed without giving any effect to the neighboring Israeli coastal islands.

Between October 2020 and May 2021, five sessions of technical talks were held, facilitated by the US mediator, John Desrocher, and hosted by the UN, but the parties failed to reach an agreement and the process stalled. For Israel, supported by the US, the talks had to be limited to the maritime area lying in between the lines deposited by the parties with the UN in 2010 and 2011, and no line located outside this area, notably Lebanon's Line 29, could be discussed or envisaged as a solution to the dispute. For its part, Lebanon called for open discussions based on international law without any constraints or pre-conditions for the purpose of reaching an equitable delimitation.

Faced with this Israeli position, the Lebanese delegation, with the support of the Lebanese Army, press, and public opinion, pushed for the amendment of the line deposited with the UN and its replacement by Line 29. However, political deciders refused to do so probably because of pressure exercised by the US with respect to this file and fear of US targeted individual sanctions. Nevertheless, even as Lebanon abstained from depositing Line 29 with the UN, it made clear in several communications addressed to the organization that the line in question was to be regarded as the southern limit of the disputed maritime area and that the Karish field was to be considered a disputed field which shall not be subjected to unilateral exploitation pending the final settlement of the dispute.[10]

On October 2021, John Desrocher was replaced as a mediator by the US Senior Advisor for Global Energy Security, Amos Hochstein. Hochstein, who had previously served as the US mediator for the maritime dispute between Lebanon and Israel, decided to replace the technical talks in Naqoura provided for in the 2020 Framework Agreement with shuttle diplomacy and separate meetings with the relevant political authorities in both states. In February 2022, he submitted to Lebanon a new compromise proposal which consisted

---

10 *Identical letters dated 18 September 2021 from the Permanent Representative of Lebanon to the United Nations addressed to the Secretary-General and the President of the Security Council*, UN Doc. A/76/351-S/2021/812, *available at* https://documents -dds-ny.un.org/doc/UNDOC/GEN/N21/266/98/PDF/N2126698.pdf?OpenElement; *Identical letters dated 28 January 2022 from the Permanent Representative of Lebanon to the United Nations addressed to the Secretary-General and the President of the Security Council*, UN Doc. A/76/675–S/2022/84, *available at* https://documents-dds-ny.un.org /doc/UNDOC/GEN/N22/248/33/PDF/N2224833.pdf?OpenElement.

of a hybrid line composed of three sections: a first section extending from the shore up to a distance of 3 M and coinciding with Israel's Line 1, a middle section of approximately 30 M corresponding to Lebanon's initial claim deposited with the UN (Line 23), and a last section of 25 M lying slightly north of the strict equidistance line. This proposal gave Lebanon 582 km^2 of the 882 km^2 historically disputed maritime triangle. Although it was considered to be a "serious" proposal by several Lebanese officials, it was finally rejected after a meeting among Lebanon's president, speaker of the Parliament, and prime minister. At this stage it became clear that, in line with its long-held position, Lebanon was not ready to settle for less than Line 23, and the US mediation stalled once again.

On 5 June 2022, a floating production storage and offloading unit (FPSO) belonging to Israel's licensee, Energean, arrived at the Karish field. This signaled that the exploitation of the gas field could begin in a matter of three to four months. On the same day, the president, prime minister and speaker of the Parliament of Lebanon issued official declarations protesting against this move which was qualified as a "provocation" and an "aggressive action" because it concerned the resources of a disputed area. On 9 June 2022, drawing upon this official reaction, the leader of Hizballah, Hassan Nasrallah, in a televised speech, warned Israel and Energean against the unilateral extraction of gas from Karish before the settlement of the dispute. He also asked for the withdrawal of the FPSO from the area and asserted that his armed group would not stand idly by and had the military capacity to prevent the exploitation of the disputed deposit. On 2 July 2022, the Israel Defense Forces intercepted three military drones that were heading to the Karish field. Hizballah claimed responsibility for sending the aircraft, and, on 13 July 2022, in another broadcast speech, Nasrallah reiterated his threats and warned that if Lebanon was not granted its maritime rights as a result of the US mediation, his group would not only prevent gas extraction from the disputed field of Karish but would also forcibly block the exploitation of other Israeli fields located further south.

The unilateral exploitation of Karish, which was scheduled for the third quarter of 2022, appeared likely to trigger a large-scale military conflict between Israel and Hizballah if it was to happen before the settlement of the dispute. This led the mediator to intensify his efforts through visits to both countries and contacts with negotiators from both sides up until 11 October 2022 when the US president announced that "after months of mediation by the United States, the Governments of Israel and Lebanon have agreed to formally end their maritime boundary dispute and establish a permanent maritime boundary between them."[11] The agreement was finalized on 27 October 2022 in a ceremony held in Naqoura during which delegations from both states exchanged letters approving the US proposal with the American mediator Amos Hochstein and submitted the geographical coordinates of the agreed maritime boundary line to representatives of the UN.[12]

The agreed line starts from a point at sea located approximately 2.9 M from the shore and corresponds to Line 23 whose coordinates were deposited by Lebanon with the UN in 2010 and 2011. The starting point of the maritime boundary line was placed offshore in order not to prejudice the location of the land boundary which remains disputed between the parties and to accommodate Israel's security interests in the coastal area. Indeed, the parties agreed to maintain the current *status quo* in the maritime area located between the starting point and the shore until such time as that section of maritime boundary is delimited in coordination with the demarcation of the land boundary. This *status quo* consists of *de facto* control by Israel up to the line of buoys that Israel installed upon its withdrawal from South Lebanon in 2000 in order to keep Lebanese ships away from the waters adjacent to the Israeli tourist site of Rosh HaNikra. The buoy line roughly follows the line deposited with the UN by Israel in 2011.

In view of the above, the decisive factor leading to the conclusion of the 2022 Delimitation Agreement appears to have been Israel's willingness to cede some maritime area in order to avoid an armed conflict with Hizballah and to secure the safe exploitation of its oil and gas resources, especially in the Karish field. This explains why, after twelve years of disagreement, Israel accepted Lebanon's initial position with respect to the course of the maritime boundary, with the exception of a limited area near the shore. In this respect, it is worth noting that in the last months of negotiations, the responsibility for the maritime border file with Lebanon was transferred from the Israeli Ministry of Energy to the Office of the Prime Minister who decided to entrust the National Security Adviser and Director of the National Security Council, Eyal Hulata, with conducting the negotiations. This move

---

11 The White House, *Statement by President Joe Biden on Breakthrough Diplomacy in the Middle East* (11 October 2022), https://www.whitehouse.gov/briefing-room/state ments-releases/2022/10/11/statement-by-president-joe-biden-on-breakthrough-diplomacy -in-the-middle-east/.

12 The White House, *Statement by President Joseph R. Biden, Jr. on the Conclusion of the Israel – Lebanon Maritime Boundary Dispute* (27 October 2022), https://lb.usembassy.gov /white-house-statement-by-president-joseph-r-biden-jr-on-the-conclusion-of-the-israel -lebanon-maritime-boundary-dispute/.

led the former top Israeli negotiator and Director General of the Ministry of Energy, Ehud Adiri, to resign from his position and confirmed that, for Israel, the delimitation of its maritime boundary with Lebanon had become primarily a matter of national security rather than a technical issue related to the division of maritime areas and oil and gas resources.

Other factors seem to have also played a role in the conclusion of the Delimitation Agreement, including the Russian invasion of Ukraine and domestic political calendars. The Russian invasion in February 2022 led Western powers to accelerate their search for alternatives to Russian natural gas. Therefore, the gas of the Eastern Mediterranean became a matter of immediate international concern. It is quite likely that the US, alongside European states, exercised some pressure on the parties, urging them to settle their dispute peacefully in order to maintain the stability of the region, develop its energy potential, and increase and secure the exportation of gas to Europe in the years to come. In his statement of 11 October 2022 announcing the reaching of a deal, President Biden thanked President Emmanuel Macron of France and his government for their support in the negotiations indicating that France had also played a significant role.

The domestic political calendar in both Israel and Lebanon was also key to the timely resolution of the border dispute. October 2022 presented a window of opportunity that might soon be closed and never opened again. The Israeli parliamentary elections were to take place on 1 November 2022, and there were no guarantees that the leader of the opposition, Benjamin Netanyahu, would move forward with the deal if he won the elections. On the contrary, he had been vocal against the terms of the US settlement proposal. It was therefore much safer for Lebanon to sign the agreement with Prime Minister Yaïr Lapid, who was eager to do so before the elections, than to push for a better deal. On the other side, the term of the Lebanese President Michel Aoun was coming to an end on 31 October 2022, and it was debatable whether the caretaker government could constitutionally sign the deal after this date while awaiting the election of a new president which could take months or even years considering Lebanon's deficient political system. Moreover, Michel Aoun, whose term was marked by the collapse of Lebanon's economy, was desperately looking for an achievement before leaving office. It was nevertheless uncertain whether the new Lebanese president would show the same openness and settle for Line 23 knowing that Lebanon had a good case to claim a larger maritime area. Here, too, it was safer for Israel to finalize the deal with Michel Aoun before the end of his term than to hope for a better deal in the future.

2 Legal Regime Considerations

The core text of the 2022 Delimitation Agreement contained in the identical letters addressed separately to Israel and Lebanon by the US refers to the establishment of a maritime boundary line without specifying the juridical character of the maritime areas delimited by the said line. However, Annexes A and B to the Agreement, which contain proposed communications to be submitted by the parties to the UN, both speak of lines of delimitation of the territorial sea and the EEZ and include a "List of Geographic Coordinates For the Delimitation of a Maritime Boundary Line Of the Territorial Sea and Exclusive Economic Zone". Nowhere in the Agreement and its Annexes is there any mention of the continental shelf. This approach is in line with the well-established Eastern Mediterranean practice of concluding EEZ delimitation agreements that do not refer to the continental shelf.[13] This practice suggests that, for the states concerned, the regime of the continental shelf is deemed to have been absorbed into that of the EEZ. This is not unreasonable since the EEZ also includes the seabed and its subsoil and the distance between the coasts of the states of the region nowhere exceeds 400 M. Therefore, there is no area of continental shelf beyond the EEZ in this region and no compelling need to distinguish the two regimes.

Lebanon has been a party to the United Nations Convention on the Law of the Sea (UNCLOS) since 1995, but Israel is not yet a party, and UNCLOS is, consequently, not in force between the two countries. Nevertheless, taking into account the fact that the agreed line follows the equidistance line in the territorial sea and that the Agreement refers to the establishment of a permanent and "equitable solution" to the maritime dispute, one could assume that the maritime boundary line was negotiated on the basis of Articles 15 and 74 of the UNCLOS which reflect customary international law. Article 15 provides for the delimitation of the territorial sea pursuant to the "equidistance/special circumstances" rule and Article 74 calls for the achievement of an "equitable solution" when it comes to the delimitation of the EEZ.

With regard to the settlement of disputes, the parties agreed that any differences concerning the interpretation and implementation of the

---

13 *See* Report Number 8-15, V IMB 3917 (Cyprus-Egypt); Report Number 8-19, VI IMB 4445 (Cyprus-Lebanon); Report Number 8-22, VII IMB 5091 (Cyprus-Israel); and Report Number 8-25 in this volume (Egypt – Greece).

Agreement are to be resolved through discussion facilitated by the US (Section 4, paragraph B).

3 Economic and Environmental Considerations

Economic considerations linked to oil and gas resources were at the heart of the maritime boundary dispute between Israel and Lebanon. Since the beginning of the Naqoura talks in October 2020, Israel insisted on limiting the negotiations to the lines deposited with the UN in order to keep the Karish field out of the scope of the dispute. For its part, Lebanon's decision to adopt Line 29 as an opening negotiating position and to call for open negations based on international law was partly motivated by the country's desire to establish a boundary that would give it full control over the Qana prospect, a very promising geological structure lying mostly in Lebanese undisputed waters but extending partially south of Lebanon's Line 23. Indeed, Israel's experience with transboundary deposits was far from encouraging, as demonstrated by the dispute over the Aphrodite gas field, a transboundary deposit discovered by Cyprus in 2011 but whose exploitation had not started yet because of a disagreement over Israel's share. Therefore, Lebanon was concerned that any solution that would split Qana could hinder the exploration and development of the prospect, if only because foreign companies would be reluctant to invest money drilling wells in a geological structure that they might not be able to exploit subsequently.

The Delimitation Agreement, without naming Qana, contains a whole section dedicated to this prospect (Section 2). This section, which acknowledges the existence of Qana and its transboundary character, stipulates that it will be explored, developed, and exploited exclusively by Lebanon's licensee, it being understood that Israel will be remunerated for its economic rights in the prospect. To that end, the parties agreed that prior to its final investment decision (FID), Lebanon's licensee will have to conclude a financial agreement with Israel determining the scope of the latter's rights. It was also made clear that the development of Qana by Lebanon's licensee was subject to the start of the implementation of the financial agreement with Israel.

On 14 November 2022, soon after the conclusion of the Delimitation Agreement, Lebanon's licensee (the consortium of companies composed of TOTAL and ENI which was granted Lebanon's Block 9 where the Qana prospect lies) and Israel signed an "agreement of principles" regarding the mechanism for compensating Israel for the cession of its rights over

Qana.[14] In line with the Delimitation Agreement, the agreement of principles stipulated that if a discovery is made in the prospect, a detailed agreement on the quantity of natural gas located on Israel's side of the border and on the amount of compensation to be paid accordingly by the consortium will have to be concluded prior to the development of the field. It was also confirmed that this development was conditional upon the transfer of the first payment to Israel. As contemplated in the Delimitation Agreement, Lebanon was not party to these arrangements between its licensee and Israel. This arrangement was meant to avoid any form of economic normalization between Lebanon and Israel.

Giving Lebanon the upper hand on the exploration and development of the Qana prospect through its licensee was instrumental in convincing Lebanon to settle for Line 23 and give up its claim to additional maritime areas to the south. It is, however, worth noting that by conditioning the development of Qana on the conclusion and implementation of a financial agreement between Lebanon's licensee and Israel, the Delimitation Agreement gave Israel "veto power" that substantially mitigates Lebanon's alleged control over the prospect. If used, which would not be surprising in view of the conflictual relationship between the two countries, this veto power might well give rise to new disputes and tensions in the years to come. For Israel, the location of the Karish field several kilometers south of Line 23 facilitated the Israeli acceptance of this line as a permanent maritime boundary with Lebanon.

In case any offshore transboundary deposit other than Qana is identified, the parties agreed to request the US to facilitate the reaching of an understanding on the allocation of rights and on the manner in which the deposit may be most effectively explored and exploited (Section 3, paragraph A).

4 Geographic Considerations

The coastal territories of Israel and Lebanon are adjacent to each other, and the full delimitation of their maritime boundary will require some connection to their land boundary. That land boundary, and the terminus point of that boundary at the coast, is in dispute, thus necessitating the creation of a maritime boundary starting nearly 2.9 M offshore.

---

14 A summary of the main points contained in the "agreement of principles" was published in Hebrew on the official website of the government of Israel: https://www.gov.il /BlobFolder/news/press_151122/he/principles_271022.pdf.

5 Islands, Rocks, Reefs, and Low-tide Elevations Considerations

The northern coast of Israel is characterized by the presence of two groups of tiny fringing islets known as the Rosh HaNikra islands and the Achziv islands. The effect that should be given to Tekhelet, the northernmost of these islets constituted, alongside the issue of the starting point, one of the main points of contention during the maritime delimitation negotiations. For Lebanon, this islet had to be ignored because of its impact on the course of the delimitation line. Indeed, if used as a basepoint for the sake of drawing an equidistant boundary, Tekhelet would have the effect of shifting the said line northward over an area of 1820 km². According to Lebanon, this effect would be disproportionate in comparison to the size of the feature (approximately 485 m²), which would justify disregarding it in the delimitation process. For its part, Israel argued that the islet of Tekhelet had to serve as a basepoint because of its proximity to the shore (approximately 1 km). Both parties invoked international case law to support their views. In this respect, it is worth mentioning that on 12 October 2021, one year before the conclusion of the Agreement, the International Court of Justice delivered its judgment in the case concerning the *Maritime Delimitation in the Indian Ocean (Somalia v. Kenya)*. This decision supported the Lebanese position since the Court decided to ignore the tiny Diua Damasciaca islands, despite their proximity to the Somali coast, citing their disproportionate impact on the course of the equidistance line.[15]

The agreed maritime boundary line corresponds to Lebanon's deposited Line 23. In the territorial sea, this line roughly follows a strict equidistance line that was drawn using the islet of Tekhelet as an Israeli basepoint. In the EEZ, however, the boundary leaves the course of the equidistance line and follows instead a straight line with a bearing of approximately 290.40°. Beyond the territorial sea neither Tekhelet nor the other Israeli islets played a role in the construction of the boundary line. Nevertheless, because the agreed line sits between the strict equidistance line and the equidistance line disregarding islands, perhaps the parties and the mediator saw it as a fair compromise with respect to the impact of small, nearshore features on the equidistant delimitation line.

---

15 *Maritime Delimitation in the Indian Ocean (Somalia v. Kenya), Judgment, I.C.J. Reports 2021*, p. 247, para. 114.

6 Baseline Considerations

No baseline considerations seem to have affected the location of the agreed maritime boundary.

7 Geological and Geomorphological Considerations

No geological or geomorphological factors seem to have affected the location or extent of the agreed maritime boundary.

8 Method of Delimitation Considerations

The agreed maritime boundary corresponds to the line deposited by Lebanon with the UN Secretariat in 2010 and 2011. In order to understand the delimitation method used to create the boundary between Israel and Lebanon, one must first understand the delimitation method used to create Line 23. Line 23 was referred to as the "Southern Median Line between Lebanon and Palestine" in the documents deposited with the UN thereby indicating that the claimed boundary was drawn using the equidistance method. However, in a report issued in 2011 upon the request of the Lebanese Government, the United Kingdom Hydrographic Office (UKHO) carried out a technical assessment of Lebanon's claimed limits and reached the conclusion that Line 23 lies to the south of the strict equidistance line over its entire length. The Hydrographic Office of the Lebanese Army (created in 2014) confirmed this conclusion in 2019 with a review of the claimed limits using the Caris LOTS software and more accurate coastline data stemming from a 2018 hydrographic survey.

In the territorial sea, the differences between Line 23 and strict equidistance were relatively minor and did not exceed a distance of a few hundred meters. According to the UKHO, this was due to the low-quality coastline data used by Lebanon. Indeed, Lebanon had defined the coordinates of the relevant basepoints by reference, on its side, to a 1:20,000 land map using mean sea level as the vertical datum to define the coast and, on Israel's side, to a 1:1,100,000 UKHO nautical chart. That is to say, the basepoints used to construct Line 23 were derived from sources using either the wrong vertical datum or a very small and inadequate scale. In the territorial sea, Line 23, and consequently the agreed maritime boundary line between Israel and Lebanon, could be considered an approximate or inaccurate equidistance line.

The situation is different when it comes to the delimitation of the EEZ. In the same 2011 report, the UKHO stated that beyond the territorial sea the Lebanese claimed maritime limit appeared to depart further from equidistance, and its most seaward point, Point 23, was located almost 4 M south of the equidistant tripoint between Lebanon, Cyprus, and Israel.[16] In May 2012, the Lebanese prime minister created a joint ministerial commission tasked with the preparation of a detailed report on the maritime limits of Lebanon's EEZ. In its report, the commission clarified that, for the southern limit with Israel, the use of the equidistance method was limited to the territorial sea, but in the EEZ the southern limit was constructed using the perpendicular to the general direction of the coast drawn between the point of Ras Beirut in Lebanon and the point of Ras Haifa in Israel.

However, subsequent verification revealed that Line 23 was located approximately 0.65 M south of the perpendicular in question. When confronted with this fact, several commission members admitted in private that the perpendicular narrative was an *ex post facto* construction aimed at providing Lebanon's claim with some kind of technical basis. According to them, in the EEZ, Line 23 was the result of an arbitrary shift of the strict equidistance line southward carried out upon the request of the country's prime minister who had demanded the adoption of a more aggressive stance than strict equidistance as an opening negotiating position with Israel. Indeed, at that time, Lebanese authorities had been led to believe, based on a 2006 UKHO report, that the maximum to which they could aim in the delimitation of the country's southern maritime border was a strict equidistance line (i.e., a line drawn using Israel's small islets). For reasons not known to this author, the prestigious British institution neglected to mention that small islets like Tekhelet are often ignored or given limited weight in a delimitation process based on international law.

Nevertheless, even the explanation that Line 23 resulted from an arbitrary shift of the strict equidistance line is not entirely convincing. It appears that the course of Line 23 in the EEZ coincided exactly with the northern limit of the Israeli oil and gas concession blocks Alon D and F that had been

---

16 It is not unusual that inaccuracies in an equidistance line between adjacent coasts will become amplified as the line moves further from shore. *See, e.g., North Sea Continental Shelf, Judgment, I.C.J. Reports 1969*, p. 37, para. 59; *Continental Shelf (Libyan Arab Jamahiriya/Malta), Judgment, I.C.J. Reports 1985*, p. 51, para. 70.

defined and granted for exploration on 1 March 2009, a year before the deposit of Line 23. This coincidence may add to the explanation why Israel accepted Line 23 as the boundary. By doing so (and contrary to the dominant narrative that followed the conclusion of the Agreement), Israel was not giving in to Lebanon's position but, rather, was agreeing to a boundary based on a line it had drawn unilaterally in 2009 as part of its offshore leasing program and which was adopted by Lebanon in 2010 for unknown reasons.

It is unclear which delimitation method Israel used to delineate the northern limit of its former concession blocks Alon D and F. Considering that this limit is straight and follows a southeast-northwest direction, it is possible that it was drawn as a perpendicular or bisector to the general direction of the coast. Another plausible explanation is that this limit corresponded to an *ad hoc* line that was established to protect Israel's oil and gas interests and activities. Indeed, these blocks were defined after the conduct of seismic surveys in the area. These surveys are likely to have revealed the existence, size and shape of the geological structure known today as the Karish field. It is conceivable that Israel drew an arbitrary northern limit to its concession blocks that would separate Karish and a buffer of Israeli waters from Lebanese maritime areas.

9 Technical Considerations

The agreed maritime boundary line consists of four points connected by geodetic lines. Their geographical coordinates appear in a table in Section 1, paragraph A of the Agreement. They are given to the nearest hundredth of an arc second of latitude and longitude and are expressed in terms of the World Geodetic System 1984 (WGS-84). Though unnamed in the Delimitation Agreement, these boundary turning points correspond precisely to Points 20, 21, 22 and 23 of Line 23 whose coordinates were deposited by Lebanon with the UN in 2010 and 2011. No official maps showing the agreed line seem to have been annexed to the Agreement.

10 Other Considerations

Due to its non-recognition and non-normalization policies, Lebanon made it clear early in the process that it was not ready to formalize a maritime boundary agreement by signing a joint document with Israel. In order to accommodate Lebanon's position, the US mediator decided to opt for a less-used treaty-making method. Once agreement had been reached on the terms of the delimitation, on 18 October 2022 the mediator sent identical letters containing those terms to Israel and Lebanon. Subsequently each party notified its acceptance of the terms by way of a formal written response addressed to the US mediator whose content was provided for in Annex C to the initial 18 October letter. In return, the US mediator replied to each side by a notice, based on the text of Annex D to the initial US letter, in which he informed them of the agreement of the other party to the same terms and confirmed the entry into force of the Delimitation Agreement establishing a permanent maritime boundary between Israel and Lebanon. All of these documents – Israel and Lebanon's letters to the US accepting the terms and the US letters to Lebanon and Israel informing them of the other's acceptance – were exchanged on the occasion of an official ceremony that took place on 27 October 2022 in the UN headquarters of the Lebanese town of Naqoura.

Lebanese authorities relied on this peculiar process and the absence of a formal document bearing the signature of both sides to comply with Lebanon's policies vis-à-vis Israel and also to circumvent the domestic rules governing the conclusion of treaties. Indeed, the letter of acceptance expressing Lebanon's consent to the terms of the Agreement was signed and communicated to the US by President Aoun without the prior approval of the prime minister, the government and the parliament as required by Article 52 of the Lebanese Constitution. The non-observance of Article 52 of the Lebanese Constitution is not without consequences. In fact, it amounts to a manifest violation of a rule of internal law of fundamental importance that could be invoked by Lebanon as a ground for invalidating the Agreement pursuant to Article 46 of the Vienna Convention on the Law of Treaties (VCLT).

Of course, the fact that the Agreement was concluded by way of an exchange of letters does not mean that it is not a treaty under international law. Indeed, Article 2(1)(a) of the VCLT stipulates that a treaty means "an international agreement concluded between States in written form and governed by international law, *whether embodied in a single instrument or in two or more related instruments* and whatever its particular designation" (emphasis added). Moreover, the involvement of a third party in the said exchange of letters does not alter its legal qualification as a treaty. For example, in the *Qatar v. Bahrain* case, the International Court of Justice recognized that an exchange of letters between the King of Saudi Arabia, who was acting as a mediator in the maritime and territorial dispute between the two states, and the Amirs of Qatar and Bahrain, constituted "an international agreement with binding force" between the two parties.[17] It is therefore unsurprising that the UN Secretary-General acceded to Israel's request to register the exchange of letters as an international agreement in accordance with Article 102 of the UN Charter and under the title "Exchange of Letters Constituting a Maritime Agreement between the State of Israel and the Lebanese Republic".[18]

III   CONCLUSIONS

The maritime delimitation agreement between Israel and Lebanon constitutes a rare instance of the peaceful settlement of a dispute between the two enemy states and is likely to have contributed to the avoidance of a new military confrontation that might have degenerated into a wider regional conflict. The extraordinary process followed to reach its formal conclusion and the unusual provisions related to oil and gas activities reflect creative solutions that could inspire other antagonists of the Eastern Mediterranean and elsewhere whose relationships are also conflictual and marked by non-recognition.

Beyond these considerations, two general conclusions can be drawn from this Agreement. First, states must establish their official maritime claims with care. Despite the sound legal and technical foundations of its new claim formulated in 2020, Lebanon did not manage to obtain areas beyond the initial claim it had deposited with the UN a decade earlier. This shows that, once formalized, it can be difficult to succeed on a more aggressive maritime boundary claim despite its relative strengths as a legal and technical matter. Therefore, states should be extremely cautious when formulating their official position with respect to the location of their maritime borders and make sure to seek technical and legal advice or support before doing so.

Second, states in a negotiation (or mediation) process have wide-ranging flexibility and, unlike a judge or arbitrator, need not provide a reason for the outcome. The adoption of Lebanon's Line 23, despite its technical inaccuracies and lack of a sound geographic or legal basis, demonstrates that maritime delimitation between states remains primarily a political process.

---

17 *Maritime Delimitation and Territorial Questions between Qatar and Bahrain, Jurisdiction and Admissibility, Judgment, I.C.J. Reports 1994*, p. 120, para. 22.
18 Exchange of Letters Constituting a Maritime Agreement between the State of Israel and the Lebanese Republic, Lebanon-Israel, 27 October 2022, UNTS (I-57582), *available at* https://treaties.un.org/Pages/showDetails.aspx?objid=08000002806029d5&clang=_en.

6216   *Report Number 8-26*

IV   RELATED LAW IN FORCE

A   *Law of the Sea Conventions*

Israel: Party to the 1958 Convention on the Territorial Sea and Contiguous
Zone and the 1958 Convention on the Continental Shelf (both ratified on
6 September 1961)
Lebanon: Party to UNCLOS (ratified on 5 January 1995).

B   *Maritime Jurisdiction Claimed at the Time of Signature*

Israel: 12 M territorial sea; 12 M contiguous zone; 200 M EEZ; continental
shelf.
Lebanon: 12 M territorial sea; 12 M contiguous zone; 200 M EEZ; continental
shelf.

C   *Maritime Jurisdiction Claimed Subsequent to Signature*

Israel: No change.
Lebanon: No change.

Prepared by Najib Messihi[19]

---

19 The views expressed in this report are the author's and do not necessarily reflect the
views of the Government of Lebanon or other organizations or institutions for whom he
worked or is currently working.

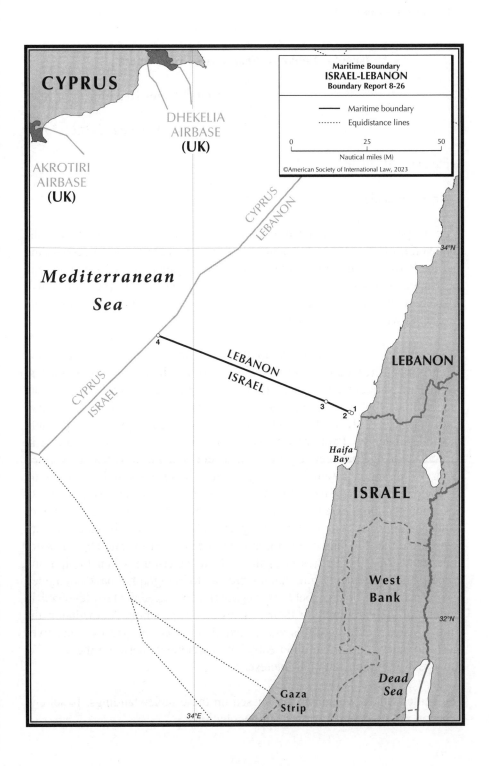

6218 *Report Number 8-26*

Israel – Lebanon Framework Agreement

United States Department of State

Washington, D.C. 20520

September 29, 2020

Your Excellencies,

With respect to the attached six points concerning discussions on the delineation of the Israel – Lebanon maritime boundary, and understanding that the Parties have agreed to move ahead to negotiate as described therein, the United States wishes to state its understanding of how the Parties will proceed with respect to certain aspects of Paragraph 5 as discussed and developed with Israel and Lebanon.

Paragraph 5 includes reference to the execution by Israel and Lebanon of agreements reached in not only the maritime boundary discussions to be held in Naqoura and which the United States stands ready to mediate and facilitate, but also in discussions with respect to the land (Blue Line) involving also UNIFIL. The discussions are expected to proceed separately and independently. Paragraph 5 should not be understood to require any particular linkage between any agreement referenced in it as being executed under Paragraph 5.1 (land) and any agreement referenced in it as being executed under Paragraph 5.2 (maritime boundary). For purposes of clarity this understanding extends to any linkage in the timing of signature or implementation by the Parties of agreements that may be reached with respect to either the land or the maritime boundary issues. The United States understands that the Parties have the right to determine when to sign and execute final agreements, and that in agreeing to Paragraph 5 have not agreed to any particular linkage between negotiation of agreements referenced in any part of the Paragraph, or their conclusion or execution. As mediator, the United States would hold this view, recognizing that the parties themselves must ultimately determine upon entry into agreements between them, consistent with their national interests.

The United States welcomes that, based on these understandings, Israel and Lebanon are prepared to engage in negotiations.

Sincerely,

<signed>

David Schenker
Assistant Secretary of State
Bureau of Near Eastern Affairs

September 29, 2020

The United States understands that the governments of Lebanon and Israel are prepared to delineate their maritime boundary as follows:

1. To build upon the positive experience of the Tripartite mechanism which has existed since the April 1996 Understandings and currently under UNSCR 1701, which has achieved progress on Blue Linc resolutions.

2. With respect to the maritime boundary issue, meetings will be held on a continuous basis at the UN Headquarters in Naqoura, and under the flag of the United Nations. The meetings will take place under the hosting of the staff of the Office of the United Nations Special Coordinator for Lebanon (UNSCOL). The United States and UNSCOL representatives are prepared to jointly take the minutes of the meetings, which will be signed by them and presented to Israel and Lebanon to sign at the end of every meeting.

3. The United States has been requested by the Parties (Israel and Lebanon) to serve as the mediator and facilitator for the delineation of the Israel – Lebanon maritime boundary and is prepared to do so.

4. When the delineation is finally agreed, the maritime boundary agreement will be deposited with the United Nations, in accordance with relevant international law, treaties and international practice.

5. Upon reaching agreements in the discussions on the land and on the maritime boundary, these agreements will be executed according to the following:

5.1) On land, for the Blue Line: after signing by Lebanon, Israel and UNIFIL.

5.2) On the sea, extending to the seaward limit of the parties' respective exclusive economic zones: The final agreed outcome of the discussions between Israel and Lebanon will be for the Parties to sign and implement.

6. The United States intends to exert its best efforts working with the two Parties to help establish and maintain a positive and constructive atmosphere for conducting and successfully concluding the above negotiations as rapidly as possible.

6220   *Report Number 8-26*

Terms related to the Establishment of a Permanent Maritime Boundary contained in Identical Letters from US Special Presidential Coordinator Hochstein to Israeli Prime Minister Lapid and Lebanese President Aoun, 18 October 2022

Excellency:

I have the honor to write you in the context of the negotiations to delineate the maritime boundary between the Republic of Lebanon and the State of Israel (hereinafter: collectively the "Parties" and individually a "Party").

On September 29, 2020, the United States of America sent both Parties a letter (Attachment 1 [*Framework Agreement reproduced above*]) to which it attached six points that reflected its understanding of the terms of reference for such negotiations, including the request of both Parties for the United States to serve as mediator and facilitator for the delineation of the maritime boundary between the Parties, and the mutual understanding of both Parties that "when the delineation is finally agreed, the maritime boundary agreement will be deposited with the United Nations."

Further to that letter, meetings were held under the hosting of the staff of the Office of the United Nations Special Coordinator for Lebanon ("UNSCOL") at Naqoura, and, in addition, the United States conducted subsequent consultations with each Party. Following these discussions, it is the understanding of the United States, that the Parties intend to meet in the near future at Naqoura under the hosting of the staff of UNSCOL in a meeting facilitated by the United States. The United States further understands [Lebanon/Israel] is prepared to establish its permanent maritime boundary, and conclude a permanent and equitable resolution regarding its maritime dispute with [Israel/Lebanon], and accordingly agrees to the following terms provided that the following is also accepted by [Israel/Lebanon]:

SECTION 1

A. The Parties agree to establish a maritime boundary line (the "MBL"). The delimitation of the MBL consists of the following points described by the coordinates below. These points, in WGS84 datum, are connected by geodesic lines:

Latitude: 33° 06' 34.15" N **Longitude** 35° 02' 58.12"
Latitude E 33° 06' 52.73" N **Longitude** 35° 02' 13.86" E 3
Latitude 3° 10' 19.33" N **Longitude** 34° 52' 57.24" E
Latitude 33° 31' 51.17" N **Longitude** 33° 46' 8.78" E

B. These coordinates define the maritime boundary as agreed between the Parties for all points seaward of the easternmost point of the MBL, and without prejudice to the status of the land boundary. In order not to prejudice the status of the land boundary, the maritime boundary landward of the easternmost point of the MBL is expected to be delimited in the context of, or in a timely manner after, the Parties' demarcation of the land boundary. Until such time this area is delimited, the Parties agree that the status quo near the shore, including along and as defined by the current buoy line, remains the same, notwithstanding the differing legal positions of the Parties in this area, which remains undelimited.

C. Each Party shall simultaneously submit a communication containing the list of geographical coordinates for the delimitation of the MBL described in paragraph A of this Section ("UN communications") in the form attached for each of the Parties (Annex A and Annex B) to the Secretary General of the United Nations on the day of the communication by the United States described in Section 4(B). The Parties shall notify the United States when they have submitted their respective UN communications.

D. The coordinates reflected in each Party's respective UN communication referred to in Section 1(C) shall supersede (i) the coordinates in the July 12, 2011 submission by Israel to the United Nations with respect to the points labeled 34, 35, and 1 in such submission, and (ii) the chart and coordinates in the October 19, 2011 submission by Lebanon to the United Nations with respect to the points labeled 20, 21, 22, and 23 in such submission. Neither Party shall make a future submission of charts or coordinates to the United Nations that is inconsistent with this Agreement (hereinafter: "Agreement") unless the Parties have mutually agreed upon the content of such submission.

E. The Parties agree that this Agreement, including as described in Section 1(B), establishes a permanent and equitable resolution of their maritime dispute.

6222 *Report Number 8-26*

SECTION 2

A. The Parties understand that there is a hydrocarbon prospect of currently unknown commercial viability that exists at least partially in the area the Parties understand to be Lebanon's Block 9, and at least partially in the area the Parties understand to be Israel's Block 72, hereinafter referred to as "the Prospect."

B. Exploration and exploitation of the Prospect shall be carried out in accordance with good petroleum industry practices on conservation of gas to maximize efficient recovery, operational safety, and environmental protection, and shall comply with the applicable laws and regulations in the area.

C. The Parties agree that the relevant legal entity to hold any Lebanese rights to exploration and exploitation of hydrocarbon resources in Lebanon's Block 9 ("Block 9 Operator") shall consist of one or more reputable, international corporations that are not subject to international sanctions, that would not hinder US continued facilitation, and that are not Israeli or Lebanese corporations. These criteria shall also apply to the selection of any successors or replacements of those corporations.

D. The Parties understand that exploration of the Prospect is expected to begin immediately after this Agreement enters into force. The Parties expect the Block 9 Operator to explore and exploit the Prospect. To do so, the Block 9 Operator will need to transit through some areas south of the MBL. Israel will not object to reasonable and necessary activities, such as navigational maneuvers, that the Block 9 Operator conducts immediately south of the MBL in pursuit of the Block 9 Operator's exploration and exploitation of the Prospect, so long as such activities occur with prior notification by the Block 9 Operator to Israel.

E. The Parties understand that Israel and the Block 9 Operator are separately engaging in discussions to determine the scope of Israel's economic rights in the Prospect. Israel will be remunerated by the Block 9 Operator for its rights to any potential deposits in the Prospect and to that end, Israel and the Block 9 Operator will sign a financial agreement prior to the Block 9 Operator's Final Investment Decision ("FID"). Israel shall work with the Block 9 Operator in good faith to ensure that this agreement is resolved in a timely fashion. Lebanon is not responsible for, or party to, any arrangement between the Block 9 Operator and Israel. Any arrangement between the Block 9 Operator and Israel shall not affect Lebanon's agreement with the Block 9 Operator and the full share of its economic rights in the Prospect. The Parties understand that subject to the start of implementation of the financial agreement, the entire Prospect will then be developed by Lebanon's Block 9 Operator exclusively for Lebanon, consistent with the terms of this Agreement.

F. Subject to the agreement with the Block 9 Operator, Israel will not exercise any rights to develop hydrocarbon deposits in the Prospect and will not object to, or take any action that unduly delays reasonable activities in pursuit of the development of the Prospect. Israel will not exploit any accumulation or deposit of natural resources, including liquid hydrocarbon, natural gas, or other minerals, extending across the MBL in the Prospect.

G. If drilling of the Prospect is necessary south of the MBL, the Parties expect the Block 9 Operator to request the consent of the Parties in advance of drilling and Israel will not unreasonably withhold such consent for drilling conducted in accordance with the terms of this Agreement.

SECTION 3

A. If there is identification of any other single accumulation or deposit of natural resources, including liquid hydrocarbon, natural gas, or other mineral extending across the MBL other than the Prospect, and if one Party by exploiting that accumulation or deposit would withdraw, deplete, or draw down the portion of the accumulation or deposit that is on the other Party's side of the MBL, then before the accumulation or deposit is exploited, the Parties intend to request the United States to facilitate between the Parties (including any operators with relevant domestic rights to explore and exploit resources), with a view to reaching an understanding on the allocation of rights and the manner in which the accumulation or deposit may be most effectively explored and exploited.

B. Each Party shall share data on all currently known, and any later identified, cross-MBL resources with the United States, including expecting the relevant operators that operate on either side of the MBL to share such data with the United States. The Parties understand that the United States intends to share this data with the Parties in a timely manner after receipt.

6224 *Report Number 8-26*

C. Neither Party intends to claim any other single accumulation or deposit of natural resources, including liquid hydrocarbon, natural gas, or other mineral, located entirely on the other Party's side of the MBL.

D. The Parties understand the US government intends to exert its best efforts and endeavors in order to facilitate Lebanon's immediate, swift and continuous petroleum activities.

SECTION 4

A. The Parties intend to resolve any differences concerning the interpretation and implementation of this Agreement through discussion facilitated by the United States. The Parties understand that the United States intends to exert its best efforts working with the Parties to help establish and maintain a positive and constructive atmosphere for conducting discussions and successfully resolving any differences as rapidly as possible.

B. This Agreement shall enter into force on the date on which the Government of the United States of America sends a notice, based on the text in Annex D to this letter, in which it confirms that each Party has agreed to the terms herein stipulated. If the foregoing is acceptable to the Government of [Lebanon/ Israel] as the final agreed terms between the Parties, the Government of the United States invites the Government of [Lebanon/Israel] to communicate its agreement to these terms by way of a formal written response as provided for in the attached Annex C to this letter.

If the foregoing is acceptable to the Government of [Lebanon/Israel] as the final agreed terms between the Parties, the Government of the United States invites the Government of [Israel/Lebanon] to communicate its agreement to these terms by way of a formal written response as provided for in the attached Annex C to this letter.

Sincerely,

<signed>

Amos Hochstein
Special Presidential Coordinator

Enclosures:

Attachment 1 [*Framework Agreement reproduced above*]
Annexes A-D

ANNEX A
Proposed Lebanese UN Submission

[Opening courtesy salutation]

[Title and name of sender] has the honour to deposit with the Secretary-General, as depositary of the United Nations Convention on the Law of the Sea, a list of geographical coordinates of points, as contained in the Exchange of Letters Establishing a Permanent Maritime Boundary, [date of entry into force per US confirmation] ("Exchange of Letters"), attached herewith, concerning:

• A line of delimitation of the territorial sea, pursuant to article 16, paragraph 2, of the Convention
• A line of delimitation of the exclusive economic zone, pursuant to article 75, paragraph 2, of the Convention

The list of geographical coordinates of points as contained in the Exchange of Letters is referenced to the World Geodetic System 1984 ("WGS 84").

The present deposit hereby supersedes in part the previous deposit made by Lebanon on 19 October 2011, which was given due publicity through maritime zone notification M.Z.N.85.2011.LOS. The points labeled 20, 21, 22, and 23 in such previous deposit are superseded; all other labeled points remain valid. The parties to the Exchange of Letters have agreed that it establishes a permanent and equitable resolution of their maritime dispute.

The Secretary-General is requested to assist Lebanon in giving due publicity to the deposit, in accordance with the aforementioned articles of the Convention, including through the publication of the deposited material and information in the *Law of the Sea Bulletin* and on the website of the Division for Ocean Affairs and the Law of the Sea.

[Closing salutation]

Attachments:
List of Geographic Coordinates
Exchange of Letters Establishing a Permanent Maritime Boundary, [date of entry into force per US confirmation]

List of Geographic Coordinates For the Delimitation of a Maritime Boundary Line Of the Territorial Sea and Exclusive Economic Zone Of Lebanon

These points, in WGS84 datum, are connected by geodesic lines:

Latitude	Longitude
33° 06′ 34.15″ N	35° 02′ 58.12″ E
33° 06′ 52.73″ N	35° 02′ 13.86″ E
33° 10′ 19.33″ N	34° 52′ 57.24″ E
33° 31′ 51.17″ N	33° 46′ 8.78″ E

ANNEX B

Proposed Israeli UN Submission

[Opening courtesy salutation]

[Title and name of sender] has the honour to deposit with the Secretary-General a list of geographical coordinates of points, as contained in the Exchange of Letters Establishing a Permanent Maritime Boundary, [date of entry into force per US confirmation] ("Exchange of Letters"), attached herewith, concerning:

• A line of delimitation of the territorial sea
• A line of delimitation of the exclusive economic zone

The list of geographical coordinates of points as contained in the Exchange of Letters is referenced to the World Geodetic System 1984 ("WGS 84").

The present deposit hereby supersedes in part the previous deposit made by Israel on 12 July 2011. The points labeled 34, 35, and 1 in such previous deposit are superseded; all other labeled points remain valid. The parties to the Exchange of Letters have agreed that it establishes a permanent and equitable resolution of their maritime dispute.

The Secretary-General is requested to assist Israel in giving due publicity to the deposit, including through the publication of the deposited material and information on the website of the Division for Ocean Affairs and the Law of the Sea.

Israel – Lebanon 6227

[Closing salutation]

Attachments:
List of Geographic Coordinates
Exchange of Letters Establishing a Permanent Maritime Boundary, [date of
entry into force per US confirmation]

List of Geographic Coordinates For the Delimitation of a Maritime Boundary Line Of the Territorial Sea and Exclusive Economic Zone Of Israel

These points, in WGS84 datum, are connected by geodesic lines:

Latitude	Longitude
33° 06′ 34.15″ N	35° 02′ 58.12″ E
33° 06′ 52.73″ N	35° 02′ 13.86″ E
33° 10′ 19.33″ N	34° 52′ 57.24″ E
33° 31′ 51.17″ N	33° 46′ 8.78″ E

ANNEX C
Proposed response from the Parties

[Excellency],

I am in receipt of the United States' letter dated [X] concerning the terms
related to the establishment of a permanent maritime boundary. The
terms outlined in your letter are acceptable to the Government of [insert].
As a result, the Government of [insert] is pleased to notify the Government
of the United States of America of its agreement to the terms outlined in its
letter dated [x].

ANNEX D
*Proposed Final USG Notification – To be sent simultaneously
to both Parties.*

[Excellency],

I refer to my letter dated [X] regarding terms related to the establishment
of a permanent maritime boundary between the Republic of Lebanon and
the State of Israel (the "Parties"). The United States confirms its receipt of
a letter from your government on [date] noting its agreement to the terms

set forth below. The United States further confirms that it received a letter from the Government of [insert] on [date] noting its agreement to the terms set forth below. Accordingly, the United States confirms that the Agreement related to the establishment of a permanent maritime boundary consisting of the following terms enters into force on the date of this letter.

[*insert terms from initial USG letter*]

Sincerely,

Israel – Lebanon 6229

Exchange of Letters Constituting a Maritime Agreement
between the State of Israel and the Lebanese Republic

October 27, 2022

Dear Mr. Hochstein,

I am in receipt of the United States' letter dated October 18, 2022 concerning the terms related to the establishment of a permanent maritime boundary. The terms outlined in your letter are acceptable to the Government of Israel. As a result, the Government of Israel is pleased to notify the Government of the United States of America of its agreement to the terms outlined in its letter dated October 18, 2022.

Sincerely,

<signed>

Prime Minister
Yair Lapid

October 27, 2022

Amos J Hochstein
Special Presidential Coordinator
United States of America

I am in receipt of the United States' letter dated October 18, 2022 concerning the terms related to the establishment of a permanent maritime boundary. The terms outlined in your letter are acceptable to the Government of Lebanon. As a result, the Government of Lebanon is pleased to notify the Government of the United States of America of its agreement to the terms outlined in its letter dated October 18, 2022.

Sincerely,

<signed>

General MICHEL AOUN

Croatia – Italy

Report Number 8-27

Exchange of Notes constituting an Agreement between the Italian Republic and the Republic of Croatia on the Accurate Determination of the Delimitation Line of the Continental Shelf

Signed: 22 and 29 July 2005 and 2 August 2005
Entry into force: 2 August 2005
Published at: Currently unpublished

Agreement between the Italian Republic and the Republic of Croatia on the Delimitation of the Exclusive Economic Zones

Signed: 24 May 2022
Entry into force: Not yet in force
Published at: Gazzetta Ufficiale della Repubblica Italiana, Serie generale – n. 129, p. 2 (5 June 2023)

I SUMMARY

The 2022 Agreement between the Italian Republic and the Republic of Croatia on the Delimitation of the Exclusive Economic Zones (the 2022 Agreement) delimits the exclusive economic zones "to which the parties are entitled." Italy has not yet completed the internal process of establishing its exclusive economic zone; Croatia has. The Agreement applies to the delimitation of the exclusive economic zone the boundary line that had been agreed upon by Italy and Yugoslavia in 1968 for the delimitation of their continental shelves, as amended by an exchange of notes in 2005 between Italy and Croatia, which contained technical adjustments to the coordinates of the 1968 boundary turning points. The 2022 Agreement currently delimits the exclusive economic zone of Croatia and will also apply to the exclusive economic zone of Italy, once this has been established.

Coalter G. Lathrop (ed.), International Maritime Boundaries, 6231-6247.
© The American Society of International Law and Koninklijke Brill BV, Leiden 2025.

6232 *Report Number 8-27*

II CONSIDERATIONS

1 *Political, Strategic, and Historical Considerations*

Italy and Croatia are located in the Mediterranean region. Their coasts border most of the Adriatic Sea, Croatia on the eastern side and Italy on the western side. Croatia and Italy are both members of the European Union and NATO, as well as of other regional initiatives in the Adriatic and Balkan regions.

Croatia became independent with the dissolution of Yugoslavia and succeeded Yugoslavia in its maritime delimitations with Italy.[1] Italy and Yugoslavia had delimited their maritime boundaries through two treaties: the 1968 Agreement between Italy and Yugoslavia Concerning the Delimitation of the Continental Shelf between the Two Countries (the 1968 Agreement),[2] which delimited the greatest portion of the seabed of the Adriatic Sea, and the 1975 Treaty of Osimo (the 1975 Treaty), which delimited their territorial sea boundary in the Gulf of Trieste, at the northern end of the Adriatic Sea, part of which now forms the territorial sea boundary between Croatia and Italy.[3]

The 1968 Agreement was based on an equidistance line between the opposite coasts of the two states, extending from Point 1 in the north, at a point 12 nautical miles (M) from the coasts of both parties,[4] to Point 43 in the south just short of the equidistance tripoint between the parties and Albania.[5] The 1968 continental shelf boundary took full account of the numerous fringing islands scattered off the coast of Yugoslavia; however, the line was adjusted to give only limited effect to the non-fringing islands, including the Yugoslav islands of Jabuka, Svetac, Palagruza, and Galijula, and to the Italian island of Pianosa, all of which were located near the equidistance line. Upon independence, Croatia succeeded to the 1968 Agreement, and the relevant portion of the boundary established in that agreement became the maritime boundary between the Croatian and the Italian continental shelves.[6]

---

1 Report Number 8-7 (3), III IMB 2437.
2 *See* Report Number 8-7 (1), II IMB 1627.
3 *See* Report Number 8-7 (2), II IMB 1639.
4 The same coordinates as Point 1, the northernmost point of the continental shelf boundary between Italy and Yugoslavia, were later used by the two states to indicate the southernmost point of the territorial sea boundary, ensuring a continuous boundary line.
5 Report Number 8-7 (1), II IMB 1627, 1628.
6 Report Number 8-7 (3), III IMB 2437. All of the 1968 continental shelf boundary was deemed to relate to Croatia except the final southern segment between Points 42 and 43 and any remaining part to be delimited south of Point 43. South of Point 42 of the 1968 boundary, in the view of the parties, Montenegro has an interest.

Following meetings of their technical experts, the parties adopted updated coordinates for their continental shelf boundary through an exchange of notes forming the Agreement on the Accurate Determination of the Delimitation Line of the Continental Shelf (2005 Exchange of Notes).

The 1975 Treaty delimited the territorial sea between Italy and Yugoslavia, starting from the terminal point of the land boundary on the estuary of the San Bartolomeo River and connecting five points with great circle arcs. The coordinates of Point 5 of the 1975 territorial sea boundary coincided with the coordinates of Point 1 of the 1968 continental shelf boundary, completing the delimitation of the maritime boundary between the two states in the north of the Adriatic Sea. The 2005 Exchange of Notes updating the coordinates of the 1968 Agreement did not concern the 1975 territorial sea boundary.

In the early 2000s, Croatia began to extend its jurisdiction over waters beyond the territorial sea. In 2003, Croatia declared an ecological and fisheries protection zone, which, in terms of substance, fell short of an exclusive economic zone.[7] Croatia's restraint was probably due to the desire to avoid direct conflict with neighboring states and possible blowback on the process for admission to the European Union. Nonetheless, Italy and Slovenia protested Croatia's ecological and fisheries protection zone.[8] Croatia eventually established an exclusive economic zone in 2021.[9]

Italy, which for decades had pursued a policy of non-extension of its maritime zones beyond the territorial sea and continental shelf, changed this approach in the early 2000s with the creation of a 24 M archeological contiguous zone in 2004 and then, in 2006, with the adoption of framework

---

7   Decision on the Extension of the Jurisdiction of the Republic of Croatia in the Adriatic Sea (3 October 2003), *reprinted in* 53 LOS BULL. 68 (2003); *modified by* Decision on Amending the Decision on the Extension of the Jurisdiction of the Republic of Croatia in the Adriatic Sea of 3 October 2003 (3 June 2004), *reprinted in* 55 LOS BULL. 31.

8   On the ecological and fisheries protection zone and the reaction of other coastal states in the region of the Adriatic Sea, *see Round Table on Fisheries Policy in the Mediterranean and the Extension of Jurisdiction in the Adriatic Sea*, 9 Croatian Int'l Rel. Rev. (Special Issue No. 32) 1 (2003); Fabio Caffio, *Zona economica esclusiva: un punto di vista italiano*, in I Rapporti di vicinato dell'Italia con Croazia, Serbia-Montenegro e Slovenia, 151 (Natalino Ronzitti ed., 2005); Budislav Vukas, *The Extension of the Jurisdiction of the Coastal States in the Adriatic Sea*, in I Rapporti di vicinato dell'Italia con Croazia, Serbia-Montenegro e Slovenia, 251 (Natalino Ronzitti ed., 2005); Davor Vidas, *The UN Convention on the Law of the Sea, the European Union and the Rule of Law: What is going on in the Adriatic Sea?*, 24 Int'l J. Marine and Coastal L. 1 (2009).

9   Decision No. 10/2021 of 5 February 2021 concerning the Proclamation of the Exclusive Economic Zone of the Republic of Croatia in the Adriatic Sea (Croatia), *available at* https://www.un.org/Depts/los/LEGISLATIONANDTREATIES/PDFFILES/DecisionEEZRepublicofCroatia.pdf.

legislation allowing for the creation of ecological protection zones.[10] The first such zone was established in 2011, comprising areas of the northwestern Mediterranean Sea, the Ligurian Sea, and the Tyrrhenian Sea. No such zone was established in the Adriatic Sea. In 2021, Italy adopted legislation authorizing the creation of its exclusive economic zone,[11] which remains to be formally established through a presidential decree. No such decree has been adopted yet to give effect to this legislation. In light of the fact that Italy is currently negotiating the application of its seabed boundaries with other neighbors to also delimit the waters, a reason for this delay might be the wish to first delimit, as much as possible, the outer limits of the future exclusive economic zone before formally establishing the zone.

The divergence of views concerning the expansion of jurisdiction beyond the territorial sea, joined with concerns over fishing activities in the Adriatic Sea, was probably the reason why Croatia and Italy did not engage in any negotiations concerning the delimitation of the water column for many years. Furthermore, both states were involved in complex negotiations with other neighbors. Croatia had to consider the pending delimitation issue with Slovenia, which also involved their land boundary, and which was eventually submitted to arbitration.[12] Italy has coasts also along the Tyrrhenian Sea and the Central Mediterranean Sea and is currently engaged in negotiations with other neighbors, which also involved evaluating whether to apply the continental shelf boundary to the superjacent waters.

Following the successful conclusion and entry into force in 2020 of an agreement between Greece and Italy on delimitation of their (future) exclusive economic zones,[13] which applies the continental shelf boundary that had been agreed upon in 1977,[14] and the creation of the Croatian exclusive economic zone in 2021, Croatia and Italy entered into negotiations with a view towards delimiting the waters of the Adriatic Sea. The Agreement delimiting their exclusive economic zones was adopted on 24 May 2022, together with a Joint Declaration on Adriatic Sea's Resources (Joint Declaration), which

---

10 Decree No. 42 of 22 January 2004 concerning the Code of the Cultural and Landscape Heritage (Italy), *available at* https://whc.unesco.org/document/155711 and Law No. 61 of 8 February 2006 concerning the Establishment of an ecological protection zone beyond the outer limit of the territorial sea (Italy), *available at* https://www.un.org/depts/los/LEGISLATIONANDTREATIES/PDFFILES/ITA_2006_Law.pdf.

11 Law No. 91 of 14 June 2021 concerning the Institution of an exclusive economic zone beyond the external limit of the territorial sea (Italy), *available at* https://www.un.org/Depts/los/LEGISLATIONANDTREATIES/PDFFILES/law9114jun21eez.pdf.

12 *See* Report Number 8-20 (Add. 1), VIII IMB 5667.

13 *See* Report Number 8-4 (2), in this volume.

14 *See* Report Number 8-4, II IMB 1591.

is mentioned in the Preamble of the 2022 Agreement, although it is not formally annexed to it.[15]

2 Legal Regime Considerations

The 2022 Agreement provides that the "boundary line of the exclusive economic zones to which the Parties are entitled to exercise, respectively, their sovereign rights and jurisdiction under international law coincides with the continental shelf boundary" as established in the 1968 Agreement (as modified in 2005) (Article 1(1)). The Agreement then reproduces the list of the coordinates of the 42 points, as incorporated in the 2005 Exchange of Notes. Presumably, the northernmost point, Point 1, is intended coincide with the limit of the territorial sea, the final point on the 1975 territorial sea boundary between Italy and Croatia, and with Point T5 of the "Junction Area" in which Slovenia enjoys certain rights in a portion of Croatia's territorial sea.[16] Finally, the Agreement provides that beyond the southernmost point, Point 42, "the delimitation line continues to a point which shall be agreed with the third State concerned" (Article 1(3)).[17]

The Agreement further contains a non-prejudice clause which safeguards the rights of the coastal states and of third states in the exclusive economic zone, as they are set out in Articles 56 and 58 of the United Nations Convention on the Law of the Sea (UNCLOS). This provision should probably be read in conjunction with the Joint Declaration, which provides for joint consultations between the two states to address conservation of marine living resources.

With regard to the settlement of disputes, Article 3 of the Agreement provides that disputes concerning its interpretation or application will be settled through direct consultations. If no settlement is reached within four months of the notice to start the consultations, either part may submit the dispute to the International Tribunal for the Law of the Sea, the International Court of Justice, or an arbitral tribunal established in accordance with Annex VII of UNCLOS. In order to decide which of these institutions will hear the case, Article 3(3) refers to Article 287 of UNCLOS. The choice of forum will

---

15 The text of the Joint Declaration can be found on the website of the Università di Macerata at https://www.unimc.it/maremap/it/JDonAdriaticSeasResources.pdf.

16 The Junction Area and the 2017 Award in the boundary arbitration between Croatia and Slovenia are addressed in Report Number 8-20 (Add. 1), VIII IMB 5667.

17 Although the 2022 Agreement does not specify which is the third state with interests in the maritime area to the south of Point 42, Montenegro is the adjacent coastal state to the south of Croatia.

6236   *Report Number 8-27*

therefore depend on the declarations made by the two states in accordance with Article 287.

3   *Economic and Environmental Considerations*

Fishing activities and the conservation of marine living resources in the Adriatic Sea have certainly played a role in the timing of the negotiations and the form in which the Agreement was eventually concluded. Traditionally, Italian fishermen had fished on both sides of the median line in the Adriatic,[18] so the extension of Croatian jurisdiction over the waters beyond the outer limit of the territorial sea was of concern to Italy. Croatia, on its side, was concerned about the rapid decline in Adriatic fisheries. The entry of Croatia into the European Union in 2013 and the subsequent application of EU law to the Croatian ecological protection zone, and now its exclusive economic zone, appeased the concerns of Croatia and Italy.

These concerns were likely at the basis of the adoption of the Joint Declaration, which is mentioned in the Preamble to the 2022 Agreement. The Joint Declaration provides for consultations to monitor "the impact that potential changes in the legal framework may have on the interests of the two Countries' populations" and to focus on the "common interest to ensure environmental sustainability in the Adriatic Sea while preserving maritime jobs and income generating activities in both Countries."

4   *Geographic Considerations*

A description of the geographic considerations that influenced the course of this boundary can be found in the original reporting on the 1968 Agreement.[19]

---

18   The 1947 Peace Treaty between the Allied Powers and Italy, which ceded the island of Palagruza to Yugoslavia, provided in Article 11 that Italian fishermen would enjoy in the nearby waters the rights that Yugoslav fishermen had enjoyed before the cession. It is unclear whether this provision has been applied in the past; *see* Fabio Caffio, *Glossario del Diritto del Mare*, 100 (4th ed. 2016).

19   Report Number 8-7 (1), II IMB 1627.

5 Islands, Rocks, Reefs, and Low-tide Elevations Considerations

A complete description of the use of insular features and how they influenced the course of this boundary can be found in the original reporting on the 1968 Agreement.[20]

6 Baseline Considerations

Baseline considerations are provided in the original reporting on the 1968 Agreement.[21]

7 Geological and Geomorphological Considerations

Geological and geomorphological considerations do not seem to have influenced the drawing of the boundary line.

8 Method of Delimitation Considerations

The method of delimitation of the earlier continental shelf boundary, on which this water column boundary is primarily based, can be found in the original report covering the 1968 Agreement.[22]

9 Technical Considerations

The delimitation line in the 1968 Agreement between Italy and Yugoslavia consisted of 43 points connected by 40 great circle arcs and two 12 M arcs measured from Croatia's (then Yugoslavia's) Palagruza and Galijula islands. The coordinates of those points were provided in two lists, one in the Italian coordinate system and one in the Yugoslav coordinate system. The boundary was also plotted twice; on an Italian chart and on a Yugoslav chart, with different systems of survey and construction. The 1968 coordinates were

---

20 *Id.*
21 *Id.*
22 *Id.*

only provided to the nearest tenth of an arc minute, a relatively coarse level of precision by today's standards.[23]

In order to bring the 1968 coordinates into a single, modern datum and to increase the level of precision of the boundary, Croatia and Italy held meetings of technical experts to convert the coordinates into WGS-84.[24] These negotiations were concluded in 2005, and the converted coordinates of the 1968 Agreement were formalized through an exchange of notes. The 2022 Agreement refers to the 2005 Exchange of Notes and adopts the coordinates specified therein. They are provided to the nearest arc second. The nature of the lines connecting the turning points is not specified, but it can be assumed that they remain the same as those described in the 1968 Agreement. The 2005 Exchange of Notes does not convert the 1975 territorial sea boundary coordinates. Nonetheless, since Point 1 of the 1968 continental shelf coincided with Point 5 of the 1975 territorial sea boundary, it is likely that if the latter were to be converted, it would coincide with the former.[25]

10   *Other Considerations*

None

---

23   The same level of precision was used for the delimitation of the territorial sea boundary in the 1975 Treaty.

24   The 2005 Italian note refers to "the technical conversion of the two different lists of coordinates" while the 2005 Croatian note refers to "the accurate determination of the delimitation line . . . utilizing the WGS-84 satellite-based survey data." The former refers to coordinate conversion, but the latter implies a reconsideration of baselines. In any event, the line connecting the coordinates agreed in 2005 now delimits the continental shelf and the water column between the parties.

25   Interestingly, the arbitral tribunal which decided the *Croatia/Slovenia* boundary case converted the coordinates of the 1975 territorial sea boundary turning points, described their coordinates to the nearest 100th of an arc second, identified a point on the 1975 territorial sea boundary (Point B), and referred to it as "the tripoint on the boundary between the maritime zones of Croatia and Slovenia, and the boundary established by the Treaty of Osimo." Reference to a "tripoint" seems rather unfortunate, as it might be read to imply that a tribunal deciding a dispute between two states may fix a tripoint which involves a third state not party to the proceedings. Furthermore, the arbitral tribunal's conversion has been questioned, as Point B, and possibly other parts of the boundary, would be located some hundred meters west of the 1975 boundary line, toward Italy.

III CONCLUSIONS

The Agreement signed on 24 May 2022 by Croatia and Italy settles all the maritime boundaries of the two states with the exclusion of the tripoint in the south, most likely with Montenegro. The 2022 Agreement applies to the delimitation of the exclusive economic zone the boundary adopted in 1968 by Italy and Yugoslavia for the delimitation of their continental shelves. The 2022 Agreement refers in the Preamble to a Joint Declaration, which addresses conservation of marine living resources in the Adriatic Sea, a matter of concern for both parties to this delimitation.

IV RELATED LAW IN FORCE

A *Law of the Sea Conventions*

Croatia: Party to UNCLOS (succeeded 5 April 1995).
Italy: Party to UNCLOS (ratified 13 January 1995).

B *Maritime Jurisdiction Claimed at the Time of Signature*

Croatia: 12 M territorial sea; 200 M exclusive economic zone; continental shelf.
Italy: 12 M territorial sea; 24 M archeological contiguous zone; continental shelf.

C *Maritime Jurisdiction Claimed Subsequent to Signature*

Croatia: No change.
Italy: No change.

Prepared by Irini Papanicolopulu

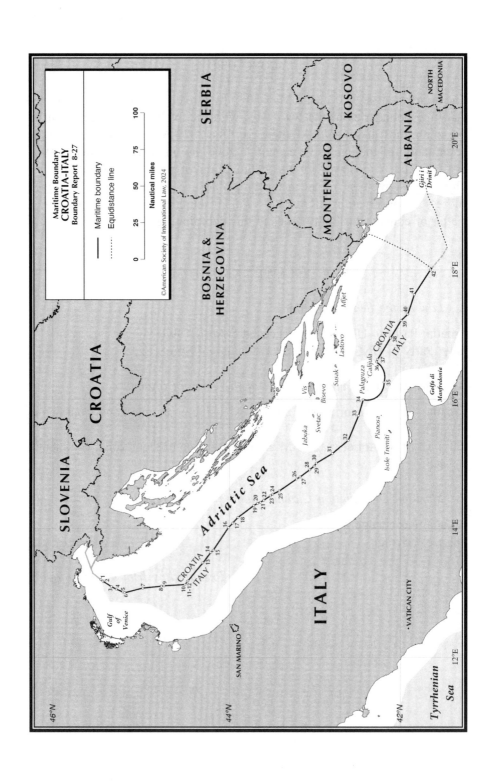

Croatia – Italy 6241

Unofficial translation

Exchange of Notes constituting an Agreement between the Italian Republic and the Republic of Croatia on the Accurate Determination of the Delimitation Line of the Continental Shelf

1. Note Verbale dated 22 July 2005

FROM THE EMBASSY OF THE REPUBLIC OF CROATIA TO THE MINISTRY OF FOREIGN AFFAIRS OF THE ITALIAN REPUBLIC

Embassy of the Republic of Croatia – Rome

Note Verbale No. 202/5

The Embassy of the Republic of Croatia in Rome presents its compliments to the Ministry of Foreign Affairs of the Italian Republic and with reference to discussions of the experts of the two States and departing from the Agreement between the Government of the Socialist Federative Republic of Yugoslavia and the Government of the Italian Republic on the Delimitation of the Continental Shelf between the two Countries, signed in Rome on 8 January 1968, which is in force between the Republic of Croatia and the Italian Republic by virtue of succession, has the honor to propose the accurate determination of the delimitation line of the continental shelf as defined in Article 1 of the Agreement, utilizing the WGS-84 satellite-based survey data. To this effect it is proposed that the delimitation line of the continental shelf between the Republic of Croatia and the Italian Republic will be considered the line defined by the following coordinates:

1	45°27'13"	13°12'40"		22	43°35'58"	14°26'16"
2	45°25'43"	13°11'07"		23	43°31'55"	14°30'07"
3	45°20'07"	13°05'55"		24	43°29'55"	14°31'49"
4	45°16'49"	13°03'40"		25	43°25'19"	14°35'07"
5	45°12'19"	13°01'01"		26	43°12'52"	14°46'01"
6	45°11'04"	13°00'10"		27	43°10'28"	14°47'52"
7	44°58'28"	13°04'22"		28	43°03'46"	14°54'40"
8	44°46'13"	13°06'07"		29	43°00'52"	14°57'49"
9	44°44'13"	13°06'34"		30	42°59'16"	15°00'37"
10	44°30'10"	13°07'46"		31	42°47'49"	15°09'28"

11	44°28'34"	13°10'43"	32	42°36'46"	15°21'46"
12	44°28'01"	13°11'34"	33	42°29'34"	15°44'46"
13	44°17'46"	13°27'55"	34	42°26'11"	15°59'32"
14	44°12'37"	13°37'52"	35	42°11'36"	16°13'38"
15	44°10'46"	13°40'01"	36	42°16'53"	16°34'30"
16	44°00'37"	14°00'55"	37	42°15'59"	16°37'04"
17	43°57'37"	14°04'49"	38	42°07'02"	16°56'37"
18	43°54'10"	14°10'07"	39	41°59'29"	17°12'54"
19	43°43'01"	14°21'16"	40	41°54'44"	17°18'42"
20	43°40'16"	14°23'31"	41	41°50'05"	17°37'03"
21	43°38'31"	14°24'34"	42	41°38'20"	17°59'51"

If the aforementioned proposal is acceptable to the Government of the Italian Republic, the Embassy of the Republic of Croatia has the honor to propose that this Note and the Ministry's note in reply will constitute an agreement between our two Governments on accurate determination of the delimitation line of the continental shelf between the Republic of Croatia and the Italian Republic, in accordance with the Agreement of 1968, which will come into effect on the date of receipt of the Ministry's note in reply.

The Embassy of the Republic of Croatia avails itself of this opportunity to renew to the Ministry of Foreign Affairs of the Italian Republic the assurances of its highest consideration.

Roma, 22 July 2005

2. Note Verbale dated 29 July 2005

FROM THE MINISTRY OF FOREIGN AFFAIRS OF THE ITALIAN REPUBLIC TO THE EMBASSY OF THE REPUBLIC OF CROATIA

Ministry of Foreign Affairs – Rome

Note Verbale No. 60-9/0313044

The Ministry of Foreign Affairs of the Italian Republic presents its compliments to the Embassy of the Republic of Croatia and has the honor to refer to the Note Verbale of the Embassy of Croatia dated 22 July 2005 No. 202/05.

Following the mixed meetings of experts from the two states about the technical conversion of the two different lists of coordinates referred to in the Agreement between the Republic of Italy and the Socialist Federal Republic of Yugoslavia on the delimitation of the continental shelf between the two countries, signed in Rome on 8 January 1968, in force today between the Italian Republic and the Republic of Croatia as a result of succession, there is agreement on the proposal contained in the above-mentioned Croatian Note Verbale of a more technically updated definition of the boundary line of the continental shelf as determined in Article 1 of the 1968 Agreement, using the geodetic satellite reference now commonly recognized and accepted WGS-84.

For this purpose, it is agreed that the line of delimitation of the continental shelf between the Republic of Italy and the Republic of Croatia shall consist of the line defined by the following coordinates:

[*see Note 1 above for coordinates of Points 1-42*]

The exchange between this Note Verbale and the Note Verbale of the Embassy of the Republic of Croatia protocol number 202/05 dated 22 July 2005 constitutes the Agreement between the Republic of Italy and the Republic of Croatia for the purpose of the technical correction of the delimitation line of the continental shelf between the two states referred to the 1968 Agreement. This corrective agreement will enter into force upon the communication by Croatia of the receipt of this Note Verbale in response.

The Ministry of Foreign Affairs, in recalling that it does not consider the line of delimitation of the continental shelf usable as the delimitation line of any marine area of functional sovereignty established by either state in the column of water overlying the continental shelf itself, takes this opportunity to renew to the Embassy of Croatia the senses of its highest consideration.

Rome, 29 July 2005

3. Note Verbale dated 2 August 2005

FROM THE EMBASSY OF THE REPUBLIC OF CROATIA TO THE MINISTRY OF FOREIGN AFFAIRS OF THE ITALIAN REPUBLIC

Embassy of the Republic of Croatia – Rome

Note Verbale No. 214/5

The Embassy of the Republic of Croatia presents its compliments to the Ministry of Foreign Affairs of the Italian Republic and has the honor to acknowledge today the receipt of Note Verbale No. 60-9/0313044 dated 29 July 2005.

The Embassy of the Republic of Croatia also has the honor to confirm that the Agreement between the Republic of Croatia and the Republic of Italy for the purpose of technical correction of the boundary line of the continental shelf between the two states referred to in the Agreement of 1968 enters into force with the date 2 August 2005.

The Embassy of the Republic of Croatia takes this opportunity to renew to the Ministry of Foreign Affairs of the Republic of Italy the acts of its highest consideration.

Rome, 2 August 2005

Croatia – Italy 6245

AGREEMENT BETWEEN THE ITALIAN REPUBLIC AND THE REPUBLIC OF CROATIA ON THE DELIMITATION OF THE EXCLUSIVE ECONOMIC ZONES

The Italian Republic and the Republic of Croatia (hereinafter the "Parties"),

DESIRING to strengthen the ties of good-neighbourliness and cooperation between the two Parties;

TAKING NOTE of the Joint Declaration on the Adriatic Sea's resources signed in Rome on 24 May 2022;

AWARE of the need to delimit precisely the maritime zones over which the two states are entitled to exercise, respectively, their sovereign rights and jurisdiction in accordance with international law;

TAKING INTO ACCOUNT the relevant provisions of the United Nations Convention on the Law of the Sea done at Montego Bay on 10 December 1982, to which the Italian Republic and the Republic of Croatia are Parties;

RECALLING the provisions of the Agreement between the Government of the Italian Republic and the Government of the Socialist Federative Republic of Yugoslavia on the delimitation of the continental shelf between the two countries, done at Rome on 8 January 1968, in force between the Italian Republic and the Republic of Croatia (hereinafter "the Agreement of 1968"), as well as the Agreement between the Government of the Italian Republic and the Government of the Republic of Croatia on accurate determination of the delimitation line of the continental shelf between the Italian Republic and the Republic of Croatia, done at Rome on 22 and 29 July 2005 and entered into force on 2 August 2005 (hereinafter "the technical adjustment Agreement of 2005");

HAVE AGREED as follows:

Article 1

1.   The boundary line of the exclusive economic zones to which the Parties are entitled to exercise, respectively, their sovereign rights and jurisdiction under international law coincides with the continental shelf boundary between

6246 *Report Number 8-27*

the Parties in accordance with the Agreement of 1968 and the technical adjustment Agreement of 2005.

2. The coordinates of the boundary line hereby agreed by the Parties and expressed in the WGS-84 datum are the following:

1	45°27'13"	13°12'40"	22	43°35'58"	14°26'16"
2	45°25'43"	13°11'07"	23	43°31'55"	14°30'07"
3	45°20'07"	13°05'55"	24	43°29'55"	14°31'49"
4	45°16'49"	13°03'40"	25	43°25'19"	14°35'07"
5	45°12'19"	13°01'01"	26	43°12'52"	14°46'01"
6	45°11'04"	13°00'10"	27	43°10'28"	14°47'52"
7	44°58'28"	13°04'22"	28	43°03'46"	14°54'40"
8	44°46'13"	13°06'07"	29	43°00'52"	14°57'49"
9	44°44'13"	13°06'34"	30	42°59'16"	15°00'37"
10	44°30'10"	13°07'46"	31	42°47'49"	15°09'28"
11	44°28'34"	13°10'43"	32	42°36'46"	15°21'46"
12	44°28'01"	13°11'34"	33	42°29'34"	15°44'46"
13	44°17'46"	13°27'55"	34	42°26'11"	15°59'32"
14	44°12'37"	13°37'52"	35	42°11'36"	16°13'38"
15	44°10'46"	13°40'01"	36	42°16'53"	16°34'30"
16	44°00'37"	14°00'55"	37	42°15'59"	16°37'04"
17	43°57'37"	14°04'49"	38	42°07'02"	16°56'37"
18	43°54'10"	14°10'07"	39	41°59'29"	17°12'54"
19	43°43'01"	14°21'16"	40	41°54'44"	17°18'42"
20	43°40'16"	14°23'31"	41	41°50'05"	17°37'03"
21	43°38'31"	14°24'34"	42	41°38'20"	17°59'51"

3. From point 42 referred to in the previous paragraph, the delimitation line continues to a point which shall be agreed with the third State concerned.

Article 2

This Agreement is without prejudice to:
a. fishing activities carried out in conformity with applicable EU rules and regulations;
b. the sovereign rights and the jurisdiction exercised by each Party in its exclusive economic zone in conformity with Article 56 of the United Nations Convention on the Law of the Sea;

c. the provisions of Article 58 of the United Nations Convention on the Law of the Sea regarding the rights, freedoms and duties of other States in the exclusive economic zone of the Parties.

Article 3

1. The Parties commit themselves to settle, through direct consultations or negotiations, any dispute which may arise concerning the interpretation or application of this Agreement.

2. If such a dispute is not settled within four (4) months from the date on which one of the Parties gave notice of its intention to initiate the procedure provided for in the previous paragraph, either Party may submit the dispute to the International Tribunal for the Law of the Sea, to the International Court of Justice or to an Arbitral Tribunal constituted in accordance with Annex VII of the United Nations Convention on the Law of the Sea.

3. For the identification of the court or tribunal to which a dispute may be submitted according to the previous paragraph, Article 287 of the United Nations Convention on the Law of the Sea and the Declarations made under the same article by the Parties shall apply *mutatis mutandis*.

Article 4

This Agreement shall enter into force on the date of receipt of the last written notification by which the Parties have notified each other, through diplomatic channels, of the completion of their internal procedures necessary for its entry into force.

In witness thereof the undersigned, being duly authorised thereto, have signed this Agreement.

DONE at Rome on 24 May 2022, in two originals, each in the Italian, Croatian and English languages, all texts being equally authentic. In case of divergence in the interpretation of this Agreement, the English text shall prevail.

For the Italian Republic
(signed)

For the Republic of Croatia
(signed)

IX

Northern and Western Europe

Denmark/The Faroes – Iceland; Denmark/ The Faroes – Norway; Iceland – Norway

Report Number 9-26 (Add. 1)

Agreement between the Government of Denmark and the Government of the Faroes, on the one part, and the Government of Iceland on the other part, concerning the delimitation of the continental shelf beyond 200 nautical miles in the area between the Faroe Islands, Iceland, Mainland Norway and Jan Mayen

Signed: 30 October 2019
Entered into Force: Not yet in force
Published at: Unpublished

Agreement between the Government of Denmark and the Government of the Faroes, on the one part, and the Government of Norway on the other part, concerning the delimitation of the continental shelf beyond 200 nautical miles in the area between the Faroe Islands, Iceland, Mainland Norway and Jan Mayen

Signed: 30 October 2019
Entered into Force: Not yet in force
Published at: Unpublished

Agreement between the Government of Norway and the Government of Iceland concerning the delimitation of the continental shelf beyond 200 nautical miles in the area between the Faroe Islands, Iceland, Mainland Norway and Jan Mayen

Signed: 30 October 2019
Entered into Force: Not yet in force
Published at: Unpublished

On 30 October 2019, Denmark/The Faroes, Iceland, and Norway signed in Stockholm three bilateral agreements implementing the trilateral Agreed Minutes on the Delimitation of the Continental Shelf beyond 200 Nautical Miles between the Faroe Islands, Iceland and Norway in the Southern Part

---

Coalter G. Lathrop (ed.), International Maritime Boundaries, 6251-6269.
© *The American Society of International Law and Koninklijke Brill BV, Leiden 2025.*

6252 *Report Number 9-26 (Add. 1)*

of the Banana Hole of the Northeast Atlantic (the Agreed Minutes) that had been concluded by the parties on 20 September 2006.[1] These three 2019 agreements must be seen in conjunction with each other. And they must be understood in the context of the Agreed Minutes in which the boundaries, now codified in the three bilateral treaties, were provisionally agreed pending consideration by the Commission on the Limits of the Continental Shelf (CLCS) of the separate submissions made to it by the three parties to the Agreed Minutes.[2]

Together, the 2019 agreements settle the delimitation of the continental shelf beyond 200 nautical miles (M) in a large area of the Northeast Atlantic Ocean situated between the Faroe Islands, Iceland, the Norwegian island of Jan Mayen, and mainland Norway. The parties followed accurately the procedural arrangements and applied the methods for drawing the delimitation lines in this maritime area that were set out in the 2006 Agreed Minutes. As a first step, this entailed making the respective national submissions to the CLCS concerning the outer limits of the continental shelf in the area as measured from the baselines of the coastlines of the four territories concerned. After due examination of all three individual submissions by the CLCS, the parties then had to ascertain whether the recommendations of the CLCS confirmed that no part of the area beyond 200 M belonged to the Area and that all three states were individually entitled to a continental shelf area sufficiently large to satisfy the assumptions made in the Agreed Minutes. This required individual entitlements that in size equalled, at a minimum, the area that would fall to each state on the basis of the provisional delimitation lines that had been tentatively set out in the Agreed Minutes.

These assumptions were confirmed on the basis of the examinations made by the CLCS of the three independent submissions. Norway made its submission for the area in 2006, receiving the recommendations of the CLCS in 2009.[3] Denmark made its submission in 2009, receiving the

---

1 Report Number 9-26, VI IMB 4532.
2 *Editor's Note*: It is the practice in this series to address each boundary agreement in its own report. Considering, however, that the earlier International Maritime Boundaries report on the trilateral 2006 Agreed Minutes covered all aspects of the delimitation process, including the negotiation of and rationale for the provisional delimitations among the parties, and considering that the 2019 bilateral agreements adopted the exact coordinates and much of the language of the Model Agreement from the Agreed Minutes, it has been preferred to address the three final bilateral agreements in this single addendum to the earlier report.
3 Commission on the Limits of the Continental Shelf, *Summary of Recommendations of the Commission on the Limits of the Continental Shelf in regard to the Submission made by Norway in respect of areas in the Arctic Ocean, the Barents Sea and the Norwegian Sea on 27 November 2006*, adopted by the Subcommission on 13 March 2009 and adopted by

recommendations of the CLCS in 2014.[4] Iceland made its submission in 2009, receiving the recommendations of the CLCS in 2016.[5]

After the assumptions made by the parties in the 2006 Agreed Minutes had been confirmed by the CLCS, representatives of Denmark/The Faroes, Iceland, and Norway held a meeting in Oslo 13-14 October 2016 where the concrete implementation of the 2006 Agreed Minutes was agreed. This meeting was followed by informal contacts to finalise the texts of the three delimitation agreements. The agreements were signed in Stockholm on 30 October 2019 in the presence of the relevant ministers or their representatives at a foreign ministerial session of the Nordic Council.

The parties agreed that the texts of the provisional delimitation treaties drafted on the basis of the 2006 Agreed Minutes were largely applicable. The three finalized agreements thus contain preambular references to the Agreed Minutes of 20 September 2006, and they replicate the coordinates and terms already indicated in the 2006 Agreed Minutes and the Model Agreement attached as Appendix II to the Agreed Minutes. Minor updating and adjustments were made to the procedural provisions in the Model Agreement concerning cooperation as regards transboundary mineral deposits, making also provision for other mineral resources than hydrocarbons. In the agreement between Iceland and Norway, transboundary cooperation provisions were deleted, as they had already been superseded by the Agreement between Norway and Iceland concerning Transboundary Hydrocarbon Deposits concluded on 3 November 2008.[6]

---

the Commission, with amendments, on 27 March 2009, *available at* https://www.un.org/Depts/los/clcs_new/submissions_files/nor06/nor_rec_summ.pdf.

A proviso in paragraph 78 as regards the use of the depth constraint line from Jan Mayen for a small triangular area bounded by the 200 M limit of the Faroe Islands had no practical consequences in light of expected, and later confirmed, overlap from the Faroe Islands.

See also Report Number 9-26, VI IMB 4532, 4541, note 23.

4   Commission on the Limits of the Continental Shelf, *Recommendations of the Commission on the Limits of the Continental Shelf in regard to the Partial Submission made by the Government of the Kingdom of Denmark together with the Government of the Faroes in respect of the Continental Shelf North of the Faroe Islands on 29 April 2009*, adopted by the Subcommission on 30 October 2013 and adopted by the Commission, with amendments, on 12 March 2014, *available at* https://www.un.org/Depts/los/clcs_new/submissions_files/dnk28_09/2014_03_14_SCDNK_REC_COM_20140521.pdf.

5   Commission on the Limits of the Continental Shelf, *Summary of Recommendations of the Commission on the Limits of the Continental Shelf in regard to the Submission made by Iceland in the Ægir Basin Area and in the Western and Southern Parts of Reykjanes Ridge on 29 April 2009*, approved by the Subcommission on 27 February 2014 and approved by the Commission, with amendments, on 10 March 2016, *available at* https://www.un.org/Depts/los/clcs_new/submissions_files/isl27_09/2016_03_10_sc_isl.pdf.

6   *See* Report Number 9-4 (3), VII IMB 5123.

The three 2019 agreements require parliamentary consent prior to their entry into force. Subsequent to the signature, the parties will initiate the necessary domestic procedures to this effect.

Prepared by Rolf Einar Fife

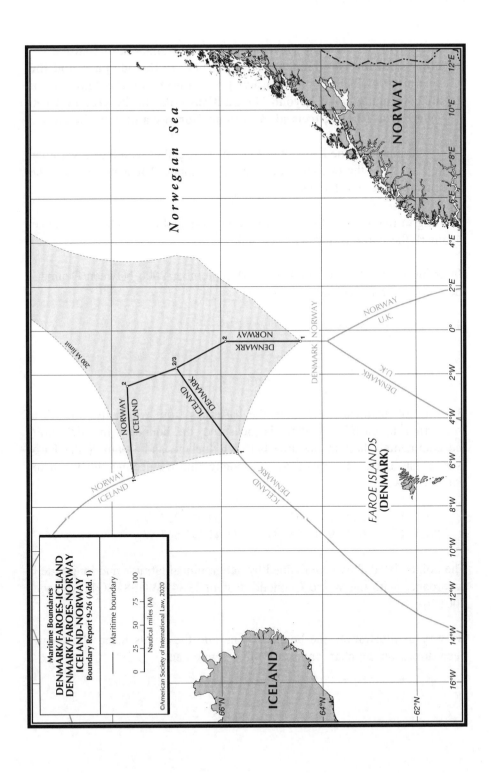

6256　*Report Number 9-26 (Add. 1)*

Agreement between the Government of the Kingdom of Denmark together with the Government of the Faroes, on the one part, and the Government of Iceland on the other part, concerning the delimitation of the continental shelf beyond 200 nautical miles in the area between the Faroe Islands, Iceland, Mainland Norway and Jan Mayen

The Government of the Kingdom of Denmark together with the Government of the Faroes on the one part, and the Government of Iceland, on the other part (hereinafter "the Parties"),

Desiring to maintain and strengthen the good neighbourly relations between Denmark/the Faroe Islands and Iceland,

Referring to the Agreed Minutes of 20 September 2006 between Denmark/the Faroe Islands, Iceland and Norway,

Have agreed as follows:

Article 1

Beyond 200 nautical miles from the baselines from which the breadth of the territorial sea of each Party is measured, the boundary line delimiting the continental shelf in the area between Iceland and Denmark/the Faroe Islands has been determined as a geodetic line connecting the following points below:

Point 1:	65° 41′ 22.63″ N	5° 34′ 42.22″ W
Point 2:	66° 49′ 15.75″ N	1° 41′ 43.56″ W

The points listed above are defined by geographical latitude and longitude in accordance with the World Geodetic System 1984 (WGS84 (G1150, epoch 2001.0)).

By way of illustration, the boundary line and the points listed above have been drawn on the chart annexed to this Agreement.

Article 2

1. If the existence of a mineral deposit in or on the continental shelf of one of the Parties is established and the other Party is of the opinion that the said deposit extends to its continental shelf, the latter Party may notify the former Party accordingly, through submitting the data on which it bases its notification.

2. If such a notification is submitted, the Parties shall initiate discussions on the extent of the deposit and the possibility for exploitation. In the course of these discussions, the Party initiating them shall support its opinion with evidence from geophysical data and/or geological data, including any available drilling data, and both Parties shall make their best efforts to ensure that all relevant information is made available for the purposes of these discussions.

3. (a) If it is established during these discussions that the mineral deposit, other than hydrocarbons, extends to the continental shelf of both Parties, the Parties shall at the request of either of them consult with a view to exploit the deposit. Exploitation of the deposit in a way that would affect the possibility of its exploitation on the continental shelf of the other Party, may not take place without prior agreement between the Parties.

(b) If it is established during these discussions that the hydrocarbon deposit extends to the continental shelf of both Parties and that the deposit on the continental shelf of the one Party can be exploited wholly or in part from the continental shelf of the other Party, or that the exploitation of the deposit on the continental shelf of the one Party would affect the possibility of exploitation of the deposit on the continental shelf of the other Party, agreement on the apportionment of the deposit between the Parties and on the unitised exploitation shall be reached at the request of one of the Parties, including as to the appointment of a unit operator, the manner in which any such deposit shall be most effectively exploited and the manner in which the proceeds relating thereto shall be apportioned. Such agreement shall be reached in the form of a Unitisation Agreement. Neither Party can exploit the hydrocarbon deposit until a Unitisation Agreement has been agreed between the Parties.

6258   Report Number 9-26 (Add. 1)

Article 3

The Unitisation Agreement to be agreed by the Parties in accordance with Article 2, paragraph 3b, concerning the exploitation of a defined transboundary hydrocarbon deposit shall include the provisions set out below:

1.   The transboundary hydrocarbon deposit to be exploited as a unit shall be defined (latitudes and longitudes normally shown in a separate attachment).

2.   The geographical and geological characteristics of the transboundary hydrocarbon deposit and the methodology used for data classification shall be described. The legal persons holding rights to exploit the transboundary hydrocarbon deposit as a unit shall have equal access to any geophysical data and/or geological data, including any available drilling data used as a basis for such geological characterisation.

3.   The estimated total volume of hydrocarbons in place in the transboundary hydrocarbon deposit shall be stated. The methodology used for such calculation shall be stated. The apportionment of the reserves between the Parties shall be set out (normally in separate attachment).

4.   Each Party shall be entitled to copies of all geophysical data and/or geological data, including any available drilling data, as well as all other data of relevance for the unitised hydrocarbon deposit, and which are gathered in connection with the exploitation of the hydrocarbon deposit.

5.   The two Parties shall individually grant all necessary authorisations required by their respective national laws for the development and operation of the transboundary hydrocarbon deposit as a unit in accordance with this Agreement.

6   Each Party shall require the relevant legal persons holding rights to exploit hydrocarbons on its respective side of the delimitation line to enter into a Joint Operating Agreement between them to regulate the exploitation of the transboundary hydrocarbon deposit as a unit in accordance with the Unitisation Agreement.

7.   The following provisions shall apply in relation to the Joint Operating Agreement:

- The Joint Operating Agreement shall refer to the Unitisation Agreement to ensure that the provisions contained therein shall prevail.

- The Joint Operating Agreement shall be subject to approval by both Parties. Such approval shall be given with no undue delay and shall not be unduly withheld.

- A unit operator shall be appointed as the joint agent of the legal persons holding the rights to exploit the defined transboundary hydrocarbon deposit as a unit in accordance with the principles set out in the Unitisation Agreement. The appointment of, and any change of, the unit operator shall be subject to prior approval by the two Parties.

8. Subject to its national laws, neither Party shall withhold a permit for the drilling of wells by, or on account of, the legal persons holding rights to exploit hydrocarbons on its respective side of the delimitation line for purposes related to the determination and apportionment of the transboundary hydrocarbon deposit.

9. In due time before the exploitation of hydrocarbons from the transboundary hydrocarbon deposit is about to cease, the two Parties shall agree on the timing of cessation of the exploitation from the transboundary hydrocarbon deposit.

10. The two Parties shall consult each other with a view to ensuring that health, safety and environmental measures are taken in accordance with the national laws of each Party.

11. Each Party shall be responsible for inspection of hydrocarbon installations located on its continental shelf and for the hydrocarbon activities carried out thereon in relation to the exploitation of the transboundary hydrocarbon deposit. Each Party shall ensure inspectors of the other Party access to such installations on request, and that they have access to relevant metering systems on the continental shelf or in the territory of either Party. Each Party shall also ensure that relevant information is given to the other Party on a regular basis to enable it to safeguard its fundamental interests including, but not limited to health, safety, environment, hydrocarbon production and metering.

12. A right to exploit hydrocarbons awarded by one Party, and which applies to a transboundary hydrocarbon deposit that is subject to unitisation in accordance with this Agreement, shall not be altered or assigned to new legal persons without prior consultation with the other Party.

Article 4

The Parties shall make every effort to resolve any disagreement concerning a transboundary deposit as rapidly as possible. If, however, the Parties fail to agree, they shall jointly consider all of the options for resolving the impasse.

Article 5

1. If the Parties fail to agree on unitised exploitation of a transboundary deposit either Party may request to solve the disagreement by negotiation. If any such dispute cannot be resolved in this manner or by any other procedure agreed to by the Parties within 6 months following such request, the dispute shall be submitted, at the request of either Party, to an ad hoc arbitral tribunal composed as follows:

2. Each Party shall within 90 days of the submission of the dispute to an ad hoc arbitral tribunal designate one arbitrator, and the two arbitrators so designated shall elect a third arbitrator, who shall be the President. The President of the arbitral tribunal shall not be a national of or habitually reside in the territory of either of the Parties. If either Party fails to designate an arbitrator, either Party may request the President of the International Court of Justice to appoint an arbitrator. The same procedure shall apply if, within one month of the designation or appointment of the second arbitrator, the third arbitrator has not been elected.

3. The tribunal shall determine its own procedure, save that all decisions shall be taken, in the absence of unanimity, by a majority vote of the members of the tribunal. The decisions of the tribunal shall be binding upon the Parties.

Article 6

If the Parties fail to agree on the apportionment of the deposit between themselves, they shall agree to appoint an independent expert to determine

Denmark/The Faroes – Iceland; Denmark/The Faroes – Norway; Iceland – Norway 6261

the apportionment. The decision of the independent expert shall be binding upon the Parties. The Parties may, however, agree that the deposit shall be reapportioned between themselves according to specified conditions.

Article 7

Each Party may after commencement of exploitation from the unitised hydrocarbon deposit request discussions to be initiated on the redetermination of the apportionment of the deposit. Any request for reapportionment must be based on substantial new information regarding factors relevant to apportionment. Both Parties shall make their best efforts to ensure that all relevant information is made available for the purpose of these discussions. The Parties may on this basis agree that the deposit shall be reapportioned between themselves according to specified conditions.

Article 8

This Agreement is without prejudice to the respective Parties' views on questions that are not governed by this Agreement, including questions relating to their exercise of sovereign rights or jurisdiction over the seabed and its subsoil.

Article 9

This Agreement enters into force when the Parties have notified each other in writing that the necessary internal procedures have been completed.

Done at Stockholm on the 30th day of October 2019 in duplicate in the Danish, Faroese, Icelandic and English languages, all texts being equally authentic. In case of any divergence of interpretation, the English text shall prevail.

For the Government of the Kingdom of Denmark

For the Government of Iceland

For the Government of the Faroes

6262   *Report Number 9-26 (Add. 1)*

Agreement between the Government of the Kingdom of Norway, on the one part, and the Government of the Kingdom of Denmark together with the Government of the Faroes on the other part, concerning the delimitation of the continental shelf beyond 200 nautical miles in the area between the Faroe Islands, Iceland, Mainland Norway and Jan Mayen

The Government of the Kingdom of Norway on the one part, and the Government of the Kingdom of Denmark together with the Government of the Faroes, on the other part (hereinafter "the Parties"),

Desiring to maintain and strengthen the good neighbourly relations between Norway and Denmark/the Faroe Islands,

Referring to the Agreed Minutes of 20 September 2006 between Denmark/ the Faroe Islands, Iceland and Norway,

Have agreed as follows:

Article 1

Beyond 200 nautical miles from the baselines from which the breadth of the territorial sea of each Party is measured, the boundary line delimiting the continental shelf in the area between Norway and Denmark/the Faroe Islands has been determined as a geodetic line connecting the following points in the order specified below:

Point 1: 64° 25' 58.14" N   0° 29' 19.30" W
Point 2: 65° 54' 43.74" N   0° 29' 13.23" W
Point 3: 66° 49' 15.75" N   1° 41' 43.56" W

The points listed above are defined by geographical latitude and longitude in accordance with the World Geodetic System 1984 (WGS84 (G1150, epoch 2001.0)).

By way of illustration, the boundary line and the points listed above have been drawn on the chart annexed to this Agreement.

Denmark/The Faroes – Iceland; Denmark/The Faroes – Norway; Iceland – Norway 6263

Article 2

1. If the existence of a mineral deposit in or on the continental shelf of one of the Parties is established and the other Party is of the opinion that the said deposit extends to its continental shelf, the latter Party may notify the former Party accordingly, through submitting the data on which it bases its notification.

2. If such a notification is submitted, the Parties shall initiate discussions on the extent of the deposit and the possibility for exploitation. In the course of these discussions, the Party initiating them shall support its opinion with evidence from geophysical data and/or geological data, including any available drilling data, and both Parties shall make their best efforts to ensure that all relevant information is made available for the purposes of these discussions.

3. (a) If it is established during these discussions that the mineral deposit, other than hydrocarbons, extends to the continental shelf of both Parties, the Parties shall at the request of either of them consult with a view to exploit the deposit. Exploitation of the deposit in a way that would affect the possibility of its exploitation on the continental shelf of the other Party, may not take place without prior agreement between the Parties.

(b) If it is established during these discussions that the hydrocarbon deposit extends to the continental shelf of both Parties and that the deposit on the continental shelf of the one Party can be exploited wholly or in part from the continental shelf of the other Party, or that the exploitation of the deposit on the continental shelf of the one Party would affect the possibility of exploitation of the deposit on the continental shelf of the other Party, agreement on the apportionment of the deposit between the Parties and on the unitised exploitation shall be reached at the request of one of the Parties, including as to the appointment of a unit operator, the manner in which any such deposit shall be most effectively exploited and the manner in which the proceeds relating thereto shall be apportioned. Such agreement shall be reached in the form of a Unitisation Agreement. Neither Party can exploit the hydrocarbon deposit until a Unitisation Agreement has been agreed between the Parties.

6264 *Report Number 9-26 (Add. 1)*

Article 3

The Unitisation Agreement to be agreed by the Parties in accordance with Article 2, paragraph 3b, concerning the exploitation of a defined transboundary hydrocarbon deposit shall include the provisions set out below:

1. The transboundary hydrocarbon deposit to be exploited as a unit shall be defined (latitudes and longitudes normally shown in a separate attachment).

2. The geographical and geological characteristics of the transboundary hydrocarbon deposit and the methodology used for data classification shall be described. The legal persons holding rights to exploit the transboundary hydrocarbon deposit as a unit shall have equal access to any geophysical data and/or geological data, including any available drilling data used as a basis for such geological characterisation.

3. The estimated total volume of hydrocarbons in place in the transboundary hydrocarbon deposit shall be stated. The methodology used for such calculation shall be stated. The apportionment of the reserves between the Parties shall be set out (normally in separate attachment).

4. Each Party shall be entitled to copies of all geophysical data and/or geological data, including any available drilling data, as well as all other data of relevance for the unitised hydrocarbon deposit, and which are gathered in connection with the exploitation of the hydrocarbon deposit.

5. The two Parties shall individually grant all necessary authorisations required by their respective national laws for the development and operation of the transboundary hydrocarbon deposit as a unit in accordance with this Agreement.

6. Each Party shall require the relevant legal persons holding rights to exploit hydrocarbons on its respective side of the delimitation line to enter into a Joint Operating Agreement between them to regulate the exploitation of the transboundary hydrocarbon deposit as a unit in accordance with the Unitisation Agreement.

7. The following provisions shall apply in relation to the Joint Operating Agreement:

- The Joint Operating Agreement shall refer to the Unitisation Agreement to ensure that the provisions contained therein shall prevail.

- The Joint Operating Agreement shall be subject to approval by both Parties. Such approval shall be given with no undue delay and shall not be unduly withheld.

- A unit operator shall be appointed as the joint agent of the legal persons holding the rights to exploit the defined transboundary hydrocarbon deposit as a unit in accordance with the principles set out in the Unitisation Agreement. The appointment of, and any change of, the unit operator shall be subject to prior approval by the two Parties.

8 Subject to its national laws, neither Party shall withhold a permit for the drilling of wells by, or on account of, the legal persons holding rights to exploit hydrocarbons on its respective side of the delimitation line for purposes related to the determination and apportionment of the transboundary hydrocarbon deposit.

9 In due time before the exploitation of hydrocarbons from the transboundary hydrocarbon deposit is about to cease, the two Parties shall agree on the timing of cessation of the exploitation from the transboundary hydrocarbon deposit.

10. The two Parties shall consult each other with a view to ensuring that health, safety and environmental measures are taken in accordance with the national laws of each Party.

11. Each Party shall be responsible for inspection of hydrocarbon installations located on its continental shelf and for the hydrocarbon activities carried out thereon in relation to the exploitation of the transboundary hydrocarbon deposit. Each Party shall ensure inspectors of the other Party access to such installations on request, and that they have access to relevant metering systems on the continental shelf or in the territory of either Party. Each Party shall also ensure that relevant information is given to the other Party on a regular basis to enable it to safeguard its fundamental interests including, but not limited to health, safety, environment, hydrocarbon production and metering.

12. A right to exploit hydrocarbons awarded by one Party, and which applies to a transboundary hydrocarbon deposit that is subject to unitisation in accordance with this Agreement, shall not be altered or assigned to new legal persons without prior consultation with the other Party.

Article 4

The Parties shall make every effort to resolve any disagreement concerning a transboundary deposit as rapidly as possible. If, however, the Parties fail to agree, they shall jointly consider all of the options for resolving the impasse.

Article 5

1. If the Parties fail to agree on unitised exploitation of a transboundary deposit either Party may request to solve the disagreement by negotiation. If any such dispute cannot be resolved in this manner or by any other procedure agreed to by the Parties within 6 months following such request, the dispute shall be submitted, at the request of either Party, to an ad hoc arbitral tribunal composed as follows:

2. Each Party shall within 90 days of the submission of the dispute to an ad hoc arbitral tribunal designate one arbitrator, and the two arbitrators so designated shall elect a third arbitrator, who shall be the President. The President of the arbitral tribunal shall not be a national of or habitually reside in the territory of either of the Parties. If either Party fails to designate an arbitrator, either Party may request the President of the International Court of Justice to appoint an arbitrator. The same procedure shall apply if, within one month of the designation or appointment of the second arbitrator, the third arbitrator has not been elected.

3. The tribunal shall determine its own procedure, save that all decisions shall be taken, in the absence of unanimity, by a majority vote of the members of the tribunal. The decisions of the tribunal shall be binding upon the Parties.

Article 6

If the Parties fail to agree on the apportionment of the deposit between themselves, they shall agree to appoint an independent expert to determine the apportionment. The decision of the independent expert shall be binding upon the Parties. The Parties may, however, agree that the deposit shall be reapportioned between themselves according to specified conditions.

Article 7

Each Party may after commencement of exploitation from thc unitised hydrocarbon deposit request discussions to be initiated on the redetermination of the apportionment of the deposit. Any request for reapportionment must be based on substantial new information regarding factors relevant to apportionment. Both Parties shall make their best efforts to ensure that all relevant information is made available for the purpose of these discussions. The Parties may on this basis agree that the deposit shall be reapportioned between themselves according to specified conditions.

Article 8

This Agreement is without prejudice to the respective Parties' views on questions that are not governed by this Agreement, including questions relating to their exercise of sovereign rights or jurisdiction over the seabed and its subsoil.

Article 9

This Agreement enters into force when the Parties have notified each other in writing that the necessary internal procedures have been completed.

Done at Stockholm on the 30th day of October 2019 in duplicate in the Norwegian, Danish, Faroese, and English languages, all texts being equally authentic. In case of any divergence of interpretation, the English text shall prevail.

For the Government of the Kingdom   For the Government of the Kingdom
of Norway   of Denmark

                                    For the Government of the Faroes

6268 *Report Number 9-26 (Add. 1)*

Agreement between the Government of Norway and the Government of Iceland, concerning the delimitation of the continental shelf beyond 200 nautical miles in the area between the Faroe Islands, Iceland, Mainland Norway and Jan Mayen

The Government of Norway and the Government of Iceland,

Desiring to maintain and strengthen the good neighbourly relations between Norway and Iceland,

Referring to the *Agreed Minutes* of 20 September 2006 between Denmark/ the Faroe Islands, Iceland and Norway,

Referring also to the Agreement of 3 November 2008 between Norway and Iceland concerning transboundary hydrocarbon deposits,

Have agreed as follows:

Article 1

Beyond 200 nautical miles from the baselines from which the breadth of the territorial sea of each Party is measured, the boundary line delimiting the continental shelf in the area between Norway and Iceland has been determined as a geodetic line connecting the following points in the order specified below:

Point 1: 67° 36' 40.54" N   6° 38' 18.95" W
Point 2: 67° 43' 06.51" N   2° 30' 45.12" W
Point 3: 66° 49' 15.75" N   1° 41' 43.56" W

The points listed above are defined by geographical latitude and longitude in accordance with the World Geodetic System (WGS84 (G1150, epoch 2001.0)).

By way of illustration, the boundary line and the points listed above have been drawn on the chart annexed to this Agreement.

Article 2

Article 1-7 of the Agreement between Norway and Iceland concerning transboundary hydrocarbon deposits of 3 November 2008 shall likewise apply for such deposits located in the area delimited by the lines drawn up in accordance with article 1 of this agreement.

Article 3

This Agreement is without prejudice to the respective Parties' views on questions that are not governed by this Agreement, including questions relating to their exercise of sovereign rights or jurisdiction over the seabed and its subsoil.

Article 4

This Agreement enters into force when the Parties have notified each other in writing that the necessary internal procedures have been completed.

Done at Stockholm on the 30th day of October 2019 in duplicate in the Norwegian, Icelandic and English languages, all texts being equally authentic. In case of any divergence of interpretation, the English text shall prevail.

For the Government of Norway   For the Government of Iceland

X

Baltic Sea

Denmark – Poland

Report Number 10-25

Agreement between the Kingdom of Denmark and the Republic of Poland Concerning the Delimitation of Maritime Zones in the Baltic Sea

Signed: 19 November 2018
Entry into force: 28 June 2019
Published at: 109 LOS BULL. 15 (2022); Folketinget, Folketingstidende Tillæg A, Beslutningsforslag nr. B69, FOLKETINGET 2018-19, at 4-7; DZIENNIK USTAW, 4 July 2019, Item 1240, at 1-12

I SUMMARY

This is the last agreement in the Baltic Sea region that settles a maritime boundary in an area where no boundary agreement, reaching at least the stage of signature, had been negotiated.[1] This agreement between Denmark and Poland, in other words, fills in the last substantial gap on the Baltic Sea maritime delimitation map by covering the area south of the Danish island of Bornholm.

Negotiations started in the 1970s, with several rounds held in 1991, 2003, and 2007. On 1 March 2018, the last negotiation round was launched, and, after nine meetings held partly in Denmark and partly in Poland, the parties reached an agreement on 17 October 2018. The present agreement was signed on 19 November of that same year. The parties consequently needed more than 40 years to finally arrive at a mutually acceptable boundary.

The agreement establishes a single maritime boundary covering the continental shelves and exclusive economic zones of the respective parties.

---

1 There are still areas in the Baltic Sea where signed agreements await entry into force, including the agreements between Latvia and Lithuania and between Estonia and Russia. Report Number 10-20, IV IMB 3107; Report Number10-22, VI IMB 4567. The author wishes to thank Henning Knudsen and Konrad Marciniak for their useful personal insights and gracious help he received when conducting the research on which the present report is based.

Coalter G. Lathrop (ed.), International Maritime Boundaries, 6273-6289.
© *The American Society of International Law and Koninklijke Brill BV, Leiden 2025.*

6274 *Report Number 10-25*

The boundary extends for about 97 nautical miles (M) and consists of 23 turning points. The agreement does not clarify the exact status of the endpoints, but, in view of the fact that all related, previously-concluded agreements provide that the tripoints should still be arrived at by means of direct negotiations between the three countries concerned, it is assumed that this also applies to Points 1 and 23 of the present agreement.[2]

The boundary divides the maritime area between the Danish island of Bornholm and the Polish mainland where the coasts of the parties are clearly opposite and the normal baseline applies as the relevant coastlines are not only smooth but also devoid of any Polish islands.

II CONSIDERATIONS

1 *Political, Strategic, and Historical Considerations*

That the present boundary took so long to conclude is closely related to the fact that the delimitation operates between an island and a mainland coast. When the negotiations began, Poland took the position that the delimitation should operate between mainland coasts, whereas Denmark was of the opinion that full effect should be attributed to the island of Bornholm. This created an area of overlapping claims of about 3,600 square kilometers (km^2).

Disagreement about the effect of large islands is not exceptional in the Baltic Sea, and Poland had already been confronted with this issue when delimiting its maritime boundary with Sweden where the exact effect to be given to the sizeable Swedish island of Gotland proved to be a bone of contention between the parties. Poland was of the opinion that the delimitation should operate between the mainland coasts, whereas Sweden was of the opinion that Gotland should be given full effect in view of its importance. The parties finally agreed to give Gotland partial effect by splitting the area of overlapping claims in a proportion of 75 : 25 to Sweden's advantage:[3] a solution already arrived at the year before between Sweden and the former Soviet Union where the location of Gotland played an even more central role.[4]

---

2 *See* Report Number 10-11, II IMB 2087, 2095, Art. 2; Report Number 10-10, II IMB 2077, 2085-86, Art. 2; Report Number 10-6 (1), II IMB 2005, 2021, Art. 4 (2).

3 Report Number 10-10, II IMB 2077, 2080.

4 Report Number 10-9, II IMB 2057, 2061-62. The agreement concluded between the former German Democratic Republic and Denmark, which delimited the area to the southwest of Bornholm, seems less relevant in this respect as the former country relied on the Island of Rügen in front of its own coast. Report Number 10-11, II IMB 2087, 2090.

A distinguishing factor with respect to the agreement here under discussion, however, is that the Danish island of Bornholm is not located in front of the Danish mainland coastline, but in front of that of a third country: Sweden.

2 Legal Regime Considerations

During the 1970s, when the negotiations were initiated between the parties, extended fishery zones were being created by Denmark[5] and Poland.[6] If the former had been the first country in the Baltic to claim a continental shelf,[7] the latter only enacted municipal legislation on that issue in 1977 on the same day it extended its fishery zone.[8]

Both countries also re-established a contiguous zone[9] after having extended their territorial seas to 12 M.[10] Denmark did so in 2005[11] and Poland a decade

---

5 Denmark enacted enabling legislation in 1976. Act No. 597 of 17 December 1976 on the fishing territory of the Kingdom of Denmark, *available at* https://www.un.org/Depts/los/ LEGISLATIONANDTREATIES/PDFFILES/DNK_1976_Act.pdf.

6 Law of 17 December 1977 on the Polish fishing zone, DZIENNIK USTAW, 22 December 1977, No. 37, Item 163, English translation *reprinted in* 7 NEW DIRECTIONS IN THE LAW OF THE SEA 168-70 (M. Nordquist, S. Lay and K. Simmonds eds. 1980). This law, by means of its Article 10, repealed the 12 M fishing zone established in 1970. Law of 12 February 1970 on the establishment of a Polish maritime fishing zone, DZIENNIK USTAW, 17 February 1970, No. 3, Item 14, Art. 2.

7 Royal Decree of 7 June 1963 concerning the exercise of Danish sovereignty over the continental shelf, *available at* https://www.un.org/Depts/los/LEGISLATIONANDTREAT IES/PDFFILES/DNK_1963_Decree.pdf.

8 Law of 17 December 1977 on the Polish continental shelf, DZIENNIK USTAW, 22 December 1977, No. 37, Item 164, French translation *reprinted in* 4 (40) DROIT POLONAIS CONTEMPORAIN 67-69 (1978).

9 Denmark had already created a customs territory of 4 M in 1972. Customs Act No. 519 of 13 December 1972 (Denmark), *available at* https://www.un.org/Depts/los/ LEGISLATIONANDTREATIES/PDFFILES/DNK_1972_Act.pdf.
   Poland created a customs zone of 6 M in 1932. Regulation of 21 October 1932 on the maritime boundary of the state, DZIENNIK USTAW, 27 October 1932, No. 92, Item 789, Art. 4 (Poland). This regulation was further elaborated in 1933. Regulation of 27 October 1933 on the Customs Law, DZIENNIK USTAW, 29 October 1933, No. 84, Item 610, Arts. 1 (3) and 5 (Poland).

10 Denmark extended its territorial sea to 12 M in 1999. Act No. 200 of 7 April 1999 on the delimitation of the territorial sea (Denmark), *available at* https://www.un.org/Depts/los/ LEGISLATIONANDTREATIES/PDFFILES/DNK_1999_Act.pdf. This law implicitly repealed Denmark's 1972 Customs Act.
   Poland had already extended its territorial sea in 1977. Law of 17 December 1977 on the territorial sea of the People's Republic of Poland, DZIENNIK USTAW, 22 December 1977, No. 37, Item 162, Art. 1 (1)). Article 8 of the 1977 law explicitly repealed Poland's 1932 regulation.

11 Act No. 589 of 24 June 2005 on the contiguous zone (Denmark), *reprinted in* 58 LOS BULL. 17 (2005); Executive Order of 29 June 2005 on the demarcation of the Danish

6276　*Report Number 10-25*

later.[12] There is however no overlap of territorial sea or contiguous zone in the area to be delimited.

As this agreement was only arrived at in 2018 and Poland and Denmark had both already firmly established exclusive economic zones by that time,[13] the agreement establishes a continental shelf as well as an exclusive economic zone boundary.

3 *Economic and Environmental Considerations*

The southern part of the Baltic is the most promising from an oil and gas exploitation perspective. To the southwest of Bornholm, economic considerations played a major role and had a direct impact on the actual course of the boundary line agreed between Denmark and the former German Democratic Republic because the Danish government had already issued licenses for the exploration and exploitation of hydrocarbon resources prior to the conclusion of the boundary agreement.[14]

In the area south of Bornholm, however, the Danish Energy Agency concluded that commercial oil and gas discoveries were unlikely to be found in the area, and in 2018 the Danish government took the decision to phase out the possibility to apply for hydrocarbon permits in the Baltic Sea.[15]

Nonetheless, the agreement contains a unity of resource clause obliging the parties to enter into consultations and seek to reach an agreement if mineral deposits were to be found extending across the boundary line in such

---

　　contiguous zone, *reprinted in* 58 LOS BULL. 18 (2005). This act and executive order entered into force on 1 and 9 July 2005, respectively.

12　Act of 5 August 2015, amending the Act on the maritime areas of the Polish Republic and the maritime administration, DZIENNIK USTAW, 19 October 2015, Item 1642 (introducing a new Art. 13(a) establishing a contiguous zone of 24 M).

13　Poland had promulgated an exclusive economic zone in 1991. Act of 21 March 1991on the maritime areas of the Polish Republic and the maritime administration, DZIENNIK USTAW, 18 April 1991, No. 32, Item 131, Art. 14. English translation *reprinted in* 21 LOS BULL. 66 (1992), *available at* https://www.un.org/Depts/los/doalos_publications/ LOSBulletins/bulletinpdf/bulE21.pdf.
　　Denmark followed suit in 1996. Act No. 411 of 22 May 1996 on exclusive economic zones, 33 LOS BULL. 32 (1997), *available at* https://www.un.org/Depts/los/doalos_ publications/LOSBulletins/bulletinpdf/bulletinE33.pdf.

14　Report Number 10-11, II IMB 2087, 2089.

15　*See* Commentary to the proposal for a parliamentary resolution on Denmark's conclusion of an agreement, dated 19 November 2018, between the Kingdom of Denmark and the Republic of Poland concerning the Delimitation of Maritime Zones in the Baltic Sea, Folketinget, Folketingstidende Tillæg A, Beslutningsforslag nr. B69, FOLKETINGET 2018-19, at 2 (sub 1 para. 9).

a way that the resource located on one side becomes exploitable from the other side. The presence of such a clause in the agreement seems to confirm a subregional practice in the southern Baltic,[16] with the exception of those countries that had signed up to the so-called Moscow declaration of 1968[17] and concluded agreements between themselves before the disappearance of the Soviet Union from the political map of the world.[18]

Since Poland became a member state of the European Union on 1 May 2004, fisheries in the area to be delimited have been under the EU Common Fisheries Policy. Considerations concerning fisheries consequently had no impact on the course of the delimitation line agreed upon between the parties.

This boundary agreement has been linked to the agreement between the same parties concluded about one month later on the Baltic Pipe Project.[19] Such a link was implied by the Polish government during discussions in committee on 30 January 2019, as it could have an indirect positive effect on the country's energy security by contributing to the timely implementation of the Baltic Pipe Project.[20] The link was formally acknowledged by the Danish Minister of Foreign Affairs a few days earlier during a parliamentary debate on this issue in his own country.[21] The project, which will connect the

---

16 *See, e.g.*, Report Number 10-2, II IMB 1931, 1941, Art. 6; Report Number 10-11, II IMB 2087, 2095, Art. 3 (both containing very similar language to Art. 2 of the agreement discussed here). The only exception is the agreement between Poland and Sweden, in which no such clause was inserted. Report Number 10-10, II IMB 2077.

17 *See* German Democratic Republic-Poland-U.S.S.R. *Declaration on the Continental Shelf of the Baltic Sea*, 23 October 1968, English translation *reprinted in* 7 INT'L LEGAL MATERIALS 1393-94 (1968). This probably has to be explained by the fact that this declaration already provided in paragraph 10 that the "Participants of the Declaration will consult among themselves concerning questions of mutual interest in connection with the use of the continental shelf of the Baltic Sea." *See also* E. SVIRIDOV, BOUNDARIES OF THE CONTINENTAL SHELF (in Russian) 40-41 (1980).

18 *See, e.g.*, Report Number 10-6 (1), II IMB 2005; Report Number 10-8, II IMB 2039.

19 In Katowice, Poland, on 11 December 2018, the parties signed "an agreement regulating the legal status of certain infrastructure elements of the Baltic Pipe project located in Denmark." Press Release, Baltic Pipe Project, *GAZ-SYSTEM Will be the Gas Transmission System Operator for the Part of the Baltic Pipe Infrastructure Located in Denmark* (14 December 2018), https://www.baltic-pipe.eu/gaz-system-will-be-the-gas-transmission-system-operator-for-the-part-of-the-baltic-pipe-infrastructure-located-in-denmark/.

20 *See* Information on the Committee work of the Sejm of the Republic of Poland, VIII session, 30 January 2019 (no. 14/2019 (402)), *available at* http://www.sejm.gov.pl/sejm8.nsf/prace_komisji_info.xsp?documentId=01A9E60DFDE09CC1C1258393004DCBFE.

21 The link between the delimitation agreement and pipeline agreement was also clearly suggested during the parliamentary discussions in Denmark and formally acknowledged by the Minister of Foreign Affairs, Anders Samuelsen. *See* Interventions by Haekkerup, Hansen, Jensen and Flyvholm, and first intervention by Samuelsen on 17 January 2019, *available at* https://www.ft.dk/samling/20181/beslutningsforslag/B69/BEH1-47/forhandling.htm#t68924C542233449782137DDB3807CA3Atab1.

Norwegian North Sea gas deposits to Poland's gas market,[22] was considered essential for Poland's energy security; Poland wanted to clarify the legal status of the area that the pipeline was planned to cross and to ensure that the operation of the part of the pipeline in the Baltic Sea between the Danish coast of Zealand and the Polish coast would remain under Polish management, even when crossing Danish maritime zones off Bornholm.[23] The discussion in the Danish parliament also clearly revealed the link between the delimitation and pipeline agreements, although none of the official documents mentioned the link. Some have suggested that express reference to the pipeline agreement would have clarified the understanding of the delimitation agreement,[24] but the link between the delimitation and Poland's energy concerns did not directly affect the location of the boundary.

4   Geographic Considerations

The coastlines of Bornholm and the Polish mainland in the area to be delimited are opposite one another. The coastlines are both rather smooth and devoid of straight baselines. Only around the smaller Danish island group of Ertholmene, sometimes also called Christiansø after the largest island of this group, located about 10 M to the northeast of Bornholm, is a system of straight baselines operational. No other islands are present in the area. A marked difference in length of the relevant coastlines on both sides, to the advantage of Poland, has finally to be noted.

5   Islands, Rocks, Reefs, and Low-tide Elevations Considerations

The exact effect to be given to the Danish island of Bornholm, measuring 588 km² with a population of 39,499 in 2020, and to a lesser extent Ertholmene, measuring 0.18 km² with a population of 83 in 2020 spread out over Christiansø and Frederiksø, proved to be the main point of

---

22 For the different components of the Baltic Pipe Project, see the official website of the project: https://www.baltic-pipe.eu/the-project/.

23 Leszek Kadej, *Jak Polska i Dania podzieliły kawałek Bałtyku*, WYSOKIENAPIECIE (4 January 2019), https://wysokienapiecie.pl/15994-jak-polska-dania-podzielily-kawalek -baltyku/.

24 See, especially, the exchange that took place between Claus Hansen and Minister of Foreign Affairs Anders Samuelsen after the latter acknowledged the link between the Baltic Sea Pipe and the delimitation agreement. *Supra* note 21.

disagreement between the parties. The most eastern skerry of Ertholmene, named Østerskær and located 0.01 M east of Christiansø, also constitutes Denmark's easternmost point, far from the Danish mainland.

The original position of Denmark was that the median line should be constructed between Bornholm and the Polish coast, whereas Poland was of the opinion that the median line should rather be constructed between mainland coastlines in the area, implying that the relevant Swedish coastline should be relied upon instead of that of Bornholm. As already noted, this resulted in an area of overlapping claims of approximately 3,600 km^2.

The political compromise finally agreed upon is that Denmark was awarded 80 percent of the area of overlap, the remaining 20 percent being attributed to Poland. This followed the somewhat similar 75 : 25 split agreed between Poland and Sweden in 1989.[25] The 75 : 25 ratio had been borrowed from an agreement concluded one year earlier between Sweden and the former Soviet Union, where the particular location of the Swedish island of Gotland between the mainland coasts of the parties had been at the heart of the negotiations.[26] The distinguishing factor between examples involving Gotland and the present delimitation is that Bornholm and Ertholmene are not backed by the Danish mainland coast but by the Swedish mainland coast.[27]

If this political compromise on the effect of Danish islands received full parliamentary support in Denmark,[28] the same can hardly be said for Poland. When finally voted upon,[29] it received a negative vote from the opposition in the Polish parliament because the agreed ratio was considered to give too much of the area to Denmark.[30]

---

25 Report Number 10-10, II IMB 2077, 2080.
26 Report Number 10-9, II IMB 2057, 2061-62. This ratio was later confirmed when Estonia and Lithuania concluded new boundary agreements in the area with Sweden after the dissolution of the former Soviet Union. Report Number 10-19, IV IMB 3089, 3096-97; Report Number 10-24, VIII IMB 5743, 5750-51. Latvia, having the longest boundary with Sweden, will probably follow suit as indicated by the location of the tripoint these two countries agreed upon together with Estonia. *See* Report Number 10-17, IV IMB 3041, 3048.
27 It should be noted that Sweden had agreed in 1984 to attribute Bornholm full effect in their delimitation with Denmark of the area to the north of the island. Report Number 10-2, II IMB 1931, 1934-35. But, as argued in a previous report, Sweden had good reasons at that time to do so. Report Number 10-11, II IMB 2087, 2088.
28 The vote was 105 in favor, 0 against, and 0 abstentions. The vote in the Danish Parliament is reported here: https://www.ft.dk/samling/20181/beslutningsforslag/b69/index.htm.
29 The vote was 280 in favor, 142 against, and 8 abstentions. The vote in the Polish Parliament is reported here: http://www.sejm.gov.pl/Sejm8.nsf/agent.xsp?symbol=gloso wania&NrKadencji=8&NrPosiedzenia=77&NrGlosowania=125.
30 *Karpinski: We Are for Baltic Pipe, but We Criticize the Deal with Denmark*, BiznesAlert (8 March 2019), https://biznesalert.com/karpinski-po-baltic-pipe-denmark/.

6280　*Report Number 10-25*

6　*Baseline Considerations*

A system of straight baselines connecting 13 turning points was first established around the smaller Danish island group Ertholmene in 1966[31] and later re-confirmed in 1999.[32] The total length of these baselines is only 2.5 M. Ertholmene has been described as "an extremely small series of rocks and islands detached from the mainland," where the major island, Christiansø, has been used as mainland around which the straight baselines were subsequently drawn.[33] Given the very restrictive nature of these baselines, their influence on the location of the boundary would have been negligible at best, even if the parties had decided to take them into account, *quod non*.

Poland does not claim straight baselines in this area, but this country clarified its normal baselines in 2017,[34] which must have helped the negotiators during the finalization of the delimitation process.

7　*Geological and Geomorphological Considerations*

The area to be delimited constitutes a shallow part of the Baltic Sea, always measuring less than 100 meters in depth and becoming deeper toward the east. Poland relied on a depression in the middle of the area of overlap as one of the reasons why special circumstances required an adjustment of the

---

31　Royal Decree No. 437 of 21 December 1966 on the delimitation of the territorial sea (as amended in 1978) (Denmark), *reprinted in* US Department of State, 19 Limits in the Seas 2 (1978).

32　Executive Order No. 242 of 21 April 1999 concerning the delimitation of Denmark's territorial sea, *reprinted in* 40 LOS Bull. 18 (1999). The description remained identical, only the coordinates were changed from the European Datum System into the World Geodetic System 1984. The latter coordinates were once more amended in 2003 representing a technical improvement reflecting more precisely the positions of the relevant geographical points but, again, without changing the description of the turning points. Executive Order No. 680 of 18 July 2003 amending Executive Order No. 242 of 21 April 1999 concerning the delimitation of Denmark's territorial sea, *reprinted in* 53 LOS Bull. 44 (2004), *available at* https://www.un.org/Depts/los/doalos_publications/LOSBulletins/bulletinpdf/bulletin53e.pdf.

33　*Supra* note 31 at 10.

34　Regulation of the Council of Ministers on the baseline, the outer limit of the territorial sea and the outer limit of the contiguous zone of the Republic of Poland, Dziennik Ustaw, 30 January 2017, Item 183, Appendix 1. It consists of the coordinates of 166 points according to the European Terrestrial Reference System 1989, which is also the standard used for the present delimitation agreement.

median line between Bornholm and Poland,[35] but this particular argument did not influence the location of the delimitation line.

8   Method of Delimitation Considerations

The line arrived at is an adjusted median line. The middle segment, running from Points 7 to 14, represents a median line between Bornholm and the Polish mainland coast and reflects the original Danish claim. The end segments between Points 1 and 2 and between Points 22 and 23, on the other hand, find inspiration in the original Polish claim. The remainder of the turning points were chosen in such a way as to attribute 80 percent of the area of overlap to Denmark and 20 percent to Poland. Most of these remaining turning points follow the contours of Bornholm, except for the segments between Points 20 and 22 that follow the contours of Christiansø and Østerskær. The segments between Points 2 and 7 and Points 14 and 22 make the link between the original Danish and Polish claims. It can be inferred that Ertholmene was not given full effect unlike Bornholm, which was at least given full effect between Points 7 and 14.[36]

Even though the agreement remains silent on the issue, the tripoints with the neighboring countries still need to be agreed upon in order to connect the endpoints of the present agreement to the already existing maritime boundaries in the area.[37]

---

35   Poland believed that a number of special circumstances needed to be taken into consideration that justified deviation from the median line, including geographical considerations, coastal length, economic importance of the area to Poland, and seabed geomorphology. Answer to interpellation No. 667 by Jan Dziedziczak, Secretary of State in the Ministry of Foreign Affairs, 12 February 2016, http://www.sejm.gov.pl/sejm8 .nsf/interpelacjaTresc.xsp?documentId=5D8AAA4B17A2AB23C1257F5D004EEE02& view=1o.
36   In the maritime delimitation agreement between Denmark and Sweden, concluded in 1984, Bornholm was given full effect while Ertholmene only received partial effect. A distinguishing factor in this case was that also Sweden had a small island, namely Utklippan, located in the area to be delimited. Report Number 10-2, II IMB 1931, 1934-35.
37   See supra note 2 and accompanying text. Point 1 is nearly identical with Point 12 of the boundary between Germany and Denmark and approximately 0.4 M from Point M of the boundary between Germany and Poland. Point 23 is approximately 0.1 M from Point S of the boundary between Denmark and Sweden and 0.9 M from Point A of the boundary between Poland and Sweden.

9 Technical Considerations

Following the example set by the delimitation agreement concluded between Lithuania and Sweden,[38] this is only the second agreement in the Baltic Sea region that uses the European Terrestrial Reference System 1989 (ETRS 89). Since the 1990s the use of WGS 84 seemed to have become the standard in this region, except for the agreements to which Russia was a party.[39] Denmark, which had concluded all of its other maritime boundaries with its neighbors in the Baltic Sea before the 1990s, steadfastly relied on European Datum 1950.[40] The technical issue of rectifying coordinates referenced to different systems will have to be addressed during any tripoint negotiations with Germany and Sweden. This is not the case with respect to the nature of the lines between the turning points that are geodetic lines like in all previously agreed maritime boundaries to which the present line will have to connect.

A map at the scale of 1:850,000 was annexed to the agreement, but the exact relation of this map to the rest of the agreement in case of discrepancies has not been specified.

10 Other Considerations

This is the sixth agreement concluded in the Baltic Sea which provides in its final paragraph that, besides the national languages of the parties involved, English is also considered to be an authentic language,[41] further confirming a new tendency in existence there since the second half of the 1990s.[42] Moreover, totally in line with this new tendency, the agreement provides that in case of discrepancy in interpretation, the English text will prevail.

---

38 *See* Report Number 10-24, VIII IMB 5743, 5759, Art. 1 (2).

39 *See* Report Number 10-23, VIII IMB 5731, 5736 (explaining more fully the Russian practice in this regard).

40 Report Number 10-1, II IMB 1915, 1925, Art. 1 (1); Report Number 10-2, II IMB 1931, 1939, Art. 2; Report Number 10-11, II IMB 2087, 2094-95, Art. 1.

41 *See also* Report Number 10-15, IV IMB 2995; Report Number 10-17, IV IMB 3041; Report Number 10-19, IV IMB 3089; Report Number 10-20, IV IMB 3107; Report Number 10-24, VIII IMB 5743. The tripoint agreement between Estonia, Finland, and Sweden is not mentioned in this list as it even goes one step further, having been drafted in a single authentic language, namely English. Report Number 10-21, IV IMB 3129.

42 Before the second half of the 1990s, maritime boundary agreements in the Baltic had solely been drafted in the respective languages of the parties, all being equally authentic.

This is the first agreement concluded in the Baltic Sea that was not signed in a city located in one of the participating states. In all of the previous Baltic Sea delimitation agreements the place of signature has been the capital of one of the participating states.[43] The present agreement was signed, out of convenience, in Brussels, the capital of Europe.

III CONCLUSIONS

The present agreement constitutes the last major piece of the delimitation puzzle in the Baltic. The only remaining issues are the entry into force of certain agreements already negotiated and signed and a number of tripoints that still have to be concluded, including on both ends of the maritime boundary established by this agreement between Denmark and Poland.

The agreement took more than 40 years to be concluded. Even though the official documents do not specifically mention it, the link with the agreement concluded between the two same parties one month later concerning the Baltic Pipe Project was specifically referred to during the discussions in both parliaments when this delimitation agreement was being considered. The legal certainty created by the conclusion of the present delimitation agreement proved to be a *conditio sine qua non* for the realization of the Baltic Pipe Project: a quintessential element for Poland to guarantee its future energy security by directly connecting it to the North Sea gas reserves. The particular timing of events, the discussions held in both parliaments, and the absence of any concrete disturbances between the parties because of living or non-living resources for over a decade prior to the signature[44] suggest that a link does exist between the breakthrough in the decades-long delimitation negotiations and the realization of the Baltic Pipe Project.

The delimitation agreement fits in well with the previous practice in the region with respect to substantial matters, such as the effect given to islands, and technical matters, such as languages and systems of coordinates used. It furthermore follows the general regional practice of giving reduced effect even to large islands, but the 80 : 20 ratio is novel. And even though factors

---

43 There is one other exception which is the agreement concluded between Latvia and Lithuania of 1999, which was signed in Palanga, a Lithuanian town of which the municipality extends to the border with Latvia. Report Number 10-20, IV IMB 3107, 3127.

44 *See supra* note 35 (stating that during the past several years no controversy over the contested area occurred in practice).

distinguishing the treatment of Bornholm from other islands in the region can certainly be noticed in this respect, the fact remains that this agreement does not seem to have attached great importance to the marked difference in coastal lengths of the parties. But all of this remains, of course, within the discretionary power of the states establishing a maritime boundary by way of mutual agreement. Finally, the formal aspect of having a signing ceremony outside of the countries involved in the delimitation is completely novel.

IV RELATED LAW IN FORCE

A   *Law of the Sea Conventions*

Denmark: Party to UNCLOS (ratified 16 November 2004).
Poland: Party to UNCLOS (ratified 13 November 1998).

B   *Maritime Jurisdiction Claimed at the Time of Signature*

Denmark: 12 M territorial sea; 24 M contiguous zone; 200 M EEZ; continental shelf.
Poland: 12 M territorial sea; 24 M contiguous zone; 200 M EEZ; continental shelf.

C   *Maritime Jurisdiction Claimed Subsequent to Signature*

Denmark: No change.
Poland: No change.

V   REFERENCES AND ADDITIONAL READINGS

Maria Dragun-Gertner, Zuzanna Peplowska, and Dorota Pyć, *The Law Applicable on the Continental Shelf and in the Exclusive Economic Zone: The Polish Perspective*, 25 OCEAN YEARBOOK 411 (2001).

Erik Franckx, *Maritime Delimitation in the Baltic Sea: An Update*, 15 TRANSNAV (forthcoming 2021).

Erik Franckx, *The Importance of Judicial Decisions and State Practice in Search of an Equitable Solution when Trying to Solve Maritime Boundary Delimitations: On Unequal Footing*, in Aktual'nye problemi teorii i praktiki morskogo prava (I Vladivostokskii morskoi iuridicheskii forum, Vladivostok, 22-23 aprelia 2021)/Actual Problems of Theory and

Practice of the Law of the Sea (I Maritime Law Forum, Vladivostok, April 22-23, 2021) 34 (A. N. Vylegzhanin, V. V. Gavrilov eds., 2021).

Erik Franckx, *Gaps in Baltic Sea Maritime Boundaries*, *in* REGULATORY GAPS IN BALTIC SEA GOVERNANCE: SELECTED ISSUES 7 (Henrik Ringbom ed., 2018).

Erik Franckx, *Maritime Delimitation in the Baltic Sea: What Has Already Been Accomplished?* 6 TRANSNAV 437 (2012).

Konrad Marciniak, *The Polish Baselines and Contiguous Zone: Remarks From the Perspective of the United Nations Convention on the Law of the Sea*, 32 PRAWO MORSKIE 49 (2016).

Dorota Pyć, *The Polish Contiguous Zone – The Exercise of the Coastal State Jurisdiction and Control*, 11 TRANSNAV 453 (2017).

Prepared by Erik Franckx

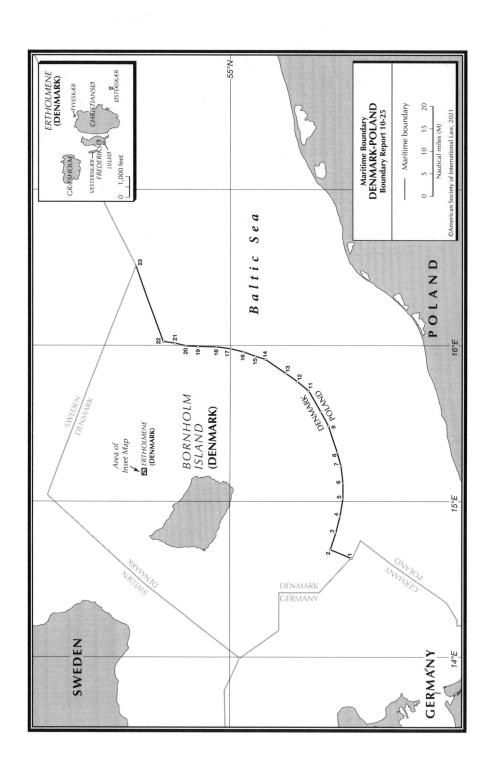

Denmark – Poland 6287

Agreement between the Kingdom of Denmark and the Republic of Poland Concerning the Delimitation of Maritime Zones in the Baltic Sea

The Kingdom of Denmark and the Republic of Poland,

hereinafter referred to as 'the Parties',

Wishing to further deepen and strengthen their good relations of neighbors and allies,

And desiring to resolve the issue of the delimitation of the area of overlapping claims of both Parties in an international agreement, in accordance with Article 74 paragraph 1 and 83 paragraph 1 of the United Nations Convention on the Law of the Sea of 10 December 1982 and taking into account relevant international jurisprudence in this respect,

Have agreed as follows:

Article 1

The boundary line between the Parties' continental shelfs and the Exclusive Economic Zones is fixed as straight lines (geodetic lines) between the following points:

1. 54° 32' 08.19"N. 14° 38' 08.28" E
2. 54° 36' 51.00" N. 14° 41' 25.00" E
3. 54° 35' 34.00" N. 14° 47' 58.00" E
4. 54° 34' 40.00" N. 14° 54' 05.00" E
5. 54° 34' 00.00" N. 15° 00' 58.00" E
6. 54° 34' 00.00" N. 15° 07' 02.00" E
7. 54° 34' 28.00" N. 15° 13' 37.00" E
8. 54° 35' 20.00" N. 15° 18' 52.00" E
9. 54° 37' 20.00" N. 15° 29' 01.00" E
10. 54° 39' 06.00" N. 15° 34' 23.00" E
11. 54° 41' 54.00" N. 15° 42' 27.00" E
12. 54° 44' 33.00" N. 15° 46' 03.00" E
13. 54° 47' 09.00" N. 15° 49' 11.00" E

14. 54° 51' 57.00" N. 15° 54' 41.00" E
15. 54° 54' 11.00" N. 15° 55' 49.00" E
16. 54° 56' 52.00" N. 15° 57' 27.00" E
17. 54° 59' 51.00" N. 15° 58' 42.00" E
18. 55° 03' 11.00" N. 15° 59' 27.00" E
19. 55° 07' 15.00" N. 15° 59' 34.00" E
20. 55° 10' 01.00" N. 15° 59' 50.00" E
21. 55° 12' 28.00" N. 16° 00' 50.00" E
22. 55° 15' 06.10" N. 16° 01' 30.00" E
23. 55° 21' 13.64" N. 16° 30' 38.17" E

The points listed above are defined by geographical latitude and longitude in accordance with the European Terrestrial Reference System 1989 (ETRS89).

Article 2

If it is established that a mineral deposit on the seabed or in its subsoil extends over both sides of the boundary line in such a way that the deposit of one Party is exploitable, wholly or in part, from the maritime area of the other Party, the Parties shall enter into consultations and seek to reach an agreement concerning the exploitation of the said deposit.

Article 3

The boundary line as referred to in Article 1 has been drawn on the map at the scale of 1:850.000 and annexed to this Agreement.

Article 4

This Agreement shall enter into force 30 days after the date of receipt of the last written notification by which the Parties shall notify each other on the completion of internal procedures necessary for the entry into force of this Agreement.

DONE at Brussels on 19 November 2018 in duplicate in the Danish, Polish and English, all texts being equally authentic. In case of discrepancy in interpretation, the English text shall prevail.

On behalf of

the Kingdom of Denmark

On behalf of

the Republic of Poland

Country-by-Country Index

The country-by-country index provides a useful reference tool, here updated to include the reports from this volume. The index below shares the basic structure of the index introduced in Volume V and used again in Volume VI and Volume VII. In addition to the countries involved in each boundary, and the *International Maritime Boundaries* report, volume, and page numbers, beginning with Volume VII the index also provides the dates of signature and entry into force, and the United Nations Treaty Series registration number where available. This information will be updated annually in *International Maritime Boundaries Online* and with each release of new volumes in this series. By including entry into force information in this index, it is no longer necessary to prepare an addendum each time an agreement enters into force. By providing the unique registration number, users will be able quickly to locate the official text of each agreement registered by the parties with the United Nations. This may be especially important if the text used for reporting in *International Maritime Boundaries* was an unofficial translation of the agreement.

In order to address the changing geopolitical landscape and still provide a useful reference tool for our users, we have applied the following treatment to the party names in this index. For the purpose of the first column ("Country A") we have identified the party to the agreement by its current, preferred name. Here you will find Russia, the United Arab Emirates, and Slovenia, but not the Soviet Union, Sharjah, or Yugoslavia. This is intended to help users find the agreements by which extant states may be bound. It is not intended to be an assessment of the legal effect of an agreement on a successor state. In contrast, we use the original party name in the second column ("Country B/C") to provide some historical context to the agreement. Parentheses after party names are used to indicate the specific subregion of a larger state implicated by a maritime boundary agreement.

Coalter G. Lathrop (ed.), International Maritime Boundaries, 6291-6344.
© The American Society of International Law and Koninklijke Brill BV, Leiden 2025.

Country A	Country B/C	Signed	EIF	Report No.	Vol.	Page	UN Reg. No.
Albania	Greece	27/04/2009		8-21	6	4462	
	Italy	18/12/1992	26/02/1999	8-11	3	2447	
	Italy			8-11 (Corr.1)	4	2869	
Algeria	Tunisia	11/02/2002	23/11/2003	8-16	5	3927	I-39821
	Tunisia	11/07/2011	16/09/2013	8-16 (Add. 1)	9	6139	
Angola	Congo	10/09/2001		4-16	6	4281	
	Congo, Dem. Rep	30/07/2007	23/07/2008	4-15	6	4270	
	Namibia	04/06/2002		4-13	5	3709	
Antigua and Barbuda	France (Guadeloupe, Saint Barthelemy)	15/03/2017	01/10/2018	2-37	9	5889	I-55817
	United Kingdom (Anguilla)	27/07/2021		2-38	9	5901	
Argentina	Chile	29/11/1984	06/05/1985	3-1	1	719	I-23392
	Uruguay	19/11/1973	12/02/1974	3-2	1	757	I-21424
Australia	East Timor	20/05/2002	02/04/2003	6-20 (1,2)	5	3806	I-40222
	East Timor	06/03/2003	23/02/2007	6-20 (3)	5	3867	I-44576
	East Timor			6-20 (3)(Add.1)	6	4366	
	East Timor	12/01/2006	27/06/2006	6-20 (4)	6	4367	I-44577
	East Timor	06/03/2018	30/08/2019	6-20 (5)	8	5547	

(*Cont.*)

Country A	Country B/C	Signed	EIF	Report No.	Vol.	Page	UN Reg. No.
	France (Kerguelen Island)	04/01/1982	09/01/1983	6-1	2	1185	I-22302
	France (New Caledonia)	04/01/1982	09/01/1983	5-1	1	905	I-22302
	Indonesia	18/05/1971	08/11/1973	6-2 (1)	2	1195	I-14122
	Indonesia	09/10/1972	08/11/1973	6-2 (2)	2	1207	I-14123
	Indonesia	29/10/1981	01/02/1982	6-2 (4)	2	1229	
	Indonesia	11/12/1989	09/02/1991	6-2 (5)	2	1245	I-28462
	Indonesia	14/03/1997		6-2 (6)	4	2697	
	New Zealand	25/07/2004	25/01/2006	5-26	5	3759	I-43985
	New Zealand			5-26 (Add.1)	6	4300	
	Papua New Guinea	18/12/1978	15/02/1985	5-3	1	929	I-24238
	Solomon Islands	13/09/1988	14/04/1989	5-4	1	977	I-26661
	Solomon Islands			5-4 (Add.)	4	2671	
	UNTAET	10/02/2000	10/02/2000	6-15	4	2753	I-36594
Azerbaijan	Russia	23/09/2002	25/06/2003	11-2	5	4034	
	Kazakhstan	29/11/2001	09/12/2003	11-3	5	4042	
	Kazakhstan	27/02/2003	09/12/2003	11-3	5	4042	
	Kazakhstan - Russia	14/05/2003		11-4	5	4055	
Bahamas	Cuba	03/10/2011	09/03/2012	2-32	7	4721	I-49590

(Cont.)

Country A	Country B/C	Signed	EIF	Report No.	Vol.	Page	UN Reg. No.
Bahrain	Iran	17/06/1971	14/05/1972	7-2	2	1481	I-11838
	Qatar	16/03/2001	16/03/2001	7-13	4	2841	N/A
	Saudi Arabia	22/02/1958	22/02/1958	7-3	2	1489	I-30248
Bangladesh	India	07/07/2014	07/07/2014	6-23	6	4403	N/A
	India			6-23 (Add.1)	7	4985	N/A
	Myanmar	14/03/2012	14/03/2012	6-24	6	4404	N/A
	Myanmar			6-24 (Add.1)	7	4999	N/A
Barbados	France (Guadaloupe and Martinique)	15/10/2009	01/01/2010	2-30	6	4223	I-47364
	Guyana	02/12/2003	05/05/2004	2-27	5	3578	I-40555
	Guyana			2-27 (Add.1)	6	4201	
	Saint Lucia	06/07/2017	01/09/2019	2-40	9	5925	I-56440
	Saint Vincent and the Grenadines	31/08/2015		2-35	8	5433	
	Trinidad & Tobago	11/04/2006	11/04/2006	2-26	5	3577	N/A
	Trinidad & Tobago			2-26 (Add.1)	6	4187	
Belgium	France	08/10/1990	07/04/1993	9-16	2	1891	I-30173
	France	08/10/1990	07/04/1993	9-16	2	1891	I-30172
	Netherlands	18/12/1996	01/01/1999	9-21	4	2921	I-35449

(*Cont.*)

Country A	Country B/C	Signed	EIF	Report No.	Vol.	Page	UN Reg. No.
	Netherlands	18/12/1996	01/01/1999	9-21	4	2921	I-35448
	United Kingdom	29/05/1991	14/05/1993	9-17	2	1901	I-31712
	United Kingdom			9-17 (Add.1)	5	4005	
	United Kingdom	07/06/2005	02/10/2006	9-17 (2)	6	4506	A-31712
	United Kingdom	12/08/2013		9-17 (3)	7	5253	
Benin	Nigeria	04/08/2006		4-14	6	4256	
Bosnia and Herzegovina	Croatia	30/07/1999		8-14	4	2887	
Brazil	France (French Guiana)	30/01/1981	19/10/1983	3-3	1	777	I-22476
	Uruguay	21/07/1972	12/06/1975	3-4	1	785	I-17411
Brunei	United Kingdom (Sarawak, North Borneo)	11/09/1958	11/09/1958	5-2	1	915	
Bulgaria	Turkey	04/12/1997	04/11/1998	8-13	4	2871	I-36204
Cambodia	Thailand	18/06/2001		5-24	5	3735	
	Vietnam	07/07/1982		5-21	3	2357	

(Cont.)

Country A	Country B/C	Signed	EIF	Report No.	Vol.	Page	UN Reg. No.
Cameroon	Nigeria	01/06/1975	01/06/1975	4-1	1	841	1-19976
	Nigeria	10/10/2002	10/10/2002	4-1 (Add.)	3	2249	N/A
	Nigeria			4-1 (Add.2)	5	3605	
	Nigeria			4-1 (Add.3)	6	4251	
Canada	Denmark (Greenland)	17/12/1973	13/03/1974	1-1	1	371	1-13550
	Denmark (Greenland)	20/04/2004	16/12/2009	1-1 (Add.1)	8	5341	A-13550
	France (St. Pierre and Miquelon)	27/03/1972	27/03/1972	1-2	1	387	1-12353
	France (St. Pierre and Miquelon)	10/06/1992	10/06/1992	1-2	1	387	N/A
	France (St. Pierre and Miquelon)			1-2 (Add.2)	3	2141	
	France (St. Pierre and Miquelon)	17/05/2005		1-2 (2)	8	5351	
	United States	12/10/1984	12/10/1984	1-3	1	401	N/A
Cape Verde	Mauritania	19/09/2003		4-12	5	3694	
	Senegal	17/02/1993	25/03/1994	4-8	3	2279	1-30956
Chile	Argentina	29/11/1984	06/05/1985	3-1	1	719	1-23392
	Peru	18/08/1952	18/08/1952	3-5	1	793	1-14758

Country A	Country B/C	Signed	EIF	Report No.	Vol.	Page	UN Reg. No.
	Peru	04/12/1954	21/09/1967	3-9	1	829	I-40521
	Peru			3-5 (Corr.1,Add.1)	4	2639	N/A
	Peru			3-5 (Add.2)	6	4235	
	Peru	27/01/2014	27/01/2014	3-5 (2)	7	4749	
China	Vietnam	25/12/2000	30/06/2004	5-25	5	3745	I-41860
	Vietnam			5-25 (Add.1)	7	4841	
Colombia	Costa Rica	17/03/1977		2-1	1	463	
	Costa Rica	06/04/1984	20/02/2001	3-6	1	801	I-37322
	Costa Rica			3-6 (Add.1, Corr.1)	4	2641	
	Dominican Republic	13/12/1978	02/02/1979	2-2	1	477	I-21042
	Ecuador	23/08/1975	22/12/1975	3-7	1	809	I-14582
	Ecuador	13/06/2012	13/06/2012	3-7 (Add.1)	7	4765	
	Haiti	17/02/1978	16/02/1979	2-3	1	491	I-18229
	Honduras	02/08/1986	19/12/1999	2-4	1	503	I-36360
	Honduras			2-4 (Add.1)	5	3561	
	Jamaica	12/11/1993	14/03/1994	2-18	3	2179	I-30943
	Nicaragua	19/11/2012	19/11/2012	2-25	5	3576	N/A
	Nicaragua			2-25 (Add.1)	6	4186	
	Nicaragua			2-25 (Add.2)	7	4683	

Country A	Country B/C	Signed	EIF	Report No.	Vol.	Page	UN Reg. No.
	Nicaragua			2-25 (2)	7	4685	
	Panama	20/11/1976	30/11/1977	2-5	1	519	I-16398
Comoros	Mozambique	05/12/2011	04/05/2012	6-26	7	5017	
	Mozambique - Tanzania	05/12/2011		6-27	7	5033	
	Seychelles	17/02/2012		6-28	7	5039	
	Seychelles - Tanzania	17/02/2012		6-29	7	5053	
	Tanzania	05/12/2011		6-30	7	5059	
Congo	Angola	10/09/2001		4-16	6	4281	
Congo, Dem. Rep.	Angola	30/07/2007	23/07/2008	4-15	6	4270	
Cook Islands	France (French Polynesia)	03/08/1990	03/08/1990	5-18	1	1175	I-27947
	Kiribati	29/08/2012	17/01/2014	5-32	7	4847	I-51976
	New Zealand (Tokelau)	04/08/2010	12/11/2012	5-43	7	4893	I-50545
	Niue	29/08/2012	06/05/2013	5-33	7	4859	II-1370
	United States (American Samoa)	11/06/1980	08/09/1983	5-5	1	985	I-28971
Costa Rica	Colombia	17/03/1977		2-1	1	463	

(Cont.)

Country A	Country B/C	Signed	EIF	Report No.	Vol.	Page	UN Reg. No.
	Colombia	06/04/1984	20/02/2001	3-6	1	801	1-37322
	Colombia			3-6 (Add.1, Corr.1)		2641	
	Ecuador	12/03/1985		3-8	1	819	
	Ecuador	21/04/2014	09/09/2016	3-8 (2)	8	5461	1-54729
	Nicaragua			2-34	7	4745	N/A
	Nicaragua	02/02/2018	02/02/2018	2-34 (Add.1)	8	5407	N/A
	Panama	02/02/1980	11/02/1982	2-6	1	537	
Croatia	Bosnia and Herzegovina	30/07/1999		8-14	4	2887	
	Italy	08/01/1968	21/01/1970	8-7 (1)	2	1627	
	Italy	10/11/1975	03/04/1977	8-7 (2)	2	1639	1-24848
	Italy			8-7 (3)	3	2437	
	Italy	29/07/2005	02/08/2005	8-27	9	6231	
	Italy	24/05/2022		8-27	9	6231	
	Slovenia			8-20	6	4455	N/A
	Slovenia	29/06/2017	29/06/2017	8-20 (Add.1)	8	5667	N/A
Cuba	Bahamas	03/10/2011	09/03/2012	2-32	7	4721	1-49590
	Haiti	27/10/1977	06/01/1978	2-7	1	551	
	Honduras	21/08/2012	11/12/2013	2-33	7	4735	1-51725
	Jamaica	18/02/1994	18/07/1995	2-19	3	2205	

(*Cont.*)

Country A	Country B/C	Signed	EIF	Report No.	Vol.	Page	UN Reg. No.
	Mexico	26/07/1976	26/07/1976	2-8	1	565	I-23255
	Mexico	18/01/2017	27/07/2018	2-8 (2)	9	5861	I-55481
	United States	16/12/1977		1-4	1	417	
	United States			1-4 (Add.1)	5	3555	
	United States			1-4 (Add.2)	6	4165	
	United States	08/02/2012	08/02/2012	1-4 (Add.3)	7	4607	
	United States	13/12/2013	13/12/2013	1-4 (Add.4)	7	4611	
	United States	31/12/2015	31/12/2015	1-4 (Add.5)	8	5395	
	United States	26/12/2017	26/12/2017	1-4 (Add.6)	8	5399	
	United States	18/01/2017		1-4 (2)	9	5819	
Cyprus	Egypt	17/02/2003	07/03/2004	8-15	5	3917	I-44649
	Egypt			8-15 (Add.1)	6	4433	
	Egypt	12/12/2013	11/09/2014	8-15 (2)	8	5651	
	Israel	17/12/2010	25/02/2011	8-22	7	5091	I-48387
	Lebanon	17/01/2007		8-19	6	4445	
	United Kingdom (Akrotiri, Dhekelia)	16/08/1960	16/08/1960	8-1	2	1559	I-5476
Denmark	Germany, Fed. Rep.	09/06/1965	27/05/1966	9-8	2	1801	I-8289
	Germany, Fed. Rep.	20/02/1969	20/02/1969	9-8	2	1801	N/A

Country A	Country B/C	Signed	EIF	Report No.	Vol.	Page	UN Reg. No.
	Germany, Fed. Rep.	28/02/1971	07/12/1972	9-8	2	1801	I-12295
	Germany, Fed. Rep.	09/06/1965	27/05/1966	10-1	2	1915	I-8289
	Germany, Dem. Rep.	14/09/1988	14/06/1989	10-11	2	2087	I-26910
	Netherlands	31/03/1966	01/08/1967	9-18	3	2497	I-8751
	Norway	08/12/1965	22/06/1966	9-9	2	1815	I-9052
	Norway	24/04/1968	24/04/1968	9-9	2	1815	A-9052
	Norway	04/06/1974	04/06/1974	9-9	2	1815	A-9052
	Poland	19/11/2018	28/06/2019	10-25	9	6273	
	Sweden	30/01/1932	30/01/1932	10-2	2	1931	
	Sweden	09/11/1984	03/09/1985	10-2	2	1931	I-23600
	Sweden	03/07/1995	03/07/1995	10-14	3	2557	
	United Kingdom	03/03/1966	06/02/1967	9-10	2	1825	I-8574
	United Kingdom	25/11/1971	07/12/1972	9-10	2	1825	I-12280
	United Kingdom	22/10/2009	22/10/2009	9-10 (2)	6	4488	A-12280
Denmark (Faroes)	Iceland	02/02/2007	29/04/2008	9-27	6	4553	I-51764
	Iceland	30/10/2019		9-26 (Add. 1)	9	6251	
	Iceland - Norway	20/09/2006	20/09/2006	9-26	6	4532	
	Norway	15/06/1979	03/06/1980	9-1	2	1711	I-19512
	Norway	30/10/2019		9-26 (Add. 1)	9	6251	
	United Kingdom	18/05/1999	21/07/1999	9-23	4	2955	

(*Cont.*)

Country A	Country B/C	Signed	EIF	Report No.	Vol.	Page	UN Reg. No.
	United Kingdom	25/04/2012	31/03/2014	9-23 (2)	7	5275	
Denmark (Greenland)	Canada	17/12/1973	13/03/1974	1-1	1	371	I-13550
	Canada	20/04/2004	16/12/2009	1-1 (Add.1)	8	5341	A-13550
	Iceland	11/11/1997	27/05/1998	9-22	4	2941	I-35941
	Iceland	16/01/2013	16/01/2013	9-22 (2)	7	5259	
	Norway (Jan Mayen)	14/06/1993	14/06/1993	9-19	3	2507	N/A
	Norway (Jan Mayen)	18/12/1995	18/12/1995	9-19	3	2507	I-32441
	Norway (Jan Mayen)	11/11/1997	27/05/1998	9-19 (2)	4	2913	A-32441
	Norway	20/02/2006	02/06/2006	9-25	6	4513	I-42887
Dominica	France (Guadeloupe and Martinique)	07/09/1987	23/12/1988	2-15	1	705	I-26854
Dominican Republic	Colombia	13/12/1978	02/02/1979	2-2	1	477	I-21042
	Netherlands (Antilles)	05/07/2021		2-39	9	5913	
	United Kingdom (Turks and Caicos)	02/08/1996		2-22	3	2235	
	Venezuela	03/03/1979	15/01/1982	2-9	1	577	
East Timor	Australia	10/02/2000	10/02/2000	6-15	4	2753	I-36594
	Australia	20/05/2002	02/04/2003	6-20 (1,2)	5	3806	I-40222

Country A	Country B/C	Signed	EIF	Report No.	Vol.	Page	UN Reg. No.
	Australia	06/03/2003	23/02/2007	6-20 (3)	5	3867	I-44576
	Australia			6-20 (3)(Add.1)	6	4366	
	Australia	12/01/2006	27/06/2006	6-20 (4)	6	4367	I-44577
	Australia	06/03/2018	30/08/2019	6-20 (5)	8	5547	
Ecuador	Colombia	23/08/1975	22/12/1975	3-7	1	809	I-14582
	Colombia	13/06/2012	13/06/2012	3-7 (Add.1)	7	4765	
	Costa Rica	12/03/1985		3-8	1	819	
	Costa Rica	21/04/2014	09/09/2016	3-8 (2)	8	5461	I-54729
	Peru	18/08/1952	18/08/1952	3-9	1	829	I-14758
	Peru	04/12/1954	21/09/1967	3-9	1	829	I-40521
	Peru	02/05/2011	20/05/2011	3-9 (Add.1)	7	4769	I-48631
Egypt	Cyprus	17/02/2003	07/03/2004	8-15	5	3917	I-44649
	Cyprus			8-15 (Add.1)	6	4433	
	Cyprus	12/12/2013	11/09/2014	8-15 (2)	8	5651	
	Greece	06/08/2020	02/09/2020	8-25	9	6181	I-56237
	Saudi Arabia	08/04/2016	02/07/2017	6-32	8	5617	I-54577
Equatorial Guinea	Nigeria	23/09/2000	03/04/2002	4-9	4	2657	I-39154
	Nigeria			4-9 (Add.1)	5	3623	

Country A	Country B/C	Signed	EIF	Report No.	Vol.	Page	UN Reg. No.
	Nigeria	03/04/2002	29/06/2002	4-9 (2)	5	3624	A-39154
	Sao Tome and Principe	26/06/1999		4-8	4	2647	
Eritrea	Yemen	17/12/1999	17/12/1999	6-14	4	2729	N/A
Estonia	Finland	20/05/1965	25/05/1966	10-4 (1)	2	1959	I-8238
	Finland	05/05/1967	15/03/1968	10-4 (2)	2	1971	I-9157
	Finland	25/02/1980	09/07/1980	10-4 (3)	2	1979	I-19806
	Finland	05/02/1985	24/11/1986	10-4 (4)	2	1989	I-24645
	Finland			10-14	3	2557	
	Finland	18/10/1996	07/01/1997	10-16	4	3019	I-33549
	Finland - Sweden	16/01/2001	12/08/2001	10-21	4	3129	I-44411
	Latvia	12/07/1996	10/10/1996	10-15	4	2995	I-33489
	Latvia - Sweden	30/04/1997	20/02/1998	10-17	4	3041	I-44412
	Russia	18/05/2005		10-22	6	4567	
	Sweden	02/11/1998	26/07/2000	10-19	4	3089	I-44413
Fiji	France (New Caledonia, Wallis & Futuna)	19/01/1983	21/08/1984	5-6	1	995	I-27963
	France (New Caledonia, Wallis & Futuna)	08/11/1990	08/11/1990	5-6 (Add.1/Corr.1)	5	3729	A-27963
	France (Wallis & Futuna)	16/09/2015	25/11/2022	5-6 (Add. 2)	9	5975	

(Cont.)

Country-by-Country Index 6305

Country A	Country B/C	Signed	EIF	Report No.	Vol.	Page	UN Reg. No.
	France (Wallis & Futuna) - Tuvalu	09/12/2014	09/12/2014	5-46	8	5539	
	Solomon Islands	11/07/2022	22/02/2023	5-49	9	6027	I-57923
	Tuvalu	17/10/2014	17/10/2024	5-48	9	6005	I-56867
Finland	Estonia			10-14	3	2557	
	Estonia	18/10/1996	07/01/1997	10-16	4	3019	I-33549
	Estonia - Sweden	16/01/2001	12/08/2001	10-21	4	3129	I-44411
	Sweden	29/09/1972	15/01/1973	10-3	2	1945	I-14443
	Sweden	02/06/1994	30/07/1995	10-13	3	2539	I-32126
	Soviet Union	20/05/1965	25/05/1966	10-4 (1)	2	1959	I-8238
	Soviet Union	05/05/1967	15/03/1968	10-4 (2)	2	1971	I-9157
	Soviet Union	25/02/1980	09/07/1980	10-4 (3)	2	1979	I-19806
	Soviet Union	05/02/1985	24/11/1986	10-4 (4)	2	1989	I-24645
France	Belgium	08/10/1990	07/04/1993	9-16	2	1891	I-30173
	Belgium	08/10/1990	07/04/1993	9-16	2	1891	I-30172
	Italy	28/11/1986	15/05/1989	8-2	2	1571	I-26933
	Italy	21/03/2015		8-2 (2)	8	5637	
	Monaco	16/02/1984	22/08/1985	8-3	2	1581	I-23631
	Spain	29/01/1974	05/04/1975	9-2	2	1719	I-14592
	Spain	29/01/1974	05/04/1975	9-2	2	1719	I-14591

Country A	Country B/C	Signed	EIF	Report No.	Vol.	Page	UN Reg. No.
	United Kingdom	30/06/1977	30/06/1977	9-3 (1)	2	1735	N/A
	United Kingdom	24/06/1982	04/02/1983	9-3 (2)	2	1735	I-21923
	United Kingdom	02/11/1988	06/04/1989	9-3 (3)	2	1735	I-26858
	United Kingdom	25/07/1991	17/03/1992	9-3 (4)	2	1735	I-29182
	United Kingdom			9-3 (4)(Corr.)	3	2465	
	United Kingdom			9-3 (4)(Add.1)	5	3943	
	United Kingdom	20/04/2011	31/03/2014	9-3 (6)	7	5115	
	United Kingdom (Guernsey)	10/07/1992	10/07/1992	9-3 (5)	3	2471	I-30858
	United Kingdom (Jersey)	04/07/2000	01/01/2004	9-24	4	2979	I-40415
	United Kingdom (Jersey)			9-24 (Add.1)	5	4006	
France (French Guiana)	Brazil	30/01/1981	19/10/1983	3-3	1	777	I-22476
	Suriname	08/11/2017	01/12/2018	3-11	8	5473	I-55757
France (French Polynesia)	Cook Islands	03/08/1990	03/08/1990	5-18	1	1175	I-27947
	Kiribati	18/12/2002	18/12/2002	5-44	8	5517	I-39386
	United Kingdom (Pitcairn)	25/10/1983	12/04/1984	5-7	1	1003	I-23067
	United Kingdom (Pitcairn)	19/01/1993	01/02/1993	5-7 (Add.)	3	2295	I-30859
France (Glorioso)	Seychelles	19/02/2001	19/02/2001	6-18	5	3784	I-37782

(Cont.)

Country-by-Country Index   6307

Country A	Country B/C	Signed	EIF	Report No.	Vol.	Page	UN Reg. No.
France (Guadeloupe and Martinique)	Antigua and Barbuda	15/03/2017	01/10/2018	2-37	9	5889	I-55817
	Barbados	15/10/2009	01/01/2010	2-30	6	4223	I-47364
	Dominica	07/09/1987	23/12/1988	2-15	1	705	I-26854
	United Kingdom (Montserrat)	27/06/1996	30/01/1997	2-21	3	2227	I-36143
	United Kingdom (Montserrat)			2-21 (Add.1)	5	3563	
	Venezuela	17/07/1980	28/01/1983	2-11	1	603	I-21969
France (Kerguelen)	Australia	04/01/1982	09/01/1983	6-1	2	1185	I-22302
France (Martinique)	Saint Lucia	04/03/1981	04/03/1981	2-10	1	591	I-20780
France (New Caledonia)	Australia	04/01/1982	09/01/1983	5-1	1	905	I-22302
	Fiji	19/01/1983	21/08/1984	5-6	1	995	I-27963
	Fiji	08/11/1990	08/11/1990	5-6 (Add.1/Corr.1)	5	3729	A-27963
	Solomon Islands	12/11/1990	12/11/1990	5-17	1	1167	I-27851
France (Reunion)	Madagascar	14/04/2005	18/06/2007	6-25	6	4405	I-46736
	Mauritius	02/04/1980	02/04/1980	6-5	2	1353	I-20620

Country A	Country B/C	Signed	EIF	Report No.	Vol.	Page	UN Reg. No.
France (Saint Martin and Saint Barthelemy)	Antigua and Barbuda	15/03/2017	01/10/2018	2-37	9	5889	I-55817
	Netherlands (Sint Maarten, Saba, Sint Eustatius)	06/04/2016	01/04/2017	2-36	8	5445	I-55222
	United Kingdom (Anguilla)	27/06/1996	30/01/1997	2-20	3	2219	I-36144
	United Kingdom (Anguilla)			2-20 (Add.1)	5	3562	
	United Kingdom (Anguilla)	04/03/2021	04/03/2021	2-20 (Add. 2)	9	5881	
France (Saint Pierre and Miquelon)	Canada	27/03/1972	27/03/1972	1-2	1	387	I-12353
	Canada	10/06/1992	10/06/1992	1-2	1	387	N/A
	Canada			1-2 (Add.2)	3	2141	
	Canada	17/05/2005		1-2 (2)	8	5351	
France (Wallis & Futuna)	Fiji	19/01/1983	21/08/1984	5-6	1	995	I-27963
	Fiji	08/11/1990	08/11/1990	5-6 (Add.1/Corr.1)	5	3729	A-27963
	Fiji	16/09/2015	25/11/2022	5-6 (Add. 2)	9	5975	
	Fiji - Tuvalu	09/12/2014	09/12/2014	5-46	8	5539	
	New Zealand (Tokelau)	30/06/2003	12/11/2003	5-30	6	4339	I-40601
	Tonga	11/01/1980	11/01/1980	5-8	1	1011	I-18960
	Tuvalu	05/11/1985	05/11/1985	5-29	6	4330	I-25964
	Tuvalu	09/12/2014	09/12/2014	5-29 (Add. 1)	8	5503	

(*Cont.*)

Country A	Country B/C	Signed	EIF	Report No.	Vol.	Page	UN Reg. No.
Gabon	Sao Tome & Principe	26/04/2001		4-11	5	3683	
The Gambia	Senegal	04/06/1975	27/08/1976	4-2	1	849	
Georgia	Turkey	17/04/1973	27/03/1975	8-10 (1)	2	1681	I-14475
	Turkey	23/06/1978	15/05/1981	8-10 (2)	2	1693	I-20344
	Turkey	06/02/1987	06/02/1987	8-10 (3)	2	1701	I-24690
	Turkey			8-10 (4)	3	2443	
	Turkey	14/07/1997	22/09/1999	8-10 (5)	4	2865	
Germany	Denmark	09/06/1965	27/05/1966	9-8	2	1801	I-8289
	Denmark	20/02/1969	20/02/1969	9-8	2	1801	N/A
	Denmark	28/02/1971	07/12/1972	9-8	2	1801	I-12295
	Denmark	09/06/1965	27/05/1966	10-1	2	1915	I-8289
	Denmark	14/09/1988	14/06/1989	10-11	2	2087	I-26910
	Fed. Rep./Dem. Rep.	29/06/1974	01/10/1974	10-5	2	1997	
	Netherlands	14/05/1962	01/08/1963	9-11	2	1835	I-7404
	Netherlands	01/12/1964	18/09/1965	9-11	2	1835	I-8011
	Netherlands	20/02/1969	20/02/1969	9-11	2	1835	N/A
	Netherlands	28/01/1971	07/12/1972	9-11	2	1835	I-12296
	Poland	29/10/1968	16/04/1969	10-6 (1)	2	2005	I-10974

(*Cont.*)

Country A	Country B/C	Signed	EIF	Report No.	Vol.	Page	UN Reg. No.
	Poland	22/05/1989	13/06/1989	10-6 (1)	2	2005	I-26909
	Poland	14/11/1990	16/01/1992	10-6 (2)	2	2023	I-29542
	Sweden	22/06/1978	20/12/1978	10-7	2	2029	I-18021
	United Kingdom	25/11/1971	07/12/1972	9-12	2	1851	I-12626
Ghana	Ivory Coast			4-18	7	4809	N/A
	Ivory Coast	23/09/2017	23/09/2017	4-18 (Add.1)	8	5489	N/A
Greece	Albania	27/04/2009		8-21	6	4462	
	Egypt	06/08/2020	02/09/2020	8-25	9	6181	I-56237
	Italy	24/05/1977	12/11/1980	8-4	2	1591	I-21048
	Italy			8-4 (Add.1/Corr.1)	6	4431	
	Italy	09/06/2020		8-4 (2)	9	6127	
Grenada	Trinidad and Tobago	21/04/2010	27/04/2010	2-31	7	4705	I-47548
Guinea	Guinea-Bissau	14/02/1985	14/02/1985	4-3	1	857	N/A
	Guinea-Bissau			4-3 (Add.1/Corr.1)	5	3621	
Guinea-Bissau	Guinea	14/02/1985	14/02/1985	4-3	1	857	N/A
	Guinea			4-3 (Add.1/Corr.1)	5	3621	

(Cont.)

Country A	Country B/C	Signed	EIF	Report No.	Vol.	Page	UN Reg. No.
	Senegal	26/04/1960	26/04/1960	4-4 (1)	1	867	
	Senegal	31/07/1989	31/07/1989	4-4 (2)	1	867	
	Senegal	14/10/1993	21/12/1995	4-4 (4)	3	2251	I-32434
	Senegal	12/06/1995	21/12/1995	4-4 (5)	3	2251	A-32434
Guyana	Barbados	02/12/2003	05/05/2004	2-27	5	3578	I-40555
	Barbados			2-27 (Add.1)	6	4201	
	Suriname	17/09/2007	17/09/2007	3-10	5	3601	N/A
	Suriname			3-10 (Add.1)	6	4236	
Haiti	Colombia	17/02/1978	16/02/1979	2-3	1	491	I-18229
	Cuba	27/10/1977	06/01/1978	2-7	1	551	
Honduras	Colombia	02/08/1986	19/12/1999	2-4	1	503	I-36360
	Colombia			2-4 (Add.1)	5	3561	
	Cuba	21/08/2012	11/12/2013	2-33	7	4735	I-51725
	Mexico	18/04/2005	30/11/2006	2-28	6	4202	I-43571
	Nicaragua	08/10/2007	08/10/2007	2-24	5	3575	N/A
	Nicaragua			2-24 (Add.1)	6	4169	
	United Kingdom (Cayman Islands)	04/12/2001	01/03/2002	2-23	5	3564	I-39224

Country A	Country B/C	Signed	EIF	Report No.	Vol.	Page	UN Reg. No.
Iceland	Denmark (Faroes)	02/02/2007	29/04/2008	9-27	6	4553	I-51764
	Denmark (Faroes)	30/10/2019		9-26 (Add. 1)	9	6251	
	Denmark (Greenland)	11/11/1997	27/05/1998	9-22	4	2941	I-35941
	Denmark (Greenland)	16/01/2013	16/01/2013	9-22 (2)	7	5259	
	Denmark - Norway	20/09/2006	20/09/2006	9-26	6	4532	
	Norway	30/10/2019		9-26 (Add. 1)	9	6251	
	Norway (Jan Mayen)	28/05/1980	13/06/1980	9-4	2	1755	I-37025
	Norway (Jan Mayen)	22/10/1981	02/06/1982	9-4	2	1755	I-37026
	Norway (Jan Mayen)			9-4 (Add.1)	7	5143	
	Norway (Jan Mayen)	11/11/1997	27/05/1998	9-4 (2)	4	2903	A-37026
	Norway (Jan Mayen)	03/11/2008	03/10/2011	9-4 (3)	7	5123	I-50378
	Norway (Jan Mayen)	03/11/2008	03/11/2008	9-4 (3)	7	5123	A-37026
India	Bangladesh	07/07/2014	07/07/2014	6-23	6	4403	N/A
	Bangladesh			6-23 (Add.1)	7	4985	
	Indonesia	08/08/1974	17/12/1974	6-6 (1)	2	1363	I-19474
	Indonesia	14/01/1977	15/08/1977	6-6 (2)	2	1371	I-19475
	Indonesia - Thailand	22/06/1978	02/03/1979	6-7	2	1379	I-19476
	Maldives	28/12/1976	08/06/1978	6-8	2	1389	
	Maldives - Sri Lanka	31/07/1976	31/07/1976	6-9	2	1401	I-15805
	Myanmar	23/12/1986	14/09/1987	6-3	2	1329	I-25390

(Cont.)

Country A	Country B/C	Signed	EIF	Report No.	Vol.	Page	UN Reg. No.
	Myanmar - Thailand	27/10/1993	24/05/1995	6-11 (Add.1)	3	2369	I-32099
	Myanmar - Thailand	27/10/1993		6-11 (Corr.1)	5	3781	
	Sri Lanka	28/06/1974	08/07/1974	6-10 (1)	2	1409	I-15802
	Sri Lanka	23/03/1976	10/05/1976	6-10 (2)	2	1419	I-15804
	Thailand	22/06/1978	15/12/1978	6-11	2	1433	I-17433
	Thailand	27/10/1993		6-11 (Add.2)	3	2377	
Indonesia	Australia	18/05/1971	08/11/1973	6-2 (1)	2	1195	I-14122
	Australia	09/10/1972	08/11/1973	6-2 (2)	2	1207	I-14123
	Australia (Papua New Guinea)	12/02/1973	26/11/1974	6-2 (3)	2	1219	I-14124
	Australia	29/10/1981	01/02/1982	6-2 (4)	2	1229	
	Australia	11/12/1989	09/02/1991	6-2 (5)	2	1245	I-28462
	Australia	14/03/1997		6-2 (6)	4	2697	
	India	08/08/1974	17/12/1974	6-6 (1)	2	1363	I-19474
	India	14/01/1977	15/08/1977	6-6 (2)	2	1371	I-19475
	India - Thailand	22/06/1978	02/03/1979	6-7	2	1379	I-19476
	Malaysia	27/10/1969	07/11/1969	5-9 (1)	1	1019	
	Malaysia	17/03/1970	08/10/1971	5-9 (2)	1	1029	
	Malaysia - Thailand	21/12/1971	16/07/1973	6-12	2	1443	
	Papua New Guinea	13/12/1980	10/07/1982	5-10	1	1039	
	Philippines	23/05/2014	01/08/2019	5-41	7	4947	I-55946

Country A	Country B/C	Signed	EIF	Report No.	Vol.	Page	UN Reg. No.
	Singapore	25/05/1973	29/08/1974	5-11	1	1049	I-45144
	Singapore	10/03/2009	30/08/2010	5-11 (2)	7	4813	I-48026
	Singapore	03/09/2014	10/02/2017	5-11 (3)	7	4827	I-54672
	Thailand	17/12/1971	07/04/1973	6-13 (1)	2	1455	I-16929
	Thailand	11/12/1975	18/02/1978	6-13 (2)	2	1465	I-16930
	Vietnam	26/06/2003	29/05/2007	5-27	6	4301	I-44165
Iran	Bahrain	17/06/1971	14/05/1972	7-2	2	1481	I-11838
	Oman	25/07/1974	28/05/1975	7-5	2	1503	I-14085
	Oman	26/05/2015	04/09/2016	6-31	8	5605	I-54173
	Qatar	20/09/1969	10/05/1970	7-6	2	1511	I-11197
	Saudi Arabia	24/10/1968	29/01/1969	7-7	2	1519	I-9976
	United Arab Emirates	31/08/1974		7-8	2	1533	
Iraq	Kuwait	21/05/1993	21/05/1993	7-11	3	2387	
Ireland	United Kingdom	07/11/1988	11/01/1990	9-5	2	1767	I-27204
	United Kingdom	08/12/1992	26/03/1993	9-5 (2)	3	2487	A-27204
	United Kingdom	28/03/2013	31/03/2014	9-5 (3)	7	5151	I-51870
Israel	Cyprus	17/12/2010	25/02/2011	8-22	7	5091	I-48387

Country A	Country B/C	Signed	EIF	Report No.	Vol.	Page	UN Reg. No.
	Jordan	18/01/1996	17/02/1996	8-12	3	2457	I-35333
	Lebanon	27/10/2022	27/10/2022	8-26	9	6197	I-57582
Italy	Albania	18/12/1992	26/02/1999	8-11	3	2447	
	Albania			8-11 (Corr.1)	4	2869	
	Croatia	29/07/2005	02/08/2005	8-27	9	6231	
	Croatia	24/05/2022		8-27	9	6231	
	France	28/11/1986	15/05/1989	8-2	2	1571	I-26933
	France	21/03/2015		8-2 (2)	8	5637	
	Greece	24/05/1977	12/11/1980	8-4	2	1591	I-21048
	Greece			8-4 (Add.1/Corr.1)	6	4431	
	Greece	09/06/2020		8-4 (2)	9	6127	
	Spain	19/02/1974	16/11/1978	8-5	2	1601	I-17429
	Tunisia	20/08/1971	06/12/1978	8-6	2	1611	I-17601
	Tunisia			8-6 (Corr.)	3	2435	
	Tunisia			8-6 (Corr.2)	4	2863	
	Yugoslavia	08/01/1968	21/01/1970	8-7 (1)	2	1627	
	Yugoslavia	10/11/1975	03/04/1977	8-7 (2)	2	1639	I-24848
Ivory Coast	Ghana			4-18	7	4809	N/A
	Ghana	23/09/2017	23/09/2017	4-18 (Add.1)	8	5489	N/A

6316   *Country-by-Country Index*

(Cont.)

Country A	Country B/C	Signed	EIF	Report No.	Vol.	Page	UN Reg. No.
Jamaica	Colombia	12/11/1993	14/03/1994	2-18	3	2179	I-30943
	Cuba	18/02/1994	18/07/1995	2-19	3	2205	
Japan	Korea, Rep.	30/01/1974	22/06/1978	5-12	1	1057	I-19777
	Korea, Rep.	30/01/1974	22/06/1978	5-12	1	1057	I-19778
Jordan	Israel	18/01/1996	17/02/1996	8-12	3	2457	I-35333
	Saudi Arabia	16/12/2007	10/06/2010	8-23	7	5105	I-47974
Kazakhstan	Azerbaijan	29/11/2001	09/12/2003	11-3	5	4042	
	Azerbaijan	27/02/2003	09/12/2003	11-3	5	4042	
	Azerbaijan - Russia	14/05/2003		11-4	5	4055	
	Russia	06/07/1998	07/04/2003	11-1	5	4013	
	Russia	13/05/2002	07/04/2003	11-1	5	4013	
Kenya	Tanzania	09/07/1976	09/07/1976	4-5	1	875	I-15603
	Tanzania	23/06/2009	23/06/2009	4-5 (2)	7	4781	I-46308
	Somalia			4-17	7	4807	N/A
Kiribati	Cook Islands	29/08/2012	17/01/2014	5-32	7	4847	I-51976
	France (French Polynesia)	18/12/2002	18/12/2002	5-44	8	5517	I-39386

Country A	Country B/C	Signed	EIF	Report No.	Vol.	Page	UN Reg. No.
	Marshall Islands	29/08/2012		5-34	7	4869	
	Marshall Islands - Nauru	29/08/2012		5-39	7	4925	
	Nauru	29/08/2012		5-35	7	4881	
	New Zealand (Tokelau)	29/08/2012	15/05/2015	5-36	7	4893	I-53058
	Tuvalu	29/08/2012		5-37	7	4903	
	United States	06/09/2013	19/07/2019	5-40	7	4935	I-57686
Korea, Dem. P. Rep.	Kazakhstan - Russia	17/04/1985		5-15 (1)	1	1135	
	Soviet Union	22/01/1986		5-15 (2)	1	1145	
	Soviet Union	03/09/1990		5-15 (3)	3	2299	
Korea, Rep.	Japan	30/01/1974	22/06/1978	5-12	1	1057	I-19777
	Japan	30/01/1974	22/06/1978	5-12	1	1057	I-19778
Kuwait	Iraq	21/05/1993	21/05/1993	7-11	3	2387	
	Saudi Arabia	02/07/2000	30/01/2001	7-12	4	2825	I-37359
Latvia	Estonia	12/07/1996	10/10/1996	10-15	4	2995	I-33489
	Estonia - Sweden	30/04/1997	20/02/1998	10-17	4	3041	I-44412
	Lithuania	09/07/1999		10-20	4	3107	

(Cont.)

Country A	Country B/C	Signed	EIF	Report No.	Vol.	Page	UN Reg. No.
Lebanon	Cyprus	17/01/2007		8-19	6	4445	
	Israel	27/10/2022	27/10/2022	8-26	9	6197	I-57582
Libya	Malta	03/06/1985	03/06/1985	8-8	2	1649	N/A
	Malta	10/11/1986	11/12/1987	8-8	2	1649	
	Tunisia	24/02/1982	24/02/1982	8-9	2	1663	N/A
	Tunisia	08/08/1988	11/04/1989	8-9	2	1663	
	Turkey	27/11/2019	08/12/2019	8-24	9	6159	I-56119
Lithuania	Latvia	09/07/1999		10-20	4	3107	
	Russia	24/10/1997	12/08/2003	10-18 (1)	4	3057	
	Russia	24/10/1997	12/08/2003	10-18 (2)	4	3077	
	Russia			10-18 (1)(2)(Add.1)	5	4009	
	Russia - Sweden	30/11/2005	17/06/2011	10-23	8	5731	I-53411
	Sweden	10/04/2014	23/12/2014	10-24	8	5743	I-53412
Madagascar	France (Reunion)	14/04/2005	18/06/2007	6-25	6	4405	I-46736
Malaysia	United Kingdom (Brunei)	11/09/1958	11/09/1958	5-2	1	915	
	Indonesia	27/10/1969	07/11/1969	5-9 (1)	1	1019	
	Indonesia	17/03/1970	08/10/1971	5-9 (2)	1	1029	

(Cont.)

Country A	Country B/C	Signed	EIF	Report No.	Vol.	Page	UN Reg. No.
	Indonesia - Thailand	21/12/1971	16/07/1973	6-12	2	1443	
	Singapore	07/08/1995	07/08/1995	5-20	3	2345	
	Singapore			5-20 (2)	5	3733	N/A
	Singapore			5-20 (2)(Add.1)	6	4299	
	Thailand	24/10/1979	15/07/1982	5-13 (1)	1	1091	I-21270
	Thailand	24/10/1979	15/07/1982	5-13 (2)	1	1099	I-21271
	Thailand	21/02/1979		5-13 (2)	1	1099	
	Thailand	30/05/1990		5-13 (2)	1	1099	
	Vietnam	05/06/1992	05/06/1992	5-19	3	2335	
Maldives	India	28/12/1976	08/06/1978	6-8	2	1389	
	India - Sri Lanka	31/07/1976	31/07/1976	6-9	2	1401	I-15805
	Mauritius	28/04/2023	28/04/2023	6-33	9	6103	N/A
Malta	Libya	03/06/1985	03/06/1985	8-8	2	1649	N/A
	Libya	10/11/1986	11/12/1987	8-8	2	1649	
Marshall Islands	Kiribati	29/08/2012		5-34	7	4869	
	Kiribati - Nauru	29/08/2012		5-39	7	4925	
	Micronesia, Fed. States	05/07/2006	24/07/2015	5-28	6	4316	I-54649
	Nauru	29/08/2012		5-38	7	4915	

(Cont.)

Country A	Country B/C	Signed	EIF	Report No.	Vol.	Page	UN Reg. No.
Mauritania	Cape Verde	19/09/2003		4-12	5	3694	
	Morocco	14/04/1976	10/11/1976	4-6	1	885	I-15406
Mauritius	France (Reunion)	02/04/1980	02/04/1980	6-5	2	1353	I-20620
	Maldives	28/04/2023	28/04/2023	6-33	9	6103	N/A
	Seychelles	29/07/2008	19/11/2008	6-22	6	4391	I-46169
	Seychelles	13/03/2012	18/06/2012	6-22 (2)	9	6047	I-49782
	Seychelles	13/03/2012	18/06/2012	6-22 (2)	9	6047	I-49783
Mexico	Cuba	26/07/1976	26/07/1976	2-8	1	565	I-23255
	Cuba	18/01/2017	27/07/2018	2-8 (2)	9	5861	I-55481
	Honduras	18/04/2005	30/11/2006	2-28	6	4202	I-43571
	United States	23/11/1970	18/04/1972	1-5	1	427	I-11873
	United States	24/11/1976	24/11/1976	1-5	1	427	I-17282
	United States	04/05/1978	13/11/1997	1-5	1	427	I-37399
	United States			1-5 (Add.)	4	2619	
	United States	09/06/2000	17/01/2001	1-5 (2)	4	2621	I-37400
	United States	20/02/2012	18/07/2014	1-5 (3)	7	4613	I-52496
	United States	18/01/2017		1-5 (4)	9	5841	

(Cont.)

Country-by-Country Index 6321

Country A	Country B/C	Signed	EIF	Report No.	Vol.	Page	UN Reg. No.
Micronesia, Fed. States	Marshall Islands	05/07/2006	24/07/2015	5-28	6	4316	I-54649
	Palau	05/07/2006	16/02/2016	5-31	6	4348	I-54767
	Papua New Guinea	29/07/1991	18/03/2016	5-47	9	5981	I-54917
	Papua New Guinea	07/09/2015	18/03/2016	5-47	9	5981	A-54917
	United States (Guam)	01/08/2014	27/09/2019	5-42	7	4963	I-55987
Monaco	France	16/02/1984	22/08/1985	8-3	2	1581	I-23631
Montenegro	Italy	08/01/1968	21/01/1970	8-7 (1)	2	1627	
Morocco	Mauritania	14/04/1976	10/11/1976	4-6	1	885	I-15406
Mozambique	Comoros	05/12/2011	04/05/2012	6-26	7	5017	
	Comoros - Tanzania	05/12/2011		6-27	7	5033	
	Tanzania	28/12/1988		4-7	1	893	
	Tanzania	05/12/2011		4-7 (2)	7	4793	
Myanmar	Bangladesh	14/03/2012	14/03/2012	6-24	6	4404	N/A
	Bangladesh			6-24 (Add.1)	7	4999	
	India	23/12/1986	14/09/1987	6-3	2	1329	I-25390
	India - Thailand	27/10/1993	24/05/1995	6-11 (Add.1)	3	2369	I-32099

(Cont.)

Country A	Country B/C	Signed	EIF	Report No.	Vol.	Page	UN Reg. No.
India - Thailand				6-11 (Corr.1)	5	3781	
	Thailand	25/07/1980	12/04/1982	6-4	2	1341	I-21069
Namibia	Angola	04/06/2002		4-13	5	3709	
Nauru	Kiribati	29/08/2012		5-35	7	4881	
	Kiribati - Marshall Islands	29/08/2012		5-39	7	4925	
	Marshall Islands	29/08/2012		5-38	7	4915	
Netherlands	Belgium	18/12/1996	01/01/1999	9-21	4	2921	I-35449
	Belgium	18/12/1996	01/01/1999	9-21	4	2921	I-35448
	Denmark	31/03/1966	01/08/1967	9-18	3	2497	I-8751
	Germany	14/05/1962	01/08/1963	9-11	2	1835	I-7404
	Germany	01/12/1964	18/09/1965	9-11	2	1835	I-8011
	Germany	20/02/1969	20/02/1969	9-11	2	1835	N/A
	Germany	28/01/1971	07/12/1972	9-11	2	1835	I-12296
	United Kingdom	06/10/1965	23/12/1966	9-13	2	1859	I-8616
	United Kingdom	25/11/1971	07/12/1972	9-13	2	1859	A-8616
	United Kingdom	07/06/2004	10/01/2006	9-13 (2)	6	4494	A-8616
	United Kingdom	03/07/2013	01/04/2014	9-13 (3)	7	5205	A-8616
	United Kingdom	06/10/1965	23/12/1966	9-13 (4)	8	5685	I-8615

(Cont.)

Country A	Country B/C	Signed	EIF	Report No.	Vol.	Page	UN Reg. No.
	United Kingdom	26/05/1992	03/03/1993	9-13 (4)	8	5685	I-30235
	United Kingdom	27/11/2013	27/11/2013	9-13 (4)	8	5685	I-51804
Netherlands (Antilles)	Dominican Republic	05/07/2021		2-39	9	5913	
	Venezuela	31/03/1978	15/12/1978	2-12	1	615	I-17901
Netherlands (Sint Maarten, Saba, Sint Eustatius)	France (Saint Martin, Saint Barthelemy)	06/04/2016	01/04/2017	2-36	8	5445	I-55222
	Saint Kitts and Nevis	04/04/2024		2-42	9	5957	
New Zealand	Australia	25/07/2004	25/01/2006	5-26	5	3759	I-43985
	Australia			5-26 (Add.1)	6	4300	
New Zealand (Tokelau)	Cook Islands	04/08/2010	12/11/2012	5-43	7	4973	I-50545
	France (Wallis and Futuna)	30/06/2003	12/11/2003	5-30	6	4339	I-40601
	Kiribati	29/08/2012	15/05/2015	5-36	7	4893	I-53058
	United States (American Samoa)	02/12/1980	03/09/1983	5-14	1	1125	I-28231
Nicaragua	Colombia	19/11/2012	19/11/2012	2-25	5	3576	N/A
	Colombia			2-25 (Add.1)	6	4186	
	Colombia			2-25 (Add.2)	7	4685	

6324 *Country-by-Country Index*

(Cont.)

Country A	Country B/C	Signed	EIF	Report No.	Vol.	Page	UN Reg. No.
	Colombia			2-25 (2)	7	4683	
	Costa Rica			2-34	7	4745	N/A
	Costa Rica	02/02/2018	02/02/2018	2-34 (Add.1)	8	5407	N/A
	Honduras	08/10/2007	08/10/2007	2-24	5	3575	N/A
	Honduras			2-24 (Add.1)	6	4169	
Nigeria	Benin	04/08/2006		4-14	6	4256	
	Cameroon	01/06/1975	01/06/1975	4-1	1	841	I-19976
	Cameroon	10/10/2002	10/10/2002	4-1 (Add.)	3	2249	N/A
	Cameroon			4-1 (Add.2)	5	3605	
	Cameroon			4-1 (Add.3)	6	4251	
	Equatorial Guinea	23/09/2000	03/04/2002	4-9	4	2657	I-39154
	Equatorial Guinea			4-9 (Add.1)	5	3623	
	Equatorial Guinea	03/04/2002	29/06/2002	4-9 (2)	5	3624	A-39154
	Sao Tome and Principe	21/02/2001	16/01/2003	4-10	5	3638	
Niue	Cook Island	29/08/2012	06/05/2013	5-33	7	4859	II-1370
	United States (American Samoa)	13/05/1997	07/10/2014	5-22	4	2673	I-52440
	United States (American Samoa)			5-22 (Add.1)	5	3734	

Country A	Country B/C	Signed	EIF	Report No.	Vol.	Page	UN Reg. No.
	United States (American Samoa)			5-22 (Add.1, Corr.1)	7	4839	
Norway	Denmark	08/12/1965	22/06/1966	9-9	2	1815	I-9052
	Denmark	24/04/1968	24/04/1968	9-9	2	1815	A-9052
	Denmark	04/06/1974	04/06/1974	9-9	2	1815	A-9052
	Denmark (Faroes)	15/06/1979	03/06/1980	9-1	2	1711	I-19512
	Denmark (Faroes)	30/10/2019		9-26 (Add. 1)	9	6251	
	Denmark (Greenland)	20/02/2006	02/06/2006	9-25	6	4513	I-42887
	Denmark - Iceland	20/09/2006	20/09/2006	9-26	6	4532	
	Iceland	30/10/2019		9-26 (Add. 1)	9	6251	
	Russia	11/07/2007	09/07/2008	9-6 (2)	6	4479	I-45114
	Russia	15/09/2010	07/07/2011	9-6 (3)	7	5167	I-49095
	Soviet Union	15/02/1957	24/04/1957	9-6	2	1783	I-4523
	Soviet Union	29/11/1957	17/03/1958	9-6	2	1781	A-4523
	Sweden	24/07/1968	18/03/1969	9-14	2	1871	I-14015
	United Kingdom	10/03/1965	29/06/1965	9-15	2	1879	I-8043
	United Kingdom	22/12/1978	20/02/1980	9-15	2	1879	A-8043
	United Kingdom	10/05/1976	22/07/1977	9-15 (2)	5	3944	I-16878
	United Kingdom	16/10/1979	30/01/1981	9-15 (3)	5	3944	I-20387
	United Kingdom	16/10/1979	30/01/1981	9-15 (4)	5	3944	I-20551
	United Kingdom	30/04/2009	30/04/2009	9-15 (5)	6	4499	A-8043

(Cont.)

Country A	Country B/C	Signed	EIF	Report No.	Vol.	Page	UN Reg. No.
	United Kingdom	04/04/2005	10/07/2007	9-15 (6)	7	5213	1-44683
Norway (Jan Mayen)	Denmark (Greenland)	14/06/1993	14/06/1993	9-19	3	2507	N/A
	Denmark (Greenland)	18/12/1995	18/12/1995	9-19	3	2507	1-32441
	Denmark (Greenland)	11/11/1997	27/05/1998	9-19 (2)	4	2913	A-32441
	Iceland	28/05/1980	13/06/1980	9-4	2	1755	1-37025
	Iceland	22/10/1981	02/06/1982	9-4	2	1755	1-37026
	Iceland			9-4 (Add.1)	7	5143	
	Iceland	11/11/1997	27/05/1998	9-4 (2)	4	2903	A-37026
	Iceland	03/11/2008	03/10/2011	9-4 (3)	7	5123	1-50378
	Iceland	03/11/2008	03/11/2008	9-4 (3)	7	5123	A-37026
Oman	Iran	25/07/1974	28/05/1975	7-5	2	1503	1-14085
	Iran	26/05/2015	04/09/2016	6-31	8	5605	1-54173
	Pakistan	12/06/2000	21/11/2000	6-17	4	2809	1-38455
	Pakistan			6-17 (Add.1)	6	4365	
	Yemen	14/12/2003	03/07/2004	6-21	5	3900	1-41170
Pakistan	Oman	12/06/2000	21/11/2000	6-17	4	2809	1-38455
	Oman			6-17 (Add.1)	6	4365	

(Cont.)

Country A	Country B/C	Signed	EIF	Report No.	Vol.	Page	UN Reg. No.
Palau	Micronesia, Fed. States	05/07/2006	16/02/2016	5-31	6	4348	I-54767
Panama	Colombia	20/11/1976	30/11/1977	2-5	1	519	I-16398
	Costa Rica	02/02/1980	11/02/1982	2-6	1	537	
Papua New Guinea	Australia	18/12/1978	15/02/1985	5-3	1	929	I-24238
	Indonesia	12/02/1973	26/11/1974	6-2 (3)	2	1219	I-14124
	Indonesia	13/12/1980	10/07/1982	5-10	1	1039	
	Micronesia, Fed. States	29/07/1991	18/03/2016	5-47	9	5981	I-54917
	Micronesia, Fed. States	07/09/2015	18/03/2016	5-47	9	5981	A-54917
	Solomon Islands	25/01/1989		5-16	1	1155	
	Solomon Islands			5-16 (2)	3	2323	
Peru	Chile	18/08/1952	18/08/1952	3-5	1	793	I-14758
	Chile	04/12/1954	21/09/1967	3-9	1	829	I-40521
	Chile			3-5 (Corr.1,Add.1)	4	2639	N/A
	Chile			3-5 (Add.2)	6	4235	
	Chile	27/01/2014	27/01/2014	3-5 (2)	7	4749	
	Ecuador	18/08/1952	18/08/1952	3-9	1	829	I-14758
	Ecuador	04/12/1954	21/09/1967	3-9	1	829	I-40521
	Ecuador	02/05/2011	20/05/2011	3-9 (Add.1)	7	4769	I-48631

(Cont.)

Country A	Country B/C	Signed	EIF	Report No.	Vol.	Page	UN Reg. No.
Philippines	Indonesia	23/05/2014	01/08/2019	5-41	7	4947	I-55946
Poland	Denmark	19/11/2018	28/06/2019	10-25	9	6273	
	Germany, Dem. Rep.	29/10/1968	16/04/1969	10-6 (1)	2	2005	I-10974
	Germany, Dem. Rep.	22/05/1989	13/06/1989	10-6 (1)	2	2005	I-26909
	Germany, Fed. Rep.	14/11/1990	16/01/1992	10-6 (2)	2	2023	I-29542
	Soviet Union	18/03/1958	29/07/1958	10-8	2	2039	I-4861
	Soviet Union	28/08/1969	13/05/1970	10-8	2	2039	I-10978
	Soviet Union	17/07/1985	13/03/1986	10-8	2	2039	
	Sweden	10/02/1989	30/06/1989	10-10	2	2077	I-27846
	Sweden - Soviet Union	30/06/1989	10/05/1990	10-12	2	2097	I-27841
Portugal	Spain	12/02/1976		9-7	2	1791	
	Spain	12/02/1976		9-7	2	1791	
Qatar	Abu Dhabi	20/03/1969	20/03/1969	7-9	2	1541	I-43372
	Bahrain	16/03/2001	16/03/2001	7-13	4	2841	N/A
	Iran	20/09/1969	10/05/1970	7-6	2	1511	I-11197
	Saudi Arabia	05/07/2008	16/12/2008	7-14	6	4417	I-30249
	Saudi Arabia	04/12/1965	31/05/1971	7-14 (2)	7	5073	I-30249
	Saudi Arabia	07/06/1999	07/06/1999	7-14 (2)	7	5073	A-30249
	Saudi Arabia	21/03/2001	21/03/2001	7-14 (2)	7	5073	A-30249

(Cont.)

Country A	Country B/C	Signed	EIF	Report No.	Vol.	Page	UN Reg. No.
Romania	Ukraine	03/02/2009	03/02/2009	8-17	5	3939	N/A
				8-18	6	4434	
Russia	Azerbaijan	23/09/2002	25/06/2003	11-2	5	4034	
	Azerbaijan - Kazakhstan	14/05/2003		11-4	5	4055	
	Estonia	18/05/2005		10-22	6	4567	
	Finland	20/05/1965	25/05/1966	10-4 (1)	2	1959	I-8238
	Finland	05/05/1967	15/03/1968	10-4 (2)	2	1971	I-9157
	Finland	25/02/1980	09/07/1980	10-4 (3)	2	1979	I-19806
	Finland	05/02/1985	24/11/1986	10-4 (4)	2	1989	I-24645
	Kazakhstan	06/07/1998	07/04/2003	11-1	5	4013	
	Kazakhstan	13/05/2002	07/04/2003	11-1	5	4013	
	Korea, Dem. P. Rep.	17/04/1985		5-15 (1)	1	1135	
	Korea, Dem. P. Rep.	22/01/1986		5-15 (2)	1	1145	
	Korea, Dem. P. Rep.	03/09/1990		5-15 (3)	3	2299	
	Lithuania	24/10/1997	12/08/2003	10-18 (1)	4	3057	
	Lithuania	24/10/1997	12/08/2003	10-18 (2)	4	3077	
	Lithuania			10-18 (1)(2)(Add.1)	5	4009	
	Lithuania - Sweden	30/11/2005	17/06/2011	10-23	8	5731	I-53411
	Norway	15/02/1957	24/04/1957	9-6	2	1783	I-4523
	Norway	29/11/1957	17/03/1958	9-6	2	1781	A-4523

Country A	Country B/C	Signed	EIF	Report No.	Vol.	Page	UN Reg. No.
	Norway	11/07/2007	09/07/2008	9-6 (2)	6	4479	I-45114
	Norway	15/09/2010	07/07/2011	9-6 (3)	7	5167	I-49095
	Poland	18/03/1958	29/07/1958	10-8	2	2039	I-4861
	Poland	28/08/1969	13/05/1970	10-8	2	2039	I-10978
	Poland	17/07/1985	13/03/1986	10-8	2	2039	
	Sweden	18/04/1988	22/06/1988	10-9	2	2057	I-27075
	Sweden - Poland	30/06/1989	10/05/1990	10-12	2	2097	I-27841
	Turkey	23/06/1978	15/05/1981	8-10 (2)	2	1693	I-20344
	Turkey	06/02/1987	06/02/1987	8-10 (3)	2	1701	I-24690
	Turkey			8-10 (4)	3	2443	
	United States	01/06/1990		1-6	1	447	
Saint Kitts and Nevis	Netherlands (Sint Eustatius)	04/04/2024		2-42	9	5957	
Saint Lucia	Barbados	06/07/2017	01/09/2019	2-40	9	5925	I-56440
	France (Martinique)	04/03/1981	04/03/1981	2-10	1	591	I-20780
	Saint Vincent and the Grenadines	06/07/2017	01/05/2019	2-41	9	5941	I-56460

Country A	Country B/C	Signed	EIF	Report No.	Vol.	Page	UN Reg. No.
Saint Vincent and the Grenadines	Barbados	31/08/2015		2-35	8	5433	
	Saint Lucia	06/07/2017	01/05/2019	2-41	9	5941	I-56460
Sao Tome and Principe	Equatorial Guinea	26/06/1999		4-8	4	2647	
	Gabon	26/04/2001		4-11	5	3683	
	Nigeria	21/02/2001	16/01/2003	4-10	5	3638	
Saudi Arabia	Bahrain	22/02/1958	22/02/1958	7-3	2	1489	I-30248
	Egypt	08/04/2016	02/07/2017	6-32	8	5617	I-54577
	Iran	24/10/1968	29/01/1969	7-7	2	1519	I-9976
	Jordan	16/12/2007	10/06/2010	8-23	7	5105	I-47974
	Kuwait	02/07/2000	30/01/2001	7-12	4	2825	I-37359
	Qatar	05/07/2008	16/12/2008	7-14	6	4417	I-30249
	Qatar	04/12/1965	31/05/1971	7-14 (2)	7	5073	I-30249
	Qatar	07/06/1999	07/06/1999	7-14 (2)	7	5073	A-30249
	Qatar	21/03/2001	21/03/2001	7-14 (2)	7	5073	A-30249
	Yemen	12/06/2000	09/07/2000	6-16	4	2797	I-43167
Senegal	Cape Verde	17/02/1993	25/03/1994	4-8	3	2279	I-30956
	The Gambia	04/06/1975	27/08/1976	4-2	1	849	

(Cont.)

Country A	Country B/C	Signed	EIF	Report No.	Vol.	Page	UN Reg. No.
	Guinea-Bissau	26/04/1960	26/04/1960	4-4 (1)	1	867	
	Guinea-Bissau	31/07/1989	31/07/1989	4-4 (2)	1	867	
	Guinea-Bissau	14/10/1993	21/12/1995	4-4 (4)	3	2251	I-32434
	Guinea-Bissau	12/06/1995	21/12/1995	4-4 (5)	3	2251	A-32434
Seychelles	Comoros	17/02/2012		6-28	7	5039	
	Comoros - Tanzania	17/02/2012		6-29	7	5053	
	France (Glorioso)	19/02/2001	19/02/2001	6-18	5	3784	I-37782
	Mauritius	29/07/2008	19/11/2008	6-22	6	4391	I-46169
	Mauritius	13/03/2012	18/06/2012	6-22 (2)	9	6047	I-49782
	Mauritius	13/03/2012	18/06/2012	6-22 (2)	9	6047	I-49783
	Tanzania	23/01/2002	23/01/2002	6-19	5	3795	I-38874
Singapore	Indonesia	25/05/1973	29/08/1974	5-11	1	1049	I-45144
	Indonesia	10/03/2009	30/08/2010	5-11 (2)	7	4813	I-48026
	Indonesia	03/09/2014	10/02/2017	5-11 (3)	7	4827	I-54672
	Malaysia	07/08/1995	07/08/1995	5-20	3	2345	
	Malaysia			5-20 (2)	5	3733	N/A
	Malaysia			5-20 (2)(Add.1)	6	4299	
Slovenia	Croatia			8-20	6	4455	N/A
	Croatia	29/06/2017	29/06/2017	8-20 (Add. 1)	8	5667	N/A

Country A	Country B/C	Signed	EIF	Report No.	Vol.	Page	UN Reg. No.
	Italy	08/01/1968	21/01/1970	8-7 (1)	2	1627	
	Italy	10/11/1975	03/04/1977	8-7 (2)	2	1639	I-24848
	Italy			8-7 (3)	3	2437	
Solomon Islands	Australia	13/09/1988	14/04/1989	5-4	1	977	I-26661
	Australia			5-4 (Add.)	4	2671	
	Fiji	11/07/2022	22/02/2023	5-49	9	6027	I-57923
	France (New Caledonia)	12/11/1990	12/11/1990	5-17	1	1167	I-27851
	Papua New Guinea	25/01/1989		5-16	1	1155	
	Papua New Guinea			5-16 (2)	3	2323	
	Vanuatu	07/10/2016	13/02/2017	5-45	8	5527	
Somalia	Kenya			4-17	7	4807	N/A
Spain	France	29/01/1974	05/04/1975	9-2	2	1719	I-14592
	France	29/01/1974	05/04/1975	9-2	2	1719	I-14591
	Italy	19/02/1974	16/11/1978	8-5	2	1601	I-17429
	Portugal	12/02/1976		9-7	2	1791	
	Portugal	12/02/1976		9-7	2	1791	

Country A	Country B/C	Signed	EIF	Report No.	Vol.	Page	UN Reg. No.
Sri Lanka	India	28/06/1974	08/07/1974	6-10 (1)	2	1409	I-15802
	India	23/03/1976	10/05/1976	6-10 (2)	2	1419	I-15804
	India - Maldives	31/07/1976	31/07/1976	6-9	2	1401	I-15805
Suriname	France (French Guiana)	08/11/2017	01/12/2018	3-11	8	5473	I-55757
	Guyana	17/09/2007	17/09/2007	3-10	5	3601	N/A
	Guyana			3-10 (Add.1)	6	4236	
Sweden	Estonia	02/11/1998	26/07/2000	10-19	4	3089	I-44413
	Estonia - Finland	16/01/2001	12/08/2001	10-21	4	3129	I-44411
	Estonia - Latvia	30/04/1997	20/02/1998	10-17	4	3041	I-44412
	Norway	24/07/1968	18/03/1969	9-14	2	1871	I-14015
	Denmark	30/01/1932	30/01/1932	10-2	2	1931	
	Denmark	09/11/1984	03/09/1985	10-2	2	1931	I-23600
	Denmark	03/07/1995	03/07/1995	10-14	3	2557	
	Finland	29/09/1972	15/01/1973	10-3	2	1945	I-14443
	Finland	02/06/1994	30/07/1995	10-13	3	2539	I-32126
	Germany, Dem. Rep.	22/06/1978	20/12/1978	10-7	2	2029	I-18021
	Lithuania	10/04/2014	23/12/2014	10-24	8	5743	I-53412
	Lithuania - Russia	30/11/2005	17/06/2011	10-23	8	5731	I-53411
	Poland	10/02/1989	30/06/1989	10-10	2	2077	I-27846

Country A	Country B/C	Signed	EIF	Report No.	Vol.	Page	UN Reg. No.
	Poland - Soviet Union	30/06/1989	10/05/1990	10-12	2	2097	I-27841
	Soviet Union	18/04/1988	22/06/1988	10-9	2	2057	I-27075
Tanzania	Comoros	05/12/2011		6-30	7	5059	
	Comoros - Mozambique	05/12/2011		6-27	7	5033	
	Comoros - Seychelles	17/02/2012		6-29	7	5053	
	Kenya	09/07/1976	09/07/1976	4-5	1	875	I-15603
	Kenya	23/06/2009	23/06/2009	4-5 (2)	7	4781	I-46308
	Mozambique	28/12/1988		4-7	1	893	
	Mozambique	05/12/2011		4-7 (2)	7	4793	
	Seychelles	23/01/2002	23/01/2002	6-19	5	3795	I-38874
Thailand	Cambodia	18/06/2001		5-24	5	3735	
	India	22/06/1978	15/12/1978	6-11	2	1433	I-17433
	India	27/10/1993		6-11 (Add.2)	3	2377	
	India - Indonesia	22/06/1978	02/03/1979	6-7	2	1379	I-19476
	India - Myanmar	27/10/1993	24/05/1995	6-11 (Add.1)	3	2369	I-32099
	India - Myanmar			6-11 (Corr.1)	5	3781	
	Indonesia	17/12/1971	07/04/1973	6-13 (1)	2	1455	I-16929
	Indonesia	11/12/1975	18/02/1978	6-13 (2)	2	1465	I-16930
	Indonesia - Malaysia	21/12/1971	16/07/1973	6-12	2	1443	

(*Cont.*)

Country A	Country B/C	Signed	EIF	Report No.	Vol.	Page	UN Reg. No.
	Malaysia	24/10/1979	15/07/1982	5-13 (1)	1	1091	I-21270
	Malaysia	24/10/1979	15/07/1982	5-13 (2)	1	1099	I-21271
	Malaysia	21/02/1979		5-13 (2)	1	1099	
	Malaysia	30/05/1990		5-13 (2)	1	1099	
	Myanmar	25/07/1980	12/04/1982	6-4	2	1341	I-21069
	Vietnam	09/08/1997	27/12/1997	5-23	4	2683	
Tonga	France (Wallis & Futuna)	11/01/1980	11/01/1980	5-8	1	1011	I-18960
Trinidad and Tobago	Barbados	11/04/2006	11/04/2006	2-26	5	3577	N/A
	Barbados			2-26 (Add.1)	6	4187	
	Grenada	21/04/2010	27/04/2010	2-31	7	4705	I-47548
	Venezuela	26/03/1942	22/09/1942	2-13 (1)	1	639	LoN-4829
	Venezuela	04/08/1989		2-13 (2)	1	655	
	Venezuela	18/04/1990	23/07/1991	2-13 (3)	1	675	I-28463
	Venezuela	20/03/2007	16/08/2010	2-13 (4)	7	4649	I-50196
	Venezuela	16/08/2010	16/08/2010	2-13 (4)	7	4649	I-50197
Tunisia	Algeria	11/02/2002	23/11/2003	8-16	5	3927	I-39821
	Algeria	11/07/2011	16/09/2013	8-16 (Add. 1)	9	6139	
	Italy	20/08/1971	06/12/1978	8-6	2	1611	I-17601

(Cont.)

Country A	Country B/C	Signed	EIF	Report No.	Vol.	Page	UN Reg. No.
	Italy			8-6 (Corr.)	3	2435	
	Italy			8-6 (Corr.2)	4	2863	
	Libya	24/02/1982	24/02/1982	8-9	2	1663	N/A
	Libya	08/08/1988	11/04/1989	8-9	2	1663	
Turkey	Bulgaria	04/12/1997	04/11/1998	8-13	4	2871	I-36204
	Georgia	14/07/1997	22/09/1999	8-10 (5)	4	2865	
	Libya	27/11/2019	08/12/2019	8-24	9	6159	I-56119
	Soviet Union	17/04/1973	27/03/1975	8-10 (1)	2	1681	I-14475
	Soviet Union	23/06/1978	15/05/1981	8-10 (2)	2	1693	I-20344
	Soviet Union	06/02/1987	06/02/1987	8-10 (3)	2	1701	I-24690
Tuvalu	Fiji	17/10/2014	17/10/2024	5-48	9	6005	I-56867
	Fiji - France (Wallis & Futuna)	09/12/2014	09/12/2014	5-46	8	5539	
	France (Wallis & Futuna)	05/11/1985	05/11/1985	5-29	6	4330	I-25964
	France (Wallis & Futuna)	09/12/2014	09/12/2014	5-29 (Add. 1)	8	5503	
	Kiribati	29/08/2012		5-37	7	4903	
Ukraine	Turkey	23/06/1978	15/05/1981	8-10 (2)	2	1693	I-20344
	Turkey	06/02/1987	06/02/1987	8-10 (3)	2	1701	I-24690
	Turkey			8-10 (4)	3	2443	

Country A	Country B/C	Signed	EIF	Report No.	Vol.	Page	UN Reg. No.
	Romania	03/02/2009	03/02/2009	8-17	5	3939	N/A
	Romania			8-18	6	4434	
United Arab Emirates	Abu Dhabi/Dubai	18/02/1968	18/02/1968	7-1	2	1475	
	Dubai/Sharjah	19/10/1981	19/10/1981	7-4	2	1499	
	Dubai/Sharjah			7-4 (Add.1)	3	2385	
	Dubai/Sharjah			7-4 (Add.1)	4	2823	
	Iran	31/08/1974		7-8	2	1533	
	Qatar	20/03/1969	20/03/1969	7-9	2	1541	I-43372
	Sharjah/Umm al Qaywayn	01/01/1964	01/01/1964	7-10	2	1549	
United Kingdom	Belgium	29/05/1991	14/05/1993	9-17	2	1901	I-31712
	Belgium			9-17 (Add.1)	5	4005	
	Belgium	07/06/2005	02/10/2006	9-17 (2)	6	4506	A-31712
	Belgium	12/08/2013		9-17 (3)	7	5253	
	Denmark	03/03/1966	06/02/1967	9-10	2	1825	I-8574
	Denmark	25/11/1971	07/12/1972	9-10	2	1825	I-12280
	Denmark	22/10/2009	22/10/2009	9-10 (2)	6	4488	A-12280
	Denmark (Faroe Islands)	18/05/1999	21/07/1999	9-23	4	2955	
	Denmark (Faroe Islands)	25/04/2012	31/03/2014	9-23 (2)	7	5275	
	France	30/06/1977	30/06/1977	9-3 (1)	2	1735	N/A

Country A	Country B/C	Signed	EIF	Report No.	Vol.	Page	UN Reg. No.
	France	24/06/1982	04/02/1983	9-3 (2)	2	1735	I-21923
	France	02/11/1988	06/04/1989	9-3 (3)	2	1735	I-26858
	France	25/07/1991	17/03/1992	9-3 (4)	2	1735	I-29182
	France			9-3 (4)(Corr.)	3	2465	
	France			9-3 (4)(Add.1)	5	3943	
	France	20/04/2011	31/03/2014	9-3 (6)	7	5115	
	Germany	25/11/1971	07/12/1972	9-12	2	1851	I-12626
	Ireland	07/11/1988	11/01/1990	9-5	2	1767	I-27204
	Ireland	08/12/1992	26/03/1993	9-5 (2)	3	2487	A-27204
	Ireland	28/03/2013	31/03/2014	9-5 (3)	7	5151	I-51870
	Netherlands	06/10/1965	23/12/1966	9-13	2	1859	I-8616
	Netherlands	25/11/1971	07/12/1972	9-13	2	1859	A-8616
	Netherlands	07/06/2004	10/01/2006	9-13 (2)	6	4494	A-8616
	Netherlands	03/07/2013	01/04/2014	9-13 (3)	7	5205	A-8616
	Netherlands	06/10/1965	23/12/1966	9-13 (4)	8	5685	I-8615
	Netherlands	26/05/1992	03/03/1993	9-13 (4)	8	5685	I-30235
	Netherlands	27/11/2013	27/11/2013	9-13 (4)	8	5685	I-51804
	Norway	10/03/1965	29/06/1965	9-15	2	1879	I-8043
	Norway	22/12/1978	20/02/1980	9-15	2	1879	A-8043
	Norway	10/05/1976	22/07/1977	9-15 (2)	5	3944	I-16878
	Norway	16/10/1979	30/01/1981	9-15 (3)	5	3944	I-20387

(Cont.)

Country A	Country B/C	Signed	EIF	Report No.	Vol.	Page	UN Reg. No.
	Norway	16/10/1979	30/01/1981	9-15 (4)	5	3944	I-20551
	Norway	30/04/2009	30/04/2009	9-15 (5)	6	4499	A-8043
	Norway	04/04/2005	10/07/2007	9-15 (6)	7	5213	I-44683
United Kingdom (Akrotiri, Dhekelia)	Cyprus	16/08/1960	16/08/1960	8-1	2	1559	I-5476
United Kingdom (Anguilla)	Antigua and Barbuda	27/07/2021		2-38	9	5901	
	France (St. Martin and St. Barthelemy)	27/06/1996	30/01/1997	2-20	3	2219	I-36144
	France (St. Martin and St. Barthelemy)			2-20 (Add.1)	5	3562	
	France (St. Martin and St. Barthelemy)	04/03/2021	04/03/2021	2-20 (Add. 2)	9	5881	
	United Kingdom (British Virgin Islands)	11/07/2005	11/07/2005	2-29	6	4213	
	United States (US Virgin Islands)	05/11/1993	01/06/1995	2-17	3	2171	I-32636
United Kingdom (British Virgin Islands)	United Kingdom (Anguilla)	11/07/2005	11/07/2005	2-29	6	4213	
	United States (Puerto Rico and US V.I.)	05/11/1993	01/06/1995	2-16	3	2161	I-32637

(Cont.)

Country A	Country B/C	Signed	EIF	Report No.	Vol.	Page	UN Reg. No.
United Kingdom (Cayman Islands)	Honduras	04/12/2001	01/03/2002	2-23	5	3564	I-39224
United Kingdom (Guernsey)	France	10/07/1992	10/07/1992	9-3 (5)	3	2471	I-30858
United Kingdom (Jersey)	France	04/07/2000	01/01/2004	9-24	4	2979	I-40415
	France			9-24 (Add.1)	5	4006	
United Kingdom (Montserrat)	France (Guadeloupe)	27/06/1996	30/01/1997	2-21	3	2227	I-36143
	France (Guadeloupe)			2-21 (Add.1)	5	3563	
United Kingdom (Pitcairn)	France (French Polynesia)	25/10/1983	12/04/1984	5-7	1	1003	I-23067
	France (French Polynesia)	19/01/1993	01/02/1993	5-7 (Add.)	3	2295	I-30859
United Kingdom (Turks and Caicos)	Dominican Republic	02/08/1996		2-22	3	2235	

(Cont.)

Country A	Country B/C	Signed	EIF	Report No.	Vol.	Page	UN Reg. No.
United States	Canada	12/10/1984	12/10/1984	1-3	1	401	N/A
	Cuba	16/12/1977		1-4	1	417	
	Cuba			1-4 (Add.1)	5	3555	
	Cuba			1-4 (Add.2)	6	4165	
	Cuba	08/02/2012	08/02/2012	1-4 (Add.3)	7	4607	
	Cuba	13/12/2013	13/12/2013	1-4 (Add.4)	7	4611	
	Cuba	31/12/2015	31/12/2015	1-4 (Add.5)	8	5395	
	Cuba	26/12/2017	26/12/2017	1-4 (Add.6)	8	5399	
	Cuba	18/01/2017		1-4 (2)	9	5819	
	Kiribati	06/09/2013	19/07/2019	5-40	7	4935	I-57686
	Mexico	23/11/1970	18/04/1972	1-5	1	427	I-11873
	Mexico	24/11/1976	24/11/1976	1-5	1	427	I-17282
	Mexico	04/05/1978	13/11/1997	1-5	1	427	I-37399
	Mexico			1-5 (Add.)	4	2619	
	Mexico	09/06/2000	17/01/2001	1-5 (2)	4	2621	I-37400
	Mexico	20/02/2012	18/07/2014	1-5 (3)	7	4613	I-52496
	Mexico	18/01/2017		1-5 (4)	9	5841	
	Soviet Union	01/06/1990		1-6	1	447	
United States (American Samoa)	Cook Islands	11/06/1980	08/09/1983	5-5	1	985	I-28971
	New Zealand (Tokelau)	02/12/1980	03/09/1983	5-14	1	1125	I-28231
	Niue	13/05/1997	07/10/2014	5-22	4	2673	I-52440

(Cont.)

Country A	Country B/C	Signed	EIF	Report No.	Vol.	Page	UN Reg. No.
	Niue			5-22 (Add.1)	5	3734	
	Niue			5-22 (Add.1, Corr.1)	7	4839	
United States (Guam)	Micronesia, Fed. States	01/08/2014	27/09/2019	5-42	7	4963	I-55987
United States (Puerto Rico and U.S. V.I.)	United Kingdom (Anguilla)	05/11/1993	01/06/1995	2-17	3	2171	I-32636
	United Kingdom (British Virgin Islands)	05/11/1993	01/06/1995	2-16	3	2161	I-32637
	Venezuela	28/03/1978	24/11/1980	2-14	1	691	I-20984
Uruguay	Argentina	19/11/1973	12/02/1974	3-2	1	757	I-21424
	Brazil	21/07/1972	12/06/1975	3-4	1	785	I-17411
Vanuatu	Solomon Islands	07/10/2016	13/02/2017	5-45	8	5527	
Venezuela	Dominican Republic	03/03/1979	15/01/1982	2-9	1	577	
	France (Guadeloupe and Martinique)	17/07/1980	28/01/1983	2-11	1	603	I-21969
	The Netherlands (Antilles)	31/03/1978	15/12/1978	2-12	1	615	I-17901
	United Kingdom (Trinidad and Tobago)	26/03/1942	22/09/1942	2-13 (1)	1	639	LoN-4829
	Trinidad and Tobago	04/08/1989		2-13 (2)	1	655	

(Cont.)

Country A	Country B/C	Signed	EIF	Report No.	Vol.	Page	UN Reg. No.
	Trinidad and Tobago	18/04/1990	23/07/1991	2-13 (3)	1	675	I-28463
	Trinidad and Tobago	20/03/2007	16/08/2010	2-13 (4)	7	4649	I-50196
	Trinidad and Tobago	16/08/2010	16/08/2010	2-13 (4)	7	4649	I-50197
	United States (Puerto Rico and U.S. V.I)	28/03/1978	24/11/1980	2-14	1	691	I-20984
Vietnam	Cambodia	07/07/1982		5-21	3	2357	
	China	25/12/2000	30/06/2004	5-25	5	3745	I-41860
	China			5-25 (Add.1)	7	4841	
	Indonesia	26/06/2003	29/05/2007	5-27	6	4301	I-44165
	Malaysia	05/06/1992	05/06/1992	5-19	3	2335	
	Thailand	09/08/1997	27/12/1997	5-23	4	2683	
Yemen	Eritrea	17/12/1999	17/12/1999	6-14	4	2729	N/A
	Oman	14/12/2003	03/07/2004	6-21	5	3900	I-41170
	Saudi Arabia	12/06/2000	09/07/2000	6-16	4	2797	I-43167